THE
ROCKEFELLER
CONSCIENCE

Also by John Ensor Harr and Peter J. Johnson

The Rockefeller Century

THE
ROCKEFELLER
CONSCIENCE

An American Family in Public and in Private

JOHN ENSOR HARR

AND

PETER J. JOHNSON

CHARLES SCRIBNER'S SONS
New York

MAXWELL MACMILLAN CANADA
Toronto
MAXWELL MACMILLAN INTERNATIONAL
New York Oxford Singapore Sydney

Charles Scribner's Sons
Macmillan Publishing Company
866 Third Avenue
New York, NY 10022

Maxwell Macmillan Canada, Inc.
200 Eglinton Avenue East,
Suite 200
Don Mills, Ontario M3C 3N1

Macmillan Publishing Company is part of the
Maxwell Communication Groups of Companies.

LIBRARY OF CONGRESS CATALOGING-IN-PUBLICATION DATA

Harr, John Ensor, 1926–
    The Rockefeller conscience: an American family in public and in private/
John Ensor Harr and Peter J. Johnson.
        p. cm.
    Includes bibliographical references and index.
    ISBN 0-684-19364-7
    1. Rockefeller family. 2. United States—Biography. I. Johnson,
Peter J. II. Title.
CT274.R59H38   1991
973.9′092′2—dc20   91-17803
[B]

Macmillan books are available at special discounts for bulk purchases
for sales promotions, premiums, fund-raising, or educational use.

For details, contact:

Special Sales Director
Macmillan Publishing Company
866 Third Avenue
New York, NY 10022

10 9 8 7 6 5 4 3 2 1

Designed by Jack Meserole

PRINTED IN THE UNITED STATES OF AMERICA

To Porter McKeever and Datus Smith

CONTENTS

Preface   xiii

Acknowledgments   xv

I   THE ROCKEFELLER DYNASTY, 1890–1952

1 The Basis of Fame   3

2 Careers   14

II   JDR 3RD, INSTITUTION BUILDER, 1951–1968

3 The Population Council   31

4 Investing in People   46

5 Population and Food   62

6 At Home in Asia   76

7 The Asia Society   90

8 Asia: The Cultural Dimension   104

9 Lincoln Center: The Concept   120

10 Lincoln Center: The Reality   138

11 Population: The "Takeoff" Stage   158

12 Leader of the Foundation   180

III   ON THE PERSONAL SIDE, 1945–1970

13 Family Affairs: The Brothers   201

14 Family Affairs: The Inner Circle   223

15 Family Affairs: The Children   236

16 Man of the Arts   249

17 The Man at Work   268

IV   "AN EXCITING TIME TO BE ALIVE," 1960–1978

18 The Fourth Field   289

19 "Wide Open for Change"   300

20 The Youth Program   318

21 The Urban Problem   333

22 The Bicentennial   346

23 Public Service Writ Large   366

24 The Third Sector   375

V   THE FINAL YEARS, 1970–1978

25 The Population Commission   395

26 New Challenges in Population   421

27 Success in Asia   443

28 Final Disposition   463

29 Family Issues   482

30 The Center and the Estate   491

31 Brothers and Cousins   502

32 Confrontation   519

33 July 1978   542

Epilogue   554

Appendix: The Rockefellers—Third and Fourth
    Generations   568

Notes   569

Index   605

ILLUSTRATIONS

(Photographs courtesy of Blanchette H. Rockefeller,
unless otherwise noted)

BETWEEN PAGES 240 AND 241

John D. Rockefeller 3rd at age forty-six

JDR 3rd with Secretary-General Trygve Lie and architect Wallace Harrison at the opening of United Nations headquarters in 1952

JDR 3rd and John Foster Dulles with Japanese Ambassador Eikichi Araki at the first annual dinner of the Japan Society, June 17, 1952

Prince Hitachi of Japan with Governor John S. Battle of Virginia and JDR at Colonial Williamsburg, September 1953

Three John D. Rockefellers—JDR; his son, Jay; and Junior—at Christmas, 1954

Junior and his second wife, Martha Baird Rockefeller, together with four of his sons and their wives at his daughter Babs's home, Christmas 1954

Blanchette and JDR entertain Prime Minister Shigeru Yoshida and his daughter and son-in-law, November 1954

JDR and Blanchette with President Ramón Magsaysay of the Philippines and his wife in Manila

JDR with President Ngo Dinh Diem in Saigon, February 3, 1957

JDR with President Habib Bourguiba in Tunisia

The six members of the third generation at Christmas, 1958

JDR and President Dwight D. Eisenhower at the groundbreaking ceremony for Lincoln Center, May 14, 1959

The President turns the first spade, watched by JDR and others

Hope Aldrich Rockefeller, 1959

Hope on her wedding day, July 4, 1959, with her father

BETWEEN PAGES 336 AND 337

John D. Rockefeller 3rd as speaker at a meeting on the performing arts in Pittsburgh, April 1961

Opening night at Lincoln Center, Philharmonic Hall, September 23, 1962

JDR with Colombian officials on a Rockefeller Foundation visit to Cali, March 1964

At a dinner in honor of Indian Prime Minister Indira Gandhi, March 1966

JDR and his office associates, January 1965

Frank Notestein

Arthur T. Mosher

Jay visiting his father's office, Room 5600, Rockefeller Center, 1966

Opening night of the Metropolitan Opera at Lincoln Center, September 16, 1966

A rare appearance of all five Rockefeller brothers in public, November 28, 1967

The eldest and youngest of the Rockefeller brothers, JDR and David

JDR visiting President Lyndon B. Johnson, May 23, 1968

JDR and Senator Edward M. Kennedy at a dinner meeting of the National Committee on U.S.–China Relations, March 20, 1969

JDR at second inauguration of brother Winthrop as governor of Arkansas, January 14, 1969

Laurance S. Rockefeller at Little Dix Bay

Another trio of John D. Rockefellers—JDR; his son, Jay; and his grandson—in Charleston, West Virginia

BETWEEN PAGES 464 AND 465

Kykuit, on the Rockefeller Estate at Pocantico in Westchester County

Three of the Rockefeller brothers—David, Winthrop, and Nelson— at a "vest pocket" park in Manhattan

John Gardner, John D. Rockefeller 3rd, and Amyas Ames in front of the bronze plaque honoring JDR on his retirement from the Lincoln Center board in 1972

Three Asia Society board members: Datus C. Smith, George Ball, and Porter McKeever (courtesy of The Asia Society)

Donal C. O'Brien, Jr., with his wife, Katie (courtesy of Don O'Brien)

Bernard Berelson

Clifton R. Wharton, Jr.

J. Richardson Dilworth

Dana Creel

Elizabeth McCormack

JDR 3rd, Grace Olivarez, and Dr. Christian Ramsey meeting with President Richard M. Nixon, May 1972

JDR with Shigeharu Matsumoto and Prime Minister Sato Tanaka in Tokyo, November 1972

JDR and Blanchette at a display of some of their Asian art

Alida Rockefeller with her brother, Jay

JDR and Blanchette in his office, 1974

JDR and William Ruder meeting with President Gerald Ford, January 20, 1975

JDR with Theodore Sorenson and Cyrus Vance at a Foreign Policy Association luncheon in June 1976

The RCA Building in Rockefeller Center (courtesy of The Rockefeller Group, Inc.)

The third generation, at Pocantico in the mid-1970s

Senator John D. Rockefeller IV of West Virginia and Sharon Percy Rockefeller, with their children

PREFACE

IN a capitalist society with an open and democratic political system, it is inevitable that great personal fortunes will continue to be amassed. It is likewise inevitable that the public will remain fascinated—or deeply suspicious—about the uses to which such wealth is put.

There is the frivolous side to this subject, as in "the lifestyles of the rich and famous" and the fulsome media attention to the doings of Donald Trump. And there is the serious side, in the role of philanthropy in society and in the moral, ethical, and political questions that are raised.

The last were aptly put in a letter I received shortly after Peter Johnson and I published our first book, *The Rockefeller Century*, in 1988. The letter was from a former mentor, the late Professor Frederick C. ("Fritz") Mosher of the University of Virginia, chairman of my Ph.D. dissertation committee many years ago. Characterizing himself accurately as "still something of a populist and a democrat with both a small and capital d," Fritz wrote: "I am still unsure of what effects the Rockefeller fortune, and others, have had on the development of our society. And although ideologically I would have preferred more public participation and accountability in their philanthropy, I have admiration for the imaginativeness, the discipline, and the wisdom the three generations of Rockefellers brought to it." He added: "Not all the very rich have much of these qualities."

Fritz went on to point to the "paradoxes" in the Rockefeller story: "Zest for making money against very high degrees of generosity and compassion for fellow people; a cornucopia of abundance in living styles versus repeated imprecations of frugality and simplicity; business practices of at least questionable ethics (in the case of Rockefeller Senior) versus religiosity and puritanical moral standards."

In the American lexicon, the Rockefeller name is as synonymous with great wealth as Benedict Arnold's is with high treason. But the Rockefellers' enduring place in American history has been earned less by the fact of great wealth than by the *uses* to which that wealth has been put by the leaders of the family. The family's powerful ethic of philanthropy and public service was established by John D. Rockefeller, Sr., significantly expanded by his only son, John D. Rockefeller, Jr., and carried on with great commitment and creativity in the third generation principally by *his* eldest son, John D. Rockefeller 3rd.

The use of family wealth was the focus of *The Rockefeller Century*, carrying the story from the first great philanthropy in 1889, the creation of the University of Chicago, to the early 1950s, when the five Rockefeller brothers of the third generation had come of age and were embarked on their adult careers. In this sequel, *The Rockefeller Conscience* (we are indebted to Jacques Barzun for suggesting the title), we cover their careers up to the late 1970s, concentrating on JDR 3rd as the brother who consciously carried on family traditions as a full-time philanthropist.

Our purpose is to document the Rockefeller story fully and to be as accurate and objective as we possibly can. Apart from our own predilection, the reason is the abundance of myth and the scarcity of objectivity in written accounts about the Rockefeller family. In this book we deal with two of the most prominent myths by presenting the facts about the scope and character of Rockefeller wealth and the origins of family traditions, and we deal at some length with two of the worst distortions in print (a *New Yorker* "profile" of JDR 3rd in 1972 and a heavily biased book published in 1976). We do this not in the naive hope that myths and distortions will disappear (they die very hard), but in the belief that there should be at least one balanced and comprehensive account in which interpretations are based on accurate information.

What we do *not* attempt to do is answer the political and social questions about the proper role and place of wealth in American society that are implicit in Fritz Mosher's comments. Elements of the story itself are suggestive in this regard—as, for example, in the work and ideas of JDR 3rd, the Rockefeller who came the closest to articulating a viable theory of the American polity in his interest in the social movements of his time and in his drive to defend, enhance, and democratize philanthropy, not to protect wealth and privilege, but as a crucial dimension of American pluralism.

In an open society that allows individuals to amass great wealth, by definition no one can tell the wealthy how to spend their money. One can only set examples. We are content to tell this story as best we know how and to let the reader judge the extent to which the Rockefeller record stands as exemplary.

JOHN ENSOR HARR
West Orange, New Jersey
August 1991

ACKNOWLEDGMENTS

OBSERVERS and analysts of the recent past depend on the expertise, assistance, and good graces of many people in assembling the diverse information needed to produce an intelligible and coherent account of their subject. The reasons are not hard to discover: the historical record has not yet fully coalesced or even emerged; the so-called facts of history are still in the process of forming; and the records of most individuals and organizations, especially governmental agencies and departments, that have played a role in the events of the past thirty years or so have not yet entered the public domain. Consequently, this book, like others of its genre, draws significantly upon the personal recollections of a number of individuals who participated in the events described.

Many of the people who shared their recollections and insights are cited in the endnotes that follow the text. However, special mention needs to be given to those individuals who shared their knowledge of the intricate relationships among tax law, investment policy, and philanthropy with us and to those who participated with members of the Rockefeller family and their organizations in the development of the programs and institutions that are dealt with in this book. Our thanks are tendered to Laurance S. Rockefeller, David Rockefeller, Dana Creel, J. Richardson Dilworth, William Dietel, Russell Phillips, Donal C. O'Brien, Jr., Joseph W. Ernst, Elizabeth McCormack, and Marsha McLean Edgar B. Young, Datus C. Smith, Porter McKeever, and the late Donald McLean patiently shared their enormous store of information and experience with us and saved us from egregious errors.

Although much of our research into the papers of John D. Rockefeller 3rd and his organizations was done prior to their transfer to the Rockefeller Archive Center, we would be seriously remiss in failing to acknowledge the importance to our work of this repository of material relating to many aspects of American social, economic, and political life. Darwin Stapleton and his staff—especially Tom Rosenbaum, Melissa Smith, and Harold Oakhill—have responded to innumerable questions from us over the years.

Our editors at Scribners, Susanne Kirk, Bill Goldstein, and Hamilton Cain, have been helpful and attentive every step of the way. The members of JDR 3rd's immediate family—Blanchette Rockefeller, Senator John D. Rockefeller IV, Sandra Ferry, Hope Aldrich, and Alida Rockefeller Messinger—granted us access to all of his papers and asked only that we write an honest appraisal of his life and work. We are grateful for the confidence they reposed in us.

Finally, we thank our wives and families for their endurance and understanding in the long years that it has taken to complete these two volumes.

PETER J. JOHNSON
Maspeth, New York
August 1991

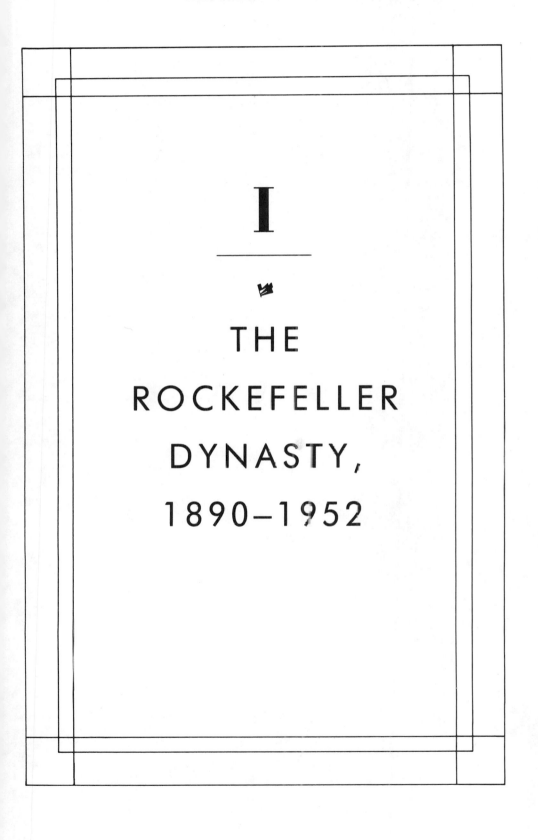

I

THE ROCKEFELLER DYNASTY, 1890–1952

1

THE BASIS OF
FAME

AMERICANS awakening to the morning news on October 31, 1989, were greeted with a story that many regarded as shocking. The Rockefellers, as one journal put it, had "sold their name" to the Japanese. Although the reality was a good deal more complicated, the public perceived that a 51 percent interest in fabled Rockefeller Center had been sold to the Mitsubishi Estate Company of Tokyo for $846 million.[1]

To many, this was the most tangible evidence to date of what they regarded as the "buyout" of the United States by Japan, even more alarming than the Sony acquisition of Columbia Pictures and former President Reagan's $2 million fee for making a sales promotion visit to Japan. At the least, the sale of Rockefeller Center offered convincing testimony to the meteoric growth of Japan from the despised enemy of the United States in World War II to the trusted ally and powerful economic competitor of the 1990s.

Some thirty-seven years earlier, there was another surprising event in New York City involving the Japanese and the Rockefellers. New Yorkers strolling along Fifth Avenue on June 17, 1952, were greeted by a startling sight—the Rising Sun flag of Japan displayed at several locations, including the entrance to the Plaza Hotel.

They might well have wondered how this could happen so soon after the end of the most bitter foreign war in American history, the Pacific war with Japan that had fanned emotions on both sides to the point of hatred.

The New Yorker indirectly responsible for the display of Japanese flags was John D. Rockefeller 3rd, eldest of the five Rockefeller brothers, known to his associates simply as "JDR." He had energetically revived the Japan Society, a bilateral cultural organization created in New York City in 1907, which had become inactive during World War II. The Society was holding

3

its first annual banquet on June 17, with the newly appointed Japanese ambassador as the guest of honor.

The revival was the first of a series of projects resulting from JDR's experience in accompanying the American peace delegation to Japan the year before. As head of the delegation, John Foster Dulles had asked JDR to come along to study conditions in Japan and propose projects in the cultural field that might help build mutual respect and friendship between the two nations over the long term. JDR undertook the assignment with zest, including the unusual step of implementing some of his recommendations personally instead of waiting for governments to act.[2]

The Japan Society revival of 1952 and the Rockefeller Group sale to the Mitsubishi Estate Company in 1989 also provide a fitting chronological framework for the careers of the Rockefeller brothers. As one article on the sale put it, they

. . . had been enshrined around the globe nearly as gods. For forty years the Rockefeller brothers had reigned as America's first family of capitalism, kings of their own circumscribed domains. But now the dynasty was confronting its own mortality . . . Rockefeller Center was sold. The magnificent art deco monoliths . . . belonged to the generational inheritors of another empire, the Mitsubishi clan.[3]

One theme in the commentary on the sale was lament over the passing of the Rockefeller family's prominence and influence, which had begun in the fourth quarter of the last century with the great business success of John D. Rockefeller. The leader of a handpicked group of associates, he created the Standard Oil Company and by the 1890s had brought it to the level of a near monopoly in the refining, distribution, and marketing of petroleum products. It was not the largest of the great trusts in the *laissez-faire* age of American capitalism, but it was the most nearly perfect. For this reason, and because he was a highly religious and very private person who never responded publicly to criticism (and thus seemed to many to be both sanctimonious and arrogant), he became the favorite target of the muckrakers and emerged indelibly in the public mind as the very essence of the robber baron.

Rockefeller owned one-fourth of Standard Oil stock when he retired in 1897, so that when the trust was split into thirty-four separate companies in 1911 (the result of a Supreme Court decision), he owned one-fourth of all of them. This, plus the great boom in the many uses of oil, made him the richest man in the United States by 1915, his fortune peaking at just under one billion dollars.[4]

If the story had stopped here, a story merely of business success and private wealth, the prominence and influence of the Rockefeller family would have dwindled into insignificance long ago. To be sure, there would have been notoriety of a sort for a time, occasioned by the public's fascination with the rich and also by the fact that the senior Rockefeller lived on as a visible and somewhat quaint icon of great wealth, giving out his shiny dimes to children until 1937, when he died just short of his ninety-eighth birthday.

There have been many private fortunes nearing or exceeding one billion dollars in the decades since 1911, yet no other family has come close to establishing a dynasty of the fame, power, and influence of the Rockefellers. The reason is the Rockefeller tradition of philanthropy—the "Rockefeller conscience," a civic and social conscience so well developed and so rigorously passed on from one generation to the next that it has no rival in American history and has come to occupy a special niche in that history.

Here is where myth enters the picture. The popular explanation for the family tradition of giving is that the elder Rockefeller, desperate to cleanse his reputation and that of his family, sought the counsel of one Ivy Lee, who was to become known as the "father of public relations."[5] Lee's advice, so the theory goes, was that Rockefeller should expiate his guilt for his years of greed and riding roughshod over everyone in building his monopoly: he could do this by becoming a philanthropist and buying his way into public favor.

The facts that make this untrue have been laid out before, yet the myth is much more powerful than the truth, possibly because it offers a neat and seemingly logical explanation that is easy to understand. Amazingly, the myth was solemnly repeated as late as the 1989 Mitsubishi sale.[6]

The truth is that John D. Rockefeller was a pious Baptist to whom giving was a natural and important part of life. He gave consistently to charity from the time of his first job, earning twenty-three dollars a month in 1855 at the age of sixteen. His giving simply increased as his income increased. As his principal biographer put it: "He had not waited to become rich before becoming generous."[7]

Nor did Rockefeller ever seek public relations advice. Far from feeling guilty, he believed he had acted responsibly; therefore he was not concerned about public opinion. His advice to his only son was to "do what you think is right and let the world wag."

Ivy Lee did not enter the picture until 1914, having been retained not by the elder Rockefeller but by the son, John D., Jr., for a specific task.[8] Far from needing Ivy Lee to tell him to become a philanthropist, the senior Rockefeller had, by this time, *given away nearly half a billion dollars*. He had created the University of Chicago, the Rockefeller Institute for Medical Research (today's Rockefeller University), the General Education Board, the Rockefeller Sanitary Commission, and the Rockefeller Foundation. Together with Andrew Carnegie, Rockefeller is credited with inventing much of modern philanthropy, in particular the foundation, in part by applying the organizing principles that the two men had independently developed in building their great business systems.[9]

The fact that Rockefeller giving was born out of religious principles, not public relations or a sense of guilt, was important in assuring its continuity from the original John D. to his son (who was known almost universally as "Junior"). There cannot be a philanthrophic dynasty without two conditions being met—a set of principles to guide succeeding generations and the presence of an heir willing and able to live out those principles. In the case of the Rockefellers, the father's moral values were omnipresent in the upbringing of the son. And, by every measure, Junior was an extraordinary individual, not so much in blindly carrying out his father's wishes but in living out the spirit of them with great commitment and originality, thereby adding to the body of good works. He was conditioned for this not only in the constant religious indoctrination of his youth and the example set by his father, but also in his educational experience at Brown University, which almost seems to have been designed to give young men of wealth a social conscience.[10] It is also likely that Junior was motivated by love of his father. In contrast to the ruthless monster depicted by the muckrakers and yellow press of the time, Junior saw in his father a warm, loving, and wise man who withstood the worst of criticism in good grace.

Junior graduated and entered his father's office in the same year, 1897, that the old man left it. He thus served his apprenticeship under the Reverend Frederick T. Gates, a formidable combination of missionary and entrepreneur to whom the father had entrusted the superintending of his philanthropies and investments outside of Standard Oil. Junior soon proved his mettle. It was his father's willingness to give money for philanthropic purposes that made the great institutions possible, but it was the son's talents that breathed life into them, especially his ability to attract experts, work with them in a supportive way, and win their respect and loyalty. Within a decade Junior had made a fateful decision: he would forgo business and make philanthropy his full-time career.

It was not until near the end of the First World War that Junior, now well past the age of forty, began to receive large transfers of financial resources from his father. The cautious old man apparently felt that not until then was his beloved son fully matured and prepared to be burdened with the responsibility of great wealth. Within the span of a few years, most of the rest of the fortune—assets worth nearly half a billion dollars—was transferred from father to son.

During the thirty-year period that followed, Junior proceeded to compile a record as a philanthrophic leader that probably will never be equaled. It is difficult to think of even a single significant aspect of life in both the United States and abroad that was not positively affected by Junior's leadership, work, or giving. A simple list of his contributions would be very long. The major fields of activity in which he showed consistent interest included conservation of natural resources, creation and improvement of national parks, historical restorations, medical research, public health, public administration, civic reform, development of the social sciences, ecumenical religion, industrial relations, support of the arts, low-income housing and urban renewal, international relations, civil rights, and support and reform of education at all levels. The complete story of Junior's involvement in any one of these fields would require a full-length book. And the picture of Junior that would emerge is that of a man true to the spirit of the Progressive era, more so than many of the avowed progressives of the time.

Junior's assets nearly doubled in the boom years of the 1920s, back up to his father's peak of nearly a billion dollars, despite his giving and full-time occupation as a philanthropist. But in the Depression he saw his net worth dwindle more than 60 percent. Nevertheless, partly to help fight the Depression, he took the enormous financial risk of proceeding with the building of Rockefeller Center after everyone else had backed out of the huge project.

Beyond all the material assets and accomplishments, Junior's growing fame and universal respect stemmed from the perception of him as a man unfailingly devoted to moral principles of the highest order, and thus an anchor of stability and reliability in a changing and troubled world. His public style was a gracious one and somewhat old-fashioned in its emphasis on formality and courtesy.

Junior's strong belief in another old-fashioned idea, that of stewardship, did much to define his character and personality. He was well aware that he had not created the Rockefeller wealth; his function was to be the steward of that wealth, to use it carefully and responsibly for the public good. This led directly to several other pronounced values. One was a healthy respect for the worth of a dollar, which at times bordered on an obsession. It was not that Junior was cheap—no man who gave away millions of dollars every year could be so considered. It did mean that his giving was not easy or frivolous, but painstaking in the extreme, and that he insisted on full value and careful accountability in every financial transaction.

A related value was the avoidance of a superior air and excessive public displays of wealth, or, to put it positively, as Junior often did when instructing his children, it was the cultivation of a certain "democratic" attitude. The basis for this was Junior's recognition that what counted was what he believed in and what he did, not that his name was Rockefeller or that he was wealthy. This led to modesty if not humility, and a readiness to deal with others fairly and equally.

Given Junior's staggering wealth, it was not easy to avoid ostentatious living. He could get carried away now and then, but on the whole it is fair to say that he avoided the flamboyant excesses that were more typical of the wealthy people of his time. This, of course, did not involve any real hardship. Junior and his family lived extremely well. Their principal residence was the nine-story house that Junior built in 1913 at No. 10 West 54th Street, near the more modest brownstone his parents lived in at No. 4 and across the street from the townhouse (No. 13) that Junior occupied for the first dozen years of his marriage. The No. 10 building was one of the largest private residences in Manhattan, though it lacked architectural distinction from an external point of view.[11] The location became even more convenient for Junior when Rockefeller Center was built in the 1930s. His office, known modestly as "Room 5600" even though it occupied the entire fifty-sixth floor of the RCA Building in Rockefeller Center (as well as the fifty-fifth and most of the fifty-fourth at one time), was only a short walk from home. The employees of Junior's office and related organizations in Room 5600 numbered in the hundreds.

There were two other important locations for the family, a summer house in Seal Harbor, Maine, known as "The Eyrie," that Junior bought in 1911 and continuously expanded until it became a vast, rambling place, and the huge Pocantico Estate just north of Tarrytown in Westchester County, New York. Junior's father first began assembling the latter in 1893, and both father and son added to it until it exceeded 3,000 acres. Except for a manicured core of about 250 acres known as "the Park," most of the estate has been left in its natural condition for riding trails and the enjoyment of nature. The country houses of various family members are scattered on the estate and the Park has four large buildings—the Coach Barn, the Orangerie, the Playhouse, and Kykuit (Dutch for "lookout"), the mansion Junior built for his parents and occupied himself after his father's death in 1937.

Junior was very fortunate in choosing his life's mate. In 1901 he married Abby Aldrich, daughter of the powerful Senator Nelson Aldrich of Rhode

Island. She was a warm and outgoing person who loved people and parties, and as such she was the perfect complement to Junior's serious and controlled nature. It was to be a useful contrast for the couple in the formidable task of raising their children to be normal and healthy despite the decidedly abnormal environment of Rockefeller wealth and notoriety.

The domestic situation was further complicated by the fact that there were six children, the first a girl, Abby, born in 1903 and called "Babs" to distinguish her from her mother, followed by the five sons who were to gain collective fame later as "the Rockefeller brothers." In chronological order, they were: John Davison Rockefeller 3rd (born 1906), Nelson Aldrich (1908), Laurance Spelman (1910), Winthrop (1912), and David (1915).[12]

The great challenge Junior and Abby faced was how to raise these children to be decent, self-reliant, and productive adults with a healthy perspective on life and wealth, but also imbued with the religious, family, and social values that were so important to their parents and grandparents. Given the wealth into which the children were born and the changing and troubled times in which they were growing up, the danger that they would turn out to be snobs or wastrels or worse was very real.

Junior soon learned how difficult it was going to be when his firstborn, Babs, turned out to be a rebel. She smoked, did poorly in school, and seemed to spend most of her time trying to find ways to outwit her chaperones. Whatever her father favored, Babs almost certainly would be against. The relationship was strained throughout their lives, easing only temporarily when Babs married in 1925. To Babs her marriage was liberation from her father and his strict household; to Junior it was a vast relief. When Babs got divorced in 1943, her father could barely speak to her; to Junior, divorce was one of the worst transgressions.

Junior was determined to do much better with his boys. He was a stern and demanding father who expected much of his sons. He never missed an opportunity to instruct them in correct behavior, and throughout his life he bombarded them with uplifting homilies and tracts. Most of all, Junior wanted his children to form good habits about money—to understand its value; keep careful accounts; learn to save; spend money properly for true needs, not self-indulgences; and use it to help others. Every Saturday the boys would keep appointments with their father in his study to go over their accounts. Allowances were kept low and increases were dependent on each boy's record of saving and sharing.

The leavening influence to Junior's serious nature was Abby's warmth and understanding. Junior adored her, and so did his sons. As for their father, each boy had his own particular mix of awe, fear, and respect. Somehow the very different styles of the parents meshed and worked well in raising the five sons. There were problems, and each son turned out to be different in personality and interests from the other four. But as far as inculcating the values of the Rockefeller family tradition in their sons is concerned, it must be said that on the whole Junior and Abby succeeded remarkably well. Each son grew up conscious of the "democratic" spirit of behavior, imbued with a strong sense of family, and determined to contribute to society in some form of public service.

For the oldest boy, John 3rd, it almost seemed that Junior's indoctrination had worked too well. John was frail, excessively serious, almost pathologically shy and self-conscious, overburdened with a sense of responsibility, and, above all, driven to please his father. He was to face a long struggle to overcome these handicaps and liberate himself from Junior's domineering influence.

The next son, Nelson, was so different from John that it is hard to imagine them as brothers. Physically, Nelson favored the Aldrich side of the family, as did Winthrop and David, while John and Laurance had the lean frame of their grandfather. Nelson was "all boy," a born extrovert who seemingly never had a self-conscious moment. He had the upbeat style and mischievous turn to go with his outgoing nature; he thus appears to have been the secret favorite of the parents. Political instinct may also have been inborn—Nelson was the one who figured out how best to manipulate the father. Because of this, he tended to be the leader of the gang.

Laurance, the middle son, was Nelson's staunchest gang member. The two were drawn to each other from their earliest years and throughout their lives. Nelson usually was the leader, but Laurance was the one person who could prick his brother's balloon and bring him down to earth. Laurance was a lover of gadgets and things technical, as in his avid interest in all forms of photography as a youth. At times, he seemed more an observer than a participant, with his keen intelligence, sardonic wit, and habit of standing back with an amused air.

Like Babs, Winthrop frequently was in trouble and seemed headed for the role of "black sheep" of the family. As a child, he grew fast and was clumsy. He was too young for the Nelson-Laurance duo and too old to get much enjoyment from playing with the baby, David. Winthrop grew up to be a handsome man with a genial, likable personality, but he failed to finish college, developed a drinking habit, drifted from job to job, and was a playboy for a time. Nevertheless, Junior never completely wrote Winthrop off for the reason that, unlike with Babs, his faults did not seem to be deliberate. He just seemed to drift into them and at the same time seemed to be trying hard to do better. There was always the chance that he might succeed.

As the baby of the family, David for a long time was too far removed from the others to be of much interest to them. He thus grew up with a sunny disposition, remarkably trouble-free except for occasional bullying by a frustrated Winthrop. David's intellectual bent and methodical, curious nature showed up early in his remarkable beetle collection; he was the only member of the family to earn a Ph.D.

These five brothers formed a special bond and developed a mystique as "the Rockefeller brothers." From time to time, they tried to include their sister in their circle and sometimes succeeded, but more often she was apart from them. The brothers were not particularly clannish. Early on they seemed to realize that each one had to carve out his own distinctive path in life. They would work together and be supportive when that made sense; otherwise they would be independent.

Certainly they had common bonds and were allies in many ways—in their love of their mother, in figuring out how to deal with Father, in sharing the notoriety of the Rockefeller name, the family venues, the support systems of the family office, and some measure of "great expectations" for future wealth, position, and prominence.

Junior was forced to face the question of sharing the wealth much sooner than he wished. Among the New Deal measures to cope with the Depression were hikes in income, estate, and gift taxes that with reason could be regarded as bordering on the confiscatory. With further increases scheduled for 1935, Junior felt forced to act in 1934. Aided by his advisers, he created what became known ever after in the Rockefeller family as "the 1934 Trusts." It was a way of transferring financial resources to his heirs, protecting those resources from frivolous use by conditions in the deeds of trust and control by Trust Committees, and paying the gift taxes at the 1934 rate. Seven such trusts were created, one each for Abby, Babs, and the five sons. The income from the trusts came to the younger recipients very slowly—Junior was reluctant to see any of his children receive unearned wealth before they were fully mature and had proven their ability to manage money wisely. In the future, there were to be more, smaller trusts and other financial gifts and measures to enhance the net worth of the sons, but the 1934 Trusts were to remain as the solid financial base and vehicle for each of the children.

Junior was not sure how the entry of his five sons into adulthood and careers would work out; in his own case, the fact that he had been an only son had simplified matters. The only one of his sons for whom a role had been ordained from the earliest days was John 3rd—the oldest son and the one with *the* name. He would enter the family office to help his overburdened father. After graduating from Princeton in 1929 and taking

2

♨

CAREERS

As was true for so many individuals and families across America, the end of World War II ushered in a period of exciting change and new beginnings for the Rockefellers. The five sons returned from wartime service full of ideas and enthusiasm for their future careers. They "invaded" Room 5600, infusing the staid family office with restless energy as they jockeyed for office space, assembled staffs, and engaged in constant meetings to find ways to cooperate even as each brother worked to carve out a distinctive career direction of his own.

It was still Junior's office. He paid the bills, and the family retainers in charge of all the central staff functions still reported to him. Within limits, he wanted to help pave the way for his sons but was not sure how to go about it. One early step he took was to hire several younger men for the office staff with the thought that they might serve the brothers.

Junior was immensely proud of the fact that all five sons had served their country with distinction during the war. A measure of his pride is the five oil portraits he had had commissioned to hang in the great baronial hall of the Playhouse at the Pocantico estate, with its dark, carved paneling and massive facing fireplaces.

The two younger brothers were the two army men, Captain David Rockefeller and Major Winthrop Rockefeller. Both had enlisted as privates and both went to Officer Candidate School. David served in North Africa and France in army intelligence, ending up in Paris as an assistant military attaché in what functioned as a military precursor to a reopened U.S. embassy. The experience intensified David's interest in international relations. As the only unmarried brother, Winthrop had been the first to join up and the only brother to be wounded in the line of duty when a *kamikaze* plane struck his troopship near Okinawa.

The next two portraits show Laurance in his uniform as a navy lieutenant and John as a lieutenant-commander. Laurance spent the war touring

14

aircraft plants to expedite production, having made himself something of an expert because of his keen interest in aviation and his many prewar investments in airline and aircraft manufacturing stocks.

At first, John found himself stuck in the Bureau of Naval Personnel because of his prior experience in industrial relations and as a recruiter and an administrator for the American Red Cross. But he soon managed a transfer to a much more exciting naval staff whose members were involved in interagency task forces engaged in planning postwar policy, including military occupation, new international organizations, peace terms, relief and rehabilitation, and return to civilian authority. Here JDR worked on plans for Japan that were to be useful later when he served on the Dulles peace mission, and he rubbed shoulders with many of the men who were to be the postwar architects and leaders of U.S. foreign affairs.

The fifth portrait shows Nelson in a blue business suit. Though the only brother not to wear a uniform, Nelson nevertheless was deeply involved in the war effort in a remarkable assignment that made use of his Latin American experience. In 1940 he had come to the attention of President Roosevelt, who named him to head the Office of the Coordinator of Inter-American Affairs (OCIAA), a new agency with 1,300 employees, $140 million, and a five-year run at countering Axis influence in Latin America through an all-out propaganda effort. As the Coordinator of this operation at the age of thirty-two, Nelson was set unswervingly on his career course of public office. He came to Washington with the inevitable aura of a lightweight because of his youth and background, but he left with a reputation as an imaginative thinker and aggressive leader.

As much as he might swell with pride as he surveyed these oil paintings of his progeny, Junior also knew at war's end that it was time to concern himself with the orderly transfer of resources and final disposition of his affairs. He was now past the age of seventy. He wanted to help his sons as they developed their postwar careers, and yet not help them too much. Despite their good wartime records, Junior still needed assurance that his sons, on their own abilities and initiatives, would become leaders in civilian life and worthy stewards of family wealth. He had been in the dominant and controlling role in both family and office affairs for so long that it was no easy matter for him to step aside. Therefore, most of the subsequent decisions he made that affected his relatives seemed to have been taken with a good deal of reluctance, often hemmed in with constraints and conditions that were acceptable to his sons at the time—they didn't have much choice—but were almost certain to cause confusion and trouble among them at a much later time.

In 1948 came the devastating loss of Abby. At the age of seventy-three, she was in the forty-seventh year of her marriage at the time of her death. As JDR 3rd expressed it in his diary, she died of "a tired heart," a condition that had concerned the family for a number of years.[1] Abby had been much loved by her husband and children, but the ensuing loneliness made the loss all the more poignant for Junior.

Junior's recognition of the need to consolidate activities and begin passing the mantle to his sons was not diverted by Abby's death, but perhaps intensified by it. He made more gifts to his heirs, and in 1952 he devoted $42 million to establishing a new series of trusts, one for each of the children of four of his sons (John, Nelson, Laurance, and David). The income from these trusts (known as the 1952 or Fidelity Union trusts) was to go to the father until the children were adjudged to be of age. And Junior began to narrow down his own focus for philanthropic giving, concentrating mainly on religion, historical preservation, and conservation.

Junior also worked out a plan for the sale of Rockefeller Center to his five sons, based on the appraised value of $2.21 million. The sale was a pivotal event in family history. In one sense, this midtown complex of a dozen varied office and theater buildings sheathed in Indiana limestone was a huge success, hailed the world over as a great innovation in urban design. And over time it was to become a great financial success as well, in fact the salvation of the family fortune, as we shall see. But when Junior sold the Center to his sons in 1948 at what seems to have been a ridiculously low price, its financial base was by no means secure.

For one thing, the Center faced an expenditure of millions to install two new technologies, fluorescent lighting and air-conditioning, required if it were to compete with new buildings in the postwar boom in New York City. Some of the major clients, including Time, Inc., Esso (Standard of New Jersey), and NBC, were threatening to move, having outgrown their space. The Center had been operating in the black for only a few years, and it carried substantial debt. Most limiting of all, the Center was built on land owned by Columbia University, and the lease provided that no portion of the Center could be sold outside of the Rockefeller family without the university's permission. Since Columbia was not about to grant this, the marketability of Rockefeller Center was severely limited.

The fact that the Center needed very careful and yet aggressive management to thread its way through all these hazards to the financial success that seemed deserved was another reason it made good sense to pass ownership to the brothers. Nelson had won his struggle before the war and had emerged as the president of Rockefeller Center. Brother Laurance, as usual, was right at his side as a member of the finance committee. They had performed well before each went off to wartime assignments. Now they were back, Nelson as chairman and Laurance as chairman of the finance committee. They were bringing in handpicked professional managers, and were readying plans to move the Center forward. The other three brothers contributed ideas and support, but in the main were content to let Nelson and Laurance run the show.

Finally, Junior's advisers had made it clear that if he were to die before divesting himself of the Center, his estate would be seriously encumbered. One element was the fact that the Center still owed Junior $75 million in 1947 (this was actual debt—monies advanced by Junior to Rockefeller Center over the years as distinct from the book value of the stock he held).

Nelson tried to talk his father into forgiving the debt, which certainly would have been good for the balance sheet of Rockefeller Center and the managerial task that Nelson and Laurance faced. Junior declined—a debt was a debt, and moreover such a transaction probably would have been viewed as a gift requiring the payment of gift tax. But several years later, Junior did make a gift of the note (now whittled down to $57.5 million) to the Rockefeller Brothers Fund. Because this was a tax-exempt foundation, no gift tax was required; the move also removed the debt as a factor in Junior's estate. And it offered Junior once again a way to signify his strong support of philanthropic activity and his approval of his sons in this regard. Up to this point, the Fund had been operating on the basis of annual gifts made to it by the brothers, which meant that its program was very limited. With Junior's gift the Fund became a more formidable philanthropic instrument and was started on its way to the upper ranks of American foundations.

The sale of Rockefeller Center by Junior to his five sons meant that each ended up owning one-fifth of Rockefeller Center for an expenditure of only $442,000 each, a value that was to increase many hundreds of times over the next forty years. As a result of the sale, the brothers also enjoyed the enhanced status of their philanthropic instrument *and* a potential tax deduction of $10.6 million each [2]

There remained one major family property to be considered in the generational transition—the Pocantico estate. Junior so loved Kykuit and the pastoral setting of his beautiful Westchester County enclave that he hated the thought of parting company with them. But by 1952 he had reluctantly come to agree with his advisers that the only sensible course was to sell the property to his sons. Again, if he died before transferring ownership, the estate taxes would be murderous. So it was that the Rockefeller boys became the owners of Pocantico at another seemingly low cost, $760,295. Again there were reasons why the valuation was low— Junior's retention of life tenancy and the restriction in the deeds that the brothers could sell only to each other. For all practical purposes, the estate was still Junior's as long as he lived—he paid the bills and made the decisions.[3]

With this transaction and more financial gifts to several of his sons, Junior completed all he was going to do in his lifetime in the process of transferring resources to his heirs that he had started in 1934. He still retained a fortune of more than $200 million, plenty to continue his favorite philanthropies, especially his beloved Colonial Williamsburg. The final disposition of what remained at the time of his death would be accomplished through his last will and testament. He had made all of his children wealthy through the 1934 Trusts, but he had expressed his values in the pattern of his gifts since then. As the oldest son and the one who most thoroughly embraced his father's values regarding wealth, John 3rd had received the most. Not appreciably far behind were Nelson, Laurance, and David, all treated about equally. Then came Winthrop, well off, but substantially behind his brothers because his father always seemed to be waiting to see if Winthrop would overcome what he regarded as his son's bad habits. They were never estranged to the degree that Junior and Babs were; she came in last by a substantial margin in the financial sweepstakes, though well taken care of for life by her 1934 Trust. The final irritation that held Junior back from giving her more gifts was that, from his point of view, she did not take a sufficient interest in philanthropy. He could easily conclude that she preferred to pay heavy taxes rather than give money away, just to spite her father. This judgment may be harsh, but the fact remains that Babs showed more interest in giving *after* her father died than while he was living.[4]

The gulf between Junior and his only daughter was so wide that she was in no position to ease his acute loneliness after the death of his wife. Junior always seemed to prefer feminine companionship, having grown up in a family with three sisters and no brothers. It fell to his daughters-in-law to try to fill this need, especially the two oldest, John's wife, Blanchette, and Nelson's wife, Mary. These two fast friends spent weeks with Junior in Seal Harbor or at his Williamsburg house, Bassett Hall.

However, Junior soon surprised everyone with the announcement that he planned to remarry. His second wife was to be Martha Baird Allen, the widow of Junior's college classmate, the lawyer Arthur M. Allen of Providence, Rhode Island. With John 3rd serving as best man, the ceremony took place in the bride's home in Providence in August 1951. The new wife was a woman of charm and distinction, having been a concert pianist before her first marriage. She was warm and gracious in her relations with the family, serving to ease any tensions that might have risen over Junior's remarrying. And Martha gave Junior the companionship he needed in his waning years.

The year 1952 was a turning point for the five Rockefeller brothers quite beyond the several decisions their father made in passing on financial resources and property to them. It was a time also for an important milestone in the life and career direction of each brother.

For David, the event was promotion to senior vice president of the Chase Bank. He had joined the bank led by his uncle, Winthrop Aldrich, in 1946, working in the foreign department. Now his responsibilities included all the New York area branches and the economic research department. He was soon to be a central figure in negotiations for the Bank of Manhattan merger (leading to the present name of the Chase) and in the bold decision to locate new corporate headquarters in troubled downtown New York, leading to revival of the area. His career directions were now set at the age of thirty-seven—prominence in the banking industry and a strong international presence.

The key 1952 event for Laurance was the purchase of Caneel Bay on the island of St. John in the U.S. Virgins, a beautiful 600-acre area of coves, promontories, and beaches where Laurance proceeded to build his idealized version of a tropical resort. The purchase ended a search of several years by Laurance and his wife, Mary, who had fallen in love with the Caribbean. It also marked the beginning of what eventually became Rock Resorts, Inc., the company through which Laurance developed other top-of-the-scale resort properties to show how it should be done. And it led within a few years to the creation of Virgin Islands National Park on St. John, a major step in Laurance's conservation work.[5]

Laurance was vigorously following in his father's footsteps as a conservationist, and was to become nationally known for it. His other major interest was in investments; in 1946 he had formed Rockefeller Brothers, Inc., as a venture capital firm with the five brothers serving as general partners and a staff of six professionals, including men Laurance had come to know during his wartime service. Laurance was by far the most active investor among the brothers, continuing his interest in aeronautics and other high-technology fields.

Winthrop's life changed drastically in 1952 when he visited his army buddy Frank Newell in Arkansas. The reason was to establish legal residency in a state that was more favorable than New York for Winthrop's purpose of divorcing his wife of four years, Barbara "Bobo" Sears Rockefeller. Far beyond the immediate purpose, the significance of the visit was that Winthrop decided to relocate permanently to Arkansas after discovering Petit Jean Mountain, a rugged plateau near the Arkansas River some sixty miles north of Little Rock. Winthrop purchased the site, envisioning his own version of Pocantico there, one that would be a working ranch.

Winthrop's father had hoped that family life would help his most difficult son settle down, but the marriage to Bobo on Valentine's Day 1948 in Palm Beach, Florida, did not augur well. It was a surprise affair, almost an elopement, with brother Laurance the only other family member in attendance. The bride was pregnant; a son, Winthrop Paul, was born seven months later. She was an aspiring actress under the stage name Eva Paul, but had been born Jievute Paulekiute, the daughter of Lithuanian immigrants in a Pennsylvania coal town. What most concerned Junior was the fact that the bride was a divorcée; her first husband, Richard Sears, was the scion of a prominent Boston family. Still, Junior hoped the match might work; almost predictably, it did not. The stormy fights, the drinking bouts, Winthrop locking Bobo out of their Manhattan apartment—all were grist for the New York tabloid press. When Winthrop repaired to Arkansas for the divorce, Bobo was demanding a $10 million settlement.

The move to Arkansas was more than a radical change of scenery for Winthrop; it smacked of a flight from a troubled past and a chance to start over again in trying to find a meaningful path in life.

Nelson's career choice in 1952 seemed more like another step in a preordained path—a return to public life. His was one of the early appointments of the newly elected President of the United States, Dwight D. Eisenhower. Nelson was named chairman of the President's Advisory Committee on Government Reorganization. It was to be an important assignment; after an absence of sixteen years from the White House, the Republicans were very serious about reorganizing federal agencies to their liking.[6]

Having been seen as something of a brash young man when he had first come to Washington as the wartime Coordinator of Inter-American Affairs, Nelson, at the age of forty-four, was now a veteran in the ways of the national capital. He had spent part of 1945 as Assistant Secretary for Latin American Affairs in the Department of State before his nonconformist policies led to his ouster.[7] As a private citizen back in the family office, Nelson's main preoccupation was economic development of Latin American countries. He created a foundation known as the AIA (American International Association for Economic and Social Development), which subsequently spun off a profit-making company, the International Basic

Economy Corporation (IBEC). The purpose of the latter was to demonstrate that capitalism could work in aiding the economies of underdeveloped countries.

It was this early concern for the lesser-developed nations that brought Nelson to the attention of President Truman. Nelson, in fact, was indirectly responsible for the "Point Four" section of the President's 1949 inaugural address in which he called for a program of aiding underdeveloped countries that would parallel the Marshall Plan's role in rebuilding the war-ravaged economies of Europe.[8] Having once fired Nelson from the State Department, Truman in 1950 appointed him as chairman of the new fourteen-member International Development Advisory Board to propose ways of bringing the Point Four idea into operation. Again Nelson was a maverick in pressing for a foreign aid agency independent of the State Department. He was defeated by the opposition of W. Averell Harriman and other Truman administration foreign affairs leaders; the aid program was constituted within the department and Nelson resigned his post.[9]

Now, back in Washington with the Eisenhower administration, Nelson exacted a measure of revenge against the State Department. Two of his reorganization plans took functions outside of State and set them up in independent agencies—the U.S. Information Agency (USIA) and the Foreign Operations Administration (FOA).[10] Another important reorganization plan brought a number of agencies and functions together within a new cabinet department, the Department of Health, Education and Welfare (HEW). This was a struggle because conservative Republicans feared the new agency would be too expensive and they disliked the way that it served to institutionalize such New Deal innovations as Social Security. The new Secretary of HEW, Oveta Culp Hobby, was so pleased with Nelson's work in creating the agency against strong opposition that she asked to have him as her Under Secretary. After a year devoted to helping Mrs. Hobby get the giant new department into working shape, Nelson moved on again, this time to the White House to succeed C. D. Jackson, former publisher of *Time* magazine, as President Eisenhower's special assistant on "psychological strategy." This was an ambiguous role at a time when the federal structure for foreign affairs was undergoing revision under the dominating influence of John Foster Dulles, the new Secretary of State. Nelson soon found himself once again in opposition to State's hierarchy and distant from the President despite his White House base, so in 1955 he resigned to return to New York.[11]

Nelson's six federal assignments under three successive Presidents constituted an extraordinary learning experience. One can never know when the idea of running for office enters someone's mind, much less seeking the Presidency. There are those who would believe that Nelson Rockefeller was not long out of diapers before the thought occurred to him. But in 1955 one thing was certain: Nelson was convinced that he would accomplish a great deal more in public life by being elected to office rather than appointed. His status as a private citizen would last only as long as it took him to find the right opportunity.

For the eldest Rockefeller brother, 1952 was a year marked not by a single decisive event in his career direction but by a whole series of events. It was in fact his year of liberation, a radical departure from his past, in which he undertook bold initiatives that ushered in a remarkable decade of institution-building.

John 3rd had suffered through a long and unsatisfying apprenticeship in his father's office throughout the 1930s, a member of many boards and committees, but always in a subordinate role, never able to shine or manage or control anything. Inhibited by his natural reserve and shyness, JDR 3rd came to believe that he was tolerated by the senior men clustered around his father only because he was the oldest son with *the* name, not because he had accomplished anything or proven himself in any independent way.

This situation was so depressing that at one point JDR came close to a nervous breakdown, as his father and grandfather had before him, barely able to come into the office or appear in public for a period of months.[12] He pulled through it with the understanding and support of his wife, the former Blanchette Ferry Hooker. Their wedding in 1932 had been a major social event, he the eldest Rockefeller boy and reputed heir to billions and she the tall, raven-haired daughter of a well-to-do and prominent family. Blanchette herself was socially at ease, but she was intelligent and sensitive enough to understand her husband's problems. The immediate family— Blanchette and the children—provided the only safe haven from a world that was inexplicably trying and difficult for John 3rd.

As was true for so many others, wartime military service marked the beginning of liberation for John 3rd—in his case, from the confines of his prewar work situation and the domineering influence of his father. In the navy he found he could work well with others and that he was regarded more for what he could do than for the fact that his name was Rockefeller. He learned a good deal about policy-making and bureaucratic struggles within and among large organizations. The planning for the postwar era that he was engaged in was a powerful stimulant to his own thinking, and there are long passages in his diary in which he speculates about the future.

For the most part, his views were prescient. For example, well before the term "Cold War" was in vogue JDR foresaw a dangerous rivalry with the Soviet Union and predicted that military preparedness and "political-military affairs" would dominate U.S. international relations for perhaps as much as the next fifty years. The most difficult problem would be the "ideological conflict" between the democracies and the Communist countries. JDR thought the United Nations would be a useful and hopeful organization, even though he expected that it would be immobilized much of the time by big-power rivalry. He also foresaw that independence for former colonial territories and economic development for these new countries would be major concerns.

JDR's somewhat gloomy overall conclusion was accurate—that the postwar era would be burdened with a great many problems of extraordinary difficulty, both domestic and international, and that governments would be hard-pressed to cope with them. Many of these problems, he wrote, "will be more difficult of solution than those of the war years." Two conclusions followed in JDR's mind: (1) there was a need to encourage highly capable people to take up government service as a career, and (2) private citizens and organizations should do everything they could to help resolve the problems, including cooperation with government.

From these analyses, JDR's own career choices flowed naturally, with much greater clarity than before the war. An immediate conclusion was that the Rockefeller Foundation should be in the forefront of efforts to solve problems in the postwar world. The Foundation had always emphasized international projects in line with the views of its founder and had gained an enviable worldwide reputation for the quality and success of its work in such fields as the physical sciences, medicine, and public health. JDR had been a board member since 1933, a very circumspect and junior member, but it was an unspoken assumption in the minds of virtually everyone involved in the Foundation that he would one day become its chairman. JDR thus envisioned this as one of his main bases for important work to be done in the postwar world.

A second conclusion pertained to Colonial Williamsburg, the total restoration of Virginia's colonial capital that had become Junior's passion in life in the years after work first began in 1926. He had already expended more than $30 million on this project and much more remained to be done. JDR was working closely with his father on the restoration and was due to succeed him as chairman. The connection to postwar needs in JDR's mind was that he had come to see Williamsburg as the perfect place for mounting a program of education and inspiration in the interest of promoting democracy as a political philosophy.

JDR believed strongly that Americans knew well what they were *against*—Nazism, communism, any totalitarian system—but were not so good at understanding and articulating what they were *for*, i.e., freedom, democracy, an open society. It was highly characteristic of JDR to approach an ideological struggle in a positive way—to promote democracy rather than simply decry communism.

Thus, two of JDR's major postwar career intentions involved organizations in which he was positioned to play a leading role—the Rockefeller Foundation and Colonial Williamsburg. The third major interest—the worldwide problem of excessive population growth—had no such organizational locus. JDR never could explain exactly why he had developed such a strong interest in the population field long before it came into vogue or was generally recognized as an area of concern. He had seen the negative effects of too much population growth in his visit to China in 1929. He had chosen population as the subject for a reading course he took at Princeton, where he studied the works of Malthus and others. He had served on the board of an organization his father had created, the Bureau of Social Hygiene, which had supported a number of projects related to the population field, including aid to the clinics of the intrepid birth control pioneer Margaret Sanger.

In fact, it was Junior's decision to terminate the Bureau that led his oldest son to volunteer to make the population field a major focus of his interest and to do what he could to carry on the work. In a letter to his father in 1934, he expressed concern that the support of population studies and projects would not be picked up by any of the other Rockefeller organizations, including the Foundation, because of "the element of propaganda and controversy which so often is attached to endeavors in birth control." JDR wrote: "I have come pretty definitely to the conclusion that [birth control] is the field in which I will be interested, for the present at least, to concentrate my own giving, as I feel it is so fundamental and underlying."[13]

For a decade, JDR was only able to play a minor role, making occasional small contributions to population projects. But now, at war's end, he saw the importance of the field as considerably heightened, and he wrote of "a logical broadening of my interest in the birth control problem." He had come to believe that the study and regulation of population was critical to "future world stability." In this, he was still ahead of his time. Awareness of the importance of the effects of population growth, especially in the underdeveloped world, was slowly growing in the immediate post-war years. But, in the meantime, JDR was frustrated in finding any meaningful way to become involved.

JDR's frustration was much more acute in the case of the Rockefeller Foundation (RF). Even before leaving the navy, JDR began pressing Raymond Fosdick, president of the RF, to begin a review to restructure the Foundation for its postwar role. In particular, JDR believed that the RF should be reorganized, that coordination among programs should be improved, and that the emphasis should shift from aiding European institutions to a focus on the "poor" countries of the world and the needs of development.

These ideas were greeted as a power play by the old guard of the RF, and JDR was thoroughly rebuffed. Although undeniably a great institution for its accomplishments over the years, the RF had become rigidified. It was organized like a university, that is, according to the major branches of knowledge, and the senior staff in each branch guarded its turf as zealously as a Chinese warlord. JDR was the only trustee born in the twentieth century, and most of the elderly gentlemen on the board liked the RF just the way it was. Contrary to popular impression, the RF was independent of the Rockefeller family. In his long tenure with the RF, Junior had cultivated this in every way he could. JDR was certainly aware of the prevailing ethos, but underestimated it, failing to realize that for a long time any initiative coming from him, the son and heir apparent, would not be dealt with on its merits but would be regarded with suspicion.

After several agonizing years of struggle, JDR fully learned this lesson. He realized it meant that the RF could never be the base of operations for him that he had once envisioned. It would still be important to him, but only in the long-term, as he outlasted the old guard, and even then only through the gentle arts of persuasion, not steamroller tactics.

With the population field and the RF holding nothing but frustration for him in the immediate postwar years, JDR turned his energies to his third major idea, that of a program of education about democracy based at Colonial Williamsburg. Here he was due for frustration of an even more agonizing kind. Although the problem began with money, the agony for JDR came from a breach with his father and a sense of betrayal.

Although Williamsburg was generating income from tourism and showed its first small operating profit in 1949, the needs of historical restoration kept mounting. JDR knew that this was his father's passion and the staff's priority, and so he donated the money himself for development of the educational program. He hired several consultants, extensive study and survey trips were made abroad, and elaborate plans were drawn up.

In his long-term view, the restoration would one day be completed and its income would partly support the education program. In several long conversations with his father and in board meetings, JDR believed he had endorsement of this in principle from everyone concerned.

Early in 1952 the breach occurred. The education program had stalled, and it is quite possible that JDR, in any case, had come to realize that it was not a viable idea. But what embittered him was the sudden revelation that his father had lost faith in him and that expressions of support for his ideas had been made only to humor him. Junior, who was nearing eighty years of age, feared that he would not live long enough to see the restoration work completed the way he envisioned it. And he now feared that his son would not carry out this trust, but would divert funds to support his own ideas. JDR believed that Kenneth Chorley, president of Colonial Williamsburg, had egged his father on in these concerns.

Father and son did their best to paper over the breach. Junior wrote an uncharacteristically candid and remorseful letter to his son: "Clearly, I have not kept my part of the agreement . . . I realize more and more that, try as I may, I cannot wholly divorce myself from any aspect of the Restoration." He wrote this "because they say confession is good for the soul."[14] But JDR's dream was clearly over. He took a leave of absence from the board and, at the end of 1952, he resigned.

Negative results in all three of his major areas of interest certainly seemed like a recipe for severe depression for JDR. But exactly the opposite occurred. Ironically, the conflict at Williamsburg had two positive effects. The first was the final act of liberation from his father's shadow. JDR now fully realized that success for him could not come from following through on any of his father's major projects. He would have to develop his own successes. The second benefit was that JDR's interest in cultural and informational programs manifested at Williamsburg was what led John Foster Dulles to offer him a role in the Japanese peace treaty negotiations.

This involvement was a tonic for JDR, and the first positive effects became evident in 1952—the revival of the Japan Society; the early work leading to the establishment of a major new institution in Japan, the International House of Tokyo; and a series of cultural exchange programs that JDR sponsored. He was well launched in his lifelong fascination and preoccupation with Japan and the Far East.

At the same time, JDR realized that he had finally reached a situation in which he could undertake significant initiatives without reference to his father. His own net worth had reached the point where he could fund new projects and organizations himself. He now had two able aides to help him. Edgar B. Young, a practiced administrator, had come from the

Rockefeller Brothers Fund to be JDR's first personal staff associate. And, to work on his Japan projects, JDR hired Donald McLean, Jr., a former army captain he had first met in Washington during the war.

Furthermore, patience finally began to pay with respect to the Rockefeller Foundation. Members of the old guard had been gradually retiring from the board and staff, and younger men more congenial to JDR's views had replaced them. In June 1952 another man JDR had met in wartime, Dean Rusk, resigned from the State Department to accept the position of president of the Foundation. In November 1952, John Foster Dulles resigned as chairman of the RF because of his selection by the newly elected Dwight D. Eisenhower to become Secretary of State in the new administration. At the annual meeting of the RF in December, JDR was elected chairman to succeed Dulles.[15]

Most important, JDR was psychologically free from his father's influence and some ideas that had proven illusory. He was ready to become highly active as a full-time philanthropist. His first target was to make something happen in the population field.

II

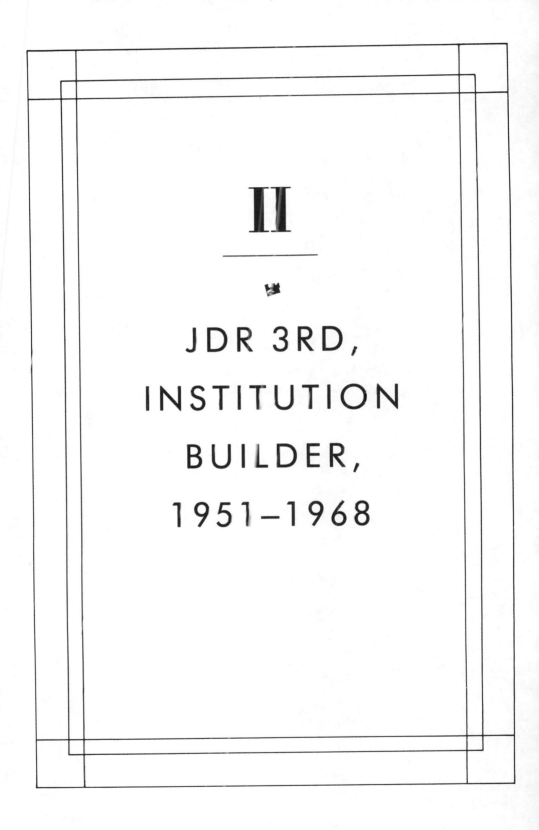

JDR 3RD, INSTITUTION BUILDER, 1951–1968

3

THE POPULATION COUNCIL

AMONG the qualities much to be desired by anyone who attempts bold new initiatives, one of the more obvious is a good sense of timing. Certainly more an art than a science, it calls for astute judgment, an ability to perceive trends, a willingness to take risks—and a good deal of luck. In these respects, JDR's ability to make decisions had improved markedly by 1952. In all the major initiatives he launched then and in the years immediately following, he displayed excellent timing.

For example, one might have thought that half a dozen years after World War II American sensitivity over Japanese behavior in wartime would still be strong enough to make a chilly atmosphere for JDR's projects aiming at friendship and help for Japan. But the altered political situation in the Far East and the general fair-mindedness of Americans made the timing exactly right. JDR was not premature in his Japanese activities: he was merely early, in fact, *first* among civilian leaders in taking such an interest, and that gave him a special kind of preeminence in Japanese affairs that never waned during his lifetime.

So it was with the population field. One could find persuasive reasons why 1952 was not a good time to attempt something new. The field was disorganized and there had been no breakthrough in the development of effective contraceptives. There seemed to be little or no interest in population control where it counted the most—among leaders of the densely populated developing countries.

Here and there, one heard ominous warnings about the effects of overpopulation. Julian Huxley, the first head of UNESCO, said: "War is a less inevitable threat to civilization than is population increase." Among the more radical voices calling for population control were individuals concerned about the conservation of natural resources.[1] But these views only served to make the whole subject more controversial than usual. The opposition of the Catholic Church became more vocal. The Communist bloc, led by the Soviet Union, was ideologically against population measures based on the Marxian tenet that the real problem was maldistribution of wealth due to capitalism, not surplus population. The complementarity of the predominantly Catholic countries and the Communist bloc on this issue was a formidable barrier to action by the United Nations.

Nevertheless, as subsequent events abundantly demonstrated, the timing proved to be perfect for a major new initiative by JDR.

Why did he choose this moment to act? There are several possible reasons. One was his bitter disappointment over the end of his dreams for a major program at Colonial Williamsburg; a natural reaction would be to busy himself in other directions, as he was already doing in his Japanese projects. And he had tested the possibility of a more active population program at the Rockefeller Foundation beyond the relatively safe research efforts it had long supported in such areas as demography, endocrinology, and sexual behavior. The major effort in this regard was a mission to the Far East in 1948 to study population problems within the context of a review of the RF's International Health Division. Two of the principals in the study were Marshall Balfour (the RF's representative in India), and Frank Notestein, a leading demographer whose Office of Population Research at Princeton enjoyed substantial RF support. The resulting "Balfour Report" stressed that the pressure of increasing population growth was mounting in the Far East and that the complex interweaving of causative factors could not be easily understood or changed. The report made a strong case for increased attention and study. JDR tried several times in succeeding years to encourage some sort of action based on the report, realizing finally that the RF was inherently too cautious to take on such a controversial field.

This created a kind of vacuum; if there was to be a bold new initiative in population, there seemed no alternative to JDR having to undertake it himself.

Finally, evidence was beginning to emerge that provided some basis for the Cassandra-like warnings being issued by Huxley and others. In part, this was due to the steady progress that had been made in developing the science of demographics over the preceding twenty years. The evidence showed that a historic change was occurring in the world as the result of birth rates increasing in less-developed countries while death rates were decreasing drastically. These were the first glimmerings of what soon would be referred to as "the population explosion." JDR was attuned

KPMG Peat Marwick

from the desk of
Mary A. Murphy

Cards

Megan

St. Patrick

A-EILEA Evelyn - Irving +

KIDS

STAMPS

Library

TRAVEL Bureau

GIFT CERT.

$$59.99 - \frac{1}{4}$$

14.9

59.99

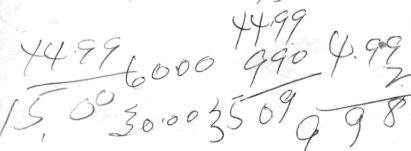

25
20
——
45

44.99
———
15.00 6000
       30.00

44.99
990
———
35.09

4.99
7.
——
998

45.00 1
5
———
5 00

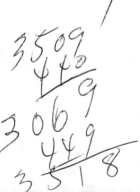

3509
448
———
9

306
449
———
3518

to this in part through his own instincts, but also through his association
with Balfour and Notestein. Another adviser was Fred Osborn, a remarkable man who had worked with JDR's father in conservation projects.
Osborn had fulfilled his ambition by making enough money on Wall Street
to retire in the late 1920s (at age forty) and devote himself to his first
love, science; he had been a strong supporter of demographic studies and
population control ever since.

Two conversations late in 1951 set JDR on the path to taking decisive
steps. The first, according to Don McLean, his new staff aide, occurred
in November when JDR ran into Lewis Strauss in the men's room on the
fifty-sixth floor. Strauss had been brought into the family office at
Laurance's suggestion to head up the investments unit. A former rear
admiral and member of the investment banking firm of Kuhn, Loeb,
Strauss had made himself a knowledgeable person about the state of the
physical sciences during his career, an interest buttressed by his most
recent experience as a member of the Atomic Energy Commission. Knowing of JDR's interest in the population field, Strauss commented to him
that few of the leading scientists in the United States seemed to have
given much thought to the population problem. He offered the suggestion
of convening a conference of scientists to acquaint them with the facts and
seek their counsel.

At JDR's request, McLean discussed the Strauss idea with Frank
Notestein, Osborn, and others. As a result, JDR held a dinner meeting
on December 9, which Strauss attended with Warren Weaver, head of the
Natural Sciences and Agriculture Division of the Rockefeller Foundation,
and Detlev Bronk, a noted scientist who was due to become a president
of Rockefeller University. When these men endorsed the idea of a conference, JDR was ready to act. As president of the National Academy of
Sciences, Bronk agreed to lead the conference under the Academy's auspices and JDR agreed to pay the bills.

To organize the conference, McLean enlisted the aid of Robert Bates,
a staff member of the Rockefeller Brothers Fund, and of Notestein's Office
of Population Research at Princeton. The group was scheduled to meet
June 20–22, 1951, at Colonial Williamsburg. Two of Notestein's associates,
Irene Taeuber and John Hajnal, were detailed to assemble the documentation for the Conference on Population Problems, as it was called, selecting
papers that stressed the "demographic transition" and the impending crisis
of world overpopulation. Hajnal, a young British demographer who had
just completed his doctorate at Princeton, also wrote an introductory
paper.[2]

Of the thirty-three participants, twenty-one were scientists. They spanned a wide range of disciplines—medicine, chemistry, physics, public health, sociology, geology, botany, economics. They came from universities, the U.S. government, and the United Nations. Among them were several past and future Nobel Prize–winners. The activists of the population field were kept to a minimum: William Vogt and Paul Henshaw of Planned Parenthood and Fairfield Osborn of the Conservation Foundation. Others who attended were from JDR's circle: Strauss, McLean, Fred Osborn, Bates, Dana Creel of the Rockefeller Brothers Fund, and Martha Dalrymple of the family public relations office. From Princeton came Notestein, Taeuber, and Hajnal; from the Rockefeller Foundation, Weaver, Marshall Balfour, and two trustees, Karl Compton, chairman of The Massachusetts Institute of Technology, and Thomas Parran, dean of public health at the University of Pittsburgh and former Surgeon General of the United States.[3]

Bronk or Notestein presided over this mixed group for the six sessions of the conference. The discussions took up food supply, industrial development, depletion of natural resources, and the dangers of political instability resulting from unchecked population growth. The transcript shows that Strauss's idea worked—scientists previously unacquainted with the population problem were now expressing concern. The activists voiced a sense of urgency, while conservatives such as Warren Weaver and Karl Compton saw solutions coming from a variety of means and methods, not a strict focus on population control. In the end there was agreement that not enough was known about rates of population growth in most parts of the world, the cultural determinants of fertility, or even the biochemical factors prerequisite to improved contraceptive technology. Well-conceived programs of study were needed.

Before the final session, Strauss worked with Notestein and McLean on the text of a resolution. It proposed that the chairman appoint a temporary committee to consider

the steps to be taken to bring about a high level . . . international council on a permanent basis, the future of that council to be to assess the facts as to the populations of the world, and the resources, cultural and material, available to give such populations a progressively improving living standard; to consider whether and to what extent these populations and resources are in balance, how such balance can be secured and maintained on a short- and long-range basis, and generally to acquaint the public with its findings and recommendations.[4]

The final session was given over to a discussion of the resolution. It was unanimously adopted, it appears, although no formal vote was taken.

To follow through, Bronk, as presiding officer, appointed a committee composed of JDR, Fred Osborn, and Notestein.

It was a fuzzy mandate, as evidenced by the contents of a second resolution passed at the Williamsburg conference, which authorized the temporary committee "to modify the basic resolution as appropriate." The verbiage amounted to a license for JDR to do pretty much as he liked. Of course, just as he did not need the authorization of the conference to take action, so no one could have objected if he had taken no action at all. But the conference had served the purpose of beginning to build a consensus on the need for population measures. A bid to do something had been uttered, and it came from a respected and influential group of people. Yet the effect on JDR's close advisers was to make them suddenly very cautious.

McLean wrote two long memoranda on July 28. The first interpreted the resolution to envisage a body that would deal with information, not action programs, and the term "international council" to mean a group that would convene once a year, literally to give counsel; it might comprise a hundred eminent persons drawn from countries around the world.

In the second memo, McLean discussed the question of JDR's participation in a variety of ways ranking from informal to formal. McLean recommended that JDR work on population "through the facilities of the Rockefeller Foundation." Though JDR was not yet chairman of the board, McLean knew that the situation seemed much improved there with Dean Rusk newly installed as president. McLean argued that if JDR did not work with the Foundation, he would run the risk of duplicating its efforts; this would be expensive and would cause friction. When the Foundation would not do something JDR wanted, he could finance the activity on his own, the right hand at least knowing what the left could not do.

As for "independent programs"—at the other end of McLean's spectrum—"there would be clear advantages to a corporation with a consequential staff" if JDR were willing to invest substantial sums in direct research. But, said McLean, "I gather you are not prepared to devote that kind of money to this project and I doubt that it could be raised from other sources. Therefore, I would suggest informality . . . at this stage." In concluding, McLean came down hard against "a corporate focal point" with a "high level" board:

. . . I personally feel that this is not the way to approach the population problem. Within the United States, for example, and elsewhere there is strong opposition . . . to birth control. This, it seems to me, should be recognized as a fact. It should be accepted as one of the problems in the area. I do not feel that a serious effort should be made to fight the problem. I think that the real effort should be made in learning more about the problem through research and the use of existing knowledge without becoming involved in political wrangles which, in my judgment, will prove very little until more is known. A corporate structure is not essential to action. It may be a deterrent.

As he soon learned, McLean was out of step with his boss on all these assessments. Quite possibly, McLean did not understand the situation at the Foundation; JDR had become so circumspect about his role there that he did not use his staff on Foundation matters or even keep them informed (as other trustees routinely did), save for the rare occasion when he deemed there was some direct and legitimate reason to do so. For the rest of his career, JDR's staff was generally in the dark about what was going on within the Foundation. Also, JDR *was* willing to spend money and face up to the controversial aspects of population.

McLean circulated his memoranda to other advisers for comment before sending them to JDR. Only those who were strong advocates of action—Balfour and Notestein—disagreed with McLean's advice. Balfour wanted an organization that would work on what he regarded as the heart of the problem—human fertility and its control. Notestein told McLean that conferences do not "prove very much and that what was really needed was some action." He also implied that McLean "was somewhat naive in feeling that the Rockefeller Foundation might do something about the population growth phases of this thing."[5]

The head of the family public relations office, Frank Jamieson, was a strong voice on the conservative side. He had been brought in to his job by Nelson Rockefeller, and he was chiefly concerned about protecting Nelson's political future from any unnecessary controversy. Jamieson wrote to JDR that he agreed completely with McLean, citing "potential political headaches."[6] Others, such as Lockwood, Creel, Bates, Strauss, and Dalrymple, also expressed caution, although Dalrymple best sensed JDR's own view in saying that if he were to go into the population field he should do it wholeheartedly, as a "vocation and not to 'play with it' as if it were one of his various avocations."[7] She believed his "capabilities would justify his full-time activity in this regard."

When JDR returned from a summer vacation in Europe with his family, it became clear that he was disposed to act. The only point of McLean's that he agreed with was the need for close coordination with the Foundation. The two men met with Rusk and Weaver in a long conference on September 4 that was dominated by Weaver, who set up criteria so stringent that he seemed to want to discourage JDR from involvement. Weaver said that a new organization to deal with population needed a budget of at least $500,000 a year for ten years, and that it should focus on the most difficult and controversial problem—human fertility and contraceptive research.

JDR on the contrary believed in working on all main aspects of population, to which Weaver rejoined that the work would suffer, the field being complex; no effort could take in everything. He stressed fertility research because that was the subject everybody else would avoid. It was vital, Weaver added, that board and staff should be of the highest quality, but he doubted that such people could be found for this new and controversial field. No less imperative, Weaver and Rusk agreed, was to make a clear distinction between a new organization and the Foundation. At the end of McLean's long report on the meeting, he wrote that it was clear

that the Foundation will not actively pursue research in human fertility, that it regards this as an important field and that if John decides to pursue it it hopes that everything will be done to avoid confusion in the minds of the outside world between his venture and the less controversial activities of the Rockefeller Foundation.[8]

Following the meeting, JDR, weekending at Fieldwood Farm, pondered his longtime concern with population and what he had learned most recently, and came to some decisions. It was time to make a move; he would form a new organization. It would take up all the issues, including the controversial. JDR drew up a list headed "Opportunities in the Broad Field of Population." It was a prescient statement of things to come:

1. Basic research relating to human fertility and the physiology of reproduction.
2. Development of a more effective, cheap and simple contraceptive, having in mind particularly the people of underdeveloped areas.
3. Studies concerning the motivational patterns relating to family size, and factors influencing them.
4. Assistance to improve the technical quality and effectiveness of selected operating programs or clinics in countries with acute population pressures.
5. An educational program.
6. Studies as to the consequences which would result from the finding of an ideal contraceptive.
7. Assistance to countries with population problems in the development of interest, research, and personnel in the population field. Such assistance might take the form of grants to institutions working in the field, fellowships to assist individuals, and the making available of scientists and technical knowledge from abroad.
8. A study of the United States population situation with the objective of obtaining information which would make long-range planning possible.[9]

Two topics on JDR's agenda were so controversial that no one was seriously proposing them at the time—technical assistance in population activities for underdeveloped countries and a national study of population in the United States. However, he had developed the principal agenda that the population field and the still unnamed Population Council would pursue for the next generation.

JDR presented the list to his advisers on September 9—Strauss, Creel, Bates, McLean, Jamieson, Lockwood, Dalrymple—and received cautious advice in return. McLean's account of the meeting tells it all:

Mr. Lockwood pointed out the importance of studying the consequences of anything which might result from research of the nature under consideration. Mr. Strauss suggested the possibility of studying migration as a screen in the event that the principal emphasis was on finding a contraceptive. Mr. Lockwood stressed the importance of flanking the contraceptive project with as many others as possible. On the question of administration Mr. Jamieson had a serious question as to whether the objective could not be achieved as effectively without a corporation.[10]

Simultaneously, McLean wrote to JDR: "At our meeting this morning you made it clear that in your judgment the population problem was important and that you proposed to do something about it." For McLean, the professional staff man, there was no more debating once the boss had made up his mind. The only question was how to get things done the best way. McLean did warn again that there would be "a substantial public relations question for the Rockefeller family, including yourself, the Rockefeller name and the Rockefeller Foundation."

JDR was aware, and was determined to go ahead. But he was also looking for a way to convey his own motives accurately. He knew that such phrases as "population control" and "birth control" sounded negative, whereas he felt his motives were positive. JDR made his first stab at clarifying this in a memo to McLean in mid-September. The population question went beyond "the relation of the food supply to the number of mouths to feed." Physical needs must be met, but "more important still are the needs which differentiate man from animal." In a redraft of this idea, JDR wrote:

Man does not live by bread alone. Consideration must also be given to his mental and emotional well-being—to education, religion, art and other forms of expression which enable man to achieve self-realization. Satisfaction and happiness come from creating and doing and a sense of accomplishment. Thus, solutions to questions of population involve ultimately not only matters of physical and material well-being, but also those of a cultural, moral and spiritual nature.[11]

These words amount to a personal credo that was deeply felt. It became more articulate as the years passed, but the basic insight did not change; it formed the basis for his actions regarding population and shaped the policies of the Population Council.

The Council was incorporated in the state of New York on November 7, 1952. Its first board consisted of JDR, Bronk Strauss, Compton, Parran, Notestein, and Osborn, all distinguished scientists except Strauss, Parran, and JDR.

An indication of the sensitivity of the population field was a controversy that erupted in New York City during the time the Population Council was being considered and launched. In March 1952, a merger took place between the Welfare Council and the Health Council of New York City, two federations of Catholic, Jewish, Protestant, and secular charities. Planned Parenthood had been a member of the Health Council. Like all organizations that had not been members of both councils, it had to apply for membership in the new organization. Opposed by Catholic Charities, Planned Parenthood was the only organization not admitted.

This brought forth sharp criticism from Jewish and Protestant leaders in a running controversy that lasted more than a year. It was not eased when Auxiliary Bishop Thomas Lynch, the head of Catholic Charities, said that the reason for his group's position was that Catholics "opposed any violation of God's law." The Reverend Adam Clayton Powell said he was "praying" that Catholics would "see the light," and the Reverend Harry Emerson Fosdick said: "I am sick at heart at the controversy. I will not lie down and take this kind of minority dictation."[12] Fosdick was chairman of the Committee for Democratic Procedures, the dissident group within the newly merged Health and Welfare Council, and his slate won in May 1953. Planned Parenthood was admitted, whereupon Catholic Charities withdrew.

The formal announcement of the Population Council's existence was not made until August 1953. On August 17 a *New York Times* editorial declared: "No organization was ever created from which so much is expected." The delay was not due to the Planned Parenthood controversy in New York, but to the time needed to fund and staff the new organization. On funding, an important question was whether or not the Council would enjoy tax-exempt status. When a new philanthropic organization was created, the Internal Revenue Service at that time normally took a year or so to assess its performance and decide whether tax exemption was justified. This meant that the first donors could be liable for both a gift tax and a retrospective raise in their income tax if the IRS ruled adversely.

Of course, in many cases a donor can be reasonably certain that an organization will qualify. But given the controversial nature of the population field, Don McLean wrote yet another warning memo when JDR made known his intention of giving the Council $100,000 for starting expenses. The Council's first year would not see much activity in any case, McLean wrote, so JDR could avoid the risk of a double tax blow on his gift if he and Blanchette each contributed the maximum tax-exempt gift of $3,000. For two years, 1952 and 1953, the Council thus would have a total of $12,000, which might suffice until the IRS ruling came through. JDR decided against this cautious route and made his $100,000 gift just before the end of 1952.[13]

The next difficulty was to find the right kind of executive head for what quickly became known as the "Pop Council." Several medical doctors were considered, but soon dropped from the running. Months passed without a paragon showing up, and JDR began to lean toward appointing Fairfield Osborn, head of the Conservation Foundation, who was close to Laurance Rockefeller. At one time it had seemed as if friction might develop between Laurance and JDR over jurisdiction in the population field, for Osborn and the Conservation Foundation already pursued a major interest in it. But it had become clear that this sprang from concern about resources and conservation, not population per se, so thereafter the two brothers considered their respective fields different but related, like the two sides of one coin.

In her study of the gradual American awakening to a population "crisis," Phyllis Piotrow divides the participants into two broad groups—the "scientists" and the "activists." There was mutual dislike, but each group needed the other. The scientists, committed to research and carefully documented progress, often benefited from the efforts of the activists in stirring up the public, the press, and the government. At the same time, most of the scientists, disliking exaggeration in general but also fearing that it could be counterproductive, were averse to the scare tactics often used by activists. The activists tended to see the scientists as too academic and conservative, but very much wanted the results of their research.[14]

JDR was one of the few leaders who functioned successfully somewhere between the two camps and could be said to have represented both. But, as Piotrow suggests, JDR was closer to the scientists than the activists. He had been schooled in the Rockefeller tradition pioneered by his father of high respect for quality, research, and science. This was indicated by the men he chose to associate himself with in his population endeavors, such as Fred Osborn and Frank Notestein and the other scientists who predominated on the Pop Council board. He shared their distaste for propagandistic tactics. But he was also a layman who felt a responsibility to speak out on the issues and exercise leadership. He admired some activists, such as Margaret Sanger, for example.

Like his father before him, JDR was to spend much time in his career figuring out how to work effectively with experts in his fields of activity without being held captive by them. Among his associates in population work, Frank Notestein was the one who worred the most about whether JDR might slip over into the camp of the activists. He was to spend much of his time figuring out how to keep JDR under control without losing his valued support. It was JDR's idea of Fairfield Osborn—very much an activist in Notestein's eyes—as head of the Council that fueled Notestein's concern. This, he believed, would make the Council primarily a propaganda organization instead of one solidly based in scientific research.

JDR was concerned that putting a scientist in charge of the Council would tip the scales too far over in the direction of research. He wanted research, but also action programs. But he acceded to the strong views of Notestein by settling on a compromise and interim candidate, Fred Osborn, Fairfield's cousin. Being just about to turn sixty-five, Fred Osborn hesitated, but was persuaded by JDR to take the post for the time being. He would have the title of executive vice president under JDR as president. The arrangement signified that JDR would be more deeply involved in this than in his other pursuits.

In September 1953, before the IRS ruling was known, JDR made two more gifts to the Council of $100,000 each. Two months later the IRS granted the tax-exempt status. In consultations about financial needs, Notestein had expressed the strong view that the annual budget for the Pop Council should be $250,000. This would support a minimal program while larger funding was sought from other sources. Accordingly, in December JDR made two more grants, one of $450,000 from his own resources and $636,000 from his 1952 trust income. His intention was that the total of nearly $1.4 million he had contributed would permit the Council to exist at the rate of $250,000 a year for at least five years. [15]

The breakthrough came almost immediately—sooner than anyone expected. Osborn and his assistant, Yorke Allen, were applying to the Ford Foundation, which in 1953 had moved to New York City with Rowan Gaither as its president. JDR had not had any luck before with Ford; but this time, on his return from another of his Asian trips in March 1954, he got the news that Ford had granted the request of $600,000 from the Pop Council. It was a jubilant moment. As JDR wrote to Gaither: "I cannot tell you how much this gift means to us."[16] What it meant was not only money, useful though it would be, but an endorsement, a vote of confidence in a nascent effort and recognition of the importance of its aims.

The request had been intelligently handled. Osborn knew better than to ask for funds in support of contraceptive research or anything suggestive of birth control; the Ford Foundation had been raked over the coals quite recently by witch-hunting congressional subcommittees. Osborn's proposal was for funds for fellowships to train scientific personnel in the underdeveloped countries, primarily in demography, during the next three to five years. The need for the program was manifest, given the flight from former colonial areas of European personnel in the field of vital statistics. The idea was to train indigenous people so that the underdeveloped countries would be increasingly able to mount their own population programs.

The Ford Foundation had exhibited a great interest in the underdeveloped world. Here was one of its obvious needs, one that was not controversial, yet had a direct bearing on the worldwide problem of overpopulation. And now there was an organization that could do the job. It had first-rate scientists on its board. It was headed by a man, Osborn, who had a reputation going back forty years as an able, intelligent, and fair-minded executive and scientist. The organization had already started a fellowship program and given its first eight training grants; John D. Rockefeller 3rd had given the new agency its basic support for the next five years. That meant that all of the Ford money would go to programs rather than overhead, something that always appeals to a foundation.

In retrospect it is easy to see all the reasons why this Ford grant was approved, but at the time it was a small miracle, a sweet vindication for JDR, and a retort to those who had said that outside funding could not be attracted.

By the time that Fred Osborn retired, having turned seventy years of age in 1959, the Pop Council had become a success. JDR continued his support at the rate of $250,000 each year (usually from the 1952 trusts), thus being the main financial pillar of the Council, but the Ford grant of 1954 had broken the ice for outsiders. In 1956, the Brothers Fund made a grant of $540,000 for the establishment of the Council's own biomedical research laboratory at Rockefeller University. In 1957 the Ford Foundation made a further grant of $1 million "to continue support of the Council's research and training activities in demography and the social aspects of population."[17]

Numerous small contributors rallied to the cause even though the

Council did not make any public fund-raising effort. Considering all the cautionary advice JDR had heard from his advisers about possible damage to the family name, he was most gratified by the fact that other members of his family contributed to the Council. In 1954, his youngest brother David donated 525 shares of Socony-Vacuum stock, and, in his letter to "Dear Johnny," said: "It is becoming increasingly clear that your idea in setting up the Population Council was a far-sighted and wise one. I feel sure that it is going to make a really important contribution to this most difficult and basic problem as the years go by."[18]

Gradually the Council's program grew and diversified. The fellowship program expanded enormously (thanks to the Ford grant), most of the fellows in demography and medicine doing their advanced training or research in the United States. They came from almost every country that felt acute population pressures. In due course, they provided the cadre of specialists necessary to undertake and staff indigenous population programs.

During Osborn's tenure the fellowship program was the major connection of the Council with the underdeveloped countries. In the 1950s the Council was able to send or provide funds for population survey missions requested by India and Pakistan.[19] But such was the political opposition of Communist and Catholic countries that sustained technical assistance was not possible until the 1960s; and not until 1964 did the Council establish its own technical assistance division.

True to JDR's vision, the Council was able to attract top people. Among new board members were Frank G. Boudreau (1953), president of the Milbank Memorial Fund, one of the pioneer organizations in population studies; Caryl P. Haskins (1955), president of the Carnegie Institute of Washington; Theodore W. Schultz, chairman of the economics department at the University of Chicago and later a Nobel Prize–winner (1957); and James B. Conant, president emeritus of Harvard (1957). When this last pair was added to the board, JDR was elected chairman and Osborn became president.

Osborn had built an excellent staff. Dr. Dudley Kirk, who had been associated with Notestein at Princeton, came in to head the demographic division. Dr. Warren O. Nelson, a leading authority on male reproductive biology, headed the medical division. Two others began long careers with the Council: W. Parker Mauldin as associate demographic director and Sheldon Segal as assistant medical director in charge of the biomedical laboratory. The demographic and medical advisory committees established by the Council included top-ranked people in each field.[20]

To try to learn what was and was not working in birth control methods,

Osborn recruited Christopher Tietze. Osborn also got permission from Clarence Gamble to take over the dormant National Committee on Maternal Health as a shell for Tietze's work, but all of its funding came from the Pop Council; a decade later the Council formally absorbed the operation. Tietze's research soon showed that population programs using existing methods "were getting nowhere fast."[21] The early varieties of the intrauterine device were ineffective and no pill had yet been invented. Conventional methods were entirely inadequate.

In 1959 Osborn insisted on retiring, although he remained on the Council board for another decade. His "interim" presidency had worked well, but JDR still thought it would be better to have a prominent lay person, one of the less vocal of the "activists," as Osborn's successor rather than another scientist. Osborn and Don McLean, who was serving as secretary of the Council, disagreed with him. JDR yielded to their entreaties and agreed on Frank Notestein as the new president. As Notestein later remarked, "Osborn and McLean pushed me with JDR."[22]

Those years during which the Pop Council was founded and began its work under Osborn have been called the "period of quiescence" in the population field.[23] Osborn preferred it that way. He even managed to talk Margaret Sanger out of holding what he feared would be a noisy, controversial conference in Washington in 1957.[24] There was no point, he thought, in provoking the Catholic Church when it seemed to be relaxing its strident opposition of a few years earlier. At the first international population conference, in Rome in 1954 (sponsored by the UN in association with the International Union for the Scientific Study of Population), Pope Pius XII had received the delegates and spoken to them mildly about the "most important problem" they were addressing. He said it was also preoccupying the Church. He went no further than urging the group, which included delegates from Communist countries and known advocates of birth control, "not to forget the moral and human aspects."[25]

On all these subjects it was a time of preparation, of endless study, of laying the ground for future work. The awesome dimensions of the problem were sinking in: it had taken mankind thousands of years of history up to 1850 to produce a world population of one billion people, but at the current rate by 1950 it would take only fifteen years to add a fourth billion to the earth's population. The studies of Tietze and others showed that despite all efforts the problem was rapidly growing worse.

By 1959 "quiescence" was over. Reports, studies, public utterances from many quarters attested to the seriousness of the "population explosion." It was General William H. Draper, Jr., who fired the loudest gun as chairman of the President's Committee to Study the United States Military

Assistance Program. From this unlikely platform Draper insisted on making recommendations on birth control, including one calling on the U.S. government, on request, "to assist other countries in their efforts to deal with the problem of rapid population growth."[26]

The Catholic Church could not stand by in silence, and in November 1959 the American bishops issued a counterblast. It led President Eisenhower, in his press conference a month later, to make his famous statement: "I cannot imagine anything more emphatically a subject that is not a proper political or governmental activity or function or responsibility."[27]

It seemed a setback, but on this issue Eisenhower was wrong. Pressure was building up. The 1960s brought events and advances no one had expected so soon, the Pop Council in the vanguard.

Because of his tenacity, JDR had succeeded in creating an organization that filled a crucial need: a private-sector, scientific organization of the highest caliber in a field that had quickly come to the fore as one of the most difficult of the fundamental problems of mankind. He had done it against the advice of many people. By the use of his name and personal fortune, he had helped to legitimize this human concern. Nor was it only leadership and money that he had contributed; he had also provided intellectual content and moral guidance to a degree remarkable for a mere layman.

Now the Council was playing a central role. Under Notestein it quickly grew tenfold in size, and the 1960s proved to be the "takeoff" stage.

4

ᴇ

INVESTING IN
PEOPLE

FROM the time he became an active philanthropist until his death, JDR showed a marked interest in investing in people as well as projects. This certainly was not a new technique—there were the Guggenheim Fellowships, for example, and fellowships had often been a feature of previous Rockefeller philanthropy. But few individuals have done as much as JDR to enable talented people to develop their gifts and further their careers.

This outlook and purpose seemed particularly appropriate for him, given his patient, low-key approach. "Investing in people" is the philanthropic equivalent of planting seeds and waiting for the harvest, though it may be years before any results are noticeable, and they are in any case difficult to measure. But the merits of the policy are real and may be seen in the difference made in the lives of individuals and the effect of their successful careers on others. Moreover, the multiplier effect of many fellowships given year after year for decades in a field or country is undeniable. In JDR's programs, as we shall see, the results were impressive.

Most often, JDR sponsored fellowship programs that were part of larger projects that he was supporting, such as research and aid in population, agriculture, and the arts. In one case, the investment in people was the entire program—the Rockefeller Public Service Awards (RPSA). It was designed to meet a genuine need—greater, perhaps, than even JDR had imagined at the outset. The program lasted nearly thirty years and evolved through three phases, each serving a different purpose. The first phase is a classic episode in the reform of public administration and cooperation between the public and private sectors.

The origin of the RPSA may be found in the concern JDR developed at the end of World War II about the quality of government service,

46

because of its vastly increased responsibilities in the postwar world. He resolved to find some way to help improve the conditions of public service and attract able young people to it. This was not some sudden impulse of JDR's, but had its grounding in a long acquaintance with the field of public administration on his part. It began at a young age with the heritage of his father's sound attitudes toward government and support of reform efforts, most notably the Bureau of Municipal Research in New York City. The BMR is justly famed for its seminal role in government reform and professional development of public administration. JDR completely subscribed to his father's view that government is not an enemy but the institutional expression of the republic—the citizen's duty is to help improve government in every possible way. JDR's education continued with his service on the board of the Spelman Fund, a small Rockefeller-created foundation totally devoted to professional support of public administration. And he learned more in his experience as, in effect, a personnel officer when he worked in industrial relations and in the Rockefeller family office, the Pocantico estate, the Red Cross, and the navy. By nature more attuned to people than to structures and processes, his thoughts about public service ran readily to such subjects as recruitment, training, career development, and morale.[1]

The RPSA program has been rightly interpreted as a vote of confidence in government service by a prominent leader of the private sector. That the program originated when McCarthyism was rampant might suggest that JDR created it as a counterweight to the senator's malicious negativism. But this was not the reason for JDR's taking action. He clearly disliked McCarthyism; after all, he undertook a program in support of government employees, and attempted another, right at the very height of the McCarthy rampage. But his intention dated back to his earlier observation of a need. McCarthyism merely provided an added incentive.

JDR had been particularly worried about the quality of State Department personnel, yet it was in State that he found his role model for excellence in the person of George Kennan; the two had met several times. Both JDR and McLean greatly admired the brilliant author of the "X" article in *Foreign Affairs* (July 1947), which first articulated the "containment policy" of the United States toward the Communist bloc.

Early in his Foreign Service career, Kennan had entered into a special training program, spending two years in Berlin studying the Russian language and culture, thus becoming one of the first of the area specialists.[2] This equipped him to serve in Moscow in 1933 as an aide to the first U.S. ambassador to the Soviet Union, William C. Bullitt. Kennan served in Moscow in wartime and returned as minister counselor of the U.S.

embassy there in 1946, the experience that led to the policy initiatives that made him famous. And he served as director of the State Department's new Policy Planning Staff in Washington from 1947 to 1950.

It was during this last period that JDR met Kennan. Then Kennan took a leave of absence in order to study and write at the Institute for Advanced Study in Princeton, New Jersey. This sparked in JDR an idea for a way to improve public service. It was simply to enable talented government servants to take sabbatical leave at the right juncture and equip themselves for expanded usefulness. Late in 1951 JDR assigned McLean to develop the idea. There was some degree of urgency, because JDR's financial means had increased substantially, and he could make a large year-end gift to start up a new program.

At first the plan was to limit the program to the foreign affairs agencies. JDR's special concern about the State Department, his own international affairs, and the link with Kennan's experience all combined to favor this limitation. Although McLean would have preferred a government-wide program, he recognized the administrative difficulties and ranged himself on the side of specializing. But as he progressed in his research and consultation with key individuals, he—and JDR—became convinced that the program should be broader.

Among those McLean met with were James Mitchell of the Civil Service Commission, Roger Jones of the Bureau of the Budget, Dean Rusk and George Kennan of the State Department, Don K. Price of the Public Administration Clearing House office in Washington, and Edward S. Mason, dean of the Graduate School of Public Administration (the Littauer School) at Harvard University.[3]

Among difficult questions, one was whether federal agencies could legally release their employees for sabbatical leave. No government-wide training authority existed. Most agencies offered only limited on-the-job training. Only a handful—including the military services, the Department of Agriculture, and the Department of State—had any legal basis for broader programs. And State, despite the Foreign Service Act of 1946, which had created the Foreign Service Institute, had no program that would have made possible something like Kennan's experience at the Institute for Advanced Study without his taking leave at his own risk and expense. Roger Jones nonetheless gave it as his opinion that the agencies could send their people off, and further, that the existence of a Rockefeller program might foster the idea of a government-wide training authority. Several bills authorizing such a thing had been introduced in Congress, following a recommendation by the Hoover Commission.[4]

Another question was whether the agencies would be willing to release their best people, the ones likely to be selected by the program, even if legal authority were obtained. The belief was widespread that government generally was going through a time of crisis, so that agencies could not spare their good people for extensive training. But again Jones took a positive view, confident that release could be arranged.

Difficult questions remained as to the selection process, the number of awards, the location of the program, the form of the sabbatical experience, and the availability of the program to senior executives or only to mid-career personnel. In the end it was decided not to impose rigid specifications of age or career level. George Kennan's views were accepted: that a candidate should have "demonstrated a superior intellectual capacity for independent thought in his field," but that the award should "be based primarily on an assessment of the candidate's "future usefulness." Kennan thought that an important criterion should be the judgment of the candidate's proposed use of the sabbatical year.[5]

Within this framework, JDR and McLean decided that the sponsoring institution should work out the details. The program would be billed as experimental for the first few years to allow for experience and observation, which would decide whether or not to continue.

As to locating the program, it seems that Harvard was almost invariably thought of first. There was the example of the Nieman fellowships and the fact that McLean had been consulting Dean Mason almost from the beginning. McLean was a member of the Visiting Committee of the Littauer School. Mason was enthusiastic about the public service idea and, at McLean's request, had his staff produce a paper describing the "Proposed Distinguished Service Fellowship Program." The paper envisioned two to five government fellows in residence at the Graduate School of Public Administration each year. They would not be required to take courses, or expected to work for a degree or to teach: they would be free to attend what classes they wished, to talk with students and faculty, and to write papers on public policy. The School was asking for only $30,000 a year "for fellowship stipends" and $5,000 a year "for overhead administration," or a total of $140,000 for a four-year experiment.[6]

It seemed certain that the program would find its home at Harvard, but it did not turn out that way. Apparently JDR felt that at least one other university should be considered as a sponsor, by way of backstop. Though it was late in the day (considering that JDR wanted to make a year-end grant), he described his idea to Harold W. Dodds, president of Princeton, when they met in Williamsburg during the first week in December for a Rockefeller Foundation board meeting. There were immediate effects. For the first time on December 6, McLean's memoranda mentioned potential sponsoring institutions by name: "either Princeton or Harvard." Dodds, a leading thinker in the subjects of government structure and public service, was understandably enthusiastic. He thought that the Woodrow Wilson School of Public and International Affairs at Princeton would be the perfect base for the program JDR had in mind. Dodds mailed a hasty note to JDR transmitting information about the Woodrow Wilson School, and followed it up on December 11 with a long letter conveying the keen interest of Dana Munro, director of the School.

On the same date President James B. Conant of Harvard was writing a letter to JDR turning down the proposal to serve as the sponsoring institution for another of JDR's initiatives, an intellectual exchange program with Japan.[7] In explaining why he was rejecting a program that one of Harvard's professors (Edwin O. Reischauer) was so enthusiastic about, Conant was trying to be gracious and polite, but ended up being stuffy. Among other things he said: "I am constantly in the position where I have to say no to propositions not unlike the one you have so generously made." And he quoted himself at length, drawing for some reason on a statement he had made in 1949 to explain why Harvard could not start a two-year college.

Having himself often been in the position of having to write stuffy letters in turning down good ideas, JDR replied on December 13, saying that he understood and respected Conant's judgment. He also told Conant about the "informal" discussions with Dean Mason on the public service program idea, and added: "The responsibility of the university in both cases is so similar that I would assume that the policy outlined in your letter of December 11 would also be applicable to the matter I have been discussing with Dean Mason."

Apparently Mason made some strong representations. On December 19 Conant wrote to JDR that the programs "are similar, but they are not identical." Deferring to Mason's views, Conant said he would welcome the public service program "on the clear understanding" that the responsibility would fall entirely on the Littauer School, even though the gift would be made to Harvard. This was still a bit standoffish, so JDR decided to respond to Dodds's warm enthusiasm. He answered Conant on December 28 to inform him that the program would go to Princeton. Again the letter was polite, but JDR was honest about his reason: "The determining factor in my decision was Dr. Dodds's enthusiasm for the program and the assurance to me that he would give it his personal attention."

When JDR wrote to Dodds to confirm the decision, he summarized his sense of purpose in one pithy sentence: "It seems imperative that every effort be made to encourage competent civilians to enter Federal service as a career and to stimulate the sustained interest, growth, and development of those already in the service." The letter transmitted a memo from McLean dated December 21 that stated the intended characteristics of the program as they were known then, but the letter pointed out that much had yet to be done to shape the program. Princeton should take the lead, subject only to the proviso that all arrangements be consistent with the objectives. JDR also notified Dodds that he was giving 7,300 shares of Socony-Vacuum stock to Princeton to underwrite costs "for roughly five years." The current market value of the gift was $253,218.75.[8]

Dodds and the staff of the Woodrow Wilson School set to work. A chairman and a selection committee were appointed. But the greater difficulties lay elsewhere. It was fortunate for JDR that he enlisted Dodds to push the program. His enthusiasm was needed in fighting political and bureaucratic resistance in Washington.

Meanwhile, JDR had not given up on the idea of a training program tailored for the State Department. While the launching of the RPSA was going on, JDR and McLean were also trying to initiate this second public service program idea. Curiously, Harvard was also unsuccessfully involved in this new effort. As the plan evolved, it combined in one program three of JDR's concerns—the adequacy of State Department personnel, the desire to promote democratic values (which he had been forced to give up at Williamsburg), and his hope of finding some way to help the American cause in the Cold War.

In pursuing these ends, McLean at first sketched a version of the RPSA tailored just for the State Department. Every year a group of State's generalists would attend a university for a program of studies "comparable in theory to the Nieman fellows at Harvard." But discussions at the Foreign Service Institute persuaded him that a more important need was to train certain specialists, the public affairs and cultural affairs officers who conducted the American propaganda effort overseas.[9]

That effort had its roots in the famous Office of War Information of World War II, which had been transferred to the State Department after the war and there had nearly disappeared. It was revived after the passing of the Smith-Mundt Act of 1948 and the outbreak of the Korean War to become an instrument of U.S. foreign policy in the Cold War. By 1952 there were 8,000 people working for what was renamed the International Information Administration (IIA), a unit within the Department of State.[10]

The IIA seemed to many at the time a vitally important agency, one of the four arms of foreign policy (political, military, economic, and psychological). In the academic community, where such disciplines as "public opinion" and "international communication" were struggling to be born, the IIA was a topic of much interest, while in Washington it was under-nourished administratively. The State Department was not a congenial host for this suddenly swollen program. Among the career Foreign Service Officers, many tended to think of IIA people as temporary and overly specialized intruders. These men and women were not accorded the high-status "FSO" personnel category, but instead were put in the (temporary) Foreign Service Reserve or the even lower class of Foreign Service Staff. Controversies swirled about the agency and the question was raised whether it should be made independent.

In 1952, JDR's interest was piqued by the fact that the public and cultural affairs officers in IIA had no way of getting training relevant to their needs. The idea was to establish a year-long seminar in a university setting for selected IIA officers. The curriculum should add to their knowledge and understanding in American history and democratic values; comparative analysis of the political systems and foreign policies of the great powers; and "international political communication, including the basic principles governing information, education exchange, and propaganda programs of the major powers; the theory and practice of various media usable as instruments of foreign policy; and finally, problems and techniques of program evaluation."[11]

JDR advised McLean to explore the possibilities at Princeton and Harvard. Although staff members at the Woodrow Wilson School were interested, Harold Dodds had little hope that the idea was realistic and felt that Princeton should concentrate on the RPSA. McLean reported: "[Dodds] stressed the hopelessness of doing anything in this field unless Ike and Dulles were willing to recognize it as an area which needed stressing. He outlined some of his frustrations as a member of one of the advisory committees in the field."[12]

At the same time, Dean Mason and his colleagues at the Littauer School were enthusiastic because of a timely coincidence. The Massachusetts Institute of Technology had received a substantial grant from the Ford Foundation for a program of research and study in the areas of international and cross-cultural communication. The program would be operated by the new Center for International Studies, which was "a joint Harvard-MIT enterprise," but was administered by MIT under the direction of Max Millikan. Mason and Millikan immediately saw the chance of fusing theory and practice if a group of IIA practitioners appeared every year in Cambridge to study at the Littauer School in the fields the Center at MIT covered through its theoretical studies. This generated a plan for two seminars to be offered to the IIA people—one on foreign policy at the Littauer School and one on international communication at the Center across the river at MIT.

Mason had already picked McGeorge Bundy of the Department of Government at Harvard to head the seminar on foreign policy.[13]

For this scheme, which sounded exciting, JDR was prepared to put up $100,000 of seed money. The Foreign Service Institute and IIA were all for it, but a new administration had come into office in Washington. The consent of the new Secretary of State, John Foster Dulles, was needed if the program were to come to life. JDR wrote several times to Dulles in January 1953, and received a favorable response. Dulles thought the department "should take advantage of your generous offer" and said that responsible officers would follow through to work out the details.[14]

Planning went ahead; JDR committed the funds to Harvard, and the Harvard Corporation gave it formal approval. But there was no follow-through by "responsible officers of the Department," so by May JDR was writing again to Dulles. On June 12 Dulles gave the bad news: "In view of our sincere feeling that this would be a most worthwhile undertaking, I am really sorry to inform you that our budgetary situation makes it virtually impossible for the Department to continue its plans for participating in this program."[15] Despite all the fanfare about the instruments of foreign policy and the Cold War, the combination of McCarthyism and GOP budget-cutting had crippled and frightened the foreign affairs agencies, IIA in particular. It now became the U.S. Information Agency (as a result of one of Nelson Rockefeller's reorganization plans), its budget was slashed, and it faced the prospect of having to cut as many as 2,500 employees. Also, it had become increasingly clear that Secretary Dulles was not interested in operational programs; he believed that the State Department should be strictly a policy-making agency. Reluctantly, JDR gave up for good trying to fashion a program to help the State Department.

The RPSA encountered difficulties, too, but its supporters managed to find ways to sidestep or surmount them and keep the program alive and growing. Before his retirement as president of Princeton in 1957, Harold Dodds was the mainstay in making the program work. Not only did he give it attention as he had promised JDR, but he did this to a greater extent than anyone had a right to expect. Dodds also repeated at every opportunity that Princeton and the Woodrow Wilson School would administer the RPSA as "a national trust," meaning selflessly and with the utmost integrity. That pledge was kept. Dodds waived the charging of overhead expenses by the university, and this, as the years passed, became a very significant contribution

Dodds and Munro appointed Professor Joseph McLean (no relation to

Donald McLean), a political scientist at the Woodrow Wilson School and a man with a long experience of Washington, as administrator of the RPSA with the title of faculty secretary. The twelve members of the selection committee were appointed soon enough to hold their organizing meeting in June 1952. Because the government-wide nature of the awards program would comprehend many professional fields, an effort was made to represent the major branches of knowledge and experience on the committee. The chairman was Karl W. Compton, distinguished scientist and chairman of MIT. Other members included Ralph Bunche of the United Nations; Dean Mason of the Littauer School; Philip Graham, publisher of the *Washington Post;* and Charles Wilson, president of General Electric.[16]

Early in 1952 Dodds and the faculty secretary made the rounds of the agencies in Washington. They found support for the principle of the program, but doubts as to its feasibility. Some agency heads and personnel directors told Dodds they could not ensure that the job or rank of a man who left for a year would be there when he returned. Needing top-level support against this attitude, Dodds enlisted the aid of Frank Pace, Secretary of the Army and an alumnus of Princeton. The result was a letter to Dodds from President Truman that strongly endorsed the plan (though wrongly attributing the gift to the Rockefeller Foundation), and said: "I am most pleased to learn of these plans and assure you of the fullest cooperation of the Executive Branch in this endeavor."[17]

The program had been referred to most often as the "Distinguished Service Fellowships," but Dodds and Joseph McLean proposed a change to the "Rockefeller Public Service Awards." From the beginning Dodds had felt that modeling the awards on the experience of George Kennan was shooting too high.[18] The boundaries should not be rigid and the target should be the mid-career level. He felt that the term "distinguished service" suggested a reward upon retirement. Because the funding came from one man, a fact that certainly could not be kept secret, Dodds thought it would be converted to an advantage if the Rockefeller name were used in the title of the program. JDR assented.[19]

To avoid any possibility of racial or other discrimination, Ralph Bunche urged that individuals should be able to nominate themselves. The other nominations would come from the agencies. The size of the award should be sufficient to cover all the expenses of six to twelve months at a university or a comparable experience. There was no requirement, Dodds had insisted, that the winners had to come to Princeton. The winner would have up to one year to start using the fellowship.[20]

The spadework in Washington led to each agency's designating a senior staff member for liaison with the administering office in Princeton. By the deadline for the first round of awards, everybody was astonished at the number of applications and nominations. In his history of the program, the third faculty secretary, Dr. Robert W. van de Velde, commented:

The fact that in the first year almost 800 applied for the five fellowships offered was an emphatic demonstration for even the most skeptical Washington agency heads that many employees felt a strong need for further training *and* that they were willing to risk a year away from their desks to get it.[21]

When JDR made the original grant, he said in his letter to Dodds that he hoped the amount would be enough to cover the expenses of the program for a trial period of five years; he added that "the funds may be used within a shorter time if experience indicates that this is necessary and desirable."[22] Figuring that each award would cost about $15,000 to cover tuition, expenses, and part of the awardee's government salary for a year, the $250,000 would thus provide three awards a year for five years. Dodds was particularly alive to the need to make an impact in Washington, so he chose instead to make five awards a year for three years, and JDR agreed. But when the flood of applications came in, Dodds went to JDR again to suggest that the way to take advantage of so much interest and make a real impact in Washington was to double the number of awards to ten. Instead of spending at the rate of $50,000 a year, the rate should be $150,000 or a total of $450,000 for three years. JDR agreed to provide the extra $200,000.

As it turned out, some agencies were able to pay the full salaries of their winners. The money thus saved was used to give additional awards in most years—as high as sixteen in one year. The eleven winners of the first year indicated the range of the program. David E. Bell of the White House staff spent a year at Harvard studying the relations between government and labor-management problems. Martin Young of the National Institutes of Health studied tropical diseases at laboratories in ten countries. Oscar Seidman, a design engineer with the Navy Department, studied supersonic aerodynamic theory at Cal Tech. Marshall D. Shulman, a researcher in the Department of State, studied current Soviet foreign policy and the French Communist Party at Harvard and in Paris.[23]

The program stirred a wave of favorable comment in newspaper editorials and in letters to JDR from government officials and leaders in public administration. Junior wrote to laud his son for the "generous gift" he had made for the "inspiration and education" of public servants. He said that he, too, had tried to do something about the lack of preparedness in the public service, but that John was carrying forward the work "in a large and effective way."[24] Still, in the first year the difficulties proved worse than expected, as Van de Velde tells us:

Two of the first-year recipients in effect lost their jobs because, or largely because, they were absent from them at the critical moment of the 1953 changeover in Administrations. One was made so "uncomfortable" when he returned "as a Truman holdover," he later reported, that he resigned from the Government six months later, and the other found that his position had been reclassified as a "political" one to be filled from a list approved by the Republican National Committee.[25]

This surge backward toward party patronage and the "spoils system," a perennial tug-of-war ever since the Pendleton Act of 1883, was perhaps understandable given the Republicans' long absence from the White House during the Roosevelt-Truman era. But there was no such excuse for what was going on in the State Department, where Secretary Dulles made little effort to combat the attacks of Senator McCarthy. In fact, Dulles appointed a heavy-handed McCarthyite, Scott McLeod, to the sensitive post of director of security.[26]

It did not appear that Marshall D. Shulman was a McCarthy or McLeod target, but probably the mood of the moment produced the bureaucratic obstacles to his taking advantage of his award. The case aroused the program's sponsors more than any other because it came to a head *before* Shulman could take up the award. Because he was on the verge of a change in status, it was ruled that he could not go away for a year unless he resigned from the State Department. This prompted one of Don McLean's colorful aphorisms. He wrote that the objective of the program was to "improve the quality of the breed. If people are forced to resign, obviously we do not achieve this objective. On the contrary, we participate in exterminating the breed."[27]

McLean felt that the Shulman affair should be given the "highest priority," because it was "basic to the whole fellowship program." He said he had "yet to see regulations which could not be modified to meet special situations."[28] Dodds wrote to Dulles, and Karl Compton wrote to Donald Lourie, Deputy Under Secretary of State for Administration, and at the last minute the problem was solved. Shulman had made no public comment and had been ready to resign and take his chances of reappointment. Now he was able to go to Harvard with the knowledge that he was still a State Department employee. In later years Shulman, who became one of the top State Department experts on the Soviet Union, said that the year of study was a critical turning point in his career.[29]

Experiences such as this gradually modified Roger Jones's early observation that the RPSA might help improve the climate for legislation to provide advanced training throughout the government. He now proposed that achieving such legislation be an objective of the program. Any reluctance to lobby for that objective disappeared after an adverse government ruling in 1955. As Van de Velde explained it:

A technically narrow interpretation of the laws by the Comptroller General raised a question of "conflict of interests" in those cases where Government salaries continued to be paid the recipient while on his study project. If a man is on Government salary, he is on "official business," said the Comptroller. And if he is on Government business, he is prohibited from receiving any "[supplement] to his salary" from a "person, association, or corporation."[30]

It was clearly important to get an endorsement from the Eisenhower administration comparable to that which Truman had given the program before it started. As the time neared when JDR had to decide whether to fund the program beyond the first three-year trial, the lack of a renewed backing troubled him. He wrote to Dodds about continuing the program:

We should be guided to some extent by the attitude of the Administration. To date there has been no endorsement, which I regret. Whether the program has actually come to the attention of the President I do not know. However, it does seem to me that there is some question as to whether it should be continued if [they are] not sufficiently interested to take an active part in promoting it.[31]

Dodds went to work. Through the President's chief assistant, Sherman Adams, he managed to get a letter from Eisenhower that concluded: "My warm congratulations go to Princeton University for its administration of the awards as a national trust and to Mr. John D. Rockefeller, III, for his dedication to the public interest."[32] JDR thought the letter was "nice," but lacking the "force and enthusiasm to really be convincing with the government agencies." Dodds said he was disappointed in "Sherman Adams' appreciation of the problem."[33] The following January Dodds got Eisenhower's agreement to receive the next batch of award winners at the White House, but this was canceled by a subsequent directive limiting the President's availability for awards and other ceremonial affairs.[34]

By this time Dodds had become a member of the second Hoover Commission as chairman of the "Task Force on Federal Personnel." He kept JDR informed, saying that the task force would come out strongly for a "senior Civil Service of top administrative officers" and "off-the-job training" as an "inescapable part of career development."[35]

Aside from Dodds and the staff at the Woodrow Wilson School, the leading lobbyists for training legislation were Don McLean and Arthur Maass, an associate professor at the Littauer School. There were also staunch advocates within the government. The career of Roger Jones, a leading supporter, had progressed—he was now head of the legislative reference service of the Bureau of the Budget. The Civil Service Commission had always been supportive, and on the White House staff Joseph Winslow was an ally.

In addition to these activists, approval came from unions, educators, land-grant colleges, the National Civil Service League, and other organizations and individuals with an interest in improved personnel and administrative practices in government. In 1957 Robert F. Goheen succeeded Dodds as president of Princeton and Robert van de Velde succeeded Stephen K. Bailey as faculty secretary in charge of the program. Both these men kept up their predecessors' efforts in support of a training bill.

But prospects did not seem good. As an issue, it had no political appeal. The first hopeful sign came in 1957 when Joseph C. Clark, former mayor of Philadelphia, took a seat in the 85th Congress as the new senator from Pennsylvania (a Democrat, Clark was the brother of Nelson Rockefeller's wife). It happened that Clark had been chairman of the Visiting Committee at the Littauer School and had heard about government training issues from Don McLean and Arthur Maass. At Clark's invitation, McLean wrote to him in detail about the powers that agencies should have, including the ability to pay the salary of an employee who undertakes off-the-job training.[36] As a freshman senator on the Post Office and Civil Service Committee, Clark introduced a bill and managed to get it passed by the Senate on April 12—all this in less than three months.

It was a different story in the House. There Edward H. Rees (R., Kansas) had introduced a similar bill, but it was stalled in the Committee on Post Office and Civil Service. Another obstacle arose when the White House objected to the Rees bill because it would lodge authority for certain aspects of training in the Civil Service Commission. This was somehow felt to diminish the executive power of the President. Nothing happened for a year, leading to concern that the 85th Congress might expire before the House acted, nullifying the Senate action. But several events occurred in the spring of 1958 that spurred the bill forward.

The first was a speech by Senator John F. Kennedy at the awards luncheon on April 30. With the aid of one of his assistants, Ralph Dungan, an alumnus of the Woodrow Wilson School, Kennedy had been induced to speak. His star was rising; he had nearly been nominated for the Vice Presidency at the 1956 Democratic convention in Chicago and he was generally thought to be in the running for the top spot in 1960. His power-

ful speech in support of the RPSA and a training bill attracted a good deal
of attention. Kennedy praised the "foresight and philanthropy" of JDR,
and said:

The Rockefeller Foundation and family have recognized—perhaps more than any
other comparable group—the usefulness of what the economists like to call
"seed capital." They have pioneered in the establishment of new projects and
programs. . . . They have established task forces or initiated ventures in order to
demonstrate what can and should be done by the rest of the Nation. These undertakings have stimulated our awareness and action in a number of fields—in medicine and public health, in education, the arts, and elsewhere. . . . But certainly
one of their finest contributions has been to the strengthening of our career public
service.

He cited the Rockefeller Foundation support of the National Institute
of Public Affairs in the 1930s as having helped to stimulate government
training activities; now, he said, the JDR initiative was another successful
experiment building on the first:

The value of this program is now undeniable. Those whom we honor today, to be
sure, are an exceptional few—but there are potentially many, many more. We
cannot expect the Rockefeller program to do the job alone—or forever. It is high
time that the Congress adopted this Rockefeller program, also.[37]

As was his custom, JDR was present at the awards ceremony and said
a few words. He was greatly impressed by the charismatic young senator
from Massachusetts and his well-researched and strong endorsement of the
program and the legislation. He was also of one mind with Kennedy when
the senator used a Cold War context for his conclusion, seemingly *de
rigueur* in those Sputnik days, in which he said that another reason for
training legislation was to help the United States "meet the single-minded
advance of the Communists."

After the ceremony, JDR and McLean went to see Speaker of the
House Sam Rayburn, who said he would try to get the training bill moving.
He said it might be effective if JDR himself testified before the committee.
Within a few days, JDR received an invitation to talk to the committee at
its bimonthly "executive meeting" on May 15. He was accompanied by
Van de Velde, Maass and McLean. A "curiosity factor" may have been at
work because eighteen of the twenty-three members showed up for what
in effect was a special hearing to decide whether further steps should be
taken toward reporting the bill—appointing a subcommittee and scheduling public hearings. At first, Van de Velde noted, there was an "apparent
air of distinct reserve" on the part of some members:

Whether this was because of suspicion toward a wealthy "outsider," or whether they had expected an aggressive "tycoon" trying to tell them what they should do, is, of course, not known. Whatever the expectation, the air of cautious suspicion began to melt away very rapidly. Observers indicated that it was Mr. Rockefeller's characteristic politeness, modesty—even self-effacement—which breached the wall of initial antipathy.[38]

After little more than an hour of testimony the committee voted to proceed with the scheduling of public hearings. Chairman Tom Murray (D., Tenn.) invited JDR to join the committee in their trip to the airport; they and other members of Congress were going to greet Vice President Nixon on his return from his famous visit to Latin America where he had been jeered and threatened by mobs. Riding in an escorted bus, JDR was able to chat informally with a number of committee members. But before Nixon arrived, JDR and McLean had to catch their own flight to New York.

Whether or not owing to JDR's charm, a subcommittee was appointed, hearings took place in June, and the full committee voted unanimously in favor of the bill. On June 27 it was passed by the House.

The one remaining hurdle was the conflict between the White House and the House version of the bill as to the location of administrative authority. It happened that some personnel changes had occurred. Philip Young had left his double role as chairman of the Civil Service Commission and special assistant to the President for personnel. Rocco Siciliano, former businessman and Assistant Secretary of Labor, succeeded Young in the White House post, but not as commission chairman. McLean reported to Dodds that he had found Siciliano "very helpful and far more interested in this bill than his predecessor."[39] In fact, he yielded far enough to permit a compromise. On July 7, Public Law 85–507, the Government Employees Training Act, was passed by Congress and signed into law by President Eisenhower. The next day a news release described the bill:

Long sought by the executive branch and recommended by both Hoover Commissions, the new law authorizes all types of employee training, including training within the Federal service and in non-Federal facilities such as colleges, universities, manufacturing plants, and laboratories.

The [Civil Service] Commission is made responsible for general administration of the law and issuance of Governmentwide regulations and instructions under which agencies will operate their own training programs. . . .

CSC Chairman Harris Ellsworth hailed the act as a new landmark in personnel administration. "The new authority establishes for the first time by law a general policy for the promotion of efficiency and economy in Government activities through employee training."

It had all happened within a very short time after Senator Kennedy's speech and JDR's testimony. Don McLean immediately wrote thank-you letters to everyone he could think of, expressing his "shock" and delight. Letters came back saying that the congratulations should be reversed. Joseph Winslow of the White House staff summed up the sentiment of others: "It is we in the Federal service who owe you and your boss a real debt of gratitude." Winslow wrote that he and Roger Jones had supported the idea since 1947, but that it was the Rockefeller awards and the work of McLean and JDR that were "really responsible for getting the training legislation moved through Congress."[40]

There was now the question of what to do about the Rockefeller awards. They could be terminated now that the much greater financial power of the federal government was behind the idea of extensive training at the mid-career and other levels. Or the awards program could be reconstituted on another basis.

While that decision was pending, JDR might very well have allowed himself to feel quite satisfied about what had happened; but he rarely permitted himself this luxury. He believed, as Senator Kennedy had noted, that a major role of philanthropy was to pioneer activities that might later be assumed by government with its greater resources and the power of law. The first phase of the Rockefeller Public Service Awards is a classic case of accomplishing exactly that.

5

POPULATION AND FOOD

JDR was a busy man in 1952 with his Japanese projects, the start-up of the Rockefeller Public Service Awards, the launching of the Population Council, and the chairmanship of the Rockefeller Foundation. Yet, amid all this, he found himself considering another new undertaking. His thoughts were fragmentary and ill-defined at first. The starting point was his realization that participation in the Dulles peace treaty mission had led him to a series of Japanese projects limited to the cultural sphere. He began to feel that he should go beyond that and find a way to help Japan grapple with her economic problems.

American policy-makers at that time worried a great deal about the state of the Japanese economy, which had been propped up since the end of World War II by payments from the American occupation and the use of Japan as a logistical base for the Korean War effort. The concern came from recognition that both the occupation and the Korean War would soon end. What would take their place in aiding the Japanese economy? It was clear that Japan, a small, overpopulated island kingdom with limited natural resources, could survive only by means of a vigorous international trade. But Japan had been shorn of her colonies and conquests, and her industrial infrastructure had been heavily damaged by B-29 raids. Moreover, Japan's natural trading partner, China, was closed to her. The result of all these factors was that Japan's exports were weak and she was importing too much, mostly foodstuffs.

To begin refining his thoughts, JDR went to Washington to see the Detroit banker Joseph Dodge, a friend of Don McLean's from their days together in the High Commissioner's office in Germany. Dodge now was serving as special representative of the Secretary of State for American assistance to Japanese economic recovery. He strongly encouraged JDR's interest in sponsoring some sort of private-sector program to aid the Japanese economy. Back home JDR formed an advisory group to consider the matter, including McLean, Ed Young, Martha Dalrymple, Stacy May (an economist in the family office, formerly with Nelson's wartime agency), and Professor Jerome Cohen of the Center for International Studies at Princeton, one of the few American experts on the Japanese economy.

The discussions of this group soon began to focus on agriculture as both a critical area of need in Japan and one that a private American philanthropic effort might be able to do something about. Dodge had cited agriculture as an area of interest and JDR first mentioned it in his diary on August 19. It was perhaps natural to see agriculture as a promising field for development now that land reform in Japan had taken place. For a long time, the reactionary element in Japanese life was strongly manifest in its agriculture; it was mired in a feudal system of land tenure, and had resisted all attempts at change. Reform became possible only when Japan lost the war, and then only at the insistence of an enlightened conqueror.

In October, Stacy May produced a paper affirming that "the field in which outside philanthropic . . . aid might have the greatest promise of usefulness is agriculture—specifically, a program designed to help the Japanese to increase their domestic production of foodstuffs." The transplanting of American techniques to Japan could boost productivity and allow imports to be cut.[1]

Soon a second paper urged an important shift in course: it would be more economical to boost agricultural production elsewhere in Asia. This would allow for a resumption of trade patterns in which Japan exported industrial products in return for food and raw materials. The major difference would be that instead of China the emphasis would be on the countries of Southeast Asia. The memo proposed the establishment of a "Far Eastern Food Research Institute," possibly located in Japan, but preferably in a Southest Asian country such as Ceylon or Thailand. The reason was that the top priority should be finding new ways to boost the production of rice, the staple food crop of the region. The memo concluded with the suggestion that JDR personally explore Southeast Asia "in a trip through the area this coming winter," and it urged that JDR be "accompanied by someone of very high competence and upon whose judgment upon agricultural matters you would rest full confidence."[2]

Apart from the fact that a valid excuse for a trip to the Far East was always well received by JDR, he was intrigued by the shift in thinking. A program of the kind suggested by May would give JDR a presence in Asian countries other than Japan, most of which he had not visited and was anxious to see. At the same time he would be helping Japan. It may have stirred in JDR memories of the General Education Board's agricultural work in the impoverished South.[3] Certainly it was akin to much of what Nelson had attempted to do in Latin America. Finally, there was a certain rightness about the idea, given the fact that JDR was in the early stages of launching the Population Council, which sooner or later would be active in Asian countries. An agricultural program would involve him in population *and* food—the two sides of the proverbial coin.

JDR knew exactly the person to take along on the proposed trip—Dean William I. Myers of Cornell, an outstanding agricultural expert and a man JDR felt particularly close to ever since Myers had sided with him in the abortive effort of 1946 to redirect the policy of the Rockefeller Foundation.

But first there came confirmation of the wisdom of the course JDR was headed on. May and Cohen told him that one of the great experts on agriculture in Asia, particularly in Japan, was Wolf Ladejinsky, the brilliant agricultural attaché of the U.S. embassy in Tokyo. Ladejinsky had been the main intellectual influence on the Japanese Land Reform Law of 1946, and had been an expert on farm tenancy in Japan since before World War II. A cable was sent to Ladejinsky, who was finishing a ninety-day special assignment in India to study land reform possibilities at the urgent request of the U.S. ambassador, Chester Bowles. En route back to his post in Tokyo, Ladejinsky was to stop in New York for a brief conference at Columbia University. Early in December he appeared in Room 5600 for a meeting with JDR. Not surprisingly, Ladejinsky was enthusiastic about what JDR was contemplating. JDR noted in his diary that his guest made "a very favorable impression."

The broad arc of Southeast Asia that JDR and Myers and their wives visited in February and March 1953 had become the prime zone of contention in the struggle between the Western democracies and the seemingly irresistible advance of communism. In the eyes of Americans, what was happening had every appearance of a vast conspiracy, an all-out offensive directed from Moscow. The Communists had taken over North Korea and China, invaded South Korea, and were stimulating revolutions throughout the region—in the Philippines, French Indo-China, Indonesia, Malaysia, and Burma.

China was gone, but Japan was stabilized and the Communists had been stalemated in Korea. The challenge now to the Americans and their British and French allies was to hold the line in the countries of South and Southeast Asia from the Philippines all the way around to India and

Pakistan. As a result, government aid programs abounded in the region. There were special U.S. aid programs in South Korea, Japan, Taiwan, and the Philippines. The European Recovery Program had started operations in another half dozen Asian countries, and the new Technical Cooperation Administration (the Point Four program) in still another group of countries. In addition, the Mutual Defense Assistance Program had started supplying military aid and advisers to several Asian countries that were hard-pressed by insurgents.

All this intensified after 1948 and the full blooming of the Cold War. Under the Truman Doctrine and the policy of "containment," the United States was ready to supply bilateral military and economic aid to any country that was trying to resist Communist influence or outright insurgency. These American efforts were colored by the disaster in China. There the postwar rehabilitation efforts and the interim aid program were replaced by the Aid to China Program of 1948, a matter of "too little, too late." The apparent lesson was that more military and economic aid in time might have reversed the situation. This thinking was prevalent in Congress, where the tendency was to favor military over economic aid— to prevent another China.

Overpopulated, with widespread poverty, disease, and illiteracy, postwar Asia was desperate for economic development. Motives for giving aid became combined imperatives—strategic, humanitarian, trade, and preserving access to resources. Even those who were the strongest proponents of economic aid almost always yielded to the higher priority of internal security and counterinsurgency. The long-term expectation from economic aid was that it would strengthen a nation's capacity to resist Communist aggression or domestic subversion.

Among types of economic aid, industrialization was favored as the surest and quickest way to economic progress. This hope rested on a faulty transfer of Western experience to Asia, although it must be said that many Asian leaders seemed more interested in this form of apparent material progress than in dealing with the difficult problems of overpopulation and rural stagnation. A minority point of view among the U.S. proponents of aid stressed precisely the problems of the peasant: overpopulation and agricultural development. After several decades, hindsight tells us that this line of thought was the wiser. Its most eloquent spokesman of the time was Wolf Ladejinsky, who wrote in 1950:

Four-fifths of the people who populate the underdeveloped areas are peasants. Agriculture, not industry, is the pivot of their lives in all of its principal manifestations. Industry has made but a small dent in the character of Asia, notwithstanding the industrialization of Japan, the oil gushers of the Middle East, the tin mines of Malaysia and Siam, the jute and cotton mills of India. The factory may bring material advancement to the Asians some day, but that day is in the future. The heart of the problem of Asia today lies in the countryside; it is on the farm where solutions must be sought and found.[4]

In the struggle against communism, Ladejinsky had no doubt that the peasant, again, was the key: "An overworked and overexploited peasantry that for centuries was inertly miserable is now alertly miserable." Land reform was crucial:

The communists, with a quick eye for the main chance, have been making the most of peasant discontent by holding out that most enticing of baits—ownership of the land. The communists succeeded in China. They have failed utterly in Japan. There, General MacArthur stole the communists' thunder and made the landless peasant's dream of a piece of land he could call his own come true. In Japan, we have forged an economic and political weapon more potent in Asia than the strongest battalions and blandishments the communists can put forth.[5]

Ladejinsky had a pithy summary of the reason for the "age-old wretchedness" of the Asian peasant—"too many people, too little land." It was a formulation that could have been a battle cry for all those concerned about the balance between population and food, reminiscent of Julian Huxley's concise statement: "Somehow or other population must be balanced against resources or mankind will perish."[6]

These certainly were slogans that JDR would agree with. He had already taken decisive steps in the population field. He had become interested in aiding Asian agriculture by a somewhat circuitous route: a cultural assignment in Japan that broadened into concern for Japan's economic woes, became focused on agriculture, and then made a logical leap to agriculture in Southeast Asia in the traditional trade pattern with Japan. Along this mental journey he could not have found better advisers than Stacy May, Jerome Cohen, Wolf Ladejinsky, and Bill Myers. He now undertook a physical journey to the region.

JDR and Blanchette were now such familiar guests in Japan that they had their "regular" rooms at the Imperial Hotel, dined with the prime minister, and had an audience with the Crown Prince (JDR's first audience with Emperor Hirohito had taken place the previous year). Now JDR's friendship with Shigeharu Matsumoto deepened. Matsumoto, whom JDR had first met as a young man at the 1929 Institute for Pacific Relations conference in Tokyo, was the key person in JDR's attempt to encourage the development of an International House in Japan. A strong group of Japanese leaders had come together in support of the plan, and progress was being made. JDR spent time making fund-raising calls with Matsumoto and discussing Asian agriculture with Wolf Ladejinsky, once again in his post as agricultural attaché.

The next stop was the Philippines, where the Rockefellers joined Bill Myers and his wife at Los Baños, about fifty miles from Manila, the site of the agricultural college of the University of the Philippines. Myers was glad to make the trip with JDR because it enabled him to visit Los Baños: his College of Agriculture at Cornell provided faculty support there under a Mutual Security Administration grant.

In the Philippines as elsewhere on this trip covering Indonesia, Malaysia, Singapore, Thailand, Burma, India, and Pakistan, JDR talked with top officials as well as local correspondents of the *New York Times* (whom he regarded highly as information sources). He also met U.S. ambassadors, opposition political leaders, academics, agricultural specialists, and businessmen, both native and foreign It was a grinding effort intended to produce insights and information about countries new to him— a lifetime of learning crammed into one intensive visit.

From his diary, it is obvious which leaders made strong impressions on him. One was Ramon Magsaysay, the dynamic Minister of National Defense for the Philippines who later in 1953 was elected president by a huge plurality.[7] JDR met him for a long conversation at the house of Gerald Wilkinson, the head of a British trading firm. A legendary figure for having broken the back of the Huk rebellion, Magsaysay was the kind of leader Americans dreamed about—forceful, honest, intelligent, a firm believer in democracy, and enormously popular—almost too good to be true. But he was real. JDR found him an "interesting, forthright, vigorous person."

One cannot help being appealed to by his crusading spirt and also by the outstanding contribution he has made handling the Huk menace. The latter has been not only a national but international contribution in that it showed that courage, determination and imagination could block a determined communist-inspired effort.

In Malaysia JDR met another fighter against insurgency, Sir Gerald Templer, a "top British general" and a "high strung, informal, aggressive man who evidently is doing a good job." In New Delhi, the leader who immpressed JDR was Prime Minister Jawaharlal Nehru. The meeting took place at the end of the day and JDR stayed only about fifteen minutes, but he wrote: "There is no question as to his strength and prestige in the country. He towers over everyone else."

By this time India had come to occupy a special status in the Cold War. The most populous country in the world, China, had fallen to the Communists, and now Americans feared that India, second in population, teeming with peasant masses, would be the next prey. Thus India came to be regarded as a battleground of democracy, the great test case to show that capitalism could work as well as communism or better, even with formidable problems of development to overcome. As a result, aid programs, both governmental and private, were proliferating in India. The Ford Foundation was making a major effort there.

Though he fully appreciated its strategic and psychological importance, JDR never took to India the way he did to Japan. He made good Indian friends, but he found the leaders aloof, at times almost rude, in contrast to the polite reserve and friendliness of the Japanese that touched him and reached into the wellsprings of his own psyche.

Once back in New York JDR invited Myers to meet with him and his advisers, to find out the recommendations Myers had framed after thinking over the trip. Present were Frank Jamieson, John Lockwood, Stacy May, and Don McLean. Myers subscribed fully to the idea of a high-level scientific institute in the Far East to tackle "the problem of increasing rice yields in the area." He thought that the Natural Sciences and Agriculture Division of the Rockefeller Foundation under Warren Weaver and J. George Harrar would be "the most promising agency" to carry out such a project, given the great accomplishments of the Foundation's agricultural research in Latin America.

Complementing this scientific effort, Myers's other recommendations dealt with subjects close to his own heart and aimed at JDR's. He proposed to put scientific advances into practical use by three means: (1) fellowships for Asians to provide in each Southeast Asian country a corps of trained persons in agricultural research, education, and extension work; (2) grants to help upgrade agricultural schools in the region; and (3) a continuing program in what Myers termed "agricultural economics," which he defined as the practical management and coordination of all knowledge and resources necessary to improve farm output and standards of living in any particular area.

It was Myers's hope that JDR might want to initiate at least a moderate amount of activity in these three areas to support whatever "basic scientific work" in Southeast Asia the Foundation might undertake. This should be done after a "thorough understanding with the Foundation" on the coordination of the two efforts. Myers further suggested that JDR have someone representing his interests accompany Weaver and Harrar on the trip to Asia they were planning for the fall.[8]

As trustees of the Foundation, both JDR and Myers knew that strong interest was developing within the staff for an Asian agricultural program based on the model developed in Mexico by George Harrar. The Weaver-Harrar trip was to be the first step toward such a program. With a chairman and a president—JDR and Rusk—who both had a strong interest in Asia, it was perhaps inevitable that the Foundation would seek expanded program interests there; it is also likely that the great and manifest needs in Asia had already attracted the interest of the staff, as was the case with the Ford Foundation.

JDR was taking pains to make sure that the staff was fully apprised of his developing interest in Asian agriculture, not because he was seeking financial support from the Foundation but to avoid friction and any appearance of rivalry or competition. George Harrar had been invited to the discussions the previous fall that were based on Stacy May's original memoranda. After meeting with Ladejinsky in December, JDR sought out Harrar and Weaver to share what he had learned and get reactions. JDR wrote that they "indicated real interest" in Ladejinsky's views and told him about their planned trip to the Far East. There was quick agreement to the proposal that a third party accompany them to make a special report to JDR on his interests. A man from a rice-producing area, Norman Efferson of Louisiana State University, was chosen to go.

JDR had also been careful to keep the Foundation informed as he had moved into the population field, but that was done because of the general tenderness of the subject, not because of the possibility of any competition. In agriculture, it was a different story. The Foundation was world-renowned for its work in agriculture. There was no point in JDR engaging in direct competition. Two factors took care of that possibility. One was that despite the Harrar-Weaver-Efferson trip of 1953, it took the Foundation nearly four years to finance the proposed rice research institute, and then only in association with the Ford Foundation. A second reason was that JDR intended to do something different, thanks to his own instincts, the formula Myers had proposed at the April meeting, and the influence of Ladejinsky.

True, research supported by the Rockefeller Foundation might result in another "miracle strain" of rice or other grain of immense advantage to Asian agriculture. But somebody had to see to it that science was applied. In actuality, this was enormously complex. Customs, land tenure, poverty, illiteracy, traditions, motivation, marketing—all would influence what a farmer would do or could be induced to do.

Part of the legacy here was the paradox of the Foundation's record in agriculture—brilliant success in research, but failure in mounting any coordinated approach among disciplines by way of follow-through. Warren Weaver had commented regretfully on the curious inability to do this[9]— as had Myers, but more perceptively, from the time he was a member of the survey team of 1941, whose recommendations had led to the Foundation's work in Mexico and Colombia. The benefits of Foundation-sponsored research gradually became manifest, but Myers and others believed this would have happened sooner and more effectively if the social sciences had been brought to bear on the problem in a coordinated approach.

Myers commented: "My admiration for Warren Weaver is very deep and profound, and my affection for him is very great. Occasionally, he would make one remark that still makes me crawl—when he said that farming is just applied biology." To Myers it was that and a great deal more—all that he grouped under the heading of "agricultural economics." There were two problems with the Foundation program in Myers's view. One was compartmentalization as bad or worse as that among departments on a university campus. "There was perfect friendship [among the Foundation's departments], but no cooperation," he said. The second problem was that the staff had not had any exposure to agricultural economics, and they were suspicious of what they didn't know.[10]

Myers added: "It seemed to me there was a place for a small foundation to supplement the work in the biological sciences by devoting itself to the human problems—to agricultural economics and sociology." He knew that the emphasis on "human problems"—the man and management on the individual farm—would appeal to JDR. His thinking also meshed with that of Ladejinsky, who had urged that U.S. government aid programs adopt the approach of the Joint Commission on Rural Reconstruction. The Joint Commission had consisted of five people, three Chinese and two Americans, all experts on Chinese agriculture. They were alert to local needs and conditions and used the limited funds at their disposal to assist the farmers, whose confidence they had won. Though the Joint Commission functioned only a year on the mainland before having to flee to Taiwan in 1948, it continued its work there and flourished for a number of years. One of the three Chinese members was Dr. James Y. C. Yen, the same Jimmy Yen whom JDR had visited at Shansi in 1929. There Dr. Yen was already famous for his model farms and the "mass education movement" among Chinese farmers.[11]

Now, nearly twenty-five years later, JDR was exercising painstaking care in developing a new program in the tradition of Yen's work. He convened a special group in June 1953 to consider with him, May, and McLean a number of detailed questions arising from Myers's recommendations. The consultants were Dr. Richard Pringle, an agricultural specialist from the Mutual Security Administration; Raymond Moyer, formerly one of the two American commissioners on the Joint Commission and now an economist with the Ford Foundation; George Harrar from the Rockefeller Foundation; Chester Bowles, former U.S. ambassador to India; and Phillips Talbot of the American Universities Field Staff. The meeting produced a set of guidelines that JDR transmitted to Efferson for his trip.[12]

With Harrar and Weaver, Efferson visited Japan, the Philippines, Thailand, Burma, and India in two months' time. Earlier he had spent six months in the other countries of the region for the U.S. Department of Agriculture. His report to JDR in November 1953 warned that no broad-scale programs, national or international, were feasible in that part of the world because "antagonism and distrust" toward Americans and Europeans still prevailed. But he believed that a small-scale program focusing on "internal farm management" could be started in most countries. He outlined a budget calling for fellowships for training in the United States, direct grants for field work, pilot project demonstrations, and conferences. Nothing of the sort had been attempted in Asia, Efferson said, and it would take at least ten years "to make a significant contribution to the area." He added that mistakes were inevitable, but if the program were built up slowly and carefully, these would be minimized.

He gauged prospects and receptivity country by country, classifying Japan, the Philippines, and Thailand as "good," Pakistan as "fair to good," India and Indonesia as "fair," and Burma and Indo-China as "poor." The problem in Indonesia was instability under Sukarno, in Burma hostility toward foreigners. In India,

the country is interested, at least academically, in improving food production and rural standards of living, but their general inertia is such that the results of assistance will be very slow to appear. . . . how much good can be accomplished by trying to help a people where many of the people do not appear to want to help themselves? However, this attitude may change.

The prognosis for Indo-China was prescient and grim; a program there Efferson judged impossible: "The lack of a stable government, resentment toward the Western World, the impossibility of traveling freely in the rural areas, and a complete shortage of individuals with a sufficient background to become effective co-operators all combine to cause this situation."[13]

The candor of the report might have deterred most potential donors, but, as was becoming evident in other areas, JDR was unique. A realistic understanding of the difficulty and long-term nature of a problem did not prevent him from becoming involved. Both he and Myers were satisfied that the Efferson report mapped out the route toward a program that JDR could sponsor. It also stimulated JDR to reflect more deeply on his role in Asia. He wrote a long memorandum on the subject, tracing the path he had taken from the cultural activities of the Dulles mission to his interest in agriculture in Southeast Asia.

He saw clearly that any effort of his "could so easily be swallowed up by this vastness and be of no long-range consequence," and resolved to keep his efforts "sharply focused" and his expectations modest. In three realms—the economic, cultural, and population fields—he could act. The political dimension would affect the others, but it was outside his reach since he had no official status. But he felt he should not shun an opportunity if it presented itself—"an occasional conversation of an informal character" or "a government assignment in the form of a mission."

Of prime importance in JDR's mind was population. The Population Council was worldwide in purview, but as a practical matter most of its work would concern Asia: "It would seem to underlie all other problems and defeat their solution unless it is somehow coped with. Because of the strong tide of nationalism that is running in this area, and because of the sensitivity and insecurity not to mention political considerations, it is one of the most difficult problems towards which a non-Asian can make a contribution."

Noticeably absent from this paper was any reference to the Cold War. JDR did not regard it as justifying his programs. Rather, his aims were the betterment of U.S.-Japanese relations and "area integration," by which he meant "a better understanding and a closer working relationship" between Japan and the countries of Southeast Asia. Most important, he agreed completely with the views of James Y. C. Yen, Wolf Ladejinsky, and others that the most effective way to promote democracy in Asia and combat communism was to deal with the basic problems that afflicted the Asian masses, rather than simply engaging in Cold War rhetoric.

If he were to meet even the least of his objectives, JDR felt he would have to become known within the various countries "and obtain the confidence of the leaders." He counted on frequent visits to Asia, receiving foreign leaders in the United States, and responding to "special and unique" opportunities that these leaders might create by requests for help on a short-term basis. Hence the need for a basic program flexible enough to accommodate any number of projects. As for getting started: "My feeling is that the program under consideration in the field of agricultural economics is ideally suited to initiate our area integration efforts. With the limited funds at present available a few projects of quality would appear to be the only sound approach."[14]

The new organization was incorporated as the Council on Economic and Cultural Affairs on November 23, 1953. Although much taken with what he had learned about agricultural economics, JDR's interest in a variety of programs was the reason for giving the organization such a broad title and not limiting it to agriculture. He was thinking of cultural projects in Japan, possibly some economic activities other than agriculture, and the "short-range" projects that might be proposed by an Asian leader.[15] Other names had been considered such as "Far East Fund" and "Rockefeller 3rd Fund," but JDR decided that the title he had chosen would do, at least for the present. He gave the organization securities worth approximately $96,000 to start with and to satisfy the IRS for a tax-exempt rating. The post of director was offered to Efferson, but he declined because of his commitment to his university. He went on the board, however, as did JDR (with the title of president), Bill Myers, Fred Osborn of the Population Council, Doug Overton of the Japan Society, and several others.

Don McLean was unhappy with the unwieldy name of the new organization and its broad mandate. He feared it would not attract enough money to make a dent on Asian problems, or indeed draw able people to the staff. He had the same fears about the Population Council and proposed various options to JDR, such as merging the two Councils or merging the new one with the American Universities Field Staff, Phillips Talbot's organization. (Both JDR and McLean held Talbot in high regard, and he was invited to serve on the board of the new Council.) The most obvious course (as McLean wrote) was simply to plunge ahead and build up the new organization and see what developed. This is what JDR decided to do.[16]

With Efferson not available, JDR hired Dr. J Lossing Buck as director of the new Council. He was the first husband of Pearl Buck, the novelist, an agricultural economist and a man who had spent much of his life in the Far East. He was nearing retirement in 1954 after having spent seven years as head of the Land and Water Use Branch of the UN's Food and Agricultural Organization. Buck's first step was to take a four-month survey tour of the region, lasting into early 1955, as a basis for proposing a program to the board. Meanwhile, at the end of the year, JDR supplied the Council with $360,000 from his own funds and $632,000 from his trust income. He committed another $258,000 early in 1955, making a total of $1,250,000 of basic financing—$250,000 a year for five years, time enough, he hoped, for other sources of funds to be found.[17]

Buck's aim was to increase production by improving the managerial ability of Asian farmers "principally through education, including the informal type of education known as agricultural extension." The programs he initiated offered fellowships for study abroad, provided visiting professors at Asian institutions, worked with the UN to sponsor regional farm management courses, and supplied books, equipment, and grants for pilot projects.[18]

Buck's budget of $550,000 was approved by the board and was made possible by a Rockefeller Brothers Fund grant of $300,000 a year for three years. The Fund continued its generous support in later years, while JDR increased his gifts. In the first seven years, his contributions averaged half a million a year.

With A. B. Lewis as his principal aide, Buck spent the three years before his retirement establishing the basic activities of the Council. But it was under the regime of his successor, Arthur T. Mosher, a Ph.D. economist from the University of Chicago, that the Council began to earn its international reputation for excellence both in scholarly accomplishment and field work. Mosher was a remarkable combination of scholar, missionary, and executive. He had specialized in agricultural economics, with fifteen years' experience in India and teaching at Cornell before Chicago. In India he had been an agricultural missionary and president of Allahabad University, a small agricultural college supported by the Presbyterian Church. Phillips Talbot, who had known Mosher in India, was the one who recommended him to JDR.

One of Mosher's first acts was to bring in Clifton R. Wharton, Jr., and Abraham M. Weisblat to form a nucleus of professional leadership that remained in charge for a long time to come.

In 1958 the Rockefeller and Ford Foundations concluded an agreement with the Philippine Republic to build and run the International Rice Research Institute at Los Baños. Ford provided the capital funds and Rockefeller the operating budget, in association with the University of the Philippines. An international board was created representing each of the countries of the region. The Institute opened in 1962.[19] The region now had the research center that Stacy May had recommended and Bill Myers thought so important.

By that time the Council on Economic and Cultural Affairs was going strong, spending nearly one million a year and maintaining personnel in five countries of Southeast Asia. Its work was almost entirely in agriculture. The "cultural" activities never developed beyond a few small grants here and there. Finally, in 1963, Don McLean's concern over the name and mandate of the organization was taken care of when it was renamed the

Agricultural Development Council. The specific cause for this reorganization was JDR's decision to launch a major new effort in Asian cultural affairs in a new organization (see Chapter 16).

Though perhaps the most respected organization in its field, the Council under any name could not be a highly visible organization. By its very nature, its work would not show dramatic breakthroughs, such as a miracle grain produced by a research institute or a new contraceptive in the population field. The result was that the Council did not attract large outside donations as the Population Council did. But by creating both the Population and Agricultural Councils, JDR established himself solidly on both sides of the development equation in Asia—population *and* food. He manifestly did not believe in the simplicity of single solutions, and he showed his innate grasp of the complexity and long-range nature of "development" and his ability to patiently remain involved over a long period of time. His background, experience, and early resolve were bearing fruit.

What is more, he had succeeded in drawing a clear line between his role within the Rockefeller Foundation and his activities as an individual philanthropist. As chairman, he would help frame the policies of the great Foundation in an open and objective way. As an individual, he would follow his own interests and instincts, supplementing the Foundation's work, doing what it could not or would not do, creating new organizations in two all-important fields where no one else showed any inclination to act, and establishing outposts that in due course attracted the support of others and gained renown for their quality and effectiveness.

6

𝕸

AT HOME IN ASIA

WHEN JDR examined the reasons for his interest in Asia and weighed the means of being effective there, he emphasized personal relations. If he were to achieve his purpose "even in a small degree," he wrote, the first step "would seem to be a personal general familiarity with the several countries and an acquaintance with at least some of the leaders." Wolf Ladejinsky agreed: "There is no substitute for the personal element. This is even more so in Asia where most activities are regulated on a man-to-man relationship."[1]

That advice to himself JDR religiously followed. His first trip to Southeast Asia in 1953 set a pattern, to the point that he began referring in letters to "my annual mid-winter visit." Usually accompanied by Blanchette and often by Don McLean, JDR would go to Japan for one or two weeks and then spend up to a month traveling in several of the Southeast Asian countries. These trips were usually made early in the year when the weather was more pleasant in the Far East than in New York. In some years there was a second trip, in summer, when the Rockefellers began introducing their children to Asia; and sometimes a short third trip for some special purpose.

These almost always were not pleasure trips in any conventional sense. As he had resolved, JDR made it his business to become acquainted with the local leaders, official and unofficial—usually entailing a grinding schedule of briefings and appointments.

At home, too, JDR met Asian leaders in Washington at official functions, in New York at the United Nations, the Council on Foreign Relations, or the Foreign Policy Association. And with increasing frequency he and Blanchette began entertaining foreign guests at their two residences in the New York area, the bilevel Manhattan apartment at One

Beekman Place or their attractive country place, Fieldwood Farm, adjacent to the Pocantico estate near North Tarrytown. It all began naturally enough, but it snowballed: an Asian notable would be host to JDR in his home country, and JDR would reciprocate in New York. The State Department began thinking of JDR when planning the agendas of foreign visitors, knowing that they would be well treated at Williamsburg or in New York. Soon visiting Asian leaders began to request that JDR be put on their agendas.

Take the year 1957, for example. When the Rockefellers had returned from their customary six weeks in Japan and Southeast Asia, JDR was consulted by the State Department about the itinerary for the prime minister of Afghanistan, soon to arrive. In June JDR and Blanchette went to Washington for the dinner given by Secretary Dulles for the new Japanese prime minister, Nobusuke Kishi. The next day Kishi and two other Japanese dignitaries arrived at Fieldwood Farm for dinner with the Rockefellers and guests, including John McCloy. The Japanese stayed overnight and made a foursome with JDR for golf at the Pocantico estate. That afternoon the visitors were guests of the New York Yankees at a game. The next day JDR attended Mayor Wagner's luncheon for the visitors, and then presided at the Japan Society dinner in their honor.

Two days later, JDR and Blanchette left for seven weeks in Asia with two of their children. Back home, their weekend guests at Fieldwood Farm included the deputy prime minister of Indonesia, the new ambassador from Pakistan, and later, a large delegation of Vietnamese led by President Ngo Dinh Diem.

JDR would go East with massive briefing books prepared by his staff. He added background papers on political and economic issues, personality sketches of leaders, recent correspondence, and information on Rockefeller Foundation activities. These trips had the trappings of official visits, though they were not. Because he was chairman of the board, there always was some apprehension on the part of Dean Rusk and the senior staff of the Rockefeller Foundation lest JDR should appear to be representing it. He often would meet with Rusk before and after a trip and carefully avoided negotiations or solicitations unless he was specifically charged before he left.

JDR could be absentminded about small things of the moment, but he had a prodigious memory for certain kinds of details about the past. He knew he had difficulty with names, so his briefing books included reminders and one-sentence biographies of Asians whom he had met previously— 686 such entries adorned his book for Japan in 1957.

In the 1950s travel in Southeast Asia could still be rugged, but JDR's concern was for safety and reasonable comfort, not luxury. He preferred hotels, though less comfortable than the guest houses maintained by local governments, the Ford Foundation, or American corporations. For a few years, an exception was the hospitable assistance of the Standard Vacuum Oil Company. Here is JDR's letter to the president of the company in advance of a trip in 1959:

If your people in the various countries could assist us as they have in the past it would be greatly appreciated. I have particularly in mind being able to turn to them for advice as to people to see and places to go. Also at times you have been particularly helpful in the arranging of appointments. On the material side, the providing of a car has been especially valuable to us, it being understood that they would rent a car for us unless they happen to have a local company car free at the time. To be specific as to a car, it would be most helpful if one could be made available in Bombay, Ceylon, Madras, New Delhi, Bangkok and Tokyo.[2]

JDR had reason to value the petroleum connection—and the chance to stay in a guest house—in Bahrain in 1957. With Blanchette, his middle daughter, Hope, and his son, Jay, he was on his way home from the summer trip to Asia. Their plane, a Qantas DC-6, developed engine trouble after stopping at Bahrain and had to turn back. The Rockefellers were facing a thirty-six hour delay in the blazing August heat of the desert sheikhdom, when JDR found that BAPCO (British-American Petroleum Company) was "a Caltex interest." He called up the local vice president "who very kindly asked us to come out to lunch at the company's most comfortable guest house and spend the night."

In 1954, JDR met Sukarno for the first time. JDR found the Indonesian nationalist, the first president of his country, to be a "very vital dynamic person; emotional, opinionated and charming; an egotistical revolutionary leader." In Singapore JDR renewed acquaintance with Malcolm MacDonald, the son of Labour Prime Minister Ramsay MacDonald, whom JDR had first met in 1929 during his postcollege trip around the world. MacDonald was serving as commissioner general for the United Kingdom in Southeast Asia. And in India, JDR met a future prime minister, Morarji R. Desai, chief minister of the state of Bombay.

JDR also saw Nehru again—a disappointing occasion, at least as described by Blanchette, who had formed the habit of writing detailed and highly readable accounts of her trips for her children.[3] The Rockefellers were among only six persons for a late dinner at Nehru's home which, Blanchette wrote, had "nothing of the simplicity of Gandhi." The prime minister "evidently was tired and did not wish to discuss anything but trivialities. Johnny made a few attempts at interesting questions which got nowhere." She found Nehru "a very difficult personality to understand," and "almost wished we had not gone there, as I left India the next morning with a negative and very bitter feeling." Part of the problem was that Indians in general were hostile to Americans at that time because of the current controversy over U.S. military aid to Pakistan. In Pakistan Blanchette was not surprised to find the atmosphere "in conspicuous contrast to that in New Delhi."

In 1959 the Rockefellers were "palace guests" of Prince Sihanouk for two days in Phnom Penh. Blanchette described the experience:

We were installed in a charming and luxurious guesthouse fully staffed with maitre d'hotel and Cambodian servants who crept in and out of our rooms with bodies bent at the waist in the manner of local court humility! Daddy and I were put in well separated double rooms, each with elaborate baths and dressing rooms and no seeming connection between. This is undoubtedly the custom in Cambodia to give visiting Frenchmen and other husbands a freer hand in their social contacts! We were also brought completely separate breakfast and tea trays both days. I think Daddy quite enjoyed his independence!

The Rockefellers had not been sure of their reception because Americans were already identified with South Vietnam and the "Cambodians and Vietnamese hate each other cordially.' Moreover, an attempted coup against Sihanouk, rumored to have been backed by South Vietnam, had just been put down. But at dinner the first night "the Prince was a thoroughly charming host and showed us every possible courtesy, including a superb dinner of blini filled with caviar, pâté de foie gras, etc., and a 16-piece orchestra (for eight guests) that played popular music throughout the evening and included some of Sihanouk's own compositions." The next day the prince sent over "beautiful gifts" of brocade and silver, but he did "cancel his appointment for a private talk with Daddy" which was "the whole purpose" in going to Phnom Penh. Blanchette added that Sihanouk had the reputation of being quixotic and temperamental, but that her husband was able to establish a "rapport" with him at dinner.

The 1950s were especially sensitive years for westerners in Southeast Asia. The Bandung Conference of 1955 launched the idea of a "third world" of countries opposed to the imperialism of both the Communist bloc and the West. The three leaders who played the most prominent roles in that "world" were Sukarno, Nehru, and Chou En-lai of China. Americans had reason to feel that the opposition was much more militant against the West than against the Communist countries, a conviction heightened as the Vietnam crisis deepened late in the decade.

Given JDR's increasing acceptance by Asian leaders and his frequent contacts with them, it might seem probable that he would transact some official business from time to time, if only as the carrier of sensitive messages. There is no evidence in his diary or other records that he ever did so. He was not likely to do anything that would jeopardize his status of private citizen, which was to him important and valuable. Being seen as such and as a trustworthy person, he could have access in Asian countries and remain above suspicion regardless of short-term crises or political currents that otherwise spoiled official relations. This in no way implied that JDR necessarily disagreed with U.S. foreign policy; in fact, American policy-makers recognized the value of such independent liaisons.

The same was true of many organizations sponsored by private sources, or "NGOs" (nongovernmental organizations) as they came to be called. They had some advantages over government programs. Their budgets were usually steadier—less apt to be affected by domestic political issues—and if they were careful of their reputations they would be accepted and could continue their work in countries whose relations with the U.S. government were less than friendly. For years the Ford and Rockefeller Foundations carried on major activities in India while official Indian sentiment was hostile to Washington. All the organizations that JDR sponsored kept functioning throughout Asia with nothing but approval despite changing political currents.

JDR does note in his diary one occasion in 1957 when he tried to give Secretary Dulles some advice. The annual trip that year had included a stop in Vietnam. JDR reminded Dulles of a remark the Secretary had made recently "to the effect that U.S. policy must be motivated by principle rather than based simply on cooperation with our friends and allies." JDR told Dulles that in his travels he had found that "Asians wanted to be friendly to the West and would be greatly encouraged in this direction if the USA followed a consistent foreign policy in regard to colonialism." There is no record of any response from Dulles or of any other such initiative by JDR. One gets the impression that his comment fell on deaf ears.

JDR had a better chance to influence policy in 1959 when President Eisenhower offered him the post of U.S. ambassador to Indonesia. He was urged to take it by Dulles and other Washington friends, and he gave the offer serious thought. In the end he declined, deciding that he could be more effective over the long term if he maintained his private status. This was only the first of a number of occasions when he had to make such a decision.

The proffered diplomatic post was not inappropriate, for as time passed,

JDR was becoming something of an expert, especially about Japan. He had also taken a special interest in India and Indonesia, and he was more and more often sought out as a speaker and writer on Asian affairs. But he accepted very few of these opportunities. He always felt a measure of humility, never making the mistake of considering himself more than a knowledgeable layman in any of his many interests.

At the same time, he was learning enough to avoid palaces and government ministries as much as possible. Otherwise he would be subjected to extensive briefings and boring tours that added little to his knowledge. He did enough official visiting to maintain the high-level contacts he had made, but he wanted to fashion his own agenda and move from capital cities to the countryside. He came to prefer meeting local leaders and common people, visiting clinics and villages rather than government bureaus.

For the trip of 1963, the publicist Earl Newsom proposed the idea of sending a writer along, convinced that the concern of this tall, wealthy American for the poverty-stricken masses of Asia was matter for a good story. JDR was no publicity-seeker, had never been, but he had come to see that publicity could help the causes he had at heart; so from time to time he tried to cooperate. The free-lancer whom Newsom produced was Lewis Lapham, a gifted writer who later became editor-in-chief of *Harper's*. Frank Notestein of the Population Council was accompanying JDR on the trip and Lapham joined them. In keeping with JDR's gingerly feelings of reluctance, Lapham's draft, intended for the *Saturday Evening Post*, never saw publication.[4] But it leaves for us a graphic account of JDR in East Pakistan (now Bangladesh), one of the worst areas of overpopulation and poverty in the world. The Pop Council was trying to assist the government of Pakistan in its efforts to mount a birth control program, one of the first in the underdeveloped world. But it was discouraging to find how very little effective action was being taken. One day JDR and Notestein took a walk down to the ferry landing on the Buriganga River in the walled city of Dacca. Lapham describes the scene:

The narrow, dusty streets cluttered with people and animals of all descriptions, smelled of bad meat, urine and sweat. Beggars leaned against the crumbling mud walls, their hands fixedly outstretched in hopes of alms. The flies on the shaven head of a sick child were as thick as caraway seeds on a roll. The few women in the streets, looking like bundles of old rags, wore veils and gold ornaments in their pierced ears and nostrils.

We reached the west bank of the river at dusk. The sun, setting through a mauve haze, squatted on the flat roofs of the town. A dhow moved laboriously upstream under oars and a red sail. On the stone stairs leading up from the shore, a holy man, his hair matted with dirt, gestured unintelligibly to an indifferent audience. The sand swarmed with people.

Rockefeller said nothing for perhaps twenty minutes. He stood beside an over-turned oil drum, confronted by the chaos so remote from the orderly presentations on the 56th floor of the R.C.A. Building. Here at last was what he had come to see, the plain reality of the so-called "population explosion." No statistics, no high-flown sentiments, no handsomely-illustrated brochures or predictions of disaster for mankind; just a lot of people pushed down to the edge of a warm river.

"The numbers," he said, "the sheer numbers of it . . . the quality, you see, goes down."

A band of staring children, baffled by the sudden appearance of the strange men wearing dark suits, had gathered around Rockefeller. He looked as wonderingly at them as they did at him. One boy, he thought, had "a really sensitive face . . . but so poor, so little opportunity."

Only when the last light of the sun had faded from the river did Rockefeller turn away from the crowded shore. "Well," he said, touching me lightly on the arm, "maybe you begin to get an idea." The children beside him, their eyes still round with amazement, stepped aside to let him pass.[5]

Even as JDR's interest broadened to all of the Far East and South Asia, it was Japan that retained his deepest affection. It was in Japan that, in one sense, it had all started, that the culture of the nation and the character of the man seemed so much in harmony. JDR rapidly came to occupy a special place in the eyes of the Japanese as the one leading American who genuinely cared about them. And his attachment was made all the warmer by the fact that his wife shared it. They developed lasting friendships; Japan came to be like a second home to them.

After six weeks in India, Pakistan, and Indonesia during the 1954 trip, Blanchette wrote of her delight in reaching Tokyo and finding herself in the same room of the Imperial Hotel: "There is the same delicious aroma of Japanese hair tonic and floor wax and the bell boys and maids seem to recognize us which always warms the heart. The air outside was about 40 degrees and we began to feel like human beings again!"

During this visit, the Rockefellers were invited to tea with the emperor and empress at the palace, an "informal" occasion lasting an hour. Blanchette was thrilled "by this great courtesy and honor." She found the royal couple "very friendly and natural" although "it is hard at best to work through an interpreter." The emperor conferred on JDR the "Grand Cordon of the Order of the Sacred Treasure" in appreciation of his work on Japanese-American cultural relations and for help during the crown prince's visit to the United States. In her account for the children, Blanchette described the decoration in "a beautiful black lacquer box with silver characters on top. Inside was a huge yellow and green ribbon to wear across his chest and two wonderful medallions of silver and colored enamel. . . . It was a complete surprise to me, although Daddy admitted that he knew about it ahead of time. In his modesty, he had not taken me in on the secret."

When it came time to end the trip, Blanchette wrote that she was "really sad" about it; Japan was her favorite place "other than home."

I dearly hope that someday we can go there to live for a few months in a house rather than a hotel. There are numbers of places I would like to visit and many leisurely hours I would like to spend with Japanese friends, looking at old and new art and architecture. We have barely scratched the surface of the possible delights. I feel at home with the people and admire them for their charming manners and thoughtfulness and for their keen aesthetic sense. They have a lot to teach us Americans.

In 1955 Blanchette got her wish: an uninterrupted stay of two summer months in Japan. It started in the same Imperial Hotel suite, but ended in a Japanese home. One of the purposes of the visit was to give Hope and Jay a thorough introduction to the country their parents loved so much. The fourth child, Alida, was too young to profit from such a trip, and the eldest, Sandra, was already well advanced in her work in art and so chose to spend the summer at an art camp.

Hope had just graduated from Brearley and Jay had finished his freshman finals at Harvard. Both of them were a year ahead of their age group in school—Jay was eighteen and Hope seventeen. It was their first trip to the Orient, and they were soon entranced. For the first few weeks their parents acted like tourists and took them to see the sights in Tokyo, Kyoto, Osaka, and elsewhere. Toward the end of the stay, the family split up. Hope went off to the mountains for a two-week program at the Kiyosato Educational Experimental Project; Jay spent the same weeks on a walking tour of the Hokkaido countryside with Lloyd Graham, a young Canadian missionary student who spoke fluent Japanese. Meanwhile, Blanchette and her husband lived in a Japanese house in the town of Karuizawa. It was a real vacation, a change of pace from JDR's normal regimen on trips abroad. As his diary shows, the Rockefellers were not lonely:

Friday, July 15: Tokyo-Karuizawa

. . . In Karuizawa we have a Japanese style house owned by Sazo Idemitsu, head of the Apollo Oil Company, a Japanese concern. It was arranged through Ichimada and Matsumoto. While not too attractive it is perfect for our needs. A staff of four is provided for us. They seem excellent. We find Mr. and Mrs.

Matsumoto are spending the weekend with us to get us organized and established.

Saturday, July 16—Monday, August 1: In Karuizawa

Our stay here really worked out very well indeed. The house was intriguing and comfortable, the staff most satisfactory and our social life in just the right amount. Golf was our main activity, we playing almost every day on the new golf course. The weather was a bit rainy in the beginning and a bit hot the last part but really very pleasant with a blanket needed at night. We kept house, Blanchette doing all the marketing, which was fun.

Our social life consisted of: two weekends with the Matsumotos in town; several meetings with the Jiro Shirazus who were most friendly; contacts with the Asos who were staying at the Kampai Hotel at the end; lunch and golf with the Kuchis: an afternoon meeting with nice Mr. Mukai who stopped in; an interesting dinner (tempura) at the home of Ataru Kobayashi whom Shirazu felt we should meet (he is President of the Development Bank in Japan and seemed able); golf with Prof. Royama 3 times and also lunch; golf also with Tokujiro Tanaka, President of the Tokyo Marine Insurance Co. and most charming (arranged with Prof. Royama); golf with Takasumi Mitsui and Tadao Watanabe, President of the Sanwa Bank of Osaka and formerly with the Bank of Japan (a very nice person); also golf and tea with young Mikimoto and some of their friends in their "art colony." . . .

That summer trip of 1955 was to have a profound impact on Jay's life and his relationship with his parents, especially his father. Jay was very tall, having shot up to six and a half feet so quickly that he had been somewhat gawky and uncoordinated as an adolescent. His father, accustomed to being known as the "tall" Rockefeller, found himself looking up nearly half a foot to his son. In personality, Jay tended toward his mother's side of the family, more outgoing and happy-go-lucky. The daughters, especially Hope, were more like the serious and introspective father.

Though never a problem child, Jay caused his parents some worry for a time. The combination of his great height and the Rockefeller identity could have produced an acutely self-conscious young man. He was not exactly a poor student, but he showed few signs of being a particularly good one, either. During his first two years at Exeter, his mother reports, he was "miserable." It was a large school, and he found it hard to get adjusted. But "socialization" took place and his last two years were happy ones, as Jay's naturally positive nature and capacity to enjoy himself gradually emerged. He did well in his studies, formed close friendships, and began to date. His father tried to steer Jay toward Princeton, but Exeter was oriented toward Harvard, and Jay followed a number of his friends there.

The question of a major at Harvard was settled for Jay after his 1955 summer trip to Japan. Backpacking through the countryside, meeting farmers and fishermen, staying in youth hostels and peasants' houses made an unforgettable impression. Jay remembers stopping at a 500-year old farmhouse and chatting with the owner, who represented the thirty-ninth generation of the family that had tilled the soil in the same place:

We sat on the floor, shoes off, and were served a simple meal. After we had finished eating, I looked at this man who was sitting across from us, this solid man who was working exactly as his forefathers had for half a millennium. He represented the backbone of Asia, of the world. He was plain and honest, no deception, no compromise. For the first time in my life I felt truly humble.[6]

Jay took Asian studies as his major at Harvard, with special emphasis on China and Japan, his adviser being Edwin O. Reischauer. The choice naturally pleased his father, but Jay did not distinguish himself. He was in no danger of failing, but was not making clear progress, either. After he finished his third year at Harvard, Blanchette remembers an evening when she and her husband were dining alone with Jay. He suddenly asked, What would they think if he dropped out of Harvard for a year and spent it in Japan?

The Rockefellers immediately felt the parents' usual fear that their son would never finish college. Jay eased their minds somewhat by explaining that the idea had come from Reischauer. Jay needed to acquire competence in either Chinese or Japanese in order to obtain the degree, and Reischauer had suggested that he might best achieve the purpose by immersing himself in the Japanese language and culture for a year on the spot. Jay enthusiastically agreed. Very likely Reischauer shrewdly perceived that a change of scene would do Jay some good. JDR was apprehensive, but he agreed. In the end, he was proud of Jay's choice and his ability to follow through on his plan. It was a unique endorsement by a son of a strong interest of his father's, and JDR was deeply touched by it.

Jay made the Eastern summer trip of 1957 with his parents and Hope, arranging in Tokyo to spend the academic year at International Christian University. Instead of continuing around the world with the rest of the family, Jay flew home to have a month there before returning to Tokyo. In mid-1958, nearly a year after he took up residence, local reporters discovered the tall young Rockefeller scion, a giant to the

Japanese, living among them as a student. Stories and photographs appeared in Asian publications and in *Life* magazine. One account described Jay's regimen:

On a budget of $27 a month, he lives in an unheated dormitory in a Tokyo university, shaves with cold water, sleeps on a thin mattress on the floor, eats rice with almost every meal and absorbs oriental philosophy by constant discussions with fellow students.[7]

The first year was a good experience, though Jay had made the mistake of agreeing to teach English eight hours a week. This had two drawbacks. It interfered with his learning Japanese, for fellow students would practice their English when speaking with him. And such deference is paid to teachers in the Japanese culture that students tended to treat Jay formally, which interfered with his effort to establish himself as their equal in a spirit of camaraderie.

As a result, Jay decided to prolong his stay; he ended up spending three years in Japan, going home for brief vacations only twice during that time. He gave up teaching English and concentrated on Japanese. During the second year he studied fourteen hours a day. To fellow students he was at first the "rich big one," but he soon became known simply as "Jay." He shared a house in Tokyo with five other students. For much of the third year, Matsumoto arranged for him to live with an artist and his family in Kyoto, where only Japanese was spoken.

Jay went on to finish his final year at Harvard, majoring in Japanese history and culture. In the fall of 1961 he entered a Chinese language program operated by the U.S. Air Force at Yale, with the intention of fulfilling the language requirement for entering a graduate program in Chinese History. But he soon decided that he had had enough of intensive language study, and he headed to Washington for a job on the Indonesian desk in the State Department and the beginnings of a career in public life. In Blanchette's judgment, the experience in Japan was an important turning point for her son. He went there a boy and returned home a man, matured and self-assured. It also helped cement his relationship with his father, in her view "a wonderful relationship." The two could sit together for hours discussing the culture of Japan and the Far East at large.

The unique status of JDR in Japan was the result of several factors—his presence during the Dulles peace treaty mission, the Rockefeller mystique, the uncanny meshing of his own personality and temperament with those of the Japanese, the obvious warmth he and his wife held for the country and the many friendships they made. There was also the important fact that this affinity was manifested in tangible projects. These were intended to build cultural bridges between Japan and the United States and gently nudge the Japanese on the path to new and enlightened relations with the other countries of the Far East—both purposes very much in Japan's interest.

In New York the Japan Society grew steadily to become the outstanding example of a successful bilateral organization in the United States. As we shall see in the next chapter, it is extremely difficult to create and sustain organizations of this kind. The Japan Society was in a particularly good position to achieve success because of the leadership and financial support of JDR and the steadily growing political and economic importance of U.S.-Japanese relations. Under Douglas Overton as executive director, the Society continually branched into new activities and attracted a growing body of members and corporate contributors.

At the same time, the International House in Tokyo flourished under the able leadership of Shigeharu Matsumoto, who secured strong local support. The House became a remarkable center of international understanding and intellectual ferment, as JDR, Matsumoto, and the other founders had intended, combining the functions of a center and hostelry for foreign students (akin to its counterparts on several American campuses) and a program similar to the Council on Foreign Relations in New York. One link between the Japan Society and the Tokyo International House was the intellectual exchange program that JDR had sponsored at Columbia University. It brought to Japan and the International House such leaders as Eleanor Roosevelt, Norman Cousins, Paul Tillich, J. Robert Oppenheimer, and David Riesman, and to the United States in return came a stream of Japanese intellectuals.

JDR also worked hard to build one other cultural bridge to Japan—the teaching there of English as a second language. To this cause he contributed considerable time over a period of fifteen years and approximately $1.5 million through a variety of channels. This effort might seem like an act of cultural imperialism; it was in fact a response to a genuine need recognized and pressed by the Japanese themselves. They had come to see English as an international language and the proper one for children in Japanese schools to learn. The Ministry of Education made it a requirement. Given Japan's political situation and commercial prospects, the move was wise. But at the outset the Japanese were unprepared for teaching English on a national scale. The language had not been a major subject in their schools before the war, and what little had been done was suspended during the war. After it, texts and methods were antiquated and qualified English teachers were few.

Several people brought the need to JDR's attention as early as 1953— Matsumoto and other Japanese leaders; Overton of the Japan Society; Edwin Reischauer; Hugh Borton, who managed the intellectual exchange program at Columbia, and Charles Woolsey Cole, president of Amherst College, who had been the first American to visit Japan under that program. But not until the summer of 1955 did JDR respond to the idea. His diary records:

As never before I am appreciating on this trip the importance of English language teaching in Japan. The lack of a common foreign language is a barrier which becomes increasingly serious with the development of modern communications. What has particularly struck me on this visit is the fact that it is not only a barrier to the West but also within Asia itself. This all makes me keener than ever to consider the further possibility of whether English language teaching in Japan can be made more effective.

Nevertheless, the project was slow aborning, delayed by the usual need for surveys and studies, both Japanese and American, and the need to steer the idea through the sensitivities of the Japanese bureaucracy and teachers' union, so that it would emerge as a home-grown product rather than something imposed by Americans. Within a few years a special steering committee assembled by Matsumoto provided a blueprint for a permanent program. The English Language Education Council, known as "ELEC" from that time on, was created with a board composed of prominent Japanese. It began work promptly, using foreign consultants, developing textbooks and other teaching and testing materials, holding summer seminars for teachers, framing university entrance requirements, and setting up teacher-training programs.

JDR was the financial mainstay, funneling his grants through the Japan Society and his Council on Economic and Cultural Affairs. Local financial support was hard to come by until the Ford Foundation became interested in supporting ELEC. An arrangement was reached between Ford and JDR to provide $600,000 each over a five-year period, $300,000 earmarked for assistance in constructing a building for the program in Tokyo. This last amount was only one-third of the building's cost, the remainder having to be raised in yen and, in the tradition of Rockefeller philanthropy, establishing that local support for the project existed.

ELEC helped to overcome bureaucratic resistance to new teaching methods. It was supported by businessmen who had become aware of the critical importance of English to Japanese commercial interests. ELEC spawned chapters in cities throughout Japan and continued to play a role in the establishment of English as the second language in Japan.

JDR's love of Japan was continually demonstrated by activities such as these and his frequent presence in the country. The affection was very much reciprocated by the Japanese. In trying to assess the importance of JDR to Japan, Douglas Overton of the Japan Society commented in his oral history that JDR belonged to "the aristocracy of those who care."

This man . . . has always struck me as a gentle and humane and very powerful person who never seeks to push himself forward but who does demand from you excellence. From the point of view of the Japanese people who got to know him from 1952 onward, he was a friend indeed. In fact, in 1952, one might say, he was the only American of prominence who showed any real and serious and continued interest in Japan. He emerged on the scene when the Japanese needed a friend abroad; and he, because he had no particular axe to grind, no economic interests, and no political ambitions, was able to fill the role with the Japanese of being what one might call something of a father figure.[8]

Even as he maintained his solid base in Japan, JDR's interest, as we have seen, was branching out to other Asian countries. He had sponsored cultural institutions to strengthen ties between the United States and Japan. Could he also do something along similar lines with other Far Eastern countries?

7

♕

THE ASIA SOCIETY

JDR's NEWFOUND INTEREST in South Asia soon inspired the thought that some kind of American organization should be created to foster cultural relations with the region in a manner analogous to the Japan Society. Aside from JDR's personal interest in this extension of his aims, a number of other reasons made such an innovation seem opportune— the wartime experience, vastly increased American presence and responsibilities in the region, and the great advances in communications and transportation technologies that made the Asian countries far less remote than formerly.

Discussions were going on in many quarters over the possibility of creating various bilateral organizations in addition to the Japan Society. The China Institute existed, chaired by Henry Luce, but its program was now confined to Taiwan. There was the Philippine-American Chamber of Commerce, a similar organization for Indonesia, an American-Korean Foundation, and a half dozen organizations pertaining to India, all of which seemed to be moribund. Chester Bowles and the writer James Michener were trying to stir up interest in a major new bilateral organization for India. Much of the debate in JDR's office centered on whether bilateral organizations should be sponsored for the larger, more populous countries such as India and Indonesia, or one organization created to encompass the entire region.

JDR and McLean tended toward the latter view, believing that the special circumstances that would make the Japan Society financially viable were not present in the case of other Asian countries, even the larger ones. And if one proceeded on a country-by-country basis, it would mean that great stretches of the vast continent would be left out.

McLean first brought up the subject in a memorandum entitled "Thoughts on the Far East."[1]

The more I think about your concern for the Far East and your desire to establish yourself as a person of distinction with a Far Eastern identity, the more I am impressed by the desirability for your establishing some kind of a focal point in this country of interest in the Far East. There is no effective center at the present time.

By this time JDR had established a policy and planning committee in his office, similar in purpose to his father's Advisory Committee on Benevolences, on which JDR had served as a young man. The members of JDR's new group were McLean, Young, Lockwood, Jamieson, and Dalrymple, with others included temporarily when they were relevant to a particular subject. One such person was Charles Noyes, a staff member of the Rockefeller Brothers Fund who had a Far Eastern background. Noyes did the initial studies for the creation of an Asian cultural organization, with Ed Young soon assigned to help him. Throughout the rest of 1954 and 1955, the subject appeared regularly on the committee's agenda, variously referred to as "Pan-Asian Society" or "Asian organization" or "one overall organization for Southeast Asia."²

Young and Noyes compiled a list of all existing organizations having something to do with one or another aspect of American relations with Asian countries. With two exceptions, they found that all were tiny or highly specialized. The two were the Institute for Pacific Relations (and its American branch), headquartered in New York, and the Asia Foundation, located in San Francisco. The immediate question was whether it would be better and easier to build up one of these organizations instead of creating a third one, just as JDR had renewed the Japan Society instead of starting something entirely new. But both the Institute and the Foundation had political liabilities associated with the bitter mood and temper of the times—the right-wing postwar backlash over presumed Communist infiltration and American "failures" in the Far East.

JDR had experienced no serious political problems in rebuilding the Japan Society because the former wartime enemy was now a most favored nation. It was a different story when it came to the rest of Asia. So bizarre and vicious was the postwar backlash in the period 1946–1954 that it is difficult today to recall and believe the excesses of the time, the wild accusations hurled about, the careers destroyed, the fear that penetrated organizations, both in government and the private sector. It was the heyday of the congressional inquisition. In his comprehensive book on the period, *The Great Fear: The Anti-Communist Purge Under Truman and Eisenhower*, David Caute provides a telling statistic. In the postwar period up to 1954 there were no fewer than 135 congressional investigations into alleged Communist activities (and hundreds more on other subjects), compared to a total of only 285 investigations in all the years of the American republic from 1789 to 1925.[3]

The most famous of the inquisitorial bodies were the House Un-American Activities Committee of Martin Dies and J. Parnell Thomas, Pat McCarran's Senate Internal Security Subcommittee, and Senator Joseph McCarthy's Government Operations subcommittee. So often did the same witnesses appear before these and other bodies that they came to be known as "professional" ex- or anti-Communists—Louis Budenz, Manning Johnson, Maurice Malkin, Igor Bogolepov, Elizabeth Bentley, Freda Utley, and many others. These were the days of guilt by association, character assassination, overworking of the Fifth Amendment, and deportation proceedings.

The right-wing atttack was fueled by a resurgence of isolationism, anger over the perceived failings of American foreign policy, and an almost paranoid fear of communism. The main target was the "eastern liberal establishment"—the Cold War internationalists and interventionists who predominated in the Truman administration, in intellectual circles, and in national media located on the eastern seaboard. As a defensive measure, the Truman administration promulgated a loyalty oath and launched its own purge of government employees. Neither this nor the staunch anti-communism of the administration and its supporters could abate the storm.[4]

It was not conceivable that tax-exempt foundations would escape the attention of the right-wing critics. As Waldemar Nielsen comments in his book, *The Big Foundations*:

Repeatedly throughout history, when nations have been under heavy stress or in the throes of social crisis, foundations have become a favorite target of official frustration and popular anxiety. . . . The United States, although unique in the modern world for the encouragement it still accords to private philanthropy, is no exception to this universal pattern. In the years before World War I, when the number of foundations was just beginning to swell following an era of great economic growth, they became a focus of bitter controversy between the forces of reckless capital and radical labor. In the agony of the great depression of the 1930s they again became a favorite object of attack, and in the hysteria of the McCarthy period after World War II they suffered the same fate.[5]

By 1950 numerous foundations had come in for a barrage of criticism from the conservative press and various congressional investigating committees. This became a focused attack in 1952 when the House of Representatives authorized still another investigating committee, this one to probe whether foundations used their tax-exempt wealth "to promote subversive activities" and "exert un-American and subversive influence on public opinion." The chairman was E. Eugene Cox, an anti–New Deal and anti–Fair Deal Democrat who had been in the House for twenty-five years. A few voices were raised in protest over this particular committee and the general proliferation of investigative bodies—the voices of Senator Wayne Morse of Oregon and Congressmen Emmanuel Celler and Jacob Javits of New York—but there was little doubt that Cox was riding the tide of popular opinion at the time. His political views are suggested by one of his more memorable statements: "If I had to have a change, I'd infinitely prefer a strong militaristic government of the type of Germany and Italy than of socialistic Russia."[6]

The animus against foundations was stirred up particularly by the perjury conviction of Alger Hiss, who had served for years as president of the Carnegie Endowment for International Peace. A favored target was the Ford Foundation, then under the liberal guidance of its president, Paul Hoffman, and his deputy, Robert Maynard Hutchins, former chancellor of the University of Chicago. Many other foundations were the objects of accusations made by the "professional" anti-Communist witnesses, who were trotted out once more by the Cox Committee. Most of the charges had to do with grants made by the foundations to organizations (or individuals associated with them) that were on the notorious list of subversive organizations first promulgated by Truman's Attorney General, Tom Clark, in 1948. A parade of foundation executives appeared before the committee to defend their organizations, most of them avowing that they had immediately ceased giving grants to organizations once they appeared on the Attorney General's list.

The Rockefeller Foundation soon came in for attention because it had been the major source of financial support for the Institute for Pacific Relations (IPR) for twenty-five years. The Institute had become a battered organization, suffering from the general attack on all those who were thought somehow to be responsible for the "loss" of China and the alleged undermining of American interests in the Far East. Already among the chief victims were a number of scholars of Asian affairs and the "China hands" in the State Department—the Foreign Service Officers who had reported their doubts about the Nationalist regime and the wisdom of trying to prop it up. The Institute was under fire on many counts. There was the past association with it of Frederick Vanderbilt Field, an avowed Communist sympathizer, as JDR had reason to know from his conversations with Field years earlier.[7]

However, the main target was Professor Owen Lattimore of Johns

Hopkins University, who had served as editor of the IPR's journal, *Pacific Affairs*, from 1934 to 1941. Thereafter, he worked for the Office of War Information and served as a policy adviser in addition to teaching at Johns Hopkins. In 1950 Senator McCarthy had denounced Lattimore for everything from being "the chief architect of our Far Eastern policy" to being the top Soviet espionage agent operating in the United States. Because of this and the fact that Lattimore vigorously defended himself, he had undergone twelve days of merciless grilling earlier in 1952 by McCarran's Internal Security Subcommittee. By the time the hearings ended in June, some sixty individuals associated in one way or another with the Institute over the years had been assailed as Communist sympathizers or actual party members. The subcommittee's report held that "but for the machinations of the small group that controlled [the Institute], China would be free."[8]

In the Cox Committee hearings, foundations sought to distance themselves from the IPR. Testifying for the Rockefeller Foundation was its president, Dean Rusk, who said he was "concerned" about allegations of bias on the part of the Institute's staff and that the prospect of future grants "was remote."[9]

With the winding down of the congressional term and the illness of Representative Cox, his subcommittee went out of business, causing the *New York Times* to note editorially its approval of the end of efforts to pillory "these great organizations that have done so much to promote human knowledge and understanding."[10]

It was not to be. In the new Republican-controlled Congress a staunch conservative from the traditionally Republican area of northeastern Tennessee, B. Carroll Reece, managed to re-create the committee with the same terms of reference and himself as chairman. It is likely that the impetus was provided by a defiant action taken by Paul Hoffman and Robert Hutchins. During the Cox Committee hearings, Henry Ford II angrily had moved in to shake up the Ford Foundation, dismissing Hoffman, moving the Foundation from Pasadena to New York, and installing Rowan Gaither as president. Some eighteen months earlier, the Foundation had appropriated $15 million to create the Fund for the Republic, with Hoffman as chairman. He delayed activating the organization for a time because of the widely publicized attack on foundations, but finally appointed Clifford Case, a moderate Republican, as president of the Fund. Case soon resigned to run for the Senate in New Jersey. With the Cox Committee hearings ended, Hoffman then named Robert Hutchins to succeed Case. Hutchins proceeded to give the Fund a

strongly liberal and civil rights orientation. This—and Hutchins himself—were anathema to the conservatives.[11]

The Reece Committee began its hearings in May 1953, opening with
publication of a staff report highly critical of foundations. A long series of
witnesses, drawn mainly from conservative members of academia, repeated
charges made to the Cox Committee and added a great many more. One
prominent theme was that foundations, particularly Ford, Carnegie, and
Rockefeller, were subverting education in the United States. The
Rockefeller Foundation was attacked again for supporting the IPR, as well
as the Kinsey sex research project at Indiana University and the General
Education Board. It was further criticized for giving fellowships to twenty-
six "leftists."

An important difference this time was that several Democratic congressmen on the Committee, led by Wayne Hays of Ohio, formed an
opposition bloc, consistently criticizing the tactics and bias of the committee majority and the staff. For months, a battle raged between Hays and
Reece, until Reece abruptly terminated the hearings and issued a report
containing scores of wild accusations against foundations. A storm of protest
came from foundation leaders over the fact that they had not had a chance
to testify to rebut the charges made by the adverse witnesses and the
committee majority report. More than a dozen foundations filed rebuttal
papers. The seventy-five-page Rockefeller paper contained a foreword by
JDR and comments by Rusk, who dismissed the charges as "bizarre
innuendoes."[12]

The foundations came out of the Cox and Reece hearings relatively
unscathed. In fact, the experience taught JDR a good deal and helped
prepare him for another time when the pressure on foundations would be
even more intense. Others were not so fortunate—the countless individuals whose careers and lives were destroyed and the organizations shattered
by the inquisition. Prominent among these were Owen Lattimore and the
IPR. The government finally dropped its case against Lattimore and the
Institute was fully vindicated in the courts, but of course the real damage
had been done. Lattimore previously had published nine books, but not
for another eighteen years would an American publisher accept one from
him. And the sources of funding for the Institute virtually dried up. Its
income dropped from $77,000 in 1951 to less than $20,000 in 1956. The
crowning blow came in 1955 when IRS commissioner T. Coleman
Andrews, a friend of Senator McCarthy's, withdrew the Institute's tax
exemption on the grounds that it had spread "controversial and partisan
propaganda."[13]

At the very time that the foundations were being accused of subversive activities, the Central Intelligence Agency was trying to infiltrate and exploit the foundations. Repeated pressure was brought to bear on Dean Rusk to make available the confidential diaries of Rockefeller Foundation executives serving at various posts around the world. He refused to do so on the grounds that to yield would destroy the usefulness of the diaries and compromise the Foundation. He was backed solidly by his chairman, JDR. A former staff member of the Foundation believes that the stand of Rusk and JDR prevented CIA infiltration not only of the RF, but also of other major foundations.[14]

For a time, the ordeal of the IPR dominated the considerations of JDR and his advisers on the subject of creating a pan-Asian organization in New York City. Even though the Institute was *in extremis* at the time, the obvious question remained whether to save it or start something new. To consider this and other issues, JDR, Noyes, and Young met on June 1, 1955, with a group of men experienced in Asia—Dean Rusk, Arthur Dean, Phillips Talbot, Edward Reischauer of Harvard, Lloyd Elliot of Standard Vacuum Oil, Douglas Overton of the Japan Society, August Maffrey of the Irving Trust, and Kenneth Holland of the Institute of International Education.[15] These men knew that the IPR was useful, though undoubtedly in need of reform, and that it had been a victim of political hysteria. Yet the prevailing opinion was that to try to save it or be linked with it was unwise. The point was made most bluntly by Dean Rusk who said that the group should not be concerned about a "garden of weeds"—some organizations will live and others will die. The consensus was that the academic functions of the Institute would be assumed by the Far Eastern Association, an organization of scholars, while the educational functions would be picked up by a number of other existing organizations.

This issue apparently disposed of, opinion was divided on the question of whether a new cultural organization should be attempted at all. Nor could the group decide whether the best means would be one comprehensive structure or a combination of bilateral groups. As usual, JDR maintained a calm exterior, let everyone have his say, and suggested at the close that there be "a quiet study of unfulfilled needs" over the summer, with no preconceptions. He also asked that the discussion be kept confidential so that "no one should think that because this group had met that it was taking over in this field."

The summer's ruminations did not heighten anyone's enthusiasm about going ahead, except JDR himself. At a meeting in September it became clear that his staff was as wary about the idea as the group of experts had been several months earlier. JDR said: "What we are really trying to do

is to create a Japan Society on a broader scale." Pressed as to whether
"you start at the IPR pole or the Japan Society pole," JDR said he was
much more interested in the latter. Noyes thought a magazine on Asian
affairs was important, but JDR and Lockwood believed it would be too
expensive for too limited a market. Besides, "It would force the organization to take positions on foreign policy issues with respect to Asia which
might prove dangerous over a period of time." The question of whether
to convene another study group gave McLean an opportunity to express
his own strong opinions:

I raised the point that anything having to do with the IPR was poison to the special
communities. That if this organization was not to be concerned with research it
could not expect much foundation support and the experience of the Japan Society
had indicated that very little individual support could be anticipated and that
therefore as a practical matter if the organization was ever to amount to anything
it would be dependent almost exclusively on corporate financing. Therefore, I said
that any group which met should be heavily weighted in favor of the corporations
and that there should be in the group a minimum of people who had been identified with the IPR or who could be regarded as university people.[16]

Noyes and Young were asked to produce another study in preparation
for convening the larger group again. Their paper specified the functions
to be performed by a new organization and analyzed advantages and
disadvantages of the different courses that could be taken. If the decision
were to proceed, the report favored the creation of "an Asia Society"
that would comprehend all of the Far East, South and Southeast Asia,
but not the Middle East. It would "parallel the activities of the Japan
Society and the China Institute," and be able to function on a budget
of $100,000 to $150,000 a year. The main disadvantage noted was that,
quite apart from domestic U.S. political differences, the inclusion of
many countries with sharply conflicting political views would prevent
the organization from playing any policy-oriented role in the manner of
the Institute.[17]
     Only two days after delivering this report, Noyes and Young wrote a
memorandum to JDR conveying their own opinion that it would be unwise
to proceed. The withdrawal of the IPR's tax exemption seemed to weigh
heavily with them. They said that starting an Asia-wide organization
"immediately upon the heels of the IRS ruling would appear to face many
serious difficulties." The new organization would look like "a successor to
the IPR, regardless of the details of its program" and would act as "a
lightning rod for politically motivated charges." This would make funding
"exceptionally difficult." They told JDR:

Even if you were willing to support the organization at a modest level during the first year, this would probably not be a satisfactory solution. An organization of the type envisaged must be a public organization in order to be meaningful and it probably would be exceedingly difficult to shift the burden of support from yourself to others under the circumstances envisaged. It was felt, therefore, that it would be unwise and probably impractical to seek to establish at this time an Asia-wide organization.[18]

JDR was not deterred. He had had a cultural organization in mind all along; that a policy-oriented role would be precluded did not bother him. JDR personally was most comfortable in cultural affairs, but he was well aware of the value of a comprehensive approach to foreign affairs, taking into account the political and economic dimensions as well. This did not mean that one could not emphasize one of these dimensions in a particular project at a particular time. JDR also knew that there were times when political factors constrained the freedom of action of philanthropy. The mid-1950s was one of those times. An organization created on the basis of cultural projects could grow into other activities in due course; if it did not exist, it could not grow.

Other points made in the Young-Noyes memo also did not deter him. Once he had set himself on a course, arguments about tax exemptions and difficult timing were not likely to sway him. Moreover, he knew he would have to support the new organization financially until other aid could be attracted; he had already done this for other organizations he had started. He proceeded with his usual caution all the same, convening the discussion group on November 21, with pretty much the same attendees as the previous June. But this time the IPR was no longer the topic of concern; now it was the Asia Foundation.

The Asia Foundation had originated in 1951 as the Committee for a Free Asia, set up by a group of West Coast businessmen, mainly from San Francisco, who were frightened by the advance of communism in Asia after the fall of Nationalist China. The aim of the Committee was to set up programs in the Far East that would convince Asians of the menace of communism and the superiority of American political values. Under the direction of one George H. Greene, the program at first was generally inept and stridently anti-Communist.

In 1953 came a decided difference in tone when Robert Blum took over. A Berkeley Ph.D., he had served with the OSS during the war, and had worked with U.S. foreign aid agencies in Europe and Indo-China. The program became more sophisticated, providing support to youth activities, book translations, scholarships for Asians to study in the United States, and Asian tours by American leaders. The new name, Asia Foundation, was adopted and offices staffed by Americans were opened up in Asian countries. Whenever JDR and Blanchette traveled in Cambodia, for example, they received the help of Leonard Overton, Douglas Overton's brother, who was chief of the Asia Foundation office there. The Rockefellers remarked several times that he was the best-informed American in Cambodia.

In 1954 Blum made a strong effort to upgrade the board of directors by recruiting nationally known figures. He approached JDR, Chester Bowles, Paul Hoffman, and two prominent university presidents, Henry Wriston of Brown and Grayson Kirk of Columbia. All except JDR accepted. The effort to keep the board at a high level continued—Adlai Stevenson became a member in 1959.

JDR's declination is interesting, considering that he was pressed to accept by both Secretary of State John Foster Dulles and CIA director Allen Dulles.[19] His refusal reveals the subtle difference that had come to mark his whole outlook, contrasting as it did with the conventional Cold War point of view. He instinctively disliked the negative, outspokenly anti-Communist posture. His purposes were to understand Asian cultures, to help fellow Americans understand them, to help solve problems in Asia, and thereby promote democratic values. As early as 1945 his diary shows his chief reaction to the ideological split in the postwar world: concern because Americans knew what they were against but not what they were for. Accordingly, JDR's response to the Asia Foundation's invitation was to decline; but he first asked his Policy and Planning Committee for advice. Jamieson summarized their feelings:

My principal reservation is the Asia Foundation's origin. It is my understanding that it has been regarded with varying degrees of resentment in Asia because it spends a lot of money and is regarded as a propaganda device of the U.S. government. Therefore, it seems to me you would not want to jeopardize your own activities in the Far East by closely associating with the Asia Foundation.[20]

Jamieson was right. The Asia Foundation spent such large sums of money and sounded so much like a propaganda bureau that many Asians believed it was a U.S. government agency. In a sense, they were right. The program expansion under Blum was financed by CIA money, channeled through the half dozen "foundations" that had been set up as CIA conduits, and the organization continued to be funded almost entirely from this source. The Asia Foundation was never allowed officially into Indonesia and only grudgingly into India, from which it was ejected in 1959. It flourished in most other Asian countries, however, carrying on many worthwhile activities in addition to propaganda. The organization lost ground and prestige when it was implicated in the 1967 revelations about CIA fronts and conduits, within and behind presumably private-sector organizations.[21]

The question is whether JDR and his advisers were aware in 1955 of the Asia Foundation's CIA connection. Nothing in the archives or in the group discussion of November 21 confirms that they did. Yet the men JDR had gathered around him were among the best informed Americans about Asia. It is likely that they suspected the CIA connection if they did not know it as a fact. Merely the suspicion would have made JDR wary, given the strong stand he and Dean Rusk had recently taken against CIA pressure for access to confidential Rockefeller Foundation files.

The issue for the discussion group was whether the sudden expansion of the Asia Foundation obviated the need for another organization devoted to Asian affairs. Ironically, the way the discussion turned, the sudden prominence of the Asia Foundation served as a spur to creation of the Asia Society. JDR voiced apprehension that in the absence of a new entity the Asia Foundation would "by default" be the leading American organization concerned with Asian interests. Overton and Talbot concurred, the latter saying that it was "tending to be the organization people look to on an all-Asia basis." Noyes said the Asia Foundation was "not the type of citizen organization to express an American interest in Asian peoples." Rusk emphasized that it was not welcome in some Asian countries.[22] In any event, JDR clearly had his sights set on a cultural center in New York City, akin to the Japan Society, not a political organization that functioned overseas.

Despite unanimity of opinion about the Asia Foundation, the group still could not reach agreement about what to do. Several doubted that business would support an Asian cultural organization to the degree that it supported the Japan Society. W. R. Herod of General Electric saw a real need for the organization, but thought that its activities would not relate closely enough to business to ensure financial support. JDR replied that the organization should not be dependent only on business support in any case.

The most difficult question in the end remained the old one whether it would be best to support bilateral organizations and not an all-Asia center. JDR conceded that the "ideal" was a bilateral unit for each country, but that this simply was not practical. One concern was that the creation of an Asia Society would delay or prevent the formation of an India Society. Dean Rusk added that although as a Foundation executive he was "professionally schooled" to take a discouraging view of new proposals, he felt that "something should and must be done." An "Asia House," as he termed it, would yield many benefits over the years.

JDR continued to solicit opinions for a few more months, but, as it seemed all along that he would, he soon decided to go ahead. On June 28, 1956, the Asia Society was incorporated in the State of New York. Dr. Grayson Kirk of Columbia was named chairman and JDR was elected president, with Phillips Talbot and Ernest A. Gross as vice presidents, August Maffrey as treasurer, and Edgar Young as secretary.

A poignant note occurred in December when the president of the IPR, J. Morden Murphy of Bankers Trust, visited JDR to find out whether the new Asia Society would be willing to take over some of the Institute's functions. JDR had to turn him down, pointing out that the Society's program would be restricted to social and cultural affairs. JDR's intention to avoid a political role was—as we have seen—genuine and unwavering from the start. The Asia Society charter stressed that it would be a place where Asian visitors and students could exchange ideas with Americans and receive assistance during their visits. Its role would be to foster cultural interchange between the United States and Asia, promote greater knowledge of Asia in the United States, and serve generally as a center of information about Asia. The emphasis on culture was reinforced when Paul C. Sherbert at the end of 1956 was named the executive director of the Society. Sherbert had a cultural affairs background and had been head of USIA programs in south India.

JDR's support of the Asia Society began at a high level: in 1956 and 1957, his largest single gifts were to the Society. They were the second largest during the next three years. All told, in the first five years he contributed an average of nearly $400,000 a year for a total of $1.97 million by 1960.

The reason for this high level of support at the outset was JDR's wish that the Asia Society should have its own home and that a building for it could also house the Japan Society, which at that time was renting offices in midtown Manahattan. In 1957 JDR bought a brownstone at 9 East 62nd Street for $290,000, and $176,000 was spent in remodeling it. But the building was on a standard twenty-five-foot New York City lot and quickly proved too small. After a year-long search, JDR acquired two adjacent brownstones at 112–14 East 64th Street, Philip Johnson was retained as architect; the two houses were razed, and in December 1959 a new seven-story, glass and steel structure with white trim was ready to be occupied by the two cultural centers. The facilities included a paneled library, a small formal garden, an art gallery, and meeting rooms, in addition to offices. The total cost was $1.168 million, of which JDR provided $1.053 million, knowing that a special fund-raising effort would have been extremely difficult at that time. His commitment to do this brought forth a letter from Grayson Kirk praising JDR for his generosity, which made it possible for the Asia Society to have a suitable home "without delay."[23]

The Society grew steadily to become a valued institution in New York, with the stress on cultural programs as JDR had intended—exhibits, publications, lectures, seminars. The Asia House Gallery under Gordon Washburn's direction earned critical acclaim for its series of exhibitions of art from various Asian countries. Much of the activity of the Society centered on "country councils"—special ongoing programs for specific Asian countries carried on largely by volunteers from the Society's membership who had an interest in a particular country. In the case of several of the larger countries, a staff member was assigned to the Country Council.

As the Society gradually grew in membership and activities, it soon became apparent that even its new home provided inadequate space, especially for the exhibition program. The Society was functioning well at a relatively low level of expectations; for a more promising future, the difficult questions had to do with developing a larger and more stable revenue base, building adequate quarters, and determining leadership and guidance for the long term. JDR worked on these and other problems of the Asia Society for the rest of his life; not until shortly before his death did he develop a plan that would lead toward a solution.

JDR created the Asia Society during a period of stormy controversy over Asian policy. In *The Best and the Brightest*, David Halberstam comments on that period: "The temper of the times was very special, notable for a kind of national timidity and dishonor."[24] The Asia Society did not become embroiled in controversy by the simple device of avoiding it; it was a cultural organization, not a political one like the IPR and the Asia Foundation. Was this the result of the same kind of timidity that permeated the major foundations for a number of years after the Cox and Reece hearings?

There is no way to tell whether this might have been an unspoken motive for JDR; as noted, all the tangible evidence shows that he was consistent in favoring a cultural organization all along. JDR was well aware, as Don McLean and others advised him, that this choice would mean that the Society would not be a very important organization in the general scheme of things. It would not be influential in American policy-making, as the Council on Foreign Relations is. And this, in turn, would make it difficult to build a broader base of financial support.

With the passing of time, as we shall see, the Asia Society gradually began to deal with the politics and economics of Asia in its lecture and seminar programs. It received government funds to operate a major program that became somewhat controversial. This trend was a natural evolution under new leadership, and one that JDR countenanced as chairman. But the Society has remained predominantly the cultural organization that JDR originally envisioned, and with his last great commitment to it (see Chapter 28) it has achieved success and the high reputation it enjoys today in that field.

8

🏴

ASIA: THE CULTURAL
DIMENSION

As STRANGE as it may seem today, there was a time when American policy-makers were deeply worried about the apparent weakness of the Japanese economy after World War II. And beyond that there was continuing worry about the economies of the lesser-developed countries of South and Southeast Asia. We have seen how JDR tried to help in this regard by establishing a technical assistance program in agriculture by creating the Council for Economic and Cultural Affairs.

He made another attempt by establishing a business firm, Products of Asia, to import Asian products into the American market. It was the only one of his major initiatives in the 1950s that had to be abandoned as a failure. Like others of JDR's efforts, this one began with a concern for Japan and gradually broadened to include other Asian countries. One motive was to help Japan overcome its image in the United States as a producer of cheap and shoddy goods by importing items of beauty and quality, such as "ceramics, furniture, textiles, lacquerware, bamboo articles, etc."[1] Not for another decade would it become clear that Japan's success in moving away from her image as a maker of cheap goods would not come from these artifacts and household items, but from becoming a world leader in electronic equipment, optical goods, automobiles, and other fields of precision manufacturing.

The error of importing the wrong kinds of goods was compounded in the other Asian countries by bringing in tourist items, the products of cottage industries. JDR began to feel that things were going astray when the executives hired to run Products of Asia started to bring in manufactured items from Hong Kong in an effort to make the enterprise profitable.[2] JDR felt these did not really represent Asian culture, thus revealing where his heart really lay and also a clash of altruistic and commercial motives that did not augur well for success. Finally, after a series of studies, JDR and his advisers were able to close everything down by the mid-1960s. He was fortunate that his cumulative losses did not exceed $3 million.

Clearly, JDR was not cut out to be an entrepreneur. He was comfortable in the nonprofit and cultural worlds, not the commercial one. In fact, if Colonial Williamsburg was the project that was most like a love affair in his father's life, it was Asian culture that came to have this sort of attraction for JDR.

He had as much trouble as anyone else in trying to come to a precise definition of the term "culture." At one point he wrote in his diary about the distinction between culture "with a capital C," meaning generally the arts, and culture in a broader, more anthropological sense of the history, ethnicity, language, and customs of a people. His goal, always, was to improve his understanding and enjoyment of Asian culture, in both senses of the term, and to do whatever he could to help others do the same.

As we have seen, this growing fascination did not blind him to the very real problems that afflicted Asia. The Protestant ethic and the missionary impulse were still present in his makeup, tempered by modern-day concepts and practices of development assistance. In this regard, his efforts settled down to working on two of the most difficult and fundamental problems of the region, excessive population growth and inadequate agricultural production. The fact that at one level he was preoccupied with Asian culture, while at another working on the gritty realism of these two problem areas, was fortunate and productive for him. His respect for Asian culture prevented him from seeking to Americanize Asians. Instead, it focused him on trying to help them deal with their own problems in the context of their own cultures. And the technical assistance organizations he formed were imbued with the founder's sensitivity to cultural differences. At the same time, having an anchor in these two problem areas kept him from "floating away" (a favored phrase of his) in the rarefied atmosphere of the cultural field.

A revealing insight into how JDR thought of his interest in culture in relation to politics and foreign policy came in his involvement in the 1956 study on Soviet-American relations conducted by the Council on Foreign Relations. The product of the year-long effort was to be a book synthesizing the research and materials prepared by academics with the comments and ideas of a broader group of experienced laymen. Given the tenor of the foreign policy establishment at the time and the hard line of Secretary Dulles in Washington, it is not surprising that the basic premise of the book was that the nation's first and most vital policy must be to ". . . prevent the world-wide establishment of Soviet Communism, even at the cost of general war."[3]

JDR was never an outspoken foreign policy critic. His inclination always was to accept the consensus of the foreign policy establishment and the decisions of the elected officials and professionals in Washington, so many of whom were well known to him. And so in this case he accepted the basic premise of the book, but he had a point of view to express, and he did so several times in the bimonthly sessions of the study group. The real issue, he felt, was how to accomplish the objective short of war. He argued that the United States had been too narrow and defensive in its approach to the rest of the world. The stress had been placed on anti-Communist purity and security requirements to the detriment of most other factors. His travels abroad, JDR said, convinced him that a good portion of the world perceived America as an immense materialistic society with little or no regard for tradition and no cultural life to speak of. If the United States was to be effective in the rest of the world, it had to begin to counter and disprove these perceptions. Americans had to demonstrate a concern for the cultural values of other societies, and they had to reveal their own traditions and belief in the importance of culture.[4]

In his growing love and respect for Asian culture, JDR in a sense was returning full circle to the beginning of his involvement in Asia—the Japan peace treaty mission in which his specific assignment had been to investigate the possibilities for cultural programs. The most tangible result of that assignment was the International House of Tokyo, an institution so unique and successful that JDR began thinking about the possibility of generating a similar effect in other Asian capitals. He reasoned that not only would such an institution be valuable within a given country, as it was in Japan, but also that the existence of additional International Houses might have the effect of stimulating intellectual and cultural interaction *among* Asian countries.

The objective of increasing regional interaction was one difference between JDR's concept of an International House and the four such institutions his father had created, three in the United States (at Columbia, the University of Chicago, and the University of California at Berkeley) and the fourth at the University of Paris. Another difference was that JDR's model was meant to be an institution in and of itself, embodying some of the functions of the Council on Foreign Relations in New York City as well as serving as a center for foreign visitors and students, but not necessarily attached to a university.[5]

Still another important difference had to do with financing. Junior had paid for his four International Houses himself. JDR had no intention of doing this. The costs would be excessive in relation to his resources and commitments already made; moreover, as much as JDR was taken with his new idea, it did not have as high a priority as his other activities. It seemed to him that this problem could be easily solved—the most likely funding source was the Rockefeller Foundation.

As he quickly learned, the idea of additional International Houses in other Asian capitals had *no* priority in the Foundation for the reason that no program existed to accommodate the idea. For sizable foundations that are run systematically, not to say bureaucratically, being "out of program" is a serious matter, requiring the changing of attitudes among staff members and action by the board. Such things do not happen easily.

This, of course, did not deter JDR, though he realized he would have to tread carefully. There were other delicate and difficult aspects to the idea. Clearly, most of the financing of capital costs would have to come from U.S. sources. At the same time, although JDR could plant the seeds of an idea here and there, an initiative would have to emerge from leadership elements within the Asian country itself. A strong local group would have to coalesce, some funds would have to be raised within the country to give credibility to local initiative, good indigenous leadership had to emerge, and the institution had to offer real prospects of becoming self-sustaining. No American donors would want to keep on supporting an institution in a foreign country indefinitely. In addition to all these difficulties, proposals of this kind faced, within the Rockefeller Foundation, a somewhat hostile staff and a generally indifferent board.

In the case of the Tokyo International House, the above conditions were met in nice order, and there were some special supportive factors that paved the way to approval. JDR was personally involved and committed to the idea by virtue of featuring it in his report on the cultural mission. Though the "old guard" was still entrenched at the Foundation, their interest in Asia and readiness to "do something" for Japan (which they had communicated to JDR) outweighed their dislike of feeling themselves under his influence. On top of all this, the architect of the peace treaty, John Foster Dulles, was still chairman of the Foundation. Therefore, the Foundation went along with this "out of program" idea despite strong feelings against it by many staff members, as reported by one who had joined the staff in 1949.[6]

JDR tried to plant the seed of the International House idea in the Philippines and Indonesia, and discussed this on several occasions with Dean Rusk. But the local leadership never coalesced in either country to adopt and push the idea and bring it to the level of a serious proposal. JDR had more luck in India. In meetings there with top officials, he managed to slip in a word about the success of the Tokyo House. The Indian vice president, Sir Sarvepalli Radhakrishnan, made it a point to stop there in 1956 and was given a tour by Matsumoto. The following year Prime Minister Nehru visited the Tokyo House.

In February 1958, JDR and Blanchette traveled eastward from New York to spend the first two weeks of their annual midwinter Asian trip in India. They met several times with top leaders—Nehru, Radhakrishnan, Defense Minister V. K. Krishna Menon, and others—and found the atmosphere to be more cordial than on previous occasions. JDR commented in his diary about how friendly Nehru was, and of his daughter, Mrs. Indira Gandhi, he wrote: "We liked her very much. Seems very capable."

Radhakrishnan told JDR how impressed he and the prime minister had been by the Tokyo House, and he raised the question of how it might be possible to create a similar institution in New Delhi. JDR was delighted that the initiative came from the Indian side, given the tendency for the Indians to be extremely sensitive over U.S. initiatives and their rigorous efforts to be neutral. When Radhakrishnan raised the subject again in a subsequent meeting, JDR decided it was a serious overture and that a possibility for a breakthrough might exist. On February 20, he sent the following cable to McLean:

ROCKJOHN NEW YORK FOR MCLEAN GETTING TRACTION HOUSE IDEA HERE STOP PLAN CANCEL CEYLON PART OF TRIP STOP COULD YOU COME RIGHT OUT ARRIVING DELHI NOT LATER THAN NEXT WEDNESDAY IF POSSIBLE STOP SUGGEST BRINGING RELEVANT TOKYO MATERIAL PLEASE REPLY ROCKFOUND NEW DELHI JOHN

Meanwhile, Radhakrishnan moved ahead to appoint a "preparatory committee" of six high-level Indians to pursue the idea. The chairman was Dr. C. D. Deshmukh, chairman of the University Grants Commission of India. The five members included two cabinet ministers, the president of the Indian Council of World Affairs, and two university presidents. Aided by the highly regarded Ford Foundation representative in India, Douglas Ensminger, JDR lobbied for the idea with various members of the committee and worked on a paper presenting the plan. After a meeting with the committee at the vice president's home, JDR told his diary that he and Ensminger were very satisfied and "felt we now had official Indian approval of the project."

During these years the government of India was widely regarded as a model of bureaucratic inefficiency by many visitors and technicians from the West. It was reputed to have learned all of the worst practices of the British Civil Service and few of the good ones. But the "preparatory committee" was another story, whether it was due to the high level of the members or the leadership of Deshmukh. On March 20, Deshmukh sent a proposal to JDR with a covering letter saying that the committee members "have the impression that you and the Rockefeller Foundation might possibly find a proposal of this kind [to be] of interest." The proposal picked up some ideas in the paper presented by JDR, McLean, and Ensminger, but went beyond it. It was a sophisticated proposal that included rationale, objectives, location, official name (India International Centre), site, local financing, leadership, type of building, costs, and maintenance.

The Indians modeled their plan very much on the Tokyo House, with the added feature of anticipating that the forty-seven universities in the country would have a membership relation with the new Centre and share ongoing costs. The paper cited the main objective to be promoting "understanding and amity amongst human communities by facilitating the exchange of knowledge and mutual appreciation of each others' cultures, using the word culture in the broadest sense."

Dean Rusk was probably relieved that JDR's efforts to excite interest in the International House idea had gotten nowhere in Manila and Djakarta. He might well have thought the idea would not sell in any other Asian capital besides Tokyo—certainly not in neutral, sensitive, inefficient India. Suddenly, however, he was confronted with a serious proposal for New Delhi. He was aware that his staff was sensitive about the idea of their chairman roaming around Asia making commitments on behalf of the Foundation. This sensitivity extended beyond rational reasons for its existence. As we have seen, JDR became a circumspect chairman after his earlier efforts to guide the Foundation's program had been rebuffed. But JDR seemed to have made up his mind that the International House idea was a proper thing for the Foundation to pursue, especially in India where it could represent a significant breakthrough in relations. But perhaps it takes only one exception to kindle and perpetuate the fear that it will happen again, perhaps often and without warning. Or perhaps the fact that the chairman had the same name as the Foundation led to exaggerated fears that innocent comments by him could be taken as commitments.

Technically, JDR had made no commitment in India, but there is no question that he created conditions that forced Rusk's hand. For Rusk, the choice was to go along or face the serious risk of alienating and embarrassing either John D. Rockefeller 3rd or the government of India—or both. It was not an enviable position, but there still was the chance that the project might break down of its own accord. Therefore, Rusk's approach was to set high standards as the project moved through the decision-making process.

Back in New York, JDR and McLean met with Rusk and his aide, Chadbourne Gilpatric, on April 7. Gilpatric terms the meeting "unforgettable." Rusk had a southerner's way of being inquisitorial without giving offense. According to Gilpatric, he was like "someone from the FBI," while JDR was "the most determined guy in the world in a most beguiling way." He would "smile and wince" at the give and take of the discussion, and "you'd never know there was a steel trap in there." Rusk and Gilpatric raised every problem and objection they could think of, but there was some sort of answer for all of them in the Deshmukh paper or from JDR and McLean. There was no choice but to carry on with the process and see what happened.

Rusk took over negotiations with Deshmukh. His letters were masterpieces of diplomatic politeness while at the same time managing to pose the difficult questions and set stringent conditions.[7] But the Indians were more than equal to the challenge. In letters back and forth and in meetings in New Delhi, New York, and Tokyo, the project inched forward. Genuine enthusiasm had developed in New Delhi under Deshmukh's able leadership. At one point an urgent call was put in for McLean's presence in New Delhi again to assist in the planning and help the Indians understand what the Rockefeller Foundation wanted. In a report to JDR from Delhi, McLean discussed all the sensitive issues and said he would not want to talk about them "with Mr. Rusk unless it is in your presence." Rusk had made it "very clear" that McLean "was not in India representing the Foundation." McLean was understandably anxious for the Foundation to appoint its own liaison so he could get out of the middle.[8]

In another memo after returning home, McLean reported more fully on the excellent progress the Indians were making. The government had provided a superb five-acre site adjacent to the Lodi Gardens. Thirty-five of India's universities had signed up to become paying members of the Centre. The Indians were committed to raising 40 percent of the capital costs, "a far larger figure than I ever dreamed possible," wrote McLean.[9]

With this sort of progress there was no stopping the project, and some enthusiasm for it developed within the Foundation. By the end of 1959, the Foundation had made grants in two stages totaling $835,000. Groundbreaking occurred the following spring, and the dedication was set for January 22, 1962. Considering all the sensitivities involved, the project

had taken a remarkably short time—less than four years from the day
Radhakrishnan first raised the subject with JDR in New Delhi. JDR
described the dedication:

Attended the inaugural ceremonies of the India International Centre at 9:30 out
of doors. Fortunately there was no wind so it wasn't too cold. It was a very
impressive occasion. The Vice President of India . . . officiated and Prime Minister
Nehru spoke, which added much to the prestige of the day. Dr. Deshmukh spoke
and presided well. I also spoke and my remarks seemed to be well received.

JDR termed the Centre "an impressive and attractive building with
beautiful surroundings." Concerned about leadership of the Centre, JDR
and McLean had long ago concluded that Deshmukh, who was due to
leave his present post, was the most likely candidate to play the sort of
role that Matsumoto performed so well in Tokyo. Radhakrishnan told JDR
that Deshmukh would become vice chancellor of Delhi University, but
would also be able to continue as president at the Centre and devote
considerable time to it.

In 1961 JDR made a grant of $50,000 to the Centre to provide
Deshmukh "with a discretionary fund." Over the next few years the Rockefeller Foundation made several small program grants to the Centre, and
in 1966 made a "terminal grant" of $50,000.[10] Apart from these funds, all
financial support and maintenance has come from Indian sources. In 1976
McLean visited the Centre again and was favorably impressed by every
aspect of it and its place in the community. An additional asset is that the
United Nations building in Delhi, formerly the Ford Foundation headquarters, is located nearby. McLean points out that if the New Delhi Centre
has never achieved the reputation of the Tokyo International House it is
for two reasons—New Delhi is not the city for international travel that
Tokyo is, and Deshmukh was able to give the Centre only part-time attention, while Matsumoto was always fully involved with the Tokyo House.
Gilpatric agrees, terming Matsumoto a "genius," a master at interweaving
the factions of Japanese society and the international community. He also
agrees that, in the end, both the Tokyo and New Delhi ventures were
worthwhile projects for the Foundation.[11]

The International House idea, as JDR conceived of it, never took root in
the Philippines,[12] but he was instrumental in getting a more ambitious
program going there, although under circumstances that initially were
tragic. JDR had become an instant admirer of Ramon Magsaysay, having
met the dynamic, able, and charismatic leader in 1953 when he was still

defense secretary. After Magsaysay became president of the Philippines, JDR and Blanchette had breakfast with him several times at Malacanang, the presidential palace in Manila. On the last such occasion, JDR wrote:

Had breakfast at Malacanang with President and Mrs. Magsaysay. There were about 18 present in all, but it really couldn't have gone better. Came away with a very warm and friendly feeling towards the President and his wife. He was jovial, frank, and relaxed. We exchanged presents.

Less than two months later, on March 17, 1957, Magsaysay died in an airplane crash. His death was all the more shocking because of the exuberance and love of life that Magsaysay projected, and the hope for a bright future for the Philippines that many saw in his leadership. He was the kind of foreign leader that Americans dreamed of—intelligent, able, honest, and a believer in democracy. On March 22, a solemn Requiem Mass was celebrated for Magsaysay at St. Patrick's Cathedral in New York City with Cardinal Spellman officiating. JDR and his daughter Hope attended.

The next day, Saturday, the Rockefeller brothers had scheduled one of their periodic "brothers' meetings" at Pocantico. Nelson had resigned his post as special assistant to President Eisenhower in the foreign affairs field at the end of 1955, and was soon to become the Republican candidate for governor of New York State. He had never met Magsaysay, but, like many Americans, he had great respect for the near-legendary Filipino leader. In the brothers' meeting, Nelson tossed out the idea that the family should do something to recognize Magsaysay. JDR had been thinking along the same lines, so he immediately seconded the idea. Since Nelson was going to be very busy as a candidate, JDR volunteered to follow up and develop a plan for a suitable Magsaysay memorial.[13] He had, in fact, already scheduled a meeting the next evening at his Manhattan apartment (One Beekman Place) with Albert Ravenholt, the American Universities Field Staff representative in Manila. Ravenholt was in the middle of his lecture tour at AUFS member campuses, and came down from Cambridge for the meeting. Like Phillips Talbot of the AUFS, Ravenholt was a former *Chicago Daily News* foreign correspondent. He and his wife, Marjorie, had become fixtures in Manila and were known as reliable contacts and sources of information. JDR had met with them on previous trips to the Philippines. In the meeting Ravenholt suggested the possibility of an annual prize of $25,000 in Magsaysay's name for outstanding democratic leadership.

Several days later, JDR discussed the interest in a Magsaysay memorial with Don McLean, who promptly consulted with several people and wrote his usual memorandum to the files:

This morning John 3rd talked with me about the idea that he and his brother, Nelson, have been considering which is to establish some sort of memorial in honor of Magsaysay. He said that Nelson had originated the idea and that the atmosphere as expressed by him was in terms of democracy and freedom but I gather from Creel more Democracy as opposed to Communism John said that as far as he was concerned this had some propagandistic overtones for which he didn't care since the words had been overused. . . . John's conclusion is that even though democracy and freedom may be the keynote, the main concern should be the well-being of the people and the improvement of their lot.

. . . John said that he had discussed the idea briefly with Ravenholt who seemed to have the idea of a Nobel Prize, the idea being that there should be some encouragement for people who have the courage to stand up and be counted on the issues of freedom and democracy.

. . . Nelson apparently has suggested the desirability of consulting people in the government. He referred specifically to Allen Dulles and Bob Murphy.

Although I gather that John has the Nobel Prize idea in his mind, I get the impression that his views are not rigid, and that the same is true in the case of Nelson. I also get the impression that Nelson is as much interested in speed and immediate impact as he is in the long-range nature of the venture. . . .[14]

Over the next ten days there was a flurry of communications as JDR sought to hasten his normally deliberate process of soliciting reactions of relevant people to any major initiative. The fact that both he and Nelson were interested in the subject virtually assured that the Rockefeller Brothers Fund would be a funding source for the project—whatever it turned out to be. The RBF board was a sort of arena in which the brothers worked out trade-offs to achieve some rough parity in the flow of funds to each one's projects.

It was almost certain that the Rockefeller Foundation would not be a funding source, although Burton Fahs submitted several ideas, one of them for an International House in Manila. Fahs told McLean that his boss, Dean Rusk, was not enthusiastic about any effort to memorialize Magsaysay, having commented that "there's nothing deader than a dead politician." W. E. Murray of Caltex and others pointed to the obvious political sensitivity of giving a "Nobel Prize" for democratic political leadership in a country and area that were notoriously unstable politically. However, Murray and Fahs both liked a variation that McLean and Dana Creel of the RBF thought up, giving four or five awards in areas "consistent with Magsaysay's ideals, such as education, civil service, civic activity, etc., to Filipinos" with the "possibility of going outside [to other Asians] on occasion."[15]

Other ideas came in. There is no record that Allen Dulles responded to Nelson, but Under Secretary of State Robert Murphy consulted with

William J. Sebald of the Far Eastern bureau of the State Department. Sebald wrote a memorandum saying that the department was entirely in agreement with what the Rockefellers were proposing and favoring a program of U.S. fellowships and scholarships for Filipinos in the name of Magsaysay.[16] However, JDR now was tending strongly in the direction of an award program to recognize human accomplishment in the spirit of Magsaysay. A working group of McLean and two RBF staff members, Dana Creel and Charles Noyes, had come together. JDR asked them to consider the idea of an annual $25,000 "Nobel Prize" being extended to all Asians instead of restricted to the Philippines. Their response pointed out the political sensitivity of this approach, and discussed the alternatives that had been advanced.[17]

JDR agreed to give up the "Nobel Prize" concept and go to the idea of smaller awards being given annually to Filipino citizens in a number of categories. The RBF board endorsed this approach at its April 11 board meeting. At the urging of Nelson, who was looking for quick and visible impact, it was agreed that a $500,000 grant would be made available immediately instead of the normal, more cautious route of smaller grants in several stages, and that this would be conveyed as soon as possible to Magsaysay's successor, President Carlos P. Garcia. The board also agreed that JDR would act as its agent in developing the precise outlines and timing of the program.[18]

To follow up, McLean got in touch with Ravenholt, who had finished his lecture at Carleton College in Minnesota, and he agreed to return to New York during the latter part of April. At Ravenholt's suggestion, McLean also brought in Colonel Edward G. Lansdale from Washington. Lansdale had been close to Magsaysay during the anti-Huk campaigns, and was soon to return to Vietnam for similar duty.[19] Wolf Ladejinsky, who was in the United States briefly, also joined the group. JDR did not attend any sessions of this working group. He was in bed at Fieldwood Farm for a week with a severe attack of laryngitis, an ailment to which he was especially prone. The group produced several drafts of terms of reference for the program, which were reviewed by Lockwood, Jamieson, Dalrymple, Creel, and Noyes.

JDR also reviewed the drafts through the medium of Blanchette, and his marginal notes shaped the outcome, which moved progressively from a program restricted to Filipinos to one in which all Asians would be eligible. Accordingly, the board and selection committee of the "Ramon Magsaysay Award Foundation" (RMAF) would include members from other Asian countries as well as the Philippines, although a majority would be Filipinos. Five categories were established for the awards. Given JDR's emphasis on "cultural" affairs, his marginal note opposite one category was interesting. The language read: "distinguished cultural accomplishments giving expression to the ideals which inspired these awards " JDR wrote: "How translate this to the specific?" In the end the five categories became: Government Service; Public Service (by private citizens); Community Leadership; Journalism, Literature, and Creative Communication Arts; and International Understanding.[20] The annual award in each category would be $10,000.

Reflecting Nelson's sense of urgency, McLean was to leave immediately for Manila to do whatever had to be done to get the program established. Ravenholt was still committed to his U.S. lecture tour so he suggested that his wife, Marjorie, travel with McLean and help him through the maze of Manila society and politics. Her inclusion turned out to be an important step in implementing the program successfully. Contacted in Seattle by telephone, she said she could not accept without meeting McLean and Mr. Rockefeller first. She flew to New York for an evening meeting with JDR and McLean on April 28. Some last minor changes were made to the terms of reference and JDR's letter to President Garcia, and then Mrs. Ravenholt and McLean left for Manila.

Once there, they were able to keep the plan secret to a surprising degree while canvassing key individuals and friends of Magsaysay to test the concept and establish the board. The first person contacted for board membership was Miss Belen Abreu, who was counsel to the Commission on Elections in the Philippines and a friend of the Ravenholts. Among the others were the chief justice of the Philippines, Pedro Tuason; Jesus Magsaysay (Ramon's brother); and Leopold Uichango, dean of the College of Agriculture at Los Baños. On May 13, McLean met with President Garcia to deliver JDR's letter and the terms of reference, and a press conference announcing the program was held. Belen Abreu agreed to be the full-time staff person in charge of the program as secretary to the board and executive trustee. In a report to JDR, McLean wrote: "She is first class and I am sure will do an excellent job. We should consider ourselves fortunate that she is prepared to leave the Commission on Elections."[21]

McLean stayed in Manila long enough to help work out some of the machinery for organizing and running the program. It was clear that Miss Abreu would have to develop contacts within other Asian countries to set up a network of correspondents. To allow time for organizing, it was decided to have the annual awards ceremony on Magsaysay's birthday, August 31, with the first awards to be made in 1958. With Chief Justice Tuason's aid, work was started to achieve changes in Philippine law that would allow the awards to be tax-free. Because the Philippine peso was always in danger of devaluation, the value of the funds for the program was protected through a trust arrangement with the Chase Manhattan Bank.

There was one other problem to solve. The RBF board wanted the program to be in Filipino hands to the maximum degree, but was also concerned about some form of liaison or representation that would assure that the program was proceeding according to the terms of reference. There had been several ideas—Nelson at first had suggested that the American ambassador to the Philippines be a member of the RMAF board, and later that a member of the Rockefeller family be on the board. These suggestions were not accepted. After his trip to Manila, McLean came up with an alternative—that the Ravenholts be retained by the RBF to be its representatives in Manila in connection with the RMAF program. They would not serve on the board, but would be supportive of Miss Abreu in every possible way and report periodically to the RBF. This arrangement was accepted on both sides.

The concept had been developed and the program established in a remarkably short time. On July 1, less than four months after the death of Ramon Magsaysay, JDR appeared in Manila, accompanied by Blanchette and Hope, to present a check for the RBF grant of $500,000 to Chief Justice Tuason, chairman of the RMAF. The following year, accompanied by his oldest daughter, Sandra, JDR attended the August 31 ceremony in which the first round of awards was made.

It became clear very early that Miss Abreu and the RMAF board were managing the program to the letter of its criteria and with the utmost integrity. Administrative costs were kept low, under $25,000 a year. The program was truly all-Asian—during the first five years, only two Filipinos were among the awardees. There was particular vitality in the journalism and creative arts category with such winners as Mochtar Lubis of Indonesia, Tarzie Vittachi of Ceylon, and Amithaba Chowdhury of India, whose careers exemplified the ideal of a free press in Asia.[22] Early winners in other categories included C. D. Deshmukh of India, Jimmy Yen and Chiang Mon-Lin of China, and Mother Teresa of Calcutta, who years later won the Nobel Peace Prize. For Filipinos there was satisfaction in the prestige throughout Asia that the program was generating for their country. As a bill introduced in the Philippines Congress in 1959 stated: "These awards already have won the Philippines international recognition. As future awards are made they are destined to substantially enhance the stature of our country, particularly throughout Asia."[23]

The intent of the bill was to give a parcel of land to the RMAF for the purpose of erecting an office building to house the foundation and generate rental income to support the program indefinitely into the future. This idea, developed by McLean, the Ravenholts, and Miss Abreu, was discussed in Manila with JDR as early as 1958. They were looking for a basis for continuing the program beyond the initial $500,000 grant, particularly for Filipino support. But they were up against the fact that there was no tradition in the Philippines for donations not related to either politics or the Church. However, on two previous occasions the Philippines Government had donated land to nonprofit enterprises.

The bill passed with the stipulation that the building had to be erected within five years or the land would revert to the government. It was a choice plot, valued at $500,000, part of the Plaza Militar on Dewey Boulevard, the most popular promenade in Manila. The land had been given earlier to the Philippines by the previous owner, the U.S. government, at no cost. For several years, the RMAF tried to find financing in Manila for an office building on the site, but to no avail. The only alternative was to go back to the RBF. In February 1962, JDR was in the Philippines to speak at the dedication of the International Rice Research Institute at Los Baños. He came to Manila for several days of talks with McLean, the Ravenholts, and Miss Abreu. The basic outline of a plan was forged, and Miss Abreu undertook the task of fashioning it into a proposal.

An important element was expansion of the RMAF beyond the awards program to provide a suitable place for Magsaysay's personal archives and memorabilia, an Asian library, and a program of seminars and panel studies related to the work of the award winners. Her twelve-page letter to JDR presenting the plan was praised by McLean. He wrote to her:

The important thing is that John was also impressed. In fact, I have rarely seen him more enthusiastic about any presentation. He in turn passed it along to Dana Creel with the suggestion that it be presented for consideration at an early meeting of the RBF. . . . the initial reaction has been excellent and I am sure that in due course you will receive a favorable and sympathetic response.[24]

McLean was correct about the favorable response, but not the timing— it took almost two years to work out the formula and the details. At its May 17 meeting the board voted a second grant of $500,000 to continue the awards program and stated a willingness to consider the building proposal. But reservations were also expressed. The key next step was Laurance Rockefeller's visit to Manila in August to attend the 1962 awards ceremony. Laurance had succeeded Nelson as chairman of the RBF. He had no firsthand knowledge of the awards program and had never been to Manila. He agreed to go at JDR's urging, and returned with enthusiasm for the program, Miss Abreu, and the Ravenholts.

After engineering studies were made, the RBF acted on November 7, 1963, by making a $1 million grant to the RMAF to help erect a building and authorizing a $2 million mortgage loan to be repaid from rental receipts at 6 percent interest. This was a risky and unprecedented form of support for a foundation to render. It was made possible by Laurance's enthusiasm, the support of Nelson and David, and JDR's commitment to personally underwrite $1 million of the costs (half of the direct grant and one-fourth of the loan).

By 1968 all of these funds were expended as the building was completed and opened to tenants. In October 1976, the RBF created a $1 million trust fund for the RMAF, the income to be used to raise the award stipends to $20,000, thereby adjusting for inflation. This action brought total contributions by the RBF and JDR to $5.18 million. At the time of the trust fund action, Russell Phillips of the RBF wrote that

the RMAF now appears to be in a stable and sound financial condition. It is extremely well administered. . . . if the Center continues to be at least 95 per cent rented (there is presently a waiting list) and if the administration of the RMAF continues to be as efficient and sound as in the past, there is no reason why the Foundation cannot continue free from further basic outside assistance.[25]

In some ways the Magsaysay Awards program seems like a strange transplant of a Western idea to an unlikely place. It was established in a unique country in Asia, the one that is most Americanized as a former dependency and which often seems like an outpost of Latin America in Asia. A further anomaly was the existence of a program based on ideals of freedom and democracy in a country where civil liberties and rights were suspended through the imposition of martial law by President Ferdinand Marcos for many years.

Yet somehow it has worked. Precisely because the Republic of the Philippines is such a unique country in Asia, Filipinos see the program as an asset that helps bind them to their region culturally. And, though certainly not equivalent to the Nobel Prizes, the program is well-known and respected throughout Asia. There has been no hint of corruption, undue influence, or political tampering with the program. The Marcos regime honored the RBF loan as a foreign debt to be repaid in dollars. It now seems that the program can be financially self-supporting indefinitely.

On a qualitative level, it is not possible to measure with any precision the impact of such a program. But any review would suggest that high standards have been maintained and the caliber of the winners has been high. Many of them have given their award money to the causes they represent. For the success of the program, McLean credits JDR's coordinating role and personal support, the willingness of the RBF to stick with the program and take risks, and the abilities of Belen Abreu and the Ravenholts. These seem like fair assessments.

9

❦

LINCOLN CENTER:
THE CONCEPT

CHARLES SPOFFORD had a special agenda item in mind when he attended a weekend conference, early in September 1955, at Tamiment in the Pocono Mountains of Pennsylvania. It was one of the bimonthly sessions of the year-long Council on Foreign Relations study group mentioned earlier. One of Spofford's colleagues on the panel of lay leaders was John D. Rockefeller 3rd. Spofford's agenda item had nothing to do with the conference—he had a special question he wanted to put to JDR.

The question arose from a series of events that had occurred over the spring and summer of 1955. One of these was the decision by the board of the Metropolitan Opera of New York to seek a new house. Spofford, a partner in the Milbank, Tweed law firm and an ardent music-lover, was one of the directors of the Met who strongly favored the move to a better home. This was not a new idea; in fact, an earlier decision by the Met board to build a new opera house, in 1927, led directly to the creation of Rockefeller Center, even though the Met was forced out of the project by the 1929 stock market crash.[1] What had seemed desirable then had now become an urgent matter. In the words of Rudolf Bing, general manager of the Met, the existing opera house was one of the "glories of the world" in its auditorium, especially the famed "Diamond Horseshoe." However: "Everything backstage was cramped and dirty and poor." The facilities were hopelessly inadequate and obsolete, and had been for decades. Now the building was beginning to fall apart as well. The neighborhood had long ago ceased to be desirable, encompassed as it was by New York's famed garment district. Worse, the new Port Authority Bus Terminal was scheduled to be built only a short distance away.[2]

All of this explains why the Met's board was excited by an overture from Robert Moses, the powerful and sometimes arrogant figure who for decades had been the master developer of New York City by virtue of his genius, his skill as a power broker, and his entrenched position as Parks Commissioner, chairman of the Triborough Bridge and Tunnel Authority, and chairman of the Slum Clearance Committee.[3] Moses and Mayor Robert Wagner had chosen a blighted, seventeen-block area on the West Side of Manhattan, between 62nd and 70th streets, for inclusion in the city's urban renewal program. This became the Lincoln Square Urban Renewal Project, so named after the double triangle formed by the intersection of Broadway and Columbus Avenue. Moses saw that the relocation of the Metropolitan Opera would be a positive force in upgrading the neighborhood, so he offered the Met a three-acre site between 63rd and 64th streets, a potentially valuable plot that could be made available at a low price under slum clearance procedures.[4]

The intermediary of Moses, Wallace K. Harrison, had been the architect for the Met for twenty-five years, and was the same "Wally" Harrison who had been one of the architects for Rockefeller Center and the United Nations, as well as a confidant of Nelson Rockefeller's for decades. Harrison was enthusiastic about Moses's idea, and he took it to Spofford.

It happened at the same time that the New York Philharmonic Society was also forced to look for a new hall, for a very different reason than the Met's. The Society was quite happy with Carnegie Hall, which it had leased since the doors were first opened in 1891. Now the new owners decided that their return on investment was insufficient. They wanted to tear down Carnegie Hall and build an office tower in its place, and so notified the Society that the Philharmonic's lease would not be renewed. Arthur A. Houghton, Jr., of Steuben Glass, a trustee of the Philharmonic who was soon to become its chairman, also turned to Wally Harrison for advice about building a new symphony hall. Harrison put him in touch with Spofford, and the two men concluded that the two long-established and world-renowned performing institutions should build new houses adjacent to each other on the Lincoln Square site.[5]

Actually, the two men were reviving an idea that had come up once before. But it had occasioned a painful incident that made the directors of both musical institutions somewhat wary of Moses. In May 1951, Moses had offered them two acres of land in the Columbus Circle Urban Renewal Project, part of which later produced the New York Coliseum. Moses insisted that the two societies had to move quickly and raise $1.5 million for the purchase of the land. C. D. Jackson, a trustee of the Met, the publisher of *Fortune*, and Nelson Rockefeller's predecessor as psychological warfare assistant to President Eisenhower, revived the old connection between the Opera and the Rockefeller family by asking John D. Rockefeller, Jr., to donate $500,000 if the remaining $1 million could be raised from other sources. Junior agreed, a rather generous act considering the problems he had had with the Met withdrawal from the Rockefeller Center project twenty-five years earlier. With Junior's pledge of one-third the needed amount in hand, the goal was in sight, but still required a great deal of hard work. Three days after the final pledge was made, Moses abruptly withdrew the offer of land.[6]

Now, four years later, it seemed that Moses was going to be difficult again. When he learned of the idea of the Philharmonic joining the Met at the Lincoln Square site, Moses was opposed. But he changed his mind a few days later after talking again with Wally Harrison, and even added another acre to the site.

Once more, it was necessary to raise $1.5 million for the land, for preliminary planning, for the relocation of tenants, and for land clearance. C. D. Jackson wrote to Junior to see if the earlier pledge of $500,000 in matching funds was still good.[7] It was, and before the summer was over the Met had succeeded in raising the full amount. But some of the directors of the paired institutions, especially Spofford, Jackson, and Houghton, were beginning to think in larger terms. They were wondering whether it would be opportune to add other elements and make an urban arts center—or at least a "musical center"—at Lincoln Square. Whatever shape the center might take, careful coordination and planning were essential. For the Met and Philharmonic alone to build new halls, a major fund-raising drive would have to take place, and the two organizations wanted to avoid going to the same sources in competition with each other. The idea then occurred of getting one of the Rockefeller brothers to lead in coordinating a grand new effort. Nelson, still located in Washington, was not a possibility, so Harrison, still serving as the catalyst, suggested John 3rd. Spofford consulted Dean Rusk, who also advised involving JDR 3rd in the effort if possible.[8]

By the time that Spofford had finished painting in some of this background, his question to JDR became obvious: would he be willing to join a small committee to probe the possibilities of a "musical arts center"? Aside from himself, Spofford said, the group consisted of Houghton, Harrison, and two other representatives of the Met and the Philharmonic. The situation was new and fluid, Spofford emphasized. The membership of the group was not set, nor were its plans.

JDR agreed to think about it. He was intrigued by the idea of the Met and the Philharmonic working closely together, and by the glimmer of a larger plan. Over the next few weeks, he discussed the invitation with Dean Rusk and Burton Fahs of the Rockefeller Foundation, Dana Creel,

Wally Harrison, C. D. Jackson, Edgar B. Young, and Lincoln Kirstein, former managing director of the City Center for Music and Drama and head of the renowned New York City Ballet. JDR attended his first meeting of Spofford's committee on October 25, 1955. At JDR's suggestion, the group was expanded to include Lincoln Kirstein, Robert E. Blum, head of the Brooklyn Institute of Arts and Sciences, and Devereux C. Josephs, chairman of New York Life and a Rockefeller Foundation trustee.[9]

At the second meeting, on November 9, JDR bound himself to the purposes of the group by agreeing to become its chairman. Even though heavily occupied at the time with his Asian projects, JDR moved quickly on this new course. He began to scout for other possible participants in a new "musical center" for New York. He held preliminary meetings with Newbold Morris, chairman of the board of City Center, and with President William Schuman and Dean Mark Schubart of the Juilliard School of Music. He interviewed representatives of management consulting firms to find staff assistance for the committee. And he paved the way with Dean Rusk for a grant of $50,000 from the Rockefeller Foundation to pay the committee's early expenses.

At the fourth meeting, on December 13, the group adopted the name "Exploratory Committee for a Musical Arts center," and agreed to meet for lunch every other Monday. A five-month budget of $50,000 was adopted, and Spofford sent off to the Foundation the formal letter requesting the prearranged grant. In it, he revealed how far the thinking of the group had gone. The mission, he wrote, was to

determine the feasibility of a musical arts center in the City not only for the opera and symphony but also for such activities as chamber music, ballet, light opera, and spoken drama, and possible educational programs related thereto. Other questions to be considered by the Committee should it reach an affirmative decision regarding the Center, will touch upon the proper organizational relationships of the various participating groups, the facilities that would be required, and the best methods of financing such a project.[10]

Thus was launched a remarkable enterprise that was to be at once controversial, frustrating, and inspiring. JDR was not known for taking on easy projects, and he had a good idea of how difficult this new one would be. He knew a great deal of the early history of similar efforts, going as far back as the original plan for Rockefeller Center. Even so, he did not know and could hardly have suspected that the Lincoln Square project would claim a major share of his time, energy, and resources for the next fourteen years and very nearly the full time of one of his associates, Ed Young. There were important accomplishments ahead—innovating the urban arts complex that would be emulated in cities around the world, the largest private sector fund-raising for the arts ever attempted, the first major involvement of government in supporting the arts in the United States, the remarkable redevelopment of a whole section of the nation's largest city. There were excruciating financial decisions to be made; disputes to mediate among the six architects who at first had the greatest difficulty working together; complex negotiations with the city, the state, and the federal government; and endless wrangles among the constituent organizations at Lincoln Center in a system that was as loosely coupled as the United Nations or the thirteen states under the Articles of Confederation. And there were the fascinating and often difficult people to deal with, such as Moses, Kirstein, Schuman, Bing, Harrison, the other architects, and that cross-section of New York's elite leadership in business and the professions whose participation was essential to success.

Why did JDR involve himself? Ed Young supplies part of the answer:

Rockefeller admired the willingness of the Metropolitan and Philharmonic leaders to sit down together to examine whether their plans for new institutional homes created an opportunity for something of even greater importance to the community. It was this potential that challenged Rockefeller then and throughout the evolution of the project.

The world Rockefeller knew best was that of voluntary, nonprofit citizen participation. He had experience and judgment in the management of such enterprises; he knew how money was raised. Rockefeller made no pretense of professional knowledge or expertise in any of the arts. He was not an opera buff, a symphony fan, or a balletomane. But he believed that opportunities to experience the arts should be available to everyone; he recognized that the arts could play a significant role in the lives of large numbers of people.[11]

JDR himself added another reason in a *New York Times* article:

For me new horizons began to open. Since the war my work had been concentrated in the international area. I had begun to think more seriously of my responsibilities as a citizen of New York . . . Therefore I accepted with enthusiasm Spofford's invitation to join his committee and to help enlist others.[12]

JDR also believed that the Lincoln Center effort was not as far removed from his international interests as it might seem. In the same Council on Foreign Relations study in which he and Spofford were colleagues, he had consistently raised the point about the low image of American culture abroad, the need to alter such perceptions, and the need for Americans to reveal their own traditions and belief in the importance of culture. In sum, Lincoln Center was a challenge large and worthwhile enough to engage JDR's devotion, and it had the virtue of combining his broad interests in culture and international affairs with his desire to play a leading role in his home city.

This last motive had been in his mind for some time. He had had two previous opportunities to become involved in a major New York City project, and both gave him some foretaste of the idea of an urban cultural center. The first was occasioned by a visionary named Albert Christ-Janner, who spent years trying to promote a "National Arts Center" that would include not only the performing arts, but also the visual arts, graphics, photography, and creative writing. An associate of Henry T. Heald when Heald was president of the Illinois Institute of Technology, Christ-Janner came to see David Rockefeller, who referred him to Dana Creel. Christ-Janner spoke with Creel and JDR several times in the early 1950s. Though Christ-Janner's idea was impractical, Creel believes it did stimulate JDR to think more broadly about the arts and the kinds of institutions that might be needed to foster artistic activity in an urban setting.[13]

Creel himself was stimulated by Christ-Janner's ideas and became an advocate of the cultural center principle. In March 1953 Creel wrote to both Junior and Laurance Rockefeller about the possibility of a "center" from 51st to 54th streets between Fifth and Sixth avenues that would include the Met, the Philharmonic, the Museum of Modern Art, a school for "postgraduate training in the creative arts," and an educational television facility. Intrigued by the idea, Laurance explored it with Anthony Bliss, president of the Metropolitan Opera Association, and Lawrence Elliman, a real estate man with extensive holdings on Sixth Avenue. They decided the plan was much too costly.[14]

The most important influence on JDR prior to his involvement with the Exploratory Committee in the fall of 1955 was his long flirtation with the City Center for Music and Drama. This experience provided JDR with an understanding of how the different creative arts might function together in dynamic fashion and how they could serve a large and enthusiastic public. On the negative side, he learned a great deal about the very difficult funding problems and chronic deficits that the performing arts almost always faced, and about the tenacity with which arts organizations defended their "turf." Many of the problems he would encounter later with Lincoln Center he observed for the first time at City Center in the early 1950s.

As was true of many cultural organizations in New York, the Rockefeller family, in the persons of Junior and Nelson, were early supporters of the City Center.[15] This began as an attempt to institutionalize the WPA's Music Project, which in the 1930s had staged low-cost concerts and provided work for unemployed musicians. Many of these concerts had been presented at the underutilized Center Theater in Rockefeller Center at ticket prices ranging from twenty-five cents to $1.10, generally to enthusiastic, standing-room-only audiences.

Early in 1943, the foreclosure by the city (for nonpayment of taxes) of the old Mecca Temple on West 55th Street provided a locale for the continuation of these low-cost concerts. The city had no authority to operate a theater or engage in artistic productions. But Mayor Fiorello La Guardia, who loved music and had a flair for the unusual, and then–City Council president Newbold Morris, the aristocratic New Deal liberal who cared for the "common man," overcame this limitation by establishing a nonprofit corporation that would use Mecca Temple, at a nominal rent, "to give performances of opera, drama, and symphony concerts to the great mass of people who cannot afford the admission charges of the Metropolitan Opera Company, the Philharmonic–Symphony Society and Broadway theaters."[16] This explicit distinction regarding both type of audience and financing was of prime importance and would later make for animosity and uncomfortable relations within Lincoln Center.

To fund the Center, Morris raised money from New York unions, a few corporations, and a number of individuals, including Junior. Existing groups, such as the ballet company founded by Lincoln Kirstein and George Balanchine, were brought into the Center and others were created. Over the next decade, the City Center achieved a mixed record. Its productions of opera and especially of ballet met with critical and popular acclaim. The policy of frequently producing new operas, ballets, and plays, often by Americans, answered a genuine artistic demand. But the difficulty of reconciling the wants of its constituent companies, poor overall management, and occasional theatrical disasters dissipated the Center's meager resources and brought it several times to the verge of bankruptcy.

The years 1952 and 1953 saw the Center at low ebb. Changes in the law enabled the city of New York to provide some housekeeping services, and these, together with grants from the Rockefeller Brothers Fund, kept City Center afloat. Late in 1953, its three leading figures—President Newbold Morris, Treasurer Morton Baum, and Managing Director Lincoln Kirstein—approached JDR with a request that he join a reconstituted board in a leadership capacity. They wanted JDR to head a new fundraising effort to be known as "the Friends of City Center." He met with Creel and Ed Young and noted in his diary: "It was generally agreed that any new activity [for me in New York City] should be in the field of culture and that it probably should be related to the City Center, which offers promise if it develops well." JDR told Kirstein that he would defer a decision until his return from the Far East in the spring of 1954. Meanwhile, he asked Ed Young to study the prospects of City Center.

In March Young reported favorably, citing the Center's plan to add or expand training facilities in opera, ballet, and drama; its intention to create a Shakespeare Theater and revive the New York City Symphony (after several years' abeyance); and its resolve to reach out more actively to the masses of New York City. City Center was in fact groping toward the establishment of a performing arts center two years before representatives of the Metropolitan Opera and the New York Philharmonic began to discuss the same possibility. Young, however, cautioned that important changes in administrative structure and board membership had to be made before the City Center plans could succeed.[17]

These findings provided the basis for negotiations between JDR and the City Center leadership that dragged on for months. What it all boiled down to was that Morris and Baum, the real powers in the Center, wanted JDR for the prestige of his name and his ability as a fund-raiser, not to yield any power or allow him to have any real say in the governing policies of the Center. But JDR always tried to avoid involvement in anything solely on the basis of fund-raising or trading on the prestige of the Rockefeller name. He was interested only if there were some genuine policy role for him to play.

The discussions, therefore, consisted largely of each side talking about its own position and not being heard by the other. Morris and Baum had plenty of ideas on how to spend Rockefeller money. At one point Morris suggested that the Rockefeller family give the City Center $2 million to build a new home. JDR proposed a new executive committee with general directive powers, and wanted an understanding that his financial involvement would have strict limits. He wanted the Center to concentrate on ballet and opera, at which it excelled, and move into new program areas slowly and only when adequate financial resources were assured. How this was received is indicated by what happened at the end of 1954 when JDR met with the Center's three leaders. According to Ed Young, it was a "frustrating" meeting "with Baum doing all the talking," including the charge that JDR's ideas amounted to "a Rockefeller takeover."[18] A few days into the new year JDR met alone with Morris and consigned this laconic note to his diary: "Morris couldn't have been nicer, more friendly— or seemingly less receptive to ideas advanced."

The discussions were muddied by the fact that Morris and Baum maintained a posture as hard negotiators at the same time JDR and Kirstein were developing a friendship. The two men were not at all alike. JDR was rational, methodical, and unflappable, while Kirstein was brilliant, erratic, and mercurial, known for the rapidity with which he could plunge from engaging personal charm to deep moody depression. Nevertheless, the two seemed to genuinely like each other. The Rockefellers and Kirsteins often saw each other socially, sometimes for dinner and attendance at the ballet and sometimes accompanied by UN Secretary General Dag Hammarskjold or some other prominent foreign visitor.[19]

JDR was inadvertently drawn into an internal dispute between Kirstein and Howard Rosenstock, head of the New York City Opera. As managing director of the City Center, Kirstein wanted unified artistic control; Rosenstock wanted to maintain his independence. JDR began to worry that Morris and Baum would think that Kirstein was using his friendship with JDR as leverage to win the raging battle. So he took pains to tell Morris that he was not trying to influence the outcome.

At lunch one day JDR was alarmed to find Kirstein depressed about his future effectiveness at City Center, to the point that he contemplated resigning as managing director, though he would still maintain his leadership of the ballet company. The next day, January 5, 1955, JDR received a copy of Kirstein's letter of resignation in the mail. He hastened to assure Morris and Baum that he had nothing to do with Kirstein's decision. But after several more meetings with the two men, JDR concluded that they would not yield to any of his ideas, so he dropped the idea of participating in City Center.

At lunch with Kirstein late in January, JDR now found his friend to be in an upbeat mood. Kirstein talked about a grand new vision of bringing the Metropolitan Opera, the New York Philharmonic, and the City Center together in a common home and common overall management. JDR said the idea had merit and Kirstein agreed to explore it without mentioning JDR's name.

This background explains a good deal about JDR's involvement later in the year in the Exploratory Committee for Lincoln Center. Though the trustees of the Met and the Philharmonic arrived at the same idea for a grand musical center that Kirstein had voiced, it appears that they did so independently. There is no evidence that Kirstein figured in their thinking. But one can see that JDR wanted Kirstein involved in the Exploratory Committee because he had specifically talked about the participation of the City Center in such a plan.

When Spofford first broached his idea to JDR, he might have been surprised at how easily receptive JDR was, but it is clear that JDR had already been thinking along the same lines. His protracted negotiations with the City Center suggest that he had no illusions about the difficulty of the task he committed himself to. But instead of the prospect frightening him, he found it attractive for two good reasons. First, there was the great advantage of the whole matter beginning with the participation of the two oldest and most prestigious musical institutions in New York City already assured. Second, the grandness of the vision and the magnitude of the task gave him at the outset the formative policy role that Morris and Baum would not yield.

There was much to be done—securing additional constituents for Lincoln Center, raising funds, acquiring the land, appointing architects and beginning the design process, solving the puzzle of achieving effective overall management consistent with the artistic independence of the constituents. Not until the first shovelful of earth was turned for the first new building would JDR feel confident that the project had truly moved from concept to reality.

These tasks obviously were intertwined, and most of them had to be carried on concurrently. But the constituents were fundamental to everything else. Adding new ones and making assumptions about others that might be added later would set the requirements of land, design, and funding. So JDR set to work achieving a final pattern of constituent members of Lincoln Center.

Because the Philharmonic and the Met were already set, there would seem to be no problems there. This was true of the Philharmonic, whose board was unfailingly cooperative and supportive throughout. It seemed certain that when ground-breaking finally did occur, it would be for Philharmonic Hall as the first building of Lincoln Center.

The Met was a different story. By any measure—staff, budget, space requirements—it was the largest constituent, and, as we shall see, an extraordinarily troublesome one.

The presence of Kirstein on the Exploratory Committee, coupled with his recent troubles within the City Center and his resignation, led everyone to assume that the New York City Ballet could be detached to become the third constituent of Lincoln Center. There would need to be a third building to house the ballet, and this came to be referred to as the "Theater for the Dance." Plans for such a building progressed through some early stages even as negotiations for a ballet constituent dragged on for years with no result. It is not clear just what Kirstein's position was through all of this or whether he even had the power to move the ballet by himself. At first he seemed to be amenable to the idea and then his institutional loyalty to the City Center reemerged. Another problem was the existence of a second respected ballet company in New York, the American Ballet Theater, which wanted to be considered. A special delegation of the Exploratory Committee tried in vain to work out a merger of the two companies, and then carried on long discussions with Kirstein about the New York City Ballet coming in alone.

Eventually it became clear that the only way to get the ballet in the new project would be to bring in all of the City Center. Therefore, JDR began new discussions with Newbold Morris that were "terminated" on both sides several times. Finally, Morton Baum and Ed Young engaged in a long, tough negotiating round that resulted in a scheme by which the City Center would enter as "primary constituent" in dance and operetta and "secondary constituent" in opera and drama. JDR and his colleagues saw no reason why the Metropolitan Opera and the New York City Opera could not coexist peacefully at Lincoln Center with different schedules and appealing to different audiences. What would be the real difference if they were next door as against ten blocks apart? The general manager and most of the trustees of the Met saw it quite differently. They were affronted by the very idea of this plebeian institution with its low-priced wares standing next door to the aristocratic Met, and they soon became very difficult to deal with. By mid-1959—more than three years after the start of discussions—things were still at an impasse.

By comparison, the negotiations to bring the Juilliard School into the complex began pleasantly. But soon awkward snags developed. An educational institution now was regarded by the members of the Exploratory Committee as an essential component of Lincoln Center, a resolve heightened by the fact that the Rockefeller Foundation made its support conditional

upon the development in the Center of a satisfactory educational activity, upon the inclusion of various forms of dramatic art and upon the achievement of cooperative arrangements among the several groups, thereby ensuring that the undertaking will be, in fact, a Center and not simply a collection of more or less isolated activities.[20]

The Ford Foundation shared this view, a matter of critical importance inasmuch as these two large foundations were being looked to for large grants to get the enterprise moving.

Juilliard, which had been founded in 1926, had a tradition and professional objectives that nearly blocked its inclusion in the nascent federation on Lincoln Square. The first snag was that Juilliard's main endowment, the Juilliard Musical Trust, limited the school's activities to training in music. But Lincoln Center had to have an institution that would also offer training in drama and the dance. The second snag was that Juilliard had a respected secondary school that was not wanted at Lincoln Center. The Exploratory Committee wanted a stream of young artists who were only a step or two away from their professional careers. This called for workshops and other forms of postsecondary training that would close the gap between formal education and professional performance

By late 1956 these obstacles seemed insuperable. However, William Schuman, the president of Juilliard and an established American composer, was a strong supporter of Lincoln Center and of Juilliard's participation. He sought the aid of members of his board, particularly its chairman John W. Drye, Jr., who was also a member of the Met board and the chairman of its "new house" committee.

The advocacy of Schuman and Drye and a strong personal appeal by JDR at a Juilliard board meeting in early January 1957 swung the full board behind the proposal to join Lincoln Center. The school transferred its preparatory department to the Manhattan School of Music, which eventually moved its headquarters to the old Juilliard building on Morningside Heights with the aid of a grant from the Martha Baird Rockefeller Fund for Music. Juilliard henceforth was to concentrate on the advanced training of persons with exceptional talent. The announcement of the decision was made on February 1, 1957, making Juilliard the third assured tenant of Lincoln Center.[21]

There was yet another hitch: where on Lincoln Square would the Juilliard School be placed? For a man who had at first opposed the inclusion of the Philharmonic, Robert Moses proved agreeable when it came to enlarging the site for other constituents. He had agreed to extend the original three-acre site to three city blocks, but he insisted on keeping the southwest corner for a park. (It subsequently became Damrosch Park with its outdoor bandshell.) However, with plans under way for three buildings (to house the Met, the Philharmonic, and the Theater for the Dance), and at least two other organizations being considered, even the enlarged site could not accommodate the complex requirements of the Juilliard: classrooms, soundproofed practice areas, recital halls, offices, and dormitories. Moses would not yield an inch of the land he had reserved for a park. Further talks finally led to the half block to the north of the original site being made available, owing to the failure of the Roger Stevens organization's plan for commercial theaters on a section of the urban renewal land.

The desire to have a drama constituent ran into two difficulties. First, despite the prominence of theater in New York City, no suitable repertory company existed to be brought ready-formed into Lincoln Center. One would have to be created. So began a long and tortuous saga featuring a parade of luminaries from the theatrical world, the first attempt being the formation of the Repertory Theater Association on February 15, 1960, under the leadership of Robert Whitehead of the American National Theater and Academy (ANTA).[22]

The second hurdle was the familiar one: money. Existing institutions in the arts tend to develop their own constituencies for financial support and they may also possess an endowment. This was true of the Met, the Philharmonic, and Juilliard. But there being no existing repertory company, there were no funds or donors for the drama component. JDR went a long way toward solving this problem by cultivating Mrs. Vivian Beaumont Allen, who had been suggested by the ANTA leadership as a possible donor. Her identity was kept secret at first while JDR met with her frequently over a period of a year to persuade her to help build a theater at Lincoln Center. She offered to contribute $2 million; he asked for $3 million and said the theater would be named after her. At last he was able to answer all of Mrs. Allen's questions and promise her that the theater would not be a second-class citizen at Lincoln Center. She finally agreed to the $3 million request and chose to give the theater her maiden name. The gift was announced on April 26, 1958. Thus, well before a repertory company was formed, the money for its home at the Center was assured.

The sixth component planned by the Exploratory Committee was a research and reference library for the performing arts, possibly associated with a museum. There was only one real candidate for this unit—the New York Public Library had the world's most extensive collection in the fields of music, dance, and drama, and these books and documents were housed in cramped and ill-equipped space in the library's main building on Fifth Avenue at 42nd Street. The library's new president, Gilbert W. Chapman, enthusiastically supported the idea of a special branch located at Lincoln Center. Here again the problem was money. The New York Public (as it is called) is a private institution, but for a long time it has received support from the City for operating funds and its branch system. A feasibility study revealed a need for $8 million to build a library-museum at Lincoln Center. Early in 1958, JDR and Spofford talked to Mayor Wagner about the possibility of city funds to support the branch at Lincoln Center. The mayor was sympathetic, but no commitment was made. A library at Lincoln Center would have to await the reality of funding.

While the search for constituents was going on, action was being taken on a number of other fronts in the effort to move from a vision to a reality. In June 1956, the development was incorporated under the name of "Lincoln Center for the Performing Arts, Inc.," a nonprofit membership corporation in the state of New York. All the members of the Exploratory Committee became directors except Wally Harrison, who was to serve instead as senior architect for the project. Three new directors were added: The Reverend Lawrence J. McGinley, president of Fordham University, for his institution was a participant in the portion of the urban renewal plan immediately to the south of Lincoln Center; George D. Stoddard, dean of education at New York University; and Frank Weil, who had been active with the Federation of Jewish Philanthropies. Ed Young served as secretary of the board, and Major General Otto L. Nelson, Jr., the retired vice president of New York Life, was a "dollar a year" man to advise on urban renewal processes.

JDR was elected president of Lincoln Center and Devereux Josephs became vice president. Later in 1956, Spofford and Houghton were also named vice presidents. These men carried an especially heavy load for Lincoln Center for years, together with Stoddard and Clarence Francis, retired chairman of General Foods, who became finance chairman and head of fund-raising for the project.

Obtaining ownership of the thirteen-acre, three-block site that Moses had reserved for Lincoln Center in his urban renewal plan was a strenuous task. It took two years of half-starts, crossed signals, and conflicts with Moses, City Hall, and officials of the Federal Housing and Home Finance Agency. Endless meetings and hearings were required to deal with the objections put forth by various critics of urban renewal. JDR testified for an hour before the Board of Estimate on behalf of Lincoln Center and was surprised to learn the next day that the meeting had not adjourned until 4:30 A.M., prolonged by argument over the inclusion of Fordham in the urban renewal plan: did it or did it not involve the separation of church and state?

One trouble developed over the existence on the Lincoln Center site of an office building in good shape that was rented by the U.S. Immigration and Naturalization Service and owned by four of the children of Joseph P. Kennedy. At lunch with the father of the future President of the United States, JDR found Kennedy amicable but wanting a great deal more than a "write-down" figure of $1 million for the building that had been offered by Moses. Finally, Lincoln Center had to agree to add $1.5 million so that Kennedy would get the total of $2.5 million he was demanding. This meant that the Kennedy property cost an average of $62.86 per square foot, while the rest of the thirteen acres came to $7.04 per square foot.[23]

On February 28, 1958, all the redevelopment sponsors—Lincoln Center, Fordham University, the American Red Cross, and Webb and Knapp, Inc.—took title to their parcels at an auction at which there were no other bidders. The total price to Lincoln Center for its thirteen acres was $3.99 million. Seven months later, Spofford, at another auction, got the half block north of 65th Street for Juilliard at a price of $850,000, or $15.03 a square foot.

Day & Zimmerman of Philadelphia, the management consulting firm retained by JDR, began the task of ascertaining space needs for the constituents and estimating construction costs. The plan now envisaged six buildings—for the opera, the symphony, the ballet, the theater, the Juilliard School, and the library-museum—even though only three of these constituents were assured. Cost estimates included the plaza and other public spaces and a garage. The first figure the consultants brought back—$90 million—shocked the directors. No one would have guessed that this would be less than half of the ultimate total.

The consultants were asked to show what could be done for $40 million. They came back with an estimate of $45 million which crept up to $48 million and then to $53 million as the architects began to be involved and as painful struggles between desire and possibility continued for more than two years. Finally, the directors reached two difficult decisions. The first was that the fund-raising goal would have to be set at $75 million. The second was that the hope of getting all the funding for Lincoln Center from the private sector had to be abandoned. Every effort would have to be made to obtain government money.

JDR, Wallace Harrison, and Anthony Bliss of the Metropolitan Opera, together with their wives, journeyed to Europe in 1956 to study opera houses and concert halls there, JDR giving up his annual midwinter trip to Asia. The group came back with some useful ideas and a keener awareness of how European governments regularly paid for the arts. Nothing like it existed in the United States; the tradition was all the other way.

As a result, there were very few sources of tax money for such projects as building the units of Lincoln Center. For a long time the directors could only think of New York City funds for the branch library and federal funds for the plaza and garage, and neither was assured. Even if these possibilities were realized, they would account for only a relatively small portion of the total needed. There was nothing to do but forge ahead and hope for the best in the private sector. In 1957 the fund-raising apparatus was put together and the campaign started in earnest. By the end of April 1958, Clarence Francis could report that $46 million had been raised in contributions and pledges. Two large gifts came from the Ford ($15 million) and Rockefeller Foundations ($10 million) along with fairly stringent matching and timing requirements.[24] Other gifts had come from sixty-two business corporations, totaling over $4 million. Junior contributed $5 million, which elicited a warm expression of thanks from his eldest son. JDR himself gave $1 million to the fund. There would be much more from him before his involvement with Lincoln Center ended.

The acquisition of land, the relocation of tenants, the razing of existing buildings, and the fund-raising effort were all directed by the Lincoln Center board acting for the whole undertaking, not by the individual constituents. One of the tricky, challenging questions in the making of Lincoln Center was the relations that should exist among the parts and those of each to the whole. What would be the functions of the Center itself as distinguished from its components, whose functions were quite clear? Certainly the dedication of the people who had been drawn to the project was not inspired merely by bricks and mortar and the workaday role of landlord. From the outset, the organizing principle of Lincoln Center was that of "a loose federation," each constituent retaining "absolute artistic and financial autonomy."[25] But the developers also expected that Lincoln Center would be more than the sum of its parts. What then was this role of the Center to be? Ed Young tells us of the understanding that grew among the directors:

There gradually emerged an organizational concept that would make the new corporation a beneficent landlord with the constituents favored tenants, that would recognize the constituents as the project's artistic endowment and place the new corporation in a coordinating role. It would enable the new organization to encourage innovations, to foster the new and experimental, to search for ways to reach an enlarging public, and to encourage international exchange in the performing arts.[26]

To make sure that these goals would be more than pious words, the directors thought it imperative that Lincoln Center have a fund of its own for programs in the arts, quite apart from the budgets of the individual constituents and the overall operating costs and physical needs of the Center. They called this the "Fund for Education and Artistic Advancement." At first, the target for this Fund was $20 million; it had to be cut back to $10 million to fit within the fund-raising goal of $75 million, though the importance of its special purpose was stressed in the submissions to Ford and Rockefeller:

The realization of these goals, and indeed the validity of the concept of the Center, depends in part upon the sound and imaginative management of the Center itself, but even more upon the nature of the constituent institutions and the readiness of their leaders to cooperate fully within the framework of the Center.[27]

In the early years the governance of Lincoln Center encountered few difficulties apart from the resistance of the Met to the inclusion of the City

Opera. The clear-cut purpose in fund-raising and site preparation and the general excitement about the grand prospect created unity. Only one foretaste of future problems was the difficulty of getting the architects to cooperate, not merely in solving questions of design for each building, but also in producing an overall design suited to the idea of a unified and unifying Center.

In recognition of his role in helping to start the project, Wally Harrison was made "coordinating architect" as well as architect for the opera house. This second role nearly obliterated the first. The house for the Met was to be the largest and most expensive of the buildings, and its requirements were difficult, so that the design solution for it was crucial. It must be right in itself, in its placing on the site, and in its relations to all the other structures.

Harrison's partner, Max Abramovitz, was named architect for Philharmonic Hall. The other architects selected resulted in an assemblage of some of the finest talents in the world—Philip Johnson for the dance theater, Eero Saarinen for the Vivian Beaumont Theater, Gordon Bunshaft for the library-museum, and Pietro Belluschi for Juilliard. Final approval rested with the directors, but JDR and his colleagues knew that none of them had the knowledge and experience to deal with this bevy of geniuses on most matters of architectural judgment. The solution was to recruit René d'Harnoncourt, director of the Museum of Modern Art, to act as adviser on design questions. According to Ed Young, he was an "ideal choice" for the job: "He enjoyed the respect of all the architects, and he regarded each of them with similar respect. Yet he was independent of them in his artistic judgments."[28]

Toward the end of 1958 Harrison convened the other five architects and d'Harnoncourt, JDR, and Young in a series of meetings, asking JDR, as a neutral nonprofessional, to serve as chairman. The agenda was simple in theory: coordination.

But matters moved slowly and great difficulties arose. Harrison seemed so overburdened by the task of designing the Met that he was "coordinating" very little. The hearts of the board members were agitated by two deep fears—about the passing of time and about the dominating building of the site, the opera house. Would it ever be designed to fit in with what the other architects were doing? A measure of the board's frustration was that JDR and Spofford met twice privately with Harrison to persuade him to take an associate architect for the Met design, either Saarinen or Bunshaft. Harrison rebuffed them.

By early 1959, the directors decided they could no longer postpone ground-breaking on at least one of the buildings. It so happened that the relocating of the hundreds of families and commercial tenants from the three-block area had not been so painfully complicated as feared. Their relocation and the demolition of existing buildings had been accomplished smoothly and ahead of schedule. But over three years had gone by during which a great deal of fund-raising and publicity had taken place. The fear now was that if no sign of tangible progress could be shown much of the collective enthusiasm might evaporate. The building chosen to be the first was Philharmonic Hall. Though plans were unfinished, its design was the most advanced. The directors scheduled ground-breaking for May 14, 1959, authorizing only excavation and foundation work. But one note of cheer was sounded—President Eisenhower agreed to turn the first shovelful of earth.

May 14 was a beautiful day, and as Ike dug his spade into the soft earth and beamed his famous smile those present could forget for at least a few moments the unresolved issues of Lincoln Center. Ike's message that Lincoln Center would stand as a symbol of cooperation between private and public organizations, of America's commitment to solve the problem of urban blight, and of the possibility of a "true interchange of the fruits of national cultures" was one that JDR wholeheartedly endorsed. Yet the wry grin of the main promoter, contrasting with the smile of the politicos in the official picture, suggests how aware JDR was of the distance still to be covered before those goals could be reached. Many years of toil and many hurdles lay ahead.[29]

10

♯

LINCOLN CENTER:
THE REALITY

IT IS FAIR to say that the best move the leaders of Lincoln Center made was to recruit John D. Rockefeller 3rd as *their* leader. The record furnishes a strong case for asserting that he was the only person in New York City at that time with the right combination of stature, resources, and personal qualities to make the enterprise succeed.

So demanding—and engrossing—was the creation of Lincoln Center that it was possible for anyone involved to forget that other things were going on in the world. But of course a great deal *was* going on, and JDR was extremely busy with other projects: Lincoln Center could only be for him a part-time occupation. Outside events also impinged on the undertaking. One of the most important, as we shall see, was the election of Nelson Rockefeller as governor of New York State in 1958. Then there was the emergence of two potential rivals to Lincoln Center. In Washington plans were announced for a performing arts complex initially known as "the National Cultural Center." In New York the razing of Carnegie Hall, which had been a spur to the fashioning of Lincoln Center, was canceled as a result of pressure brought to bear by citizens anxious to preserve the music hall as a historic landmark. As a result, competitive fund-raising started, with the slogan being "Save Carnegie Hall."[1] With the theory that the country needed more rather than fewer cultural resources and that opposition from Lincoln Center would have been a public relations disaster, JDR refused to worry about these competitors, and he turned out to be right. Yet another factor was the decision to hold a World's Fair in New York City in 1964; by a strange turn of events, it proved the salvation of Lincoln Center in one of the crises that threatened its existence.

The vicissitudes and perplexities tended to fall into three groups, and they will be described thus clustered for the sake of clarity, but it is obvious that they occurred not separately but in complex interrelations. The three divisions of trouble came under the heads of: (1) completing the roster of constituents and the bizarre funding solution that made it possible; (2) skyrocketing costs that required endless fund-raising; and (3) management, in the sense of physically completing the project as well as combining the parts into a unique new institution.[2]

The ideal of autonomous but intermeshing components that would form a unity greater than the sum of its parts did survive in the end, although it was rudely battered along the way. Fresh constituents were created (or aborted) in such fields as film, chamber music, and musical theater, but basic planning for Lincoln Center always regarded the six constituents already described as primary, each to have its own building. The Metropolitan, the Philharmonic, and the Juilliard were already assured, each with strong funding. Mrs. Allen's gift made possible the building of a theater, and the Repertory Theater Association was soon created to become the fourth constituent. So much was clear. The uncertainties had to do with the library-museum building and the ballet company that was to occupy the dance theater. There were two needs in each case: officially signing up the constituent and securing the funding.

As far as the first need was concerned, the library-museum was the easier hurdle. The trustees of the New York Public Library were very much in favor of joining the Center. But they could not accommodate the cost of a new building within the existing pattern of financial support from the city of New York. New money would have to be made available. To keep the 1956 fund-raising target of $75 million intact, one measure adopted by JDR and his colleagues was simply to deduct from that budget the costs of the library-museum and the public spaces such as the plaza and garage, on the assumption that government support for these purposes would materialize. JDR kept after City Hall to allocate the new money needed for the library-museum, but, as he soon learned, Lincoln Center was now in the political business of competing for the scarce resources available to New York City and nothing was going to be easy. As it turned out, there was no resolution until the problem of the dance theater was solved.

Compounded by the animosity between the City Center and the Metropolitan Opera, the problem of the sixth primary constituent for Lincoln Center dragged on for nearly eight years of tortuous maneuverings and negotiations. At the very time of ground-breaking there was a disturbing omen in the form of a letter on JDR's desk in Room 5600. It was

Lincoln Kirstein's letter of resignation from the Lincoln Center board. There being no discernible reason for Kirstein to resign, JDR kept trying to find out what the trouble was. Finally he wrote a warm letter reminding Kirstein of their common vision and years of friendly cooperation. Referring to Lincoln Center as "Lincoln Square," Kirstein replied rather darkly:

I had no notion of the powers needed for Lincoln Square. Working so long with artists, I imagined it might answer their possibilities—fantasy, imagination, selfless capacity.

Four years taught me; the criterion is manipulation of real-estate sweetened by the education-business. Your associates are not inimical to art; to them it is not real. Their habit is compulsive charity to maintain dynastic prestige.

Is there any mastery, patronage or grand-design? For me and my kind, Lincoln Square frames that moral vacuum which makes Europe and Asia wary of American pragmatism.[3]

Discussions with the leaders of the City Center had been stalled for some time; Kirstein's resignation made the prospects of lining up the New York City Ballet or all of the City Center as the sixth constituent of Lincoln Center seem all the more bleak. Even worse tidings arrived shortly after ground-breaking: the financial needs of Lincoln Center had been greatly underestimated. Chuck Spofford, now serving as vice president, sounded the alarm in June 1959 and called for a new detailed study. By the end of the month, Ed Young produced figures showing that the gap between the budget of $75 million and the actual need was $37 million. Young suggested such means of bridging the chasm as increasing the fund-raising goal, eliminating certain buildings, deferring the construction of others, exploring the possibilities of increased government support— and borrowing.[4]

All these devices had to be resorted to over the next few years. At the time most of them were regarded as much too radical. That summer of '59 marked the first of a series of crises, and it took awhile for its full import to sink in. An immediate result was a fit of unrealistic budgetary thinking in regard to the problem of the sixth constituent. Only $7 million had been earmarked within the $75 million budget for the dance theater, a very low estimate in itself. Now the directors decided to renew negotiations to bring in all of the City Center as the sixth constituent, in the hope that the small city subsidy it received would ease the funding problem. On this note the directors cut the $7 million for the dance theater in half.

The board continued to agonize over the budget until May 1960, when more realistic estimates for the entire project were finally produced and approved, raising the total all the way up to $142 million. It was a staggering increase, nearly a doubling of the previous forecast. Of this new figure, $35.2 million was now to be sought from the various levels of government. This government funding target now included a much more plausible $17.5 million for the dance theater; the remainder was accounted for by new estimates for the library-museum and the public spaces.

During this period JDR resumed his lengthy and difficult negotiations to solve two problems—to get the needed funds from government sources and to include the City Center as a constituent. It had become clear that these two desiderata were inseparable. The flinty negotiating posture of the City Center leadership was not eased by their awareness that for a considerable time Lincoln Center had been interested in stealing the New York City Ballet away from them. Still, Morris and Baum had their reasons for engaging in the discussions. For one, circumstances could still be imagined that would allow the ballet to slip away from one Center to the other. For another, the City Center was still deeply mired in its own financial problems and needed some sort of breakthrough.

Part of the problem of government funding was solved when Robert Moses changed his original stand against any federal money for Lincoln Center beyond the subsidy for the land under urban renewal procedures. Lincoln Center was ultimately able to get more federal funds for the public facilities (the plaza and the garage); but the efforts required were excruciating, owing to the unfriendly, even bitter, feelings of the federal officials responsible for the urban renewal program toward Moses. They resented his always getting the lion's share of urban renewal funds for his New York City projects, and they suspected that financial irregularities had occurred in several of them.[5] This still left the problems of the library-museum and dance theater; the only hope of money for these was New York City and New York State.

To realize that hope, it was of enormous help that Nelson Rockefeller had been elected governor. He was known to have supported the arts for his entire adult life, and it was natural that he would be solidly behind the Lincoln Center concept. But, according to John Lockwood, one of his closest associates, it gave Nelson pleasure and amusement to know that now the tables were turned—his older brother coming to him "to bail out Lincoln Center."[6] During late 1959 and 1960 Nelson, JDR, Moses, Mayor Wagner, and a varying cast of aides met on the question, usually at Nelson's Fifth Avenue apartment. At one point JDR presented a long list of items that Lincoln Center needed from the city and left the meeting in a euphoric state thinking everyone had approved. The truth was that

Moses, who was beginning to have trouble hearing, had nodded benignly without really following what had been said. Afterwards he made it plain that he disagreed with most of JDR's proposals.[7]

All efforts at first were bent on getting the needed money from the city. But when JDR and Nelson got together at Christmas in 1959, they came to realize that the city could not do everything and that the state would have to do its part. They asked John Lockwood to look into the legal problems and suggest a way for state action.[8] An unlikely solution in the form of the 1964 New York World's Fair soon emerged from talks between Lockwood and Moses. Plans for the fair had been announced the previous summer and gained the support of the New York political and business establishments. To become president of the World's Fair Corporation and thus cap his career, Moses had to resign most of his public offices. He had great hopes that "his" fair would succeed financially as Grover Whalen's in 1939 had not.

The "unlikely solution" was this: Lincoln Center would be designated as the performing arts unit for the fair and the state's contribution to the fair would take the form of money to build the dance theater. Lockwood's research had shown that the state constitution forbade the allocation of funds for building any facility that was not owned by the state or city, though a leasing arrangement could sidestep the prohibition. On July 21, 1960, JDR met with Mayor Wagner and Newbold Morris to present the scheme. By this time Morris had succeeded Moses as the Commissioner of Parks. The proposal was to have the state provide $15 million for the dance theater if the city would match the amount. The city's money would go for several purposes: to complete the sum needed for the dance theater, pay for the library-museum building, provide some maintenance reserve, and repurchase the land on which the two buildings were to be erected. The last provision was necessary because Lincoln Center would turn over the ownership of the two buildings to the city after the fair in order to comply with the constitution, and then would recover them on a long-term lease.

Morris and the Mayor liked the idea. With all the forces finally lined up behind the plan—the governor, Moses, Morris, Lincoln Center, City Center, and the mayor—the unlikely solution had become likely. But there was to be another grueling two-year period before the city's part was assured—approval was delayed by political interference, opposition at lower levels, and the need for city and state to pass enabling legislation. When the last step was taken on August 30, 1962, Lincoln Center had at last $15 million from the state for the dance theater (now appropriately renamed the New York State Theater); $4.4 million from the city toward that same theater and its land; and $7.6 million from the city for the library-museum and land.[9]

Success entailed another emergency: the State Theater had to be completed in time for the opening of the fair on April 23, 1964. That condition had been set by Governor Rockefeller. But this pressure could almost be considered a trifle compared to the problem of getting City Center formally signed up as a constituent. Although not a written condition of the deal, it was strongly implied. By that time, it was hard to imagine Lincoln Center as complete without the New York City Ballet as one of its residents. And there seemed to be no realistic hope of splitting the ballet away from City Center. Fortunately, Lincoln Kirstein had turned amiable again, and at lunch with JDR in October 1961 he expressed the view that the whole of the City Center should be located in the State Theater, with the calendar assigned one-third to ballet, one-third to opera, and one-third to foreign companies, with Lincoln Center undertaking to manage the last. JDR had held similar views for a long time. He knew that the ballet was indispensable, that the City Opera would not compete with the Met but simply give the genre a broader appeal, and that it was appropriate for the Lincoln Center management to fill the free time in the State Theater.

The board of the Metropolitan Opera passed a resolution stating that it would be "pleased" to have the City Center join Lincoln Center and expressing confidence that detailed questions "will be satisfactorily worked out between the managements of the two organizations." This was accomplished by the strong influence of Chuck Spofford; Rudolf Bing, general manager of the Met, remained "furiously opposed" to the idea of having two opera companies on the same spot.[10] Other members of his staff as well as some trustees and patrons of the Met shared Bing's feelings. Still, the Met *was* on record as accepting City Center. Not that this was the end of the difficulties for JDR. The leaders of City Center wanted independence from Lincoln Center—complete control of the State Theater. The main reason for this position was the fear that the City Opera would be dominated by the Met owing to the Met's weight in Lincoln Center councils. Moreover they disliked the elitist aura of the Met just as much as the Met's leaders looked down upon the plebeian character of the City Opera. In a word, there was predictable paranoia on both sides, and JDR was in the middle with his goodwill and a desire to find a compromise as his only allies.

The City Center's position became apparent as early as November 1961, when Newbold Morris pressed for language in the various pieces of legislation that would enable City Center to lease the State Theater directly from the city, bypassing Lincoln Center altogether. If Lincoln Center *had* to be the lessee, Morris wanted a provision to achieve the same effect, one that would have required Lincoln Center to sublease the building to City Center. Morris was backed by the mayor and JDR by the governor. JDR argued that any such provision would go against the very principle of Lincoln Center, reducing it merely to a real estate operation. The result was language permitting the sublease but not requiring it. JDR had won a round. But feelings ran so high that it was not possible to advance any further by the opening of the World's Fair, so the temporary solution was a contract providing for the New York City Ballet to appear at the State Theater for twenty weeks during each of the two years of the fair.[11]

From the time the financing of the State Theater was secured, it took more than three years of protracted and agonizing negotiations for JDR to bring City Center fully into Lincoln Center. Despite the Spofford resolution, animosity within the Met was so acute that at one point it nearly withdrew from Lincoln Center, and later the Lincoln Center board was so wearied that it seriously considered proceeding without the Met. Coexistence with a rival opera company was but one issue; others involved planning delays and changes, cost overruns, and demands for special treatment by the Met. As time passed, JDR grew testy. One day at lunch he told Anthony Bliss, president of the Metropolitan Opera Association, that he could understand why some people used words like "smugness," "arrogance," and "defensiveness" to describe the Met.

The City Center desire for complete freedom from Lincoln Center was equally intense. As parks commissioner, Newbold Morris no longer played an active role in negotiating, and Lincoln Kirstein was being very cooperative. He and JDR had resumed their periodic lunches together, and JDR found Kirstein "his old self" of several years earlier, "relaxed, friendly and genuinely enthusiastic." So Morton Baum, once again, was JDR's interlocutor in the protracted talks. We have his description from Ed Young:

. . . chairman of its Finance Committee and the most influential member of its board, Baum wielded a power far wider than his title suggested. He shunned the spotlight and ruled by the force of his tight grip on the purse strings. He was a frugal manager, a stern taskmaster, and in negotiations, as hard as nails. A respected member of New York's legal community, he had been an advisor to Mayor Wagner and his predecessors on city financial matters. Moreover, he loved music and ballet, and held an incontestable belief in the low-priced ticket policy of City Center. As a result he had achieved a supportive attitude toward City Center on the part of a succession of mayors and their administrations.[12]

JDR had learned about this the hard way in his dealings with Baum over the years. For once JDR warmly supported a political candidate, John V. Lindsay, the man he thought would be the next mayor of New York.

In the process, JDR made sure that candidate Lindsay knew all about Lincoln Center. Here he had in mind not so much the City Center puzzle, which he thought would be resolved long before the election, but a host of housekeeping relations with the city, among them zoning, tax status, security, city sidewalks and streets. In the end, Lindsay disappointed him on some of these issues, including those affecting City Center: Lindsay, like all previous mayors, tended strongly in the direction of supporting whatever Morton Baum said.

The City Center problem was only the worst of those stemming from the relation of part to whole at Lincoln Center. Hard as JDR and his fellow board members tried, they could not keep these relations from degenerating into adversary roles at times. The founders wanted to make sure that Lincoln Center was more than a real estate developer and a managing agent, that it would have a coordinating and innovative role in promoting the performing arts above and beyond what the individual constituents could do, but in a way that did not compete with them. Each constituent would occupy a new building designed expressly for its needs, would have no debts to carry and no rent to pay. Lincoln Center would bill the constituent for operating costs and upkeep on a break-even basis. Yet these straightforward necessities led to a host of wrangles, from ordinary housekeeping problems to policies such as the allocation of costs and the right to book a hall when a constituent did not use it.

In the end, no single scheme was followed. For example, the Philharmonic had priority in choosing dates for Philharmonic Hall for 35 to 40 percent of the year, Lincoln Center being free to run and use the building the rest of the time. Contrariwise, the Met insisted on keeping total control of its house and booking any outside attractions. The only concession was that it would do this "in collaboration" with Lincoln Center. For the State Theater, JDR and his colleagues wanted what Kirstein had indicated—the City Ballet and City Opera would each have its season and Lincoln Center would book the hall at other times. Baum wanted Lincoln Center to stay out altogether. JDR appealed to Nelson, who assigned his aide William J. Ronan to mediate. Nothing worked. A typical parley at breakfast in Nelson's apartment on the last day of 1964 went as follows, as JDR reported in his diary:

Its purpose was to try to somehow get Morton Baum to be willing to give a little in order to meet Lincoln Center's minimum request in connection with the leasing of the New York State Theater to City Center. Lincoln Center has really met all of the requirements of City Center and now is only asking that five weeks each year of State Theater time be set aside for allocation by Lincoln Center. Also that the New York City subsidy for the State Theater be allocated to offset maintenance costs throughout the year and not just for the period when City Center will be using the Theater. Nelson was fine the way he handled the situation; the Mayor said nothing. Baum was his usual uncompromising self, only not quite as violent and unreasonable as he sometimes is.

After almost daily meetings early in January 1965, an agreement was reached and announced to the press on January 11. Baum had finally given way a little. The lease would be concluded with Lincoln Center, which could book the State Theater to outside groups for five to ten weeks each year. City maintenance money would be allocated for costs computed over the full year. And the Music Theater, a new constituent for American musicals, organized by the composer Richard Rodgers, would occupy the theater for twelve weeks each year. [13]

In his mild way, JDR had characterized Baum as "a bright and able man, but also extremely difficult to deal with." Now JDR could sigh with relief. Baum and other City Center leaders took seats on the Lincoln Center board, while Lincoln Kirstein of the New York City Ballet and Julius Rudel of the New York City Opera became members of the Center Council, composed of the professional and artistic managers of the constituents.

Even so, contention was not over. As JDR put it, Baum "kept right on negotiating" the points of the agreement. It took another year and arbitration by Father McGinley, the president of Fordham University and a Lincoln Center trustee, before a contract was finally signed. Never satisfied, Baum kept raising several of the points with Mayor Lindsay at City Hall. But this was now only a minor irritant; the matter of corralling all the large and essential constituents of Lincoln Center *was* settled. As JDR had always believed would happen, the City Opera and the Met were able to coexist amicably. Years later Rudolf Bing stated: "It now seems clear to me that I was wrong in fighting the entry of the City Opera to Lincoln Center. There have been no particular difficulties. They have helped us and we have helped them." [14]

During the financial crisis of 1959–1960, when the total budget took the astounding leap upward to $142 million, the portion to be raised from the private sector rose to $102 million. This news was enough to dampen the enthusiasm of the campaigners, led by Clare Francis, retired chairman of General Foods. By the time the revised budget was accepted, the effort had yielded nearly $65 million in cash and pledges. But this was the "easy" money collected from individuals, corporations, and foundations in the first round of solicitations. It included the large gifts from the Ford and Rockefeller Foundations, other substantial gifts from smaller foundations, Mrs. Allen's pledge of $3 million for the repertory theater, $1 million from JDR, and a total of $10.5 million from his father in three separate gifts.

Thereafter, the state of fiscal crisis was chronic as costs inexorably rose. The campaign goal was hiked to $120.6 in 1963, revised again in 1966, and lifted again to its final figure of $141.4 million in 1969—by far the largest amount ever raised for the arts from the private sector. With income and government funding added, the final capital cost for Lincoln Center was $184.8 million.[15]

JDR's diary is peppered for almost ten years with anguished notes about cost overruns, emergency meetings, fiscal crises, and fund-raising burdens. Tremendous pressure was exerted on the constituents by the Lincoln Center board to keep costs down. Honest efforts were certainly made. For example, dormitories were eliminated from the Juilliard plan, and the library-museum and repertory theater were combined into one building. Still the rise in costs was relentless, the result of faulty estimates, escalating building costs, design changes after construction had started, and above all the very size and scale of Lincoln Center. The best and most modern buildings imaginable were being tailor-made for the various performing arts, and, as one committee report expressed it, this required facilities for audiences and performers "far in excess of the traditional provision for these purposes in New York." Space requirements "both backstage and in front of the house have grown tremendously." The total cubic footage of Lincoln Center construction increased 72 percent in five years of planning.[16]

Many people worked hard and capably at fund-raising, but through it all the real heavyweight was JDR. He knew it and everyone else knew it. When it was all over, he was primarily responsible for about 70 percent of the $141.4 million raised from the private sector, either directly from Rockefeller sources or indirectly from others whom he influenced strongly, such as the Ford Foundation and Mrs. Allen. And, of course, most of the government money came as the result of collaboration between JDR and Nelson. But at the same time, how could JDR discharge the responsibility that was rightly his to shoulder and yet keep Lincoln Center from being permanently dependent on the Rockefellers? The dilemma was like that which his father and grandfather had faced in creating the University of Chicago. There was only one answer—hard work until the job was done and then a firm withdrawal.

As long as the burden lay upon him, JDR was a relentless fund-raiser. At one point he guaranteed to raise half of a $16 million deficit and succeeded. At another he closed a gap with a $5 million gift of his own, half of it anonymous. He wanted by his example to spur the other directors to give, but not be so lavish himself that they would just sit back and applaud.[17]

As chairman of the trust committee for one of his cousins, Mrs. Muriel McCormick Hubbard, JDR managed to give most of the trust, some $8.9 million, to Lincoln Center, designating it for the Juilliard building. The trust was the residue of one that Senior had set up in 1917 for his daughter, Edith Rockefeller McCormick, with 12,000 shares of Standard Oil stock, then worth $13.6 million. The trust was split among her children, and the resulting trust for her daughter Muriel was worth $9 million at the time of Muriel's death in 1959. The terms of the trust provided for it to be liquidated and shared among her legal issue. If she had no children the trust committee could give the proceeds to charity. Mrs. Hubbard had four adopted children all under the age of seven, technically not legal issue. The executor's action was challenged in court on behalf of the adopted, and by the time the matter was settled, in 1965, the trust was worth more than $13 million. Thus the children received not only Mrs. Hubbard's own estate, but also a share of the trust after the court awarded $8.9 million of it to Lincoln Center.[18]

JDR had many more successes than failures in his fund-raising, but the failures and near failures generally proved the most interesting. He once tried to get a gift from the Ford Motor Company on the principle that General Motors and the Chrysler Corporation were already contributors. He wrote to Henry Ford II who, as expected, wrote back declining and citing the large gift from the Ford Foundation. JDR retorted by drawing the parallel between, on the one hand, Standard of New Jersey and the Rockefeller Foundation, and on the other, the Ford Motor Company and the Ford Foundation. Though linked by investments, the Rockefeller Foundation and Standard Oil functioned independently in making grants and both had given to Lincoln Center. But the Ford heir remained unmoved.[19]

JDR had as little success with the Kennedy family. The fact that John F. Kennedy was in the White House made him everyone's target for help in publicizing projects in order to share in the glamour of "Camelot." The President's wife, Jackie, was an enthusiastic patron of the arts, and she responded to JDR's invitation to grace the opening night of Philharmonic Hall on September 17, 1962. He escorted her as an estimated audience on 26 million Americans watched on CBS television. The First Lady had written to him

that anything under the sun you want me to do—now or in the future—I will do with the greatest pride and pleasure. You have only to tell me what it is. I will be on any committee you wish, cut any ribbon, dive off the high diving board at the Aquacade if that will help.[20]

But JDR also wanted Kennedy money, specifically a $1.5 million grant from the Kennedy Foundation for Lincoln Center. Here the First Lady's lively enthusiasm was of no avail, nor was an intervention by General Maxwell Taylor, who had been recruited by President Kennedy as special assistant on national security in April 1961, after only six months as president of Lincoln Center. JDR was mystified as he was repeatedly turned down by the Foundation. Among wealthy donors, a quid pro quo is sometimes helpful, so JDR made a donation of $106,000 to the National Cultural Center in Washington, a project the President favored. It was only in talking by telephone with R. Sargent Shriver, then the steward of Kennedy family interests, that JDR learned the cause of the refusal: the long memory of the patriarch of the Kennedy clan, ex-ambassador Joseph P. Kennedy. Shriver said that Kennedy's unshakable "no" was based on "the situation which developed in relation to the price to be paid for the Kennedy building. It would seem that Mr. Kennedy still feels very strongly in regard to the handling of this matter and associates his unhappiness with the Lincoln Center leadership."[21]

The reference was to an incident five years earlier, which JDR thought had been taken care of and had forgotten. It will be recalled that Lincoln Center had agreed to the $2.5 million price that Kennedy had demanded for the family-owned building at Lincoln Square, but subsequently the New York City Board of Estimate rejected the deal under urban renewal procedures and set the figure at $1.5 million. Kennedy sued, and it took several years before the court set the final payment at $2.4 million. Kennedy felt he had been swindled out of $100,000 by Lincoln Center.

To redress the grievance—or try to—JDR sent his personal check for $100,000 to the Kennedy Foundation. Kennedy thanked JDR for the check and "the spirit in which it was tendered," but added: "For me to accept $100,000 for the Foundation might make it appear that my 'annoyances and worries' are a matter of dollars and cents. They are not."[22] Still, Kennedy kept JDR's check. Bemused by this behavior, JDR later read Richard Whalen's biography of the Kennedy "founding father" and learned something about his penchant for holding a grudge, especially if some real or fancied slight from the WASP establishment were involved.[23]

But JDR was nothing if not tenacious. He kept after the Kennedy Foundation, now seeking $1 million for the Juilliard Library. In June 1965, Mr. and Mrs. Stephen Smith (she was the President's sister Jean) stopped in to see him and announce that the Kennedy Foundation would contribute $100,000 to Lincoln Center. JDR found this "most disappointing." Mrs. Smith had said "she hoped something distinctive could be found for which the money could be used as a memorial to President Kennedy. I said that I was concerned that this might be difficult in terms of the amount proposed." JDR wrote to Maxwell Taylor the following spring and pointed out that the junior senator from New York, Robert Kennedy, had done nothing to assist the Lincoln Center project. He continued:

I do honestly feel that the family has not done very well by us. It is interesting that they have not hesitated to press my family interests to support their family projects. At the moment there is strong pressure on the Rockefeller Foundation for support of the Kennedy Center at Harvard even though they have raised twice as much as they had originally in mind. Forgive me if I sound slightly annoyed, but I really am![24]

Another nearly dry well might have been known to be such. There had been a notion that foreign governments might want to contribute to Lincoln Center. Oddly enough, the only countries that responded were the former enemies of the United States in World War II. The first effort by Clare Francis, in Latin America, drew a blank. JDR got nothing in London and Paris despite a persistent push. He worked on the French for several years, visiting Paris and having meetings with a future president, Finance Minister Giscard d'Estaing ("I like him so much"), Foreign Affairs Minister Couve de Murville ("friendly but in fact cold and uninterested"), and Minister of Culture André Malraux ("could not have been nicer or more friendly"). In July 1964 JDR met with President De Gaulle, who spoke "warmly of my family's interest in France." But in the end no gift was forthcoming.

Despite worse financial problems than those of the French, the Italian government responded to JDR's request with a gift of the travertine marble for the Juilliard building. The West German government contributed $2.5 million to the completion of the Metropolitan Opera, and the Austrian government contributed the crystal chandeliers and other light fixtures for the Met.

JDR decided it was probably time that the Japanese should feel able to respond to such suggestions. On the advice of Matsumoto, he initiated a request for $1 million from the Keidanren (Japan Federation of Economic Organizations), a uniquely powerful institution in the business and government of Japan. Word came from Douglas Overton of the Japan Society, who said he had heard that the Japanese were "appalled" at the request. Fearing that he had misread the situation, JDR asked Edwin Reischauer and Matsumoto whether he should withdraw the request. Both counseled patience. Matsumoto reported that the Keidanren had formed a committee to raise the money from among its members without going to the government.[25]

The committee politely asked through U.S. State Department channels for information on the Rockefeller Foundation and family contributions to Japan during the years 1952 to 1962, thus indicating that any Japanese gift would be made as a token of gratitude to the Rockefellers and not as a response to Lincoln Center. Having learned Japanese ways, JDR just as politely had the Foundation and family office list all the contributions, not from 1952 but from 1913 so as to obscure his own share. The total was nearly $20 million. When the Keidanren finally announced its $1 million gift in July 1963, it simply stated that the "donation will be made as a token of gratitude for a variety of aids given by the Rockefellers, either individually or through the Rockefeller Foundation."[26] It was the first foreign gift from Japan in the postwar years.

Given the magnitude of the funding needs, it is not surprising that some ill-considered, not to say naive, efforts would be made. These were variations on a single idea: to find one or several wealthy donors so taken with the Lincoln Center plan that they would give all the money needed for an entire building. JDR put out some feelers toward Huntington Hartford, Doris Duke, and others, but came away empty-handed.

The most bizarre version of this idea was the notion that the seven best-known Greek shipowners might each be willing to give $1 million in honor of their country, "the birthplace of the arts." The sum would be used to build the dance theater (then estimated to cost $7 million). David Rockefeller agreed to help, and he saw or wrote to six of the mysterious and reputedly wealthy Greeks—Niarchos, Andreadis, Nomiros, Livanos, Goulandris, and Onassis. Only Stavros Niarchos pledged his $1 million. Nicholas Goulandris would contribute if everyone else did, but David added that Goulandris "may have had his tongue somewhat in his cheek, as he seemed very skeptical that so large a sum could be raised from the Greeks."[27]

On a trip to Europe in the summer of 1965, JDR and Blanchette spent several days with Mr. and Mrs. Niarchos on their 2,000-acre Greek island, Spetsopoula, having been flown from Athens to the island in Niarchos's helicopter. With some difficulty, JDR was able to pin Niarchos down and talk business:

. . . he indicated an interest in Lincoln Center, provided the suit of the U.S. Government against his interests was resolved, which he anticipated would be next month, and provided he could develop business interests in the U.S.A. which would generate money which he would be prepared to give to Lincoln Center. He pointed out that in Greece there is no tax deduction for philanthropic gifts. . . . he made reference to the one million dollars which he had pledged four or five years ago, and indicated that if what he had in mind should be possible he would be glad to give substantially more than this.

As the conditions Niarchos was setting foreshadowed (despite the pledge), a gift from him was most unlikely, and none ever came. JDR had to be content with a pleasant and interesting visit.

The strangest undertaking among the fund-raising efforts was JDR's attempt to make a philanthropist out of J. Paul Getty, who stood at the head of the list *Fortune* published in 1958 of the ten richest men in the world. Having learned that Getty had no standing as a philanthropist, JDR decided to go after him. Through a friend of David Rockefeller's, JDR arranged a meeting with Getty in Paris in February 1958. The diary is laconic about the outcome:

In the afternoon went to see Paul Getty, the wealthy oilman, about a possible contribution to Lincoln Center. Has a modest apartment at the George V. Was most friendly and chatty and enjoyed my visit with him which lasted 3½ hours. Not too encouraged as to the results of my mission.[28]

The two men had hit it off and formed a genuine liking for each other. It was a time, incidentally, when JDR was deliberately trying to protect, enhance, and expand the practice of philanthropy as a positive social force in the United States, so it would be quite a coup to convert Paul Getty while benefiting Lincoln Center. Unfortunately, JDR's hunch about Getty was correct. But JDR, as we know, did not discourage easily. The Paris meeting was only the beginning of a ten-year campaign. JDR's suasion to turn the old man into a generous giver produced a fascinating "Dear John" and "Dear Paul" correspondence and became a pursuit by JDR and Blanchette: they visited Getty again at the George V, in Rome, in Vienna, and at Getty's English country place in Guildford, Surrey.

Soon after the opening salvo, JDR asked Getty for $7 million to pay for Philharmonic Hall and was turned down. JDR's grandfather was something of a hero to Getty, so JDR sent over a copy of Allan Nevins's biography of Senior. Getty wrote back, remarking that Senior "was unquestionably the most successful businessman of all time, a very good, ethical, kindly, generous man." He added: "He was a philanthropist on a titanic scale, and his benefactions have made the world a better place to live in."[29]

This expansive vocabulary sounded promising. Getty did make a gift of

$75,000 to the Asia Society in 1961; he never gave to Lincoln Center. In 1964, after a visit to the English country house, JDR commented ruefully:

Could see that my various talks with Mr. Getty have really gotten us nowhere insofar as changing his attitude in favor of making major gifts himself. While he agrees that philanthropy is important in our American way of life, he also thinks that business is and that the successful businessman is as respected as the philanthropist. Said I agreed to all this but that we needed both. Said I felt our only real disagreement was as to our individual and personal responsibilities in this connection and that obviously each of us had to make our own decision.

In the Center's financial crisis of 1967, JDR tried one more time. Getty responded by asking forgiveness "for being so negative about a project which I know is so close to your heart." The letters continued to be cordial, though JDR did not refrain from blunt comments about his "sadness" and "disappointment." At one point he expressed concern that Getty's sons were being "brought up in such an atmosphere." He wrote: "If only for their sake, I would think that an atmosphere of public responsibility would be valuable quite aside from the personal satisfactions which you would derive."[30]

Small wonder that JDR was glad to deal with more orthodox sources of money such as the large foundations. Ford and Rockefeller ended up giving totals of $25 million and $15 million respectively. Practiced givers, too, were a comfort. Alice Tully made possible a chamber music recital hall (bearing her name) in the Juilliard building. JDR described her as "a fine person of the old school," meaning one who listened carefully, saw a need, considered it rationally—and made the right decision.

Deciding how to use the money in building Lincoln Center was as difficult as raising it in the first place. By invitation, JDR and Ed Young (interim president of the Center after General Taylor left) sat in on many of the meetings of the architects, usually exhausting free-for-alls. JDR staggered out of one and groaned in his diary about "six hours with six architects." The group generally jumped on any design presented by one of their number. But as the years passed the crucial decisions were made one by one. Design unity for the project was achieved—by the use of travertine marble throughout, the massive use of glass, of spacious public areas, of outside balconies at promenade levels. The entire complex was turned around to face east instead of north, with Philharmonic Hall and the State Theater, of equal mass though of different facades, flanking the entrance. Philip Johnson's design of radiating spokes was accepted for the Plaza. For space reductions, economy, and design unity, Gordon Bunshaft and Eero Saarinen proposed combining their two buildings, the library-museum and the repertory theater.[31]

First to be completed was Philharmonic Hall, designed by Max Abramovitz. It was widely acclaimed after its gala opening, seen on nation-wide television in September 1962, but it soon became clear that there was a major flaw—the acoustics were bad. The science of acoustics is notoriously inexact, and several expensive attempts to improve the sound availed little, until in 1976 the entire interior was gutted and rebuilt. The hall was renamed in honor of Avery Fisher who had donated $10 million. There was considerable improvement of the acoustics, but not to the rank of the great halls of the world.

Philip Johnson's task was to get the State Theater designed and built in time for the opening of the World's Fair in April 1964. He succeeded magnificently with a hall that was widely praised for its beauty and utility, though the acoustics were judged to be less than desirable. The Met was supposed to be ready for the Fair as well, but there was no chance of it. Harrison was encountering massive difficulties, and it took a full decade, from the first sketches of 1956 to the grand opening in September 1966, to complete the building that had become the grueling test of his long and distinguished career. In the end he conquered all the problems and pro-duced a richly beautiful building with fine acoustics.

The building combining the library-museum and Vivian Beaumont Theater was also acclaimed. The problem for the theater has been the inability to maintain a successful repertory company. Half a dozen attempts failed, keeping the theater dark much of the time since it opened in 1965.[32]

The scale and technical requirements of Pietro Belluschi's Juilliard building had grown to the point where it was nearly as complex as the Met; it called for complete soundproofing, various kinds of studios and classrooms, several auditoriums, and offices. The site for all this was no longer big enough, and construction had to await the purchase of the rest of the block from the city and the razing of the high school located there. Not until 1965 was ground broken. But the building turned out to be a masterly achievement when the Juilliard School occupied its new quarters in 1969.

As Lincoln Center gradually passed from construction to programs and performances, the trustees decided that they needed as president an artist-administrator instead of a professional executive. The ideal man was quickly found—William Schuman, one of the foremost American compos-ers and a man of reputed administrative abilities as the president of the

Juilliard School. He took office late in 1961 and Ed Young became his executive vice president.

Schuman had no difficulty grasping the principle so dear to the heart of JDR and his coadjutors that Lincoln Center should lead and coordinate as well as present the arts through each of the constituents. Schuman's "fault" was that he took the idea too much to heart—his reach exceeded his grasp. His excesses in this direction and their financial consequences became JDR's last great crisis at Lincoln Center. It was an excruciating dilemma for him, because he basically believed in what Schuman was trying to do. For just such purposes as Schuman's, JDR had backed the "Fund for Education and Artistic Advancement" and had fought to protect it over the years. But a sense of the possible, of material limits, had to prevail. The trouble with Schuman was that he saw his mission to create arts programs and arts components as an open-ended enterprise; it would be the role of JDR and others to find the money, however large the cost. In the end, it was not a course that JDR, who was also fighting to phase out Rockefeller dependency, could accept.

Much of what Schuman did was brilliant. Some programs were unexceptionable and continue to this day, such as the outreach program for schoolchildren and the "Mostly Mozart" summer series, an outgrowth of his initial summer festivals that were great artistic and popular successes but financial disasters. The available funds dwindled down to the point that Lincoln Center verged on technical bankruptcy. Relations with the major constituents worsened and the very idea of a federation was threatened. The constituents were wary of a central impresario, and Schuman's energetic initiatives created the fear that they would end up picking up the costs. In 1967, David Keiser, one of the strongest financial supporters of the Center and the chairman of the board's program committee, came out in opposition to Schuman's impresario role.

JDR counseled with Schuman frequently. If JDR's associates had any criticism of him, it was that in such situations he waited too long to cry halt, had too much trust, and was too confident of his ability to get the other party to change course. At one point JDR tried to get Schuman to involve the board more creatively in decisions instead of only seeking rubber-stamp approval of his own ideas. In 1965, JDR tried the tack of giving Schuman even more responsibility on the theory that this might cause him to deal more prudently with financial limitations. JDR's idea was to make a "terminal" gift and withdraw as much as possible without cutting every tie. For a start, he stepped down from the executive committee. But Chuck Spofford and Dev Josephs pointed out that this would not work unless Ed Young left also, Young appearing inevitably as JDR's man. It was not an easy step to take for either of them, but Young returned to Room 5600, though he remained on the board and as JDR's link with the Center. In Young's other roles, the board put John Mazzola, a former Milbank, Tweed lawyer who had been brought to Lincoln Center years earlier by John Lockwood.

Still the situation kept worsening. It seemed hopeless after JDR and the other trustees learned what Schuman had said in a speech at Princeton University on December 8, 1966. He had entitled his speech "The New Establishment," meaning the new cultural centers such as Lincoln Center, which he said could be a force for good or evil, "pro-art or anti-art." He articulated "Schuman's Law" which stated: "Nonprofit institutions in the performing arts compromise their reason for being in direct proportion to the programs and policies which are adopted for fiscal reasons extrinsic to artistic purpose." Schuman added: "Basic to our problem is not that our deficits are too large, but that they are too small." He criticized "fiscal pressure" and any "compromise with artistic standards." Schuman also criticized performing arts institutions in the United States as being "at dead center. They haven't changed and they aren't moving." Although there is no certainty that he had his constituents in mind and that dead center might mean Lincoln Center, in the inflamed situation one could pardon his New York colleagues for suspecting that this was the case.

None of these thoughts and surmises were of a kind to soothe weary fund-raisers who had exhausted themselves reaching unprecedented heights in attracting funds for the arts at Lincoln Center. Schuman's words suggested a bottomless pit and no restraints. When he himself allowed that his comments might have been "rash," he surely understated the case. He had by that time lost the confidence of most of the trustees, yet even then JDR was not ready to give up. He and Schuman maintained good communications and frequently discussed their differing views, but the debate indeed was at dead center. Schuman had to be on leave during the summer of 1968 for medical reasons. Returning in the fall, with Lincoln Center near bankruptcy, he tried to work out an austerity budget, but after a series of meetings in November, JDR obtained Schuman's resignation. Schuman was "fine" about it. He was given a year's salary and named president emeritus.

This paved the way for JDR to end his association with Lincoln Center by resigning from the board in 1969. Before stepping down he worked hard in yet another round of fund-raising to restore Lincoln Center to a viable financial position. In this effort he enjoyed working with realtor Lawrence Wien, who for years had helped JDR in setting up meetings with leaders of the Jewish community and of the real estate world. At the last meeting on the capital campaign a gap of $2.5 million still yawned. After the meeting and a few words together, JDR and Wien decided to split the difference, each contributing $1.25 million.[33]

After fourteen years, a new leadership had emerged: men such as Wien and Amyas Ames and Hoyt Ammidon on the board and John Mazzola as president. JDR was glad he had borne the burden, but also glad to lay it down. He had been the prime mover, but had always underplayed his role, trying to involve and give credit to others whenever possible. He particularly enjoyed something he had rarely had in his life, camaraderie under pressure with men like Chuck Spofford, Dev Josephs, and the rest, that "fine group on the board and staff."

To play down the "Rockefeller factor" in the Center, there would be no building there with his name on it. But it was as fitting as it was unavoidable that the trustees and staff should place in the North Plaza at a ceremony on May 11, 1970, a bronze plaque honoring him. Amyas Ames, who succeeded JDR as chairman, said: "Without John Rockefeller, Lincoln Center could not have been built. It was his leadership and inspiration that carried us through to its completion." On the plaque are JDR's own words from a speech he had made to the American Symphony Orchestra League in San Francisco in 1963:

The arts are not for the privileged few, but for the many. Their place is not on the periphery of daily life, but at its center. They should function not merely as another form of entertainment but, rather, should contribute significantly to our well-being and happiness.

11

✠

POPULATION:
THE "TAKEOFF" STAGE

IT WAS during the 1960s that JDR became the best-known figure around the world in the rapidly escalating movement to curb population growth. This was not the sort of fame in which one's face was instantly recognizable to everyone, as was the case with Nelson and domestic politics. But no one anywhere in the world who was seriously involved in working on the population problem could fail to know about John D. Rockefeller 3rd.

As an individual making a difference vis-à-vis a major worldwide problem, what JDR did over the span of a dozen years bordered on the incredible—in providing moral leadership, in spurring leaders in developing nations to take action, in helping to provide them with the means to do so, and in moving his own government from a situation in which one could scarcely mention the population problem to an impressive level of commitment and action on all fronts.

Of course, he did not do all of this alone or by the force of his personality. But he was ready, with his unique attributes and his relentless commitment, when world conditions suddenly began to favor action and an end to the "period of quiescence." Some important changes signaled the beginning of a new era.

For one, the papacy of John XXIII, who was elevated in 1958, seemed to promise a liberalizing of Roman Catholic doctrine. At the same time, world attention focused more on the dire problems and legitimate needs of the developing world and less on the confrontational aspects of the Cold War as the end of European colonialism neared and new nations emerged on the world stage. More and more, the United Nations had a genuine role to play in technical assistance, contrasted to its helplessness in the face of big-power rivalries. And the developing world caught the imagination of many Americans, encouraged by the enthusiasm of the Kennedy administration, as typified by the creation of the Peace Corps and the revamping of foreign assistance programs into the new Agency for International Development (AID).

With the spotlight on the developing nations of Asia, Africa, and Latin America, awareness of their unprecedented rates of population growth—soon termed by the press the "population explosion"—became part of the popular consciousness. In country after country around the globe, leaders began to understand that the dramatic increase in births and the steady decline in death rates due to better public health programs and nutrition might have serious economic consequences that could undermine their newly won independence. Although levels of hostility toward former colonial powers may not have eased much in many cases, there was a definite awakening of interest in the advice, know-how, and technology of the West, in population as in other fields.

Through a combination of foresight, patience, and luck, the Population Council was uniquely qualified to respond. JDR, in a sense, had anticipated these trends and had created the ideal private assistance agency. It was the only one in the world that combined nongovernmental status, an absence of ideological strings, specialization in the population field, solid scientific credentials, and an international program of grants-in-aid. Although it did not have the level of funding one associates with a government agency, the Pop Council nevertheless was giving grants for biomedical, demographic, and contraceptive research, and awarded fellowships for young professionals from developing countries to take advanced studies in relevant disciplines.

Since its inception in 1952, the Council had been carefully nurtured along these lines by Frederick Osborn, with a staff numbering not more than a dozen professionals. The restrained, low-key style of the Council only enhanced its reputation. We have seen how Osborn talked Margaret Sanger out of organizing a big population conference in Washington in the mid-1950s. In his judgment, it was much better to move along quietly, basing one's action on sound scientific evidence and accomplishment, instead of energizing the opponents of population control by talking too much about the "population explosion" or engaging in any form of what Osborn called "scare tactics." In this, Osborn's style was sharply differentiated from those he regarded as activists or propagandists—not only those of the recent past such as Margaret Sanger and Clarence Gamble, but also such newer figures as Dixie Cup magnate Hugh Moore, Planned Parenthood president Cass Canfield, and General William Draper. Osborn's low-key approach was strongly supported by his board, especially by such scientists as Detlev Bronk and Frank Notestein.

When Osborn retired in 1959, JDR somewhat reluctantly came around to accepting Notestein as the new president. Osborn and Don McLean both favored Notestein. Osborn was a sort of elder statesman, but JDR and Notestein were more nearly contemporaries. Notestein certainly had the credentials for the job, as one of the pioneers in the science of demography and the head of the Office of Population Research at Princeton for twenty-three years. But he and JDR had what might be called a "like-dislike" relationship (a milder version of a "love-hate" relationship).[1] A tall, homely, balding man, Notestein could be "one of the boys," a chain-smoker and martini drinker. But he was also a consummate professional, a man of strong opinions who sometimes could be blunt in expressing them. Theirs was a relationship between a professional and a lay leader, and it was a touchy one.

From JDR's side, there was often an attitude of impatience toward the Council—he wanted to see more energy and action to take advantage of the sudden burgeoning interest in population. On Notestein's side, there was a frequent tension over the desire to keep JDR properly involved and yet to restrain him at the same time. Notestein wanted to find things for JDR to do so that he would not bother the professionals at work in the Council, but also would not lead him astray into the camp of the propagandists or away from badly needed leadership and support of the Council. In short, Notestein wanted to control JDR.

The more one looks back and examines the record of their collaboration, the more clear it seems that each was extremely fortunate in the other. In Osborn and Notestein and the people they attracted to the Council, JDR had exactly what the population field needed—first-rate professionals of the kind that Warren Weaver had feared would never be drawn to it. On the other side, it would be impossible to imagine a lay leader for the Population Council who could have been more generous, responsible, and effective than JDR turned out to be.

What saved the relationship was the importance of each side to the other and their ability to recognize each other's best qualities. Notestein and his colleagues knew how indispensable JDR was to them and what a singular role of leadership he could play in the population field generally if given the right kind of help. And it was in keeping with all of JDR's experience and everything he had learned from his father to have high respect for the professionals. Moreover, he was a believer in their view that it would be a disservice to use exaggeration or scare tactics in the tensely ideological atmosphere that permeated the population problem. At the same time, he recognized that part of his responsibility as a leader was to try to exercise vision—to push the professionals and stay one step ahead of them.

Sensing the rapid expansion of opportunities for action, JDR began pressing Notestein, almost as soon as he took office, to expand the Council. But Notestein would do this in his own way and at his own speed. By 1961 JDR was pressing hard, as this diary entry indicates one day in March after the two men had lunch at the Century:

I wanted to talk to [Notestein] particularly about the question of increasingly broadening the area of usefulness for the Population Council. I do feel that the Council is in a unique position and has great opportunities before it which it can only fully meet if we keep pressing ahead in the expansion of our staff and the augmenting of our resources. I am somewhat concerned that Frank Notestein is not building and expanding as rapidly as is possible and, in my judgment, essential.

Numerous times JDR made this point, in Pop Council board meetings and privately with Notestein. Two years later he was still at it, writing in his diary in August 1963: "I personally wish we could move somewhat faster as I feel to a certain extent the Council is not meeting the challenge which the rapidly moving field presents to it." He added: "However, I cannot push Frank Notestein too hard without undermining his position or morale." Almost another year passed before JDR expressed any satisfaction, this after a board meeting in which favorable comments were heard from such trustees as World Bank president Eugene Black, career ambassador Ellsworth Bunker, and *New York Times* columnist James Reston:

The Population Council program really is moving into high gear in a way that is most gratifying to me. For a long time I have been concerned that events were overtaking us, but I really feel now that we are building an organization that can do the kind of job I hoped for.

In these first five years under Notestein, the Council's expenditures had quadrupled, from less than $1 million in 1959 to more than $4 million in 1964. In the following seven years, they were to quadruple again, to more than $16 million in 1971. A variety of new donors had been attracted. In addition to the two early standbys, the Ford Foundation and the Rockefeller Brothers Fund, other foundations were now making significant grants to the Council—the Rockefeller Foundation, the Carnegie Corporation, the Commonwealth Fund, and the Avalon Foundation. JDR, of course, remained the mainstay, contributing not only his leadership and personal involvement but also funds averaging close to $750,000 per year. Also, his sister Abby and his stepmother (Martha

Baird Rockefeller) began contributing on the order of $50,000 per year. At one point, David Rockefeller donated $100,000.

The most significant new individual contributors were members of the Scaife family of Pittsburgh, a branch of the Mellon family. Cordelia Scaife May had been referred to Frank Notestein by Dean Rusk. Notestein found her to be interested in the population field "for all of the wrong reasons," so he took her on an Asian trip to show her the realities of the problem firsthand. She came home a different person, taking a seat on the Pop Council board and persuading other members of her family to join her in contributing. At one time, members of the May, Scaife, and Mellon families were responsible for nearly $2 million per year of the Council's funding.[2]

The staff expanded. Christopher Tietze's evaluation studies were fully integrated into the Council. A technical assistance division was created in 1964, with field personnel soon representing the Council abroad in nine countries. The fellowship and research programs were stepped up, with the Council's own laboratory under Dr. Sheldon Segal expanding at Rockefeller University. The Council contributed to research on the birth control pill, but placed its main reliance on perfecting the intrauterine device (IUD). This was the position strongly urged by Dr. Alan F. Guttmacher and Dr. Howard Taylor. The Council anticipated that the improved IUD would be more effective than all previous methods and would have several advantages over the pill for widespread use in developing countries—it would be cheaper, would not require the individual to remember to take a pill every day, and would have fewer or no side effects.[3]

In 1963 Notestein took an important step by recruiting Dr. Bernard Berelson as vice president. Barney Berelson's degree was in library science, but he had become recognized as a leading social scientist specializing in public opinion and communications studies. He was head of the social sciences at the Ford Foundation at the time the first Ford grant was made to the Pop Council. In 1958 he joined Paul Lazarsfeld and Robert K. Merton at the Bureau of Applied Social Research at Columbia. Notestein first brought Berelson in to advise on a communications program for the Council. Everything else seemed in readiness—the manifest need on the part of millions of women for family planning assistance, a promising contraceptive method (the improved IUD), a newly supportive attitude among leaders in key countries, and an agency to channel assistance (the Pop Council). Were there communications techniques that could solve the problem of getting the idea across to masses of women in developing countries?

"It sounded like glorified market research," Berelson said, recalling that he knew nothing about the population problem at the time other than what he had read in the *New York Times*.[4] For two months he immersed himself in the literature and made a field trip. He became aware that the Pop Council had done no communications work, not even preparing sample materials for use abroad. It was clear that the actual communicating would have to be done by the host countries. Berelson prepared the first kit of materials for the Council to use as models in its technical assistance work. But he concluded from his study that communications techniques as such would not solve the problem, that the conditions of life for poor people would have to change in directions favoring smaller families, and that the most potent communications tool would be "a few success stories." At this point he joined the Council staff as a general program and research officer and began to design research programs for use in the field to try to measure the progress of family planning efforts.

Berelson quickly became recognized as a major figure in the population field, and he was in the right position to succeed to the presidency of the Pop Council in 1968 when Notestein would retire. In the later years Notestein felt he and JDR were not communicating well, but he observed that Berelson, an articulate man with a lively sense of humor and an ability to present a subject "in bold outline," had good rapport with JDR. Because Notestein and Berelson were as one on the scientific side, Notestein concluded that he had found exactly the right man as his successor.

At the same time, JDR made an important change in his personal staff. The steady expansion of his activities over the past decade had left his two-man staff of Ed Young and Don McLean seriously overburdened, especially with Young spending virtually all of his time at Lincoln Center. JDR became interested in finding a younger person to join the staff with special responsibility for the population field. He found his man when his son, Jay, who was then working for the Peace Corps in Washington, brought a friend, Ray Lamontagne, home on a visit. It turned out that Lamontagne was well known to Don McLean, being an alumnus of the same prep school, Andover. Lamontagne had won a scholarship to the prestigious school, and had been a star athlete there. A strapping, good-looking man, Lamontagne had flirted briefly with a professional baseball career, but decided on attending Yale and Yale Law School before joining the Peace Corps. Bright, articulate, and gregarious, Lamontagne made the perfect addition as JDR's third associate. Taking over McLean's liaison work with the Pop Council, Lamontagne quickly became effective in improving communications among all the key figures.

Soon a fourth person was added to the staff. He was John McNulty, a member of the public relations staff at Lincoln Center who several times had been drafted to assist JDR in preparing speeches. JDR's activities and visibility had grown so much that he was receiving a steady stream of speaking invitations. Sorting these out, selecting the best ones, and preparing for the event became a major preoccupation for the small staff, so it was decided that JDR needed a full-time person to assist in this role. McNulty was a practicing Catholic, and JDR liked the idea of having someone on his staff with whom he could debate population issues and improve his understanding of the Church's thinking.

Prior to the 1960s, the only field work overseas had occurred when the Pop Council responded to invitations to do limited studies in India and Egypt. As attitudes began to change, JDR's stature abroad, especially in Asia, was invaluable in creating and expanding opportunities for the Council. Almost in terms of wonderment, Notestein recalled what happened when he and JDR visited President Ayub Khan of Pakistan in Lahore early in 1963. For a year, the Pop Council had been administering a large Ford Foundation grant for a family planning program in Pakistan, but a major problem was that the Pakistani government had placed the local leadership of the program in the wrong ministry and at too low a level. JDR spoke bluntly: "I'm sorry to say it, Mr. President, but you're only ten percent of where you ought to be." He then described exactly what he thought was wrong. The surprised Pakistani leader responded that it made little difference because there was no effective contraceptive available. At this point, Notestein pulled out the new, improved IUD and explained its benefits. Khan said he would have every midwife in the country inserting them within two weeks. Notestein tried to slow things down, pointing out that more research was needed, but the president said, "I'm in a hurry." Two months later, the best administrator in the Pakistani government was put in charge of the family planning program, according to Notestein, who said: "Only JDR could have spoken to Ayub Khan that way."

In Tunisia two years later, a tired president, Habib Bourguiba, reluctantly granted JDR a fifteen-minute interview to exchange pleasantries, but became enchanted by his visitor's earnestness and the fact that he seemed the antithesis of the capitalist profiteer his name suggested. The interview lasted ninety minutes, with Bourguiba using such a slow, lucid French, with much use of the hands, "that even I could understand," Notestein said. He said the resulting program in Tunisia was "truly international, with Bulgarian physicians inserting American-made IUDs in Tunisian peasant women."

Moving on to Cairo, JDR and Notestein found President Nasser to be a weary man completely uninterested in talking about population at first, according to Notestein, but JDR "charmed" him. Nasser had just received a picture of the king of Thailand, and he made the comment that the king seemed to be anti-American. "Yes," JDR responded, "but he's a friend of mine."

Also in 1965, Kenya became the first black African country to request Pop Council assistance. JDR had first spoken to Jomo Kenyatta about population problems when visiting Nairobi in 1963. According to Notestein, JDR's personal touch also paved the way for closer relationships and more attention to family planning requirements in South Korea, Taiwan, India, Thailand, and Turkey. For years, the Council was the only resource for population work in developing countries. Gradually, with Pop Council encouragement, the World Health Organization of the UN and the foreign aid programs of several Western nations began to participate. Another sign of progress was the extending of Pop Council fellowships beyond the biomedical and demographic fields to include public health, valuable because many developing countries already had public health networks in place.

Another mode of leadership for JDR was public advocacy. It will be recalled that in the late 1940s he became the first Rockefeller to be openly identified with the population field—his father's support of population-related activities had always been anonymous. As population control entered its "takeoff" stage in the 1960s, JDR became a frequent public speaker on the subject. One of his early speeches was a major one, before the Second Biennial Conference of the Food and Agriculture Organization (FAO) in Rome in 1961. He delivered the second lecture in a special series that had been inaugurated by historian Arnold Toynbee two years earlier. FAO's director-general, B. R. Sen, called JDR "a person of world standing" as chairman of the Rockefeller Foundation, which had done such great work in assisting the less-developed countries of the world in agriculture. But the emphasis of JDR's talk, entitled "People, Food, and the Well-Being of Mankind," was on population. He said it "is sad, if not shocking, that man knows so little about so vital a subject as the relationship between population growth and economic and social development." He scored those who let fear of "birth control" dictate their actions:

I submit that we must grow up to our responsibilities. Let the world first learn the facts on population growth and their broad implications. Then, on the the basis of full knowledge, let our responsible leaders, country by country, decide whether population stabilization is required, and whether acceptable means can be found.

It is unfortunate that too few nations—including the United States—are fulfilling their responsibilities to their people by obtaining this knowledge.

JDR called for government action. He said that private groups could contribute much, but that population problems were so great that only governments, "supported and inspired by private initiative, can attack them on the scale required." He stated the challenge bluntly:

To my mind, population growth is second only to the control of atomic weapons, as the paramount problem of our time. All of us hope and pray that the world's nuclear suicide can be avoided. But there is a cold inevitability, a certainty that is mathematical, that gives the problems posed by too-rapid population growth a somber and chilling cast indeed.

The grim fact of population growth cuts across all the basic needs of mankind and, more than any other single factor, frustrates man's achievement of his higher needs.

On this last note, JDR was touching on the "quality of life" theme that had occupied his mind at the time he was creating the Population Council in 1952, the moral philosophy that argued that "population control" was not negative, but positive in nature. It was wrong, he said, to see the problem in Malthusian terms as numbers of people versus quantities of food because this equated man with animal and food with fodder. "There is a third dimension," he said, "an aspect that touches the very essence of human life. This overlooked dimension concerns man's desire to live as well as survive."

Stated in many ways, this theme was a fundamental element in the speeches JDR made frequently on the population question over the next decade, speeches in Denver and Dallas, before the New York Economic Club and to congressional committees, at the University of Michigan and the University of North Carolina. As chairman of the Population Council, JDR was well aware that his words could be taken as expressing the policy of the organization, so he was always careful to check his drafts beforehand with Notestein or Berelson. But he did not always accept changes they proposed.

The "takeoff" stage of the population program seemed to be having some effects in three of the most powerful seats of public opinion in the world—the White House, the Vatican, and the Kremlin. The first Catholic in the White House, John F. Kennedy, made several mild statements in support of population research, and former President Eisenhower explicitly reversed the statement he had made against government programs in pop-

ulation at the time of the 1959 Draper Report.[5] As noted, momentum also
seemed to be building for a liberalizing trend in the Vatican under John
XXIII. And Marxist spokesmen, normally opposed to any birth control
measures on the international scene (while in many cases countenancing
their practice at home), seemed to be softening their rhetoric.[6]

In 1963 came the deaths of President Kennedy and Pope John XXIII.
With both of their successors, prospects seemed good for lobbying for
greater acceptance of population measures, and in 1964 JDR began actively
working to do exactly that. What happened in the Vatican could matter
very much in the White House, and vice versa, so JDR pursued action in
both. In his FAO speech he had quite rightly singled out his own government as a leading example of those that had done nothing about the population problem. The main inhibition in the United States had been the
reluctance of most Democratic politicians to risk the enmity and opposition
of the urban Catholic voters and the wrath of the Catholic bishops (this
was still a time when many Republican leaders were supportive of family
planning). Similarly, the opposition of Catholic countries, particularly the
Latin American voting bloc, had always forestalled the UN from moving
beyond population research to more activist programs of technical assistance and the dissemination of contraceptive information and techniques.

On August 19, 1964, JDR took the first step in what was to be a long
and persistent effort to involve the U.S. government in the population
problem:

Ray Lamontagne went with me to see Messrs. Notestein and Berelson at the
Population Council. I wanted to discuss with them our taking initiative in
approaching President Johnson after the election in regard to a statement from him
concerning the population problem and possibly as to his establishing a presidential
commission to make recommendations as to the field of population. They felt that
the idea was worth exploring and agreed that during the weeks immediately ahead
we should pull together a statement pointing up the questions which such a commission might consider and indicate the direction of the answer.

The four men met a number of times over the next several months
while JDR continued to press on other fronts. In September he went to
see writer John Gunther to propose that he do a book on the population
problem. JDR wrote in his diary that Gunther seemed taken with the idea.
JDR also flew to Washington to participate in a special meeting on the
population problem that had been organized by General William Draper
for the Organization of American States. Present were all the OAS ambassadors and ambassadors from the Latin American countries to the United
States. JDR wrote:

I sat next to Dr. John Rock, Professor Emeritus at the Harvard Medical School, who is really quite an amazing person and a character at 75. He is a scientist, Catholic, and deeply interested in the population problem [as one of the developers of the birth control pill] and his book of some months ago caused quite a sensation in regard to the problem of birth control and Catholics.

Only a few days after President Johnson's landslide victory in November 1964, JDR and Berelson went to Washington to press their ideas for a Presidential statement and population commission, meeting first with White House aide McGeorge Bundy and then with Secretary of State Dean Rusk and "six of his experts." Their efforts to see the President had not succeeded. JDR and Berelson found everyone to be cordial, but also extremely cautious. In many meetings with officials over the next several years to press for government action, the greatest frustration for JDR was that almost everyone agreed with his point of view, but very few were willing to take any risks. Even among such committed men and close JDR acquaintances as Dean Rusk and John Gardner (soon to be named HEW Secretary), the dominant concern was to protect the President's political flanks.

Yet Rusk did lead to the first breakthrough. Although he came out against the idea of a commission in the first meeting with JDR, he thought that a reference to population in a speech by the President might be possible. The result was one sentence in the State of the Union message, delivered on January 4, 1965: "I will seek new ways to use our knowledge to help deal with the explosion in world population and the growing scarcity in world resources." This strongest statement to date gave encouragement to population activists in Washington officialdom, and later would be looked back upon as a decisive turning point. But action was to be agonizingly slow in coming.

However, there was no reticence on Capitol Hill among a dozen or more senators, including William Fulbright of Arkansas and Ernest Gruening of Alaska. Gruening in particular was highly vocal in calling for population action, especially in the foreign aid program. In September 1965, JDR testified before Gruening's Subcommittee on Foreign Aid Expenditures of the Government Operations Committee. These hearings, called Population Crisis Hearings by Gruening, extended intermittently over a three-year period and were ultimately successful in goading the government into action.[7]

Recognizing that a breakthrough in Washington was not going to come easily or quickly, JDR decided to try his luck with the Vatican. It seemed possible that the new Pope, Paul VI, might continue the liberal trend of his predecessor. He had appointed a special commission in Rome to study the position of the Church on population questions. In a series of meetings with the Reverend Theodore Hesburgh, Rockefeller Foundation trustee and president of the University of Notre Dame, JDR had raised the question of whether it might be possible for him to have an audience with Paul VI in which the population problem could be discussed seriously and at length. Hesburgh was decidedly liberal in his own views on population, although he would not go as far as JDR on some aspects. He thought such an audience was quite likely, and in letters and telephone calls to Rome during the spring of 1965 he worked to arrange it through a close friend of his, Monsignor Paul Marcinkus, assistant secretary of state in the Vatican.

In briefings by Georgetown University professors arranged by Frank Notestein, JDR began to learn something of the complexities of the Roman Catholic Church that curtailed the freedom of action of any Pope. On his trip to Rome, JDR took along his Catholic speechwriter, Jack McNulty. The audience was set for July 10:

Monsignor Marcinkus had suggested we arrive at the Vatican for our appointment half an hour ahead of time which we did. We were received very formally. . . . We were passed from one official and dignitary to another as we advanced toward the inner sanctum room by room. Every now and then we would be left for a brief period in one room and then advanced another room or two towards our objective. The area was all attractively done but to me cold and severe. After a while, Monsignor Marcinkus joined us and was with us the last few minutes and last few rooms.

Jack McNulty stayed outside when we went into the Pope's office at about 12:00 o'clock. It was an extremely large room and relatively bare but friendly and pleasant around His Holiness's desk where we met. His Holiness could not have been more warm and cordial.

JDR spoke at length in the meeting about his moral position on the population question, the urgency of the problem, new research and methods the Church might find acceptable, and the concerns of various world leaders he had met in his travels. The Pope, he said, listened attentively and commented quite often. "He spoke warmly of my family and the work and objectives of the Rockefeller Foundation. He more or less said that we really had common objectives."

When the session was over Marcinkus, in a nice touch, took McNulty in for his own private audience with the Pope. Then Marcinkus escorted the guests on a tour of the Vatican and back to their hotel where he and JDR had a final talk:

He seemed to feel, as I did, that the morning's meeting had gone well. We discussed together some of the things that I would have liked to have said to His

Holiness if we had had more time and he urged me to write and to speak out forthrightly. He said that if I would send the letter to him, he would see that it reached His Holiness, indicating that the Pope was an avid reader. This suggestion pleased me very much as I do feel now, knowing the Holy Father, that there are things I could say that might be meaningful.

Monsignor Marcinkus is an American who has now been at the Vatican for fifteen years. I liked him, was impressed by him and would have confidence in him.

JDR immediately wrote a long and comprehensive follow-up letter. He saw the Pope again and was able to introduce Blanchette to him when the Pontiff visited New York and the UN in October 1965. Over the next three years, JDR wrote five more times to the Pope on the population question—in the end to no avail. In 1966 Paul VI issued an encyclical (*Populorum Progressio*) that seemed to suggest a tolerant view of population measures for non-Catholics in one passage. But in reality he rejected all proposals for change from his special commission on population and closed the door on any liberalization with his 1967 encyclical, *Humanae Vitae*.[8]

JDR continued to press for more action wherever he could, at home and abroad. Only six weeks after his visit to the Vatican, he and Blanchette stood at the head of a receiving line in Geneva where two hundred delegates from thirty-five countries were attending an international conference sponsored by the Pop Council. JDR was also the keynote speaker. The gathering occurred just a week before the second United Nations conference on population in Belgrade, which, JDR wrote, "was to be so broad and general that it was felt desirable to have ours come first."

Several months later he headed a "population panel" as part of the White House International Cooperation Year conference. A week later he met with John Gardner again to press his idea for a Presidential commission on population. Gardner thought one step toward that would be to select a small group of key people both in and out of government who could have a series of informal meetings to consider "the important next steps in the population field." Gardner said his Under Secretary, Wilbur Cohen, would be "a useful member of such a group." JDR followed through, and he and Cohen did form a group that met together every few months.

All during this time JDR knew that officials at the second and third echelons in the State Department and AID had been doing what they could to move their agencies toward population activities. Rusk had approved designating a "population officer" in State, and AID staff members found they could support research and information activities in developing countries without arousing Catholic ire—as long as they stayed away from anything having to do with contraceptives. But, as one observer termed it, this amounted to "the peculiar anomaly of a talked-to-death policy with no program at all."[9]

JDR kept on pressing wherever he could, meeting repeatedly with figures on Capitol Hill, with Vice President Humphrey, with White House aides Bill Moyers and S. Douglass Cater, Jr., with Rusk and Gardner, and with other cabinet members such as Willard Wirtz of Labor and Stewart Udall of Interior, who both supported his views strongly. In March 1966 JDR had a private meeting with Rep. Clement Zablocki, a staunch Catholic who headed the House subcommittee on foreign aid expenditures. He then testified before Zablocki's committee, supporting population activities by AID in such a gentlemanly way that he managed to avoid alienating the chairman. That same day he met with AID administrator David Bell, who told him that "he had studied the whole question carefully and was convinced that the existing rules and regulations did make possible the carrying forward of the Agency's sincere desire to be helpful to countries that really wanted United States help in relation to their population problems."

Despite such expressions, JDR's calls on important people in Washington seemed to produce very little in the way of tangible action. He was beginning to feel discouraged, and by the summer of 1966 turned his sights on the Population Council again. In a series of meetings with Notestein, Berelson, and Lamontagne he expressed the view that the Council was "not moving fast enough, not living up to its responsibilities." Partly in defense, Notestein said it would be helpful if JDR would travel more and try to stir the leaders of developing countries as he had done successfully before in a number of cases, instead of continuing to use so much time pushing in Washington for a Presidential commission that was very unlikely to come about. Tension on this point continued until Berelson came up with an idea that, he later confessed, was born out of a desire to divert JDR and keep him busy elsewhere so he would leave the Council alone and free to go about its business.

The idea was both simple and audacious. It was to persuade heads of state in countries around the world to sign a statement that expressed the seriousness of the population problem and urged action to resolve it. It was audacious to expect world leaders to find any reason why they should go out on such a limb, and particularly audacious to expect a private citizen, JDR, to have the time, energy, entrée, and stature to persuade presidents, prime ministers, and kings to do so.

Somewhat to the surprise of everyone concerned, JDR took this idea seriously. With the help primarily of Ray Lamontagne, JDR embarked eagerly on this new mission. After much reworking, a suitable draft was achieved. It began with a preamble stating how "too rapid population growth" seriously hampered efforts to raise living standards and "frustrated and jeopardized" human aspirations for a better life. It then expressed a series of "beliefs" that bore JDR's unmistakable stamp:

We believe that the population problem must be recognized as a principal element in long-range national planning if governments are to achieve their economic goals and fulfill the aspirations of their people.

We believe that the great majority of parents desire to have the knowledge and the means to plan their families; that the opportunity to decide the number and spacing of children is a basic human right.

We believe that lasting and meaningful peace will depend to a considerable measure upon how the challenge of population growth is met.

We believe that the objective of family planning is the enrichment of human life, not its restriction; that family planning, by assuring greater opportunity to each person, frees man to attain his individual dignity and reach his full potential.

Recognizing that family planning is in the vital interest of both the nation and the family, we, the undersigned, earnestly hope that leaders around the world will share our views and join with us in this great challenge for the well being and happiness of people everywhere.

A close reading reveals that this statement does not commit the signatory to any specific action. Earlier drafts did so, but JDR's advisers warned him that he would never get any signers that way. It was difficult enough as it was. In the fall of 1966, JDR sent his personal letter and a copy of the statement to leaders in fifty-two countries and began arduous follow-up efforts to convince them to sign. He lobbied by letter, on the telephone, in travels abroad, and with ambassadors of target countries in Washington and at the UN. Naturally, he considered it very important to get President Johnson to sign on behalf of the United States, and he began pressing this idea through every channel available to him.

There were some easy victories at first, countries long supportive of population control such as Sweden and Finland, and newer countries where family planning programs were firmly in place, such as South Korea, Malaysia, and Singapore. A major step forward occurred when Indira Gandhi, now the prime minister of India, agreed to sign. Nasser of the United Arab Republic and Bourguiba of Tunisia soon agreed. There was some elation when Tito of Yugoslavia signed, but then it was realized that this maverick among Communist countries would not attract others to follow, in fact might have the opposite effect.

In October, JDR, Blanchette, and Ray Lamontagne left on a planned three-country trip to Latin America. The "population problem" was the main reason—"am anxious to see the situation first hand in Catholic countries," JDR wrote. He also hoped to get at least one Latin American country to sign his "World Leaders Statement." His advisers were pessimistic about this, and so was the former president of Colombia, Alberto Lleras Camargo, when JDR saw him in September to talk about his trip and also about becoming the second non-American trustee of the Rockefeller Foundation (after Lord Franks of Great Britain).[10] However, JDR found his man in the person of Carlos Lleras Restropo, the current president of Colombia. After seeing him in Bogota, JDR wrote: "It was about the most satisfactory meeting I have ever had with a chief of state." Colombia became the tenth signator of the World Leaders Statement.

JDR had no further luck on this trip, however. President Frei of Chile was ill, and JDR had to cancel the Mexican portion of the trip because of laryngitis.

But with the Colombian signature and some encouraging signs from Washington, JDR was feeling sanguine about his statement. It appeared that the only way to get the prime ministers of Japan and the United Kingdom to sign would be to get President Johnson's signature first. The French, always fearful that the Germans would outbreed them for the next round, had already declined. JDR felt that the statement needed some official platform or status, so in November he went to see an old friend, Secretary General U Thant of the UN, to suggest that the statement be released at the UN with the support of the Secretary General on Human Rights Day, December 10. Both U Thant and Philippe de Seynes, Under Secretary for Economic and Social Affairs, endorsed the idea. So JDR sent letters to his best prospects, citing the UN auspices and urging them to sign up. On December 6 came bad news—a phone call from Doug Cater to let JDR know that President Johnson had decided not to sign:

He said that Bill Moyers, Walt Rostow, and Harry McPherson, like himself, were all distressed but that they were afraid it was final and that there would be no use my trying to bring further pressure on the President. This of course was most distressing news to me particularly since in our letters to invite the other world leaders to participate we had with the knowledge of the White House indicated that the statement had been submitted to the President and that we had every confidence that he would endorse it provided there was a representative group of other leaders.

As a result, JDR canceled his trip to Washington for the Rockefeller Public Service Awards luncheon in order to meet with his advisers and UN representatives to decide what to do. It now seemed clear that Japan would not sign as hoped. U Thant sent word that he was prepared to go ahead with the ceremony in any case. So a cable was sent to all remaining prospects merely listing the ten countries that had agreed. This yielded only two more signatories, Nepal and Morocco, making twelve in all for U Thant's December 10 announcement.

Although there had been disappointments at the end, a surprising amount had been accomplished in less than three months. And there were some near misses. So U Thant readily agreed to JDR's proposal to allow another year to gain more endorsements. JDR also found he had an articulate supporter in Lord Caradon (the former Sir Hugh Foote), the head of the British delegation to the UN, who praised the World Leaders Statement in his speech to the International Planned Parenthood convention in Chile in 1967.

Despite his failure to sign the World Leaders Statement in December, President Johnson in January came out more strongly than ever before in support of population activities. In his 1967 State of the Union address, he said:

Next to the pursuit of peace, the really great challenge to the human family is the race between food supply and population increase. That race tonight is being lost. The time for rhetoric has clearly passed. The time for concerted action is here, and we must get on with the job.

The pace indeed was quickening. In 1966 LBJ had proclaimed the "War on Hunger," and this served to strengthen the case for population activities as well. In mid-1966 a major step occurred when two key agencies both appointed population officers who took their roles very seriously, and, with quite different styles, pushed hard for action. They were Philander P. Claxton, Jr., at the Department of State and Dr. Reimert T. Ravenholt at AID. JDR's friend at HEW, Wilbur Cohen, also pushed for action in domestic programs. In 1967 Congress took the initiative, passing the Foreign Assistance Act of 1967, which, in Title X ("Programs Related to Population Growth"), authorized population activities in broad language, clearly including family planning assistance, and earmarked $35 million in economic aid funds to support them.[11]

JDR was in touch on these developments—for example, testifying before congressional subcommittees on the foreign aid bill—but he was devoting most of his energies to the two top items on his agenda: getting more signatories for the World Leaders Statement and getting LBJ's agreement to a U.S. commission on population. He felt he was making good progress on both. In separate meetings early in 1967, both Rusk and Gardner now said they thought a commission was a good idea and agreed to raise the question with the President. JDR himself met with the President in May, and spent half an hour selling both the statement and a commission, but found LBJ to be noncommittal. In June, however, JDR heard from Phil Claxton of the State Department that the President had agreed to a request from Rusk to sign the statement.

This good news brought on another flurry of activity, and by the fall JDR had another dozen signers—Australia, Barbados, Jordan, Iran, Pakistan, Trinidad-Tobago, Norway, Denmark, the Netherlands, the Dominican Republic, Ghana, and New Zealand. With the United States lined up, he also felt certain he would get Great Britain and Japan.

However, nothing was happening on the commission idea, and in October JDR had reason to feel the anxiety sometimes associated with pressing on too many fronts. With his friend Mary Lasker, a noted philanthropist in the medical field, JDR had arranged an appointment with the First Lady in the White House. He related in his diary what happened:

The three of us had a good session and Mrs. Johnson could not have been nicer. Our subject was population and the purpose was to arouse Mrs. Johnson's interest in the hope that she could stir the President to greater action. Mrs. Lasker raised the question of the Presidential Commission on Population and Mrs. Johnson agreed to speak with the President about it. I was a little concerned as to the possibility of wire-crossing by this approach, but neither Mrs. Johnson nor Mrs. Lasker seemed to be perturbed. I left with Mrs. Johnson a copy of my May 26th letter to the President and accompanying memoranda.

While we were talking with Mrs. Johnson, first Lynda Bird dropped in and then the President himself. The President seemed aware of my presence and the subject of our discussion. He was cordial and friendly, but stayed only briefly between appointments.

It was now time for the stretch drive to get more signers for the World Leaders Statement. The names of the new signers were to be made public on Human Rights Day at the UN again, although in a more elaborate ceremony for what was agreed would be the final such occasion. Two more attempts by mail to enlist the Pope had failed. For a time, JDR thought the U.S.S.R. might come in, which would have been an exciting achievement, not as good as signing up the Vatican perhaps, but the next best thing. The reason he was hopeful was that the Soviet leadership was taking the request quite seriously. Soviet ambassador Anatoly F. Dobrynin carried messages back and forth, and on several occasions he and JDR had thoughtful talks on the subject. The first response, in April, from Aleksei N. Kosygin, chairman of the Council of Ministers in the Kremlin, was a cable that read:

WE CONFIRM THE RECEIPT OF THE LETTER IN WHICH YOU EXPRESS THE OPINION THAT IT WOULD BE DESIRABLE IF THE SOVIET UNION JOINED THE OTHER COUNTRIES IN ENDORSING THE WORLD LEADERS STATEMENT ON POPULATION. WE CONSIDER THIS QUESTION AN IMPORTANT ONE AND IT IS UNDER CONSIDERATION.

There were several more letters from JDR elaborating his arguments, but in September Kosygin finally wrote to him declining to endorse the statement. It was a reasoned letter that discussed the issue at some length, but in the end based the negative response on good Marxist doctrine— that only "a radical solution" was possible to end the disparity between swift population growth and slow economic growth, a solution that would require "fundamental socio-economic reforms." The chairman also took issue with the statement that the preservation of peace could well depend on how the population problem is resolved. He wrote that the causes of wars "lay not in the population growth but in the imperialist policies of certain developed States."[12]

Late in the game there was sudden concern that President Johnson might not actually have agreed to endorse the statement, but some frantic double-checking resolved this doubt. Thailand, Great Britain, and Japan all signed, bringing the total up to twenty-eight nations—twelve the previous year and sixteen new ones. The UN representatives of the twenty-eight nations were on hand in the flag-decked hall of the Economic and Social Council on Human Rights Day (December 11) when U Thant welcomed the new signers and publicly complimented and thanked JDR, who was in the gallery. Speaking on behalf of the signers, Lord Caradon said the twenty-eight countries accounted for one-third of the population of the world. He said the World Leaders Statement was "a decisive document in history" and that governments everywhere had to make up for lost time. He added: "If we avoid or neglect the problem of population any longer we shall utterly fail in everything else."[13]

On that same day, JDR was able to add two more signatories, both of which pleased him immensely. Just as the UN ceremony was starting, a messenger brought JDR a cable from Indonesian Foreign Minister Adam Malik saying that Suharto would sign. And back at his office after the ceremony, JDR received a cable from President Ferdinand Marcos of the Philippines saying that he concurred in the statement.

Adding populous Indonesia and the Catholic Philippines to the list, for a total of thirty nations, topped off a triumphant day for JDR. His impressive accomplishment as a private citizen was widely covered in the press and praised editorially Yet the peculiar anonymity he had with the general public was still there. For example, a feature in the *This Week* Sunday newspaper supplement reported in tones of wonderment about the "precedent-breaking" act of signing up President Johnson and twenty-nine other world leaders in support of "voluntary birth control," and added: "All of the work was carried out by one private citizen acting on his own, John D. Rockefeller 3rd, the least prominent of the five remarkable Rockefeller brothers." The article was headlined: "The Unknown Rockefeller Also Can Win."[14]

As we have seen, JDR was not one to rest on his laurels. In fact, he had felt for some time that getting a Presidential commission on population was the most important of his two goals. This was clear as far back as June 1967 in a letter JDR wrote to Bill Moyers:

I hope so much that the President does not feel that by agreeing to sign the World Leaders Statement we will not feel disturbed if he does not agree to the appointment of the Commission. At this point as I see it, the Commission is the more important of the two.[15]

So it was not surprising that soon after the UN ceremony for the World Leaders Statement at the end of 1967, JDR resumed his campaign to get a Presidential commission appointed. As a Presidential election year, 1968 was an important time of transition. Harassed by the Vietnam War protest movement and the urban riots, LBJ announced that he would not be a candidate for reelection. For the Democratic Party, the mantle would fall to Vice President Humphrey. Richard M. Nixon had made a remarkable comeback and was the leading contender for the Republican nomination. Nelson Rockefeller soon began organizing for his third and last try for the GOP bid. In the spring, Ray Lamontagne announced he was leaving JDR's employ to work on Nelson's campaign staff—it was to be almost a year before a successor was found as JDR's population associate.[16] In the meantime, the transition occurred within the Pop Council from the retiring Frank Notestein to Barney Berelson.

In his contacts with Doug Cater and Joseph A. Califano, Jr. ("one of the President's closest special assistants and also a Catholic"), JDR learned that lists of names were being formulated in the White House for a commission. When several months passed, he wrote a strong letter to the President implying that LBJ's follow-through efforts for family planning did not match his "strong and helpful" public statements.[17] As a result of this letter, JDR and Berelson were invited to meet with the President in the Oval Office on May 23.

There LBJ announced that he was establishing not a commission but a "task force" of mixed public-private membership with JDR and Wilbur Cohen as cochairmen. The President handed JDR a paper that set forth an impressive mandate for the task force:

(1) To define the Federal Government's direct role in research and training in population matters, including the physiology of human reproduction and fertility control, and to develop a five year program plan for research and development of safe, effective, acceptable and inexpensive means for fertility regulation; (2) To define the responsibility of the Federal Government, in cooperation with state, community, and private agencies in assuring that all families have access to information and services that will enable them to plan the number and spacing of their children; (3) To suggest actions which the United States should take in concert with other countries and with international organizations to help the developing countries of the world to understand and to deal effectively with their high rates of population growth.[18]

The issuance of such a mandate was dramatic evidence of how far acceptance of the population field had come in the 1960s. A decade earlier, the key words in the mandate could not even have been mentioned in the White House. But the work of the Cohen-Rockefeller group was doomed to anonymity. Not only was LBJ's power fading fast, but JDR discovered to his dismay at the end of June that the "commission" he had asked for, which had been downgraded by the President to a "task force," was now downgraded even further to a mere "committee." JDR wrote: "Just how it will work out, I am not sure, but at this point it would seem desirable to go through with it. Even if the results are not substantial, at least I will learn considerably more than I now know about the inner workings of government."

This proved to be about the only tangible benefit of the effort. JDR had only praise for the members of the group who met numerous times, organized into four subcommittees, and produced what he considered to be an excellent report. After one of the meetings, the committee met with LBJ in the Cabinet Room, and JDR wrote:

He made a very nice general statement as to the importance of the population problem and exhorted us to do a job for him. He seemed to address his remarks more to me, so at the end I replied briefly.

A symptom of the futility of the effort came when the report was finished toward the end of 1968 and the ceremony for presenting it to the President was rescheduled no less than four times. It finally took place on January 7, 1969, only a few weeks before LBJ's term ended. There was almost no press coverage, and JDR wrote gloomily in his diary about the "unfortunate factor" of coming at "the end of an administration."

Nothing daunted him for long, however. JDR kept pushing for a Presidential commission in the next administration. He was to achieve a more impressive mandate and platform for his efforts, from *both* the White House and the Congress, than even he could have imagined.

12

⚑

LEADER OF THE
FOUNDATION

DESPITE his famous name, it was often necessary for JDR to identify himself beyond merely citing it (as in the opening line of Congressional testimony: "My name is John D. Rockfeller 3rd and I am . . ."), or for others to do so—journalists who wrote about him or program chairmen who introduced him as a speaker. In some cases, the appropriate designation would be "chairman of Lincoln Center" or "chairman of the Population Council." But most often it would be: "chairman of the Rockefeller Foundation."

This was his most visible institutional link to his family's famed heritage, one of the heaviest burdens of responsibility that he bore, and at the same time a precious opportunity to vary and expand his own influence in his chosen career as a full-time philanthropist.

For forty years the Rockefeller Foundation (RF) was an important part of his life in these ways. For the first half of that period, his service as a trustee in the main was frustrating. He survived his apprenticeship and suffered mutely through the criticism of an older trustee in the 1930s for not having earned his position on the board other than happening to bear the name of Rockefeller. And, in the 1940s, he lost a power struggle to the men who dominated the RF after his father had retired—Raymond Fosdick, Walter Stewart, and Chester Barnard.[1]

But he outlasted them all. For the latter part of his time on the board, JDR gradually became the effective leader of the Foundation as its chairman. During the 1950s he shared power with Dean Rusk, who was a strong figure as president. By the 1960s, JDR and his ideas had matured, he had brought in new trustees over the years, he selected his man as president—and he unquestionably shaped the agenda of this most prestigious of foundations.

Even more impressive, he not only did this without the RF suffering any loss of prestige, but he modernized and improved the Foundation to a significant degree. He did this carefully, with in the boundaries of propriety and due process, quite conscious of the painful lesson he had learned in the power struggle of the 1940s about the proper limitations of family influence.

The RF has been unique among major foundations for the way in which it has combined a towering reputation for excellence and a prominent role of leadership for a member of the founding family, always the individual who would be thought of as the "head" of the family. It began with Senior, whose vision and principles were as important as his financial contributions in creating the RF. Junior was president for the first four years of the RF's existence, 1913 to 1917, and then took the new post of chairman until his retirement in 1939. JDR came on the board in 1931 and served as chairman for nineteen years, from 1952 until his retirement in 1971. Jay became a trustee in 1968, but resigned early in 1977 when he was elected governor of West Virginia.

Among other major foundations in which the founding family has been so prominent, performance in almost all cases has been erratic, peculiar, or so constrained and limited as to be of little value.[2] The RF was able to avoid these pitfalls because of the high ideals and ambitions of Senior, Junior, and the men with whom they associated themselves. They gave the RF a "public character" from the beginning and insisted on bringing in only the most eminent and respected men for the staff and board of trustees. Such men would not tolerate for long the whimsicalities of personal or family control. Only when this is understood can one appreciate the fact that JDR's position of influence in his later years as chairman of the RF came about not because he controlled anything, not because he inherited or was given power—but because he had earned it.

For most of the postwar years, the acknowledged "big three" of the foundation world were the Ford and Rockefeller Foundations and the Carnegie Corporation. This was not just a matter of size, although Ford and Rockefeller for many years ranked first and second in the value of their assets. In 1968 the assets of the Ford Foundation totaled $3.66 billion, followed by the RF with about one-fourth as much, $890 million. But the Carnegie Corporation was in eleventh place with assets of $334 million.[3] Rather than sheer size, the high reputation and leadership role of these three foundations were based on the quality and significance of the work they were doing, the independent character and stature of their boards of trustees, and the caliber of their staffs.

Each of the three foundations is distinctively different from the other two. In part, their leadership role has stemmed from the fact that all three have been headquartered in New York with a good deal of communication and cooperation occurring among them. Carnegie and Ford have cooperated in the fields of higher education and public television. Ford and Rockefeller have cooperated in overseas programs, particularly in India, and in agriculture, population, and Lincoln Center. JDR was close to John Gardner, who became president of Carnegie in 1955, and to Alan Pifer, who succeeded Gardner when he went to Washington in 1964 as Secretary of HEW. Although JDR had no luck with the Ford Foundation when it first began operating in Pasadena under Paul Hoffman, he developed good working relationships with the succeeding presidents in New York—H. Rowan Gaither, Henry Heald, and McGeorge Bundy—and with such key staff people as W. McNeil Lowry of the fine arts and humanities program and David Bell, head of international programs.[4]

One difference among the three foundations was that the RF earned a reputation for excellence almost as soon as it was created in 1913 and maintained it over the years. Although created two years earlier, the Carnegie Corporation did not become a distinguished foundation until the post–World War II years, and the Ford Foundation, of course, was not activated until 1950. Writing in 1972, Waldemar Nielsen in *The Big Foundations* characterizes Carnegie during its first forty years as "by turn profligate, precious, and meandering." Its rise to excellence, as "probably the best of the large foundations" in Nielsen's view, occurred under Gardner and Pifer:

Under the leadership of Gardner the Carnegie Corporation became a highly professionalized operation. Under Pifer it has now also become responsive to contemporary social concerns. . . . it has skillfully defined a set of programs for itself that fall within its financial and other capabilities and at the same time are of national benefit. . . . it has a less bureaucratic and more personal approach than many foundations. It has acutely sensed the possibilities of spurring public action on major national problems through study projects and public commissions. In organizing these projects it has consistently shown tactical skill and good timing.[5]

In evaluating the Ford Foundation, the "prodigal young giant of philanthropy," Nielsen has this to say:

In its brief career, it has had triumphs as well as conspicuous failures. It has careened from bold attack to indecisive floundering, from conservatism to activism. It is an adolescent that has had great trouble growing up.[6]

The Ford Foundation was activated on the basis of a report done by a special study group, led by H. Rowan Gaither, which labored for two years and conducted hundreds of interviews with leaders in all aspects of American life. The purpose was to recommend how the foundation should be organized and the fields of activity it should pursue. Nielsen described the results in glowing terms:

The report, the finest statement of the case for modern creative philanthropy yet produced, aroused great excitement when it was distributed. It began with the premise that the most important problems of contemporary life lay in man's relation to man, not his relation to nature. The foundation would therefore not concentrate on science or technology but would give priority to five areas.[7]

The five areas were world peace, the problems of democracy, problems of the economy, education, and the scientific study of man. It tells us a great deal about JDR and about the rigidity of the Rockefeller Foundation to recognize that in 1946—two years *before* the Gaither study was undertaken and four years before it was made public—JDR had come to essentially the same conclusions and had articulated them in his unsuccessful effort to redirect the course of the RF to meet postwar needs. His language was not as sophisticated, but his views were based on his own observations and instincts and with very limited consultation not on a comprehensive study effort. He urged a transition from research to the application of knowledge, the coordinating of programs across divisional lines, a shift of program focus from the advanced countries to the "backward areas of the world," and the adoption of three "areas of concentration" to give the Foundation clearer definition and a framework for coordination.[8] Two of the three areas of concentration—"international understanding" and "human behavior"—correlated closely to the first and last areas of the Gaither report, as is evident in the specific language explaining the areas. JDR's exposition of his third area, "our national life," clearly comprehended the other three areas in the Gaither report—democracy, the economy, and education.

In the Ford Foundation's erratic course, it has functioned at its best, in Nielsen's estimation, when it reflected this original mandate of "strong concern for the human problems of a democracy" and a determination to be "a relevant philanthropic force in a time of controversial social and political change." One standard Nielsen uses in evaluating the worth of foundations is their courage in addressing "the race question." His assessment: "As of 1970, only four foundations—Mott, Rockefeller Brothers Fund, Carnegie, and above all, Ford—have a high degree of interest in and an activist approach to the problems of blacks."[9]

Nielsen had high praise for the RF:

. . . the Rockefeller Foundation has been a great foundation: it has set high standards for itself; it has preserved its integrity; it has persevered in its efforts to fulfill its objectives; and it has major achievements to its credit. Indeed, judged by the magnitude of its contributions to human well being over the years, the Rockefeller Foundation has accumulated an unrivaled record. In many ways it has been the standard against which the other "modern" foundations have measured themselves.

But Nielsen also listed criticisms of the Foundation, the same ones that JDR was trying to change: overemphasis on science and medicine and relative neglect of the social sciences and humanities, a certain rigidity, inhibitions growing out of long traditions and a sense of self-importance, and an organizational pattern that reflected divisions of knowledge rather than problem orientations. Nielsen pointed out that over the years the RF has embraced some of the characteristics of a university—emphasis on academic degrees and research backgrounds of staff members, organization according to branches of knowledge and disciplines much as a university is organized (medicine, natural sciences, social sciences, humanities). The result:

It may well be that [the RF's] great productivity in the advancement and application of scientific knowledge over the years has been due to its disciplinary structure and professionalism. But the same organizational staffing philosophy may explain its inability to achieve similar results in dealing with social issues and creativity in the arts and its inflexibility in changing program directions.[10]

Given the strength of this pattern and related ones within the RF, the failure of JDR's early efforts to bring about change is no surprise. His blush of postwar enthusiasm caused him to misread the situation when he tried to redirect the program of the Foundation in 1946, and he was outmaneuvered in selecting a new president to succeed Raymond Fosdick in 1948. It is quite possible that these defeats were good for him in the long run. This conclusion seems warranted in considering what the situation might otherwise have been *and* in the light of what actually transpired in the 1950s.

At war's end, JDR had chosen the two family responsibilities—the RF and Colonial Williamsburg—because they appeared to be the ideal instruments for doing what he thought was needed in the postwar world. If he had succeeded in having the direct influence on their programs that he had sought, he probably would have been fully occupied in those institutional roles and might not have taken initiative elsewhere—certainly not to the remarkable extent that he did in the 1950s. In other words, his failures within the RF and at Williamsburg and the resulting break in the ties that bound him so closely to his father had the effect of forcing him out on his own.

JDR's surge of activity and institution-building in the 1950s resulted in a much more variegated and influential posture for him as a philanthropist than would have been the case if he had stayed within the more narrowly circumscribed boundaries of the two institutions. He got out of Colonial Williamsburg altogether, but continued within the RF, realizing that it could still be an important base for him, a different one than he had first envisioned, but one recognized everywhere in the world. In addition, he could bring a substantial share of the resources of another major foundation—the Rockefeller Brothers Fund—to bear on program needs. He had his own wealth and the trust fund income he controlled as further philanthropic tools. He created his own philanthropic staff. Most important, the half dozen organizations he developed gave him stature in new circles, often in mutually reinforcing ways. Having all these resources to draw upon gave JDR unusual independence and flexibility as a philanthropist.

The one resource that had to be handled most carefully was the RF. When JDR became chairman at the end of 1952, he did not make any concerted effort to redirect the Foundation. There were other constraints besides his earlier frustrations. By this time he was busy developing his outside organizations. Although the men who had opposed him most directly in the RF were gone—Fosdick, Stewart, and Barnard—others of the old guard remained, men such as Alan Gregg and Warren Weaver. Lindsley Kimball, who was almost fanatically devoted to Junior and Barnard, was still executive vice president.

Dean Rusk assumed his post as president of the RF in June 1952, six months before JDR was elected chairman of the board. They were contemporaries, but not close friends; they first met in wartime Washington and then encountered each other occasionally as a result of their mutual interest in the Far East.

Having served on the RF board for several years before being named president, Rusk was well aware of the touchiness of the staff and many trustees over anything that could be seen as family influence. After he accepted the presidency, Rusk was invited to lunch by Junior at Bassett Hall. Rusk feared he was going to get his marching orders, but Junior said it was the first and last time Rusk would get any advice from him—and that advice was "to go off and think afresh."[11] According to Rusk, the other Rockefeller brothers never set foot within the RF. Thus, the issue of sensitivity to family influence was specifically with JDR 3rd and no one else.

Rusk and JDR approached each other somewhat warily. Despite his soft Georgia drawl and low-key manner, Rusk was a strong-willed individual. He girded for problems, but found that his chairman "played it very straight." Their relationship got off to a good start when they saw eye to eye in defending the Foundation against the charges of the Cox and Reece Commissions and the CIA attempt to see internal documents that was mounted by Allen Dulles. Rusk said he had never met anyone who was as "clean" and had "such high standards" as JDR. He said: "John was a gentle, soft-spoken man who never used four-letter words, never lost his temper—but he was persistent, he gnawed at it, he was stubborn, much stronger than he appeared."

There were only a few cases when grants were made to something in which JDR was directly involved. The assistance to the Tokyo International House had been prearranged with the old guard, despite staff resistance, and Rusk was merely following through. The one time JDR nearly provoked a rebellion was the case of the India International Centre, but here, as we saw, JDR (or more accurately, the Indian leadership) simply outmaneuvered Rusk and the RF staff. In the case of Lincoln Center, Rusk felt some responsibility for having been the one who switched Spofford's attention from Nelson to JDR. RF grants to Lincoln Center were delicate, Rusk said, only because JDR was so heavily involved personally, not because anyone on the RF board or staff questioned the merit of the project.

Lacking pressure from JDR, Rusk's cautious approach as president of the RF did not contemplate any drastic revisions in program. During their time together, the main accomplishment that he and JDR made was to shift program emphasis to what JDR had called the "backward countries of the world," known in contemporary jargon somewhat more diplomatically as the "lesser-developed countries" (LDCs). On this the two men agreed emphatically. Once the International Health Division was terminated in the early 1950s, the only significant RF activity in the developing world was the agricultural program in Latin America. Under JDR and Rusk, program commitments steadily grew in Asia and Africa. The International Rice Research Institute in the Philippines, created in cooperation with the Ford Foundation, was one major example.

The two men also agreed on the role of the board and the need for trustees to participate actively. There was always the danger, Rusk said, of "the phenomenon of boredom" if the staff had too much control so that the trustees felt they were looking at the same items and dockets at every meeting. He said JDR was an excellent chairman, skilled and evenhanded in eliciting the views of others and getting them to participate. Sometimes he did not even express his own views, and he did not "politick" among the board members. One of the problems in foundation work, Rusk said, is the temptation to play God, but JDR had none of this about him. He had an appealing style, Rusk said, "shy in manner, but not under the skin."

As a veteran member of boards of directors, JDR had a highly developed view of the role and responsibilities of a chairman, which he applied at the RF and the half dozen other institutions where he served in that capacity. Once he articulated that view in what any personnel officer would acclaim as an excellent job description. This happened on vacation in Maine during the summer of 1970 when JDR met with C. Douglas Dillon, who had been nominated to succeed him as chairman of the RF. Dillon asked JDR for his thoughts on the chairmanship:

These I was glad to give him, pointing out that I thought the job was much more than presiding at board meetings—that it included working with the nominating committee on new trustees, planning for board meetings with the president, serving as advisor to the president as called for in the by-laws as well as working closely with him on policy and program matters, working with the president to make the trustee participation more meaningful and vital not only in meetings but generally, and finally having a sense of responsibility before Washington and even the public in connection with foundation matters broadly.

JDR indeed worked carefully with the nominating committee on new trustees, anxious to maintain the high level of quality on the board and at the same time to find men likely to be sympathetic with the broad directions he thought the Foundation should be taking. JDR had paid close attention to this ever since the success of his first experience at bringing in new members in 1947. The men he helped recruit then were John Dickey of Dartmouth, Henry Van Dusen of the Union Theological Seminary, and Robert F. Loeb, professor of medicine at Columbia. The trustees always seemed to fall into a number of occupational categories— college presidents, business and financial executives, scientists and medical doctors, media executives, and internationalists.

During the 1950s two of JDR's strongest supporters on the board retired—Bill Myers and Tom Parran. Arthur Sulzberger of the *New York Times* and Robert Sproul of the University of California also retired, and John J. McCloy resigned to become chairman of the Ford Foundation. JDR worked with the nominating committee to bring in the first black to serve on a major foundation board, Ralph Bunche of the United Nations, and Chester Bowles, Barry Bingham of the *Louisville Courier-Journal*, Arthur Houghton, Lee DuBridge of Cal Tech, and Benjamin McKelway of the *Washington Star*.

Dean Rusk said that the RF board during the 1950s was outstanding: "Any President would've been happy to have it as his cabinet." These words might have seemed prophetic when 1960 came and President-elect John F. Kennedy began to raid the RF board. Douglas Dillon had just been recruited to the board as he returned to his brokerage firm after serving as Under Secretary of State in the Eisenhower administration. He was plucked by JFK as his nominee for Secretary of the Treasury. Chester Bowles was recruited to be Under Secretary of State, and then Dean Rusk was asked to be Kennedy's nominee as Secretary of State. The breeding ground of the RF board for service in foreign affairs was as potent as ever.

JDR and Rusk had developed great mutual respect during their years together, as became evident at the annual meeting of the RF in Williamsburg in December 1960. There was some excitement in the air, as JDR commented in his diary: "A special note was added to the meeting because of various telephone calls from Washington in connection with Cabinet posts, there being several of the candidates present." After two days of sessions, JDR wrote: "Everybody seemed to feel that they were among the best we have had. Dean Rusk, as always, did a first-rate job, and he has brought together a really good group around him." JDR also noted that one of the new trustees, Douglas Dillon, had been "particularly helpful." He could not have known that Dillon and Rusk would soon both be gone to Washington as members of the new cabinet.

It was a time of considerable turnover on the board. Aside from the three who resigned to take posts in the new administration, a number of men retired during the next year or two, including Loeb, McKelway, Henry Allen Moe, Wally Harrison, and Robert Lovett. New men brought to the board in the early 1960s included Orvil Dryfoos of the *New York Times*, Clark Kerr of the University of California, Lowell Coggeshall of the University of Chicago, Frank Stanton of CBS, Father Hesburgh of Notre Dame, George Woods of the First Boston Corporation, Clifford Hardin of the University of Nebraska, and the first foreign member, Lord Franks of Headington, the chairman of Lloyd's Bank, Ltd. Frank Stanton and Ted Hesburgh in particular were men who were to become close to JDR and whom he would rely upon in many ways.

By all odds, however, the most important personnel matter at the beginning of the new decade was the search for a replacement for Dean Rusk as president of the Foundation. A special committee was established, consisting of John Dickey, Robert Lovett, Orvil Dryfoos, and JDR. For almost the first six months of 1961, this group carried on an executive search that was considerably more extensive than any that had been conducted by the new administration in Washington for the cabinet posts.

One consideration that occurred as a matter of course was promotion from within. The turnover had included the last prominent members of the old guard on the RF staff. Dr. Alan Gregg had retired in 1956, and Lindsley Kimball reached retirement age in 1960 and went on a consulting status. Warren Weaver, who had been a strong candidate for the presidency when Raymond Fosdick retired in 1948, had retired himself in 1959 and went over to be vice president of the Sloan Foundation. This left vice president George Harrar as the senior member of the RF staff and the only possible candidate for promotion from within. He became acting president while the search was conducted.

There was no doubt who the key decision-maker was—a parade of RF trustees and other luminaries marched through Room 5600, some to suggest candidates and others to help JDR evaluate those already under consideration. JDR also went down to talk to Dean Rusk about finding a successor. At least two candidates were being lured away by the State Department—Ken Young to be ambassador to Thailand and Phil Talbott to be Assistant Secretary for Near East and South Asian Affairs. The problem was that the RF selection process could not come to a head before these men had to respond to the State Department bids. At one point the list of candidates for what President Truman had called "the best job in the U.S." read like a *Who's Who* of the outstanding men in the country. Some other candidates were lost to university presidencies as the process wore on.

By May the choice had been narrowed down to two candidates, Clark Kerr, president of the University of California system, and, surprisingly, George Harrar. Some people who had been negative about Harrar at first, such as Lindsley Kimball, reversed themselves on the basis of the excellent job he was turning in as acting president. Warren Weaver came to see JDR to endorse Harrar strongly. JDR perhaps recalled his own prescient thought back in 1951 that Harrar might make a good candidate for the presidency of the RF "once he had a chance to grow a bit more in stature." They were on a trip to Colombia, and JDR had been very impressed when Harrar voiced a strong belief in the "human ecology" approach that JDR liked so much. The point was to deal with human problems by considering all of the major interacting forces instead of viewing them from the narrow perspective of one discipline. As far as the RF was concerned, the idea was to find ways to mount coordinated programs across divisional lines.

Ever since he had joined the RF in 1942 to staff a new agricultural program in Mexico, Harrar had been identified with the most outstanding postwar success of the Foundation. In 1970 the RF's Norman Borlaug won the Nobel Peace Prize in what was generally understood as a gesture honoring all those who had worked on the "miracle" strains of corn and wheat and rice in the "war on hunger" (the RF itself or Harrar might just as well have been the winner). Harrar did not regard himself as a farmer but as a researcher and organizer. He had earned his Ph.D. in plant pathology at the University of Minnesota. Harrar felt that one of his main contributions was finding the right people for the program, such as Borlaug, for example. "Many resisted me because they thought they would disappear professionally," Harrar said.[12] An important step forward in the program occurred at the 1945 Williamsburg meeting of the RF board when Harrar was brought up from Mexico to report on progress after only three years. His report completely sold the board and put the program on a sound footing. It was at this time that Harrar first met Junior and JDR 3rd.

In one of his last acts as RF president in 1952, Chester Barnard brought Harrar up from Mexico to run the program out of New York, against the wishes of Warren Weaver, who was Harrar's nominal superior. By the end of the decade, Harrar had moved out of his specialized field to a broader administrative role as vice president, having shown an ability to run a specialized program and at the same time think more broadly about problems, as in his support of the "human ecology" approach. In particular, he was an advocate of population activities, believing strongly that the RF should move beyond the "safe" areas of demographic and biomedical research to family planning assistance. Harrar was an admirer of JDR for his "courageous" stand in the population field. He said he thought JDR was wise to set up a separate Population Council instead of continuing to try to get the RF to be a population agency. Because of Harrar's agricultural background, JDR had consulted him about the speech he was to make to the Food and Agriculture Organization (FAO) of the UN in Rome in 1961. Harrar praised the strong stand on population that JDR intended to take. "The FAO tried to get him to tone it down," Harrar said, "but he went right ahead."

JDR was highly impressed with Clark Kerr; in fact, he was the only member of the selection committee who had been able to spend any appreciable amount of time with Kerr. He made a trip to the West Coast for this purpose, but when he returned he found the boom for Harrar had progressed. The sense of the committee was that there were two outstanding men to choose from, but that the value of promoting from within tipped the scales in Harrar's favor. On June 20, JDR asked Harrar to come to his office,

where he told him that the committee was going to recommend him as
president to a special meeting of the RF board called for the following week:

He obviously was pleased and moved, and we had a very nice talk which made
me even surer that we would be able to work happily and closely together. I
particularly stressed to him that he would be the chief executive officer and my
role was only that of adviser; also that I thought of my job as principally to back
him up in such ways as I could.

These were well-intentioned words, but they overestimated JDR's ability to restrain himself from pressing the RF to meet what he considered
to be great opportunities for action *and* Harrar's ability to move rapidly in
directions JDR wanted. As soon as Harrar took office, JDR suggested that
he begin a program review process, one emanating from the staff that
Harrar would direct instead of a more formalized committee of the board
such as the one in which JDR had participated back in 1946.

JDR realized that the time was propitious for new initiatives and
priorities for the RF. Not only was the old guard gone, but there was also
a new president with whom he saw eye to eye. Harrar's great success had
been in science-based agriculture, which JDR had vigorously supported
for fifteen years. In turn, Harrar was a supporter of JDR's two principal
objectives for the Foundation—expansion of population programs and
coordination across divisional lines. JDR's stature and influence as chairman
had grown immeasurably. And the world and domestic situations in the
1960s seemed to cry out for new initiatives.

For all these reasons, JDR was anxious to get moving. But he waited
patiently for a year for something to come back from Harrar. Then he
began applying serious pressure, as he had to Frank Notestein at the
Population Council and as he had in many directions at Lincoln Center.

Finally, in August 1962, Harrar showed him a first draft of program
review ideas for submission to the board. "I was much disappointed when
I read it," JDR wrote. He told Harrar his three main criticisms: there was
too much orthodox staff thinking reflected in the document and not enough
of Harrar; it did not present a "concentrated" program; and it did not
make the case for the use of substantial principal, which Harrar was advocating. JDR wrote: "We had a good frank talk which pleased me, and he
agreed to rewrite the memorandum on a personal basis to me, stating his
own ideas and not trying to include—at this point at least—recommendations of the other officers."

A month later the two men had lunch and JDR reported:

We concentrated on program and had a really very good discussion, both of us
speaking frankly and directly. I do appreciate being able to talk with him in this

way on almost any subject. My concern about his program presentation is the lack of focus. I am keen about his main ideas, but wish we could more effectively clear the decks of other carry-over items.

He kept hammering at this point with Harrar and found some support when a version of the Harrar plan was presented to the board in December: "The trustee comments were most helpful and I was pleased the way they took to the idea of concentrating the program and was particularly gratified at the reaction of several who indicated that they felt that what had been presented to them would not really permit the kind of focus that seemed desirable."

The following April JDR applied some more pressure by making the case publicly for program change in his remarks at the Fiftieth Anniversary Dinner of the RF at the Plaza Hotel. He said:

The fact is that we always face the need for self-examination. If it seems more urgent at the present moment, it is because our next half-century will most certainly be quite different from the one just closed. Increasingly, I have come to the conclusion that we will need a new sense of direction—perhaps even a new definition of purpose.

I believe we must begin by being less complacent about our past achievements, most of which are beyond question. Rather we must be concerned about our response to the challenges of the impatient future.

I am convinced of the need of regularly re-examining and updating our own conception of our task and our approach to it. On our ability to do this may depend the continued usefulness of philanthropic foundations.

JDR certainly represented the "impatient future" to Harrar. After another session two months later, JDR wrote: "I must say I am very much bothered by the fact that we still have no approved program for the Foundation even though Harrar will have been president for two years at the end of this month." However, Harrar shortly produced a statement of program reorientation and objectives that JDR liked and the board approved. Entitled "Plans for the Future," the statement was made public on September 20, 1963, with an aura of fiftieth-anniversary celebration. Noting that much of the work of the foundation during its first half century, in medicine, public health, and agriculture, had been absorbed on a vastly increased scale by governments, the statement said the time had come to redirect the Foundation's priorities:

As we advance our traditional interest in the welfare of all mankind, we see great possibilities for effective effort in this country and increasing opportunity for constructive action abroad—especially in the developing countries. With such consid-

eration in mind, the Foundation will, during the foreseeable future, concentrate
its effort in the following five areas of pressing human need:

    I. Toward the conquest of Hunger
   II. The Population Problem
  III. Strengthening Emerging Centers of Learning
  IV. Toward Equal Opportunity for All
   V. Aiding Our Cultural Development

In a creative way, this statement combined elements of continuity with
new program interests and cast them all within a problem-oriented framework of objectives that represented a marked departure from the past.
Only the agricultural program was vigorously reendorsed in its entirety.
The other four areas of concentration all contained something new that
reflected, in every case, a belief strongly held by JDR for many years. His
imprint was unmistakable. This was most obvious in the population and
cultural development programs. The RF had considerable history in both,
with its humanities division and its record of grant-giving in the "safe"
areas of the population field. But there were important new elements.
Both areas were raised in status by being singled out, with an implicit
commitment for increased resources. The mandate in the population field
was clearly broadened to include family planning assistance. And the program in cultural development, which formerly had been international in
character, was now oriented to the United States.

The third area, "Strengthening Emerging Centers of Learning," was a
decisive shift toward the increased commitment JDR had consistently
urged for the lesser-developed countries of the world. A great portion of
the Foundation's efforts had always been directed toward strengthening
colleges and universities as bastions of research and learning that were
vital to the progress of mankind. In the main, it was institutions in Europe
and the United States that benefited. The new idea was to concentrate
that aid on building up great indigenous universities in selected areas of
the lesser-developed world.

The new area was the fourth one, "Toward Equal Opportunity for All."
It was dedicated to the goal of racial equality, with initial emphasis by the
RF to be directed toward what was seen as a vital key—improved opportunities in higher education for blacks. Like the cultural development program, this was clearly oriented toward the United States. The fact that
two of the five areas of concentration were for the domestic scene was a
significant change in course for a foundation that had always been predominantly international in character. The equal opportunity program was a
frank recognition of the fact that although the General Education Board
(GEB) and the Laura Spelman Rockefeller Memorial (LSRM) had been

absorbed into the RF many years earlier, their activities to improve the life of black citizens had been allowed to lapse.[13] The historic interest of the Rockefeller family in aiding blacks had been maintained strongly by the Rockefeller Brothers Fund, but, in JDR's view, that was not enough. The new program resulted from his belief that it was time for the RF to reenter this field in a major way.[14]

The achievement of new program priorities and announcement of them in 1963 was a great step forward in JDR's view. But he soon became concerned over an apparent gap between stated objectives and program realities, and he began to press Harrar unmercifully. After several discussions, JDR tried a withdrawal technique one day at lunch with Harrar, as noted in his diary in July 1964:

After speaking of my satisfaction in working with him and my gratification that we could exchange ideas frankly, I said to him that I felt the way things were going at the present time I had to tell him that I felt we had less than a 50 per cent chance of developing the kind of program that would bring real distinction to the Foundation and that he and I had envisioned when he first came in as president. Also said that I felt I could not push him any more as chairman and hence that I thought I should pull back insofar as taking initiative was concerned. He, of course, was concerned and the rest of the lunch we had a good and useful talk.

A few months later JDR tried another way of applying pressure when Harrar came in to see him to talk about a proposed major grant for the Council on Foreign Relations:

I had taken the position that it seemed to me that the item was really out of program now in view of our new and focussed program. While he did not really disagree, he said that the officers were keen to do it and that the emphasis would be on the basis of a terminating grant. Of course I went along with him, as this is obviously a matter for officer decision. However, I had wanted to emphasize my concern in order to further focus attention on my belief in the importance of a really concentrated program if the Foundation is to have an exciting and truly meaningful program in the years ahead under Harrar's leadership.

Almost a year later, in June 1965, JDR was still harping on the problem in no uncertain terms:

George Harrar had invited ten of his top people to a luncheon as I had wanted at some point to talk a little with them about program. For a long time now I have expressed to George my concern that we were not focussing enough on the new program. At the luncheon, I said that perhaps today we were operating both in terms of the new five-way program and also on a divisional program basis which was the old pattern of operation. Said that I did not feel we could do both and have a truly distinctive record of accomplishment. There was not much discussion. George suggested we have meetings such as this from time to time.

JDR had achieved a long-sought goal—programs organized across divisional lines. But this diary entry sounds as if he had decided that that was not enough, that he would need to force a reorganization of the RF to do away with the divisions. Yet no such reorganization occurred. There would have been some difficult problems in attempting it, apart from the heavy hand of tradition and Harrar's deep-rooted faith in professionalism. As the 1963 "Plans for the Future" announcement indicated, the RF employed more than one hundred professionals in its various divisions at home and abroad. Certainly there could be no wholesale firing of these people. Presumably most of the specialists could be redeployed to one of the new programs, such as population or the effort to strengthen universities in the developing countries. Citing the traditional method of organizing by disciplines, the 1963 announcement said: "Today increasing emphasis is placed on the development of programs in which several disciplines are associated for maximum effectiveness." It went on to say that in a time of rapid change it was "impossible for the Foundation to lay out a detailed blueprint for the future."

On the other hand, the RF specialists might simply be doing the same old things, only under different labels. This apparently was JDR's concern as he lectured Harrar and his ten staff people in 1965. In *The Big Foundations*, Waldemar Nielsen is skeptical on the same point, expressing doubt that the RF "would ever break out of its well-set patterns and become a fully problem-oriented, innovative institution in nonscientific areas."[15]

It is a difficult issue to judge. Nielsen also points out that these same patterns helped give the RF unusual stability among foundations. This could have been threatened by mass turnovers in staff and an organizational structure based on shifting problem areas. Veteran managers and students of administration agree that the purpose of reorganization often turns out to be reorganization. More important is clear articulation of purposes with vigorous follow-through efforts by top management to get the needed performance in every area that can contribute to the achievement of those purposes—possibly including reorganization. In their own ways, this is what JDR and Harrar were in the process of doing, and as time passed it apparently began to work well enough so that JDR did not press for more formal shifting of people and boxes.[16]

JDR doubtless was premature in registering such impatience on that occasion in 1965—but it probably was good executive technique. And

Nielsen's evaluation admittedly was written close in time to the events in question and without the benefit of in-depth research on the functioning of the RF. Whatever the case, JDR clearly began to feel better about the way the Foundation was progressing. He kept the pressure on, but moderately, and several times he expressed satisfaction.

At the end of 1968 the RF published a five-year review consisting of reports by the directors of the five programs. It showed that nearly $120 million in grants had been made cumulatively in the five areas. The agriculture and equal opportunity programs each received more than $30 million, with the latter showing a substantial shift from the more traditional education activities to ghetto projects. Population received some $18 million, with 62 percent of that going to family planning assistance (more than 46 percent to the Population Council). The university development program focused on universities in Colombia, the Philippines, Thailand, Nigeria, and East Africa, with grants totaling $23 million. And the cultural development program spent over $16 million in support of music, theater, dance, writing, television, film, and general humanities projects throughout the United States.[17]

Without question a very significant difference had been made in what the Rockefeller Foundation was attempting to do. More than twenty years after JDR had first expressed his views on that subject, much of what he had foreseen as necessary had indeed come to pass. He had never given up—convincing evidence of his consistency and patience. And his pressure for change had been entirely proper, done in the interest of worthwhile purposes that were not self-serving, strongly supported by his board and prevailing opinions of the time.

Nielsen's final comments on the RF in the late 1960s seem most appropriate. He cites the "unique aspect" of the RF: the fact that it is "highly institutionalized and independent" and yet a family member continuously has played a prominent role. But, Nielsen points out, the family "is by no means dominant," the trustees are "probably the most eminent and diversified group" of any foundation in the country, and "there has never been any question about the professional competence and influence of the staff." If there has been any concern, "it has been over the possible excess of staff influence vis-à-vis the trustees." It was JDR who confronted this issue in an effort to make the RF responsive to the problems and challenges of its time. Nielsen refers to JDR's early attempts to change the course of the RF and then comments:

But these efforts to stimulate new thinking were initially seen by the staff as an aggressive thrust of family influence and they were resisted.

Nevertheless, after forty years of continuous involvement in the foundation's affairs, . . . [JDR's] imprint on the foundation's program is unmistakable. The substantial alteration of its program priorities since the 1950s has on the whole been in the direction of concerns with which he is especially identified: population, the fine arts, and the blacks. Undoubtedly, events in America and the world have helped to bring about the general change in course, as have the efforts of non-Rockefeller trustees and members of the staff. But it would appear that John D. Rockefeller 3rd is a much underrated force not only in the affairs of the Rockefeller Foundation but in other aspects of American philanthropy as well.[18]

III

ON THE PERSONAL SIDE, 1945–1970

13

❦

FAMILY AFFAIRS:
THE BROTHERS

BEFORE World War II there was intense public curiosity directed toward
the five Rockefeller brothers. Numerous magazines articles and newspaper
spreads appeared about them, dealing mainly with their unusual heritage
and potential accomplishments, not actual ones. Nelson was the only
brother who stayed prominently in the public eye as a result of his activities as Coordinator of Inter-American Affairs during the war, with the
State Department in 1945 during the Truman administration, and with the
Eisenhower administration in the early 1950s The other brothers were
not seeking publicity, and, in fact, had done little to merit it. For years
they did not appear much in the public prints except for the notoriety
attached to Winthrop's marriage to "Bobo" Sears.

By the late 1950s, the other four brothers were being rediscovered by
the press. They were beginning to do things that caught attention—JDR
with Lincoln Center, Laurance with his support of conservation and cancer
research, Winthrop in his new life in Arkansas, and David progressing in
his banking career. In 1958 the *New York Journal-American* ran a series
on "The Fabulous Rockefeller Dynasty," consisting of an introductory article on Senior and Junior followed by installments on five successive days on
each of the brothers in turn—"Shy John, Outgoing Nelson, Venturesome
Laurance, Maverick Winthrop, and Dogged David." The growth to prominence might be measured by another spread five years later in *Look* magazine entitled "The Rockefellers' New York." The article focused on the five
brothers and began: "The Rockefellers are the first family of New York
City by any yardstick—civic, cultural or commercial. A fog of superlatives
swirls around their contributions to the life of the city."[1]

This was a period—the mid-1950s to the early 1960s—of great transition
for the family. Junior's era passed from view, all five brothers became

recognized for their accomplishments in varying degrees and in different circles, and members of the next generation, the sons and daughters of the brothers and their sister, the generation known as "the Cousins," attained adulthood in growing numbers and became a force to be reckoned with.

As usual, Nelson led the way. If he had been well-known before, he now was famous. His rise to national prominence as a politician was meteoric, occurring in the brief span of several years, 1958 to 1960, and his fame and some of his subsequent actions had profound effects on Rockefeller family members and their relationships.

In leaving the Eisenhower administration at the end of 1955, Nelson professed an eagerness to get back into family affairs, but he was already thinking of running for office. He resumed the chairmanship of Rockefeller Center, and showed his knack for getting publicity by making an effort to keep the Brooklyn Dodgers from moving to Los Angeles. Nelson offered "to acquire some percentage of ownership in the club" and "to participate in building a stadium." It was prominently mentioned in the newspapers that Nelson had no history as a baseball fan. His interest in the Dodgers was attributed to his "UN mood," his penchant for coming to the rescue when his home city needed something, as he had done eleven years earlier in persuading his father to purchase and donate the UN site.[2] More likely, it was Nelson's "political mood."

As soon as he left Washington, Nelson began pressing to take over the presidency of the Rockefeller Brothers Fund (RBF) from his older brother, who had served for fifteen years. At first reluctant, JDR finally agreed, recognizing that he was overburdened in any case, with half a dozen projects in Asia plus the chairmanship of the Rockefeller Foundation. He commented in his diary that he agreed that the RBF now "should not be just an orthodox foundation but has a real opportunity to do something more."

After taking over at the trustees' meeting of March 1956, Nelson quickly showed what his idea of "something more" would be. As a foreign affairs adviser in the White House he had organized special study groups at Quantico, Virginia, in connection with the 1955 Geneva summit meeting. One of the products of these brainstorming sessions was the "open skies" proposal made by President Eisenhower at Geneva, despite the opposition of the State Department hierarchy.[3] Now Nelson wanted to apply the "Quantico technique" in private life to a larger task. His idea was to assemble a group of experts to examine America at midcentury, look ahead for the next ten to fifteen years, and develop a blueprint for the problems and needs that would arise. Nelson conceived the idea of a "Special Study Projects" staff as a regular administrative division of the RBF. It would provide staff and logistical support for large-scale inquiries of the kind he was contemplating. The trustees agreed, and Nelson hired Nancy Hanks, who had worked for him in Washington at HEW. He was also able to persuade Henry Kissinger, whom he had first met at the Quantico seminars, to take leave from Harvard University to be the director of the first major inquiry, the "America at midcentury" project.

As chairman of the "overall panel," Nelson selected some thirty panel members, including Dean Rusk, John Gardner, Father Hesburgh, economist Arthur Burns, businessman Charles Percy, physicist Edward Teller, publisher Henry Luce, and such close Rockefeller friends as Dev Josephs, John Dickey, and Chuck Spofford. A "panel" was formed for each of six subjects—foreign policy, defense policy, foreign economic policy, domestic economic and social concerns, education, and "the democratic idea." The membership of the overall panel was split up among these substantive panels, and other experts and leaders were recruited to serve on them. For example, JDR and Rusk were among those on the foreign policy panel. Laurance served on the defense panel, and its report was written by Kissinger. David Rockefeller was a member of the foreign economic policy panel.[4]

The "panel reports" were published separately as they were ready, from 1958 through 1961, a technique designed to enhance the publicity they received. Then all six were published together in book form under the title *Prospects for America—The Rockefeller Panel Reports*. The RBF appropriated a total of $755,000 over a five-year period in support of the effort, the largest sums of $340,000 and $220,000 coming in 1957 and 1958.

Nelson's timing was excellent. The material, for the most part, was well done, and this sort of high-level, nongovernmental, comprehensive policy analysis seemed to strike a responsive chord, aided by the successful Russian launching of Sputnik in 1957 and the onset of a Presidential election season in 1960.

Somewhat controversial was the defense panel report, which took issue with the moderate tone and fiscal restraint of the Eisenhower administration in its later years. The Rockefeller defense panel took a hard line toward the Soviet Union and called for a substantial increase in the defense budget. The foreign policy panel report was somewhat more elevated in tone, although it, too, had its Cold War basis. But it took a moderate stance toward China, warning of the danger of pushing mainland China into the arms of the Soviets. And it struck an optimistic note regarding the possibilities of creative and constructive change, holding out the prospect of a new world order that might transcend the negativism of the Soviet-American bipolar rivalry.[5]

An example of the attention the series of panel reports brought to

Nelson was a *Newsweek* cover story headlined "The Rockefeller to Keep Your Eye On." The story said that Junior had established "the Rockefeller tradition of public service" and that Nelson was "the Rockefeller who today epitomizes" that tradition. The reason was that it was Nelson "who inspired the Rockefeller reports" and who might become "the first Rockefeller in politics." The writer of the article did not seem to understand that a career in politics would be very different from Junior's brand of public service.[6]

Shortly after this article appeared, Nelson did indeed decide to run for governor of New York State in the 1958 campaign. Laurance took over as chairman of the unfinished panel reports effort. Nelson had passed up a chance to run for the Senate two years earlier. Seemingly, he had his eye all along on the post that served so well as a power base for such figures as Al Smith, FDR, and Tom Dewey. But Nelson was given little chance of defeating Averell Harriman, the incumbent Democrat who was running for reelection. It would be an off-year election, and as such was expected by most analysts to be a strong Democratic year.

However, in 1956 Harriman unwittingly had done Nelson a favor by appointing him chairman of a temporary state commission to study questions relating to a possible constitutional convention. Nelson handled the difficult assignment with great skill, thereby earning the respect of political figures throughout the state and learning a great deal about state government. This experience paved the way for him to win the GOP nomination in 1958.[7]

The campaign pitted two wealthy patricians against each other. Nelson already was being labeled as "too liberal" by many Republicans, but he gained some support from the conservative wing of his party by taking Assemblyman Malcolm Wilson as his running mate. Frank Jamieson functioned as chief of staff for the campaign. Dr. William J. Ronan of New York University, who had been director of the constitutional convention study for Nelson, served as chief speechwriter. A significant new addition to Nelson's inner circle was veteran political adviser George Hinman.

It was the first time a Rockefeller had ever run for political office. Junior might have opposed such an idea in earlier years, but he made no objection now. The reactions of Nelson's brothers reportedly varied from attempts to discourage him to enthusiasm. However, they all responded favorably to a proposal by Frank Jamieson and John Lockwood that each contribute a total of approximately $18,000 for the campaign, to be divided among various Republican committees, including several for Nelson.[8]

Nelson waged an energetic and aggressive campaign, barnstorming through the state and showing political skill, personal charisma, and typical

Rockefeller stamina. It did turn out to be a "Democratic year" elsewhere in the nation, but not in New York. Nelson won his race with a plurality of 557,000 votes, a stunning victory that immediately catapulted him into the ranks of Presidential contenders. His inaugural address dealt mainly with national and international themes, suggesting that Nelson indeed might have his eyes on the White House. But he took charge of state government in no uncertain terms, solving problems, meeting needs, and innovating state services at a breakneck pace that has few rivals in American history.

In March 1954 the Rockefeller brothers held a "family dinner" at Laurance's house on the Pocantico estate in honor of their father's eightieth birthday. Junior's love of music had been rekindled by his marriage to former concert pianist Martha Baird Allen, so it was fitting that after dinner the group moved up to Junior's residence, Kykuit, for a recital by opera singer Ezio Pinza. The party was held in March instead of on Junior's actual birthday, January 29, because it was the earliest time that the five brothers could coordinate their schedules to be together. JDR, for example, was on an Asian trip in January.

Junior lived on another six years, an old man with parchment skin smiling benignly at his grandchildren and great-grandchildren when they came to Kykuit for dinner. He was still a formidable man, still possessed of a substantial fortune, paying the bills at the family office and engaging in acts of philanthropy, still shepherding along his beloved Colonial Williamsburg.

But it was a mellow period in his life. His marriage to "Aunt Martha," as his sons came to call his second wife, was a pleasant one, giving him the companionship and care that he needed. Junior seemed relieved of worries and responsibilities, at peace with himself as he basked in the glow of his justly earned fame and the accomplishments of his sons. His long-term associate, Raymond B. Fosdick, published his biography of Junior in 1956, generating a cover story in *Time* magazine. Headlined "The Good Man," the article termed Junior "an authentic American hero" because his life had been dedicated to "constructive social giving."

Rockefeller's life is simply, quietly and uniquely dedicated to his fellow men. . . . he is a symbol of the stern conscience that has long been the heritage of the same Protestant American ethic that sparked U.S.-style capitalism—a conscience that made a virtue of work and its rewards, but likewise saddled the successful with an awesome compulsion to regard his wealth as a trust, to redistribute one's gain for the benefit of many men. . . . "Giving is the secret of a healthy life," he says. "Not necessarily money, but whatever a man has of encouragement and sympathy and understanding."[9]

Junior had won national and international recognition, but he was honored in his own hometown as well, the area of Tarrytown and the Pocantico estate in Westchester County. At the age of eighty-four, Junior gave a grant of $300,000 for recreational facilities to the Pocantico school district. This prompted the local paper to say: "Our good neighbor on the hill has done it again."[10] It was estimated that Junior's gifts to his immediate neighborhood totaled $50 million over the years.

Junior's attitudes toward his six children had not varied much by these later years.[11] The long patriarchal role he had played prevented him from being really close to any of them. He had disapproved of the behavior of Babs and Winthrop; that feeling remained strong in her case, but Junior had become more accepting of Winthrop. The most complex relationship was probably that between Junior and his oldest son, John, who had come to occupy a special category, as we shall see. Junior was satisfied with his other three sons, indeed proud of them. Nelson had always been a favorite, and Junior certainly was proud of his second son's election as governor of New York State. He would have agreed with a *New York Times* assessment that it gave the "final stamp of approval to a name that was once hated and feared in America."[12] Laurance had the Rockefeller business acumen and he was a staunch conservationist, something dear to Junior's heart. David had earned higher degrees; he was showing perseverance at the Chase Bank and was rising rapidly, clearly destined for important things.

The gulf between Junior and Babs was never quite bridged. He felt that she remained defiant; she was uncomfortable with anything that smacked of his authority. Like Winthrop, Babs needed physical distance from her father. She and her first husband, David Milton, had built a home on the western edge of the Pocantico estate on land given to her by her father, just as Junior had given JDR and Blanchette the acreage they had staked out for Fieldwood Farm on the northwestern edge. After divorcing David Milton in 1943, Babs sold her home, Hudson Pines, to her brother David. She lived thereafter in her Manhattan apartment and had a "country home," called Laurel Hill, in Oyster Bay on Long Island. She remarried in 1946, to Dr. Irving H. Pardee, who died in 1949. She then married a third time, to Jean Mauzé, in 1953.

In contrast, Junior saw Winthrop as a flawed and troubled person, but a basically decent and well-meaning one. They remained distant, but not necessarily antagonistic, as indicated by the fact that Junior entrusted the chairmanship of Colonial Williamsburg to Winthrop.

In the case of JDR, Junior could scarcely disapprove of a son who was so earnest and hard-working and who had tried so hard to follow in his father's footsteps. JDR's moral conduct was exemplary. He had a fine wife and family. He certainly had taken to heart his father's views about the caretaking of money and the obligation to serve—he was a frugal man and a full-time philanthropist. But he simply did not arouse any enthusiasm in Junior. Despite some scattered successes, JDR's career did not add up to much in Junior's estimation. He had not assumed Junior's place and influence in American society, but perhaps that was too much to expect of anyone. There is no evidence that Junior held the disagreement with JDR over policy at Colonial Williamsburg against his son. But he probably was influenced by the way that the "old guard" at the Rockefeller Foundation had regarded JDR during the time they had opposed his initiatives in the late 1940s. Chester Barnard and his supporters thought JDR was not very bright and was "mulish" in his behavior. According to Lindsley Kimball, Junior thought his son was "too sweet" to count for much.[13]

We have seen JDR's remarkable burst of creative activity in the 1950s in a number of fields. But unless one looked closely and realized how difficult were the causes he was trying to serve and the patient, long-term effort they required, it was still easy to see him as somewhat ineffectual. This was Junior's impression up to the time of his death in 1960. He tended to see his son's occasional success, but not the long-term underlying commitment.

His son had passed fifty years of age and what had he done? He apparently had helped Mr. Dulles in Japan and had revived the Japan Society. That was nice, but in the past now. The Rockefeller Public Service Awards had had a significant result in the Government Training Act, but Junior thought that that, too, was over. It was praiseworthy of JDR to dedicate himself to the population field, but it seemed to be going nowhere. Other activities—Asia Society, Magsaysay Awards, CECA, and so on—were too new to mean much. The one great exception was Lincoln Center. Here, Junior was convinced that his son had become involved in something truly important, so much so that Junior was willing to make significant financial contributions to it himself. But even Lincoln Center was far from a success by the time Junior died. The maturing and flowering of many of JDR's activities did not occur until the 1960s, after his father was gone, and one major contribution—in which JDR surpassed his father—had not even begun (see Chapter 18).

Junior was necessarily distant from all his sons during the last few years of his life, given their busy schedules and his age and failing health. He and Martha spent the spring at Williamsburg, the summer in Seal Harbor, the autumn at Pocantico, and the winter in the same small inn in Tucson that he and Abby had enjoyed. It was at the last city that he succumbed on May 11, 1960, of a weakened heart and pneumonia. Nelson and Laurance were present, having gone out the night before. JDR got the news back in New York and "spent the rest of the afternoon notifying members of the family." Three days later, services were held at graveside at the cemetery in North Tarrytown with only family members present, and JDR wrote: "There were about forty in all and it really was quite beautiful with the sun slanting in the late afternoon and the dogwoods out in full."

Jay, who had flown in from the Far East to be present, remembers it as a moving experience, not so much emotionally, but with a sense of history passing on. The same mood prevailed at the public service and memorial at Riverside Church, one emotional moment coming when bass William Warfield sang "Going Home."

Junior's gross estate was valued at $157 million. Junior left the vast Manhattan apartment and contents to Martha, the "Eyrie" and other property in Maine to Nelson and David (because they were the two brothers who had adjoining property and vacationed there), and the JY ranch in Wyoming to Laurance. Junior had already given Bassett Hall in Williamsburg to JDR and Kykuit was already owned by the brothers by virtue of the 1952 sale of the Pocantico estate to them. Out of the "marital deduction" half of the estate, $48 million went to Martha after various small debts and administrative, tax, and funeral expenses were covered. Some $12 million went for state and federal taxes. The residual, eventually valued at $72 million, went to the Rockefeller Brothers Fund. Coming on top of the $58 million gift from Junior in 1951, this strengthened the RBF as a major foundation, able now to make annual grants in a total of from $7 million to $9 million per year.[14]

Junior left the substantial amount to Martha in the same spirit of the trust fund he had given her before their marriage—so that she could experience "the joy of giving" that he had known. She followed his intent faithfully, dividing her generous giving in ensuing years between the field she loved, music, and causes identified with Junior's sons.

As far as Nelson was concerned, there was only one cause that really counted—his political career. Martha supported this "cause" to a surprising degree, contributing in excess of $10 million to five of his campaigns through the establishment of trusts, and donating another $1.45 million directly to two of these campaigns. "Whenever we needed money, we'd call on Martha Baird," said Hugh Morrow, Nelson's longtime press secretary. He added that Nelson's handling of Martha was a "triumph of charm and diplomacy."[15]

There were many campaigns because Nelson ran for governor four times and was a candidate three times for the GOP Presidential nomination. Martha accounted for 78 percent of the family's total of $14.8 million contributed to all of Nelson's campaigns. Morrow characterized JDR's contributions as "parsimonious" at $405,000. David gave $592,000, Babs $509,000, and Laurance $1.36 million. Campaign costs were rising steadily, especially with the increased use of television. Nelson was one of the first politicians to make extensive use of that medium, in his 1958 campaign. But he also needed increased funds because each election was a greater struggle for him than the one preceding it.[16]

For a while it seemed inevitable to many observers that Nelson Rockefeller would be President of the United States. He came the closest of anyone in the Republican Party of his time to having the personal appeal and political skill of a Franklin Delano Roosevelt. There were other similarities—the towering ambition, the sense of destiny, the wealth and status, the liberal image, the New York power base. Moreover, Nelson seemed to have limitless energy. He was an excellent administrator and could draw talented people to him. His intellect was of surprising range and depth and intuitive grasp. But all of these impressive attributes were steadily undermined by some sort of flaw that was hard to identify, almost as if Nelson were an actor in a Greek tragedy who continually took steps to put out of reach the prize he wanted so much. Some would say the flaw was a tendency toward lapses in judgment that would crop out sporadically. Others would say it was an underlying character fault, a lack of consistent principles. And still others would identify it as an overweening ego that took the form of Nelson believing that he could do almost anything he wanted and get away with it.[17]

Whatever the reason, Nelson's political career, from 1958 all the way through to 1976, was one of almost unrelenting personal and political drama. The first great error occurred in 1960. Too new on the scene to head off Richard Nixon, heir apparent to President Eisenhower, Nelson had enough political clout after Nixon had won the nomination to force the candidate to come to him instead of vice versa. Nixon needed at least a show of support from the man who had won such an astounding plurality in New York State only two years earlier. So he traveled to Nelson's Manhattan apartment for a meeting that the press termed the "humiliating compact of Fifth Avenue." This alienated many party conservatives, who saw Nelson as arrogant, especially after Nixon lost to JFK in the general election. It also seemed to confirm their suspicion that Nelson was too liberal for their taste, a view that was heightened when the Kennedy administration adopted some of the ideas in Nelson's "Prospects for America" exercise.[18]

In November 1961 Nelson and his wife, Mary ("Tod"), announced that they were separated and seeking a divorce. It was clear that the initiative was his. Although the inner circle of family members knew the marriage had not been a close one for some time, the news still came as a shock, all the more so to the unsuspecting public. Aside from the personal trauma involved, there were bound to be political repercussions, though Nelson and his aides expressed confidence that these could be overcome. Nelson and Tod had been married for thirty-one years and had five grown children. No divorced man had ever been elected President, and this seemed an especially poignant case of jettisoning a wife after nearly a lifetime together, an image that was heightened the following March when Tod fought back tears as she left the Reno courtroom with her divorce decree, accompanied by sons Rodman and Steven.

The death of Junior removed the most formidable barrier against Nelson's going ahead with the separation and divorce. There is no question that he waited until his father's death before proceeding. Another restraint disappeared with the death of Frank Jamieson of lung cancer, also in 1960. Quite apart from Junior's moral strictures, Jamieson was a strong influence against divorce for Nelson on political grounds.[19]

The divorce was hard on Nelson and Tod's children and on her many friends within the family, especially her close friend Blanchette. But Tod's wit and wisdom would still be available—she would keep the Fifth Avenue apartment and a residence at Pocantico. Ironically, tragedy struck Nelson and Tod only a few days after their separation had become public knowledge. Tod was having lunch at Fieldwood Farm with JDR and Blanchette on Sunday, November 19. JDR wrote in his diary: "While we were with her she got word through the Dutch Ambassador to Washington that Michael was missing off the southern coast of New Guinea. We stopped by afterward to see Nelson, who had decided to go out to West New Guinea with Mary to be close to the situation." Michael and Mary were twenty-three-year-old twins. He was on an anthropological expedition and was lost when he tried to swim to shore after his small native boat drifted out to sea. He was never found.[20]

In 1962 Nelson ran for reelection. His opponent was Robert S. Morgenthau, U.S. Attorney for the Southern District of New York. It was a measure of Nelson's strength as a candidate that he overcame his divorce and the tax increases required by his innovations in state government to win by 518,000 votes. He had hoped for a plurality of one million votes to put him in an unassailable position to win the GOP nomination for the Presidency in 1964. Indeed, the defeat of Nixon in the California gubernatorial race seemed to leave the field wide open to Nelson. But in May 1963 he completed what he had started with his separation and subsequent divorce by marrying Margaretta Fitler Murphy, known to everyone as "Happy," an attractive thirty-six-year-old mother of four who had just been divorced a month earlier from Dr. James "Robin" Murphy.

This was the culmination of an affair that had been going on for some time, an open secret within the Rockefeller family. The Murphys were family friends. They lived in a house they had built on the Pocantico estate, and Robin worked as a microbiologist at the Rockefeller Institute.[21] The wedding was widely regarded as political suicide for Nelson. He would listen to no advice on the subject; he was in love and he refused to believe that he had to give up either his love or his political career. He thought he could have both. But the public saw what had happened in stark terms—a husband rejected, young children abandoned, unseemly haste.[22]

There had been press speculation that Nelson would remarry. To avoid the press, the ceremony was hastily scheduled and held in private at Laurance's home on the Pocantico estate. He was the only one of Nelson's brothers in attendance and the only other family member present was Martha Baird Rockefeller, Junior's widow. David and Peggy knew Robin Murphy particularly well and were devastated by what had happened. Because other writers have stated that John and Blanchette refused to attend the wedding, it is worth tracing in some detail what actually happened.[23] The family members knew that a wedding was imminent, but were not certain when or where it would take place. Blanchette's first concern was for her close friend Tod, so she invited Tod to get away from the scene entirely by staying with her at Bassett Hall in Williamsburg.

Left alone at home, JDR conceived the idea of taking thirteen-year-old Alida on a trip to Washington to see the sights and visit her brother, Jay: "She had never been there and I had been wanting to take her for some time." It was a lovely May weekend, and Alida and her father covered the standard tourist sights—the FBI, Capitol Hill, the Wax Museum, the monuments, the Smithsonian—some of them seemingly "firsts" for JDR as well. On Saturday night they came back to their rooms at the Sheraton-Carlton Hotel, and JDR described what happened:

At 9:00 p.m. Alida and I got through to Blanchette, she having called earlier in the day from Williamsburg. It was from her that we first heard that Nelson and Happy Murphy had been married at noon that day. I am sure it was the fact that we were away and the belief of a number of people that others had told us that resulted in our not being informed in advance. Certainly I know that Nelson was most anxious not to have the date, hour and place get out to the press in advance.

Instead of snubbing the wedding, it seems that JDR, in effect, was forgiving Nelson for not having told him in advance of his plans. As far as JDR was concerned, it was Nelson's decision and he had done it. JDR seemed more interested at the moment in his daughter having a good time on her trip. The next day they had lunch with Jay at the rented house he was sharing in Georgetown, a house that "is relatively modest in size but does have a swimming pool in back, which has great appeal for Washington summers." Jay then took his father and sister to the National Gallery of Art and through Arlington Cemetery on the way to the airport and home. JDR wrote that he and Alida "could not have had a nicer time together."

Despite the enormous handicaps he was now bearing, Nelson decided to enter the contest for the 1964 GOP Presidential nomination, a decision that he made after the assassination of President Kennedy in November 1963. Whether or not Nelson was trying to assume something of the Kennedy mantle, he chose a difficult course within his own party. He took a decidedly liberal tack, perhaps to offer a contrast to the front-runner, Senator Barry Goldwater of Arizona. The climax of this unsuccessful attempt came with Nelson's memorable appearance before jeering delegates at the Cow Palace in San Francisco. He outlasted them, and it was a courageous performance, his finest hour in politics to some observers. Others felt that he got what he deserved after baiting the party's conservatives for months in the campaign.

In 1966, his political fortunes seemingly at low ebb, Nelson ran for a third term as a decided underdog against Democrat Frank O'Connor, the Manhattan district attorney. Nelson fought a hard and expensive campaign, taking on some of the conservative coloration of his party, and won by 400,000 votes. In 1968 he made his third try at the national prize after President Johnson withdrew and the campaign of Nelson's candidate, Governor George Romney of Michigan, fell into disarray.[24] Nelson lost on the first ballot at the GOP convention in Miami. In 1970 came his fourth and last campaign for the governorship. Again, he seemed like an underdog at the beginning, but he defeated Arthur Goldberg by 700,000 votes, his biggest plurality ever.

*   *   *

The relationships among the Rockefeller brothers were as complex as those among any group of siblings, prominent or otherwise; only they themselves had any truly intimate knowledge of them. Yet it is possible to characterize those relationships to some degree. All of the brothers wanted family unity. As a result not one of them ever spoke disparagingly of any of his brothers in public, and probably not very often in private. JDR, for example, hardly ever spoke to his staff members about his brothers, and when he did he praised them or spoke in neutral tones, never negatively.

The boyhood affinity between Nelson and Laurance continued throughout their adult lives; no other relationship among the brothers came close to rivaling the love between these two. To Nelson, Laurance was a wry, wise friend, the person who knew him most intimately in the world, the one who could always be counted on. To Laurance, it was a privilege to be Nelson's brother. Not only was he a wonderful brother in Laurance's estimation, but he also was a genuinely great man who very nearly could do no wrong.

Otherwise, the brothers were cordial, but not especially close. In fact, had they not been brothers sharing a unique heritage, one suspects that they would not have been more than casual acquaintances. One underlying factor was their father—the family traditions he embodied and transmitted and the wealth he dispensed. With his death, the institutions he had created continued to exert a unifying influence. These included the philanthropic institutions, Rockefeller Center, the Pocantico estate, and, most importantly, the family office and the various trust funds that tended to bind succeeding generations together, at least within a broad framework.

Beyond this, the brothers had two institutions of their own to coordinate their activities—the RBF and the periodic "brothers' meetings." The latter seemed to occur about six to eight times a year, not on a rigorous schedule, but whenever a quorum was available, usually at Pocantico on a Saturday or Sunday afternoon. The usual group was JDR, Nelson, Laurance, and David, though Nelson attended less frequently after he became governor. Winthrop was present only rarely, whenever a trip back east happened to coincide with a meeting. As a member of the brothers' generation, sister Babs was not excluded, but she rarely attended a meeting.

Once the RBF came into big money, with Junior's 1952 gift of $58 million, it began to lead a sort of bifurcated existence. Its original purpose continued—to serve as the philanthropic vehicle for the brothers, both for their "citizenship" giving and their larger interests. At the same time, the RBF increasingly developed a program and direction of its own as one of the nation's major foundations. Both of these purposes were served by

Dana Creel and his small, growing professional staff. Throughout the 1950s and 1960s, Babs and her five brothers were all members of the board of trustees. Junior's widow, Martha, was placed on the board after his death and served until her death in 1971. Two members of the Cousins' generation were added, Abby M. O'Neill (Babs's oldest daughter) in 1958 and Laura Rockefeller Case (Laurance's oldest daughter) in 1963. The effort to broaden the RBF began to be an important factor by the 1960s, and one symptom of it toward the end of the decade was the addition of more "Cousins" and nonfamily trustees. Up to this time there had been only two nonfamily trustees, Detlev Bronk, president of the Rockefeller Institute, and Nelson's old friend, architect Wally Harrison.

The RBF was created originally with funds contributed by the brothers. Even after the large gift and the bequest from Junior made the RBF a major foundation, Babs and the brothers continued to give periodic gifts to it, as if to further legitimize the grants made by the Fund to the philanthropic interests of each family member. Over his lifetime, for example, JDR contributed $2.16 million. Of course, the nonprofit institutions and causes he supported received a total of much more than this in grants from the RBF, and this was true for all of the brothers.

In the mid-1970s the pattern of giving to causes identified with individual Rockefellers and the amounts given became a sharply divisive issue (as we shall see in later chapters) within the family. But until that time, the RBF operated amicably and with what seems to have been a rough parity in grants to interests identified with various brothers—they could be reasonably sure that their causes would receive their fair share sooner or later. This was not an automatic process, but one that occurred within a broad consensus covering such areas of sustained family interest as the arts, international relations, civil rights, projects in support of New York City, and others.

Up to the late 1960s, the largest single recipient was the Museum of Modern Art with a total of $6.65 million grants. MOMA, of course, was Nelson's major philanthropic interest, but also had always been important to Blanchette and became increasingly so to David. The Jackson Hole Preserve received $2.3 million, and every year smaller grants would go out to a number of Laurance's conservation interests. JDR seemed to do quite well with $2.5 million going to Lincoln Center, $2.2 million to the Population Council, and frequent smaller grants to the Asia Society and to his Asian agricultural program. The Magsaysay Awards program was of interest to all the brothers, but was mainly identified with JDR.

Apart from the forums of the brothers' meetings and the RBF board and such occasions as Christmas and weddings, the brothers did not see

much of each other. Each had his own interests and for the most part
these were widely separated. Although JDR, Laurance, Nelson, and David
each had a suite of offices in Room 5600, the latter two were almost never
there. Nelson was busy being governor, and when he came to New York
City he used offices in a brownstone on West 55th Street, just off Fifth
Avenue. David spent most of his time at Chase Manhattan headquarters
in downtown Manhattan, and Winthrop was in Arkansas.

As for the two who were headquartered in Room 5600, JDR and
Laurance, the degree of interaction is suggested by a 1957 entry in JDR's
diary: "Had lunch with Brother Laurance—a sort of 'get acquainted' talk."
In 1964 JDR reported that he and Laurance had "a nice talk" at lunch:
"He does have a very ranging mind and an imaginative approach to problems and situations." In 1967 there was a rare item of business between the
two that caused several meetings. JDR described what happened: "Brother
Laurance stopped in to talk to me further about joining up in regard to the
family airplane plans. Feel badly not cooperating but just do not believe I
would use a plane enough to justify the considerable expense."

Two of Laurance's three main areas of activity—venture capital investments and cancer research—were quite distinct from any of JDR's interests. And in the third, conservation, Laurance had long ago moved away
from any possible conflict or overlap with the population field. Aside from
the development of vacation resorts, Laurance's interests were pretty much
in the same orthodox conservation mold as those of his father. In 1958
Laurance began a long string of official posts in Washington when
President Eisenhower appointed him chairman of a commission to study
outdoor recreation. The recommendations, delivered to President Kennedy, resulted in the establishment of a Bureau of Outdoor Recreation in
the Department of the Interior. Then President Johnson appointed Laurance chairman of the Citizens Advisory Committee on Recreation and
Natural Beauty, and here he found a deep kinship and became fast friends
with the President's wife, Lady Bird. President Nixon appointed Laurance
chairman of the Citizens Advisory Committee on Environmental Quality.
These roles provided Laurance with a base for involvement in a whole
series of studies and environmental policy issues.

The resorts numbered seven at the peak of development, and Laurance
created a company called Rock Resorts to manage them. He wanted to
develop the finest possible resorts according to the dictates of his own
taste, and he succeeded admirably. His resorts have been enormously
popular, and also returned substantially on the investment. Caneel Bay on
St. John in the U.S. Virgins and Little Dix Bay on Virgin Gorda in the
British Virgin Islands set the standard of excellence for luxury resorts in

the Caribbean. Other projects—Dorado Beach and Cerromar in Puerto Rico, the Mauna Kea Hotel on the big island of Hawaii, and Estate Fountain River on St. Croix—were undertaken by Laurance at the request of local leaders who were anxious to promote tourist development. Woodstock in Vermont had many of the same elements for Laurance, plus the additional one of doing something for his wife's hometown.

The only one that JDR and Blanchette patronized was the Dorado Beach, for many years taking their midwinter vacation there, usually only one week in late January or early February. They went there not so much because it was Laurance's hotel but because it met their needs. They enjoyed the anonymity they found in this large complex. They could play golf and JDR could relax in the balmy climate in a facility where it was easy to avoid prolonged exposure to the sun, something he was never able to stand.

Next to Nelson, the brother who became the most famous during the 1960s was the youngest one, David. He was elected vice chairman and a director of the Chase Manhattan Bank in 1956, having worked in international banking, planning, bank development, and branch operations. In 1961 David advanced to president when George Champion vacated that position to succeed John J. McCloy as chairman, but such was David's importance within the bank that he and Champion divided the leadership responsibilities and were regarded as "co-chief executive officers." In actuality, Champion held the title of CEO, but David was chairman of the executive committee of the board. Champion was eleven years David's senior, and he was highly experienced in such traditional banking areas as corporate lending and government securities. In contrast, David's strengths were in nontraditional areas, such as management, sales, and strategic planning, in addition to his high visibility in international banking. All of these represented important needs as American banking changed significantly in line with postwar demands and the great banks expanded and modernized to meet the opportunities afforded by enormous economic growth at home and unprecedented American responsibilities around the globe.

The dynamic tension and divided authority between Champion and David did not work well in the end. Each stressed a different area of banking. Chase, consequently, did not choose a definite course. As a result, despite spectacular growth in the 1960s—by the end of the decade the bank had 25,000 employees, 800,000 shareholders, $21 billion in deposits, $35 billion in assets—Chase was not as well-positioned as its principal competitor, Citibank, to deal with the tumultuous 1970s.

David had been the leader of the rejuvenation of Lower Manhattan's financial district, with the turning point being the decision he urged for the Chase to build a new $140 million headquarters building there. He was also a leader in urban renewal for the Morningside Heights area. He served as chairman of the Rockefeller Institute for Medical Research and presided over its conversion to Rockefeller University. A major collector of modern art, he created the Business Committee for the Arts in 1966 to promote corporate patronage. A champion of racial justice, he helped bring the Urban Coalition into existence after the 1966 and 1967 urban riots. David was also a major real estate developer, playing a leading role in such projects as L'Enfant Plaza in Washington, the Embarcadero Center in San Francisco, and Interstate North in Atlanta.

But it was as a businessman, economist, banker, inveterate globetrotter, and spokesman for the private enterprise system that David became the most famous. He always seemed to be in motion, making his well-staffed and publicized visits to financial leaders and heads of state all over the world. His credits in international affairs were numerous—comfortable in two foreign languages (German and Spanish) and fluent in French, chairman of the prestigious Council on Foreign Relations, a founder of the International Executive Service Corps in 1964 (the so-called "paunch corps"), participation in the high level and secretive Bilderberg Meeting every year, cosponsorship of the annual Dartmouth Conference (of U.S. and Soviet citizens), and participation in a series of official U.S. commissions and committees dealing with aspects of foreign affairs, world trade, and the domestic economy.

Unlike his brother John, who had a close identification with Asia, David Rockefeller regarded the whole world as his oyster. But he felt a special kinship with Latin America, the area in which he began his own work in international banking. This led him to create the Center for Inter-American Relations as the base for the Council of the Americas (now known as the Americas Society) and a number of smaller multilateral organizations.

It was during the bank's great growth period of the 1960s that David's reputation was established as the premier American banker and spokesman for capitalism. Particularly as Nelson seemed to falter with his divorce and remarriage, David was seen in some circles as the most powerful and influential of the Rockefellers. Writing in 1977, Warren Moscow said: "In the financial community, he is one of a handful at the very pinnacle. . . . In a list of world leaders, he is always there. Some pointed to him as the most powerful and influential man in America outside of the man in the White House."[25] A standard joke for a time was that for David Rockefeller to be President of the United States would be a demotion.

Through it all, David remained genial and unflappable, still a bit pudgy, always ready with a friendly greeting in his thin, reedy voice. He had no special relationship with any one of his brothers, but was equally cordial to all, and for a time in later years this cast him in the role of trying to ameliorate disputes between the Nelson-Laurance duo and JDR. For JDR there was somewhat more interaction through the years with David than with Laurance. One factor was that David's wife, Peggy, was one of the relatively few family members who seemed to understand JDR and appreciate what he was trying to do, especially in the population field, and she had great respect for him.

Another factor was the mutual interest JDR and David had in international affairs. JDR's prominence in Asia was an asset to his brother on occasions when David would entertain financial leaders from Asia at Pocantico. JDR and Blanchette were guests every fall at a luncheon David would give at the Playhouse for members of the World Bank and International Monetary Fund. On one occasion JDR had a delegation from Afghanistan to lunch at Fieldwood Farm. He wrote: "After lunch took the Prime Minister over to meet brother David at his home as Afghanistan is having negotiations with the Chase Bank."

After moving to Arkansas in 1953, Winthrop had thrown himself into his first big project, the building of Winrock Farms atop Petit Jean Mountain, sixty miles northwest of Little Rock, with a commanding view of the Arkansas River and the surrounding countryside. It was a breeding farm for Santa Gertrudis cattle, the best equipped and most modern one imaginable, a showplace in poverty-stricken Arkansas.

Win soon turned his attention to the problems of his adopted state, setting up the Winthrop Rockefeller Foundation and siphoning a share of RBF grants to a range of needs in Arkansas in such fields as the arts, medical care, education, and rural development. Orval Faubus, who started his string of six two-year terms as governor of the state in 1954, appointed Win as chairman of the newly formed Arkansas Industrial Development Commission in 1955, and Win's energetic and successful performance in this role "changed the face of Arkansas for all time," in the words of his biographer.[26] It also made him visible throughout the state. His big frame and gregarious nature were not what Arkansans expected in a Rockefeller, and these attributes and his generosity made him a popular figure. As columnist Doris Fleeson noted, he was widely regarded as "better for Arkansas than 20 years of good cotton crops."[27]

In 1956 Win married for the second time, to Jeanette Edris, daughter of a wealthy Seattle industrialist and theater owner. Like Win, Jeanette had a difficult earlier life, having had three prior husbands. She and Win came together as veterans and equals, and were good for each other for a time. Her two children by her second husband, Bruce and Anne Bartley, lived happily at Winrock Farms. Win's only child, Winthrop Paul, had been born in 1948 and had spent his growing years mainly with his mother, becoming something of a jet-setter. In the late 1960s he began spending more time at Winrock Farms. Once past the age of twenty-one, he declared his intention to settle down there, and was warmly received by his father.

In addition to different interests, the physical distance that Win had put between himself and the rest of the family tended to limit interaction. The warmest relationship was probably between Win and John. He and Blanchette went out for a weekend visit in 1962, taking a scheduled flight to Memphis "where Win's Beechcraft met us and took us to the airstrip near his farm on Petit Jean Mountain. Win and Jeanette met us in my family's old 1916 Crane Simplex, which was really quite intriguing." They then spent so much time inspecting the farm and Win's projects around the state that JDR said his only regret was that he and Win did not have much time to talk together.

Win inevitably was drawn into politics in Arkansas. He strongly opposed Faubus's racist posture in the 1957 Little Rock school integration crisis, but he absented himself from the state in order to avoid the appearance of fanning the flames of controversy. Win refused to declare himself a Democrat, which would have been the most direct route to office in solidly Democratic Arkansas. Apart from adhering to family tradition and his own predilections, he believed that building up the minuscule Republican Party was at least as important as any office he could win. By 1964 he was ready to take on Faubus. In March he was in New York and had lunch with JDR at the University Club. JDR wrote of Win: "He has lost 35 pounds since I last saw him and seems to have his own personal situation well in hand, which is much to his credit. It would appear that he is very seriously thinking of running for governor of Arkansas."

Despite his hearty nature, Win was somewhat shy and enjoyed his privacy. The "personal situation" JDR referred to was Win's drinking problem. Since he was a true alcoholic, it never left him, and he was known to slip backward on occasion. For a man with these inhibiting characteristics, he must have been powerfully motivated to take on all the problems that came with public life. Win's biographer speculates about several possible reasons, and on one of them quotes Harry Ashmore (then the noted editor of the *Arkansas Gazette*): "[Win's] brother Nelson was doubtless his model, and symbolic goad."[28] It was too late to prove anything to Junior, who had never accepted an invitation to visit Winrock Farms. But it is likely that Win wanted to be governor not only to help the people of Arkansas and create a two-party system but also to prove to the rest of his family that he was not a "black sheep," that he could accomplish important objectives on his own and be recognized for them outside the family orbit.

Win lost to Faubus in 1964. In March 1966 he was in New York again and came to see JDR at the latter's request for a "nice talk" about his "problems and plans for the future," as JDR put it. "He seemed generally in good shape and on top of his situation. He appeared to have some question as to whether he really wanted to be Governor of Arkansas, but at the same time was going ahead full speed to win the next election."

This time he won by 55,000 votes, an astounding plurality under the circumstances, becoming the first Republican governor of Arkansas in ninety-four years. Even Win appeared staggered by what had happened. Two weeks after the election he visited New York, and JDR wrote:

Stopped in to see Win at his apartment at One East End Avenue. He is having a bit of a letdown after his campaign and we felt needed a bit of family backing and encouragement in terms of the future. His New York doctor came in while I was there and we had a positive talk together, Win being aware of his problems and his need to face up to them particularly now that he is in the national spotlight.

JDR was a loyal supporter. He contributed $110,000 to Win's several campaigns, a considerable amount in a state where campaigning was much less costly than in New York. And he and Blanchette attended the inauguration in January 1967. The other brothers had prior commitments, Nelson of course for his own inauguration for a third term, so JDR was the only brother to make the trip to Little Rock. By all accounts, Win performed heroically for the people of Arkansas, modernizing state government and reforming or innovating numerous services. This was an uphill struggle all the way, against the arch conservatives who formed the backbone of his own party and the Democratic conservatives who controlled the state legislature. In 1968 Win won reelection handily, and once again JDR was the only brother to attend the inauguration.

In 1970 Win yielded to the pleas of his followers and decided to attempt a third term. He was tired and already ill with the cancer that would kill him. Orval Faubus tried a comeback, but was defeated in the Democratic primary by Dale Bumpers, an attractive young liberal who in turn defeated Win in the gubernatorial election. Unquestionably, it had been Win's reforms that made it possible for a man like Bumpers to become prominent in Arkansas politics.

As for Win, he also lost Jeanette, who had tired of public life and divorced him. But Win's last years, until his death of cancer in early 1973, were cheered by the presence of young Win and his bride at Winrock Farms.

The most complex relationship among the Rockefeller brothers was that between JDR and Nelson. As noted, they were so unalike in so many ways that the fact that they were blood brothers almost strains credulity. They had been genuinely affectionate toward one another back in the early days when each served as best man at the other's wedding and presented a united front to Junior in the family office. But even back then the characteristics of each that would irritate the other were evident. As their paths diverged and the years passed, their relationship seemed fine externally with each properly appreciative of the accomplishments of the other, but the deeper irritations also developed and came more and more to the surface.

For Nelson it was the feeling that he should be the head of the family in fact as he so often was in practice, as the one who had been the favorite of the parents, who had the energy and talent, who had become famous, and who so often took the initiative in family matters. But blocking his way was an older brother who, in Nelson's view, lacked all of these attributes and who had the *name* and a prior claim on family institutions only because he happened to have been born first, not because he deserved it. Nelson did not like having to be a supplicant to this older brother in such matters as asking for the RBF chairmanship.

For his part, JDR often found Nelson to be impetuous, so sure of himself as to seem smug, a man with an overly large ego who had developed an irritating habit of command from his years in high office. JDR was a highly controlled person so that he was rarely known to lose his temper. But Blanchette remembers one occasion when he "hit the roof" over an action by Nelson. It was the kind of project in which Nelson seemed to "bathe himself," Blanchette recalled, once he got going on it, and the incident was made worse for JDR by the fact that Nelson had enlisted Blanchette's aid in it. He wanted to redo the Japanese garden and to renovate the superb teahouse his father had built in 1913 on the hill just below Kykuit. The result was a beautiful and authentically Japanese structure perched on the shore of a tiny lake that overlooked carefully manicured trees and shrubs and immaculately tended gravel paths. The spot has the serenity of a Japanese temple or Hiroshige print. It also cost a lot of money, which Nelson attempted to apportion among his brothers without prior consultation.

What is surprising about JDR and Nelson is not that there was occasional friction between them but that they got along as well as they did for so many years. This was no doubt helped by the fact that they were not in proximity to one another during Nelson's long tenure in Albany. JDR often would shake his head in amazement over Nelson's undoubted talents and accomplishments. At the same time, many of JDR's projects began to become manifestly important and successful during the 1960s, and Nelson was genuinely impressed.

It was not until very late in life for both men that they came sharply into conflict, a time when the generation of the "Cousins" became important in family councils and the surviving four brothers were torn by the effects of the "generation gap" and several extraordinarily difficult family issues they were trying to resolve.

14

☙

FAMILY AFFAIRS:
THE INNER CIRCLE

IN MANY WAYS, life for the family of John and Blanchette Rockefeller was much like it was for countless other American families in postwar decades—the Rockefellers were by no means immune to the changes affecting family and social life generally during these years. By and large, John and Blanchette had the same cares and concerns and confusions that other parents did. In other respects, of course, the famous name, wealth, and position made for some decided differences.

JDR was perhaps even more frugal and practical than his father had been. His family lived well and he always insisted on quality, but he avoided any ostentatious display. Family vacations in private railroad cars, of course, were very much a thing of the past. A diary note in the summer of 1965 described the modern way of transporting the family:

Blanchette, Alida, and her friend Cynthia Saltzman, Sigried, Margo, and Lyka, our German Shepherd puppy, left for Maine in our already over-loaded station wagon at 5:30 A.M. We had extra springs put in the car so everything worked out well indeed. We reached Rockland an hour ahead of the 3:30 ferry which was good time under the circumstances.[1]

The driver of the station wagon was JDR himself. As the diary entry suggests, he was not a man who wanted to waste any time on the road. The destination was Millstream Cottage, a summer home on North Haven Island, which the Rockefellers had purchased from four members of the Lamont family in 1955 for $20,000. It was a comfortable, two-story house with seven bedrooms, but still a far cry from Junior's huge place at Seal Harbor, some thirty miles up the Maine coast.

A slow decline in churchgoing was another sign of changing times that the Rockefellers shared with other families. Like many people of strict religious upbringing, JDR began to question the efficacy of organized, formal religion, once he was free of family strictures himself. However, like most parents, he and Blanchette thought it was important for their children to go to church regularly, so for years the family dutifully attended the Riverside Church when in Manhattan and the Pocantico Hills Union Church when at Fieldwood Farm.

Then the family began to lag. JDR would be the first one in the car on a Sunday morning, fuming, waiting for the others to straggle out. Soon he got to be the hardest one of all to get to church. The family decided to go to church two Sundays a month, then it became a matter of *which* Sunday, and finally it was everyone on their own. For JDR, Sunday became the time for reading the *New York Times*, watching "Meet the Press" and other news interview programs (about the only television shows he ever watched), and perhaps taking his children to a movie. Generally, these were movies of a serious or uplifting quality, or war movies. Just as he loved war books, JDR was fond of war movies.

The parents were "Mummy" and "Daddy" to their children for many years. Jay never changed the terms, but Sandra did, and she remembers "the almost hurt look" on her father's face when she began calling him "Father."[2] In one important respect, the home was very much like other homes: Daddy worked hard at his office and traveled a lot; Mummy sometimes traveled with him, but frequently stayed home to take care of the children.

As parents, John and Blanchette were eerily reminiscent of his parents, Junior and Abby. Like his father, JDR was excessively serious, earnest, stiff, somewhat formal. He had a sense of humor, but he was so burdened with serious concerns and so quiet a person that most of the time he was scarcely noticeable. To his friend and art adviser Sherman Lee, the most memorable note about JDR was the way that "serious reticence could be punctured by an appeal to dry wit." There would be "discussion, argument, persuasion, counter-argument," and then for JDR "a leaning forward, an extended hand, sometimes a touch, a quizzical beneath-the-eyebrows look, with a wry remark embodying either triumph or capitulation."[3]

The children remember how rarely their father laughed out loud. On the rare occasions when he did so, they were so excited and happy that they laughed all the harder. More often, as Jay recalled it, JDR would sit through an entire meal with his family and never say a word.

In marked contrast, Blanchette was lively and outgoing, much as Abby had been. Her husband was highly controlled, but her emotions were much nearer the surface—she could be "eruptive" at times, as one of her children expressed it, or she could easily see the humorous side of something. These natural tendencies were accentuated on occasion because of the vacuum left by her husband's lack of expressiveness.

Because Blanchette was lively and responsive, the children naturally gravitated to her; whole conversations could occur at supper as if the father were not present at all.

JDR sometimes was jealous of the way the children flocked to Blanchette, and he sought equal time. However, this often would take the form of solemn meetings in the library—at both One Beekman and Fieldwood Farm, the library was the father's sanctum. The children would file in one by one for a discussion. Their father would have a lined yellow pad in his lap with the notes he had made for the discussion. He was always organized and prepared. This allowed little room for the natural spontaneity or the lively imagination of a child, so that memories of the discussions were mostly somber ones.

It was not that JDR was harsh or cruel or lost his temper very often. He was gentle, and he tried hard to be supportive. The children never doubted that he loved them. Yet Sandra always felt the "Rockefeller anger and aggression" were there below the surface.

To a rebellious child, JDR would talk about how *he* had coped as a child. "You can either spiral up or you can spiral down," he would say. If a child was having a problem figuring out how to deal with other people, JDR would explain how they would have to take the lead and put other people at ease because "we are Rockefellers."

There was, of course, the all-important subject of learning how to handle money and to see the family wealth as a trust to be used responsibly instead of in a self-indulgent way. Each child had three little white boxes for apportioning allowances to savings, giving, and spending. JDR started out with the intention of being as rigorous as Junior had been with him, but, in Blanchette's words, it "sort of petered out." He sometimes would forget to give the children their allowances. Blanchette would upbraid them when their spending went off in the wrong direction. Blanchette thinks that her husband had perhaps "an overdose" of this sort of training in his own youth and was subconsciously reacting against it. In the beginning there were account books of the kind that had been so important to Junior and Senior, but they soon "faded out," according to Jay. But JDR worried the subject earnestly for a time, to the point of having lengthy discussions in the office with a staff aide about the possibility of writing a slim book with a modernized version of Junior's precepts for teaching children to handle money responsibly.[4] JDR had no problem with Junior's goals—he lived them out every day himself. But there might be a better way to help children achieve them.

For training in charitable giving, JDR would use the *New York Times*'s "100 Neediest Cases." He would convene the children in the library and read the cases aloud so that each child could pick a few. Alida remembers agonizing so much that she sent her contribution in with a letter asking the *Times* to give it to the family that needed it the most.

The father may have been silent much of the time, but, as Jay put it, he was "very much a presence or force in the household—he'd pick his moments to intervene." Sandra remembers the feeling that her father was constantly suppressing emotions, that he was "a powerful person," very controlled and methodical. All of the children felt that their father provided a safe and reliable context for the family, that "you could count on his integrity and values," as one of them expressed it. But there wasn't much warmth. For that, they turned to their mother. Small wonder that each of them treasures in memory the less formal moments with their father— going to the movies with him on Sunday afternoon, taking a walk to observe the progress in construction of the UN building not far from One Beekman, horseback riding or chopping wood up in the country (his two favorite ways to be outdoors and exercise).

The parents experienced the common feeling of suddenly becoming aware that time was passing by quickly. The children were growing up rapidly. The youngest, Alida, was born in 1949, eleven years after the birth of the next youngest, Hope. "We were elderly parents," Blanchette said, "but Alida helped keep us more understanding of young people." In 1959 JDR attended the thirtieth anniversary of his Princeton graduating class. "Was really glad I went," he wrote in his diary. "It was a pleasure to have a chance to meet again with some of my classmates after 30 years. On the whole it was quite a responsible and impressive group." In 1962 came the thirtieth wedding anniversary of John and Blanchette. "Really quite amazing!" he told his diary.

Blanchette continued to play the role of a "good Rockefeller wife," which meant that she was not unlike other wives of her generation— supportive of her husband's career, subordinating herself to the extent necessary, and taking care of the home and the children as a first priority. The comment of Jay's future wife, Sharon, on the phenomenon of marrying into a famous family is apt: "When you marry a Rockefeller you are an in-law, but you often feel like an outlaw."

It was expected, of course, that Blanchette would find ways to be of service to society that would be consistent with her fundamental duties.

Like her mother, she had the energy, intelligence, and administrative ability to be very good at this. For a time, her interests were absorbed by the social work she was engaged in at the time of her marriage, but then she followed her natural interest and the lead of her mother-in-law and brother-in-law Nelson by becoming active with the Museum of Modern Art. JDR was just as puzzled at this as Junior had been by Abby's great interest in modern art, which was instrumental in the creation of MOMA and the building of the museum on West 53th Street on property formerly owned by the Rockefellers.

Blanchette's career with MOMA began at the end of the war. In 1948 Nelson challenged her to create and lead a Junior Council, which she did very successfully. She became a hard-working trustee, serving on the executive committee, the collections committee, and the exhibitions committee. Then in 1956 she took on another tough assignment, the chairmanship of the International Council, the latest incarnation of a MOMA function that could be traced back to 1939 and the "Department of Circulating Exhibitions." The original purpose was to proselytize—modern art came as a shock to many people, and it often took considerable time and exposure for them to become educated. In Blanchette's time, the revamped International Council was also structured as a means of involving well-to-do patrons, both here and abroad, in the doings of MOMA, at the dues of $1,000 per year. Only a few years later, in 1959, Blanchette was tapped for another role, as Russell Lynes explained in his book on MOMA:

At the urging of her brothers-in-law, Nelson and David, and somewhat to the dismay of her husband, who was up to his eyes in the affairs of the new Lincoln Center and wished her at his side, Mrs. John D. Rockefeller 3rd let herself be elected President of the Museum. She could scarcely decline. The Museum had since the beginning been a Rockefeller responsibility, a protectorate, one might also say . . . in a sense [the Rockefellers] groomed John's wife to assume a somewhat matriarchal position in the Museum much like that once occupied by her mother-in-law. Not, to be sure, that she was the sort of woman who could be manipulated against her will, but when she became a Rockefeller she was quite aware that she was assuming a role with very stringent demands, a public aspect that was inescapable, a private aspect that was clannish, and she had shared "the boys' " admiration and affection for their mother.[5]

Lynes presents a good portrait of Blanchette in his book. He quotes Aline Saarinen's description of her as "a cool, pale beauty with a regally poised head." A view attributed to an unnamed curator has been oft-quoted, perhaps because it is so apt: "If there is ever a natural aristocracy—I don't mean an aristocracy of money but of pure quality—she would be my candidate for the queen." Something about Blanchette brings out these images of royalty, but one should quickly add that in person she is gracious and charming with a fine sense of humor and without any hint of being overbearing or pretentious. As Lynes puts it:

She has a quiet voice which has assurance without insistence and an easy but not casual manner. When you have her attention, you have her full attention, and she speaks with what for her is frankness, though she is used to being careful of what she says. . . . When those who have worked with her and for her speak of her, it is almost always with extravagence—a combination of respect and admiration, far more tinged with affection than with awe.[6]

In part, Blanchette's value to MOMA stemmed from the depth of her commitment to modern art and the institution. When she first affiliated with MOMA she became an active student and collector of modern art herself, and she created her own unique institution, a "guest house," as an expression of her commitment. The idea came to her when she realized she would have to find a place to house the objects of modern art she had started to acquire with the benefit of advice from some of the experts at MOMA. She ordered a Marino Marini bronze sculpture of a man on a horse from Italy and when it arrived at One Beekman Place, with the nose of the horse sticking through the door, she was astonished to see how large it was. Clearly, it could not fit in the apartment, and her husband in any case was rebelling. He did not want modern art in his home, and Blanchette agreed that it would not go very well with their traditional furnishings. One of her art advisers, Philip Johnson, who then was on the architectural staff at MOMA, suggested that she build a place that could be used for out-of-town guests and for housing her art. He said he would design it for her. This was in 1947 and Johnson did not yet have an architectural license, but he could work through a friend. It was the first commission received by Johnson, who was to become world-famous as an architect in the ensuing years.

A lot where a brownstone had been torn down was found at 252 East 52nd Street, not very far from One Beekman. Blanchette had a small trust fund from her father's estate. It was this that gave her the wherewithal to purchase modern art and build her guest house. Before going ahead with the idea, Blanchette consulted with her husband's mother, Abby. It is clear that Abby was especially fond of this particular daughter-in-law and thought that her eldest son had married very well. Abby warmly endorsed the idea of the guest house. She said that a wife needed space of her own, and pointed out that she had had the same problem with her husband that Blanchette was having with hers. Junior would not allow modern art throughout the household, and the solution was for Abby to create her own private gallery on the sixth floor of the family home at 10 West 54th Street. Since there was no such room at One Beekman, the guest-house idea was a perfect solution for Blanchette.

The project went forward and the guest house was built. "It was as impeccably modern on the inside in Johnson's spare manner," Lynes wrote, "as it was impeccably unostentatious on the outside. . . . The guest house became an informal arm of the Museum. It was there that small parties were held and committees of trustees and staff frequently met."[7]

JDR even came to some functions at the guest house, and on one occasion Blanchette succeeded in persuading him and the children to stay there overnight. But over the years he became increasingly nettled by the guest house and the amount of Blanchette's time that it took. He complained that she was "running two households." Blanchette reluctantly agreed. She had enjoyed the experience thoroughly, but it was becoming too much, and now it was time to give it up. She already had begun giving some of her art pieces to MOMA. The problem now was to dispose of the guest house. The obvious solution was to give it to MOMA, but Blanchette's finances had been depleted and she could not afford to pay the gift tax. JDR "bailed out" Blanchette by buying the guest house from her in 1959, giving it to MOMA, and paying the gift tax. This plus other gifts, including a major one at the time of MOMA's twenty-fifth-anniversary fund drive, yielded a lifetime total of $760,812 that JDR gave to MOMA—not bad for a man who disliked modern art.[8]

It was perhaps as a "tradeoff" for giving up the guest house that JDR acquiesced in Blanchette's becoming president of MOMA in 1959. Despite her heavy involvement with the Museum and JDR's concern, Blanchette continued to play her role as a Rockefeller wife very well. She did not spread herself thin—MOMA was her only major activity. She enjoyed the work, the stimulation, and such activities as the annual trip she made for the International Council. The demands of being a wife and mother did cause her to withdraw from the MOMA presidency in 1964, but she returned to that office again in 1972.

It was obvious that Blanchette was an unusually accomplished person, and that JDR indeed had married well, as had his father and grandfather before him. But nothing makes Blanchette quite so angry as any suggestion that she was really the power or the intellect behind her husband. His strong principles, his good instincts, and his perseverance were all very much his own, she stresses. She played a supportive role. He sometimes would seek her counsel, but he was totally in charge of his own decisions and life.

Again, the marriage of John and Blanchette was like that of many other couples in that it had its high points and low points. There was strain and tension stemming from their very different personalities, the burden of expectations that he carried, and his nearly total concentration on his work. Blanchette understood the importance of the population field intellectually, but never could develop the deep emotional commitment to it that her husband had. And she was not happy when he worked on such related fields as abortion and human sexuality. As noted, he had no interest in modern art and tended to be jealous of the time she committed to MOMA. They were very much together in their interest in Japan, the arts generally, and Lincoln Center. But she could never be as unrelentingly serious as her husband. Once, on the first trip to Asia, she and Don McLean got into a giggling fit when visiting an Indian ashram, to the stern disapproval of JDR, who was taking it all quite seriously.

They each seemed to have a physical manifestation of underlying tension. With Blanchette it was headaches so painful and persistent that they could knock her out for days or even weeks. There seemed to be no predictable pattern for when these attacks would occur. Once a much anticipated trip to Europe and the Soviet Union was ruined for her by her headaches. Ordinarily, Johnny, as she called her husband, was sympathetic, as his diary entry over the Christmas holidays of 1967 shows:

[Blanchette] really has been miserable since last Thursday with persistent and debilitating headaches. As always she is a good sport about it, but this time felt she had no choice but to stay in bed. She did hate to miss the family Christmas party after having worked so hard in planning things for everybody.

For JDR, the recurring disability throughout his life was laryngitis, which also seemed to strike in a random way. It did not seem related, for example, to appearing in public—he frequently made major speeches to very large audiences and was forced to cancel because of laryngitis only on a few occasions. There was some irony in this for him because the only cure was a few days' rest at home, where he was usually a silent person anyway, as against the office where he would talk a great deal in meetings and in dictating and telephoning. The enforced rest usually restored his thin voice to normal functioning without much delay, but on one occasion in 1965 he wrote glumly in his diary that the condition was just as bad on the tenth day as it had been on the first.

Social life for the Rockefellers necessarily revolved around their Asian interests and New York cultural affairs, especially Lincoln Center. They were the kind of people who would have the king and queen of Thailand as weekend guests at Fieldwood Farm, *en famille*. Little time was available for anything but these interest-related social occasions. There was the occasional chic dinner party, as for example one given by the John Gunthers, who invited John and Blanchette along with Jackie Kennedy, Adlai Stevenson, the John Kenneth Galbraiths, and the Leonard Bernsteins. And there were the occasional White House invitations. JDR wrote about one in 1964 for the visiting president of the Philippines:

I really enjoy very much our occasional White House functions. Since President Kennedy, the seating has been on a small table basis, which does make it more informal. This time there were so many guests that some, including myself, were in a smaller adjoining room. However, was reassured when I found Mrs. Johnson and President Macapagal there also.

Once in a while John and Blanchette would try to break out of their routine by having a dinner party for people with whom they had no functional or interest-based relationship, a dinner party "to develop new friends," as JDR once expressed it. But these occasions never seemed to have any lasting significance. Blanchette had Tod and other intimate friends, but her husband was too reserved and formal to have close friends. He was completely unlike Nelson or Winthrop in that he never surrounded himself with cronies with whom he could totally relax and be himself. There were many men he saw frequently and admired, men such as John Gardner, Bill Moyers, Frank Stanton, Sherman Lee, Phillips Talbot. These men and many others were certainly friends but not close and intimate ones. The only two nonfamily members invited to John and Blanchette's fortieth-anniversary dinner party were Gardner and Lee.

In this regard, JDR and his father were very much alike. JDR also was like his father in learning that he could relax and enjoy himself in the company of women friends in a way that he could not with men. Junior discovered this early in life when he realized that his sisters shared his values and problems vis-à-vis the outside world and that he therefore could be frank with them and trust them. He rediscovered this late in life after Abby was gone, finding solace in the company of Tod and Blanchette and several of his granddaughters—Sandra, for example, was his guest at Seal Harbor for two weeks one summer. Then his marriage to Martha solved his problem of companionship.

The outlet of spending time with women friends began for JDR in the late 1960s, a time when he was beginning to become somewhat more relaxed generally. He came to believe, for example, in the changed attitudes grouped under the heading of "women's lib" and in some of the values emerging in the so-called youth revolution of the time—including the view that it is foolish to allow conventional barriers to prevent a man from having good friendships with women and vice versa.[9]

JDR's near-romances of his youth had all faded long ago. He ran into his sweetheart and pen-pal of prep school days, the former Catherine Robb, when visiting Alida at her prep school, the Concord Academy, located in the hometown of Catherine's parents. It was worth only a bare diary mention. His Vassar friend of League of Nations days in Geneva, the former Elizabeth "Pete" Peterson, continued to correspond for a number of years, but it was all a thing of the past. The person of whom he had been most fond, his cousin Faith, died in 1960 at the age of fifty-one. Her husband, Jean Model, had died five years earlier at the age of forty.

JDR's friendships with women late in life were not unlike those of his youth, in the sense that they were "safe" for one reason or another. He took a great interest in the next generation of Rockefellers, the "Cousins," making it his business to spend time with one or another of them whenever an opportunity arose. Two-thirds of the Cousins were women. The only male among them with whom JDR established a close relationship was Nelson's second son, Steven, who had a philosophical turn of mind and became a faculty member at Middlebury College in Vermont after studying at the Union Theological Seminary and Columbia. But JDR met on occasion, often for lunch, with such other Cousins as two of Laurance's daughters, Laura and Marion, and two of David's daughters, Neva and Peggy, and his diary contains warm references to them.

Much of JDR's time spent with women was in his self-appointed role as counselor to a friend who had undergone some trauma such as a bad divorce, the death of a husband, or another death in the family. In some cases the friends were professional women whose accomplishments JDR admired. In one case, the friend was one of JDR's own cousins.

All of this quite naturally gave Blanchette considerable pause for a time. It was not easy to accept a husband who tended to be quiet and remote at home, wanted her to stay in her place, and yet could go off for a pleasant luncheon with one of his women friends, or even off to visit one of them on the West Coast or in Maine. JDR was not secretive about it, but this had the effect of being thoughtless about Blanchette's feelings at times. However, the very fact that he was not secretive about his friendships—plus the fact that he was into his sixties when most of them began—suggested that these were not marriage-threatening liaisons, but were what they purported to be, simply friendships. Blanchette also could recall from personal experience how important friendships with women had been to Junior during his period of loneliness after Abby's death. For all of these reasons, Blanchette relaxed in the end, too; that was the way her husband was, and that was that. It was helpful that JDR's agreement with values associated with "women's lib" brought on a measure of regret over having suppressed Blanchette's outside interests earlier. He was supportive when she resumed the presidency of MOMA in 1972, and he spoke admiringly of her accomplishments there to others.

JDR's nature did not make family life uniformly dour any more than Junior's had in his household. There was Blanchette's outgoing personality, for one thing, and Jay grew up with a lively nature very much like his mother's. The house was sometimes filled with friends of the children, and there were the vacations, which were pleasant times. JDR's regular annual pattern remained fixed for years—three weeks in the summer in Maine, a week in the winter at the Dorado Beach, and a week at Bassett Hall in the spring and another one in the fall, over Thanksgiving. Of Millstream Cottage in Maine, JDR wrote: "We do like our little house . . . it is an ideal size, although even with the guest house may seem somewhat small when married children and families come to visit as they may want to do later on. We do have fun also working around the house on the small piece of property which is ours."

After Junior's death, in the summer of 1960, John and Blanchette interrupted their stay at Millstream Cottage for a poignant trip to the Eyrie in Seal Harbor. Nelson and David had decided to tear down the huge old house rather than trying to maintain it—each already had his own summer home nearby. And the family was gathering there for the first time since summer days of long ago—for a last look and to choose from among the furnishings and art objects.

The sentimentality of the occasion was directed more to the mother of the Rockefeller boys than to their father, for it was Abby who had dominated the decor of the Eyrie through her great love of Oriental art. She was known for her love of modern art and also for her collection of American folk art at Williamsburg; less known was the fact that she had been a steadfast collector of Oriental objects throughout her adult life. She purchased many Japanese prints by the great masters—among them Hiroshige, Utemaro, and Toyohiro—as well as many porcelain figurines, services of the Kakaemon, Kutani, and Imari styles, and other examples of the decorative arts. Most of these objects were brought to the Eyrie, which, as a result, was decorated almost completely in an Asian motif.

Two areas of note were the "Buddha" room, containing a number of exquisite bodhisattvas, and Abby's sculpture garden. To elements of an English formal garden, she added carefully selected Asian sculpture—Chinese votive steles and shrines, Japanese snow lanterns and stone figures, and large Korean tomb figures flanking a spirit path leading to a Buddhist shrine.

JDR described the last visit to the Eyrie:

The purpose of our trip to Seal Harbor was to participate in the distribution of the contents of the family's house which had been left by Mother to her six children with a life interest to Father. The first two days we spent looking at the many lovely objects, a high proportion of which were Oriental, deciding which ones we would like to choose under our rotating selection plan. . . . It was difficult in two days to really do justice to the collection. . . .

The system really works out very well with a minimum of friction. . . . Blanchette and I got many beautiful things but, of course, missed many others that appealed to us, as under the system each member of the family only has one choice out of every six. Fortunately, there were many items in each category so we all came out very well.

The Nelsons and Davids were very hospitable as the two members of the family living in Seal Harbor. We had meals with each of them. . . . We had a brothers' meeting at Nelson's.

It was good to see the family's house again before all the contents are removed. All of us grew up there as far as our summers are concerned and hence have many memories of the place. We had a professional photographer come and take pictures, which will be good to have for the future.

Hopie and John [Spencer] came up for the weekend as we wanted them to see the house before it was torn apart. Unfortunately, however, we could not spend much time with them. I took them around the house and then out into Mother's garden, which really looked as beautiful as ever. I think they were glad that they came.

Back at Millstream Cottage, JDR commented that the rest of the vacation

worked out very nicely. Alida enjoys the sailing very much, so we went out several times. Also I played a bit of golf, including some practice. The days somehow went by fast, even though we did not do very much. I really enjoyed just puttering around the grounds and reading on the porch. Actually I did quite a bit of telephoning in connection with Lincoln Center matters.

Bassett Hall, in the center of the restored area of Colonial Williamsburg, always provided a pleasant interlude as well. JDR described the ambiance in 1964 when Alida came down from Concord to join him and Blanchette over Thanksgiving week:

It was good to have her with us and she seemed to enjoy being on her own a bit after the constant companionship of boarding school life. . . . Blanchette and I had a leisurely time during the week and enjoyed our stay. . . . I rode a number of days, which I enjoy very much, and am grateful to the Restoration for loaning me one of their horses. Also Alida and I rode together a couple of times. Blanchette and I played golf twice, which was fun although my game is still at a rather low ebb.

Our Bassett Hall set-up is really very appealing. The house is most attractive, the garden is lovely, and the back woods provide an area where one can walk or ride without being interrupted. As a matter of fact, the whole property is very private and provides a retreat which is meaningful after the busy life of New York. Having Colonial Williamsburg assume general responsibility for the property on my behalf is of course a great help. It is in their interest, as my holding of the property is a protection for the restored area and I am sure they hope eventually to get it.

An interesting note in JDR's diary, during the Thanksgiving 1967 visit, records a report by Carlisle Humelsine, the president of Colonial Williamsburg, about what happened when President Lyndon B. Johnson and his family stayed at Bassett Hall:

We had the Humelsines for lunch and they told us about President Johnson's visit to Williamsburg for the Gridiron Club. The question had come up as to his spending the night and the problem was where. Mr. Humelsine suggested Bassett Hall, and of course we were pleased to cooperate. Along with the President were Mrs. Johnson and Lynda Bird and her fiancé, Capt. Charles S. Robb. It seems that they really enjoyed the place, staying on all of the following day. The only problem, from our point of view, was that changes had to be made in terms of tearing out our security system and putting in a rather massive telephone hookup, not to mention changes in furniture to make the President more comfortable. However, everything has now been put back as before, with only one small porcelain bird as a casualty.

As the years passed, JDR became much less remote and formal with his children. As noted, he was easing his own rigidity in general, but there was also a simple and specific reason: his children were growing up. He could interact with them as adults instead of infants. To him, small children were another species entirely, one he could never relate to satisfactorily. In the years ahead he would derive much pleasure from coming to know his adult children better than he ever had before.

15

✠

FAMILY AFFAIRS:
THE CHILDREN

THE CLOSER RELATIONSHIP between JDR and his children as adults was not the result of proximity—none of the children lived with the parents after college. Sandra moved to the Boston area, choosing a very private life-style, and Hope was the first of the children to marry and live with her own family. Jay lived where he worked—first in Washington and then West Virginia—and Alida lived in California for a number of years after college.

All three of the girls went to Brearley. Sandra followed in her mother's footsteps by going on to Vassar, but Blanchette thought it might be better if her daughters went to different colleges so she influenced Hope to go to Smith. Like her mother, Sandra was interested in music while at school, but gravitated to art afterward. For several summers she went to the Norfolk music school in Connecticut. With a mother long devoted to the piano, all of the children were musically inclined. Sandra remembers Jay playing the slow movement of the "Moonlight Sonata" beautifully, but giving up when he came to the fast movement.

The only time the life of one of the children was seriously threatened by illness was when Sandra had a mastoid operation as a child. She nearly died, and she believes the pain of that experience accentuated her sensitive nature. Sandra had her debut at a St. Regis Roof dinner dance in Manhattan in 1953. She graduated from Vassar in 1957 and went on an Experiment in International Living trip to England that summer, staying with an English family in Plymouth.

As it came time to return home, Sandra encountered the problem that every one of the Rockefeller "Cousins" had to experience in one way or another—how to cope with *the* name and the image of great wealth. She talked to English reporters and was widely misquoted as saying that life as a rich girl was "boring" and "artificial," that she "loathed" wealth and would like to live as "a working girl." When the parents read these accounts in the New York newspapers they knew it was not their daughter talking. A delegation was on hand to meet Sandra when her boat docked September 18—her parents, her sister Hope, her Vassar roommate Mitsao Matsumoto (daughter of the Rockefellers' close friends in Tokyo), and a mob of reporters. JDR told his daughter that she would have to talk to the press or they would never let her alone. Somewhat frightened by now, Sandra faced up to the interview—and found out that she did very well and enjoyed it. All the New York papers carried big stories of the interview with photos showing Sandra, her parents, and Mitsao all looking pleased and happy.

But Sandra's method of coping from then on was to be a very private person on her own. She loved the Boston area, knowing a number of her mother's "wonderful friends" there. She took an apartment and did become a working girl for a while, serving as a receptionist at Children's Hospital. Then she took up painting. Her father liked one of her paintings so much that he hung it in the office along with original works by American masters.

Sandra's privacy became more complete when she dropped the Rockefeller name. Some five years after graduating, she took a trip to Ireland to see her aunt Helen, and she only used her middle name to see how differently people would react in dealing with Sandra as just another person, not as a Rockefeller. She liked the difference and soon decided to adopt the change permanently. She remembers screwing up her courage for five days before a scheduled visit to Boston by her father when she would tell him what she had done. She was vastly relieved when he responded that he understood completely and thought it was probably a wise thing to do. That experience typified their relationship ever after. As an adult she found her father invariably gentle and understanding, and her pride in him and respect for him grew steadily. Whenever he was in the Boston area and had time, JDR would stop in to see Sandra. A diary note in 1965 reads: "Had dinner with Sandra at her apartment. Is really a very nice way to see her and be with her and she enjoys so much preparing the dinner herself."

Hope also had her "coming out" at a St. Regis Roof dinner dance given by her parents after she graduated from Brearley in 1955. Like many young women, she went through a period of questioning and uncertainty, having long, earnest discussions with an Episcopal priest while at college. Early in life Hope showed a talent for descriptive writing, something noticed by Junior, who complimented his granddaughter on the quality of the letters she had written to him.

One way JDR had of interacting with his grown-up children was to visit them at school, often by himself if he were traveling in the vicinity or for a "fathers' weekend." On one such occasion in 1957 he went to see Hope at Smith, staying at the home of the president of the college, attending chapel, watching a crew race, going to a father-daughter dance in the gym, and having dinner with Hope and her roommates. JDR chatted with Senator Mike Mansfield, whose daughter also attended Smith, and called on Mary Ellen Chase, a writer and retired English professor who had written a biography of his mother.[1] JDR wrote: "Thoroughly enjoyed the whole weekend—being with Hopie, meeting her student friends and the faculty members with whom she is working."

After graduating *cum laude* in 1959, Hope married John Spencer in a Fourth of July ceremony at St. Barnabas Episcopal Church in Irvington, New York. The son of the Boylston Professor of Rhetoric at Harvard, Spencer was eight years older than Hope. He had graduated from Princeton in 1953 and served as a marine captain in the Korean War. He tried law school, but decided in favor of a business career with the National Sugar Refining Company. After five years, Spencer wanted to move out of the business field. For a while he served as an aide to David Rockefeller, then got the chance he was looking for to move into area studies and writing, with an Institute of Current World Affairs assignment to East Africa in 1962. The program was set up to study the emerging nations by sending out field personnel who would write periodically for the ICWA newsletter.

In July 1963 JDR, Blanchette, and Alida traveled to Nairobi to see the Spencers, and found it to be a fascinating visit. There was a joyous reunion and the visitors were put up in a house in the suburbs rented from people who were on home leave. It was next door to where Hope and John lived with their baby son, David, the first grandchild. JDR wrote: "The Spencers' house seems just right for their needs and in terms of his work. It is not as large or attractive as the one we have, but that is for the best in my opinion."

There were trips to game preserves and visits to schools. JDR was pleased to see his old friend, Malcolm MacDonald, who was serving as governor. He told JDR he was "cautiously optimistic" about the independence of Kenya. With the assistance of his son-in-law, JDR had visits with such notables as President Julius Nyerere of Tanzania; Tom Mboya, the minister for justice and constitutional affairs; and Prime Minister Jomo Kenyatta. Of Mboya, JDR wrote: "An interesting person: very young, very able and very self-assured and arrogant." Of Kenyatta: "Were much impressed with him; seemed alert, intelligent and certainly was friendly."

Never one to miss an opportunity, JDR spoke about population and recorded Kenyatta's response: "Seemed quite receptive to planned parenthood but felt its acceptance would depend on further education." JDR summed up the trip: "We were very pleased as to Hope and John's general state of mind and the positions which they seem to have made for themselves in the community; and we were encouraged as to the future of Kenya although obviously there are many tough problems ahead."

When the Spencers returned to the United States in 1964 it was Hope who produced a book about their African experience. Entitled *The Way to Rehema's House: An East African Diary*, it was published by Simon and Schuster in 1967. The book was compiled from the letters Hope had written.

Soon after the Spencers arrived home, JDR had dinner with them and wrote in his diary: "Very fine couple if I do say so." But there was trouble coming. Two more sons were born and then the parents began to drift apart. John was trying to settle on a career path. He took a job with the Ford Foundation program office for northeast and central Africa in 1964 and resigned three years later. He did some lecturing and writing, and served as a consultant to the Population Council. He taught some courses at the New School in Manhattan as an African historian and area specialist. With her book published, Hope began turning her writing skill to magazine articles, thinking about a possible career as a journalist. Finally the couple separated amicably, and Hope got a Mexican divorce decree in October 1969. John took a faculty position at Middlebury College and Hope became a reporter for *Newsday* on Long Island, moving later to a newspaper in New Mexico.

JDR saw it happening and did his best to help. He was genuinely torn with sympathy for both Hope and John. Most of the female Cousins married, losing their Rockefeller identity by taking another name—and most of them ended up divorced at least once. JDR was sensitive to the problems that seemed to occur whenever a young man married a young woman who happened to be named Rockefeller. He had observed this closely in the case of his sister Babs and Dave Milton. Figuring that Junior was part of the problem, JDR had tried delicately to intervene, but to no avail. A number of times JDR had lunch with John Spencer, noting in his diary only that the purpose was to talk about "his problems." But this was to no avail, too.

About the time that Hope was beginning seriously to contemplate divorce after nearly ten years of married life, her older brother Jay was beginning to think seriously about getting married. After his remarkable three-year experience in Japan, finishing college at Harvard, and deciding against staying on in graduate work, Jay went to Washington in 1962 looking for a job. He ended up as a special assistant to Sargent Shriver, head of the Peace Corps, and then became operations officer for the Republic of the Philippines. At that time, the Peace Corps seemed to epitomize the idealism, optimism, and youth orientation of the Kennedy administration. One of the friends Jay made there was Ray Lamontagne, who later was to join JDR's office as a specialist in the population field. During one weekend visit to Fieldwood Farm in 1963, he and Jay announced to Jay's startled parents that they were going to enlist in the U.S. Army's Special Forces, which were then being sent to Vietnam by President Kennedy. They tried, but Jay was an inch too tall and Ray a year too old.

Jay wanted to see if diplomacy would be the right career for him. To find out, he was not above using a bit of "drag" as his father had before, at Princeton and in the navy. JDR found an occasion to speak to Secretary of State Dean Rusk, and Jay soon was offered his choice of assistant desk officer for Vietnam or Indonesia. He chose the latter, serving there awhile and then becoming a staff aid to Roger Hilsman, Assistant Secretary for the Far East. During this period Jay might best be described as leading the life of a swinging bachelor. He was certainly tall, dark, and handsome. In addition, he was smart, well-to-do, had a famous name and an open, gregarious nature, and he enjoyed a good time. Jay was one Rockefeller who had no problem with the name. At age twenty-one, as prescribed, he had exercised his choice by taking the full, formidable name, John D. Rockefeller IV, choosing the Roman for his numeric designation rather than the Arabic his father had favored—but he remained known to everyone as "Jay." As his future wife, Sharon, put it: "He loves being a Rockefeller, loves whatever advantages it gives him to do something important or something good."

JDR was much more like his grandfather than his father in relating to a son. That is, he was interested, responsive, and supportive whenever Jay wanted to talk about life and responsibility and what he should do with himself. He did not try to influence Jay in any one career direction, nor did he press any preordained role and memberships on boards. As a result, they talked often, and, as Blanchette expressed it, "they had a wonderful relationship." In Sharon's opinion, this strong support and avoidance of second-guessing by the parents gave Jay "super confidence," but also for a time "made him somewhat blithe and naive."

Jay joined his parents during their Dorado Beach vacation several times and often brought friends home for a weekend at Fieldwood Farm. On one occasion, Jay's presence and knowledge of Japanese was very helpful— the crown prince and princess of Japan spent a weekend at Fieldwood

John D. Rockefeller 3rd at age forty-six in 1952, the year in which he broke free of his father's dominant influence and began his innovative career in philanthropy

JDR 3rd with Secretary-General Trygve Lie (*left*) and architect Wallace Harrison at the opening of the new United Nations headquarters in 1952, built on land donated by the Rockefellers

JDR 3rd and John Foster Dulles with Japanese Ambassador Eikichi Araki at the first annual dinner of the Japan Society at the Plaza Hotel, June 17, 1952. JDR took the lead in reviving the Society as an early step in his long-term interest in Japan.

Prince Hitachi of Japan is flanked by Governor John S. Battle of Virginia (*left*) and JDR at Colonial Williamsburg, September 1953.

Three John D. Rockefellers—JDR 3rd; his son, Jay; and Junior—meet at Christmastime, 1954.

Junior and his second wife, Martha Baird Rockefeller (*center*), are the senior couple at the family Christmas gathering at Babs's home, 1954. Three of the brothers are visible in the back row, David (*2nd from left*), Nelson (*4th from left*), and Laurance (*7th from left*). Seated in the next row are (*from left*) Blanchette, Jean Mauze, Martha Baird, Junior, Babs (Mrs. Mauze), JDR 3rd, and Mary "Tod" Rockefeller (Mrs. Nelson Rockefeller).

Fieldwood Farm became a familiar stopping place for distinguished Japanese visitors. Blanchette and JDR entertain Prime Minister Shigeru Yoshida and his daughter and son-in-law, Mr. and Mrs. Takakichi Aso, November 1954.

A gift from JDR and Blanchette proves entertaining for President Ramón Magsaysay of the Philippines and his wife at Malacanang Palace, Manila, in January 1957.

JDR meets with Ngo Dinh Diem, president of the Republic of South Vietnam, and an aide to the president in the palace in Saigon, February 3, 1957.

One of JDR's important contributions to the Population Council was his ability to discuss population issues with heads of state in the Third World, as in this visit with President Habib Bourguiba in Tunisia.

The six members of the third generation at Christmas, 1958. *From left:* Nelson, Winthrop, Babs, JDR, Laurance, David.

JDR and President Dwight D. ("Ike") Eisenhower at the groundbreaking ceremony for Lincoln Center, May 14, 1959

Ike turns the first spade, watched by (*from left*) JDR, board member David M. Keiser, Commissioner Robert Moses, Manhattan Borough President Hulan Jack, Mayor Robert F. Wagner, and Lieutenant Governor Malcolm Wilson.

Hope Aldrich Rockefeller, 1959

Hope on her wedding day, July 4, 1959, with her father

Farm *en famille*. In December 1965 Jay brought a new girl home to One Beekman—Sharon Percy, the very attractive blond daughter of Mr. and Mrs. Charles H. Percy of Illinois. JDR wrote that he had known Sharon's father "slightly for a number of years now." Chuck Percy had become well-known as the "young president" at Bell & Howell. He had become chairman of the company, and, as JDR wrote, "is now prominent in the Illinois political sitution as a promising young Republican."

There were already some important changes under way in Jay's life. In the wake of the Kennedy assassination and President Johnson's "Great Society" program, a cultural phenomenon of the times among many young people was a decided shift away from the glamour of foreign affairs to the hard reality of domestic problems. Jay decided against a State Department career. In the fall of 1964, he left Washington to take a field assignment in rural West Virginia with Action for Appalachian Youth, a product of the President's Commission on Juvenile Delinquency and Youth Crime. West Virginia had become an important state politically—it had been a key to John F. Kennedy's success in his struggle with Hubert Humphrey for the Democratic nomination in 1960 and now was regarded as the leading example of all that the words "Appalachia" and "poverty" had come to evoke. Jay now was showing the serious and purposeful side of his nature, and he threw himself into his work, trying to help the people he met in the hollows of West Virginia's mountainous countryside. After a year, he had come to a crucial decision. The right career for him would be public life. That was the basic decision. It immediately brought to the surface two more difficult choices—should he run for office as a Republican or a Democrat, and should he stake out his career in West Virginia or in California?[2] He had friends who were taking all sides of these questions. Jay had long discussions with his father on both issues. In the end, he knew that his heart lay with West Virginia and the Democrats. He had too many friends in both the state and the party to choose otherwise. The Democratic Party was closer to all of his instincts and beliefs than the GOP. JDR was sorry about this break with a century of Rockefeller tradition, but he understood Jay's reasons and did not try to argue with him. He never wavered in his support of his son. Jay's decision was to run for a seat in the West Virginia House of Delegates as a Democrat in the November 1966 election.

For a time, JDR tended to confuse North Carolina and West Virginia, and he once wrote in his diary about Jay's work: "I'm still not entirely sure as to just what he does there." He soon began to learn, however. On one occasion, Jay brought five couples from West Virginia home to Fieldwood Farm for a house party over Memorial Day weekend. "They were a nice group of people and we enjoyed being with them," JDR wrote. In

September 1966 JDR accepted an invitation to be the speaker at a dedication ceremony in Emmons, West Virginia. The local Community Improvement Association had acquired a piece of property on which they planned to develop a community center to be called "Rockefeller Center." JDR described the occasion:

Jay and I motored out to Emmons, his hollow, where [community leaders] were waiting for us to join the parade which was led by a local school band with smart costumes and drum majorettes. . . . There was a speaker's stand on the hillside and a lot of chairs below us . . . where the people from the hollow sat along with quite a few from Charleston and the surrounding area who had been invited because of the special occasion. The program was run off very well indeed and Jay seemed to feel that my remarks which he and I had planned together were well received.[3]

After the ceremonies for an hour or so mixed with the people who were most cordial and friendly. Quite a few came up and spoke with me and so many obviously felt very warmly towards Jay and so appreciative of what he had done for the community. It was really a moving occasion when one realizes that it really all came about as a result of Jay's efforts in the hollow. The fact that the area is being called Rockefeller Center is of course a tribute to him.

JDR had a personal interest in no fewer than four candidates in the November 1966 election. Two of his two brothers were running for governor of their respective states, Jay was seeking election to the West Virginia state legislature, and Chuck Percy was the Republican candidate for the Senate from Illinois. All four won. The personal interest in Percy was there because by the time of the election the Rockfellers knew that Jay and Sharon would soon announce their engagement. In December JDR and Blanchette flew to Chicago to meet with Jay and Sharon and the Percys to talk about wedding plans. They stayed at the Percy home in Kenilworth and then attended services Sunday morning at the Rockefeller Chapel at the University of Chicago. This was where Jay and Sharon planned to be married. Her father was an alumnus of the university and a trustee, and, of course, the Rockefeller connection was obvious. The wedding date was set for April 1, 1967.

During the preparations, JDR contributed an amusing sartorial note and a commentary on the state of his health. His frugal nature extended to replacing his clothes only when they wore out, not for reason of any fashion changes. Because he bought fine-quality suits, usually at Brooks Brothers, they seemed to last forever, leading to speculation among irreverent younger personnel at Room 5600 that they were spun out of steel thread. JDR's suits easily outlasted such design stratagems as changing the

width of a lapel. For Jay's wedding, JDR realized that the cutaway he had
worn at his own wedding thirty-five years earlier would be quite appropriate in terms of style. He had not gained much weight over those years,
so that only minor adjustments would be needed. He wrote: "Went to
Brooks Brothers for a revamping of my 1932 cutaway for Jay's wedding on
April 1st. It would appear that the operation is feasible."

As might be expected, the wedding was a major social event. The press
did not make quite as much fuss over the dynastic implications as it had
the last time a Rockefeller scion had married the daughter of a senator—
when Junior and Abby were wed in 1901. But the coverage was massive.
There was a color spread in *Life* with the cover photo showing the radiantly
handsome couple. The Matsumotos from Tokyo were there, as were such
notables as Maurice Chevalier, actor George Hamilton and Lynda Bird
Johnson, Governor Romney of Michigan, and Mayor Lindsay of New York.
Winthrop came up from Arkansas and Laurance was on hand, but the
other uncles were tied up elsewhere. Officiating at the ceremony was
Dr. Robert J. McCracken of the Riverside Church in New York. John
Spencer was Jay's best man, and Alida was a member of Sharon's bridal
party.

JDR described the reception:

As we feared, the numbers who came were so large that our main concern was
just to get them through the line. Finally after nearly two hours Jay and Sharon
decided to walk up the line, greeting people as they went, inasmuch as in this
fashion they could better control the amount of time per person. Mr. Percy and I
followed along behind them, although at a slower pace. . . .

It has been a real pleasure working with [the Percys] in regard to the wedding,
and we do have high regard for them. As to Sharon, we feel that she is an outstandingly fine girl and she and Jay bring a great deal to each other—that as a team
they should really go far together.

The newlyweds left with Winthrop and Jeanette in Win's personal airplane for Arkansas before heading out the next day on their Far Eastern
honeymoon. Once back in West Virginia, Jay and Sharon began building
a home, a family, and a career. Sharon was a good match for Jay in energy,
intellect, and articulateness. They were an attractive couple with the look
of destiny about them, an irresistible magnet for the nation's press. It
seemed that scarcely a month passed without a major magazine or newspaper spread about them. Jay was concerned about the next incremental step
of running for his first statewide office, secretary of state, in November
1968. He won handily, and the next year the first of Jay and Sharon's four

children was born. Named John, he would have the same option of choosing his name at age twenty-one, and in the meantime would be known to everyone as Jamie.

After the assassination of Senator Robert Kennedy of New York in June 1968, it was up to Governor Nelson Rockefeller to appoint someone to fill out the remaining two years of the term. He offered the post to Jay in a gesture that was apparently sincere and even magnanimous, but represented one of his aberrations in judgment. Nelson reasoned that he would be replacing a Democrat with a Democrat and helping a nephew at the same time. Jay turned the offer down. Having been in the Kennedy administration, the idea of profiting from Bobby's death in such a way was anathema to him. Moreover, he realized that to accept such an offer would have been political suicide for him. Nelson then appointed Rep. Charles Goodell, who failed to win reelection in 1970.[4]

If anything, the press attention to Jay and Sharon increased after his 1968 victory and as their family grew. More than ever, the reporters were envisioning Jay and Sharon in the White House. It was a case of too much too soon. Jay and Sharon realized this, but could do nothing about it. Jay's next objective was winning the race for governor in 1972. He got the nomination and found himself facing a tough campaigner in Republican Arch Moore. Jay's commitment to West Virginia was firm and genuine, but Moore kept charging him with being a "carpetbagger." It might have helped if Jay had been able to reveal how he had turned down his uncle's offer of a Senate seat in 1968, but he did not because of possible damage to Nelson. It was a disastrous year for the Democrats with George McGovern as their standard-bearer. President Nixon crushed him in the election, and Jay was but one of many promising Democrats whose careers suffered a setback. Another factor was that his stand against strip-mining had hurt him with the mine owners and many of the workers in West Virginia. Arch Moore became the first Republican governor of the state since Reconstruction days.

With all of the publicity and his political ambitions now in ashes, Jay demonstrated once and for all his commitment to West Virginia by staying on. He declined an offer of the presidency of New York University, instead accepting the post of president of West Virginia Wesleyan. And he began thinking about 1976.

By the time Jay was married and settled into his political career in West Virginia, the Vietnam War protest and the "youth revolution" were in full sway. As the youngest of the Rockefeller children by eleven years, the impressionable, sensitive Alida grew into adulthood during this decade of turmoil and rioting and challenges to authority.

Unlike her two sisters, Alida did not finish at the Brearley School, but spent her prep school years, 1963 to 1967, at the Concord Academy in Massachusetts. JDR always seemed to enjoy his visits there, coming away impressed with the varied talents of his daughter. On one occasion, Alida participated in both a glee club performance and a concert, the latter, she told her father, only because "they desperately needed a second cellist." On another visit, JDR went to the art department to see Alida's works. "She has done some very imaginative and attractive paintings, ranging very widely as to character and subject matter," he wrote. "I was much impressed." And, later, in the senior class play, JDR found that his daughter "had quite an important role which she did very well."

During Alida's senior year, JDR spent two days at Concord as "Hall fellow," lecturing and teaching on the subject of population. Each of the two mornings he addressed the entire school body on an aspect of the population problem, followed by two forty-five-minute classroom sessions for questions and general discussion. "These sessions were quite fun," JDR said, "and the girls' questions were generally thoughtful and to the point."

Given the tenor of the times and the questioning that was stirring within Alida, she was adamantly against following the traditional pattern of going to one of the women's colleges such as Vassar or Smith. Early in 1967 she and her father, accompanied by William McChesney Martin (chairman of the Federal Reserve) and his daughter, visited the campus of Stanford University in Palo Alto, California. The girls disappeared into a freshman dormitory, but for the fathers it was a high-level visit, meeting with Stanford president J. E. Wallace Sterling and various heads of schools and departments. Stanford became Alida's choice, and she was thrilled when she was accepted on an early-admission basis.

At her graduation ceremony at Concord in June, JDR wrote of how proud he was of his youngest daughter. In addition to the parents, Jay and Sharon and Alida's two sisters were there. A few months later, after Alida's eighteenth-birthday party, JDR wrote:

It is hard to believe that she is that old, although unquestionably she is a much more mature and developed person now after her years at Concord. She really has her feet on the ground and is in good shape to take on Stanford, even though this will be a major change for her.

Another sign of changing times was waning interest in debutante parties and the whole idea of presenting a young lady to society. Alida was against this, but she yielded to her mother's urgings for a pleasant substitute—a dinner dance her parents gave for her at Fieldwood Farm shortly before she was to leave for Stanford. A tent was erected in the garden, and about

130 people came, the group "being built around Alida's girl friends who each brought her own beau," as JDR put it. "It was really a very nice group which gave a warm and friendly atmosphere to the occasion."

Once at Stanford, Alida needed all of the maturity she could muster. It was a very difficult time for someone with the last name of Rockefeller to be a student at a great liberal university. To the radicals in the student body, the Rockefellers were among the enemies. They epitomized the greedy capitalists who were carving up the world and oppressing the masses. It was both a frightening and an exhilarating experience, and Alida managed to find her way through it without losing her head. She came to know many of the radicals, but did not go to radical excesses herself. She learned a great deal and adopted liberal attitudes and opinions. She also found many of her own questions sharpened and accentuated.

During her visits home, Alida probed her parents relentlessly. On one occasion, her mother left the dining room in tears over the questions Alida was asking about Rockefeller wealth and influence and values. "My father was calmer," Alida said. "We discussed it. We could always talk." In fact, JDR was avidly interested in what his daughter had to say. He was trying to understand the war protest and "youth movement" himself. Alida was not exactly a guide for him because she was too confused herself. But she was a genuine representative of much of the ferment that was going on, and as such she was an important touchstone to her father, as we shall see in later chapters.[5]

In managing his financial affairs, JDR's family was an important consideration for him in three respects: the financial well-being of his wife and four children now and in the future, philanthropic giving closely associated with individual family members, and gifts to the community in which the family resided. In all cases, JDR lived up to the best teachings and example of his father and his own beliefs. He was generous, scrupulous, and thoughtful. He gave to every institution that had benefited a member of his family. Aside from the churches the family attended, an important local charity for him was the Phelps Memorial Hospital in North Tarrytown, only a few miles from Fieldwood Farm. He served on the board there for a long time and was proud of the way the hospital was managed and the volunteer services it attracted. Over the years his gifts to Phelps totaled $365,376.

We have seen how JDR contributed $760,812 over the years to his wife's favorite institution, the Museum of Modern Art. In addition, he gave Vassar College, of interest to both Blanchette and Sandra, a total of slightly more than $1 million. For his own alma mater, Princeton, on whose board he served, his gifts totaled $6.8 million, slightly less than $3 million of this for the Rockefeller Public Service Awards. He also gave $1.5 million to the Loomis School. To the various schools attended by his children, he gave the following: Brearley School, $343,100; Buckley School, $151,225; Concord Academy, $125,362; Harvard University, $312,575; the International Christian University in Japan, $252,662; Phillips Exeter Academy, $130,032; Smith College, $112,192.[6]

JDR's relationship with his trusts was also exemplary. It will be recalled that Junior created two sets of trusts for the benefit of his children and grandchildren, the first in 1934 and the second in 1952. The conditions attaching to each set of trusts were quite different. The 1952 Trusts were placed with the Fidelity Union Trust Company of Newark for each of Junior's grandchildren. Those created for JDR's children were each funded with 20,300 shares of Standard of California and 22,700 shares of Jersey Standard, with a total market value on the date of gift in 1952 of $2,876,000. Initially, these trusts produced collectively about $1.3 million a year in income, and of course they appreciated greatly in value in the following years. JDR, and his brothers, had the power of assigning a portion of the income to each of their children.

For a number of years, JDR enjoyed the benefits of these trusts, designating some $7.2 million to charity, most of it to the Population Council. But he also passed the income to his children in the most straightforward manner possible—increasing the amount of income each received from his or her trust by 10 percent each year after age twenty-one, thus reaching a level of 100 percent by age thirty.

The much larger 1934 Trusts were the major holding of Rockefeller wealth for the benefit of future generations. The value of JDR's trust in the beginning was $12 million. Junior added to this on several occasions, JDR inherited a portion of Abby's trust, JDR sold his share of Rockefeller Center to the Trust in the 1950s, and the whole appreciated steadily in value throughout the prolonged postwar economic boom. As was the case with his sister and four brothers, JDR received all of the income from this trust throughout his life—this was his main source of income. Upon his death, the income would be divided among his four children, and the principal remaining in the trust eventually would be inherited by their children.

Each trust was governed by a committee, with Devereaux Josephs of New York Life serving as chairman for many years. The annual meeting of each of the Rockefeller brothers with his trust committee in December was always important—and most amicable. Under the terms of the trust, each brother could draw out principal, some portion or even all of it in theory, if his trust committee agreed. To the extent that principal was taken out, of course, the estate for that particular brother's children and grandchildren would be diminished (unless the principal was used to produce other income that the brother would then will to his heirs).[7]

In 1967 JDR spoke to John Lockwood about the possibility of withdrawing some principal from his trust fund. Lockwood said there would be no problem. Learning to his surprise that he was the only brother who had never taken out any principal, JDR proceeded with his request to take out slightly more than $12 million and the committee approved. Out of this sum he created a new trust for Blanchette of $5 million and added the same sum to Jay's 1952 Trust (in each case, the amount was slightly more than $5 million). The balance of nearly $2 million was used to pay gift taxes on these two transactions.

JDR felt that Blanchette should have more funds available to her personally: the trust also would provide her with ample funds in the event of his death and before his will took effect. In the case of Jay, there were several considerations. He had turned thirty years of age and gotten married in 1967. He had also embarked upon a career in public life in West Virginia and would need funds for that. Being thirty years old, Jay would begin to receive all of the income from his now-augmented 1952 Trust, and also could invade the principal if he desired.

With these moves, JDR felt that he had made adequate provision for the two family members who needed special attention at the time. For the future, his four children would be well taken care of by their share of his 1934 Trust upon his death and his wife by her share of his personal estate.

16

♕

MAN OF THE ARTS

DURING all his busy years of institution-building in the 1950s, JDR simultaneously developed a deep personal appreciation of the arts. It began with his involvement in cultural programs in Asia and was intensified during his leadership in creating Lincoln Center. These were quite different experiences, yet they reinforced each other and led him to a wide range of new activities. Considering all that he did, JDR must be regarded as a man of the arts to an extraordinary degree.

This contrasts with the jocular comment voiced by friends and critics that the man who made Lincoln Center for the Performing Arts possible was not particularly known as a devotee of any of the arts performed there. JDR acknowledged it. In an early interview, he said: "I never had any great knowledge or particular ability in the arts." He said wryly that his study of the violin as a youth was done "with parental encouragement," adding: "I'm not sure why the lessons stopped, but it may have been a certain lack of proficiency on my part."[1]

At times the point would be made with a sarcastic intention, as if lack of devotion to the ballet, the symphony, or the opera should disqualify a man for the role he assumed in Lincoln Center. Even his erstwhile friend Lincoln Kirstein implied that JDR's interest was in bricks and mortar and personal glory rather than art.[2]

The truth is that the reward for JDR was endless problems, heavy responsibilities, unremitting work close to drudgery, and a steady drain on his resources. As for glory, it may be measured by the fact that in relating the history of Lincoln Center on the occasion of the twentieth anniversary of Philharmonic Hall, the *New York Times* managed to omit any mention of JDR.[3]

Yet, despite all frustrations, he undoubtedly derived much inner satisfaction from his effort. The closest thing to self-satisfaction we find in JDR's diary is an entry he made after standing anonymously in Lincoln Center

Plaza one fine summer evening, savoring the obvious pleasure of the throngs of people congregating there before the performances in the various halls. Far from being a love of bricks and mortar, his interest stemmed from a deep conviction of the value of art to human life. He saw that value as made up of personal pleasure, communication and understanding, and a sense of existence as something higher and finer than mere survival. He became determined to do everything he could to enhance and propagate those values.

This outlook had already led JDR away from a predominantly Cold War attitude to a cultural one in his Asian programs; next came Lincoln Center as his main activity for the good of his home city. These endeavors then brought him to pioneer in expanding the means of support for the arts. He also wanted to use art for international understanding and enlarge its place in education; finally, he became a notable collector of works of art, for his own pleasure first and then for the public benefit.

As far as "a passion for art" was concerned, JDR's was for the visual arts. Given his lifelong environment, this was not surprising. He grew up surrounded by his father's medieval tapestries and Chinese porcelains and his mother's collection of modern art and Oriental art. JDR almost majored in art history at Princeton, he witnessed the restoration of Colonial Williamsburg, and saw his mother amass the great variety of American folk works that are housed there. The Museum of Modern Art was an influence on him, if only because of the devotion to it of his mother, his wife, and two of his brothers. Given that his mother was a lover and collector of three great types of art—modern, Oriental, and American folk art—she undoubtedly was the greatest influence on JDR.[4]

The real cause for surprise, given this background, is that it took JDR so long to become a serious collector. From their first visit together to Japan in 1951, he and his wife began collecting Oriental objects, but on an intermittent and amateur basis. They acquired paintings, too, but for the conventional purpose of adorning bare walls. Blanchette remembers that except for pictures of their children they had little of interest or value. With her husband immersed in his board memberships and projects, it was she who began pushing him to acquire good paintings. She pushed toward the French Impressionists—a school of modern art that JDR found acceptable. Up to a point JDR would buy any work his wife liked even if he didn't. Blanchette adds with a smile that he was always kind enough *not* to buy things she didn't like.

These purchases remained few and casual for a long time. JDR's first priority for disposable income was philanthropy. Beyond this, his native frugality made it difficult for him to spend the large sums needed to buy good works of art when he was unsure of himself and thought that it might be frivolous, or at least a self-indulgent thing to do. Of course, the prices JDR paid for various works of art make them all seem like fantastic bargains today, but prices are always relative; at the time they were in fact expensive.

Not until the early 1960s, when he was nearing sixty years of age, did JDR seek advice and commit the resources necessary to become a serious collector. Yet, within a dozen years, he had put together two important collections—one of Asian art, the other of American art. Both were acclaimed as intrinsically valuable and significant. Why did he start so late in life? Not until this point did his personal means allow for both philanthropy and art collecting. After the hectic institution building of the 1950s, he may well have felt that he deserved a respite in the form of personal pleasure. Knowledge of Asia and Lincoln Center stimulated him, and the collector's "disease," as Blanchette put it, became his major avocation. And, like his father had before him, JDR rationalized his new passion on the grounds that he would be but a temporary custodian; the objects would ultimately serve the public.

By the early 1960s, JDR realized that he needed professional guidance if he were to go beyond the gifts and purchases of Oriental art that he and Blanchette had amassed during the previous decade. At Asia Society functions JDR had met Sherman Lee, director of the Cleveland Museum of Art and an outstanding expert on Asian art. It was in October 1963 that JDR asked Lee to advise him on collecting during a one-year trial. Because the Cleveland Museum was very active in the Oriental field itself, Lee obtained approval from his museum board; a year later JDR was so pleased with the arrangement that he extended it.

The Asian pieces already acquired by the Rockefellers were regarded by Lee as "mostly indifferent." Blanchette was more blunt in saying that many of them were "terrible." She and JDR began weeding out while JDR and Lee began to canvass the market. JDR set up an annual budget and tried to stick to it, though expenditures naturally varied according to what was available. Connections were established with the finest dealers in New York, London, and Tokyo, and once a month JDR and Lee spent several hours together discussing acquisitions. The two worked on a mutual veto system: if either disliked a piece, whatever the reason, it would be passed up.[5]

JDR's understanding of Asian art began to advance under Lee's tutelage. According to Lee, JDR was "curious," a "good listener," and one who "asked good questions." And Lee began to learn about the character and interests of his new client. Art collecting was one Asian interest in which JDR did not start out with the idea that he would limit himself to Japan. His acquisitions ranged in provenance beyond Japan to the great cultures of China, Korea, Southeast Asia, and westward to India and Pakistan. At the same time, he made no concerted attempt to achieve a "representation," either in chronology or cultures. His most important criterion was taste. As Lee put it, JDR bought if he found the object to be both significant and emotionally stirring.

For example, JDR did not care much for Chinese painting or Japanese screens. Like his father, he found solid objects most appealing—sculpture, ceramics, jade. But his interest went far beyond his father's, which was concentrated almost entirely on Chinese ceramics. Lee informs us that JDR was "very responsive to mysterious, gentle, compassionate themes in Oriental art," including religion. All art was to him "one of the highest manifestations of a culture," and his collecting "reflected a deep love and reverence for Asian civilization."

The two men developed a rating system, with each assigning a grade to a piece under consideration, ranging from "A" to "C," with plus and minus signs sometimes used—an "A" for an object that was unique, the best of its kind, a "B" for one of good museum quality, and a "C" for one of average museum quality. Lee recalls only one occasion when he thought that JDR had made a bad mistake: it was in passing up a piece of Cambodian sculpture that Lee regarded as the finest in the world outside Cambodia itself. It was somewhat damaged, and as it did not appeal to JDR, Lee bought it for the Cleveland Museum.

Art dealers, naturally, were delighted to have a Rockefeller as a customer. Knowing of his choosiness and of Lee's presence, they tended to show him only quality. JDR did not haggle, nor was he niggardly, but the dealers found out that he would pay a fair price and nothing more. They were quite happy to loan pieces to him for days or even weeks at a time. Often, JDR had to live with a piece for a while before making up his mind, and Blanchette's opinions were very important to him. As the collection began to grow, JDR had a special, temperature-controlled storage and viewing area constructed on the second floor of the Beekman Place apartment. A young woman, Bertha Saunders, was hired as full-time assistant to help the Rockefellers manage their collection.

JDR and Lee grew to have great mutual respect. A measure of this was the fact that they were able to collaborate successfully despite the complicating fact that the Cleveland Museum continued to be a buyer of Asian art. JDR noted in his diary that the four main buyers in that particular market were two individuals (himself and Avery Brundage) and two institutions (the Cleveland Museum and the Freer Gallery in Washington).

On at least one occasion, at the request of the Freer, JDR dropped out of competition for a piece he wanted. With Lee he had a clear-cut arrangement that spared Lee the danger of conflict of interest. Whichever man was first approached about a piece by a dealer or first became aware of it in any way had the right of first refusal. There was a "tie" in only two cases out of hundreds, according to Lee. One was decided by the flip of a coin, JDR winning. The other, JDR settled by paying half the purchase price and having the object go to the Cleveland Museum.

In Lee's estimation, JDR grew to be the ideal collector, serious, with a deep love of the objects he sought and very sound judgment, but never compulsive—wholly free of a "Toad Hall, *Wind in the Willows* approach that I *must* have that piece." Lee saw the two sides of JDR's personality in his collecting: "the *emotional, aesthetic* reaction to particular pieces of art that led him to select some over others and to eschew a comprehensive collection, and the *practical, rationalistic* side which forced him to adduce substantial reasons, well beyond the personal, for purchasing art—its historical importance, its ability to uplift and teach large numbers of people, for example."

After a decade of collaboration, JDR's collection numbered more than two hundred pieces ranging in date from about 2,200 B.C. to the early nineteenth century. It was particularly strong in Chinese and Japanese ceramics and in Indian and Southeast Asian sculpture. One piece that JDR bought for $30,000 was valued a few years later at more than $1 million. The most valuable single piece, according to one expert, is an Indonesian bronze figure, eighteen inches high, of the bodhisattva Maitreya, dating from the eighth century.[6] By the mid-1970s, only two of the earlier, pre-1960 acquisitions remained in what had become one of the finest private collections of Asian art in the world.

In 1964 JDR also began to purchase American paintings. The impetus was his recognition that there was something odd in showing to the steady stream of Asian visitors at Fieldwood Farm or One Beekman Place only Asian and European art—nothing American. He decided that representative works of his native land should also be on view.

He thereupon bought *Twilight*, a landscape by Frederick Church (circa 1856), and *Ship and an Approaching Storm off Camden, Maine* (1860), a striking work by Fitz Hugh Lane. Sherman Lee was ready to advise JDR on American art occasionally, but thought that if this new interest were to continue, a specialist should be retained. He recommended Edgar P. Richardson, who was nearing retirement as director of the Winterthur Museum in Wilmington, Delaware. In the years immediately before World War II, Lee had worked for Richardson when the latter was curator of painting at the Detroit Institute for the Arts. In December 1964, Richardson accepted an invitation to One Beekman, for the purpose JDR describes in his diary:

We told him we had just realized our basic collection was Asian art and that our paintings were mainly European and hence had concluded we would like to add 20 or so paintings by the best American artists which would fit in with our other items. Presumably this would mean they would be from the late 19th and 20th century period. Agreed to go ahead with Mr. Richardson for a 1-year trial period. As to an honorarium, he said he had never operated outside his Museum for pay, so we agreed to consider this again after we saw how much time was involved.

By then, JDR was experiencing shock at the escalating value of French Impressionist paintings. He considered the prices out of all reason. Not only did he stop buying these and works of other French schools, but he began selling some of those he owned, until an outcry by Blanchette and the older children caused him to stop. In buying American paintings, JDR found that he had stumbled onto a field where bargains were still to be had. American art was practically virgin territory for collectors. Before World War II, only the Brooklyn and Boston Museums had extensive collections.

Before going to Winterthur, E. P. Richardson had spent thirty years at the Detroit Institute for the Arts, learning his trade under the great German curator Wilhelm Valentiner. In the days when experts in American art were largely self-taught, Richardson patiently built up the Detroit "American" collection and thereby made his own reputation. He was given the freedom to do this by Valentiner, whose interest was largely in the German moderns.

In his meeting with JDR, Richardson termed the acquisition of the Church and Lane paintings as "darn good purchases." He and JDR set out to find more, and soon the initial goal of twenty paintings was exceeded. Almost from the beginning, collecting American art became "an absorbing interest." Richardson was "surprised at how adventurous" JDR was and what a "natural eye for quality" he had. He never bought anything "he [had] not himself enjoyed and found significant, often after long study."[7] The collection, said Richardson, "thus represents a thoughtful, personal view" of American art:

The collection interests me both for the works of art themselves and for its choices. It passes by works representing a purely esthetic impulse or mode, in favor of those expressing a response to human life and to nature. Included are realists and dreamers, artists of only an artisan's skills and those of great sophistication, famous names and unknown or forgotten figures.[8]

The famous names are amply represented in the collection—John Singleton Copley, Charles Willson Peale, Thomas Cole, Albert Bierstadt, Winslow Homer, Eastman Johnson, Childe Hassam, Grant Wood, Andrew Wyeth. But JDR and Richardson's special delight was to find the best work of a little-known painter or one who had gone out of fashion—George W. Maynard, Thomas Hovendon, William Morris Hunt, John F. Peto.

According to Richardson, JDR was able to acquire the best still life by Raphaelle Peale and the best Charles Burchfield watercolor in existence. As for works by little-known painters, Richardson points to *Oranges in Tissue Paper*, by William J. McCloskey, who was active for only a few years in the late nineteenth century, and *The Guitar Player, 1885*, by Dennis M. Bunker, who died at a very young age.

JDR and Richardson disagreed at times, but JDR was "so remarkably courteous" that it was a "very satisfying relationship." JDR would love to go "arting" on Saturday mornings, making the rounds of New York galleries: "He would pay good prices, but not exorbitant ones. He would take a painting home and study it. If it spoke to him, he would buy it."

In contrast to the Asian market, hundreds of American works that might be worth considering could be seen at any moment in the galleries of New York. JDR and Richardson used the same grading system that Lee had worked out. To the A, B, and C grades, Richardson added another—"X" for an excellent painting by an unknown or by an out-of-fashion painter who might make a comeback. An "A" painting, say a Hopper or Copley, or a Hicks *Peaceable Kingdom*, might cost JDR anywhere from $80,000 to $195,000, while an "X" painting could be picked up for $2,000 or $3,000.

Meeting Richardson from time to time and consulting him frequently by telephone in the evening, JDR proceeded to build an American collection of nearly two hundred paintings. He slowed down in the mid-1970s when prices for good works began to climb steeply. The rise was due in no small measure, Richardson points out, to the influence of JDR's own presence in the market. But the taste had also spread and long-neglected Americans were now being eagerly sought by museums and private collectors. JDR had long since overshot his original purpose. He had, in fact, assembled in a very short time one of the finest private "shows" in existence.

JDR chose works from among his Asian and American pieces to decorate Fieldwood Farm, One Beekman, and his corner of Room 5600. In these settings, works from these two very separate traditions of art seemed to harmonize well. Indeed, the gathering of two such different groups of artifacts during the same years of JDR's life suggests something about his character, as Sherman Lee pointed out:

One learned to respect [JDR's] deeply felt response to the often contemplative ideals of Eastern art and to understand the creative tension existing between these ideals and the more pragmatic and concrete achievements of his other artistic love, American painting. This tension was a true meeting of East and West, and to me it epitomized the character of the man, rooted in the traditional American virtues, but increasingly aware of other transcendental realms.

There is no doubt that JDR found great personal pleasure in assembling these two impressive collections. He was spending at the rate of about $1 million to $1.5 million a year during the most active period, when his income was averaging slightly more than $8 million. But by the 1970s, he realized that he had reached the age when he must grapple with the difficult question of what should be done with the collections after his death. His decisions gave rise to fascinating stories that are reserved for later chapters.

Concurrently with building his two art collections, JDR took an important step to expand his support of Asian cultural work. To do this he revamped the Council on Economic and Cultural Affairs (CECA), relieving it of responsibility for cultural programs and assigning them to a small new foundation. In 1963 the CECA was renamed the Agricultural Development Council, and the new foundation was called the JDR 3rd Fund.

The CECA's agricultural program had become so successful under Arthur T. Mosher's presidency that for all practical purposes it was an agricultural organization and not the flexible instrument for various Asian interests that JDR originally had envisioned. Grants for cultural activities had amounted to only a small fraction of the CECA's budget, and by the early 1960s this fraction had become routine—annual grants in support of the Japan Society for English language teaching in Japan ($60,000) and Phillips Talbot's American Universities Field Staff ($10,000), plus two or three small grants for miscellaneous purposes.

Abe Weisblat, who had previously managed exchange programs for the Ford Foundation, spent part of his time supervising these cultural doings. His particular interest being India, he decided to make grants to a few Indian artists for travel to the United States. Such was the beginning of what became a major activity. Mosher told Don McLean that the CECA really was not competent to develop such a program. As this question coincided with JDR's desire to expand cultural activities in Asia, the decision was made to spin off the CECA's cultural work. Mosher was pleased with the result—at one stroke he got rid of the cultural program, got a new and much more suitable name for his organization, and received assurance from JDR of ten more years of financial support.

JDR's original wish to have a flexible means of serving a variety of modest programs was thus fulfilled. The support of culture in Asia was to be the first but not the only function of the new organization. On this account it was called the JDR 3rd Fund instead of being given a more descriptive title. To be sure, JDR was mildly uncomfortable with the new name—it was a bit too personal, almost flippant, he felt. Hence every other year or so he would ask his staff if anyone could think of a better name. No one ever did.

A CECA paper issued in 1962 gave the Fund some guidance in its beginnings. Entitled "Asian Arts—Who Is Doing What?"[9] it pointed out that a considerable amount of cultural exchange with Asia was being done by the U.S. government, the Asia Foundation, and other organizations, but that it was scattered: it lacked depth and rarely aided indigenous cultural resources. Personnel and budgetary fluctuations adversely affected the programs, which often suffered from political influences. The paper argued that a stable program and steady effort were needed that would locate and assist cultural leaders in each Asian country.

This paper is an example of the high standards the CECA upheld under Art Mosher; his influence undoubtedly played a part in the success that the JDR 3rd Fund was to achieve. JDR's own standards and steadiness led in the same direction and so did the qualities of the man chosen to head the cultural program. He was nominated by Abe Weisblat, who had decided to stay in agricultural economics instead of taking the JDR 3rd Fund post. Weisblat had heard good things about a man he did not know, Porter McCray, who had made an unusual career for himself in the management of cultural exchanges. Weisblat mentioned his name to JDR and he was hired. Weisblat became fond of saying that this act was one of his claims to fame.[10]

A soft-spoken but strong-minded Virginian, McCray, a graduate of the Virginia Military Institute, taught school for six years during the Depression before saving enough money to study architecture at Yale. There he became friendly with Wally Harrison. When Harrison became deputy cultural coordinator in Nelson Rockefeller's Office of Inter-American Affairs, just before World War II, he took McCray with him. That office was the pioneer in the modern style of cultural exchange programs, and it was there that McCray gained his experience. There also McCray met René d'Harnoncourt, who later became the president of the Museum of Modern Art. The end of the war found McCray driving an ambulance in India, his first exposure to Asia. Afterward, he joined Wally Harrison's architectural firm in New York City. Next he was appointed by d'Harnoncourt to direct the Circulating Exhibitions Program of the Museum, which in 1951 was given a push toward international scope by Nelson Rockefeller's urging the Brothers Fund to make a five-year grant. When the grant was delayed, McCray took leave for a year to work for the Marshall Plan in Paris. Back in New York, he worked energetically at MOMA's International Program, soon to generate an "International Council" of which Blanchette became the first president.

By the end of the 1950s, the large and successful International Council became a focus of dispute among the heads of the museum departments, and McCray, shaken by this, resigned in 1961. He accepted a temporary assignment from the State Department Bureau of Cultural Affairs to travel to African and Asian countries and assess arts activities there. An airline ticket to thirty-eight countries—the fattest ticket McCray had ever seen—and $10,000 of his own money took him on an extended tour that lasted nearly a year.[11]

He returned home in August 1963 to find himself invited to lunch by JDR, on Weisblat's suggestion and "in the nick of time," as McCray later said, for he had to find a new job. He and JDR had a nodding acquaintance, and McCray knew Blanchette well from their work together on the Museum's International Council. Our faithful witness, the diary, reports:

I told McCray that I had for several years now been interested in fostering better understanding between the U.S. and Asia and that I had long felt that the cultural—the arts—could play an important part in this objective. Indicated that through the Asia and Japan Societies and through CECA as well as directly a number of grants had been made towards this end as well as programs initiated. Expressed concern, however, that I have never approached the subject on a really thoughtful and organized basis. Told him that I was planning to set up a new Fund and that I had in mind under its aegis at least making a survey as to the possibilities in this direction and hopefully to develop a program. Asked whether he might be interested in heading up such an effort, at least in the survey stage. He seemed to feel he would, and we agreed to meet again shortly. Liked him and was impressed with him.

Five days later the two lunched again and decided to join forces. Both Blanchette and Don McLean had supported McCray's appointment. JDR incorporated the JDR 3rd Fund on September 17, 1963, and, in line with his desire to keep it flexible, stated the purpose broadly in the charter—"to stimulate, encourage, promote, and support activities important to human welfare." In two grants before the end of the year, JDR gave the Fund $250,000 for initial work in the field of Asian culture.

To McCray, the idea behind the grants was no mystery. Drawing on his experience and particularly his recent tour, he was in a good position to complete the survey JDR wanted. He went further and delineated the scope of a possible program by the time the first board meeting of the Fund was held in January 1964. The program would take in the visual and performing arts in all Asian countries from Afghanistan eastward. To these standard art forms it would add architecture, archaeology, art history, cinematography, arts and crafts, and museology. In any of these branches four objectives were to be aimed at: (1) to foster opportunities for Asians to travel and study through fellowships; (2) to encourage the assessment and preservation of Asian cultural traditions through aid to museums, documentation, conservation, and research by both Asian and western scholars; (3) to promote the exhibition and performance of Asian works both in Asia and the United States; and (4) to promote the exhibition and performance of American works in Asia.

McCray's recommendations and list of grants were approved by the trustees at that first meeting. JDR's approval may be measured by his gift a month later of $2 million, and six months later of $509,000 more. JDR had learned the wisdom of forward financing and the building up of a reserve. During the first nine years of the JDR 3rd Fund's existence, he fed it an average of $1.2 million a year, which built up a reserve of approximately $4 million by the late 1960s.

Because the JDR 3rd Fund was to serve other philanthropic purposes of JDR's, no support was expected to come from any source but him; in this regard the Fund contrasted with the Asia Society, the Japan Society, the Population Council, and the Agricultural Development Council. These had distinctive identities and public boards and could look beyond JDR to the Brothers Fund, the Foundation, and yet other foundations, to say nothing of membership dues, government grants, contracts, or other sources of funding. The only outside grant that came to the JDR 3rd Fund was given under unusual circumstances. It was a $200,000 grant from the estate of Michael Clark Rockefeller made in his memory by his mother, who was executor of the estate. It was earmarked for assisting in the preservation of Asian culture with particular attention to the Indonesian and West Irian regions.

The Fund was thus, in a sense, a "personal" foundation, though JDR did not want it to be—or even appear to be—subject only to one person's whims. Among other things, he wanted to make sure that the cultural program maintained high standards, so the Fund published an annual report and soon broadened its board of trustees. The three original members were JDR (president), Don McLean (vice president and secretary), and Kenneth Young, former State Department official and ambassador to Thailand. In the fall of 1964, two others were added—Phillips Talbot and George Kennan. The latter, now fully retired from the Foreign Service and serving as professor at the Institute for Advanced Studies in Princeton, was suggested by McCray, who saw in him "the ideal trustee."

JDR was fond of citing two experiences that confirmed his hope and purpose in establishing the Fund:

One occurred in 1958, well before the [Asian cultural] program itself was started. I was visiting Kuala Lumpur, and I accompanied the U.S. Ambassador to Malaysia one evening to a concert given by a young American baritone, William Warfield, whose fine voice was matched by his warm personality. It was an exciting and moving evening. Afterward, the Ambassador said to me: "He has accomplished more for U.S.-Malaysian relations in two hours than I do over a period of many months."

The second incident occurred years later when George Kennan . . . was invited to become a trustee. . . . He accepted with some enthusiasm, stating: "All my life my efforts have been on the economic and political fronts and we have not been too successful. I am challenged by the thought of working with a program that relates exclusively to the third front—the cultural, involving respect and understanding among peoples."[12]

Four other trustees were soon added: JDR's daughter, Hope; Sherman Lee; Samuel B. Gould, president of Channel 13 in New York and then-chancellor of the State University of New York: Douglass Cater, former journalist and aide to President Johnson. After Don McLean left JDR's employ, he was succeeded on the board by Datus Smith (president of Franklin Books, who joined JDR's staff in 1967).

Porter McCray very quickly brought the Asian cultural program to full speed. In grants that frequently totaled more than $500,000 a year, McCray served the goals he had articulated. With this sum, as many as eighty to one hundred individuals, mostly Asians, received fellowship, research, or travel grants. Approximately twenty "project grants" would also be made, usually to institutions, for things ranging from archaeological digs in Thailand to bringing a Japanese Kyogen group to the United States, from purchasing recording equipment for the performing arts center in Bombay to providing travel for Asian delegates to the World Crafts Congress in Peru.

A review of any of the annual reports of the JDR 3rd Fund reveals a wide array of grants in support of every modern and traditional art form in virtually every Asian country, as well as to every kind of organization and institution serving the arts. Like the Agricultural Development Council, the Asian cultural program of the JDR 3rd Fund soon became known as a gem in the world of foreign assistance, an example of how much can be done with a relatively small amount of money. The arts in Asia were served for their own sake, not for any political purpose. Administrative expenses were kept low; at its largest, McCray's staff numbered three assistants. Care was taken to make sure that Asian grantees coming to the United States felt that they had a home base in the JDR 3rd Fund offices in Rockefeller Center and that any help they needed was forthcoming.

Many grantees came to the United States for graduate study; others went to Europe for research and travel. European and international organizations with Asian interests received support, conferences were sponsored, and grants given to Asians for travel in Asia. The operation was unique in the world and it earned great respect in Asia. To have been a JDR 3rd Fund grantee is recognized in many Asian countries as a mark of distinction, and former grantees constitute a body of leadership in the arts in each country. They also serve as scouts to recommend new grantees.

For JDR, the Asian cultural program was not only a declaration of faith in the value of the arts for international understanding but also another example of the value of investing in people, like the Rockefeller Public Service Awards, the Magsaysay Awards, and the fellowship programs of the Agricultural Development and Population Councils.

On the same day that JDR decided to hire Porter McCray, he also discussed with Dana Creel, director of the Brothers Fund, and Nancy Hanks, head of its Special Studies Project, another major program in the arts. The purpose of the meeting, as JDR expressed it, was to allow them to "bring me up to date on the performing arts study project. It increasingly looks as if I should assume the chairmanship of the panel. Actually they are assuming that I will."

A little over a year later, still another undertaking in the arts was discussed by JDR and his staff—"the pilot project idea in several smaller communities to determine what might be possible to do in the way of effectively exposing young people to the arts so that they could decide for themselves whether art was to be an important factor in their lives."

Both projects came out of JDR's immersion in Lincoln Center. He had learned from firsthand experience what difficulties face the arts in a modern democratic society. One was: How to broaden support for the arts? That was the task in Project No. 1, beginning with a two-year study by a distinguished group, which resulted in a seminal report on the problems and prospects of the performing arts. Project No. 2 sought to answer: How to enhance the understanding and appreciation of the arts among people generally? This concern produced the Arts in Education program of the JDR 3rd Fund, which made substantial grants to selected school systems for developing new ways of fostering artistic awareness and appreciation among schoolchildren.

The plight of the performing arts in modern times has been made glaringly evident by the history of Lincoln Center. Costs rise inexorably, yet there is no significant way to retrench, streamline performance, or increase productivity. It takes one hundred or so first-rate musicians and a conductor to make a symphony orchestra go, and it always will. There are no shortcuts, no way of raising the speed at which the musicians play.

By the 1950s, American performing arts companies were unable to subsist on the traditional means of support—patronage and admissions tickets. New means and sources had to be found—the business community and the government.

It was Chuck Spofford who in 1962 began pressing for a study that would throw light on the predicament and make a case for soliciting new types of patrons. But time passed, and Spofford seemed neither able nor willing to lead the effort. JDR felt the responsibility devolving on him, since he had the means at hand to provide both financial and staff support, the latter in the Special Studies staff of the Brothers Fund, which Nelson Rockefeller had formed to work on the "Rockfeller Panel Reports." In addition, Dana Creel and Nancy Hanks were themselves deeply interested in a study of the arts.

Others were, too, which showed the spread and genuineness of the concern. Congressional inquiries were being mounted and bills were being offered. Government's role was argued pro and con. Nelson Rockefeller was vigorously continuing his lifelong interest in the arts as governor of New York State. President Kennedy had created a White House Council on the Arts, of which JDR was invited to become a member. Plans were progressing for the National Cultural Center in Washington (it became the Kennedy Center after the assassination of the President). President Johnson evinced a modest interest in the arts, and also invited JDR to participate in White House meetings on the subject. JDR declined both opportunities by reason of his heavy burden at Lincoln Center.

In March 1962, President Kennedy appointed August Heckscher as his special consultant in the arts, and a year later Heckscher published his report recommending an advisory council on the arts in the White House and a national arts foundation to administer grants-in-aid. Heckscher called for "an across-the-board effort to encourage and assist the development of facilities for the performing arts throughout the country."[13]

Heckscher then returned to his presidency of the Twentieth Century

Fund with the intention of sponsoring an economic study of the arts in modern times. At that point, Creel and Hanks pressed JDR to take the chairmanship of the long-contemplated Brothers Fund study. Consultation with Heckscher showed that the two studies would be complementary rather than redundant. One would be a professional analysis of the economics of the subject by two Princeton economists, William Baumol and William Bowen; the other would be an inquiry by a panel of distinguished citizens and artistic leaders into managerial needs, sources of funds, and the roles of government, foundations, business, and universities. To make sure that the studies did not overlap, Heckscher agreed to join the Rockefeller panel.

Among the thirty on the panel were individuals well-known to JDR— Spofford, Dev Josephs, Sam Gould, Henry Allen Moe, and Frank Stanton. The others came from business, academia, and the arts, and represented the several regions of the country. Research papers were commissioned, some thirty papers in all; frequent day-long meetings were held, continuing through 1964 to hear presentations and testimony.

One meeting was devoted to the issue of the government's role in the support of the arts, the reports covering federal, state, and local governments. The idea of a State Council on the Arts had been pioneered, not surprisingly, by the governor of New York, Nelson Rockefeller. North Carolina had also taken steps, with California coming third. John MacFadyen of the New York Council and Governor Terry Sanford of North Carolina addressed the panel. JDR had already testified before the Special Subcommittee on the Arts of the Senate Labor and Public Welfare Committee, endorsing the concept of government support. Although he had had the experience before, he was still irritated at what is the usual course of such hearings:

I was somewhat disappointed in that [the senators] did not seem too interested either in the initial testimony or the questions and answers. The questions were mainly from Senator Javits. Stayed on for the balance of the morning to have lunch with Senator Pell. As the morning wore on increasing pressure was put on the witnesses to be brief. The net impression I had was that the Subcommittee was primarily interested to get good names on the record as supporting the bills rather than really probing the ideas and opinions of those who took the time and trouble to prepare statements and to appear.

The drafting of an acceptable final report, when a panel is large and distinguished and when the subject is anything but clear-cut, can be an awesome task. The sponsors of the performing arts study soon found themselves facing a crisis in this regard. High hopes had been vested in Alvin

Toffler, who later became well-known as the author of *Future Shock*, but he could give only part of his time during the early months. Other writers dropped out for various reasons as time passed and the deadline approached. The sponsors were saved when they recruited Richard Schickel, film critic of *Life* magazine. Schickel, who later would have an unhappy association with JDR, had done two of the research papers, and he agreed to step in and write the final report.

It was published by McGraw-Hill in 1965 under the title *The Performing Arts: Problems and Prospects*. To help launch the book, JDR held a press conference, appeared on NBC's "Today" show, and spoke at a *New York Herald Tribune* book luncheon. Something of the flavor of the report is suggested by excerpts from the final chapter:

This study of the performing arts is made with the conviction that the arts are one of the central elements of a good society, an essential of a full life for the many, not a luxury for the few. . . .

Few can take issue with the objective of making the arts available to everyone who wishes to enjoy them. But an important cautionary note must be added if the actions discussed in this report are to be meaningful. We must never allow the central focus on quality to weaken or shift. . . . Democratization carries with it a peril for the arts, even as it does for education. . . .

It is a bold venture to envision a great enlargement of the mission of the performing arts—opera, instrumental and choral music, the dance, and theater—when all of them are in deep economic difficulties in carrying out their present programs. However, the basic resources, human and material, for the full development of the arts do exist in the United States. The problem is to mobilize them and to use them effectively for the pleasure of the many. . . . We believe the challenge is worthy of the nation and that the nation is equal to the challenge.

The Rockefeller panel report and its companion, the Twentieth-Century Fund economic study, together made a powerful case for more, and more continuous, support of the arts by foundations, business, and government. Action followed more swiftly than even the most optimistic promoters might have imagined possible. The time was ripe, as these two efforts themselves suggested and as the flurry of activity on Capitol Hill confirmed. JDR testified again before Senator Pell's subcommittee, and in the fall of 1965 the National Foundation on the Arts and Humanities bill was passed by Congress and signed into law by President Johnson. Under its provisions, the separate National Endowment for the Arts and National Endowment for the Humanities were established.

Shortly thereafter, JDR went to Washington for one of his periodic luncheons with Roger Stevens, the prominent theatrical producer who had tried in vain to include a cluster of new theaters in the Lincoln Square scheme. Stevens was now White House arts adviser and director of the National Cultural Center. He was scheduled to become chairman of the brand-new National Endowment for the Arts. Having put so much effort into creating a basis for government support of the arts, JDR was now worried that the government might go too far. But Stevens put his fears to rest—so says the diary:

. . . I wanted to urge him to go slowly in making commitments as to grants until he had a greater chance to study how best Federal money could be used for the arts. He said this was exactly what Congress had told him too

I also urged him not to undertake programs that would be in competition with private efforts. Said that I had been concerned by the President's comments when he signed the Arts and Humanities Foundation bill and also other reports emanating from Washington to the effect that the Federal Government might be launching or sponsoring national companies itself. Was reassured by Stevens' statement that this was not at all what was contemplated. Then we went on to discuss a number of types of programs to which he was giving thought and on which he wanted my reaction. On the whole was encouraged by our discussion.

After Richard Nixon's election as President in 1968, a Republican was slated to be appointed chairman of the Endowment to replace Stevens. By March 1969 it was clear that the post was going to be offered to JDR.[14] He passed word that he unfortunately could not accept, so the White House made a move that pleased both Nelson and John Rockefeller— Nancy Hanks got the appointment. The new institution flourished under her administration. Strongly backed by the White House, its budget rose steadily from $7 million to $157 million during her eight-year tenure.

Having helped to create the performing arts report, JDR demonstrated his support of its objectives by following it up with the aforementioned Project No. 2—the Arts in Education program. The panel study had found that even though the arts were a growing force in American life only a small percentage of adults was actually involved. Nor was any sustained effort being made in the public schools to equip the average student with an understanding of art and its relation to other subject matters.

The idea of repairing this deficiency was not easy to translate into programmatic terms. After the staff discussion of 1964, nothing much happened for several years, except references by JDR to such a purpose when he met people prominent in the world of art. Finally, Ed Young was assigned the task of developing a program. At the end of 1966, he and JDR met a small group assembled by Young. JDR described the meeting:

Spent most of the day in a meeting at the Princeton Club which Ed Young and I had called to discuss the desirability as well as the feasibility of developing pilot projects in three or four American communities to test the possibility of exposing all of the young people in the schools to the arts in sufficient depth so that they themselves might be in a position to determine whether the arts might be a meaningful factor in their lives. We had a very good group present including Miss Kathryn Bloom, Director, Arts and Humanities Program, Department of Health, Education and Welfare, and Dr. Samuel B. Gould, President of the State University of New York. There were about a dozen others and the discussion was interesting and helpful although in a way by necessity not conclusive.

Nothing, of course, would be "conclusive" until JDR decided how much money to venture on such a program and how he and his associates could structure it. In addition, they had to choose where to place it and who would run it. Ed Young said that he did not have the background or training to head the program; a specialist would have to be retained.

Decisions were soon made to hire Kathryn Bloom, who had attended Young's planning group, to direct the Arts in Education project, to lodge it within the JDR 3rd Fund, and to underwrite it at approximately the level of the Asian cultural program. Early in 1967 Bloom accepted on condition that she could phase out of her Washington post gradually and serve part-time at first. By 1968 she was fully engaged.

This left the JDR 3rd Fund with two programs of comparable size, each headed by a director and with no administrative officer above them. Porter McCray was not pleased at the arrangement. With Don McLean gone, the difficult task of keeping the peace fell to Datus Smith, who had completed his part-time phase and was now joining JDR's staff as a full-time associate. One of his assignments was to supervise the JDR 3rd Fund as vice president and secretary.

Kathryn Bloom proceeded energetically to set up the pilot projects JDR had talked about, giving grants to the school system of University City, Missouri, a suburb of St. Louis; to schools in the Long Island community of Mineola; and to the Bank Street School in Manhattan. The aim was not to revamp the arts curriculum as such, but to create an environment in which appreciation of the arts would be enhanced throughout the entire educational process. Small grants were given for teacher training, for mobilizing the arts resources of the community, and for research and evaluation.

There is no precise way to measure the value of all these involvements in the arts on the part of JDR. The panel study on the performing arts was clearly a force in the groundswell that led to government action, but no exact weight can be assigned to the impetus. Nancy Hanks thought it the most important contribution, and that JDR's leadership had been decisive.

On the tenth anniversary of publication of the report, in 1975, she wrote to him:

My mind is filled with many memories on this occasion. First and foremost are not the "old" memories, but living ones: namely, your vision in creating the panel; your persistence in keeping our collective noses to the grindstone to obtain a strong report; and your constant dedication to "quality."[15]

One cannot assess, either, the benefit that the thousands of people derive who attend cultural events at Lincoln Center or who see JDR's two art collections now that they are available to the public. Nor can the ripple effect of the JDR 3rd Fund's cultural program in Asia or Arts in Education in the United States be weighed concretely.

Yet one conclusion does seem warranted about JDR himself. Far from being a wealthy philistine going through the motions of obligatory patronage, he was a man with a genuine conviction and a plan for the arts. Few in his time rivaled him as a man who combined appreciation with specific action to advance them. And this activism was one of the three driving forces in his life, side by side with his commitment to freedom and individual initiative, and with his concern for the worldwide problem of population growth.

17

♨

THE MAN AT WORK

IN YEARS PAST on typical weekday mornings, New Yorkers hurrying to work might have noticed a tall, slender gentleman striding purposefully along 50th Street in a westward direction toward the RCA Building at Rockefeller Center. And again, they might *not* have noticed him because there was nothing about the man that suggested anything unusual such as the fact that his name was also Rockefeller—John D. Rockefeller 3rd. We know he could afford a limousine to take him to work, but he much preferred the half-hour walk from his apartment at One Beekman Place on the East River. On inclement days he might take a taxi, but more likely would board the 49th Street crosstown bus. The walk to and from work was just the exercise he needed to keep his figure spare. His deformed ankle, the badge of his tennis days at school, did not hinder him until late in life when he injured it again.

As he strode along, JDR could pass for any midlevel bank or insurance executive; his bladelike nose and prominent chin led the way under the omnipresent felt hat that always seemed a little large. The profile was distinctive, but not familiar. On winter days he would wear a muffler, black leather gloves, and a dark blue-gray Harris tweed overcoat, cut longer than most so as to extend below his knees. Once indoors, JDR tended to be a bit thin-blooded and chilled easily. During staff meetings in the conference room, he would jump up several times to make minute adjustments of the thermostat. On a really cold day when the wind howled outside the windows of his corner office, one might find JDR wearing the overcoat while seated at his desk.

For a man bearing one of the most famous names in the world, a man extremely well-known in certain circles, whose stature could open almost any door, JDR had a peculiar kind of anonymity with the general public. In part, the famous name itself was the cause of his paradox. It evoked a confusing image in the minds of many people, with the specific identity of the wearer of the name lost in a haze of generational succession. Many people would think first of a spry old gentleman who handed out shiny new dimes. Then they would realize that *that* one was no longer around and would wonder who *this* John D. might be. The anonymity began with Junior who, despite all he had accomplished, was largely forgotten after his death in 1960. Neither he nor his son had any eccentricity or flamboyance to make them memorable in the public eye. Both were soft-spoken, formal, modest men who deliberately avoided the limelight.

It was easier to remember a Rockefeller named "Nelson" or "Laurance" or "Winthrop" or "David"—there was no previous Rockefeller with any such first names. So if one spoke of John D., the natural question for many people would be, *which* John D.? To ease the puzzled look, one might make a stab at explaining—"Nelson's older brother," "the oldest of the five brothers," "Jay's father," "the *third* John D.," or one might mention Lincoln Center or the population field or the Rockefeller Foundation as an identifier.

For a variety of reasons, the *fourth* John D. does not have this problem—because of his great height, his outgoing personality, his style as a politician, because he has done some things that tend to stick in the memory (became a Democrat, moved to West Virginia, married Sharon Percy), but, probably more than all of the other reasons, because he has always been called "Jay." One does not confuse "Jay" with any previous "John D."

For his part, JDR enjoyed the privacy that his anonymity brought him, especially when traveling. He would always fly first-class, but frequently under the name of "John Davison." He hated to arrive at his destination and find a huge limousine waiting for him or a luxurious suite in the most expensive hotel. Those who made his travel arrangements soon learned not to err too much on the other side either, but in general JDR preferred a smaller car or taxi and a modest suite or large room in a modest hotel.

JDR combined personal frugality with extraordinary generosity in his philanthropic work. This, plus his legendary name and passion for anonymity, produced in him an intense dislike of being overcharged or cheated or being taken as a man who threw his money around. It irritated him to find on entering his hotel room a basket of fruit and a bottle of wine. When checking out, he would scan his bill to make sure that the offending items, which he had not ordered, were not charged to him. More than once they were. Anything on the bill that was not clear he would question. Tips would be calculated with mathematical precision. This process could be so agonizing that any of JDR's associates traveling with him would try to beat him to the cashier's window on checkout morning to sign for the bill. JDR did not scrutinize the expense accounts of his associates in a penurious way.

On one occasion such a companion was especially glad that anonymity was the rule. He and JDR had finished dinner in their hotel and taken the elevator to their rooms to go to bed, one on the eighth floor and the other on the ninth. Just as the elevator door closed, two young women slipped in, one of them black, the other white. By the eighth floor, it was clear that they were prostitutes, and the associate had a moment's concern, but he decided that JDR was a grown man who could take care of himself. As he left the elevator, the white prostitute slipped out to follow him, attempting all of the usual ploys. Safe in his room, the associate broke into laughter, wondering what would be going through the black prostitute's mind if she had known she was alone in an elevator with John D. Rockefeller. The next morning at breakfast, a remark by JDR showed that he had been amused by the same thought.

For a man who was monumentally patient in dealing with great problems of world scope, JDR could be very impatient over small things. For example, he liked to get where he was going in an efficient way, without any unnecessary loss of time. This was why in a city away from home he preferred a taxi to the limousine that a host organization might provide. Chances were good that the taxi driver might drive as fast as JDR liked to go, but chauffeurs, knowing who was in the back seat, tended to be supercautious. Once in New Orleans, an elderly black chauffeur was so determined that nothing was going to happen to Mr. Rockefeller in *his* limousine that he came to a full stop at each intersection, whether or not there was a light or sign, and would wait patiently for cars a block away to pass by before proceeding. JDR was so beside himself with frustration that it was all his associate could do to hold him down.

On another occasion, a two-day visit in Los Angeles, with appointments at a downtown clinic, a community group in Watts, lunch in Westwood Village, appointments at UCLA and USC, and so on, began to look like an attempt at the impossible. But JDR's associate knew the Los Angeles freeway system fairly well. Using a rental car and having studied the map, he drove at breakneck speed back and forth across the area, barely making each appointment. The driver was nearly a basket case, but JDR beamed the whole time and said he had never had a better trip.

JDR's penchant for speed did not overwhelm his frugality, however. As will be recalled, he did not join his brothers in sharing the costs and use of the family airplane. He also declined to share in the large helicopter that Nelson, Laurance, and David often used, especially to go between

Manhattan and Pocantico. To JDR, it was extravagant to use a private plane to go, say, to Washington. His way was to leave the office in the late morning, catch a taxi to La Guardia, have a hot dog and glass of milk (preferably buttermilk) at a lunch counter (he considered this "a fine lunch"), and take the Eastern Airlines shuttle. He also passed up the converted PT boat in which, for some years, brother Laurance commuted during the warm months from Tarrytown down the Hudson River to a West Side dock in Manhattan. JDR did ride once with Laurance, enjoying breakfast aboard and a chat during the one-hour trip. But during the summer he used the Hudson River Line of the New York Central just like any other Westchester commuter.

Although JDR owned a town car with a full-time chauffeur, its use was primarily for Blanchette, not for him. Tom Kissick, the chauffeur hired (in 1973) by the Rockefellers, was interviewed by Blanchette alone and did not meet JDR until he had been on the job three weeks. The car was a small Lincoln, JDR not liking anything suggestive of a limousine, such as extra length or opera windows, and dark blue was the color JDR insisted on. He saw no reason to trade in a car until it got good use for three or four years.

About the only time JDR would use the car and driver was when he and Blanchette had an evening engagement in Manhattan, or on a Friday afternoon when the chauffeur would fight the rush-hour traffic to take them to Fieldwood Farm, with JDR's brothers no doubt soaring overhead in the helicopter. When the car approached Tarrytown, always a heavily congested place in the late afternoon, JDR's liking for speed would desert him even further. Instead of taking the quick route around the town, he sometimes insisted on going straight ahead, bumper-to-bumper, to the dismay of Blanchette. It was his way of seeing what was happening in town, what people were doing, what shops were new.

When weekending in later years, JDR got in the habit of returning to the Manhattan apartment on Sunday afternoon. Several times Tom Kissick offered to come up to the farm and get him, but JDR would remind the chauffeur that Sunday was his day off, and JDR would take the train. He would spend the evening alone at One Beekman, reading and preparing for the week's work. Blanchette usually came down on Monday after the morning rush hour.

The office that JDR reached after his walk across town had its own kind of anonymity. When all the brothers returned after the war, it became known officially at the "Office of the Messrs. Rockefeller," and it was so listed on the board in the lobby of the RCA Building. In the mid-1960s, as the generation of the Cousins was coming along, the office designation was changed to "Rockefeller Family and Associates." The office was also known by its mailing address, "Room 5600," meaning the entire fifty-sixth floor of the RCA building, comprising some three dozen offices plus reception areas, conference rooms, and a library. There the four brothers, their associates, the legal department, the head of the office, and the office manager were housed. But "Room 5600" was something of a misnomer for it also included the fifty-fifth floor where all the services were (standard investments, venture capital investments, accounting and payroll, public relations, personnel, security, travel), and the fifty-fourth floor, where the headquarters of the Rockefeller Brothers Fund, the American Conservation Association, and Rock Resorts, Inc., were found.

The three Rockefeller floors were served by the highest tier of the building's elevator system, the first stop on the way up being the top executive floor for RCA, the fifty-third. The visitor alighting from one of the eight elevators on the fifty-sixth floor would face a glass wall and door behind which sat a man at a desk. For several decades, this receptionist was a distinguished-looking black man, Howard Douglas. There was no sign or placard—the visitor who did not know whose office it was didn't belong there. After Douglas retired, his post and its counterparts on the two floors below were filled by retired New York City policemen.

The pattern that emerged after the war stayed put. Each brother had a small number of associates, and the central management staff and service units were available to all of the family. The entire group, numbering over 200 people, would forgather once a year at the office Christmas party, a rather sedate affair lasting several hours of the late afternoon in one of the large rooms of the Rockefeller Center Luncheon Club on the sixty-fifth floor. Champagne and hors d'oeuvres were served and all the Rockefellers that could attend formed the receiving line. Each year a different member of the family would say a few words of appreciation to the assembled staff.

Three men in senior positions were important counselors to the brothers. One was J. Richardson Dilworth, who served as head of the office and also of investments from 1958 until his retirement in 1981. John Lockwood had succeeded Thomas Debevoise as senior legal counsel after the war; in the late 1960s Lockwood withdrew progressively to be replaced by another Milbank, Tweed partner, Donal C. O'Brien, Jr. The third counselor was Dana Creel, president of the Brothers Fund until his gradual retirement in the late 1970s. He was succeeded by William Dietel.

Other important advisers were the senior tax lawyer, Howard Bolton; senior investments adviser Peter O. Crisp; and the head of accounting, David Fernald. The public relations office lost some of its importance after the death of Frank Jamieson. He was replaced by Emmett Hughes, former editor of *Life* and speechwriter for President Eisenhower, and Martha Dalrymple resigned. Later occupants of the office were Stephen David and George Taylor. For many years the office manager under Dilworth was Carl Siegesmund, who retired in the early 1970s to be replaced by Edward Burdick.

The practice of carefully choosing associates and reposing great trust in them had been started by Senior in the Standard Oil Company. It had been continued by Junior in building up the family office, and it remained in force under the brothers. It worked extremely well. JDR acknowledged the fact in a speech to the National Institute of Social Sciences in 1967, when he quoted and confirmed his grandfather's formula for success: "My associates; I have been very fortunate in my associates." The brothers respected and trusted their staff and received in return integrity and professionalism. JDR commented on this occasionally in his diary. For example, he wrote of Dana Creel: "He is a very wise and helpful individual and I do greatly respect his judgment."

JDR had the northwest corner suite of "Room 5600," a fairly large office, an office for his two secretaries, four adjoining offices for his associates with areas for their secretaries, and a large reception room. To the south of this space, his father's large office was preserved just as it had been when Junior died in 1960, with its antique paneling, furniture, and chandeliers. It was dark, gloomy, museumlike. When JDR's needs for space expanded toward the end of the 1960s, Junior's office was carefully dismantled piece by piece and put in storage, later to be restored in the Rockefeller Archive Center at Pocantico. Three small offices and room for a secretarial pool were made out of the resulting space.

JDR's office had an Early American air about it, with its antique sofa and chairs and walls painted Williamsburg blue. Behind his walnut desk and leather chair was the Eastman Johnson portrait of his grandfather in middle age. It was the only work of art in JDR's suite of offices that stayed in its place, for the outstanding feature of the decor was the changing selection of works from his Asian and American collections. The Asian pieces were usually shown in the large reception area, along with a few American paintings, perhaps the Hicks *Peaceable Kingdom*, a Hopper, and some landscapes, possibly something from the Hudson River School. There would be paintings in all the other offices, a unique fringe benefit for JDR's associates. JDR took great pleasure in planning the changeovers (which occurred about once a year), as we learn from the diary for 1965:

In the course of the day all my art objects here in the office were removed and a new group brought in. I had, of course, planned the location for all of the principal pieces so that the change-over was made without too much trouble. However, I had fun working out the exact location and heights. Feel that the new pieces do tie together in a meaningful way. Having the art here has, I think, been significant not only in terms of visitors but also those in the office seem to enjoy it. Have, generally speaking, brought only first-rate pieces.

The 1960s ushered in a period of change and expansion in JDR's activities, and consequently in his office staff as well. Aside from the JDR 3rd Fund in 1963 and a number of minor initiatives toward the end of the decade, his great period of institution-building was over. His concern now was to make the institutions he had already created successful and to continue being a leader in his major fields of action—the arts, population, Asian affairs, and philanthropy. We have seen how his activities in the arts grew, most conspicuously in his work for Lincoln Center, which took all of Ed Young's time and much of JDR's. The 1960s, as we shall see, was the great "takeoff" period in the population field, marked by JDR's massive participation. The wide variety of his Asian interests, especially the Asia Society, became ever more demanding. In addition, his concern for the care and preservation of philanthropy as a unique social force in the United States suddenly became highly active.

Earl Newsom, whom JDR still occasionally consulted, not about public relations as such but about his career and his interests, warned his client that he was understaffed for handling the demands on him and the things he wanted to do in his four major fields. Back in 1954, JDR had formed his Policy and Planning Committee to advise him. It consisted of his two associates, McLean and Young, plus Frank Jamieson, John Lockwood, and Dana Creel. Jamieson was now gone, Lockwood was nearing retirement, and Dana Creel, although still at hand when needed, was busy with the much-enlarged Rockefeller Brothers Fund.

Moreover, Young was giving full time to Lincoln Center, physically located there, and Don McLean was growing restive. He had enjoyed field work, negotiating, institution-building, so that in a sense his glory days with JDR were over. After more than a decade as an associate, he was close to having had enough of staff work. He had already turned down an offer to head a medical institution in Cleveland, but it seemed likely that he would soon be leaving Room 5600.

In 1963 JDR talked to Donal O'Brien about joining his staff, but in the end O'Brien decided he wanted to stick with the law. JDR kept searching and, by the end of the year, he had decided on two new associates. One was Ray Lamontagne, Jay's Peace Corps friend, who had a law degree. He was warmly endorsed by Don McLean. The second man was John W.

McNulty, who had been on the public relations staff at Lincoln Center and had been helping JDR with some of his speeches for several years.

Both decisions were fruitful. Lamontagne was hired to spend most of his time in the burgeoning population field, but soon proved effective as a counselor in other areas as well. As for the hiring of a speechwriter, it signified the beginning of a subtle change in JDR's orientation, away from institution-building and toward public advocacy. Slowly, JDR was becoming more philosophical, intent upon forming a legacy of ideas. He was now much sought after as a speaker, and he carefully sifted these requests for the best opportunities to influence events or set a policy direction.

Within a year another new associate was brought in, Kenneth T. Young, Jr., whom JDR had known when Young served in various posts in the State Department Far Eastern Bureau, most recently as ambassador to Thailand. But Ken Young was in Room 5600 only a short time. JDR succeeded in making some desired changes at the Asia Society, and Young moved over to become its president. By this time, Don McLean had also left Room 5600 to become head of the Lahey Clinic in Boston.

In 1966, Jack McNulty was "borrowed" for three months by Robert Kintner of President Johnson's staff to bolster the speechwriting crew in the White House. But McNulty caught "Potomac fever," and when asked to stay remained in Washington.[1] To replace McLean and McNulty, JDR recruited two more new associates. One was his college classmate, Datus C. Smith, who took hold gradually as he phased out of his role as president of Franklin Books. Smith assumed McLean's role of liaison with the Asian programs and the JDR 3rd Fund and also served as the administrator of JDR's small staff group. The other new associate was John E. Harr, a former journalist who most recently had been director of the Office of Management Planning in the Department of State. Harr took over the writing assignments from McNulty, liaison with the Rockefeller Public Service Awards program, and responsibility for developing programs in several new fields. Both men were fully on board by mid-1967. By then, Ed Young had returned to Room 5600, although he still spent most of his time on Lincoln Center matters. He also took over liaison duties with the Japan Society and was responsible for the preparation of JDR's annual program of personal giving.

This, then, was JDR's staff by the end of 1967: Young, Smith, Lamontagne, and Harr, each with well-defined duties and also expected to meet as a group, usually once a week, to advise JDR on any appropriate subject. From time to time, consultants would join the group. For a while in the late 1960s, one of these was JDR's summer neighbor in Maine, the former actor Robert Montgomery, who served as speech consultant to JDR as he had to President Eisenhower. Another participant, for a time, was Kathryn Bloom of the Arts in Education program of the JDR 3rd Fund. For a longer term, beginning in 1968, a new man was engaged to fill the void left by the death of Earl Newsom. This was Bill Ruder, of the New York public relations firm Ruder & Finn. As with Newsom, Ruder's role was not to work on conventional public relations lines but to counsel as a friendly critic of JDR's policy and career choices.

A tradition from the earliest days of Rockefeller philanthropy had been to respect the integrity of organizations that were created and to give executives a full opportunity to play an autonomous role within them. The Rockefellers and their associates normally refrained from interfering from day to day, trying to exercise influence only in a manner appropriate to an officer or director when important matters affecting the organization required it. JDR was a strong believer in the right interplay of independence and advice. As early as 1954, when he established his Policy and Planning Committee, he had taken pains to make clear the division of responsibility between his associates and the staff of organizations in which he played a part. He declared that it was not the function of his associates to influence "the substantive programs or projects."

I feel strongly that the organizations should be autonomous and that we at Room 5600 should become involved in their operations only to the extent that we have responsibilities as officers or directors. This is essential if the integrity of the organizations is to be maintained and if the personnel of the organizations is to feel a real sense of responsibility for the units with which they are associated. In short, it is my feeling that [my associates] should be advisory to me and not to the organizations themselves.[2]

As a result, relations among JDR's office and staff and the numerous organizations in which he played a role were in general excellent. JDR leaned over backward to act with correctness toward the Rockefeller Foundation and the Rockefeller Brothers Fund. None of his associates were assigned liaison roles with either foundation. Thus, in JDR's office only JDR himself really knew what was going on within the Foundation. And his staff did not normally see or discuss the dockets that were prepared for RBF board meetings.

This sense of correctness permeated all staffing arrangements. A person being hired as an associate would be told that salary would lie somewhere between the amounts that one might earn in an academic position and in the business world. Because the office was a nonprofit one serving worthwhile causes, one was expected to have a motive beyond that of making money. At the same time, one had to be compensated enough to live well in the New York City area. Fringe benefits and working conditions were good, but normally there were no bonuses or other perquisites except for the prestige associated with this unique window on the world. The staff had the sense that JDR was a sort of national resource, and their challenge constantly was to find the best way to use that resource to the greater advantage of the country and the world.

Although it was one man's staff, there was security for the employees. JDR was not an employer who lost his temper or made unreasonable demands. On the other hand, the relationship was not a close, personal one. There was always some sense of distance between JDR and his staff members, although JDR clearly was especially fond of Lamontagne, in some ways almost as a father toward a son. JDR rarely asked his staff for anything to be done during evenings, weekends, or holidays, although he frequently made late-evening telephone calls to discuss some office matter. There was little socializing within the staff and almost none between JDR and staff members. Although he was ready to help if someone had a serious problem, JDR did not make a practice of giving extensive loans or gifts to his associates the way that Nelson did.[3]

Over the years JDR had developed an effective personal style, both in small groups and on the platform. He had the politician's gift of making the individual he was talking to feel as if he or she were the only person in the world. His sincerity and modesty tended to disarm people who otherwise might be suspicious of him, young radicals, for example, or Third World statesmen such as Bourguiba or Nasser. A visitor to his office would usually come away charmed, having found JDR courteous, thoughtful, attentive, and genuinely interested in what the other person had to say. When he was anxious to make a point, he would not override someone else or interrupt, but he had a way of sending out signals to get attention—holding a clutched hand in the air or leaning forward with an intent gaze.

JDR had become an effective public speaker thanks to three factors. He had conquered his fear by facing it frontally—by debating and taking speech courses at Loomis and Princeton and in not running away from opportunities to face an audience. He projected sincerity, no doubt because he *was* sincere. And he was always well prepared—extremely well prepared. He marveled at the politicians in the family, his brothers and his son, who had to make eight or ten speeches a day when campaigning and could take copy handed to them by a speechwriter with only a moment's review. For JDR the only way was to take a great deal of time, certainly weeks and even months, in preparing for a speech. He would never accept an important speaking engagement unless it was at least three months off and was astonished if an organization asked on shorter notice. He liked to live with a draft for days on end, to fuss with it, go over it with experts, agonize over a word, sentence, or paragraph. He was not so much a "nitpicker" as he was a natural editor who could afford to take his time. He had a good sense of organization, and he refused to utter any statement he did not fully understand or that did not fit exactly the purpose and the architecture of his speech.

Life was made bearable for those who worked with JDR on his speeches or magazine articles by several conditions. One was that patterns tended to recur in the problems presented by the speeches, and these usually would be solved by about the third draft. That draft, very often, would be about 90 percent "in the ballpark," so that the time and trouble from then on were a burden on JDR himself and the typist, not the speechwriter. Bill Ruder chided JDR for spending 10 percent of the time doing 90 percent of the job and then 90 percent of the time fussing over the remaining 10 percent. JDR agreed and tried to change, but it was a hard habit for him to break, although Ruder, as was his style and in a sense his role, kept reminding him of it. What Ruder was talking about, of course, was the syndrome of the perfectionist. True, JDR could afford to spend his time on whatever he wanted to, and this partly explained his behavior. But when it came to the written word, he also yielded to the passion of the painstaking reviewer. This was especially pronounced in the speeches, where JDR alone was in charge and responsible for the product. After all, it was he who would be standing up facing an audience and uttering the words. The next most arduous task was composing magazine articles, but in these an editor was involved who would set some limits to the process. Next came letters of great importance or considered to be such, which required much labor; they went through many drafts. Only routine correspondence and JDR's diary were released at first draft.

The point of Ruder's gentle jabs was not just the unproductive use of time; also implicit in them was the belief that achieving the "right words" on paper was not the same as achieving the desired result in the real world. Experience also kept reminding JDR of this truth, but that did not help him to break the habit of overdrafting and revising.

On the positive side, the endless fussing with a draft was JDR's way of keeping in touch with others and their ideas, of learning and internalizing this knowledge. As he grew older, he was reading less. His most important source of ideas and insights consisted in talking with other people. In effect, when JDR accepted an invitation to speak or a request for an article, the speechwriter's task often amounted to setting up an adult education course in the subject for one student. This might include trips out of town, visits to sites in New York, and bids to a stream of interesting visitors who were knowledgeable about the subject. With them JDR would hold long discussions of the forthcoming topic. One would see people such as Martin Luther King, Jr., visiting Room 5600; or former Chief Justice Earl Warren soon after his retirement; Daniel Patrick Moynihan; the writer Alex Haley; the anthropologist Margaret Mead—to cite but a few out of many. An unforgettable sight was that of two "living institutions" walking down the corridor of Room 5600: JDR escorting Miss Mead out after their meeting, walking slowly past the Asian and American art, his tall, craggy profile leaning solicitously over the short, squat outline of his guest, who was making progress with the aid of a staff as tall as she was.

So important to JDR was the interaction with people that on occasion he liked to vary his collaborators, sometimes retaining an outside consultant. At other times, the speechwriter would come in at the end, to serve as the "doctor" to the final draft. Occasionally, JDR, the speechwriter, and a consultant would work together throughout. There were times when the results could be proportionate to the effort, if the work on the speech led JDR to make an important shift in policy or to undertake a new program or activity.

JDR's notion of the power of the written word was part and parcel of his belief in logic and rationality. This was shown again in what might be called his "personnel officer" mode. When he dealt with people who were not performing up to his expectations—something that happened fairly often—JDR had almost boundless faith in his ability to counsel them, to get them to see the error of their ways and take the correct path henceforth. One form this took was the phenomenon of "year-end shape-up letters" that JDR wrote to the heads of the organizations of which he was founder or chairman. This was dreaded by the secretaries because the letters literally would be written on the last day of the year, with many revisions, which could cut into private plans for New Year's. Another form was personal counseling in which JDR kindly but bluntly would give another person feedback about his faults and shortcomings. No one seemed exempt, from brother Nelson on down—the diary is filled with examples.

Usually, there would be two results. One was that most people would agree with JDR's critique. Given his high status and grandfatherly manner, it was hard not to agree with him, and JDR would often conclude his diary entry with a comment about "how nice" the other person had been. The second result was that nothing would change, or very little. Despite constant examples in life's experience to the contrary, JDR never lost faith that he could improve people by sweet reason.

The subdued elegance of Room 5600 and the lofty position of its occupant could be overwhelming for some visitors. He was good at putting people at their ease, but his status still kept some in awe, even individuals who worked with him. This was less of a problem on his immediate staff. JDR was wise enough and secure enough to want people around him who would tell him the truth as they saw it, not "yes men." McLean's characteristic bluntness had set the tone in the beginning. JDR's understanding of the need is evident from the diary note on the hiring of Datus Smith: "He always tells me what he really thinks and does it simply and directly." The staff was not troubled by excessive deference; familiarity helped to create a sense of ease. For when he was not traveling, JDR was in the office every day—often the first one in and the last to leave—and he was very accessible to the staff. Seeing JDR virtually every day reduced the status barrier to a comfortable level for his associates, something the executives in JDR's many organizations located elsewhere in New York City did not have.

For the sake of an even better understanding, JDR and his staff decided to work specifically on their ability to communicate with one another. After months of talking about it, a "staff retreat" was held in January 1968. The thought was that getting away from Room 5600 to a new setting, even for a short time, would facilitate communication. Unfortunately, the site finally chosen was still JDR's "turf"—Bassett Hall at Colonial Williamsburg. Harr and Lamontagne made arrangements to bring Chris Argyris from Harvard University as a consultant on the communications process within the group. Argyris was perhaps the foremost exponent of the "human relations" school of management and an expert in the small-group training developed under the aegis of the National Training Laboratories.[4] In this approach the group works to create a temporary new environment in which status and communications problems can be addressed frankly and new behavior tested. Spouses were invited along on the trip to Williamsburg, but were not included in the group sessions, which were held morning and afternoon over a three-day period. It was an eight-person group: JDR, his four associates, and three consultants—Robert Montgomery, Kathryn Bloom, and Professor Argyris. JDR described the group sessions in his characteristically understated and bland way:

Another all day Bassett Hall session. Professor Argyris has encouraged each of the participants to speak out frankly. This has certainly stimulated discussion. His interest in such sessions is particularly on the human relations side, having in mind the importance of inter-relationships in terms of effective operation. This approach means of course developing situations that might not otherwise come to the surface in an ordinary staff conference, even one of this duration. Certainly much of it is helpful and to the good. The feeling seemed to be that the discussion had been useful.

The entry suggests that JDR understood what the sessions were intended to do and was vaguely satisfied at the time. Possibly Argyris was a bit overawed himself and was not as penetrating as he normally was in such exercises. Whatever the reason, the "retreat" did not "take" with JDR on an emotional level and his longer view was to see it as disappointing because the group spent three days and did not accomplish much. By this, he meant the actual work of the office.

In truth, JDR was rarely satisfied for long by evidence of progress or accomplishment in any endeavor. He would not allow himself to savor success. His mind immediately would jump to the next task or challenge. In this he was very much like his father, wearing the Protestant ethic like a shawl. This was of a piece with JDR's general working style, his patient, behind-the-scenes approach, his refusal to become discouraged, his unwavering pursuit of objectives. Ray Lamontagne's favorite image of JDR was to see him as a Sherman tank. No matter what obstacles and disappointments might be strewn in his path, he would keep coming, not in a swift or fancy way—but relentlessly.

An example of this dauntlessness occurred when JDR took up a suggestion by Ray Lamontagne—that it was time to break the barrier against black members in the clubs he belonged to in New York City and Washington. One way to fight this prejudice was to resign in public protest, as several members of President Kennedy's administration had done in Washington and as Nelson had done in New York. JDR thought this was the politician's way; it tended to occur at election time, and it seemed to make no difference—the clubs kept on discriminating. He made up his mind that the way to fight this battle was from within—patiently and persistently, without necessary recourse to public fanfare.

JDR first talked to the officers of the clubs to find out what the practice was and to begin to make the case for a new policy. A diary entry covering a trip to Washington in 1966 suggested how useful this approach was going to be:

Next went to see Livingston Merchant, the President of the Metropolitan Club . . . to talk with him about the Club's racial problems. Found that they had not changed at all since I last talked with the president five years ago. Still not only do they not have a Negro member but if a member brings in a Negro [guest] he is later told that this is counter to Club policy. Told Livie that I was not only sad at the continuation of the status quo but also that he as a leader in our government's foreign service had not felt compelled to take some leadership as President of the Club working towards a more liberal approach. His main reply was that he felt that Washington still being basically southern, the raising of the issue would split the Club right down the middle and he indicated he enjoyed the Club too much to see that happen.

So JDR decided on another stratagem—to propose a black candidate and force the club to deal officially with the proposal. He needed a highly qualified man who would agree to the attempt and be secure enough to endure rejection. Lamontagne proposed to him the ideal candidate: Clifton Wharton, Jr., the vice president of the Agricultural Development Council. A tall, handsome, gregarious man, Wharton was the son of a career Foreign Service officer who had served in ambassadorial posts. Clif Wharton graduated from Harvard in 1948 and became the first black student admitted to the School of Advanced International Studies at Johns Hopkins. But instead of following his father's footsteps in the U.S. Foreign Service, young Wharton's interest was development assistance abroad. He had been in the audience when General George Marshall made the Harvard commencement address announcing what came to be known as the Marshall Plan.

Wharton went to work for Nelson Rockefeller's American International Association, specializing on development in Latin America. After a few years, this kindled an interest in economics, and he went to the University of Chicago to earn his Ph.D. He also met Art Mosher there. When Mosher was called to New York to succeed J. Lossing Buck as head of JDR's Council on Economic and Cultural Affairs (which became the Agricultural Development Council), he hired Wharton as his assistant. Wharton gained field experience as resident program officer in Malaysia. Both there and in New York he quickly built an enviable reputation for both research and administration in his chosen field.

When Lamontagne first brought Wharton in to discuss the subject of club membership, JDR spoke of both the University Club and the Century Association. "You know, they discriminate," he said to Wharton very solemnly. Wharton allowed as how he knew that, and said he would go along with the plan if JDR wanted to propose him. He said he knew more people at the Century, but JDR seemed to want to go after the University Club, so they agreed on that. For a club that required a college degree as one criterion for entry, Wharton obviously was overqualified.

JDR then opened the campaign:

Mr. Charles Saltzman came to 5600. I had asked to see him because he is President of the University Club. Wanted to advise with him about putting up Clif Wharton, an outstandingly fine Negro with the ADC, for membership in the University Club. We had a good talk lasting about an hour and I felt that he was sympathetic. He told me about the Club's handling of the Jewish situation not too many years ago in which he was involved as Chairman of the Club's Membership Committee. He agreed to take up the matter informally but indicated it would take time to reach a conclusion as to the best of his knowledge no Negro had ever been presented for membership before.

A month later, Saltzman reported back to JDR on his informal soundings. JDR wrote: "The feeling seemed to be that proposing a Negro for membership at this time would be somewhat premature " The only thing to do now was to press the issue, so JDR went ahead with the formal proposal. It was 1967 by the time all the paperwork and the rounding up of the required number of members to support the nomination were done. Two years later, the matter was still unresolved despite frequent pressure by JDR. He stepped up his campaign with more phone calls, letters, and the buttonholing of members. Then Clif Wharton was offered and accepted the presidency of Michigan State University.

The officers of the club were delighted. They called up JDR with a solution to their predicament. The by-laws of the club allowed any college or university president to enjoy privileges when nominated by a member who was a graduate of the institution. Among the seven or eight members of the New York University Club who were graduates of Michigan State, one could be found who would so nominate Wharton. But the president (Wharton) would not be an actual member of the club; he would merely enjoy its privileges and only so long as he was president. The club officials thought they had put an end to JDR's pressure without having set the precedent of accepting a black as a member. JDR conferred with Wharton and they agreed not to let the club off the hook with this nonsolution. It was to be full membership or nothing at all. Faced with this strong stand, the club officials finally capitulated, and Wharton became the first black member in 1970.

In contrast to his patience in achieving this result, JDR was often impatient over details. He often fretted at mealtimes if there were some business to be performed, as when he hosted a luncheon meeting or had a guest to discuss some current topic. JDR did not like to waste much time on cocktails and dining, wanting to move right along to the discussion. For him, eating was for sustenance, not pleasure. He did frequently enjoy a glass of beer or sherry before lunch, but was never known to take two. He always had his coffee served demitasse, and his favorite dessert was butter pecan ice cream.

Once when JDR took a new associate to lunch, one of the appetizers on the menu was Oysters Rockefeller. The guest said he had never known exactly what they were. JDR told him they were oysters baked on the half shell with a dressing made primarily of spinach. When the associate still looked puzzled, JDR said soberly: "Green, you see. Like money."

On another occasion an associate spent a Sunday night at JDR's Manhattan apartment because he and JDR had hours of work still to do on testimony that JDR was to present the next day in Washington. When dinner with JDR and Blanchette was served he found that on Sunday evenings the Rockefellers had a light meal. He was starving by the time the work session broke up hours later. JDR asked if he wanted anything before going to bed, and the underfed collaborator confessed that he would like a midnight snack. JDR took him to the kitchen, told him to see what he could find, and then went padding about the apartment to turn off the small lights above the paintings on the walls. Meanwhile, the victim of malnutrition was lost in a maze of pantries and preparation rooms that were all immaculate, with no sign of ordinary glasses and tableware or even a refrigerator. Finally JDR came to the rescue, locating a glass of milk and a piece of cake. As his associate eased his pangs, JDR shook his head. "Just like Alida," he said.

All of JDR's associates naturally have their favorite stories about him, his habits and foibles, what it was like to travel with him, and so on. These are told with amused shakings of the head and with great affection. Those who worked with him every day in his office probably knew him better than anyone else, in some respects better than members of his family. From their near vantage point, they could see the faults and weaknesses, the exasperating habits, but they could also see the great qualities that far outweighed the foibles.

They were drawn to him and were loyal because he was doing important work, because he was dedicated, because he was willing to attempt new things and to take risks. They were not cronies or intimates and knew that the relation was better and more professional that way. They were not sycophants, dependent on a rich man's whims; the bond was always one of mutual respect. They knew that their man would never be found wanting in matters of principle; his integrity was impeccable. It was an article of faith with him to treat others equitably and fairly. He could be angry and upset like anyone else, but he never showed it in outbursts of temper, in behavior that humiliated or degraded another person.

When everything was weighed and recalled, it was clear that one great quality of JDR's towered above all the others, a quality that drew people to him and made working with him exciting. Despite his old-fashioned upbringing and stilted ways, he was an open-minded man. He was refreshingly ready for new ideas and when these were good, eager for change.

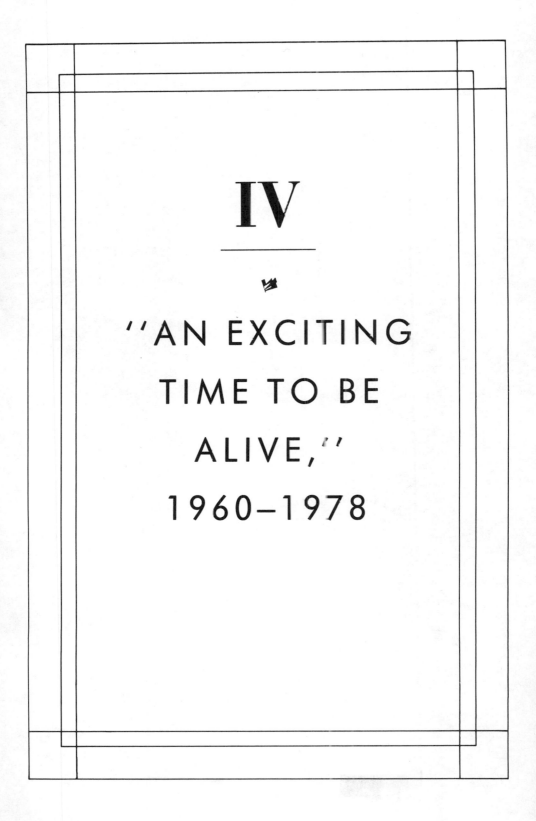

IV

"AN EXCITING
TIME TO BE
ALIVE,"
1960–1978

18

ꚷ

THE FOURTH FIELD

ONE OF the more remarkable aspects of JDR's career was his self-appointed role as the caretaker of philanthropy. Many wealthy people engage in philanthropic activity, and some even make it a full-time occupation, as JDR and his father did. But JDR was unique in his time in the extent to which he exerted leadership to protect, reform, and enhance philanthropy generally in the United States.

In this he was following a pattern set by his grandfather and father, but he varied that pattern to meet new problems and contemporary needs. Historians credit John D. Rockefeller and Andrew Carnegie as the most prominent leaders in creating modern American philanthropy around the turn of the century. Rockefeller's only son, John D., Jr., devoted his life to further developing and expanding his father's vision of the role of philanthropy as a basic institution in American society. Together with a host of able associates, Junior worked tirelessly to adapt philanthropy to the modern world in the reformist ideology of the Progressive Era. Their goal was to make philanthropy more efficient, economical, democratic, and responsive to modern needs. In their view, philanthropy could no longer be merely charitable and conservative, but must become reformist, liberal, and scientific. Thus conceived, the modern charitable trust, along with the modern business corporation, would lead the way to a bright, shining future.[1]

In his turn, JDR perceived that philanthropy had fallen far short of this vision. Battered by the Depression and increasingly dominated by tax considerations, philanthropy was far from being an equal partner of the other two major sectors of American society, government and business. Its role was not well understood by leaders of those sectors, nor by the public generally. Developments in the postwar years threatened its viability and integrity. For all these reasons, JDR determined to take responsibility himself for trying to conceptualize philanthropy anew, broaden its base, and enhance its value and stature as a major bastion of the American polity.

As a youth, JDR worried that he would never be able to live up to his father's example—he never commanded more than a fraction of the resources Junior did. Yet, in this case, JDR clearly exceeded expectations in moving beyond the tending of his own philanthropic activities to a concern for the well-being of the entire field of philanthropy. Junior was aware of his son's interest, but had no idea of the proportions it would assume. As in so many other areas of JDR's career, there is irony in the fact that the important services he rendered in philanthropy all occurred too late to earn his father's approbation.

As was often the case with JDR, his initial interest in philanthropy as a field that needed attention was largely instinctive, not something he had thought through deeply. It was as if he had thought that there must be some special significance to his spending his life in philanthropy beyond what he could do personally with his own limited resources.

JDR began thinking of philanthropy as his fourth field of activity in the 1950s, having been stimulated by becoming chairman of the Rockefeller Foundation and dealing with the Reece investigation. His three other main fields—Asia, population, and the arts—had all become quite operational, characterized by institution-building and specific programs. But for years JDR's involvement in his fourth field, literally, was limited to talking; with surprising frequency, according to his diary, JDR met with wealthy individuals or new foundation executives to discuss their opportunities and responsibilities in philanthropy. His thoughtful counsel became recognized, and people began to seek him out for advice.

The events of the 1960s gradually moved JDR to activate his relatively neglected fourth field of interest. His participation in Lincoln Center deepened his knowledge of some of the important issues, such as the financial plight of many nonprofit institutions. At the same time, he became more sensitive to the value both of large donors to major campaigns and of having many givers from all elements of society. The personal visits and letter-writing in his long-term effort to convert J. Paul Getty into a philanthropist honed JDR's thinking about the moral and social obligations of the wealthy in a democratic system.

Philanthropy has a long and honorable history in other countries, but seems to have occupied a special place in the American experience, perhaps because of the openness of the frontier and the economy. The modernizing of philanthropy at the turn of the century, including the invention of the foundation, were specifically American developments.

Obviously, philanthropic motivations existed long before the income tax was invented. Yet so important has taxation become as a multifaceted instrument of public policy that it tends to be a dominating feature of modern-day philanthropy. It is not possible to engage in charitable contributions to any significant degree without reference to the tax laws. Generally, American law has favored charitable giving. Even though tax laws might become stringent for a time, as during the worst years of the Depression, this is usually followed by a swing of the pendulum, as in the 1954 amendments liberalizing the "unlimited charitable deduction."[2]

This particular development had an important effect on JDR. In the early 1960s he learned that he had met the new qualifications—for eight of the ten preceding years the combination of his charitable gifts and income taxes had exceeded 90 percent of his income. This meant that henceforth there was no limit on the deductions he could take for charity. He could give away 90 percent of his net taxable income to legitimate causes and pay *no* income taxes. The immediate effect of this was that it greatly enlarged the amount that he could shift from the category of taxes to the category of charitable gifts—nearly tripling the latter, in fact. But JDR felt as a matter of principle that it would be wrong to pay *no* taxes (even though he would be giving away at least 90 percent of his net taxable income to worthwhile causes), so he made certain every year that he paid 5 to 10 percent of his income in taxes, still allowing a vastly increased amount that he could devote to charitable giving. Though he obviously had good intentions, this practice of JDR's erupted into a minor controversy at precisely the wrong moment later in the decade.

Despite being one of the growing number of wealthy Americans who qualified for the "unlimited charitable deduction," JDR did not think of philanthropy as a province of the wealthy. To the contrary, he was adamant in his belief that the success of the American system depended on the philanthropic impulse being widespread, rather than narrowly restricted. He was always much more concerned with how to "democratize" philanthropy than with maintaining a privileged position for the wealthy.

It was for this reason that he disliked the very term "philanthropy," even as he continued to use it for years for lack of a better alternative. He felt it was a complicated word that was little understood, and that it probably had an inescapable association with great individual wealth, or worse, with the idea of the "do-gooder," as in the Helen Hokinson cartoons in the *New Yorker* featuring rich, fat society ladies with empty heads. To JDR, philanthropy was a hard, pragmatic business that was vital to the successful functioning of a democratic society, and thus should be taken very seriously.

This conviction deepened within JDR as philanthropy increasingly came under fire from many quarters during the 1960s—and the result was that his somewhat inactive "fourth" field now became a major preoccupation. The attacks on philanthropy—mainly directed at foundations, which had grown steadily in number—were a manifestation of the social turbulence of the 1960s. In *The Big Foundations,* Waldemar Nielsen points out that foundations have become a favorite target in the United States during times of stress or social crisis such as the Depression of the 1930s and the McCarthy era after World War II: "Not surprisingly, therefore, as another massive social crisis began to unfold during the 1960s, foundations again found themselves caught in the political crossfire. The shooting came from all ideological directions."[3]

The man who kept the pot boiling most consistently throughout the decade was the redoubtable old Populist from Texas, Congressman Wright Patman. Ever since he had entered Congress in 1928, Patman had been inveighing against the evils of concentrated economic power, which he saw lurking everywhere. In 1961 he focused his attention on foundations. Although he conceded in the beginning that some foundations had great accomplishments to their credit, Patman's probe increasingly took on the characteristics of a crusade. Many of his charges were exaggerated and much of his data unreliable, but his work also began to uncover genuine examples of abuses and misconduct by foundations. And in hearings before Patman in 1964 came the first revelation that the Central Intelligence Agency was using foundations and other nonprofit institutions as conduits and "front" organizations.[4]

Goaded into action by Patman's continuing pressure, the Treasury Department did a study of private foundations in 1965. It rejected some of the more exaggerated charges (such as that foundations represented a "disproportionately large" segment of the national economy and were "dangerous" concentrations of economic power). But the study also effectively analyzed certain growing abuses, and it proposed legislative remedies. The abuses had mainly to do with "self-dealing" (transactions that could result in improper diversion of foundation assets to private advantage), slow payout (resulting in delays of the benefits to charity for which the foundations were granted tax-exempt status in the first place), and various improper relationships between donor families and foundations, and between businesses and foundations.[5]

Not surprisingly, the sound ideas for reform in the Treasury report were largely ignored by the foundation world, dismissed as completely inadequate by the critics of foundations, and editorially praised by the *New York Times.*[6] The pressure increased as Patman stepped up his efforts, releasing a particularly juicy example of foundation misconduct every now and then. Foundation executives such as John Gardner began to worry that all foundations might be penalized because of the misconduct of a relative few.[7] By 1967 foundations were under widespread attack. Conservatives were incensed by some programs such as the Ford Foundation's support of voter registration drives in the South and school redistricting in Manhattan. Left-wing critics increasingly saw foundation grants and think tanks as the fount of U.S. policies they regarded as repressive. CIA links to nonprofit organizations, many of them well-known and respected, erupted into a series of major revelations and scandals

A general sense of public outrage boiled over when Treasury Secretary Joseph Barr released specific figures on the number of wealthy individuals who had paid no income tax in 1967 (including 155 with adjusted gross incomes of more than $200,000 and twenty-one with incomes in excess of $1 million). The animus against foundations became part of a general and growing public demand for tax reform. It was clear that private philanthropy was approaching a crisis as lawmakers on Capitol Hill began gearing up to meet the demand. Early in the decade, JDR sensed the negative trend coming, and very soon he moved well beyond his avuncular habit of dispensing advice to new philanthropists. He began laboring ceaselessly for sensible reform and the preservation of incentives for philanthropic giving. He began speaking in public on the subject—for example, to the "One Per Cent Plan" group in Cleveland and the Federation of Jewish Philanthropies in New York City.[8] He formed an internal office group to meet periodically and discuss strategy for meeting the assault on philanthropy. In addition to his associates, the members were lawyers John Lockwood and Howard Bolton, Dana Creel and Robert Scrivner of the Rockefeller Brothers Fund, and J. Richardson Dilworth. Later, JDR also gradually brought together a larger informal group composed of some of these men plus some outside advisers. And he became an inveterate lobbyist, traveling frequently to Washington throughout the 1960s for round after round of meetings with leaders in the tax field. These included former IRS commissioners, prominent lawyers, three succeeding Treasury Secretaries (Douglas Dillon, Henry Fowler, and Joseph Barr), and the two key chairmen in Congress—Russell Long of Senate Finance and Wilbur Mills of House Ways and Means. JDR also met on occasion with other lawmakers, including a pleasant chat in 1964 with Wright Patman, and with men at the second and third echelons, both on the Hill and in the agencies. One of JDR's most helpful contacts in Washington was Lawrence N. Woodworth, at that time the chief counsel to the Joint Internal Revenue

Committee. A voluminous correspondence piled up between JDR and these Washington figures, covering almost every conceivable aspect of policy that might affect philanthropy.

One advantage of lobbying is that the lobbyist becomes well informed—JDR was in a good position to know how ominous the prospects in Washington were. Revision of the jerry-built Internal Revenue Code was long overdue in the minds of almost everyone, but it was hard to find any two people who would agree about just how it should be done. Every special interest that might be affected was fighting for its own welfare. Philanthropy seemed to be the weakest of them all. It was constantly getting bad publicity. It had no visible constituency back in the home districts of members of Congress. Aside from the strenuous efforts of JDR and the few people he was able to mobilize, no one seemed agitated about the fate of an area that tended to be identified with the wealthy and was not well understood by the general public. Lobbyists from some special-interest groups were not above working to divert attention away from their own areas toward the easy target of foundations and their tax privileges.[9]

There were several reasons for the weakness of the philanthropic lobby. It was an ill-organized field with little or no consistent communication among groups with a stake in charitable giving. Foundation executives, who must say "no" to grant requests ten times for every time they are able to say "yes," are not necessarily popular with those who do the asking—there was little rapport and poor communication between what came to be known as "donor groups" and "donee groups." Individuals who might have been effective back on the hustings—college presidents, museum directors, religious leaders—were not energized. Many seemed simply unaware of how serious the trend was. As early as 1964, in a speech to the Federation of Jewish Philanthropies, JDR had been pushing for some sort of "association" in the field to help get it better organized, but to no avail.

He could not even get unity at home. The damaging publicity about rich people who paid no income tax in various years seemed to go on endlessly. To counter it, JDR came up with the idea of proposing a minimum tax of 10 percent on incomes above a certain level, no matter what combination of deductions and exemptions an individual might be entitled to—JDR was even willing to sacrifice the "unlimited charitable deduction" for this. He tested the idea in a brothers' meeting one time when Nelson happened to be absent. David was in favor, but Laurance rejected it.

There also were rivalries and antagonism among various classes of donee groups. Conservative groups such as the United Way, health organizations, and old-line institutions were aligned against groups that seemed to be radical, or at least new, representing new problems and interests, particularly those associated with minorities. JDR and other moderate leaders in philanthropy had long recognized two broad areas of responsibility: the *maintenance* function of continuing to assist long-existing causes and institutions, and a *creative* function of helping new organizations and approaches to deal with new needs and problems. But seemingly nothing could be done to stop the infighting between the various factions or the growing disfavor in which philanthropy seemed to be held in general. In a time of pressure upon philanthropy, it was always the riskier activities— the new and creative ones—that suffered the most. Thus, many representatives of the conservative side were content to sit back and let events unfold.

As matters worsened, JDR's informal advisory group met more often. In addition to the internal figures, the members now included Douglas Dillon; John McCloy; Julius Stratton, chairman of the Ford Foundation; Alan Pifer, president of the Carnegie Corporation; and William Warren, dean of Columbia Law School. With proposals being aired in Washington that would seriously cripple foundations, JDR decided to press ahead with an idea that had emerged from the advisory group to create a formal and independent commission that would make a major study of philanthropy.

Datus Smith, the associate who was JDR's staff man in the field of philanthropy, worked with him to plan the commission. They agreed that Bill Moyers, by then the publisher of *Newsday* on Long Island, would make an excellent chairman. When Moyers had to decline, JDR turned to Peter G. Peterson, a highly regarded businessman who was following in Chuck Percy's footsteps as the president of Bell & Howell in Chicago. In early February 1969, Peterson stopped to see JDR at Fieldwood Farm while en route from Chicago to Boston in his company plane. The two men agreed that the commission should be representative of various interests and be totally independent if its conclusions were to carry any weight. A month later Peterson met with the advisory group in New York to discuss his ideas fully. He then agreed to take on the task.

The commission was given the formal title of "Commission on Foundations and Private Philanthropy." Peterson selected fifteen members in addition to himself, a highly distinguished group representing business, labor, education, the arts, law, and the media. The members all had one thing in common—no official connection with any foundation. Foundations were not asked to fund the effort. JDR gave the first $25,000, followed by Bell & Howell and the AFL-CIO (through the good offices of commission member Lane Kirkland, then the second-ranking executive of the AFL-CIO). Additional funding came from similar grants by individuals and corporations. Peterson selected his own staff and consultants, mostly from the University of Chicago. Throughout the life of the commission, JDR and Datus Smith restricted themselves to merely maintaining a liaison with it.

Meanwhile, the House Ways and Means Committee began hearings on an omnibus tax reform bill. The matter of tax-exempt foundations was considered first and nothing seemed to go right. McGeorge Bundy, the new president of the Ford Foundation, did not make a good impression on some committee members, who regarded him as arrogant and uncaring. The most controversial issue had to do with the grants given by Ford to eight members of the staff of the late Senator Robert F. Kennedy. Bundy had personally approved these grants.

A week later, on February 27, 1969, there followed JDR's earnest testimony for two hours before the committee. The burden of it was a plea "not to throw the baby out with the bath"—a phrase JDR and his advisers favored at the time to make the point that all foundations should not be penalized because of the misconduct of a few. JDR urged Congress to see the difference between actual misconduct and honest mistakes or matters of judgment. Afterwards, JDR worried about a communications gap, writing in his diary that none of the questions from committee members "related to the basic work of foundations or the importance of foundations in relationship to our society today, but almost all to special points of concern to the individual Committee member."

Still, JDR felt that the atmosphere had been "basically friendly" during his testimony. But the committee members had failed to notice or comment on one reference in JDR's statement that led to caustic criticism in the days that followed. In his prepared statement, JDR happened to mention that although he had qualified for the unlimited charitable deduction every year since 1961, he had "deliberately paid a tax of between five and ten percent of my adjusted gross income in each of those years." The fact that this meant that JDR was *giving away* a huge share of his assets each year was lost in the negative reaction that followed. What came across was that a man named Rockefeller was paying a smaller percentage of his income in taxes than the average person and paying any taxes at all only because he *chose* to do so. To many people, this was condescending at best; Congressman Patman registered his "shock" and "disgust" at what he considered to be the worst of the statements "coming from persons who offer self-serving defenses of privileged positions."[10]

As 1969 wore on the situation became worse. The image of foundations suffered another blow that summer in the revelations that Supreme Court Justice Abe Fortas received an annual retainer from the Wolfson Family Foundation and Justice William O. Douglas was on the payroll of the

Parvin Foundation. Louis Wolfson was a notorious stock manipulator and Albert Parvin owned interests in Las Vegas hotels and casinos. Fortas was forced to resign his seat, but Douglas survived efforts to oust him that were led by House Minority Leader Gerald Ford.

Then the Ways and Means Committee reported out a bill that contained harsh and punitive measures against foundations, and the bill soon passed the House. The atmosphere was hostile on all sides. The only person in the Nixon administration who spoke out strongly in defense of foundations was HEW Secretary Robert Finch.[11] As Nielsen described the situation: "Handicapped by a dubious public, an irritated and harassed Congress, and an unsympathetic Administration, the foundations in September prepared to face the Senate Finance Committee."[12]

This time, leaders of donor and donee groups rallied to testify, stimulated by a House bill that could have meant the virtual end of charitable giving. The Peterson Commission made available its interim findings. JDR's testimony on September 27 was strong and forceful. He supported measures to end abuses and questionable conduct by foundations, but beyond this he said that foundations should be strengthened and made "more venturesome" instead of supercautious:

A foundation that never makes mistakes is not worth very much, for this is a sure sign that it never attempts to deal with the really tough problems. Philanthropy must provide the venture capital for attacking such problems. It must pioneer new fields, take calculated risks, identify new needs. These are the historic functions philanthropy has performed best in our pluralistic system. It must perform them more vigorously now than ever before.

JDR concluded with a plea for a more effective partnership between government and philanthropy:

Philanthropy is a valuable resource to government because of its ability to do what government cannot do or is not ready to do, its ability to supplement government efforts, its ability to move quickly and take risks. To me, it would be tragic and self-defeating to cut back this resource.[13]

The Senate committee did leave out several of the worst provisions of the House bill, but added one of its own that placed a forty-year limit on the life of a foundation. This, however, disappeared in the final version of the bill. It was difficult for the philanthropic world to get attention when the conference committee went to work—the measures affecting philanthropy were, after all, only a small part of a huge bill that touched on almost every aspect of taxation. Again the Peterson Commission proved to be a valuable resource.

On December 23 the conferees agreed on the final bill. Present were the expected measures against "self-dealing" and for better reporting, payout, and divestiture, all of which JDR applauded. But also present were measures that could only be regarded as damaging and punitive. Instead of a fee for audit, the bill set a tax on foundation income which, of course, amounted to an indirect tax on charitable recipients. Some measures served to reduce incentives for giving (including the elimination of the "unlimited charitable deduction"). But the worst were the provisions that inhibited foundations from cooperating with government or engaging in activities that might be construed as affecting public policy. These included a dubious distinction between "private" and "operating" foundations and extremely harsh penalties for violating the vague and ambiguous prohibitions.

The bill was not nearly as bad for foundations as it might have been, and some of the onerous provisions could be and were eased by subsequent interpretations by the administrative agencies. There is no way to know how much more damaging the Tax Reform Act of 1969 might have been had it not been for JDR's efforts. But former Treasury Secretary Douglas Dillon was quite certain about one aspect. On January 6, 1970, he wrote to JDR:

Now that the tax bill is law I must tell you how much the charitable world and the entire nation is in your debt. If you had not conceived the idea of the Commission to study the role and operations of foundations, pushed it through to fruition and obtained Peter Peterson to head it up, I don't know where we would be today.

Largely through [Peterson's] efforts, we were successful in knocking out the iniquitous allocation of deductions provision that would have dealt a death blow to private charity as we have known it in this country. And under pressure Congress found an entirely different way to get at tax sheltered income, a way that will not do any harm to charitable giving.

As to foundations, while his success may not have been total, I am sure that the results would have been far, far worse if it had not been for his efforts. And all of this was the result of your original idea of a Commission to study foundations.

My congratulations and thanks. You should be proud of yourself.

In May 1970 the Peterson Commission made its findings public in a trenchant report that was not sparing in its criticism of abuses and misconduct, but also put these in perspective as affecting only a tiny percentage of foundations. The real problem, it said, was that the nation's organizations that depended on charitable support increasingly were operating at deficits and faced serious financial crises in the years ahead. The need, therefore, was to greatly increase charitable giving—especially by improving the tax-incentive system to democratize giving.[14]

The Peterson Commission was handicapped by limits in time and funding, and by the fact that the subject it was considering was undergoing
revision by the Congress at the time. Nevertheless, the report soon was
to become regarded as a landmark contribution. It presented information
on philanthropy never before developed, and a series of recommendations
designed to preserve and improve "a dual system of private giving and
government funding," as Peterson expressed it at the May 1970 press
conference. He said this "was a better way to allocate resources for the
general welfare than the alternative of relying solely on government
allocations."

To JDR, the struggle had only begun. For the better part of a decade,
he had finally been active in his fourth field, that of philanthropy—but it
had all been on the defensive. Now it was time to take the offensive. To
him, it was astounding to learn how little philanthropy was understood
generally, and how little it was appreciated, even by leaders of government
in Washington. There were no courses taught in philanthropy at universities as there were in the fields of business and government. There were
no scholars in the field, no body of research, not even a common terminology. The field was scattered and disparate, lacking identity. At the very
time that the spirit of giving was needed the most, JDR believed, philanthropy was neglected, taken for granted, under fire. Much needed to be
done to reverse those trends—and JDR was determined to do what he
could.

The Peterson report had little impact at the time of its publication. Its
true importance lay in what it helped to get started—an entirely new
appreciation and recognition of the importance of the private nonprofit
sector in American life. In achieving that, JDR was to be the foremost
leader and catalyst.

19

※

"WIDE OPEN FOR CHANGE"

THE LAST DECADE of JDR's life—from 1968 to 1978—was a turbulent and exciting period for him, one filled with change and conflict and personal growth.

It was the time of life when most men think of retirement—he became sixty-five years old in 1971—and indeed he worked hard to complete some of his responsibilities and resign some of his chairmanships. But he replaced these with new interests and added even more. If anything, he was more busy than ever before.

By the 1960s, as we have seen, JDR had become highly active in his previously neglected "fourth field" of philanthropy. At the same time, he continued his support of projects in the arts. He was trying to resolve the problems of the Asia Society as well as other Asian interests throughout his final years. He continued unabated his leadership in population, finding exciting new challenges. All the while, he worked toward the final disposition of his projects and resources—*and* some of those of his extended family.

All or most of these activities could well have been expected of JDR. What was unexpected was the zest with which he went beyond them to new interests. This period of activism late in life ran counter to such conventional formulations as "change of life" or "the ages of man." It seemed to well up from deep and powerful motivations within him and in response to the profound changes he saw taking place in society around him.

In becoming more concerned with leaving behind a legacy of ideas than in continuing to build institutions, JDR developed a deep interest in the social movements and problems of the time—civil rights, the "youth revolution," the urban riots, the environmental movement, "women's lib,"

Watergate. Primarily an internationalist up to this time, JDR now became concerned with the domestic scene as well, just as he had led the Rockefeller Foundation in this direction to a degree. A latent interest in American history began to come alive for him. He became more concerned than ever before about family affairs generally and his family's place in history. Although this eventually led him into conflict with his brothers, especially Nelson, on some issues, it also brought him close to the younger generation.

JDR was not an intellectual, nor did he ever think of himself as one. But he did have great curiosity, good instincts, an open mind, and an ability to pursue his interests relentlessly. During this last decade of his life, he would select a new subject and begin to probe it almost as if he were undertaking an expedition. Indeed, the notion of "making a journey" in this fashion became a metaphor that appeared frequently in his speaking and writing. Although he did not think of it in so many words, his engrossing interest in the later years became American political theory—how his ideas and experiences fit in, how the system functioned best, how it could adapt to new needs. In this process he was finding a unifying concept for all of his philanthropic interests as he worked toward his own interpretation of American political theory and his vision of a just and good society. Despite all of the world and domestic problems of the time, it was the vision which led him to say on several occasions that "this is an exciting time to be alive."

The moment of decision between this marked level of activism and a more conventional climax to JDR's career probably came when he was offered the post of U.S. ambassador to Japan in 1969 by the Nixon administration. The first offer of an ambassadorship, to Indonesia, had come to him from the Eisenhower administration. Dean Rusk said that during eight years as Secretary of State in the two Democratic administrations of the 1960s he had always considered JDR to be the ideal envoy to an Asian country— any Asian country. Rusk said that many times during these years JDR had been offered posts abroad, including Tokyo, but he had always declined because of his heavy current responsibilities.[1]

By 1969 the situation was different. Being close to the customary retirement age, JDR was under some pressure by his immediate family to ease up for his own good. Taking a post abroad would provide a gracious way to exit from many responsibilities, especially board chairmanships—otherwise not an easy matter for JDR. No one could argue with the reason for resigning, and, in any case, one's absence abroad would settle the matter.

JDR considered the offer very seriously. His successes in life had begun with his exposure to Japan, and so the Tokyo embassy would seem to form a fitting capstone to his career. Given the love he and his wife had for Japan and the veneration for him there, he would have good reason to think that he could be an effective U.S. ambassador, especially in promoting his long-term goal of greater Japanese responsibility for Southeast Asia and more generous assistance to the region. Blanchette was all for going. JDR polled his advisers. Those who regularly attended his staff meetings, his four associates and Bill Ruder, came independently to the same conclusion—that he should accept. They all agreed that he had earned the post and that it would be a fitting change in his life at the right time.[2]

For some time JDR's staff had been counseling him to relax more and enjoy life. Ray Lamontagne was the first to speak to him in these terms. After his departure the leader became Bill Ruder, whom one staff member described ecumenically as "JDR's rabbi and expert on the Protestant ethic." Ruder had been telling JDR that it was not sinful to enjoy life and that he should begin to choose his activities at least as much for reasons of personal pleasure as for any contributions to society they might make. Given JDR's particular background, being ambassador to Japan seemed to offer just such a combination.

Nevertheless, after several weeks of agonizing, he decided to decline the offer. There were two reasons. He believed the more responsible way to exit from his obligations would be to stay at home. He knew he would have to be firm about his decision to resign in the case of each board chairmanship, but at least he would be on hand to work with the particular organization to make sure he was leaving it in the best possible shape. The other reason was that he was deeply fascinated by what was going on in the domestic society. In fact, he had already moved ahead to take on new interests and activities.

During this final, active decade, JDR demonstrated more clearly than ever before that he was the most liberal of the Rockefeller brothers. "Liberal" and "conservative" are gross terms at best, but they are at least broadly suggestive of different patterns of belief and attitude. On almost every issue of the day, from abortion to recognizing Red China, JDR was over on the "liberal" side of the spectrum. He supported social programs designed to deal with the effects of poverty and discrimination, and he came to accept many of the "new values" being espoused by young people. He was a strong believer in the First Amendment. In the case of pornography, for example, JDR believed it was better to let the banality of the product serve to diminish it instead of trying to control it by tampering with freedom of expression.

At the same time, JDR lost none of his innate personal caution. Several times he cited to his staff examples of wealthy persons who had gone beyond liberal ideas to radical ones and ended up as ineffectual persons, dismissed as eccentrics. This was not a cowardly point of view, but a pragmatic one. Unless a constituency existed or he believed he could generate one, JDR normally would figure that an idea or cause simply was not worth pursuing on practical grounds. Although he was willing to take on very difficult tasks against odds, JDR did not care to tilt at windmills.

His liberal attitudes tended to be instinctive at first, and he could be uncomfortable defending them unless he had studied them personally. For example, one weekend his brother Nelson spoke to him with particular vehemence about welfare and unemployment programs creating an army of drones who would rather live on the dole than do honest work. This shook JDR's instinctive beliefs, coming as it did from the governor of a great state, a man who generally was thought to be quite progressive. JDR discussed the subject with several members of his staff. One of them brought to his attention a report of a new and impressive body of research showing that attitudes associated with the work ethic were just as strong among welfare and unemployment compensation recipients as among employed people. JDR was happy to return to his instinctive belief that lack of motivation to work had little to do with unemployment.

Not surprisingly, the ideological complexion of JDR's staff changed from moderate Republican to liberal Democrat as the years passed. The original three—JDR, Don McLean, and Ed Young—were all registered Republicans, although Young styled himself as "the kind of Republican who always votes for Democrats in presidential elections." JDR appears to have been more of a loyalist, although he noted in 1976 that he had voted for Jimmy Carter over Gerald Ford. This was the only time that JDR ever revealed his vote in his diary.[3]

All of the associates hired in later years were political liberals. This was more the result of natural selection than it was of any deliberate process. No prospective employee was ever asked about political beliefs or party affiliation. People with a certain mix of attitudes tended to be drawn to JDR and vice versa. And to the extent that staff members aided in recruitment, they naturally tried to replicate themselves.

This is not to suggest that there was ideological unity within the office. There were many shades of opinion among staff members. At times they seemed to reflect the views of Kennedy Democrats or New Dealers or even prairie populists, but JDR's brand of liberalism escaped any such classification. It was peculiarly his own. He was liberal on matters of social and political policy, but he also had his conservative personal and fiscal habits and his streak of pragmatism. However, there was enough of a common point of view about most things in JDR's offices to assure a good level of harmony—debates tended to be about priorities or methods rather than objectives. The associates worked fairly independently in their areas of interest and assignment. There was no liberal cabal ensnaring JDR. In general he influenced his staff members more than they influenced him.

There was one great issue of the times over which JDR, like millions of other Americans, was markedly ambivalent—the Vietnam War. He had always been uncomfortable about American military commitments in Southeast Asia. At one early point he expressed the view to his mentor, Secretary of State John Foster Dulles, that the United States should take a tolerant attitude toward anticolonial movements. He had been rebuffed in this, as he was later when he suggested to Prime Minister Indira Gandhi that she take a conciliatory position on the Kashmir issue. Whether or not such incidents were the cause, JDR rarely expressed an opinion in public about specific foreign policy issues. It was as if he had decided that this was not his province. We have seen how Cold War terminology disappeared from his letters and utterances at an early point as he concentrated his energies abroad on population control, agricultural development, and cultural understanding.

JDR was uncomfortable about the Vietnam War, but he also believed in the "domino" theory—he was sure that Indonesia would have gone Communist had it not been for the strong U.S. presence in Vietnam. Moreover, he was intimately associated with such prime incubators of American foreign policy leadership as the Rockefeller Foundation and the Council of Foreign Relations. At any given time, those officially in charge of foreign policy were men he had known and respected for years. He was never likely to come out publicly in opposition to these men, even in the Nixon years as the war protest movement grew and his own misgivings increased. Always his dispensation was to have faith that the wisdom and good intentions of those in charge of foreign policy would eventually make things turn out all right.

Moreover, JDR's style was anything but confrontational. His successes in political maneuvering came when he persistently promoted something he believed in strongly, usually in a behind-the-scenes and personal way. He was an optimist and a believer in persuasion and rationality. He was at his most politically inept when these things broke down and he found himself in confrontation. As a result, he tended to avoid such situations whenever he could.

JDR had another reason for caution. During the years that the Vietnam controversy was intensifying, his efforts to promote a positive policy and action in the population field by the U.S. government were at their zenith. His instinct was that it would make no sense for him to cut the ground out from under himself in population by criticizing the administration's foreign policy. This was not really a conflict of principle—JDR was never sure what the correct policy in Vietnam should be, but he was emphatically sure about what it should be in population.

The result of all of this for JDR, as for so many others, was that he simply tried to avoid the subject of Vietnam as much as possible, and when he could not he did little more than refer to the war as a "tragedy."[4] But this problem did not hamper him in moving ahead vigorously in other areas as he found himself profoundly stirred by new problems and social ferment on the domestic scene. This was most clear in his decision to investigate the "youth revolution"—and in the impact that had on his decision to write a book.

JDR did not often surprise his staff. But one morning in the spring of 1968 he began a staff meeting with two surprises. The first was his announcement that he had decided to accept the annual Gold Medal award of the Society for the Family of Man. He would be expected to deliver the principal address at the Society's annual banquet in New York City the following October.

This perhaps would not have been much of a surprise in most offices, but in JDR's it was. It was unheard of for him to accept a major speaking engagement without consulting his staff, so tentative and selective was he. Serious invitations invariably were discussed at great length.

The surprise was heightened by the nature of the occasion. The Society for the Family of Man was one of those organizations that seemed to flourish in New York City in which the entire function appeared to consist of giving an award to a famous person at an annual banquet attended by a cross-section of Manhattan's civic leadership. JDR almost always turned down honorific bids routinely. It was true that he had made an exception the year before when he had joined with his four brothers in accepting awards from the National Institute of Social Sciences.[5] But that had happened only because the brothers were taken with the novelty of appearing together in public.

The fact that previous medalists of the Society for the Family of Man included Presidents Kennedy and Johnson would not have deterred JDR from declining the award. Clearly, something was up, and the staff soon learned what it was. JDR's second surprise of the morning was that he had decided to accept the Society's invitation because he thought it would make a good platform for talking about the "youth revolution."

From the perspective of many years later, it is not easy to recall the fervor with which the phenomenon of youthful protest swept the nation in the 1960s, spreading from its beginnings in the "free speech" movement at Berkeley in 1963 to virtually every college campus and city and home in the nation. The core of concern for serious issues had emerged rapidly— the Vietnam War, environmental damage, racism, sexism—as had the cultural manifestations of the movement such as rock music, "flower power," hippie dress, and long hair, which were so unsettling to almost everyone past the advanced age of thirty. And there was the ugly side—drug abuse, manipulation of the media, violence by the radical fringe.

In retrospect, it is not surprising that 1968 was the time JDR chose to somehow become involved in what was happening on the domestic scene. It was the year of the assassinations of Dr. Martin Luther King, Jr., and Bobby Kennedy. It was the year when the youth movement showed political muscle in aiding the campaign of Senator Eugene McCarthy and precipitating the decision of President Johnson not to run again. And it was a year when matters threatened to get out of hand. The student uprisings seemed to gain in strength, forcing Columbia University, for example, to shut down before the spring semester ended. There were the huge uprisings throughout the summer in Paris, the slaughter of students in Mexico City just before the Olympic Games, and the ugly mood at the Democratic Party convention in Chicago.

But the power and prominence of the youth revolution in 1968 did not explain why JDR would suddenly take an interest. He was not one to adopt any popular cause or cultural phenomenon that came along, and even at its strongest one suspected that the youth movement was transitory—nothing could sustain such fervor indefinitely.

Was JDR somehow trying to recapture his own lost youth? The thought vanishes as soon as it arises—that would have been very unlike him, and there was no other evidence, no change of behavior, to suggest it. Was he trying to understand his youngest daughter? This may have been a contributing factor, but does not seem to have been the primary motivation. Alida was exposed to young radicals at Stanford at this time, and she was questioning her parents' values. JDR did consult with her occasionally, but, as Alida later commented, she was too confused herself to be very useful as a guide for her father.

JDR's interest in youth was not quite the aberration it seemed. His concern for young people was evident as early as the 1930s when he had devoted himself for several years to a study of juvenile delinquency and was instrumental in producing a highly progressive report about what to do about the problem. He and Blanchette had spent many hours with young foreigners at the International House in New York. He had tried for years to bring some dynamism to the American Youth Hostels, to no avail. And in his service on the Princeton board, JDR was always most interested in matters that directly affected the life of students on campus.

But his fascination for the youth revolution of the 1960s did not stem merely from a sentimental interest in young people. The probable answer lay in JDR's most obvious characteristic—his straightforward concern for substantive issues. Outwardly, JDR appeared to be a calm and composed person, even a withdrawn one at times. But inwardly he was a man of strong passions, with a sense of urgency concerning the issues he cared most about. He was frustrated by the apathy and defensiveness he encountered so often—in foundations, among business and political leaders, in government agencies. In the student rebels, JDR at last has found individuals as passionate about the issues as he was, if not more so—and they were a good deal more effective at goading the Establishment.

The thought of relating the youth revolution to world problems in a constructive way first came to JDR early in 1968 when he was having lunch at the Century with Lord Caradon, the British representative to the United Nations. As noted earlier, the two men had a mutual interest in pursuing action in the population field. They were engaged in a gloomy discussion of the lack of progress when Caradon suddenly began talking about the youth revolution. He pointed to the energy and moral fervor of young people on the one hand and to the existence of great world problems on the other. Caradon said that young people seemed particularly concerned about what he considered to be the three underlying problems of the world—overpopulation, racism, and poverty. There should be some way, Caradon said, to relate the idealism and energy of the young to practical work on these great problems.

JDR brooded over this question as urban riots and student unrest came close to home—in Harlem and Newark and at Columbia University. Occasionally a staff member would find him in an uncharacteristic pose—standing at one of the north windows of his fifty-sixth floor office and staring out over the city toward Harlem and Columbia as if physical evidence of the problem could be seen from that distance.

Jack Harr, the associate responsible for assisting JDR in writing projects, had passed the age of forty and declared himself to be hopelessly out of touch as a guide to the youth phenomenon. He could help on the final stages of drafting the speech, but this was one of the cases in which JDR clearly needed a third party, a younger person, for the educational phase.

Harr recruited James A. Carney, a former Foreign Service officer who was not yet thirty and had an inquisitive mind and an engaging manner. Carney had found the Foreign Service too confining for his interests and was in the process of broadening his horizons in preparation for a career as a writer and management consultant. He attacked the JDR assignment with zest, setting off on his own investigation for a month and then arranging a long string of experiences for JDR—visits to campuses, meetings with experts, and encounters with youth leaders of every description, singly and in groups.

For four months JDR immersed himself in the problem. He was a participant in a weekend sponsored by Columbia University to examine the protest movement on its campus. JDR and Alida went to see a performance of *Hair*, then in the midst of its opening run on Broadway, and he declared that he enjoyed it, especially the music.

On October 23, JDR stood up before a capacity audience in the Grand Ballroom of the Americana Hotel in Manhattan and delivered what was one of the two or three most successful speeches of his career. He held the rapt attention of the audience as he presented a view of the youth revolution that few expected, but many found stimulating and challenging. As suggested by JDR's initial motivation, he took a basically positive view of the youth phenomenon, but he criticized its excesses and abuses in unequivocal language. He confessed his bias in favor of young people to his audience, and said that his positive convictions had become strengthened in the course of his "adventure of trying to understand the world of the young."

Saying that "there is nothing new about youthful idealism and youthful protest" and that "every generation has its gap," JDR nevertheless held that the contemporary movement was "deep and intense" and that it offered an opportunity: "I am convinced that not only is there tremendous vitality here, but there is also great potential for good if we can only understand and respond positively." It was for this reason, JDR said, that he realized early in preparing his remarks that he would be addressing them not so much to young people as to "my fellow members of the older generation."

He examined the youth movement in respect to three traditional moral bastions of society—the law, the family, and the church—and in each case his conclusion brought him back to his basic theme: "The crucial issue is not the revolt of youth but the nature of our response to it." One response would be to attempt to suppress the youth rebellion as had happened in Mexico City and Chicago; another would be to simply ignore it and hope that it would go away. JDR said that neither response was productive nor would work in the long run:

The greater tragedy will be the opportunity we will have lost. For we know all too well that time *is* running out on the great problems the world faces. It seems to me that we have a choice. By suppression or apathy, we can make the youth revolution into yet another problem—in which case the burden will become crushing. Or we can respond in positive ways so that the energy and idealism of youth can be a constructive force in helping to solve the world's great problems.

This is the third possible response. It is simply to be responsive—to trust our young people, to listen to them, to understand them, to let them know that we care deeply about them.

Next came the most oft-quoted passages of the speech:

Instead of worrying about how to suppress the youth revolution we of the older generation should be worrying about how to sustain it. The student activists . . . perform a service in shaking us out of our complacency. We badly need their ability and fervor in these troubled and difficult times.

In my judgement, the key to sustaining the energy and idealism of youth is more direct and effective action on the problems about which young people are concerned—the problems of our cities, of our environment, of racial injustice, of irrelevant and outmoded teachings, of overpopulation, of poverty, of war.

JDR ended to a standing ovation. The speech proved immensely popular, forming the basis for numerous articles. It was reprinted several times, most conspicuously with a lead-in cover in the *Saturday Review* of December 14, 1968, under the title "In Praise of Young Revolutionaries." The speech was reported in both *Time* and *Newsweek*, in the latter under the headline, "The Establishment: Feelin' Groovy," and with the comment that JDR was an "Establishmentarian with a difference" for his ability to see positive value in the youth revolution.

Despite the success of the speech JDR's staff still thought his interest in youth was a "one-shot" phenomenon that would soon pass. It seemed rather far removed from his four avowed fields of interest. But not to JDR. It was not immediately apparent, but for him the involvement marked a beginning, not an end. The invitation for him to become the U.S. ambassador to Japan came and went. But JDR's interest in youth continued, and in fact became one of the reasons for turning down the Japan assignment.

JDR's involvement with the youth movement was to have a profound effect on his life and work. Among other things, it made a decided difference in the book he was attempting to write, leading to a sweeping change of course in that effort.

*   *   *

Ray Lamontagne was the staff aide who first proposed that JDR write a book. This happened in 1966 when JDR was gearing up to try to counter the attacks being made on philanthropy. Much of his effort was directed toward Washington lobbying, but there was recognition of a broader need to educate the public about the benefits of philanthropy. Lamontagne thought that such an effort should include a book to popularize the subject and to be written by the nation's leading philanthropist—JDR.

Specifically, Lamontagne's model was President Kennedy's book *Profiles in Courage*. If a book could be assembled out of a series of stories of heroism in political life, why could not the same be done about the great accomplishments of philanthropy? It was an appealing thought, but as usual when presented with a new and unfamiliar idea JDR neither approved nor disapproved. He asked Lamontagne and speechwriter Jack McNulty to "play with it for a while" to see what particular stories of philanthropic accomplishment they would propose for such a book.

JDR then turned for advice to Datus C. Smith, who was in the process of winding up his responsibilities as president of Franklin Books before joining JDR's staff. It was intended that Smith would become the associate who would be responsible for assisting JDR in the field of philanthropy. Smith also liked the idea of the book and said that JDR needed a senior and established writer to work with him. McNulty had not done any book projects, and, in any case, was being "loaned" to the White House speechwriting staff. Smith had his candidate—Richard Schickel, the movie critic for *Time* and *Life*, who had done such an excellent job of writing the final report of the Rockefeller Brothers Fund panel on the performing arts. The three men discussed the project at lunch at the end of September 1966, and soon thereafter Schickel agreed to assist JDR. The contract called for a stipend on an annual basis, although the two men expected that the book would be finished in less than two years.

The first problem arose with the "profiles" approach. All those involved in thinking about the book agreed that there were some excellent stories from the Rockefeller experience—the eradication of hookworm by the Rockefeller Sanitary Commission, for example, or the work of the General Education Board in aiding the education of blacks in the South. And Lamontagne thought that the story of the Population Council was a good example of how private initiative could lead to governmental action. But it had become clear that JDR was extremely uncomfortable about using more than one or two Rockefeller examples for fear of being seen as self-serving.

Then Schickel found that in seeking non-Rockefeller philanthropic stories, particularly contemporary ones, it was very difficult to get all the facts and to find stories with a beginning, a middle, and an end. One of the great problems of foundations was, and is, that of evaluation—finding out exactly what does happen when grant money is given, particularly in a difficult and complex area. And in such cases, foundations are not always helpful to outside writers. The Ford Foundation's great support of educational television was an obvious candidate for the book, but it was a story that was a long way from finished, and it did not even seem near a turning point or climax that one could describe or evaluate.

Finally, the "profiles" approach was abandoned, but not the idea of a book. JDR and Smith agreed that there was, after all, a need for a straightforward presentation and advocacy of philanthropy in book form, a policy-oriented book that would build understanding and appreciation for this important dimension of American life—in short, a book that would express in extended form all of the positive themes about philanthropy that JDR was using in his speeches and lobbying activity.

The second approach also ended in failure. The "chemistry" simply was not there in the effort by Schickel and JDR to collaborate. Moreover, Schickel had taken on too much—he was involved at the time in finishing no less than two books of his own, biographies of Goya and Disney (both ultimately were successfully published). The fundamental problem was that the subject had not been thought through for presentation as a book in terms of structure, style, and audience. As a result, Schickel and JDR held long rambling conversations about philanthropy and Schickel would go off to try to fashion his notes into chapters, bedeviled constantly by the higher personal priorities he had set for himself. Very soon he began to find the subject of philanthropy to be a monumental bore. His draft chapters showed it, and JDR was not happy.

Smith tried his best to intercede and make the collaboration a fruitful one, but to no avail. The project limped on for several years, degenerating steadily. In desperation Schickel tried several times to resign, but JDR would not let him go. The reason, he said, was not so much because of the book, but for Schickel's sake—he hated to see Schickel fail to do something he had committed himself to doing. Smith finally was able to convince JDR that this attitude was doing Schickel no favors.

Schickel delivered his final compilation in July 1969, a 179-page double-spaced draft that he himself described as "turgid" to Smith.[6] The project ceased, seemingly never to rise again. But Smith, now fully on board as an associate, still believed that it was important for JDR to write a book about philanthropy. The effort had two strikes, but a third try might succeed. Smith's plan for accomplishing it was to have his colleague, Jack Harr, successor to Jack McNulty, assigned to assist JDR in the project.[7]

Harr was happy to find that JDR was not anxious to take up again so soon in an area where failure had been so conspicuous. But by mid-1970 JDR's interest had revived, and a number of planning sessions ensued with an emphasis on avoiding the mistakes of the past. By now experienced in helping JDR with his speeches, Harr pointed out that it would be impossible to approach a book at the same deliberate pace. A book on contemporary issues would have to be done no slower than one chapter per month or it would be outdated before it was finished. Paradoxically, JDR would have to spend more time on a book project than he had contemplated, and yet would have to "sign off" on draft chapters at a faster pace than he was accustomed to. JDR agreed and pledged that he would try his best, consistent with his need to understand and believe in every sentence if he were to put his name on the book.

JDR had followed up his "youth revolution" speech of 1968 by inaugurating a "youth program" that involved a variety of activities and a number of interesting consultants (see next chapter). In this Harr saw an opportunity to make the book a more interesting project, not only for himself and JDR, but perhaps ultimately for readers as well. Instead of a book about philanthropy, he suggested that only one or two chapters be devoted directly to that subject with the rest dealing with the *substance* of philanthropy—the substantive issues that were so engrossing to JDR and with which philanthropy tried to cope. JDR could draw on forty years of experience as a philanthropist in commenting on population, the environment, the youth revolution, civil rights, the role of government and of the business sector as well as philanthropy, and any other subjects that appealed to him.

To help think through the basic concepts, Richard W. Barrett was brought in as a consultant. Already a consultant on JDR's "youth project," Barrett had resigned from the federal government after nineteen years during which he had earned an unusual reputation for being innovative and taking initiative. He had served with the Bureau of the Budget, the task force that helped create the Agency for International Development, the Kennedy White House, and the State Department. His last assignment had been as President Johnson's appointee as staff head of the American Revolution Bicentennial Commission. For the next two years, Barrett remained involved as a third party in the creating of JDR's book. He made content suggestions and did first drafts of several chapters, but his main contribution was to serve as a sort of buffer or balance wheel between the other two participants. Harr's role was to do the writing while JDR decided on content and reviewed, amended, and approved drafts. The three-man process was so useful that the participants commented on it to each other several times. Opinion was either unanimous for or against a substantive point or it was two against one—never a standoff of one against one. Votes were not taken, but arguments occurred with minds frequently being changed, and the process never broke down as it might have if only two persons had been involved.

JDR remained true to his word. He devoted a great deal of time to the effort, usually several long meetings a week with Barrett and Harr and additional hours at home devoted to reading successive drafts of chapters.[8] But he also was willing to sign off on chapters at Harr's recommended pace of about one a month. The nineteen-chapter book was finished in less than two years and was published by Harper & Row in early 1973.

The title, *The Second American Revolution*, stemmed from JDR's thesis that the nation was currently in a period of "profound and far-reaching social change," which fully merited being called "a humanistic revolution." JDR worried about using the term "revolution," but finally decided to go ahead. He explained in this way:

Let me say that in trying to understand the forces at play in our society, I was not looking for a revolution. The name Rockefeller does not connote a revolutionary, and my life situation has fostered a careful and cautious attitude that verges on conservatism. . . .

But once one accepts that a revolution of positive potential is emerging, it is time to stop worrying about scare words and to start thinking about what one can do to help ensure that positive outcome. Without a sense of purpose, the explosive forces of change in our society could easily become disintegrative. But a revolution that has a humanistic focus, which is concerned about the quality of life for all people, can provide that sense of purpose. It can give direction to the runaway locomotive of change.

Central to JDR's thesis was the view that the revolution was one of fulfillment rather than overthrow—"to fulfill the ideals and promises that were articulated two hundred years ago" in the Declaration of Independence and the Constitution. He wrote:

The humanistic values stated at the founding of our society and the materialistic ones which have predominated throughout our history have often been in conflict. The outcome of the revolution will depend on how that conflict is resolved.

Although it had been the youth movement that spurred JDR's involvement in contemporary social issues, he quite correctly identified the civil rights movement as the prime initiating and moving force: ". . . this revolution, like every revolution, had its beginnings in issues of justice and freedom." It was on this subject that JDR's words became the most impassioned:

More than a century ago, blacks were freed from physical and legal slavery, but in the last two decades they have freed themselves from psychological slavery. The change in the verbs is important: *they have freed themselves*. They are casting off their feelings of inferiority, of low self-esteem, and instead are saying to the world that black is beautiful. And any time that a person insists on his own dignity as a human being, takes pride in his own uniqueness, says that he will not be imposed upon nor taken advantage of any longer, that is indeed a beautiful thing. On the whole this is happening with dignity and restraint and a faith in American ideals which ought to give us all great pause for reflection.

Terming the black experience "at once the agony and drama of America," JDR analyzed its "profound historical significance," the obstacles still in the way, and the impact of the movement in encouraging other groups to "assert their identity and seek equality." He concluded by citing the famous "I have a dream" speech of Martin Luther King, Jr.:

I share that dream. It is a vision not of Utopia, for that can never be. And perhaps fulfillment is to be found not in the happy state itself, but in the knowledge that one is striving to attain it. It is a vision of making it work, of rising above what divides us to what unites us, and finding out in that process that we are all members of the same human family.

Next JDR turned to the youth movement. "If the humanistic revolution began with protest and self-assertion by the blacks, the vanguard of the revolution soon became American youth." Through several chapters, JDR cast much of the discussion in the context of analyzing the clash and mix of the founding American values and those that arose during the Industrial Revolution. He saw them synthesizing into "the new values" in a complex process of social change:

. . . the emergence of the "new values" has gone far beyond the point at which they can be dismissed simply as the idealism of the young. The process of diffusion is under way, and the "new values" are spreading throughout our society. In determining how far this process will go, and whether in the end it will succeed, the role and response of the moderates—the vast American center—is crucial.

JDR discussed at length "this pattern of radical beginnings followed by a moderating influence," and then analyzed the agenda for change in a series of chapters—on population, the environment, business, government, the nonprofit sector, the "politics of humanism." He called for a "giving society," a "learning society," and a "planning society." In a concluding section, JDR presented his view of "the quality of life," and he defined the "true meaning of private initiative" as the key to a successful and peaceful revolution:

The essence of private initiative is the decision by individuals to become involved and committed to something larger than themselves. It is their deliberate determination to put aside the temptations, distractions, and pressures for conformity which press in on all of us in our everyday lives. It is their belief that the moral and ethical transcend the selfish and the material. And it is having the courage to take actions based on those beliefs.

Once again JDR anchored his argument in "the fundamental strength of our democratic ideals and values," citing democracy as the "political philosophy most compatible with human nature, the system that is most flexible and most conducive to humanistic values and human growth." The basic reason for optimism was to be found "in our extraordinary good fortune in having a firmly rooted democratic system . . the only conceivable environment for a successful revolution of the twentieth century." He wrote:

I do not speak of democracy in this way merely for patriotic or ideological reasons. The concern is not whether a democracy is capitalistic or socialistic, whether it is rich or poor, small or large. The only concern is whether it in fact assures access to information, freedom of choice, opportunities for human growth, and other basic human rights. . . .

All depends now on how the present generation of Americans uses its good fortune. A democratic system is not some lifeless thing, an edifice, an institution, a museum object. Its lifeblood is the vitality and initiative and understanding and commitment of its members.

JDR expressed his personal optimism in strong terms:

I feel this is an exciting time to be alive. Virtually everything seems to be wide open for change. I look upon this positively for to me it means that everything is wide open for improvement and progress. It means to me that each person has the opportunity to influence the course of events, in however small or large a way. I would much rather be alive during a time of challenge such as this that during a sedate and static period of history.

In the final sentence of his book, as if expressing the core of his personal philosophy, JDR wrote of the "need to reach beyond the material and concern ourselves with what makes life worth living—and loving."

In the course of working on his book, JDR particularly enjoyed long conversations with two of the most interesting social philosophers of the time—Carl Rogers and Abraham Maslow. He also profited from counseling by Willis Harmon of the Stanford Research Institute, economist Kermit Gordon, and sociologist Daniel Yankelovich. James B. Shuman, a former correspondent for the *Reader's Digest,* was another consultant. JDR circulated chapters for comment to his office advisers and to members of his immediate family, particularly Blanchette, Jay, and Alida. At one point Dick Barrett asked if JDR intended to show the manuscript to his brothers before the book was published. After thinking about this for a while, JDR said that the problem in asking for comments was that then one had to accept or reject them, and he did not want to go through too much of that. Obviously, JDR felt more comfortable in dealing with advice from the office and his own family than from his brothers.

An amusing footnote to this was reported by Joseph Persico, former speechwriter for Nelson, in his book *The Imperial Rockefeller.* Only after JDR's book was published did he bring a copy in to give to Nelson. Persico recorded what happened:

Nelson sat down, scanned the table of contents, and dipped into a few pages. "Johnny, this is terrific," Nelson exulted. "But you don't say anything about the brotherhood of man under the fatherhood of God."

"But, Nell, that's not my kind of statement. Though I appreciate it's one of yours."

"And I don't see anything about labor either."

"But Nell, I don't know anything about labor."

"Hughie, come here." Nelson gestured for Hugh Morrow to join them. "Johnny, I want you to meet the greatest editor in the country. Hughie, I want you to take a look at Johnny's book. See where we can fit these things in." Edit his already published, widely praised book? John's response was his customary hurt silence before Nelson's overpowering effrontery.[9]

Morrow, Nelson's longtime press secretary, dutifully devoted some time to finding places in JDR's book where a few sentences could be inserted. When the copy was delivered to JDR with Morrow's carefully inked inserts, JDR brought it into Harr's office with a bemused expression on his face. What to do with it? Call Harper & Row and start the presses rolling again? Obviously not. Harr kept the copy as a souvenir.

An example of JDR's innate honesty occurred earlier when the page proofs were ready to be returned to the publisher, one of the last steps before the book would be printed. JDR said that because Harr had done so much of the writing it was only fair that they both be listed on the cover as coauthors. He asked Harr to think about this. The next day Harr declined, saying that he felt the situation was similar to what occurred when he and JDR worked together on a speech—that he aided the process, but the final product very definitely was JDR's. Harr also said that others, particularly Barrett, had helped, and that if names other than JDR's appeared on the jacket it would dilute the impact of the book. He said he could be given due credit in the acknowledgments in the beginning of the book. JDR agreed—and then asked Harr to draft the acknowledgments!

The book sold over 15,000 copies in two hardbound editions and 10,000 more in paperback, surprisingly good for a book of personal philosophy.[10] As Persico noted, it was widely praised, although JDR, as a typical New Yorker, was somewhat hurt and could never understand why the *New York Times* ignored it.[11]

There is little doubt that JDR derived some rare satisfaction from the writing and publishing of his book—if judged only by the fact that before long he was prepared to contemplate doing another one. Working on the book helped to crystallize his thinking in some areas and stimulated him to further inquiry in others. The content was very much related to new activities that he took on in the mid-1970s. But like many of his efforts, it represented a beginning for him, not an end. It did not fully articulate his deeper feelings about the value and position of philanthropy in the American polity. And so his mind began to focus on this subject even as he busied himself with his current activities.

20

✄

THE YOUTH PROGRAM

MORE THAN ONCE in his lifetime JDR heard a familiar vulgarism: "Put your money where your mouth is." He commented on this to his staff with a wry smile at one point, allowing that it was rather sound advice—he believed that people often talked too much and did too little.

He heard words to this effect from his son soon after Jay read the text of his father's 1968 speech on the youth revolution. In that speech JDR said that the ferment of youth offered "great potential for good if we can only understand and respond positively." He said that "the key to sustaining the energy and idealism of youth is more direct and effective action on the problems about which young people are concerned." This prompted Jay to say to his father: "All well and good. But what are *you* going to do about it?"

JDR agreed that having spoken so forcefully on the subject he now had a responsibility to do everything he could to "understand and respond." This commitment was a major reason why he passed up the ambassadorship to Japan; it served to spawn instead the so-called youth program in his office.[1] This grew over the next four years to considerable proportions and a variety of activity, involving a host of youthful consultants and a great many encounters between JDR and opinion-makers of all kinds, from young activists to prominent business leaders. Although there were several attempts at programs of action, much of the effort consisted of JDR's continuing quest for knowledge and understanding of both current problems in the society and the attitudes of the young. It was during this same period that he worked on his book, *The Second American Revolution*, so that his program of self-education served both endeavors.

In particular, JDR was fascinated with the "new values" he discerned in young people and which he wrote about in his book. He found these values to be congenial with his own basic views, some of which he had suppressed over the years. These values not only infused his youth activities, but, as we shall see, also led him off in other new directions as well,

318

and in some cases influenced his style of operating within his traditional interests.

One example of these values leading JDR in a new direction occurred in the first activity he undertook after his Family of Man speech—an inquiry into new attitudes toward love, sex, and what JDR referred to somewhat quaintly as the "boy-girl relationship." He accepted the invitation from *Look* magazine to write an article on this subject, and so set off on another "journey," again with Jim Carney as a consultant and his principal aide. The new attitudes were a revelation to JDR. They simply made a great deal of common sense to him as he contrasted the more open and relaxed approach to sexuality and human relationships generally that he perceived among young people to the uninformed and furtive process that characterized growing up in his own generation, with sex a subject ridden with taboos, fear, and guilt.

The resulting article, published in the October 7, 1969, issue of *Look*, was entitled "Youth, Love and Sex: The New Chivalry." It was a wide-ranging and surprisingly sophisticated analysis of how prevalent attitudes toward sex can distort human relationships and how the new values might improve them, with JDR probing the parent-child relationship, marriage, and friendship. JDR explained his title as follows:

Everyone knows what the old chivalry was: a code of elaborate manners and courtesy, but at the core, it consisted of placing the woman on a pedestal and glorifying her, while the man went off to do knightly deeds to win her favor. The result of course was that instead of being raised up, the woman was being put down. The man was encumbered with false notions of masculinity, and the woman, although idealized, was in fact dehumanized.

One might be a little wistful about the manners; I am not in favor of discarding those, but in other respects the new chivalry, as I envision it, is quite different from the old. The emphasis is on the specifically human characteristics of man and woman. Romantic love gives way to human love, a relationship in which each appreciates what the other brings to it, each person feels responsible for the development of the other, and each feels the need to make the other's life fulfilling to the extent that he or she can. . . . Sex finally finds its perspective as one key element within the full, rich range of human association.

Much of the prose was epigrammatic: "The best ally of the pornographer is the puritan." "Even so healthy a concept as sex education in our schools is somehow made to be controversial." "Premarital sex was not invented by this generation." "Love is much, much more than sex . . . it is natural for a person to be loving, in the finest sense, toward many other persons of both sexes."

JDR made a strong case for sex education: "I am amazed that in an area of human behavior that is common to us all, where so much ignorance and secrecy abounds, some people seek to destroy an effort to bring more honesty, understanding, and sensibility." JDR followed through on this belief by coming to the financial aid of the Sex Information and Education Council of the United States (SIECUS), whose founder, Dr. Mary Calderone, had become the focal point of opposition to sex education and was constantly under attack by the John Birch Society and right-wing publications. The view of Calderone and her associates was that responsible sex education was one important way to begin to assuage such problems as teenage pregnancy, illegitimacy, divorce, venereal disease, promiscuity, and sexual violence—and JDR wholeheartedly agreed. In 1969 the Rockefeller Brothers Fund proposed a $25,000 grant to SIECUS, but JDR asked that it be doubled, and then contributed $50,000 of his own.

For about a year after the *Look* article was published, JDR was pursued by an editor of *Playboy* who wanted him to do another article or agree to an interview. JDR was intrigued by this, but the members of his immediate family had been uncomfortable with his first foray into print on the subject of sex. So he finally turned *Playboy* down and contented himself by continuing to support SIECUS on an annual basis until, as we shall see, he ventured into a more ambitious project on human sexuality some years later.

Meanwhile JDR had moved ahead to search for more concrete projects involving youth by retaining Dick Barrett as a consultant. Barrett proceeded to study a number of possibilities while at the same time arranging a series of encounters between JDR and groups of young people— Columbia University dissidents, suburban high school students, Peace Corps and VISTA volunteers, a group at a New York Boys' Club, a group of young Washington civil servants, and numerous others. JDR learned a great deal, and there were some amusing incidents. For example, in a session with a group of young black professionals JDR was trying to stay up with the animated conversation, but he was puzzled by frequent references to "the man." He finally got his question in: "Who is the man?" This was met with blank stares and then laughter as one of the participants said, "*You're* the man!" The participant then explained that this was a generic reference to anyone who had some form of status, control, or authority over another person, especially a white person over a black person. JDR was still puzzled.

One major line of inquiry pursued by Barrett was whether or not JDR should take the lead in endorsing some form of a national service program concept for young people or commission a Rockefeller Panel to study the subject. Several variations of such a concept had been proposed. JDR discussed this subject with a special group of educators, businessmen, and social analysts convened by Barrett. JDR found opinion to be highly favorable, provided the program was voluntary and not a universal service idea akin to the draft for military service. The prevailing view was that there were enormous needs for service manpower in such fields as health care, education, and conservation, and that there were large numbers of young people who would respond to such an opportunity.

The latter point was supported in a national survey conducted by pollster Daniel Yankelovich for *Fortune* magazine and CBS, which classified college youth on the basis of responses to questions measuring alienation, rebelliousness, and attitudes toward social issues. The survey results categorized 23 percent of campus youth as "reformers" and 48 percent as "moderates," compared to only 1 percent as "revolutionaries" and 10 percent as "radical reformers." This verified JDR's view that there were very large numbers of young people who were both concerned about social problems and positively oriented toward doing something about them— potentially a large reservoir for a voluntary service program.

In the end, however, JDR decided against pursuing the service idea. One reason was that it simply seemed impractical given the huge cost and administrative structure that would be required and the fact that the Nixon administration was already cutting back on such existing programs as the Peace Corps and VISTA. Perhaps more important, however, was the instinctive view of both JDR and Barrett that a large-scale, somewhat regimented program just was not in keeping with the times, that young people would be more responsive to activities that were decentralized and local, and also more self-directed than imposed. It was for these reasons that JDR opted for an approach suggested by Barrett—providing the initial stimulus for small-scale, local projects to show what might be done in the private sector and open up the possibility that the projects might be emulated by others. The leitmotiv of the approach was the creation of communication between young people and the "establishment," and, if possible, cooperative action on social problems. The "establishment" was defined primarily as business leadership. JDR decided to fund these activities through the JDR 3rd Fund,[2] initially with a grant of $100,000 on November 10, 1970, "to plan, develop, and test projects which it is hoped will lead to creation of constructive youth-Establishment relationships." In 1971 he provided a further $160,000 and approximately $200,000 in 1972.

A five-man planning group for the overall effort was formed and became known in the jargon of the office as the "Youth Task Force." The members were Barrett, Harr, Ruder, Yankelovich, and Paul Ylvisaker, a Harvard Ph.D. and former Ford Foundation executive who had just made a transition in 1970 from his post as commissioner of the New Jersey Department of Community Affairs to the faculty of the Woodrow Wilson School at Princeton.

Yankelovich was involved both because of deep interest in the effort and a commitment to provide partial funding to his firm for annual updating of the research on the attitudes of young people that he had first done for *Fortune* and CBS. The idea was to generate longitudinal data to see if the "new values" had staying power and how they might be assimilated elsewhere in the society.

The first Yankelovich survey under the new arrangement was administered to a sample of businessmen as well as students, and was entitled, appropriately enough, "Youth and the Establishment." It showed that, if anything, student attitudes had intensified, especially in opposition to the Vietnam War. The sample of 408 businessmen, drawn randomly from a list of 2,000 executives of the *Fortune* 500 companies, showed a surprising level of agreement. Three out of four of the businessmen said they would be glad to work with young people on almost any project and two out of three said they would be interested in sponsoring projects and devoting personal time to them. The survey presented a list of five hypothetical projects and asked the students and businessmen which one appealed to them the most. The winner was an idea in which students from several colleges would form a group to draw on faculty resources and local business to undertake an important environmental project in the area.

This message seemed so clear that the Youth Task Force set out to turn the hypothetical project into a reality, and this in turn led to a celebrated incident at Hampshire College in Amherst, Massachusetts. An arrangement was made to offer a $25,000 grant to Five Colleges, Inc., a consortium composed of Smith, Mt. Holyoke, Amherst, and Hampshire Colleges and the University of Massachusetts. The purpose was to fund an environmental study of the Connecticut River Valley by a fifteen-member student group, three from each of the five schools, which would be advised by a ten-member faculty group and draw on local business resources.

In the course of developing this project, JDR was invited to speak to the students by Franklin Patterson, president of Hampshire, a college that was somewhat avant-garde in nature and a hotbed of youthful ferment. JDR accepted with the plan in mind that he would speak and the members of the "Youth Task Force" would follow as a panel to answer questions, discuss possible activities, and present the latest results of the Yankelovich research. The speech was scheduled for 1:00 P.M. Sunday afternoon, December 6, 1970, in a large lecture hall at Hampshire. Accompanying JDR to Amherst for the weekend were his wife, Blanchette; all the members of the Task Force; David Lelewer (JDR's population associate who was becoming heavily involved in the youth program); Jerry Swift, a young man Barrett had taken on as an aide; and several youthful recruits who, together with Swift, were to form the nucleus of an operational staff on the youth program in JDR's office.

By the time the group arrived in Amherst for a wintry weekend the atmosphere had become somewhat tense. There were rumors that there would be demonstrations, the students would turn down the grant, and JDR would be heckled and perhaps not allowed to speak. Ylvisaker did some scouting and reported to JDR on Sunday morning that there would be a skit attacking the Rockefeller family and JDR outside the auditorium before the speech. Ylvisaker said he thought JDR should arrive in time to see part of the skit. He also said that the students insisted that JDR appear alone on the stage to make his speech and answer questions with no other members of his entourage involved. Ylvisaker added that he discounted the rumors of possible violence that were floating around the campus.

Some members of JDR's group thought he should not give in to demands and should simply go home, but JDR thought it was important to stay and see it through. Moreover, he had worked hard on his speech, and he always hated to give up on anything in which he had invested time and thought unless absolutely necessary. The speech, entitled "Youth and the Establishment: A Unique Opportunity," restated some of the basic views he had expressed in his Family of Man speech two years earlier, but in the main was devoted to explicating his approach of trying to build bridges between generations for constructive purposes. President Calvin Plimpton of Amherst told JDR he initially had been opposed to the $25,000 grant, but changed his mind when he read the text of JDR's speech.

As advised, JDR and Blanchette went early to see some of the skit being performed by the University of Massachusetts "Guerrilla Players" outside the lecture hall. There were five actors each portraying one of the Rockefeller brothers and all wearing hats in the form of oil wells. They were playing a version of Monopoly on a world scale, and David Rockefeller had just won South Africa when JDR and Blanchette arrived. The player representing JDR began to mimic him as he prepared to roll the giant dice. Blanchette was appalled, but JDR was amused and at his disarming best. He told one of the players: "You put on a good show. I don't think I can put on one as good." But he did. JDR described the afternoon's happenings in his diary:

The Gorilla [sic] Players had a light touch with a resulting less offensive approach than could have been. The hall which seats 250 was packed, mainly with students, including many sitting in the aisles and standing in the rear. Dr. Patterson did a good job with his introduction, I thought, and my speech seemed to be well received. In any event there were no interruptions as we had feared there might be. Afterwards for more than an hour I answered questions from the floor, some of which were obviously hostile, but the general atmosphere was one of concern and responsiveness. Somehow I quite enjoyed the two hours, at no time feeling that the situation was in any way out of hand. It was a good and interesting experience and was helpful in understanding the students' approach to the Establishment. . . .

After my speech Dr. Patterson announced that . . . the grant had been turned down by the student group involved earlier in the morning. I said to the audience that from my point of view this was entirely sound and reasonable, that the project must be the students' own project and that they should not take money from outside sources until they were convinced that everything was reasonable and sound from their point of view. . . .

. . . on the way out we were verbally accosted by a group of extremists who would have nothing of the Establishment. They followed us for a way to our cars, shouting abuses. When I suggested talking to them, I was told it would serve no useful purpose.

In characteristic fashion, JDR somewhat understated what had happened—it was a courageous performance. President Patterson left the stage after his introduction so that JDR was entirely alone. The tension in the hall was palpable. One of JDR's associates described the event as being "like a performance of *Hair* except that all the hair was out in the audience." JDR clearly won over the great majority of the audience and received a standing ovation.[3]

Afterwards the affair of the grant threatened to escalate into a full-scale reprise of the "tainted money" episode of 1905[4] with the interesting difference that the press this time was all on the side of the Rockefellers. A *New York Times* editorial called the students "young ingrates." The *Boston Globe* said JDR was "unruffled" and *Time* said he had performed "gamely." *Newsweek* asked: "If there's an award to anyone as best sport of the year, how about John D. Rockefeller 3rd?"[5]

Telegrams and phone calls poured into JDR's office from student groups across the country saying they would be glad to accept the grant, but it turned out that the Five Colleges committee had merely deferred the grant instead of turning it down. In due course, it was accepted. The committee's problem was that it was under criticsim from radicals on the five campuses who accused the members of being "coopted" by the establishment. The situation remained anarchic enough so that the project was never well organized, and no useful product resulted.

The second idea emerging from the Youth Task Force was for a series of "youth-establishment dialogues" described in the 1971 JDR 3rd Fund report as

two- or three-day meetings between leading businessmen and youth from the same community. . . . The intent is to give business and community leaders a better understanding of youths' diagnosis of society, and to give young people greater insight into the process of getting things done within the constraints of established institutions.

With this program, the Task Force became less active as an operational staff took over, occupying the space made available in Room 5600 by the removal of Junior's old wood-paneled sanctum. There was some irony in the contrast between the former decorum of that space and the new atmosphere provided by a revolving band of young consultants. Datus Smith, who served as administrator of JDR's office in one of his roles, occasionally caught a whiff of marijuana coming from the youth headquarters and was moved to exert a presence to cool things down.

Leader of the crew was Jerry Swift, a thirty-four-year-old former Jesuit scholastic with an engaging manner. Swift was an articulate man in speech and writing, able to move easily between the young activists he recruited and business leaders. Yet he had strong feelings and an independent mind; so noncomformist was he that he had parted company with the Jesuits only a week before his scheduled ordination. His good nature and competence in promoting the "dialogues" led to a good relationship between Swift and JDR, but this was to be damaged by unfortunate circumstances later on.

Swift recruited a band of young operatives that expanded or contracted as the needs dictated. There were two more former Jesuit students, Jerry's younger brother, Paul "Porky" Swift, and Roger Guettinger, who had been ordained but was not active in the Church. One of the first recruits was Rob Lilley, an engaging young man thoroughly steeped in the counterculture whose father was president of New Jersey Bell (and later president of AT&T). Lilley brought in his roommate, Steven Haft, at nineteen the youngest of the band, whose particular interest was studying and relating to blue-collar families and youth. Later recruits included a young black man, Ron Heath, and two women, Eloise Hirsch and Peggy Blumenthal.

JDR showed his commitment to the youth program not only by retaining and supporting the Task Force and Swift's youthful crew, but also by taking the lead in establishing contact with business leaders. He hosted a dinner for twenty chief executive officers of large corporations, and out of this several projects grew. The most interested participants were Robert Lilley, Sr., and Bruce Dayton of the Dayton-Hudson department stores headquartered in Minneapolis. The latter's interest led to the first "dialogue" project. The pattern was to locate a businessman who would take the lead in enlisting other executives in his community to meet with a youth contingent organized by Swift or one of his consultants. What happened then was up to the participants, in some cases a retreat of several days, in others a once-a-week meeting, sometimes with an environmental or social service project resulting. Swift's agent would continue to be available in the community as needed.

In this manner, projects were initiated in a number of cities in addition to Minneapolis, including Louisville, Chicago, Cleveland, San Francisco, and Jackson, Mississippi. Prominent business leaders accepted the role of convener—for example, A. W. Clausen, president of the Bank of America, in San Francisco, and Reuben Mettler, president of TRW, in Cleveland. The "dialogues" differed in most respects, but one common feature was the need to overcome an initial level of hostility between the generations. Swift's organizers did not take the easy route of recruiting young people who were likely to be seen as models of behavior by the businessmen, but rather sought those who seemed to be genuinely representative of the "youth revolution." This made the establishing of effective communication more difficult to achieve, but more rewarding in the long run.

There were many cases of a young activist and a prominent businessman developing a personal relationship of trust and mutual help and criticism, elsewhere a rare occurrence in those days of the exacerbated generation gap. A young man in Louisville who slept on friends' floors and ran a soup kitchen for the hungry was able to bring home to a proud Kentucky manufacturer some of the reality of poverty, including the fact that within a mile of his plant a woman had recently starved to death. A gruff retailer showed a radical community organizer quicker ways of "spreading the word" and involving, rather than alienating, local opinion-makers. Even where the dialogues did not result in a joint, ongoing project in the community, they established lines of communication that took the edge of suspicion and bitterness away from relations between important groups in the local society. In some cases, the "dialogue" lasted for a period of only a few months, in others for several years.

In addition to the "dialogues," JDR's youth staff became involved in a variety of other services linking youth groups to the resources of the business world and exposing establishment organizations to dedicated and articulate young leaders. These efforts included arranging financial support for youth-controlled organizations (often through small grants by JDR or the JDR 3rd Fund), technical assistance in fund-raising or communications or internal organizing, and introduction to influential forums such as the Foundation Luncheon Group in New York City. On the establishment side, the efforts included responding to many and varied requests for help, suggesting candidates for corporate assistance or grants, and spreading understanding (for example, in producing and distributing an attractive report on the White House Conference on Youth).

As the Hampshire experience illustrated, it could be perilous to offer funds and help when there was no preexisting organization already pursuing its own goals with proven commitment and some success, at least in coping with hard times. In contrast, the JDR staff found its best success in assisting groups that had already fought their way into existence and some measure of recognition—from the East Kentucky Health Services Center started by the two young Appalachians, to Tie Line, a community network in Los Angeles, to Project Interface, a student-business group in Dayton, to the Ripon Society of young Republican moderates, to the notorious Black P Stone Nation in Chicago.

Swift and his organizers believed that the "dialogue" process in general was working, leading in some cases to exciting breakthroughs in communication and relationships between generations. JDR's experience in attending some of the group meetings in several of the cities led him to share this view and continue his support of the effort. But over time it became clear that the approach suffered from several factors—the difficulty of measuring exactly what *was* happening, the fact that the approach was not replicable elsewhere without the presence of a third party and the hard organizing work done by the staff of JDR's youth program, and the growing expectation among youth groups and individuals that there were endless grants to be had.[6]

The strain in the relationship between JDR and Swift occurred over the publication of a "profile" of JDR in *The New Yorker* magazine of November 4, 1972. The profile, a *New Yorker* staple with several appearing each year, is always intended as a major piece based on months of research by the writer. The writer in this case was Geoffrey T. Hellman, in the twilight of his career as a *New Yorker* contributor and leading practitioner of the art of the profilist. Since he had first started writing for the *New Yorker* in 1929, Hellman had cultivated something of the reputation of a bon vivant and "man about town." He had profiled Nelson Rockefeller as early as 1942, and then went to work for Nelson in the Office of the Coordinator for Inter-American Affairs in Washington for two years.[7]

As noted before, JDR was such a private person that he was always wary of press attention focused on him rather than on one of his projects. He was going to decline the honor of being profiled, but was persuaded to change his mind by Bill Ruder, who argued that *New Yorker* profiles were serious and honest and that the exposure would do all of JDR's interests some good. This was a case where JDR's initial caution was warranted—Hellman's piece turned out to be what is commonly known in the trade as a "hatchet job."

Although unexceptionable in some parts, as in dealing with JDR's early years and some of his activities, the bulk of the article had an unmistakably snide and mocking tone about it, referring variously to JDR as "the underprivileged monarch," "Pop's pop" (as the founder of the Population Council), and "the disappearing artist." The last was Hellman's way of characterizing JDR's sometime practice of gradually cutting back on his own contributions to organizations he had created. There were sound reasons for this practice, as we have seen, with the desire to avoid overdependency on JDR and encourage self-reliance for the organization's own good being only the most obvious. However, Hellman did not explore any such motivations; instead, despite all evidence to the contrary, he inferred that JDR's "doctrine of phasing out" meant that he was stingy. Hellman wrote:

To the student of John Rockefeller as an innovative philanthropist—to use an adjective that is much in vogue in humane circles—the Asia Society is of particular interest, because its finances offer a clear-cut example of a technique he has perfected. In line with this, the worthy patron, trinketed in Bloomingdale's best, puts up "seed money" *ab initio*, and then, by dint of bringing in other donors, begins to phase himself out.

In tracing the finances of Lincoln Center in a later section Hellman concluded that "it *looks* as though the citizen-at-large helped bail the Center out with around eleven million dollars, in bites." By italicizing the verb, Hellman managed to cast some doubt on the total of JDR's contributions. He went on: "Alas for the doctrine of phasing out! Alas for hurty [*sic*] feelings along the way to mass culture!" Hellman then reported that men prominently associated with the building of Lincoln Center today "purse their lips and avert their gaze" when JDR's name is mentioned, and he quoted one of them, unnamed, as saying: "The goddamn monument is there. It's paid for." Hellman did not explore the reasons for these alleged negative feelings about JDR at Lincoln Center, leaving the implication that he deserted the cause after his "monument" was built. It would be difficult to more grossly distort the truth about JDR's involvement in Lincoln Center.[8]

Clearly, Hellman did not like JDR, and why this was so is not easily apparent. JDR detected a faint atmosphere of animosity in their interview sessions, but he put this down to the fact that he was not willing to commit to more than a few interviews of several hours each. Hellman complained that he had practically lived with the last man he had profiled (Francis T. P. Plimpton) for an entire week. Hellman also interviewed all of JDR's associates, many friends and colleagues, and several family members. Whenever he put a negative twist on a quotation from one of these interviews he did not make a direct attribution. The one big exception had to do with Jerry Swift.

For their interview, Hellman and Swift had agreed to meet after office hours one day in the Promenade Café on the concourse level of the RCA Building. Swift brought along one of his young colleagues, Rob Lilley. After a few drinks, Hellman confided that he thought JDR was a snob. He explained that he knew the Rockefeller brothers personally, especially Nelson and Laurance, but that one time at the Century Association checkroom he had said "Hello" to JDR and JDR ignored him. Swift suggested that JDR simply must not have heard the greeting, that he would never intentionally insult anyone. As the evening progressed, it became clear to Swift that the checkroom incident was not an isolated one, that whatever the cause Hellman had a strong personal bias against JDR. Swift thereupon set out, in the best Jesuitical fashion, to educate Hellman about JDR. It turned out to be a serious mistake.

Swift's approach was to candidly present his own first impression of JDR, one that any young activist might have had, an image that sounded negative, but then to contrast that with the reality of the man as he had come to know him. The first impression was that JDR was remote, not serious, not intellectual, had little going for him except his money and his name, was interested in young people only for his own benefit or for other dubious reasons, and was outclassed by his more dynamic brothers. Unless one took pains to probe beneath this image to understand JDR, Swift said, he could easily be dismissed as ineffectual and unimportant. The reality that he had come to know, Swift said, was that JDR had qualities of greatness. "A hundred years from now, who will know or care who the Vice President of the United States was in 1972?" he asked rhetorically. "JDR may not be remembered either, but the good effects he had on people in his lifetime will still be felt." In reality, Swift told Hellman, JDR was very serious and very frank, a man who genuinely cared about what he was trying to do, and one of the most honest men Swift had ever met.[9]

Hellman told Swift that this was his best and most useful interveiw since he had started working on the JDR profile, and he wanted to continue it if Swift and Lilley would join him for dinner. They agreed, and Hellman took them to his brownstone residence in Manhattan where his wife prepared dinner. The discussion continued in animated fashion for several hours. For a time it turned on the concept of "the best and the brightest," the title of David Halberstam's book, which was then a best-seller. Hellman said JDR was *not* one of the "best and the brightest," and Swift agreed entirely. But then it became clear that this was a criticism to Hellman, while Swift saw it as a compliment. Hellman saw JDR as a sort of doddering dilettante. He seemed vaguely disappointed that JDR was not a mover and shaker of men and events like his brother Nelson or Robert McNamara. Swift argued that this was exactly what made JDR great, that he was not power-hungry and manipulative, but humane and supportive of what people really wanted, much more a man for the times than "the best and the brightest."

By the time the evening was over Swift believed that the debate had helped Hellman move beyond his dislike of JDR to a better understanding of the innate qualities of the man he was profiling. He thought his Jesuitical approach was working just as it had worked once before, in the case of another writer who was all set to "destroy" JDR in print because of his suspicions about JDR's motives for involving himself in a "youth program."[10]

But in the case of Hellman, the approach backfired. Hellman did not credit the positive view offered by Swift, but instead concentrated on the negative, as this passage indicates:

The director of the seven-man Task Force is Jerry J. Swift, a friendly, somewhat youthful ("Rockefeller liked me because I was young—I'm thirty-five") ex-Jesuit with bobbed orange hair and an eager expression, whose affectionate devotion to his employer is entirely devoid of awe. "I think he's sort of conscience-ridden," Swift says. "So earnest and moral and concerned and anguished. He never wants to be congratulated. He hasn't had any education—four years at Princeton!—but he has a most tenacious mind. I don't mean intellectual. We bring young people into the office to talk to him. He's an almost savage interrogator; he may go on for three hours. Relentless questioner. Terrible memory. Never remembers names, faces, facts. . . . He disarmed the young people: 'I'm so happy you could come. The Establishment is really doing nothing; I hope you'll take some initiative.' In five minutes, he was their grandfather: 'That poor old man. How can we help?' He never attacks. He is entirely defenseless. I can imagine Nelson going over him like a steamroller. David sometimes puts him down. He's a real underdog, in a funny kind of way. He fusses with us all day long—'Have I done the right thing? Is that all right now?' I think he's still looking for an identity. He's in a cocoon. He can't call people up—he'd be asked for a million dollars twenty times a day. He has to rely on his staff. We're all involved in moving him around the spectrum a little bit, which is the way he wants it."

Not only did Hellman fail to accept Swift's central point, but, according to Swift, he exaggerated and distorted the prefatory negative points. Swift's account of what happened is that Hellman "selected out of context a string of negatives from five hours of conversation and fabricated them into a breezy monologue of his own making." Swift likened Hellman's techniques to those later denounced forcefully by the *New Yorker* itself in a controversy involving the writer Alistair Reid.[11]

Other consultants on the youth project, such as Dick Barrett, Paul Swift, and Steve Haft, strongly support Jerry Swift's point of view, pointing out that he loved JDR and would never have been a party to sabotaging him in the manner Hellman recounts.

Proofs of Hellman's article, which he had worked on for more than a year, were available in JDR's office before publication date, and of course they provoked a mood of gloom. JDR and Swift met several times to discuss what had happened. Swift explained what he had tried to do, but it was not easy and his version was complicated and a little bizarre. However, JDR was sensitive enough to note in his diary that Swift "did not want to be put in the position of being apologetic." He accepted Swift's statement that he had not intended to be negative, and that Hellman had misused and misquoted him. Swift felt that Bill Ruder had failed as a professional in public relations by not screening Hellman in the first place and then not pressing the *New Yorker*'s editors on the matter of Hellman's faulty tactics, which he felt could be demonstrated simply on the basis of internal evidence in the article itself.[12] If JDR shared this assessment of Ruder, he said nothing about it.

JDR and Swift agreed that their mutual trust had been shaken, but, as JDR put it, "not shattered." They decided to continue working together. Swift stayed on in charge of the youth program for another six months, but finally resigned early in 1973. "No matter how hard we tried," he said, "it could never be quite the same again."

Swift's departure was not inappropriate because the "youth revolution" was beginning to wane in any case—and JDR's youth program with it. Three members of Swift's staff—Ron Heath, Peggy Blumenthal, and Eloise Hirsch—continued to work on the "dialogue" program. Some of the groups continued to do well. Others had lapsed, and a few of those revived. In some cities additional groups of young people and businessmen were spawned. In mid-1973, a two-day conference was held in San Francisco of a youth and business delegate from each of the groups across the country. JDR attended and found the meeting rewarding and impressive—"The program has something special about it," he wrote.

But by 1974 the program had ground to a halt. The reason was not

Hellman's poison pen but the changing attitudes of young people. The "youth revolution" was over, with the ending of the Vietnam War as probably the most decisive turning point. The change was amply documented in Yankelovich's fifth and last youth survey, the most ambitious one of the series in which other social groups in addition to college youth were surveyed.[13] Published in mid-1974, the burden of the study was that the ferment of youth had not been a mere "aberration" nor was the end of it a simple "return to normalcy," but rather a complex process involving both the diffusion of "new values" from college youth to noncollege youth and other sectors of society, and society's efforts to accommodate and adapt those values with older, more traditional beliefs. The discussion was reminiscent of JDR's analysis in his book of the "role of the moderates" in social change.

In short, the fervor had abated, but the society would never be quite the same again—nor would JDR. However his youth activities might be evaluated, for him personally they were enriching and broadening enough to lead him to other new experiences.

21

☙

THE URBAN PROBLEM

JDR loved to quote Alexis de Tocqueville, the French political scientist who wrote *Democracy in America* after traveling through the United States in the 1830s. Tocqueville wrote in wonderment about the propensity of Americans to become involved in the work of their communities, to form associations to take action and meet problems or needs without any instructions from higher authority.[1] To JDR this was the essence of democracy, and as time passed it became clear that it was this quality that excited him so much about all of the social ferment of the 1960s and early 1970s.

Everywhere he looked he saw individual Americans who were passionately concerned about something to the point that they were moved to become involved in efforts to achieve change for the better—whether they were environmentalists, young activists, feminists, civil rights workers, or those concerned about such issues as the urban problem, education, population, or war. While he disliked some of the tactics and excesses in these movements, in the main he agreed with the diagnoses. But the unifying theme for JDR was the activism itself, the fact that people cared enough to take action on their own initiative. In the final section of his book, he referred to this phenomenon as "private initiative," taking care to make clear that he was not using a code phrase to denote the business sector. In speeches and articles he began using the term "individual initiative" and then "citizen participation" and "citizen involvement." As he thought through concepts about how American democracy worked best and what he felt needed to be done, he finally adopted the phrase "the third sector" in an effort to distinguish citizen activism of all kinds from the business and government sectors of society.

It was this interest that caused him to stay home instead of becoming U.S. ambassador to Japan, and to say that "this is an exciting time to be alive." It was an interest that permeated his book and motivated his youth activities. There were other ways in which he tried to stimulate and sup-

333

port individual initiative and participation. Although he did not always have great success, he never lost faith in the basic concept. Two of his involvements offer small case studies with particular insight into the times, JDR's commitment to the ideal of citizen participation, and the frustrations of dealing with officialdom—in this chapter the urban housing problem, in the next the Bicentennial of American Independence.

The urban housing problem did not seem a likely field for involvement by JDR. When residential areas of a great city begin to degenerate, normal economic conditions no longer apply and the downward spiral worsens, resulting in a problem of such massive scale, requiring so great an infusion of capital, that seemingly only government has the resources to deal with it. The business sector is constrained by the absence of normal market conditions, and the sheer scale of the problem inhibits philanthropic involvement.

The housing problem was a prominent factor in the wave of urban riots that began in Watts in 1965, spread elsewhere, and reached a crescendo in Newark and Detroit in 1967. All levels of government sought to understand and eliminate the causes of these unprecedented civil disorders. In the housing field, for example, new initiatives were announced by New York City, New York State, and the federal government. Prominent among the responses of the private sector was the creation of the Urban Coalition. David Rockefeller joined with twenty-two business, labor, and social leaders who came together to launch the organization, and JDR's friend John Gardner became its chairman after leaving his post as Secretary of the Department of Health, Education, and Welfare in 1968.

At Gardner's request, JDR good-naturedly joined in the making of a television commercial promoting the Urban Coalition. More than one hundred celebrities convened in a studio to sing lyrics from the Broadway musical *Hair* ("Let the sun shine in . . .") as Mitch Miller conducted an orchestra and cameras whirred. Pictures were taken for magazine ads. JDR found it an "interesting" experience to stand between "Myrna Loy and a girl from the cast of *Hair*" and join in the singing.

Voluminous files in the Rockefeller Archive Center testify to the long involvement of the Rockefeller family in the housing field, going back nearly a century to the days when Senior helped to finance the City and Suburban Homes Company, an effort to provide good, inexpensive housing for New York City's poor in the 1880s and 1890s.[2] Junior became involved in the battle for tenement house reform in association with the Citizens

Union in the late 1890s, an effort that resulted in the Tenement Reform Law of 1901 and created the New York City Housing Commission to enforce the new and stricter regulations regarding size, light, and sanitation. Junior maintained strong contacts with many prominent individuals in the housing reform movement, including Jacob Riis, Robert De Forest, Lawrence Veiller, and Lillian Wald of the Henry Street Settlement.

In the early 1920s New York State passed a law allowing 6 percent limited-dividend corporations for the purpose of stimulating new and affordable housing. Under the terms of this law, Junior helped finance the City Housing Corporation, which built Sunnyside Gardens in Queens and Radburn in New Jersey. He also provided all of the financing for the Paul Laurence Dunbar cooperative apartments in Harlem where W. E. B. Du Bois and Bill "Bojangles" Robinson lived. Junior also was instrumental in convincing Standard Oil of New Jersey to provide adequate housing for employees in Bayonne, an activity in which his wife was very much involved. Some of Junior's projects defaulted during the Depression, and in the late 1930s he managed to sell off his interests for about thirty cents on the dollar, though recouping most of his investment because of the tax loss.

Activity in the private housing field virtually stopped during the Depression, although JDR worked hard for a time with the Rockefeller Foundation in an effort to develop new construction methods, noting that housing construction would be especially beneficial because it would create jobs as well as dwelling units. But nothing came of this.

Creating housing for lower-income groups was one of the main activities of the International Basic Economy Corporation (which Nelson created), first in Latin America and later in IBEC's U.S. operations. David Rockefeller has been the most active of the five brothers in housing, serving as chairman of Morningside Heights, Inc., which attempted to rejuvenate the area around Columbia University. He also helped to found the New York City Housing Partnership, which brings all elements of the housing picture together in an effort to generate collaborative projects. From the time of the Urban Coalition, David consistently played a leading role in citywide programs to increase the quantity and improve the quality of housing in New York.

As governor of New York, Nelson was necessarily involved, and was the moving force in creating the Urban Development Corporation, a state corporation with unusual power to override local governments in mounting projects to meet urban problems.[3] Laurance sponsored an attempt to make a breakthrough in housing rehabilitation involving the total gutting of an apartment building interior to be replaced by a complete new modular interior lowered in from the top. This turned out to be so expensive that Laurance abandoned it.

The Rockefeller Brothers Fund (RBF) reflected these activities of the brothers by helping to underwrite the efforts of the Urban Coalition and the work of other groups that sought to understand the causes of the urban crisis and come up with solutions for it.

Given this history of family and RBF involvement and his "full plate" elsewhere, there was certainly no compelling reason for JDR to try to do anything in a field that had become notorious for complexity, frustration, and failure. And yet JDR helped sponsor a new organization that was on the firing line, in the sense of actually producing housing projects. It became one of the most innovative and enduring efforts of the time. He did this for several reasons. One was that the approach offered a chance for lower-income families to participate in solving their own housing problem. It also exemplified another favored JDR theme—public-private cooperation. The approach was designed to provide private, nonprofit, professional resources to help make government programs work where it counted—in the community and the neighborhood. Finally, the effort was explicitly intended to be self-supporting after being launched with the aid of philanthropic funds. Once its "pipeline" of housing projects was sufficiently advanced, it would cover its ongoing costs and overhead through legitimate fees for its professional services and role as a housing sponsor. This last was an essential feature because no philanthropic source can afford to subsidize housing projects indefinitely.

The new organization, which came to be known as the Urban Home Ownership Corporation (UHO), was incorporated in 1968 under the name of CENDEVCO (Center for the Development of Cooperatives). The name was changed to UHO about two years later when the first project was being developed. The idea of UHO came from Jerome and Evelyn Boxer of Scarsdale, two of the owners of the buildings that became UHO's first project. Evelyn's family had been very proud of these buildings back in the days when the Grand Concourse area of the South Bronx had been one of the finest Jewish residential areas in New York City, and she and her husband were now watching the deterioration of the buildings with dismay. They were moved to action one day when their daughter came home from school and asked if it was true that her father was a "slumlord."[4]

Stated succinctly, the UHO approach was deceptively simple—to locate basically sound apartment buildings in "fringe" areas of New York City (not hard-core "inner city," but low-income neighborhoods where buildings are degenerating and heading for eventual abandonment unless something

By diligent application, John D. Rockefeller 3rd became an effective public
speaker, as in the case of this meeting
on the performing arts in Pittsburgh,
April 1961.

Opening night at Lincoln Center, Philharmonic Hall, September 23, 1962: JDR with
First Lady Jackie Kennedy and Maestro Leonard Bernstein

The critical connection between food and population growth. JDR discusses the subject with Colombian officials on a Rockefeller Foundation visit to Cali, March 1964.

At an Economics Club dinner in honor of Indian Prime Minister Indira Gandhi, JDR is seated between Ambassador B. K. Nehru and Mrs. Gandhi, March 1966.

JDR and his office associates, January 1965. *From left:* Ken Young, Jack McNulty, Ray Lamontagne, and Don McLean. Not present when the picture was taken was Edgar B. Young, JDR's first associate.

Under Frank Notestein's presidency, the Population Council entered its "takeoff" period in the 1960s to become a worldwide resource.

Arthur T. Mosher brought the talents of missionary, scholar, and executive to his successful presidency of the Agricultural Development Council.

A contemplative moment between father and son when Jay visits his father's office, Room 5600, Rockefeller Center, in 1966. The Eastman Johnson portrait of his grandfather hangs behind JDR. Jay had served as a VISTA volunteer in West Virginia and was now a candidate for his first political office in the state's House of Delegates.

Opening night for the Metropolitan Opera at Lincoln Center, September 16, 1966: *From left:* William Schuman, composer, president of Lincoln Center; President Ferdinand Marcos of the Philippines; Rudolf Bing, general manager of the Metropolitan Opera; Imelda Marcos, Lady Bird Johnson; and JDR.

A rare appearance of all five Rockefeller brothers together in public, when they were honored by the National Institute of the Social Sciences (NISS) at the Plaza Hotel, November 28, 1967: *From left:* David, Winthrop, JDR, Nelson, Laurance.

The eldest and youngest of the Rockefeller brothers at the NISS dinner, JDR and David

Population policy was the subject when JDR visited President Lyndon B. Johnson in the Oval Office, May 23, 1968.

JDR and Senator Edward M. Kennedy urged an opening to China at the dinner meeting of the National Committee on U.S.–China Relations in New York, March 20, 1969.

JDR traveled to Little Rock for the second inauguration of brother Winthrop as governor of Arkansas, January 14, 1969.

Laurance S. Rockefeller at Little Dix Bay on Virgin Gorda in the British Virgin Islands, one of the luxury Rock Resorts that he developed, in the mid-1960s. (*Richard Meek*)

Another trio of John D. Rockefellers—JDR 3rd; his son, Jay; and his grandson, who was known as Jamie at this stage of his life—Charleston, West Virginia, July 16, 1969, when Jay was serving as West Virginia secretary of state 'is done), to selectively acquire and substantially rehabilitate the buildings through the medium of a government interest-rate subsidy and mortgage-guarantee program, and to turn over ownership of the buildings to the tenants in residence in a housing cooperative. The theory was that successful cooperatives of this kind would provide "anchors of stability" that would help reverse the deterioration of a neighborhood.

In practice, UHO faced formidable obstacles. Despite all the new housing programs being announced, New York State and New York City had nothing that could be adapted to the UHO approach. The only recourse was the federal programs of the Department of Housing and Urban Development (HUD), but here there were difficult biases to deal with. The great postwar housing boom stimulated by VA and FHA mortgages had been oriented to the middle class, to new construction, and to single-family home ownership. HUD was now pointed toward the urban problem, but the biases lingered. In particular, the overwhelming emphasis was on tearing down old buildings and building new ones, *not* on rehabilitation—"rehab" was the stepchild of HUD programs. Moreover, there had been little experimentation with the idea of cooperatives. Co-op apartments are commonplace in New York City, of course, but chiefly for the well-to-do, not families with low incomes. The unspoken bias—the legacy of public housing—was that poor people could not or would not take care of their housing. Moreover, though no HUD official would ever say it publicly, the agency did not like to work with nonprofit groups because all too often they were church or community groups that offered no professional skills, but could be strident and demanding. HUD much preferred profit-motivated private developers despite the existence of a good deal of greed and corruption in this particular business.

With all these handicaps, putting together the basic fund for UHO was no easy matter. JDR provided the money for the planning phase, and Robert T. Bonham of Washington, D.C., was recruited to lead the effort. He brought with him as his aide a young former Foreign Service Officer, James F. Ragan, Jr. A measure of their commitment to the idea was that their assignment could have been very brief if the plan were not attractive enough to amass the basic funding needed until UHO could become self-sustaining.

Bonham had a folksy, hayseed approach, but he was in fact an aggressive, smooth-talking executive, the perfect choice for the UHO assignment. Trained as a lawyer, he had long experience in Washington agencies, including government housing programs. And he had a lifelong devotion to the cooperative movement, having been raised during the Depression in a low-income family living in a housing cooperative. He had administered co-op activities in the foreign aid program and had been the success-ful president of a chain of Washington food cooperatives. He fervently believed that the cooperative idea was the best way for "poor folks" to amass a degree of economic and social power and take more control over their lives. From his own experience he knew that a stake in ownership would make a crucial difference in how low-income families maintained their apartments and buildings.

Bonham and Ragan refined the basic plan, and obtained an option on the first project, known as "Crotona Park East," a set of three related buildings with 197 apartments on the Boston Post Road in the South Bronx. The level of rehabilitation would be "substantial," as distinguished from merely cosmetic work at one extreme or the total job known inele-gantly as "gut rehab" at the other extreme. By "substantial," Bonham meant: new heating, plumbing, wiring, security, and elevator systems for the building, new windows and doors, public space for meetings and social events, coin-operated laundries, modern kitchens and bathrooms, com-plete redecorating in every apartment, and beautification of corridors, lob-bies, and the exterior of the building. Thus, $2 million might be spent to rehabilitate a building that was acquired for $1.5 million. The resulting $3.5 million mortgage, guaranteed by HUD, would be repaid over a long term by the monthly payments made by the residents for their co-op apartments. Because of the federal interest-rate subsidy and tax abatement by New York City, the monthly payment would be only marginally more than the rents formerly paid. But the building would be as good as new, the residents would own it, and it would be less expensive than a new building.

UHO's biggest problem was to be bureaucratic red tape. HUD's processing time for the pilot project stretched out to eighteen months. Construction took another year. Bonham hoped that processing time would diminish as UHO built a track record, but to keep the operation going the goal for the basic fund was set at $1.2 million. JDR was the initial contribu-tor, and others followed. The Rockefeller Brothers Fund was an obvious target. Laurance Rockefeller, with his own unhappy experience in housing behind him, was chairman of the RBF. When the grant request was consid-ered, according to a staff member present, Laurance groaned and threw up his hands. Then he said, "Well, if they want to try, let them go ahead." The third major contributor was the Ford Foundation, the only large foun-dation to consistently support efforts in the urban housing field. The fourth major contributor was the New York–based Glen Alden Corporation, whose president, a southerner named Paul Johnston, simply decided that his company owed something to the city of New York. Smaller grants came from the New York Urban Coalition, the Maremont Foundation, and the Edna McConnell Clark Foundation.

In the early 1970s UHO proceeded to develop another half-dozen projects, and Bonham and Ragan continued to innovate. The view was unanimous that Bonham's idea of rehabilitating a building while the tenants were still in occupancy would never work. but he insisted on trying in the belief that it was important to retain whatever social fabric and leadership elements might already exist in a building instead of evicting and relocating everyone. He developed a system of accumulating enough vacant apartments so that tenants could be moved within the building to free up one vertical row of apartments at a time. This allowed the heavy work—plumbing, heating, and wiring—to be done in that vertical line. These apartments then would be occupied, freeing up another vertical line. The process worked.

Another example of UHO's innovation had to do with the legal requirements for housing cooperatives that had grown up over the years in New York State. These were designed to protect the affluent, and the paperwork for a single cooperative project could be a foot thick. Bonham knew that all of the legal complexities would never work for "poor folks" so he badgered Attorney General Louis Lefkowitz's office until new and simplified regulations were issued.

Bonham soon realized that the fees allowed by HUD for nonprofit sponsors were not sufficient to sustain UHO's overhead. The basic fund was melting away as each new project was taken on. So he talked HUD into allowing a fee of 6 percent of the mortgage for the nonprofit sponsor. Even though this was only one-third of the return allowed to a profit sponsor, there was no precedent for it.

Bonham had one other commitment—to work himself out of a job. Because UHO's housing projects were populated by black and Hispanic families, he believed that the staff and board of directors should also be drawn predominantly from these minority groups. Over time this was done by attracting outstanding blacks and Hispanics to the board and able and committed minority group employees to the staff. In particular, Bonham wanted the president to be a black, and he was able to groom his successor, Preston Moore, a young man who combined architectural training with a flair for management and leadership.

The story of UHO over more than a decade resembled *The Perils of Pauline*. Within a few years, the basic fund was gone, having served its purpose of starting up the organization and keeping it alive until sufficient projects were in development. UHO was existing primarily on the 6 percent fee, but the interminable HUD processing time made this extremely difficult. There were frequent financial crises. During one three-year period there were no salary increases for the staff and on at least half a dozen occasions there were insufficient funds to cover the following month's payroll. A measure of the dedication of the staff was that all through this time only one person resigned because of the economic hazards of the job.

Particularly difficult was the problem of "seed money," which refers to all the expenses that UHO (or any developer) must cover between the time a project is identified and a HUD mortgage commitment secured—funds to cover locating the project, negotiating an option, assembling the financial data, providing information to tenants and community groups, and costs of architectural design, construction estimates, and the paperwork and legal fees necessary to making an application to HUD. Once the commitment comes through, the developer is reimbursed out of the mortgage, but "seed money" is high in risk because it may be lost if HUD turns down the project. Just at the point that UHO's basic fund was nearly exhausted, Bonham discovered an almost-secret New York State "revolving fund" of $10 million specifically set up to make the high-risk "seed money" loans. But this turned out to be a catch-22 operation, with requirements so demanding that its processing took as long as HUD's, meaning that when the "seed money" loan became available it was no longer needed. No amount of importuning and logic was able to change this "no risk at all cost" operation. When the official in charge of the fund finally said that processing could be speeded up if Bonham could get insurance to cover the loan, Bonham left the man's office in shock, never to return. The "seed money" problem was solved only when a courageous urban affairs officer of the Chase Manhattan Bank agreed to set up a revolving loan fund for UHO.[5]

Through it all, UHO built up an impressive track record in a field strewn with failures. In its first eight years it produced ten projects valued at more than $30 million, which provided clean and modern housing for 1,200 low-income families in Harlem and the South Bronx. The UHO board had hoped to do much more—the volume was limited only by the number of projects that HUD would approve. Even so, UHO had become the largest nonprofit sponsor of low-income housing in the United States. Construction work on all of its projects was completed on time and within financial estimates, with some even coming in at less. There were no defaults on UHO projects.

The high point for UHO came when HUD tried to overcome its weakness in rehabilitation (as against new construction) by mustering a special effort known as "Project Rehab." Only a limited number of developers were to be selected. A measure of UHO's progress was that, against heavy competition, it was one of three sponsors (and the only nonprofit) designated by HUD in New York City. For a time conditions improved. One project was even processed by HUD in less than six months. But then the processing began to stretch out again, to as long as three years in some cases.

This was the primary cause of the failure that was most grievous to all of those associated with UHO—it was not possible to bring most of its projects to the "co-op" stage. They remained as rental buildings, with UHO unhappily forced to serve in the role of landlord. The problem was that the financial conditions discussed with tenants at the inception of a project changed significantly by the time HUD processing was completed a year or eighteen months or two years later, primarily because of rising costs. By this time, many tenants would lose interest in the "co-op" idea or become suspicious of it. This problem was worsened by the oil embargo, the recession that followed, and the Nixon "freeze" on HUD programs (which UHO survived only because several projects it had submitted before the freeze were eventually honored). It was also worsened by new ideologies that crept into successive housing legislation, making each HUD program less workable than the one that preceded it—from "Section 221d3" to "Section 236" to "Section 8."[6]

The most telling blow came in 1976 when HUD sent a special task force to the New York area to see how things could be made more efficient. The task force made two decisions, both inimical to UHO. One was to eliminate the "Project Rehab" staff in the area office, and the second was to eliminate UHO's 6 percent fee on the grounds that it was not specifically provided for in the legislation. This left UHO with only one way to get new projects—to enter into tax-shelter arrangements. As long as it could hold out, the UHO board refused to do this for several reasons. There was an ideological dislike of the idea of wealthy people getting enormous tax benefits from projects that provided housing for poor people. Even worse, the tax-shelter route evaded the issue of dealing directly with the housing problem and getting workable legislation and programs. Still worse was that the nature of real estate tax shelters specifically eliminated the possibility of a cooperative.[7] Worst of all, in a tax-shelter deal UHO would be largely reduced to the status of a conduit or a "cover," working *for* the financial people, lawyers, contractors, and architects instead of the reverse. In short, the loss of the 6 percent fee confronted UHO with the choice of closing its doors or going the tax-shelter route. And the latter would erode UHO's independence, eliminate any hope of achieving home ownership as propounded in its very name, and endanger one of its most precious assets—the protection against corruption provided by its nonprofit status and the presence of an uncompensated, public-spirited board of directors.

All of these points were pressed by UHO directors in impassioned meetings in the HUD New York area and regional offices and in one pilgrimage to Washington to meet with high-ranking HUD officials. There was no change. The 6 percent fee was not restored. Because Section 8 was virtually unworkable, the HUD efficiency experts saw tax shelters as the way to get housing done, easier for HUD than its existing programs and certainly easier than trying to get new legislation or adequate appropriations through Congress. The loss of revenue to the U.S. Treasury from overdependence on this method was not HUD's concern.

UHO kept trying. Bonham, who had returned to Washington several years earlier, was brought back to do a special study to distill needed elements for a national housing policy from UHO's experience. He presented his results in testimony before congressional committees. UHO's board produced an eloquent "white paper" that chronicled its experiences and problems and proposed elements that should be present in new housing legislation.[8]

Through all of these years JDR stood by UHO. It was very clear in the begining that he had no commitment beyond helping to create the original funding, and it was an article of faith for UHO's board not to go back to the donors in the light of the pledge to stand or fall on the basis of the viability of government housing programs. Nevertheless, JDR voluntarily made small grants to UHO at critical times, and on two occasions he cosigned loans. After the initial funding period he made five more grants to UHO for a total of nearly $250,000. On two occasions he toured UHO projects in the South Bronx and Harlem, meeting with UHO staff members and project residents.

JDR wrote letters about UHO to every Secretary of HUD from Robert Weaver in the Johnson administration to Patricia Harris in the Carter administration. Usually his purpose was merely to cast some light on UHO's innovative approach at a high level, and for the most part the letters elicited turgid responses written by staff aides. But when the 6 percent fee was disallowed, this gave JDR a specific issue, one that disturbed him. All of his life he had tried to promote public-private cooperation, and in recent years had become something of a missionary on the unique values in the American system of the private, nonprofit, "third sector." He saw the disallowance of the fee as an act of unknowing discrimination not only against the participation of citizens in housing cooperatives, but also against a professional nonprofit agency specifically set up to do what the government ostensibly wanted done.

Despite the fact that he had no obligation to UHO and was inordinately busy, JDR tried to do something about this. He wrote an Op-Ed page article in the *New York Times* of October 4, 1976, entitled "Success in Salvaging." The article succinctly told the story of UHO and focused on the most successful of its cooperatives, a ninety-five-unit project known as "Malcolm X" on 146th Street in West Harlem. The hardy residents of Malcolm X had risen above every disincentive provided by processing delays and cost increases to insist on forming their cooperative and owning their building. It was an outstanding success in every way, and as if to prove it the residents of Malcolm X had recently voted to increase their monthly payments by 20 percent to cover increased fuel and other costs. The fact that they did this themselves in contrast to the fruitless, age-old battle with a landlord was impressive. JDR concluded his article:

Malcolm X is a small beacon of hope, a low-income project that has worked in the city with the toughest housing problem in the nation. If this is possible on a small scale, there should be no valid reason why it cannot be done on a large scale.

I do not believe that the housing problem need be out of control, that it is beyond the range of human ingenuity and will. It is time to learn from the experience of the past and to fashion a national housing policy that works and includes all needed elements. Home ownership projects must be promoted, for they encourage residents to take responsibility. Processing time must be rigorously held to six months or less. Modest fees are essential to enable nonprofit talent pools like U.H.O. to do the job. Many more such nonprofit organizations should be created.

Will this happen? The only certainty is that until it does the housing problem in New York City—and elsewhere in the nation—will grow steadily worse.

JDR's continuing efforts on UHO's behalf constituted an object lesson in the frustrations of trying to deal with official Washington. HUD Secretary Patricia Harris had been a prominent black leader, and JDR knew her slightly and respected her highly. Shortly after she took office in the new Carter administration, he wrote her a letter about UHO and the canceling of the 6 percent fee, enclosing copies of the UHO "white paper" and a document summarizing Bonham's congressional testimony on the elements needed in a new approach to the urban housing problem. Nearly four months later she responded that she had designated Assistant Secretary Harold Simons to investigate the matter.[9] It was this that ultimately led to the trip to Washington by UHO president Preston Moore and four board members to meet with Simons and his group, which availed nothing. At the end of 1977, JDR decided to try again this time writing to his friend Daniel Patrick Moynihan, by now the new Democratic senator from New York State. Two months later Moynihan wrote back saying that he had been trying to get a response from HUD with no success: "I am in complete agreement with your position, and shall press HUD until that behemoth produces a decision."[10] Nothing came of this, either. JDR's staff tried to follow through with Moynihan's staff, but his office turned out to be as impenetrable as the HUD "behemoth."

Never one to give up easily, JDR tried again in May 1978, somewhat fired up on the "third sector" theme and believing that President Jimmy Carter's celebrated walk on Charlotte Street in the South Bronx suggested the possibility of positive action in Washington after all the dismal years of the Nixon freeze and Section 8. JDR wrote to Secretary Harris again, this time pressing hard on the "third sector" theme:

The "third sector," as I have come to call it, has been a distinctive and positive force throughout our entire history as a nation. Yet today housing is the only major social problem we face in which the third sector is virtually absent. Why should this be, I ask myself? I cannot help wondering if it is not a situation which should be of concern to you.

JDR enclosed a new document prepared by the UHO board, which presented the case and stressed the value of nonprofit organizations in producing housing cooperatives as an alternative to the tax-shelter approach:

The rationale can be seen in comparing what happens when a co-op project works as against when it does not work. When it works, the co-op creates a better sense of community, a greater possibility for "sweat equity" involvement, a sense of responsibility on the part of residents, better long-term caring for the property, and an anchor of stability in the neighborhood. When a co-op project does not work, it simply falls back to the highest level that HUD can now achieve under present conditions, namely a rental project.

In other words, there is nothing to be lost and much to be gained. For this reason it makes eminent good sense to try the co-op idea with as much official support and the building in of incentives as possible.

Secretary Harris wrote back only a month later, saying: "I, too, think that the start we made last year toward the exploration of this matter did not go far enough." She proposed that she and JDR meet "to explore ways in which the 'third sector' can play a highly visible role. . . ."[11]

JDR was convalescing from major ankle surgery (see Chapter 33). On June 22, 1978, he responded to Secretary Harris, saying that he was not able to travel yet, but he hoped that the meeting might be arranged in New York City if she were to be traveling there in the forthcoming weeks. A follow-up telephone call to Secretary Harris's appointments secretary produced the surprising news that the meeting could not be arranged until the following fall because Harris would be spending so much time over the summer campaigning for Democratic candidates in the off-year election. It was an appointment that JDR would not be alive to keep.

Meanwhile, UHO's directors reluctantly agreed to enter into tax-shelter projects in order to keep UHO alive while waiting for new housing policy to be created in Washington with workable legislation and programs. They are still waiting.

22

⚜

THE BICENTENNIAL

IT IS a considerable leap from the grime and red tape of the urban housing problem to the potential splendor of the Bicentennial of the American Revolution, but JDR made it on the connecting link of citizen participation and opportunities for the "third sector." JDR had set the stage for his involvement in the Bicentennial in his book, *The Second American Revolution*:

It is purely a coincidence that we are witnessing the emergence of the *second* American Revolution during an era in which we are celebrating the Bicentennial of the *first* American Revolution. Yet it is an interesting coincidence, and a fitting way to celebrate the Bicentennial, for the driving force of today's movement is to fulfill the ideals and promises that were articulated two hundred years ago.[1]

JDR cited the fervor of the thousand young people who met in Estes Park, Colorado, at the White House Conference on Youth in 1971. This was not a gathering of Young Republicans arranged by the Nixon administration, but an apparent representative sample of articulate young people. The preamble to their conference report began: "We are in the midst of a political, cultural, and social revolution." The delegates spoke of "a rage of love" for the founding ideals and principles of the United States, and said: "It is time now to affirm and implement the rights articulated in the Declaration of Independence and the Constitution." JDR wrote:

These young people are patriotic in the deepest sense of that term. It is no accident that they choose the Declaration of Independence and the Constitution as the philosophical bases for their report. Clearly, they believe in this country and its historic ideals. They are concerned with the substance of patriotism, not the symbols.

In comparing the founding of the nation with the conditions of today, JDR articulated his view of the Bicentennial:

346

Today, just as then, we are in a time of profound social change involving masses of people. We are dealing with the very root and structure of society. The first American Revolution did not occur on July 4, 1776, or even in the year 1776, but worked out its full course over a period of several decades. That will be just as true of the Second American Revolution.

Our need today is to summon within ourselves the energy and wisdom to influence our destiny just as our forefathers did two centuries ago. This is what the Bicentennial should be all about, not just festivities or a review of the past. I have nothing against fireworks and parades. And I believe the renewed interest in our history is extremely important. But I submit that the ultimate test of our vitality and spirit will be the extent to which we come to grips with today's problems and the setting of goals for the future, just as the founding fathers did in their time. The Bicentennial will be meaningful and productive if it becomes an era during which the power of private initiative is rediscovered.

Having said this, JDR felt an obligation to become involved himself in supporting Bicentennial activities, just as he had felt obliged to develop his youth program in the wake of his Family of Man speech. Although JDR had not even thought of the Bicentennial when he began working on his book, it now seemed a timely opportunity to promote citizen involvement with a private-sector effort to supplement what the government was doing.

This turned out to be a tall order because the efforts of the government were floundering badly by the time JDR's book was published in early 1973. A review of the somewhat bizarre history of the official Bicentennial effort is essential to understanding JDR's involvement.

Seemingly, the federal government had gotten off to a good start by acting early on the basis of an intelligent piece of legislation, Public Law 89-491, signed by President Johnson on July 4, 1966. The bill established the American Revolution Bicentennial Commission (ARBC) for the purpose of planning and coordinating federal activities and helping to generate activity in the fifty states. By authorizing the ARBC to stay in existence until 1983 (the two-hundredth anniversary of the Treaty of Paris which ended the Revolutionary War), the law implicitly established the concept of the "Bicentennial Era" instead of a one-year celebration in 1976 or a one-day party on July 4, 1976. It was a difficult concept to establish because of the overwhelming tendency of people to be aware of such events as the signing of the Declaration of Independence or the winter at Valley Forge, but not a Revolutionary War that lasted for more than eight years or a thirteen-year span between the Declaration and the Constitution. And the nation's press was of little help, never ceasing to refer to the Bicentennial as "the nation's birthday party" throughout the whole period. The bill tried to get past pure celebration by stressing that the Bicentennial had a serious side and should be concerned with the "ideas" of the American Revolution.

President Johnson appointed a distinguished and representative group of members to the Commission, with Carlisle Humelsine, president of Colonial Williamsburg, as chairman, but nothing happened for nearly two years because the Congress had neglected to provide any funds. When the first appropriation of $150,000 was secured in 1968, Humelsine recruited Dick Barrett as executive director. But this was the time of LBJ's fall from power, the bitter 1968 election, and the peak of discontent over the Vietnam War. Barrett could do little but think and plan. With Nixon's election, he realized his days were numbered, so he resigned in 1969 to set up a consulting firm in New York City. But he managed to replace himself with a friend who shared his thinking, career Foreign Service Officer Melbourne L. Spector, who took the position on detail from the State Department. Also present as program director of the ARBC was R. Lynn Carroll, whom Barrett had recruited.

President Nixon appointed a new Commission, including only one woman (an elderly conservative), only one minority group member (also elderly), and no young people. The rest of the members shared several characteristics: Republican, male, conservative, white, and over fifty years of age. There was early enthusiasm for goal-setting in the Nixon administration, and this led to a seriocomic episode when the President asked his cabinet members each to suggest a goal for achievement by 1976. Vice President Agnew proposed landing a man on Mars, not realizing that it would be impossible to reach Mars in the time available even if the technology were already in place. Attorney General John Mitchell, soon to find himself in a federal prison, opined that an absence of crime would be the best Bicentennial gift for the American people.

Under the benign leadership of the first Nixon appointee as ARBC chairman, Dr. J. E. Wallace Sterling, retired president of Stanford University, Spector and Carroll were able to produce the ARBC report and plan which had been mandated in the law. It was necessarily a limited document because the White House was paying little attention to the Bicentennial and no policy guidance was forthcoming. Nevertheless the document did reinforce the "Bicentennial era" as against a birthday party, stressed a grass-roots approach and a plan for small grants to stimulate activity in each state, and established three program areas corresponding to the past, present, and future—Heritage 76, Festival USA, and Horizons 76. The ARBC staff was organized according to this format. The organization moved into two of the handsome restored Federal-period homes on Lafayette

Square, and began issuing an annual commemorative medallion bringing in several millions of dollars a year, not much less than the appropriations the ARBC now was receiving from Congress.

From the time of its initial report, the path of the ARBC was steadily downhill, the result of a combination of official indifference, poor management, and political conflict. Shortly after the report was delivered in July 1970, President Nixon appointed David J. Mahoney as the new chairman of the ARBC. As chairman of Norton Simon, Inc., a large conglomerate, Mahoney had built a reputation as a dynamic executive, and he came to the Bicentennial assignment with zest and a "take charge" attitude, but he soon found himself frustrated on all sides. He had a staff largely borrowed from other agencies, inadequate appropriations (about one-tenth the amount the Canadians had provided for their Centennial, exclusive of Expo 67), little discernible interest in either the White House or the Congress apart from occasional rhetoric, a stodgy and unrepresentative Commission (with Mahoney at forty-seven the youngest member), and an organization that seemed to be a lightning rod for dissension and criticism. Mahoney also had the knotty problem of the Bicentennial expo on his hands. Among four competing cities, the ARBC 1970 report had designated Philadelphia as the site, but the tide of opinion was running against having an expo at all.[2]

In the face of all this, Mahoney could only function on a part-time basis because his role was uncompensated (as were all public commissioners) and he was still running Norton Simon. Mahoney also made his share of mistakes—for example, in converting the good idea of moving the quarterly meetings of the ARBC around the country "to take the Bicentennial to the people" into a bad idea by deciding to keep the meetings closed to the public. Mahoney wanted closed meetings because the ARBC was in a weak position and there were problems to discuss—it lacked a coherent theme and workable program ideas, in particular a "big idea" to provide a national focus in the event an expo proved unfeasible. But closing the meetings provoked press criticism and was part of a perceived arrogance that alienated a potential ally, the Bicentennial Council of the Thirteen Original States.[3] There was one other significant organization in existence at the time, the People's Bicentennial Commission (PBC), headed by youthful activist Jeremy Rifkin, which was implacably hostile toward the "Nixon Bicentennial" and anything the ARBC might try to do. But the closed-meeting policy and other gaffes made it all the easier for the PBC to heap scorn on the ARBC.

With little prospect for significant federal money and political turmoil in the City of Brotherly Love, the outlook for the expo idea was dim as the Philadelphia planners kept changing the location for their fair. The ARBC finally administered the *coup de grâce* by withdrawing its designation in May 1972. By this time Mahoney had unveiled his own version of a "big idea" for the Bicentennial, a plan to create a Bicentennial park in each of the fifty states with the help of $1.3 billion in federal funds. However, even this initiative was fumbled. The announcement came in a press conference after one of the closed ARBC meetings, in February 1972. It was a "trial balloon" that was nearly shot down at the outset by the thirteen-state group and various federal agencies. They were upset because they had not been consulted beforehand.

Mahoney's worst mistake was the appointment of a former business associate, Jack I. LeVant, to the top staff position of the ARBC, replacing Mel Spector. LeVant had been serving as an unpaid adviser to Mahoney from the outset. A former Colgate-Palmolive executive, LeVant had a managerial style that alienated almost everyone, and he soon came under attack. The People's Bicentennial Commission had been seeking transcripts of ARBC meetings through the Freedom of Information Act with little success, so it received purloined ARBC files from a disgruntled mail clerk. These formed the basis for a caustic article in the *Progressive*, and, with the material now in the public domain, a devastating three-part article in the *Washington Post* followed.[4] The series portrayed the ARBC as fumbling, inept, and rife with political and commercial favoritism. There was also a whiff of scandal and the breaking of government regulations. The result was oversight hearings by two congressional committees and an investigation by the General Accounting Office. LeVant received no solace from a study he had commissioned by the Arthur D. Little management consulting firm, which concluded that the problem of the ARBC was management that was "overbearing, unsympathetic, insensitive and punitive." In the midst of all this, LeVant prudently resigned in a letter to Mahoney on July 31, 1973, "so that my own continued service will not serve as a controversial and distracting issue." Mahoney replied that LeVant had been made "a scapegoat," and praised his "immense" contributions.

By this time the winds of Watergate were gathering in earnest. Even though the ARBC was but one small embarrassment in a sea of troubles for the Nixon administration, the White House early in 1973 introduced legislation to scrap the organization and start over again. With strained relations between the Congress and the Executive, it took a year to produce the new legislation, during which the ARBC became moribund. Mahoney, somewhat embittered, resigned after his fifty-state Bicentennial parks idea was quietly killed in the wake of negative reports by several federal agencies. The Congress seemed to be taking out some of its animus against the administration by curtailing the official Bicentennial agency. Although the bill raised it in status, from a "commission" to an "administration," other provisions weakened it. The fifty-member Commission was replaced by an eleven-member governing board composed of heads of federal agencies, and the twenty-five public members were placed in an advisory council. The administrator was specifically barred from serving as chairman of the governing board. Appropriations did not go above the $8 million level. Despite the pleas of scores of witnesses, Congress dealt a blow to the "Bicentennial era" concept by specifying that the organization, now known as ARBA (American Revolution Bicentennial *Administration*), would cease to exist after 1976. A measure of the times was that some of the outgoing commissioners thought that the word "revolution" should be expunged from the title of the organization because it was too suggestive.

In April 1974 the new administrator was appointed. He was John Warner, a quiet, pipe-smoking man who had been Secretary of the Navy and whose future distinctions were to include becoming the sixth husband of actress Elizabeth Taylor and U.S. senator from Virginia in the 1980 election. With little power, too little money, a hostile Congress, and a disintegrating Presidency, Warner was to serve out his term as a caretaker.

In brief, such was the short, unhappy history of the official Bicentennial effort.[5] Even if it had been a splendid success, JDR would have seen reason to become involved to further his "third sector" interest. But with the Bicentennial a yawning vacuum, it almost seemed his duty to do so. This was the sense of the matter when it was first discussed in October 1972, as three of JDR's advisers, Bill Ruder, Dick Barrett, and Jack Harr, journeyed up to Fieldwood Farm on a Saturday to meet with JDR and Blanchette. She joined the meeting because of her view that JDR should start cutting back instead of taking on more new involvements. He was sixty-six years old and was in the late stages of two time-consuming activities, the writing of his book and chairmanship of the Population Commission. She thought he now had the perfect opportunity to devote his time to the organizations he had long supported to make sure they were in shape to be self-sufficient, and otherwise to begin to relax and enjoy life more and spend more time with his family.

It was a potent argument, and JDR said he agreed, that he looked forward to curtailing his time in the office, taking a day off now and then and more short vacations. The three advisers also agreed. But the fact was that JDR was not yet constitutionally able to avoid filling his time with activities. The upshot of the meeting was that JDR would consider undertaking limited involvement. One of the problems of the Bicentennial was a shortage of funding sources. Corporations and foundations had virtually ignored it, and, as we have seen, the federal government was being niggardly. So in the weeks that followed JDR decided to establish a new program within the JDR 3rd Fund to make small grants for worthwhile Bicentennial projects. Secondly, he would explore the wisdom of setting up some sort of national citizen's committee to promote Bicentennial activity. The idea was not to compete with the federal effort, but to help shore it up and supplement it. His assurance that all of this would be limited satisfied Blanchette.

At the beginning of 1973 JDR began a remarkable odyssey of discussing the Bicentennial with leaders in American society that extended over a three-year period. He went to Dallas to meet with former mayor Erik Jonsson, whose highly successful "Goals for Dallas" program had won national attention. One of the first group of Nixon appointees to the ARBC, Jonsson had tried to sell city-based goal-setting as the centerpiece of the "Horizons 76" component of the Bicentennial, with no success. JDR went on to San Francisco to meet with A. W. Clausen of the Bank of America; Arjay Miller, dean of the Stanford Business School; and Wallace Sterling, the first Nixon chairman of the ARBC. Then JDR went to Washington to meet with Senator Charles McC. Mathias, one of the coauthors of the original Bicentennial bill in 1966. Back home, former Chief Justice Earl Warren warmly endorsed the idea of a citizens' committee for the Bicentennial, as had all the others, but counseled JDR that he should seek some sort of White House blessing so that he would not be seen as mounting a rival effort. At a breakfast meeting, Robert McNamara of the World Bank had the same advice.

The idea had evolved that the citizens' committee would only work if it were headed by a nationally known person who could give it full time in a vigorous campaign across the nation. One day Dick Barrett and Jack Harr ventured the opinion that a man like Nelson Rockefeller would be ideal—charismatic, energetic, visionary, certainly a vigorous campaigner. JDR agreed, but pointed out that Nelson would not finish his fourth term as governor of New York State for almost two more years. Barrett and Harr had speculated to each other that such a Bicentennial role might be an attractive platform for Nelson if he were contemplating another timetable for seeking the Presidency, one that would have to center on 1976, the year that Richard Nixon presumably would be finishing his second term in a blaze of Bicentennial glory. Their motive was not so much to get Nelson elected President as it was to get the right man for the Bicentennial. They wondered aloud if Nelson might conceivably resign his office early to take on the Bicentennial, a step that would certainly put the whole project on the map. JDR said he thought not, but that it would be a good idea to discuss the Bicentennial generally with Nelson.

By the time JDR arranged for himself and Jack Harr to have lunch with Nelson and several of his advisers, it was clear that Nelson had come up with his own platform for launching his next try at the White House. The luncheon took place early in February in the building that JDR referred to in his diary as "Nelson's so-called club," 13 West 54th Street, the townhouse that Junior and Abby had occupied in 1901. It was connected by a passageway to the brownstone on West 55th that Nelson used as the governor's New York City office. On the way to lunch, Nelson and JDR tarried for a moment and reminisced in the room where JDR had been born in 1906. It was also the room in which Nelson Rockefeller was to die almost exactly six years later.

The year before, Nelson had created a state body called the Commission on the Role of a Modern State in the Changing World. He then conceived the idea of expanding this into a national commission on America's future, but he wanted to keep control of it as governor of New York State. At Camp David, he tried the idea on President Nixon, who had just won his landslide reelection, and the response seemed favorable. At lunch Nelson told JDR that he was going to Washington to follow up his prospects at the White House. JDR talked about the Bicentennial, and Nelson responded that his futurist project could fit beautifully into the Bicentennial era concept, with studies to be published in 1976 setting goals for achievement by 1989, the Bicentennial of the Constitution. He also agreed that JDR should seek White House sanction for his citizens' committee idea, and offered to act as go-between. The two men agreed to meet in Washington on a date in March.

When JDR arrived there he found that Nelson "unfortunately" had already seen the President "on certain political matters." But, Nelson also reported, the Bicentennial had come up and the President had "responded warmly to the suggestion" of JDR taking initiative in the private sector. The two brothers then met with three Presidential advisers, Anne Armstrong, Leonard Garment, and Kenneth Cole, to discuss "the current unsatisfactory state of the Bicentennial and the need for a greatly augmented citizen effort." JDR handed over a letter he had written to the President, along with a suggested reply, the idea being merely an exchange of positive letters on the subject rather than some official sanction. JDR wrote: "The consensus seemed to be that I should consider that I had the White House's blessing and to proceed with my efforts."

The "certain political matters" that Nelson discussed with the President, of course, dealt with the expansion of Nelson's state-based exercise into a national commission. Very shortly Nelson had a letter from the President asking him to head "a national commission which would be bipartisan and broadly representative of all Americans." Nelson soon came up with a suitable name: "Commission on Critical Choices for America." It was a typical Nelsonian effort, very reminiscent of his "Prospects for America" project of the late 1950s. He recruited thirty-eight distinguished Americans to serve on the Commission, raised $1.6 million to finance it, assembled a staff, and, on December 11, 1973, did in fact resign as governor more than a year before his term was up to plunge into his new preoccupation with typical gusto.[6]

Meanwhile, JDR was not having as much success with Presidential letters. A few weeks after the Washington visit, Leonard Garment came to New York to have lunch with JDR and Harr. It was a strange and confused encounter, with Garment apparently under some sort of pressure. He talked about reasons for delay, and then suggested that perhaps a Presidential letter to JDR would not be necessary. JDR finally cut through by saying that he regarded a letter "as in no way essential," that he had been advised to "touch base with the White House" before launching a citizens' effort, and he felt that that had been accomplished with Nelson's chat with the President, JDR's letter, and the meeting with the three White House advisers. He said the best thing would be to just forget about the letter: "Mr. Garment seemed quite agreeable to this suggestion— maybe even relieved." In retrospect, it seems clear that Garment had been given the uncomfortable assignment of telling JDR that there would be no White House response, and he was trying to do it as politely as possible. From that point on, whenever JDR tried to open a line of communication and cooperate with federal efforts, he did not receive a positive response. And whenever he did something independently, one could almost feel the paranoia emanating from Washington.[7]

JDR proceeded to launch his personal Bicentennial campaign by making an impassioned speech at the University of Arkansas in Fayetteville on May 2, 1973. Six months earlier his dying brother Winthrop asked JDR if he would deliver the first "Governor Winthrop Rockefeller Distinguished Lecture," a series that was being established in his honor. This was the occasion for JDR's Bicentennial speech, entitled "Of Anniversaries and Celebrations." He began by speaking with deep feeling about Winthrop, who had died on February 22. He then summarized his "Second American Revolution" thesis, analyzed the nature of anniversaries and celebrations, and presented his vision of how to celebrate the Bicentennial, beginning by saying that it should draw its inspiration from American history and the founding ideals:

If the Bicentennial counts for nothing else, Americans generally should come away with at least a better understanding of their country's heritage. The plain fact is that except at a certain abstract level most Americans are remarkably ignorant about their own history. I can say this because I am one of them. Not until I became concerned about the Bicentennial did I sense more fully the rich drama of our past, of its relevance to our situation today and our prospects for tomorrow. Only by knowing our heritage better can we fully understand our unfinished agenda. For the past is never really past: it lives within us and around us, and we ignore it at our peril.

He made the case for the Bicentennial era concept from 1976 to 1989, spanning the Declaration of Independence and the Constitution. This, he argued, would provide the time span needed to make the Bicentennial what it should be—a Bicentennial of achievement. JDR cited a range of areas for goal-setting and accomplishment. As far as celebration was concerned, he said: "If we dedicate the Bicentennial Era to these ends, we will have earned the right to celebrate as never before." The indispensable ingredient, JDR said, was a rebirth of individual initiative: ". . . the Bicentennial will be meaningful and productive only to the extent that it becomes an era during which the power of individual initiative is rediscovered." Citing Tocqueville once again, JDR elaborated his point in a way that suggested some of his own pique at the unresponsiveness of official Washington:

Today the situation is somewhat different. We have developed the distressing habit of referring far too often to government. I believe the well-publicized difficulties of the Federal Bicentennial Commission are at least partially explained by a curious lack of initiative from the private sector. Everyone seems to be looking to Washington, while Washington has been looking primarily to the grass roots. . . .

The fact of the matter is that we have heard virtually nothing about the Bicentennial from our great corporations, from the labor unions, from the foundations, from many of the largest nonprofit organizations, indeed from our universities.

Clearly, unless we greatly reinvigorate our tradition of initiative—both as individuals in our own right and as members of organizations—our 200th anniversary is going to be a charade, and the opportunity it offers for moving our society forward will be lost. Hanging back and waiting for government approval before doing anything is sheer nonsense. If we had done that 200 years ago, we would still be a British colony.

JDR had continued canvassing a wide range of opinion leaders—Frank Stanton, Bill Moyers, Dr. Jonas Salk, Margaret Mead, Burke Marshall, former ambassador Sol Linowitz, black leaders Vernon Jordan and Roy Wilkins, labor leaders George Meany and Leonard Woodcock, businessmen Walter Haas and Ruben Mettler, Ladonna Harris of Americans for Indian Opportunity, Monsignor Gino Baroni of the National Center for Urban Ethnic Affairs, Cyrus Vance, Walter Cronkite, Joseph Papp, Joan Ganz Cooney, and a group of university presidents including Kingman Brewster of Yale, Father Hesburgh of Notre Dame, William Friday of the University of North Carolina, and Terry Sanford of Duke. Everywhere he had the same positive response. He invited a dozen of these people to dinner at One Beekman, including the university presidents, and reported the result in his diary:

There seemed to be a unanimous feeling that the Bicentennial could be tremendously significant to this country, particularly now with Watergate; and, second, that we should take initiative in creating a national private group. The balance of the meeting really was spent discussing the question of finding the right person to head up the project and then the general nature of the organization. It was recognized also that adequate funding was essential but it was believed this was obtainable.

By the time of the second meeting a month later, the consensus had formed in the group that Father Hesburgh was the ideal person to head up the citizens' Bicentennial effort. Hesburgh clearly was intrigued by the notion. JDR was still concerned enough about trying to get along with the Nixon administration that he expressed reservations in his diary over the fact that Hesburgh currently was at odds with the White House, having been asked to resign as chairman of the Civil Rights Commission. JDR was not sure what the problem was so he took the trouble to find out, and concluded that Hesburgh was in the right. Then JDR met privately with Hesburgh to persuade him to accept the Bicentennial challenge. To do so, Hesburgh said, it was clear that he would have to step down as president of the University of Notre Dame. He had held that post for twenty-two years, and he told JDR that it might well be time for a change, not just for himself, but for the institution as well. But he had investigated the matter and found that his order did not have a successor in line, so he simply felt he could not leave.

Over the summer JDR approached another half-dozen prominent people, and the story was always the same—they felt they could not relinquish what they were currently doing. During this time JDR joined millions of other Americans in watching the Senate Watergate hearings on television.

Although Richard Nixon's resignation was still almost a year away, JDR had no doubt about what was happening: "While the whole thing is really tragic," he wrote, "I believe that it can end up a plus by alerting Americans to the dangers of what happened and encouraging them to take a fresh look at the fundamentals on which our society was built."

This became the theme of JDR's second major Bicentennial address, this time at West Virginia Wesleyan College on September 28, 1973. The occasion was the installation of Jay as the president of the eighty-three-year-old school, a post Jay had accepted after his loss in the race for governor of West Virginia the year before. JDR marched in academic robes, and watched his son's investiture with pride. Then Jay presented his father as the inaugural speaker. JDR began with some good-natured quips:

I am honored to be present at this ceremony today and grateful that my son, Jay, and West Virginia Wesleyan College invited me to take part in this important occasion. Usually when a son is away at college and gets in touch with his father he has a different request in mind.

It is probably not very often that a father is invited to be a speaker when his son is installed as a college president. It must be a testimonial either to the father's longevity or to the son's outstanding qualities at a young age. In the present case, I suspect it is a mixture of both.

In any event, I am pleased, as any father would be, that my son has entered into a relatively stable line of employment. There is something about the very idea of being "installed" which sounds much more secure than Jay's most recent other endeavor.

Then JDR moved quickly into the serious theme of his speech, which was entitled "New Beginnings: Watergate and the Bicentennial." He said: "I want to talk today about two subjects which are very much on my mind. One is negative and depressing—the Watergate crisis. The other is positive and full of hope—the forthcoming Bicentennial of American independence." He continued:

I do not speak of Watergate gratuitously, merely to add my voice to a chorus of critics. Rather I am compelled by my belief that the totality of what we have come to call Watergate is of crucial importance, that we must try to understand what it means, learn from it, and begin to consider what we are going to do about it.

What has happened is now fairly clear. Men who have sworn to uphold the law and who have spoken much of law and order, have apparently broken the law. These same men, sworn to uphold the Constitution of the United States, have apparently infringed upon the Constitution. They managed to infuse the White House with a mood and style that is secretive, suspicious, fearful, and mistrustful—

a mood and style alien to the concept of an open society. It is this closed and conspiratorial atmosphere that provided the seedbed for Watergate.

JDR then explored the possible positive effects of Watergate, making the point that everyone soon was to be making, a celebration of the elements of the American system that functioned "to correct the abuse of power—the press, the courts, the Congress, public opinion. And, to these I would add the Federal bureaucracy because although several agencies were compromised, the overall resistance to improper pressure was remarkable." He continued:

It is not often in our daily pursuits that we pause to think about freedom of the press, individual rights, the separation of powers, the integrity of Federal agencies and of the courts, what the Declaration of Independence and the Constitution really say. I wonder how many Americans during the course of the Senate Watergate hearings either searched for, or wished they had available, a copy of the Constitution so that they could see exactly what the First Amendment says, or the Fourth, or the Sixth. We tend to take our basic values and institutions for granted. Watergate has made us think about them anew, and it has helped us realize how precious they are.

From this he moved into his favorite current theme of individual initiative:

We have grown too accustomed to allowing and even encouraging power and responsibility to shift to the Federal Government. We are too used to focussing our attention on our own narrow self-interest. But perhaps now we recognize better than before that politics in this country can only be as good as you and I make it, that this democracy only functions well when the people are involved and committed. If Watergate serves to regenerate the great American tradition of individual initiative, then I will truly agree with a famous quotation of Shakespeare's—"sweet are the uses of adversity."

This provided the bridge to the subject of the Bicentennial:

Certainly, I do not regard Watergate as providential, sent to test us so we could prove our mettle once more. We could have done without it. . . . In this regard, I do think it is providential that we are entering the period of commemoration of the 200th anniversary of American independence and the forming of our nation. . . . I submit that the Bicentennial could well be the antidote to Watergate if we can seize the opportunity for renewal and rededication it offers and make the most of it.

JDR observed that it was "perhaps not surprising" that the Bicentennial efforts of the government had made little progress:

The mood and style which produced Watergate has deterred the present
Administration from providing any real leadership for the commemoration of 200
years of an open society. The result is that many people are virtually unaware of
the advent of the Bicentennial, while others fear that it will be a kind of charade,
a superficial celebration of a national birthday party or July 4th, 1976, and nothing
more.

He then presented his prescription for the Bicentennial, by now honed
to four points—drawing inspiration from the founding values, the concept
of a Bicentennial Era lasting from 1976 to 1989, the keynote of achievement, and "a resurgence of the American tradition of individual initiative."
This, he said, held the prospect of new beginnings: "Let us here dedicate
ourselves to new beginnings, for West Virginia Wesleyan, for its new
President, for ourselves, for all our institutions, for our great country in
its time of need."

In this speech JDR distanced himself from any possibility of cooperation
with the Nixon administration, not that there was much chance of that in
any case. Late in 1973 JDR went even further when he finally found the
person to lead the citizens' Bicentennial effort or at least thought he
had. He was William Ruckelshaus, who had come suddenly into national
prominence in October when he joined Attorney General Elliot Richardson
in resigning from the Department of Justice rather than follow instructions
from the White House to dismiss Watergate Special Prosecutor Archibald
Cox. It was the famous "Saturday night massacre." JDR, who had known
Ruckelshaus slightly as director of the Environmental Protection Agency,
regarded him as a "vigorous, attractive person, with a great sense of
humor." The two men met several times in Washington and New York,
and Ruckelshaus told JDR that he was contemplating setting up his own
law firm in Washington. Nevertheless, he proposed an exploratory phase
to see if he could come up with a plan and program that would meet the
Bicentennial challenge. Underwriting was provided by the JDR 3rd Fund,
and a temporary office was set up in Washington for Ruckelshaus and his
three staff aides. Dick Barrett joined this group, as did Mel Spector, who
had retired from the Foreign Service not long after his tenure at the
Bicentennial Commission had ended. Also participating was Richard
Gibbs, one of the most prominent Bicentennial leaders at the state level,
who had been ousted as head of the North Carolina Commission by the
incoming Republican governor.

A number of "brainstorming" sessions followed, with various
Bicentennial figures brought in to meet with the Ruckelshaus group. It
gradually became clear that the group was divided between two positions.
JDR's men were adhering to his view of a vigorous national effort on

many fronts, while Ruckelshaus and his aides favored a limited approach. Ruckelshaus finally lighted on an "issue of the month" idea first proposed by Walter Cronkite of CBS News almost a year earlier in which all of the media would focus at the same time on a succession of great issues to be examined and discussed all across the country by Americans in their homes, schools, and workplaces. It had been rejected by the ARBC and the National Endowment for the Humanities (NEH).[8]

By the spring of 1974 the situation was different. The Nixon Presidency was visibly unraveling, and John Warner came on board as administrator of the newly organized American Revolution Bicentennial Administration (ARBA). One of his first acts was to meet with Ruckelshaus and then come up to New York to see JDR. It was an amicable meeting, with Warner suggesting that he be a member of the board and executive committee of whatever private sector organization JDR might be creating.

Urged by Ruckelshaus, Warner and NEH picked up on Walter Cronkite's idea. The new program was given the name "American Issues Forum," officially endorsed by ARBA, and funded by a $750,000 grant from NEH. JDR had been supportive of Cronkite's idea from the first time the newsman had talked to him about it, and his aide, Jack Harr, had participated in an informal planning group set up by Cronkite. But now NEH had control of the agenda for the American Issues Forum, and despite lobbying by the Cronkite group and JDR's aides to base it on the founding values of the nation, the result was a calendar of nine bland and broad topics ("Business in America," "Working in America," "Growing Up in America") to be promulgated one a month from September 1975 through May 1976.[9]

JDR was disappointed that nothing more had come out of Ruckelshaus's efforts. He wrote in his diary that he was not happy with Ruckelshaus's "limited time involvement and seemingly somewhat limited personal feelings as to the contribution of the Bicentennial. . . . It is all somewhat disturbing to me. What is toughest is that we don't have an alternative in terms of top leadership." It was now clear that Ruckelshaus was disengaging and that his first priority was setting up his law firm, which he did in June 1974. In defense of Ruckelshaus, he had never committed to more than an exploratory phase, and his exploration convinced him that the depressing effects of Watergate were too powerful to have hope for much more than something like the American Issues Forum. He was also concerned about the availability of funding in the private sector in the light of the many grant requests that had come in once it became known that JDR had set up an office with Ruckelshaus in charge. From his point of view, his withdrawal was a prudent move, and it was to be proved right by subsequent events.[10]

From this point on it was clear to JDR and his staff that there would be no knight on a white charger to rescue the Bicentennial. All JDR could do was keep on trying to help within the personal limitations he had set. He continued his missionary work with opinion-makers, including the media, in a series of meetings with the heads of the television networks, the wire services, and leading publications. He was a guest at editorial board luncheons at *Time, Newsweek,* the *New York Times,* and the *Washington Post.* The meeting at *Time* was dominated by Hedley Donovan's view that American history was the only proper subject for Bicentennial activity. At *Newsweek* and the *New York Times,* the subject of the Bicentennial elicited spirited discussion, but at the *Washington Post* the atmosphere was considerably different. Publisher Katherine Graham and her editors had been so emotionally involved in their Watergate exposés that they could not work up much interest in the Bicentennial. The prevailing mood was gloom that the resignation of Richard Nixon had produced nothing more than Gerald Ford as President.

During this period the JDR 3rd Fund was providing "seed money" grants for a number of Bicentennial projects, such as $25,000 to the National Academy of Public Administration for a study intended to lead to "a third Hoover Commission" to reexamine the workings of American government and $25,000 to the University of Virginia to assemble "the best minds in America" to create the "New Federalist Papers." JDR also served as convener to bring together potential funding sources for an idea proposed by former Labor Secretary Willard Wirtz to form a network of community organizations that were engaged in various forms of goal-setting. The plan was to aid these projects with small grants, conduct research to find which techniques worked best, and to build a program of information exchange and other services. This project earned a $250,000 grant and endorsement from ARBA, with the sum being matched by the JDR 3rd Fund and the Lilly and Kettering Foundations. Wirtz created a nonprofit organization, the Citizen Involvement Network, and Dick Barrett returned to Washington to join Wirtz's staff. Some twenty varied community organizations were selected to participate in a three-year pilot program from among 220 who applied.[11]

By late 1974 it was clear that the Ford administration was not prepared to make any major Bicentennial effort of a national character. There were plenty of small-scale projects in communities all across the nation, and there would be a celebration on July 4, 1976, and not much more. JDR and his advisers therefore decided that their last effort would be to sell the Bicentennial Era concept so that something might be in place from 1976 on leading toward the two-hundredth anniversary of the Constitution. Bill Ruder took charge of a communications effort to do this. An organization was created, the National Committee for the Bicentennial Era (NCBE), with a small staff and a board including such members as JDR, Frank Stanton, Ted Hesburgh, William Friday, and historian Merrill Peterson of the University of Virginia. A "Bicentennial Declaration" was drafted, based on JDR's four points, and discussions were held with John Warner and other ARBA officials about the possibility of joint sponsorship of it.

Meanwhile, JDR labored to raise $1 million to pay for producing a one-hour television show and for presenting the Declaration in a series of advertisements in major publications. He talked to John Knowles, president of the Rockefeller Foundation, who declined to help. The foundation had its Bicentennial project, involving the cataloging of American music, and was not prepared to make any other grants. Knowles said he thought that funding should come from business and labor. JDR solicited a number of major corporations and heard many reasons why they could not participate, but in the end found five that were willing to join the JDR 3rd Fund in making up the sum needed.[12]

In January 1975, JDR and Ruder went to see President Ford to enlist his support. JDR reported that it was "a good, friendly chat," but "unfortunately the President had not read our Bicentennial Declaration and hence didn't really have the feel of what we have in mind. . . . He said he was not sure just how he could be helpful but he wanted us to know that he wholeheartedly supported what we were doing." However, everything was straightened out in subsequent conversations with Warner and Presidential adviser John Marsh. The President introduced the NCBE televsion program, and ARBA officially endorsed the Bicentennial Declaration, which was presented at a press conference in New York in February. In the weeks that followed, the Declaration appeared in ads in major magazines and newspapers, signed by forty of the prominent people JDR had met with over the preceding two years.[13]

There was one small sour note afterward. The twenty-five-member advisory council of ARBA, led by film producer David Wolper, decided it wanted to create its own version of the Bicentennial Declaration. JDR had been hoping that ARBA's efforts would be directed toward planning for operational follow-through to a Declaration that already existed, rather than mounting a rival one. There were some conversations back and forth between New York and Washington on this subject, but the advisory council was feeling its own independence and persisted in spending months in what turned out to be a fruitless exercise. Although this did not mean that ARBA was withdrawing its "official" endorsement of the Bicentennial Declaration, it *did* mean that nothing more was done in support of it.

This probably made little difference inasmuch as ARBA was not in a position to do much in the way of follow-through in any case. JDR had found out how dry the financial well was in the private sector with very little interest in the Bicentennial among foundations and corporations. In Washington, the only significant Bicentennial funding was coming from NEH, but it was being spent very conservatively and stolidly by its head, Dr. Ronald Berman. ARBA administrator John Warner was exaggerating only slightly when he made a gloomy comment during a visit to JDR's office in early 1975: "Sometimes I think that you and I are the only ones who really care about the Bicentennial."

At best, the publicizing of the Bicentennial Declaration could be called a modest success, eliciting a considerable volume of mail, favorable press commentary, and a faint stirring of interest in Congress. However, with no operational planning or funding to back up the Declaration, interest soon died down.

The congressional interest was being manifested by Senators Mathias, Pell, and Javits, and in the House by two Democrats, Representatives Patricia Schroeder of Colorado and Paul Simon of Illinois. With considerable help from Gary Knisely, executive director of the NCBE, they worked on drafting a bill that would proclaim a Bicentennial Era from 1976 to 1989; activity would be stimulated by an "American Constitution Bicentennial Foundation" to be modeled on NEH, NEA, and the National Science Foundation, except that it would cease to exist at the end of the Bicentennial Era. Their reasoning was that a government foundation would operate with less fanfare and a longer view than an ARBC-ARBA type of organization which seemed to promise too much and delivered too little. In particular, their emphasis was on generating activity in the private sector by providing the new foundation with $35 million in annual appropriations, but specifying that this could be spent only on the basis of a two-to-one match by private funds. Mathias said: "The whole focus of this legislation is to have the federal government act as a catalyst to increase citizen participation—not overwhelm it." Schroeder said she hoped the bill would cause Congress to see July 4, 1976, as the logical starting point rather than the culmination of the Bicentennial: "Once the birthday party is over, it will be time to get down to business." Despite these hopes and supportive testimony by a number of witnesses, including JDR, the bill quietly died in committee.[14]

In June 1975, at what turned out to be the final meeting of the NCBE board, JDR told the group that he had "regretfully come to the conclusion that I didn't feel the Bicentennial would become a major factor in terms of lifting our country and moving it forward as I had hoped when I originally decided to get involved. Indicated that it would mainly be a celebration but that much that was useful could and would happen . . . such as the inspirational, based on our past."

In this assessment JDR was exactly right. It was quite a celebration. The weather was beautiful all across the country on July 4, 1976, and everywhere there were festivities with many memorable images, but perhaps none more so than the tall ships of "Op Sail 1976" parading in New York harbor and the Statue of Liberty bathed in an ethereal glow in the great fireworks finale. JDR was right, too, that much was done that was useful. Although almost all the national projects had fizzled out for lack of funds, there were activities in virtually every community across the nation apart from the birthday party itself. And JDR was right that the "inspirational" was there. The USA—200 story about the July Fourth celebration in New York City referred to "an almost giddy spirit of joy among six million participants" and a "lovely quality of human kindness and deep emotion over the meaning and reality of America."

The inspirational was there for JDR, too, in the awakened interest in American history he had spoken about in his Fayetteville speech. Never much of a television-watcher except for news programs, JDR had become enthralled by "The Adams Chronicles," the lengthy miniseries broadcast by public stations, which topped anything the three commercial networks had done. JDR was moved to go out of his way to meet and chat with a modern-day descendant of the Adams clan, Charles F. Adams, chairman of the Raytheon Company.

Peter Johnson, a Ph.D. candidate in history at Syracuse University, was in the process of being recruited as a research assistant in the JDR office at the time, and was nonplussed by the first question when he was ushered into JDR's office for an interview: "What do you think of 'The Adams Chronicles'?" Johnson wondered if this was some sort of test. He replied cautiously that as a historian he could see much about the series that was superficial, but that nevertheless it was a good introduction and very well done as television. He said he enjoyed it. JDR agreed.

JDR did not waste any time lamenting the small yield of the time and resources he had put into the Bicentennial. Rather, he told his diary that he would be ready to help if anything got going later on that would lead to the Bicentennial of the Constitution. All of the frustrations of trying to work with officialdom in the Bicentennial and the urban housing problem did not make him cynical—he continued to believe that it was important for the citizen to do everything possible to try to help government programs become effective. And he had learned a few things that honed his thinking about the "third sector," which was becoming a major preoccupation for him.

23

⚑

PUBLIC SERVICE
WRIT LARGE

JDR's EXPERIENCES in the youth, urban, and Bicentennial fields all helped him to develop his thinking about the "third sector." This probably explains why he was not discouraged by the fact that those activities, for the most part, were considerably less than successful. In fact, the short-comings seemed to spur him on. A specific indication of this was the surprising decision he made in 1975 to revitalize the Rockefeller Public Service Awards (RPSA) program just as it was on the point of expiring. He did this because the new concept for the program appealed to him and fitted well into his evolving philosophy of the "third sector."

The RPSA program was almost terminated once before—after passage of the Government Training Act of 1958. Earlier we saw how the RPSA earned a niche in American administrative history by saluting federal employees at their time of low ebb under the McCarthy attacks and by contributing directly to the creation of the 1958 Act. Because the Act gave the government the authority for such major training experiences as those the RPSA had been set up to provide—a "sabbatical" year of training at the mid-career level—the RPSA could be discontinued. JDR was inclined to do this, but he was persuaded to keep the program going by the Woodrow Wilson School at Princeton, which liked running it, and by the public administration establishment in Washington, which liked the morale value of "outside" recognition and the association with the prestigious Rockefeller name. As Robert van de Velde, faculty secretary for the program at Princeton, described attitudes in Washington:

. . . the very fact that the RPSA were administered by a *private* university and were supported by a *private* individual, had done much to restore morale and self-respect among many careerists. Here was evidence that respected nongovernmental people and institutions did have regard for the work of dedicated, but largely anonymous public servants. In short, they said, change the actual program however you must change it, but keep some sort of awards program going and keep the name, Rockefeller Public Service Awards, because that has come to mean something quite special for us.[1]

For its "second phase," the focus of the RPSA was changed from mid-career development to honoring distinguished career service by federal employees. Beginning in 1960, awards of $10,000 were given annually in each of five categories—foreign affairs; administration; law and legislation; welfare and resources; and science, technology, and engineering. Otherwise the RPSA remained the same—continuing impartial administration by Van de Velde and Princeton, the same high-level independent selection committee, and a similar process of soliciting nominations, reviewing dossiers, announcing winners in the fall, and giving the awards at a luncheon in Washington in December.[2]

The program generally was regarded as successful for a number of years. The awardees certainly were outstanding individuals. There was no hint of impropriety in managing the program. The worst case of overt pressure Van de Velde could recall was when Treasury Secretary John Connally telephoned to push Treasury's nominee and "practically threatened me." JDR enjoyed his Washington connection and attended every December awards luncheon except one. He usually was prevailed upon to speak briefly, and he heard other speakers over the years, including several cabinet secretaries and Vice President Hubert Humphrey, lavish praise upon the program and on JDR for creating and supporting it.[3]

Despite all these positive factors, the RPSA was losing its luster by the early 1970s. It never earned significant public attention, even in the Washington newspapers, although still regarded as highly prestigious in official circles. In fact, one of the problems was that the program became so much the province of the senior ranks of federal employees that it began to seem routinized despite hard work by Van de Velde to avoid this. At one point a study showed that the winners averaged over twenty-seven years of government service. Van de Velde and the selection committee always hoped that the winners would have at least a few years of government service left, but there were instances of winners retiring within a year after receiving the award and one case of a winner's retirement being announced just before the awards ceremony. Van de Velde's toughest battle was to keep the awards from becoming the "captive" of the administrative machinery of the various federal agencies. This problem was not the result of any improper tactics, but simply of the fact that the agencies were in the best position to staff out the nominees they wanted to win. Creating a good, complete dossier for a nominee required considerable work, and agency administrators were willing to go to the trouble because of the prestige that winning an award would bring to the agency.

Van de Velde did his best to compensate for this by soliciting letters and conducting interviews to fatten the dossiers of nominees who were not the beneficiaries of internal agency support. But this was an uphill struggle, all the more so in the case of mavericks or "whistle-blowers" who were at odds with agency hierarchies.

The most routinized category over the years was "foreign affairs." It almost always was won by the most prominent Foreign Service Officer of the Department of State in any given year, usually one who had attained the rank of Career Ambassador or Career Minister. Although the RPSA selection committee kept on the lookout for a winner from another foreign affairs agency or program, it was hard to resist the likes of Charles "Chip" Bohlen, Llewellyn "Tommy" Thompson, U. Alexis Johnson, Foy Kohler, Livingston Merchant, and other top diplomats who were winners over the years.

JDR was aware that the program was losing its vitality, and so once again he began to consider terminating it. His ability to give money away had been curtailed by the elimination of the "unlimited charitable deduction" in the Tax Reform Act of 1969. The new charitable deduction limit was 50 percent of net taxable income. JDR began looking for places to cut, and the RPSA, which was costing him about $90,000 a year, was an obvious candidate.[4] But terminating the RPSA was the kind of thing that JDR would never do unilaterally and peremptorily. He would seek other opinions and some degree of consensus. He started this process by deciding that there should be a formal review of the RPSA after twenty years of operation, so in 1972 President Robert Goheen of Princeton appointed a review committee chaired by John Gardner. The other two members were John Lewis, dean of the Woodrow Wilson School, and Elsa Porter of the Department of Health, Education and Welfare. The tone of their twenty-page report was somewhat lukewarm about the program as it addressed a number of options. But it concluded that the RPSA should be continued because of the importance of "private sector recognition of outstanding public service" and because no other awards program had the "prestige or political independence of the Rockefeller awards."[5]

In a subsequent private meeting, JDR pressed Gardner for his personal opinion, and Gardner responded that he thought the awards were important, but not of top-rank priority for JDR's attention and resources in the manner, say, of the population field. But Gardner became concerned when JDR said he thought the program could not go on "indefinitely" and that he was considering terminating it. Gardner said that was "bound to have a serious negative impact." The problem, as JDR's staff had also pointed out to him, was that the morale of the federal service was at low ebb once again, under attacks and political infiltration from the Nixon White House. If the initiation of the program had boosted morale at the time of McCarthyism, it would be wrong to damage morale now by withdrawing it when the federal service was once again under attack. It was primarily for this reason that JDR subsequently decided to fund the program for another three-year period.

At the time of the 1973 awards ceremony in Washington, JDR held a special meeting with the selection committee at the invitation of the chairman, Robert Wood, president of the University of Massachusetts. The members of the committee were inclined to think that the program should be continued, but JDR explained his concerns, as recorded in his diary:

Said I felt in a way that the awards had run their course and maybe today had less meaning and value than they did in the earlier days. Said that to me while the appointees each year were unquestionably fine people that possibly there was some lack of originality in the selection. Also said that I thought the lack of publicity had largely vitiated a major reason for the program, namely the encouraging of fine younger people to choose public service as a career.

JDR's thought was that the RPSA be terminated after two more years (when the current funding would expire) unless "some fresh thinking develops as to [its] nature and focus." He recorded that "the group seemed quite responsive" to the idea of ending the program "unless something exciting should develop during the interim."

For a considerable time it appeared that nothing "exciting" was going to develop. Bob van de Velde retired, and the RPSA seemed to lose even more of its vitality with his departure. Dean Lewis soured on it and agreed that it should be terminated. Finally, at the time of the selection process for the 1974 winners (September 1974), Robert Wood happened to visit JDR's office on Bicentennial business, and took the opportunity to mention to JDR that he had been disappointed in that year's field of RPSA nominees. JDR reported: "His conclusion was that we should wind up the program with this year's awards, it being best to terminate it while it was doing reasonably strongly and not let it peter out."

In December JDR attended what he thought would be his last RPSA awards luncheon. Ironically, for the first time a President of the United States, Gerald Ford, took the trouble to come over to the Mayflower

Hotel to speak at the ceremony. There were some other fresh faces at that luncheon. William Bowen was the new president of Princeton, replacing Bob Goheen, who had become U.S. ambassador to India. And Donald F. Stokes, formerly dean of the graduate division at the University of Michigan, had succeeded John Lewis as dean of the Woodrow Wilson School. Stokes felt strongly that the RPSA program should be continued, and he was in search of some "fresh thinking" to revive it. At the luncheon he spoke to JDR in these terms, putting his emphasis on "achievement" as the key concept for the program. Stokes recalls JDR being "mildly startled" that anyone was speaking positively about the RPSA by that time. Stokes and JDR learned that Bowen also was in favor of finding a basis for continuing.[6]

JDR agreed to hold off announcing the termination of the program for a while, and Stokes went to work to develop a concept, aided by Jay Bleiman, assistant dean of the Woodrow Wilson School. For their planning sessions they soon recruited Rufus Miles, a senior fellow at the school who was an RPSA winner of the 1955-56 class. Recently retired from the federal service, Miles early in his career had established a reputation as a brilliant and innovative thinker. A fourth member joined the group: Ingrid Reed, who was resuming a working career after some years spent at home raising her children. She was to be the faculty secretary for the RPSA program if it survived.

This group produced a plan that was certainly fresh and exciting, indeed radical when compared to the existing program. A selection committee would make the same number of awards at the same stipend on the same schedule as before—but everything else would be different. The awards would be given on the basis of achievement instead of career-long distinction, in an effort to bring some drama into the program. But the big difference was the extension of the concept of "public service" to include *everyone* instead of only federal employees. The expectation was that government employees, whether federal, state, or local, would probably still win one or two of the awards, but that most of them would go to private individuals making a significant achievement on their own or as members of nonprofit organizations. It was also thought that occasionally a person in a profit-making business might qualify by reason of some unique and significant public service.

Expanding the RPSA to cover the whole society was a breathtaking leap, but it meshed squarely with JDR's Bicentennial focus on citizen participation and his growing concern for recognition and support of "the third sector." The concept also fitted into JDR's emerging thinking in another significant way. His view of how American democracy worked best involved not only a healthy third sector but also good working relationships among all three sectors. Indeed, this came close to his definition of pluralism—a variety of ways to achieve what needed to be done through one sector or any combination of them working together. In the new RSPA approach, most of the winners would be *located* in the third (private, nonprofit) sector, but their work might have benefited from help from the other two sectors (business and government), and indeed an individual from one of those two sectors might also be a winner. In any case, there were no rigid barriers and the entire program had a "third sector" orientation in the linking theme of "public service"—achievement for the public good instead of private gain.

This close meshing of concepts was coincidental to a degree. The Stokes group was aware of JDR's Bicentennial focus on achievement and individual initiative, but not his "third sector" thinking, which he was only then in the process of developing. The ideas of Stokes and his colleagues stemmed more from their own perceptions of needs and opportunities than from a conscious effort to mold something just to fit JDR's predilections. Thus, the immediate receptivity from JDR and his staff came as a pleasant surprise to the Princeton group when the approach was first discussed in the spring of 1975.

However, both sides immediately recognized some formidable problems. One was the difficulty of administering such an expanded program. The Gardner report had cautiously suggested enlarging the RPSA to include employees of state and local governments and the legislative and judicial branches of government, in addition to federal executive branch employees. But the administrative problem in doing this seemed so staggering that the Gardner report said it would require another whole program alongside the existing one. Now Princeton was proposing expanding the program to the entire society. How could this be administered? Could the program be communicated broadly enough so that enough people would submit nominations and help build up the dossiers to the point that the selection process could be adjudged as legitimate? This burden would fall primarily on Ingrid Reed, and she began examining ways to get the job done.

Meanwhile, the Princeton innovators were not yet finished. Another problem was identifying the categories within which awards would be made. The previous functional breakdowns of government service areas would no longer suffice. Jay Bleiman offered a solution, an ingenious one even though it complicated the program further. He proposed convening another committee at Princeton early in the year for the purpose of identifying the priority problem areas in American society. Ingrid Reed and her staff (one secretary and several students working part-time) would then spread information about the program (including the problem areas chosen) as widely as possible, receive nominations, work to fatten the dossiers over the summer, and prepare everything for the meeting of the selection committee to choose winners in the fall.

Bleiman's idea was adopted, and the new committee was called the "ad hoc committee" because its membership would be subject to change each year. The rules were that at least two members would be drawn from the Princeton faculty and there would be some overlap with the selection committee, with two or three persons serving on both. Other participants would be knowledgeable persons recruited from the outside. Not all of the problem areas would change each year, and not all areas would necessarily have winners. The idea was to keep the program flexible so that it could reflect changing priorities in the society.

Finally, the new plan incorporated ideas designed to achieve long-desired goals that the former versions of the program had lacked—to give the RPSA an educational component and more of a link to the Princeton campus. Graduate students at the Woodrow Wilson School would be used to do research, especially on the problem areas, and the winners would be invited to visit the Princeton campus each year to meet with students and make other appearances in the area.

A final problem was that the new program would cost more money than the old one. The size and number of awards would not change, but the broader selection base, additional committee, and educational component would all add to the administrative costs. It was a measure of JDR's commitment to the third-sector concept that he agreed to contribute nearly twice as much annually as the $90,000 he had been on the verge of saving to put to other uses. The new plan had been presented to JDR as an "experimental" one in a realistic sense, not merely to help sell it. No one knew if the administrative problems could be surmounted, so JDR agreed to three-year funding with provision for a review at the end of two years. That decision inaugurated the "third phase" of the RPSA.

The planning process had taken considerable time, so it was announced that no awards would be given in 1975, and that the awards would be resumed in 1976 under the new and expanded concept. There was considerable regret over the change in the RPSA voiced by the Washington administrative fraternity. But there were "old Washington hands" who warmly applauded the new concept, men such as Roger Jones, Robert Nathan, and Elmer Staats.[7] In fact, Nathan, who had succeeded Robert Wood as selection committee chairman, agreed to remain as chairman under the new concept.

The ad hoc committee held meetings late in 1975 and early in 1976, producing a list of problem areas dealing with such subjects as unemployment, energy policies, crime reduction, economic adjustment, the role of public-sector employment, protecting the international environment and resources, and redefining the role of the United States in the world order. During the spring and summer, Ingrid Reed and her assistants worked overtime to convey information about the new program through every imaginable channel, including government agencies at all levels, trade and professional associations of every description, colleges and universities, foundations and nonprofit groups, Princeton alumni, and former RPSA winners. To everyone's relief, the process worked well, bringing in a sufficient number and variety of nominees to make for a good selection process. The selection committee did its job, picking seven winners in five of the problem categories (there were two shared awards).

The results of the first year immediately suggested that the RPSA "third phase" had all the fresh appeal and dynamism the planners were hoping for. The accomplishments of the winners included a successful campaign of combating discrimination against women; mobilizing government and union support to open apprenticeship opportunities for minority workers; reform of overcrowded penal and mental health institutions in Alabama; reform of unjust bail practices and new methods to help ex-offenders find employment; a successful metropolitan approach to providing low-income housing in Ohio; and a long-range development and investment plan proposal for the drought-stricken Sahel region of Africa.

The winners turned out to be a fascinating group of people. JDR enjoyed meeting and chatting with them at the awards ceremony in December. Years later one of his aides remarked in a memo: "I have never seen JDR enjoy himself so much."[8] President Ford received the winners at the White House. Fittingly, JDR was the speaker at the luncheon to a large audience composed of the winners, their families and colleagues, previous RPSA winners, and longtime Washington supporters of the program. After briefly recounting the history of the program and its recent change, he explained the rationale for the "third phase":

This change was inspired by an increasing awareness that the grave problems that confront us can only be solved through the initiative of individual Americans, both within and outside of government service. It was stimulated by the public service activity of recent years in such fields as civil rights, the environment, consumerism, and women's rights. It recognizes that the essence of public service is individual initiative—and that it can occur anywhere in the nation, and on the part of any citizen.

JDR then uttered some memorable words that seemed to those present to capture the spirit of the revitalized program:

This Awards Program has not in the past received much attention from the media because the people it honors have not been known celebrities. At times, we Americans seem captivated by the star system, by the doings of celebrities. But that is not the real story of America or of public service. The names of the seven individuals we honor here today are not household words. But I submit to you that they have probably accomplished more than a whole roomful of celebrities. They have acted not in the expectation of reaping fame or power or money, but because they cared—and because they had it within themselves to take the initiative that was crucial to meeting a genuine need in our society.

It was these qualities of caring and individual initiative which formed a free nation 200 years ago—and which remain our best hope of maintaining a free and just society now and in the years ahead.

In particular, JDR's statement that the winners "have probably accomplished more than a whole roomful of celebrities" struck a responsive chord. Subsequent winners were just as inspiring as the first group—a utilities executive who devised a successful means of mediating between the Mohawk Indians and the state of New York, two black women from the Deep South who pioneered child care centers, a geophysicist who battled the bureaucracy for years in trying to convey understanding of the limits of oil and gas reserves, two young Kentuckians who established a model health care center in the poorest county of Kentucky without soliciting any government assistance, and so on down a long list.[9] Almost all of the winners were able to spend a few days and sometimes longer on the Princeton campus, and, according to Ingrid Reed, these occasions were always satisfying and sometimes inspiring. As the time neared for the two-year review of the "experimental" program, in 1978, everyone involved knew that it was a remarkable success.

24

⚓

THE THIRD SECTOR

THERE WAS no grand design, only instinct—but the many new activities JDR branched into from 1968 on were elements of a process by which his "fourth field" of lifetime interest became converted into the "third sector."

As we have seen, JDR's "fourth field"—his concern for the well-being of philanthropy and voluntarism in American society—had become highly active for him in the period leading up to the Tax Reform Act of 1969. His performance—in organizing support, lobbying, testifying before Congress, and creating the Peterson Commission—was credited with blunting the worst excesses of the antifoundation sentiment of the time.

Far more disturbing to JDR than the negative features of the Act itself, however, was what the ferment stirred by it revealed about the status of philanthropy and prevalent attitudes toward it. He was shocked to learn that something he had always regarded as one of the pillars of American democracy was poorly understood, especially in Congress, and generally was either taken for granted or regarded as of minor importance. He was distressed over the lack of any sense of identity and unity in the nonprofit world. And, as a result, he saw in the wake of the Tax Reform Act of 1969 a need for a long-term campaign to change attitudes and build understanding and support.

But how to do this? What kind of campaign? It can be said that from 1969 on JDR was operating on two levels. One was obvious and specific— a renewed effort in Washington to try to improve the climate of opinion for philanthropy within the executive and legislative branches and bring about more favorable tax and regulatory policies. The second level was perhaps a means to the first, but it was just as difficult and certainly more diffuse—to conceptualize anew the place and role of philanthropy in the American system so that it would be better understood and actively supported throughout the society. In this, JDR was groping for new ideas and insights, trying to rethink a lifetime of experience. The writing of his book was a good beginning—the seeds of his new thinking were there, but they were not conceptualized to his satisfaction. JDR's commitment to himself to rethink philanthropy helps explain why he broadened out to the new activities and experiences that involved some form of experimentation with public opinion and citizen participation.

Meanwhile, JDR moved ahead on the more tangible task of new representations in Washington. Pursuing this took him to the nation's capital many times during the early 1970s for meetings with Treasury Secretary John Connally, his successor George Shultz, and Deputy Secretary William Simon (who later succeeded Shultz). JDR's best contact and adviser was Lawrence N. Woodworth, whose expertise was suggested by the fact that he had served with the Joint Congressional Committee on Internal Revenue Taxation since 1944. Currently chief of staff of that committee, Woodworth was a Rockefeller Public Service Award winner in 1972. JDR frequently had breakfast meetings with Woodworth, and on some of those visits he also was able to see the two men who guarded the approaches to the Internal Revenue Code, Senator Russell Long and Congressman Wilbur Mills.

There was no sense of imminent danger since the Congress had already vented itself on the subject of philanthropy in 1969. Back then, the Peterson Commission had been severely handicapped by the crisis situation and the lack of time. JDR wanted another study commission on philanthropy created, one that would be better positioned with support in Washington so that it could do a more thorough and effective job than had been possible for the Peterson Commission. He hoped for a White House or congressional commission or some sort of joint public-private study, but he soon recognized that chances were slim. There was no interest in the White House, and JDR commented in his diary about "how discouraging" it was that President Nixon had never uttered a public word in support of foundations or philanthropy. It was clear that a study group would have to be initiated and supported once again in the private sector, so JDR's Washington representations became geared to creating as receptive an atmosphere as possible for that kind of effort.

Back home he once again pulled together a group of advisers who met with him frequently to discuss strategy. Included were Dick Dilworth, family tax lawyer Howard Bolton, Bob Goheen of Princeton, and an eminent tax attorney in Washington, Leonard Silverstein, who was to play an important role in the effort. Also joining the group several times were two businessmen, Walter Haas of Levi-Strauss and Bruce Dayton of Dayton Hudson. They were exemplars of corporate responsibility and men whom JDR admired. Among the many others with whom JDR consulted were

John Gardner, Douglas Dillon, and Kingman Brewster, the president of Yale.

In this effort, the key staff person for JDR was Porter McKeever, who had taken over the retired Datus Smith's responsibilities for the Asian programs, philanthropy, and office management. Another important resource for JDR was Elizabeth McCormack, who had resigned from her order and the presidency of Manhattanville College, a Catholic women's school in Westchester County, to join the staff of the Rockefeller Brothers Fund. In due course she moved out of the RBF to head up a revived family philanthropic office in Room 5600. (This office had gone out of existence after the death of Arthur Packard in the early 1950s as the RBF became prominent and the brothers all took on personal staff.) A small unit in the RBF continued to provide assistance for family members in their "citizenship" giving. The provisions of the Tax Reform Act of 1969 made it clear that this function would have to be managed separately from the RBF. Also, the coming of age of many of the Cousins' generation created a greater need for a philanthropic advisory function. As manager of the new philanthropic office, McCormack was to become an influential adviser to many members of the Rockefeller family.

By late 1972, JDR and his advisers were working in earnest on the plan to bring a new commission into being. As always, the key consideration was finding a leader, and by mid-1973 the JDR group had their man—John H. Filer, chairman of the Aetna Life & Casualty Company of Hartford, Connecticut. The planning and organizing work took the balance of the year, and by the beginning of 1974 the panel, known inevitably as the Filer Commission, was ready to launch a two-year program of research and debate leading to a final report. Its formal title was the "Commission on Private Philanthropy and Public Needs." JDR, Aetna, and the Ford Foundation each contributed $25,000 to get the project started. Before it was over, $2 million was raised from some seven hundred contributors, mainly due to the efforts of Philip Klutznick, a commission member and philanthropic leader from Chicago, and the American Association of Fund Raising Counsel.

This sum was needed because of the determination of the organizers to begin filling one of the critical needs of the nonprofit world—for research and hard information as a basis for building understanding and making recommendations. The Filer Commission funded eighty-five separate research studies by scholars from many different institutions and universities, at a cost of $1.5 million. JDR's efforts in Washington paved the way for close working relationships with the government. The effort had the blessing of Mills, Shultz, and Simon, and a Treasury official was given a two-year leave of absence to serve as the Commission's research director. Several government agencies cooperated extensively in some Commission projects, and Washington lawyer Leonard Silverstein became executive director.

A broadly representative group of twenty-eight persons formed the Commission. Among those well-known to JDR were Douglas Dillon, George Romney, Walter Haas, Elizabeth McCormack, and Alan Pifer, the president of the Carnegie Corporation. As in the case of the Peterson Commission, JDR himself was not a member.

If nothing else of a positive nature, the Tax Reform Act of 1969 had served the purpose of getting the attention of all of the diverse elements of the nonprofit world. JDR could hardly muster a constituency for the hearings in 1969, but the Filer Commission had no such problem. There was widespread interest in what it was setting out to do, and many points of view were represented in the makeup of the Commission and its staff, in the research it sponsored, in the public hearings it conducted, and in its relationships with outside groups. There was considerable divergence of opinion, even controversy, on many issues the Commission considered. In effect, the nonprofit world was going through a "consciousness-raising" period in the wake of the Tax Reform Act, and there were issues to be worked out before there could be more of a united front on behalf of the third sector as a whole, or before the kind of broad representational organization that JDR had long advocated could be brought into being effectively.

From a short-term point of view, it could be said that the Commission was sharply constrained, nearly immobilized, by conflicting points of view and the complexity of many of the issues. A longer view suggests that its historical mission was to be an integral part of the process of working out the issues as a precondition to greater unity. From this perspective, the Commission and its report played a seminal role, as subsequent events indicated.

True to the spirit of the times and JDR's own personal bent, the Commission's operations were conducted on as open a basis as possible. This extended to providing support for some of its most severe critics, the leaders of a group of "donee" organizations (recipients of philanthropic giving as contrasted to the "donors" or givers). These particular donee groups tended to be new, small, concerned with social issues, and to have political orientations ranging from moderate-liberal to radical.

A major consideration, obviously, was tax policy. Here the Commission was up against the centrist thinking that had grown up in Washington as the tax code became an increasingly powerful instrument of federal policy. Implicit for years, this thinking became more and more manifest by the

1970s as the doctrine of "tax expenditures" became firmly implanted—the process by which the Internal Revenue Code is rejiggered to create "tax shelters" in order to influence the flow of capital toward societal needs favored in Washington. Although undoubtedly effective in some respects, this also has its dysfunctional aspects. We saw one in the discussion of the urban housing problem—the weakening of a direct approach to dealing with a social problem. Another is that many tax expenditures become highly politicized, subject to whatever pressure is strongest. A third is that the logical extension of this approach is for Washington technocrats to see every deduction as a "tax expenditure" at best and a "loophole" at worst. Columnist George Will engaged in an exercise of *reductio ad absurdum* by suggesting that this approach means that the entire Gross National Product belongs to the federal government and that citizens should feel grateful for whatever the government lets them have.[1]

The "tax expenditure" doctrine and its implications were particularly damaging for the nonprofit world. It could eventually make tax considerations the overwhelmingly dominant consideration in charitable giving and reduce the nonprofit sector to the status of continual supplicant for government's favor instead of retaining a substantial degree of independence. A variation on the theme became a divisive issue for the Filer Commission. The donee groups and some Commission members and consultants took the position that there was an equity issue in the deduction for charitable donations. A wealthy person paying taxes at the 70-percent rate who makes a charitable contribution gets a 70-percent deduction, or, stated another way, 70-percent of his contribution is "subsidized" by Uncle Sam. But a low-income person paying taxes at the 14-percent rate would get only a 14-percent "subsidy" for his contribution. The Commission was slowed down for months as many proposed "solutions" to this problem were debated, involving special deductions, tax credits, and supplemental credits. All of them had logical imperfections.

Equity was one issue. A related one was the desire to "democratize" charitable giving by creating stronger incentives for persons of average or low income. Because this includes the great majority of taxpayers, such moves would also serve to increase the total of giving. But ideas for resolving this need were nearly as divisive for the Commission as the equity issue. Serious consideration was given to the idea of proposing the abandonment of the charitable deduction altogether, and one research paper estimated that no more than one-third of giving was specifically motivated by tax considerations. This approach, which would wipe out all of the complex tax questions at one stroke and put everyone in the same situation, had considerable appeal, but the more conservative members of the Commission were too concerned over the uncertain effect on total giving (and, presumably, their own personal giving) to allow such a recommendation.

So wide was the Filer Commission's ideological net that it included among its consultants the foremost theorist of the "tax expenditure" school, Harvard law professor Stanley S. Surrey, who had been Assistant Secretary of the Treasury for Tax Policy in the Nixon administration. Another consultant was Paul Ylvisaker, dean of the Harvard Graduate School of Education and former member of JDR's "youth task force." Ylvisaker was inclined to believe that philanthropy had lost as much as it had gained through its association in the public mind with tax advantages. A third consultant was Wade Greene, former social sciences editor of the *Saturday Review*, whose unhappy task it was to write the final report for a divided and stalled Commission. In an article written for the *New York Times Magazine* after the Filer Commission had completed its work, Greene analyzed the tax policy issues and the pros and cons of various proposed solutions. With the punning title "A Farewell to Alms," the article took the gloomy view that philanthropy was "disintegrating" as the result of a changing society and the blurring of its role, especially in its relationship with government and the complex tax issues. The article did not offer hope that these issues would be resolved in a way that would be very helpful.[2]

JDR did not speak out publicly on these tax policy questions. He had been "burned" when he had done so in 1969—provoking a storm of criticism over his statement that he "arranged" to pay some federal income taxes every year even though he qualified for the unlimited charitable deduction. Moreover, JDR did not have a strong ideological position on tax policy. For a man born into wealth, he had always been supportive of policies of redistributing income through government tax and spending policies, as long as they were gradual, reasonable, and not directed toward the goal of a totally egalitarian society, which he regarded as utopian. In any case, he was more concerned at the moment over the fact that the Filer Commission was immobilized by divided opinions. By no means did JDR regard the tax issues an unimportant, but he recognized that the Commission was not going to resolve them. He felt it should concentrate on illuminating the issues, make what recommendations it could, and then get on with other important matters, including the broader philosophical questions and the overall welfare of the third sector. JDR was more interested in these than in debating mathematical formulas for the tax code.

This was the burden of JDR's message to Chairman Filer in an hour-long private meeting they held in late August 1975, only a few months before the final report was to be completed and made public. JDR normally refrained from interceding so directly, but had been urged to do so by McKeever, McCormack, and others. Filer was a moderate and so interested in achieving consensus that he had taken no positions on the issues himself. This praiseworthy stance, one that JDR himself often adopted, was beginning to look like a lack of leadership after nearly a year of agonizingly slow progress. Writer Wade Greene was foundering under a lack of direction. Because of time pressure he had produced a first draft that JDR found too wishy-washy, or in his own words as recorded in his diary, "weak and unconvincing." JDR wrote: "I went quite far with Mr. Filer in my comments, only stopping short of telling him that if the report went through substantially as it is I could not support it."

Filer agreed to JDR's suggestions, and work proceeded at a brisker pace for the next few months, though not without moments of trauma and anxiety for those involved, especially Wade Greene. The result was a vastly improved document that was presented December 2 in a ceremony at the office of Congressman Al Ullman of Oregon, who had succeeded Wilbur Mills as chairman of the House Ways and Means Committee.[3] Also present were JDR, Filer, other Commission members, Treasury Secretary Simon, Senator Russell Long, and members of the press.

The title of the 240-page report was *Giving in America: Toward a Stronger Voluntary Sector*.[4] Following the ceremony, Filer was the guest of honor and luncheon speaker at the National Press Club. JDR wrote: "Filer did a good job in his statement and in handling questions, and we were all impressed with him."

On the vexing tax deduction issues, the report followed JDR's suggestion of a limited approach, making only two recommendations (with many dissents recorded), one calling for a "double deduction" for low-income taxpayers and the second for allowing those who use the short form to itemize charitable giving in addition to taking the standard deduction. Beyond this, the report also followed JDR's lead in addressing the broader themes related to the welfare of the third sector as a whole. It contained eloquent passages attempting to describe the third sector in all of its great diversity, establish its historic importance in American pluralism, and present in compelling terms its precarious financial position in the face of a relative decline in private giving and rapidly rising costs. It then made a series of recommendations for broadening the base of philanthropy and strengthening the philanthropic process. In the latter category, the report made a strong case for easing the discriminatory restrictions against nonprofit organizations engaging in the influencing of legislation, pointing out that businesses and trade associations were allowed to deduct the costs of lobbying and that analyzing and attempting to affect the processes of government had become an increasingly important role for the nonprofit sector.

The report also focused on corporate giving. Recognizing that the "primary, if not only, business of business is still business," the report nevertheless argued that a potent case could be made for corporate philanthropy in terms of the environment for business and long-term survival. The problem was that the allowed deduction of 5 percent of pretax net income, originally established as a constraint, had become a distant goal. Only 20 percent of the nation's corporations made any contributions at all, and only 6 percent contributed more than $500 a year. The report quoted President Johnson when he chided a group of business leaders: "In spite of the fact that your federal government has seen fit to allow a charitable deduction of 5 percent of your profits, the record is quite clear that you business leaders still feel that the federal government can spend this money more wisely than you can." The Commission considered a number of tax-law changes that would provide stronger incentives for business to increase its giving, but in the absence of consensus settled for a recommendation that encouraged corporations to set "as a minimum goal" a 2 percent level of giving by 1980.

The final recommendation was one that had been suggested by JDR, calling for the establishment of "permanent national commission on the nonprofit sector" by the Congress. JDR's reasoning was that although the work of the Filer Commission had turned out to be good and useful, it also fell considerably short of initial expectations. He felt that the recommendation would at least set the idea forth as a goal, even if it was not likely to be taken up in the form proposed. The report supported the proposal by pointing out that the Filer Commission's own temporary span allowed only a "modest beginning" in examining many complex issues, despite all of the research that had been sponsored, and that the importance of the nonprofit sector and its critical situation required a permanent organization "if the voluntary sector and philanthropy are to become as well understood, as well mapped, as the government and business worlds."

The report had some influence on the Tax Reform Act of 1976, which was not a major creative piece of legislation, but rather one that clarified and eased some of the murky provisions of earlier acts, including the 1969 one. The major provision for the nonprofit sector had to do with the lobbying issue. It was generally recognized that the 1969 Act and its harsh penalties had tended to dry up sources of funds from donors who were uncertain about the law. The 1976 Act provided that gifts to "grass roots and lobbying" nonprofit organizations would be tax-exempt if the organization did not spend more than 30 percent of its budget on efforts to influence legislation.

But the major benefit of the Filer Commission was the effect its report and research had in raising consciousness and stimulating new initiatives in the years that followed. Many of these were mounted or supported in JDR's office, including a variety of Washington initiatives, a search for "university underpinnings" (JDR's phrase) for the third sector, a major effort to promote corporate philanthropy, a quest for an umbrella organization for the third sector as a whole, and a stepped-up speaking and writing effort for JDR. For several years, all of these activities were referred to generically in JDR's office as "Filer follow-up."

The Filer experience revived JDR's effort to solve the semantic problem that had dogged him for years, ever since he had recognized that "philanthropy" was too limited a term to denote what he had in mind, and unattractive to boot, for its inevitable association with wealth. How could one successfully promote the welfare of a huge field of activity if one could not even find a decent name for it? The Filer Commission had wrestled with this problem, too, and failed to solve it, using the term "voluntary sector" in the title of its report and frequently in the text, then shifting to "nonprofit sector" and finally to "third sector." Writing about his experience with the Filer Commission in his *Times* article, Wade Greene touched on the problem, referring to the "dissatisfaction . . . with the very term 'philanthropy' and the diligent if unsuccessful effort to find an alternative. This dissatisfaction, I believe, was more than semantic."

JDR certainly agreed with the last thought. But he had to solve the problem semantically, at least for himself, if he were to get on with his speaking and writing. He disliked "voluntary sector" because, like philanthropy, it referred to only one aspect of the phenomenon under consideration, and it smacked of "do-goodism," at least in JDR's mind. "Private sector" was no good because it could include business, just as "nonprofit sector" could include government. The entire, more accurate term, "private nonprofit sector," was simply too long. In a conversation with John Gardner one day, Gardner said he liked "independent sector." JDR did not. Independent of what? Gardner responded: independent of government and of the profit motive. True—but JDR was more interested in *inter*dependence. JDR finally made up his mind, and explained his reasoning in a basic paper he drafted, which subsequently served as a basis for his speeches and articles. Pointing out that the problem was broader than semantics, JDR wrote:

There is a conceptual problem as well. Instead of struggling to make the word "philanthropy" intelligible to everyone, we should place the focus on the much larger dimension of American life of which philanthropy is a part.

Let me make myself clear. Broadly speaking, our society is composed of three sectors. Two of them are obvious—government and business. The third is the non-profit sector. It includes hundreds and thousands of institutions—churches, museums, hospitals, libraries, private colleges and universities, performing arts groups, foundations. It includes social service groups as diverse as the Red Cross, the Boy Scouts of America, and the newer activist groups working on social problems in virtually every community across the country. It is in the third sector that we have seen the pioneering efforts to solve social problems in so many fields—civil rights, the environment, population, the "green revolution," women's rights, the administration of justice.

Government is supported by taxes, business by its profits. The third sector is supported principally by contributions; in short, by philanthropy. Thus, philanthropy should be seen as a means to an end. It is the support mechanism which makes possible the third sector as we know it today.

JDR stressed that the third sector was indispensable to American pluralism, to the diversity and energy and creativity that made American society distinctly different, citing supportive quotations from historians Henry Steele Commager and Daniel Boorstin and the old standby, Tocqueville. JDR then addressed the semantic issue directly:

How does one convey, in a word or a phrase, a mental picture of this rich and diverse tradition in American life? . . . I have been mistaken in using the term philanthropy over the years when what I really meant was the much larger third sector itself. Other terms have been used and found wanting. Recognizing that there is no perfect wording, I have simply begun . . . to use the term "third sector." On first hearing this might provoke some curiosity, if no substantive meaning. This was the case with "Point Four" when it was introduced by President Truman in his 1949 inaugural address. The substance of what he meant soon became understood by almost everyone.

There is value, also, in the fact that a reference to "the third sector" immediately brings to mind the other two. It suggests that in addition to government and business there is another—a third—major dimension to our society which is critical to the maintenance of our way of life and to the resolution of the many difficult problems we face today.

I believe that the third sector is clearly suffering from a lack of identity. We simply have failed to conceptualize it as a coherent and readily identifiable phenomenon in our society. Government and business do not have this problem. There is instant identification when one speaks of events or issues within these two sectors. Not so with the third sector. There is no framework of recognition. Individual Americans know of their own contributions . . . or their participation as a volunteer. . . . But they tend not to see this for what it is—one small part of a broad and crucial dimension of our national life.

If all were well within the third sector, the problems of concept and wording might not matter so much. But the fact is that the third sector is eroding before our eyes, and very few people seem to be aware of it.

JDR analyzed the causes of the decline, and drew a picture of what would happen if it continued:

. . . the results would be tragic. We would have lost the essence of what makes our system distinctive, scarcely being aware of it until it is too late. I have said that the obvious problem of the third sector is the growing shortage of funds. But this stems from a deeper problem—the lack of understanding and recognition of the third sector by leaders in government and business. In part at least, this comes back to the matters of concept and wording. I am afraid that to all too many of these leaders the third sector might as well be the invisible sector.

JDR concluded by wondering "what would happen" if government and business leaders fully appreciated the importance of the third sector and acted accordingly, not only in specific measures such as tax policy and corporate philanthropy but also in providing leadership and moral support:

If such a change of attitudes were to come about—and I believe it is possible— we would be ready to embark on an American renaissance. We would become a giving society, one in which the power of individual initiative is rediscovered and revitalized. We would surprise ourselves and surprise the world, for American democracy, which all too many observers believe is on a downward slide, would come alive with unimagined energy and creativity. Nothing less than this is at stake.

It was all somewhat high-flown and idealistic but written with un- doubted passion and conviction. From 1976 on this basic draft would be rewritten many times, extended in various versions with argumentation and examples to support the main points, to serve as the basis for JDR's speeches and magazine articles, and finally as the germination of a second book. Meanwhile, there were specific initiatives to be dealt with in the broader campaign of "Filer follow-up."

One proposal came in from Yale when Kingman Brewster asked JDR for a grant of $10,000 to underwrite a feasibility study for an academic program in the third sector at Yale. JDR complied. The completed study called for a Program on Non-Profit Organizations to be headed by law professor John Simon and based in the Institute for Policy and Social Studies. The planned scope for research, publication, and attracting lead- ing scholars to Yale was ambitious, with the funding need estimated at $10 million. JDR's advisers were dubious about the prospects for raising such a large sum, but so intent was JDR on developing "university underpin- nings" that in December 1975 he made the first commitment to the pro- gram—$250,000 over a five-year period contingent on $1.5 million being raised from other sources. Brewster met with a mixed response as he made the rounds of the foundations, and then he dropped out when he became the U.S. ambassador to the United Kingdom in the Carter administration. Not until late 1977 did John Simon succeed in raising enough money to begin drawing down on the JDR commitment.[5]

As usual, much of JDR's effort was centered in Washington. He and his advisers agreed that an organization should be established there to promote follow-up to the Filer Report. The first step would be to set up a committee to explore the possibilities. On the recommendation of McCormack and McKeever, JDR discussed this with Walter McNerney, president of the Blue Cross Association of Chicago, who had turned in a strong performance as a member of the Filer Committee. McNerney agreed to head up the effort.

Early in 1976 JDR resumed his Washington visitations, and he found Treasury Secretary William Simon, Lawrence Woodworth, and Congressman Al Ullman to be warm and receptive. Simon in particular was responsive, having set up an Advisory Committee on Philanthropy within Treasury, headed by one of his assistant secretaries. However, the prevailing advice to JDR was not to count on much of significance happening in Washington during the Presidential election year, and even longer if the election resulted in a change of administrations.

JDR was intrigued with the candidacy of Jimmy Carter. He liked the way Carter had seemingly come out of nowhere with a great deal of grassroots appeal and voluntary citizen support. He also liked Carter's religious faith and his apparent combination of keen intellect and a deep sense of caring about people. Carter's persistent attacks on the government bureaucracy seemed promising, too. As we have seen, there was no sense in which JDR was antigovernment, but he, too, had come to feel—and had stated it publicly many times—that something was out of balance, that the federal government had become too controlling and bureaucratic in many of its domestic policies and programs. His answer, as he had outlined in his book, was not to dismantle the government but to reorient it in major ways to a role that would facilitate the efforts of citizens in solving their own problems. The congruence of this with a revitalization of the third sector was obvious. Although JDR felt that Carter was sometimes overzealous in campaigning against the Washington establishment with which he would have to work if he were elected, he put this down to pardonable campaign and rhetorical excesses. In the tradition of the New Deal, the Fair Deal, the New Frontier, and the Great Society, Jimmy Carter would need an organizing theme for his own Presidency. JDR did not have the right words for a slogan, but he felt he knew what the substance should be. There was much about Jimmy Carter that suggested he would understand what the third sector was all about.

These were the reasons JDR did not vote for a man he personally liked, Gerald Ford, and instead voted for Carter.[6] In a staff meeting after the election, JDR and his aides talked about possible points of entry into the new administration. There was Secretary of State Cyrus Vance, another in the long list of Rockefeller Foundation trustees to hold high office in foreign affairs. Commerce Secretary Juanita Kreps, a known advocate of corporate social responsibility, looked promising. And the new Treasury Secretary, W. Michael Blumenthal, former president of Bendix, had the reputation of a progressive. Du Pont chairman Irving Shapiro, with whom JDR had been discussing the third sector and corporate philanthropy, was high on Blumenthal.

Toward the end of the Ford administration, Treasury Secretary Simon made one last gesture toward the third sector—upgrading his philanthropy committee by giving it joint public-private membership, with former Treasury Secretary Douglas Dillon as chairman. This could be a step toward the permanent organization for the third sector in Washington that JDR and the Filer Report had envisioned. It was something to pursue with the new administration.

JDR happened to discuss the Carter administration with Bill Friday, chancellor of the University of North Carolina, who had been a member of JDR's National Committee for the Bicentennial Era. Friday suggested that a point of entry on the third sector theme might be Stuart Eizenstat, assistant to the President for domestic affairs and policy. Friday had known Eizenstat as a student at North Carolina, and felt he had the intellect and insight to grasp the potential of what JDR was talking about. At JDR's suggestion, Friday paved the way by talking to Eizenstat, and JDR followed up with a letter proposing a meeting. He sent along a copy of his basic third-sector paper, and wrote:

It has occurred to my associates and me that there are areas of our efforts which are supportive of President Carter's goals and objectives. Therefore we have been thinking for some time of establishing contact with the White House. Mr. Friday's suggestion was therefore most welcomed.

Eizenstat wrote back proposing a date for a meeting, and on April 21, 1977, JDR and his aide Jack Harr went to the White House. On the walk up the driveway JDR confessed some misgiving to Harr about going in to talk philosophy and ideas to a Presidential aide overloaded with work and problems, especially in the early months of a new administration. JDR said that in all his previous experience in the White House he had found very little interest in ideas. "All they want to know is what they can do specifically, right now," he said.

The visitors found Eizenstat indeed to be harassed. At one point he had to leave the meeting for a prolonged period, and JDR and Harr were left making small talk with two Eizenstat aides who seemed in awe of JDR. When Eizenstat returned, JDR had his chance to make his case. Eizenstat seemed attentive and understanding. He said he had read the paper and found it very interesting. The ideas were appealing, but—was there anything he could do specifically, right now?

JDR did have one request. There had been considerable publicity about President Carter's desire to wipe out government commissions and committees in wholesale numbers in his drive to cut down the size of the federal establishment. A review process was already under way. JDR said that Treasury's Advisory Committee on Philanthropy should not only be saved but reoriented and upgraded in line with the ideas just discussed.

Back home, JDR got off a gracious letter to Eizenstat, thanking him for the meeting. In it he wrote:

Of particular importance, I believe, is the salvaging of the Advisory Committee to the Secretary of the Treasury. It represents the only organized channel of communication between the third sector and the administration and as such can fill a very useful role for all concerned.

Eizenstat wrote back:

I have been informed by the President that in his desire to dramatically reduce the number of advisory committees and commissions, it would not be advisable to make an exception and continue the Advisory Committee on Philanthropy. Nevertheless, we recognize the important role which that sector of our society plays and the special contributions it makes. What we are trying to do is simplify the institutional structures without losing the advantage which regular contact and consultation can bring.

The letter concluded by suggesting that Eizenstat's office be the place "where your contributions take place, and concerns [are] aired," an informal arrangement that "might be more efficient and productive than an advisory committee."

The administration went ahead with its elimination of commissions and committees, a move that did not reduce the size of government appreciably, but did manage to cut off many channels of contact with the citizenry. JDR wrote a final letter to Eizenstat saying he was "understanding" of the administration's position, but a close reading reveals that JDR came about as close to sarcasm as he could. On the "direct approach" to Eizenstat's office, JDR said, "I am concerned as to the very heavy load which you carry." In other words, it was a totally unworkable idea. JDR also commented that it would "please" him if the relationship were "on a two-way basis." This could be read as saying that JDR had spoken his piece and that if the White House wanted to do anything more it could contact him.[7]

Of course, JDR never heard again from Eizenstat, nor did JDR ever attempt to press his point of view with the White House again. It seemed that he finally was growing weary of the frustrations of dealing with official Washington, although he continued to make occasional representations on some of his interests to several cabinet members. There was some sentiment within JDR's staff that perhaps he had given up too quickly on the Carter White House. But then again his instincts may have been right once more, almost prescient in regard to a President who would become a technocrat and curiously remote despite his occasional public relations forays into the homes of citizens, and who would end up suggesting that the problem was with the people and not the leadership in his famous and self-defeating "malaise" speech.

While not giving up on government entirely, JDR turned his main attention to the remaining sector—business. JDR had always been somewhat reluctant to try to influence businessmen. He was not a businessman himself, and even his investments, for the most part, were managed for him. He could overcome his reluctance in seeking support for a specific cause such as Lincoln Center, the youth program, or the Bicentennial, but in trying to sell the third-sector concept he was addressing corporate policies more generally. But he now felt that the stakes were high and that he had a good case. He believed that the time was past when great family fortunes could be amassed that could lead to great private philanthropies. The main repository of wealth in the private sector was corporate America, and in JDR's mind it should begin to fill the need.

There were plenty of comments from his advisers along the way about the realistic limitations to what one could expect business to do, given that its core reason for being was to make money, not give it away. But, as Datus Smith commented, JDR saw "gold" and began "a typical JDR pattern of long-term effort, hanging in, looking for incremental progress." With the help of Bill Ruder and Porter McKeever, JDR began engaging in a long series of meetings and luncheons with the chief executive officers of major corporations. He corresponded with others invariably sending a copy of his basic document. Over an eighteen-month period, he made a considerable dent in the *Fortune* 500, at least in terms of contacts made. He began pressing leading business organizations, such as the Business Roundtable and the Conference Board. As McKeever expressed it, the objective was "to energize the field, discover where there were successful programs and why, and to make businessmen more aware and responsive." McKeever said that JDR believed "if he kept probing long enough he would find the right formula for energizing business." As far as the cautious nature of most corporate giving was concerned, McKeever said JDR's view was that any increase in giving to "safe" causes such as the arts and the Boy Scouts would mean more foundation money available for innovative purposes.[8]

One individual who was very responsive to JDR's ideas was his former loyal ally at Lincoln Center, New York realtor Larry Wien. He bought one hundred shares of stock in one hundred leading corporations, and then persistently showed up at annual meetings to serve as a "gadfly" to press for increased corporate giving.

Throughout 1977 McKeever worked on plans to give the corporate philanthropy program an organizational base in the JDR 3rd Fund, using as a consultant the former Rhodes Scholar and Ford Foundation executive Waldemar Nielsen, whose writings included the book *The Big Foundations*. Nielsen produced a paper proposing a wide range of activities—creating an advisory board of business leaders, specific research ideas, several variations on the continuing effort to persuade business leaders, awards and incentives programs, encouraging noncash giving, and professionalizing and upgrading the philanthropy function within corporations.[9] At their October 12 meeting, the JDR 3rd Fund trustees approved the program and appropriated $100,000 for initial costs. Nielsen was retained to manage it.

While JDR sought increased corporate giving, he always cast his argument within the framework of the third-sector concept, seeking understanding, leadership, and moral support from businessmen as well. He made this case in speeches at the Stanford Business School, to a Conference Board meeting, and in a special seminar at Duke University for top corporate executives, sharing the platform with Commerce Secretary Juanita Kreps and John Filer of Aetna. A rewritten and expanded version of his basic paper became an article in the March 1978 *Across the Board*, the Conference Board magazine, and, by prearrangement, was reprinted in the April *Reader's Digest*.

JDR took a particular interest in one speaking engagement, in Minneapolis in June 1977. Fewer than fifty of the 1.7 million American corporations were giving the full 5 percent allowed by law. Of these, no less than twenty-three were located in the Twin Cities—one of the reasons for the high quality of the arts and civic life in the region. Such a phenomenon obviously did not occur by accident, but was the result of persistent efforts by local business leaders. Prominent among the organizers of the Minneapolis Five Per Cent club were Kenneth and Bruce Dayton. An added reason for JDR's interest in the occasion was the fact that his youngest daughter, Alida, had begun dating Mark Dayton, Bruce's son, and it was beginning to look serious. Again, JDR shared the platform (the Greater Minneapolis Chamber of Commerce) with Juanita Kreps. He delivered his message, praised local leadership, and paid Minneapolis perhaps the ultimate compliment by referring to it as "the emerald city."

During this period, efforts on the organizational front were proceeding. Walter McNerney had incorporated the Committee for the Third Sector in Washington and hired an executive director. There was a movement toward a merger of the National Council on Philanthropy and the Coalition of National Voluntary Organizations. A meeting to discuss that was held at the Ford Foundation in May 1978. A second meeting was scheduled for July 11, with John Gardner slated to play a prominent role.[10]

Throughout all this activity, with new experiences and insights gained, the conviction grew among JDR and his staff that he should do a second book, this time specifically on the third-sector concept. Various ideas were discussed. One was to do a straightforwardly descriptive and philosophical book, much like his first one. Another was to assemble some intellectual weight behind the subject by doing an anthology—different aspects to be examined by prominent leaders with JDR doing the introduction and final chapter. Jack Harr and Bill Ruder worked with JDR in outlining these approaches. Ruder brought in Robert Bernstein of Random House, who said he would like to publish a personal, semiautobiographical book on the subject by JDR. Other approaches, such as an anthology, could follow.

This, of course, ran into JDR's lifetime aversion to doing anything that could be considered by anyone as self-glorification. For example, JDR would not listen to talk by any of his associates about a biography. But the archival record of all of JDR's activities was already immense, and Porter McKeever thought that at least some work should be started to sift through and organize it. It was for this reason, as he later admitted,[11] that he engaged in the "semideception" of persuading JDR that the hiring of a research assistant in the office was necessary. Peter Johnson came on board in 1976 and spent about half of his time doing research to help McKeever and others in their activities. The other half was spent in combing the JDR historical record. The retired Edgar B. Young was engaged in compiling the saga of Lincoln Center for no compensation other than some research help from Johnson and the provision of a secretary. McKeever agreed to pay a consulting fee to have Don McLean come in and do some reminiscing about his early work for JDR, with help from Johnson. All of this was going on with no one talking to JDR about a biography.

On the matter of the third-sector book, however, Bernstein was persuasive that he was emphasizing the "semi" in referring to a semiautobiographical approach. He convinced JDR that it was perfectly legitimate for him to draw on his own experiences, that as long as they were cast in the context of explicating the third sector they would not be self-serving. JDR, for example, could tell the story of the population field to illustrate how private initiative could grow into a major public-private endeavor, or the story of the Rockefeller Foundation and the "green revolution." Some of the stories of the winners in the third phase of the Rockefeller Public Service Awards could add human interest and illustrate what individuals acting on their own could do. Other similar examples could be found that had nothing to do with JDR, or he could choose a subject such as the work of the Ford Foundation and Carnegie Corporation in supporting public television.

There remained the question of just how to do this. Bernstein was enamored of the interview method and finding someone to work with JDR on it. At one point he made the somewhat bizarre suggestion of trying to enlist Chicago author Studs Terkel, who had perfected the interview method to an art form, to work with JDR. As months passed with no further suggestions from Bernstein, JDR asked Jack Harr to begin looking for a writer. They had agreed long before that because they were both so close to the subject it would be desirable to have someone new come in to work with them on the project. They wanted to preserve the triumvirate arrangement that had worked so well in the case of JDR's first book, with Dick Barrett playing the role of the third party. This time Harr would do that and the new person would be primarily responsible for the drafting.

All of the new activities undertaken by JDR from 1968 on could seem to be a large collection of miscellany. But they all came together in his intellectual process of trying to convert his "fourth field" of lifetime interest into the "third sector." As we have seen, all of this was a major endeavor for him in the 1970s. But he still had formidable challenges to meet in his other fields, especially in Asian affairs and population. And he had difficult family issues to work out with his brothers and a strong motivation to do what he could to "pass the baton" to the next generation, the Cousins.

He was intent on doing all of this—clearing the decks so that he could devote two years to working on his third-sector book.

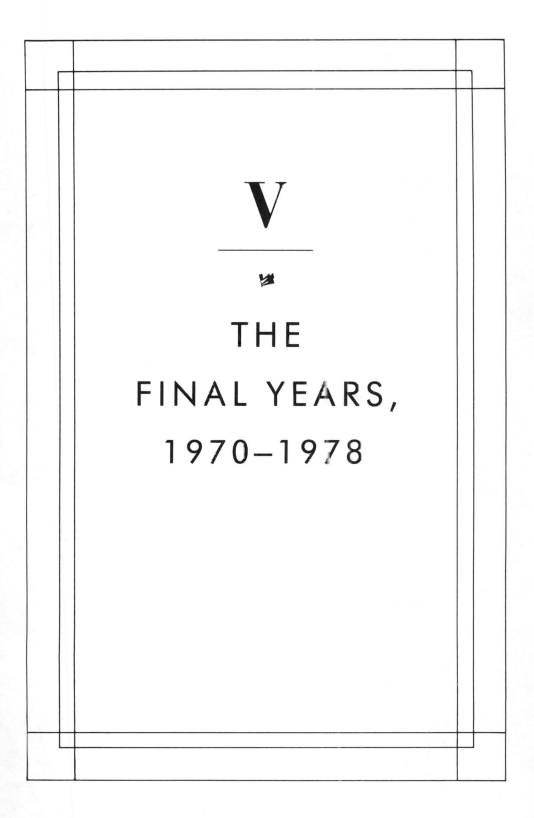

V

THE FINAL YEARS, 1970–1978

25

❦

THE POPULATION COMMISSION

ON MONDAY, MARCH 16, 1970, President Richard M. Nixon stood in the Roosevelt Room in the White House before a gathering of legislators, administration officials, news people, and guests. He apologized that the Cabinet Room was being redecorated and could not be used for the occasion—the signing of a new bill into law. The bill was Public Law 91–213 of the 91st Congress, which established "a Commission on Population Growth and the American Future."

The President had requested the legislation from Congress in a message he had delivered the previous July, a message couched in far stronger language than any U.S. President had ever uttered before on the subject of population growth. In structure the new Commission would be similar to many other such bodies—the President would appoint twenty members, including a chairman and a vice chairman, and the two houses of Congress would each appoint two members, representing both major political parties. An executive director and staff were authorized, as well as the payment of staff salaries and Commission expenses. The bill called for an interim report after one year and a final report after two years. The Commission would terminate sixty days after submission of the final report.

It was the mandate of the Commission that was striking—to study "a broad range of problems associated with population growth and their implications for America's future . . . between now and the year 2000," and to "provide information and education to all levels of government in the United States and to our people."[1]

In his remarks the President called the event "an historic occasion," and he congratulated the Congress for acting in a "bipartisan" manner— the bill had passed both houses by overwhelming margins. Nixon referred to "broad support in the Nation" for the effort, and then, with these words, he introduced the man he had chosen to be chairman of the Commission:

An indication of that broad support is that John D. Rockefeller has agreed to serve as Chairman of the Commission. The other members of the Commission will be announced at a later time. Of all the people in this Nation, I think I can say of all the people in the world, there has been no man who has been more closely identified and longer identified with this problem than John Rockefeller. We are very fortunate to have his chairmanship of the Commission and we know that the report he will give, the recommendations that he will make, will be tremendously significant as we deal with this highly explosive problem, explosive in every way, as we enter the last third of the 20th Century.[2]

It was a moment of triumph for JDR. For years he had been convinced that the United States must mount such an effort, not only for valid domestic reasons, but also to legitimize American efforts to persuade leaders in more densely populated countries to undertake population programs. He had pursued that goal relentlessly. The "commission" that had been downgraded to a "task force" and then further downgraded to a mere "committee" by President Johnson had been a barren victory, delivering its report almost unnoticed in the waning hours of the Johnson administration. Now JDR had the best possible auspices—a full-fledged commission strongly backed by both the President and the Congress, maximum public visibility, a mandate not only for addressing a wide range of population issues but also something as breathtaking as the "American future" out to the year 2000, two years within which to work, and the prospect of twenty-three more commission members, a professional staff, and federal funding on the order of two to three million dollars.

Yet there was much about what had happened that was sobering and would allay any temptation to celebrate—not that JDR would have yielded to such a temptation in any case. For one thing, he now had primary responsibility for a tremendously difficult task over the next two years, and he was shortly to find out just how difficult it was going to be. For another, there were signs that President Nixon's enthusiasm, so manifest the previous July, had tempered considerably by March 1970. There was no question that JDR had been the prime mover in achieving the Commission. He had worked very hard toward that goal, using every bit of influence and prestige he could muster. Except for the unexpected and welcome emphasis on "America's future" to the year 2000, the design of the Commission and its mandate followed closely the recommendations he had made. But so sensitive had the population issue become within the White House that JDR had not been certain he would be rewarded with the chairmanship until three days before the March 16 ceremony.

*   *   *

The fourteen months that elapsed between January 1969, when JDR and Wilbur Cohen delivered their almost-secret report to President Johnson, and March 1970, when JDR stood at the pinnacle of triumph, was a tumultuous period generally for the population field and an extremely busy one for JDR. His main energies, of course, were directed toward the goal of creating a new commission. But he also had to complete the population study he had taken on for the United Nations Association. He played the leading role in two population conferences sponsored by the Rockefeller Foundation. He supported studies of abortion and urged reform of laws affecting abortion, which became a hotly controversial issue by early 1970. And he continued his search for a population assistant to replace Ray Lamontagne, who had left his staff in May 1968.

In retrospect, it seems fair to say that this was a period in which public interest in the population field reached its zenith. There was scarcely a prominent American who did not have something to say about the population problem. Four of the powerful social movements of the time—civil rights, the environment, women, and youth—all impinged in some degree on population, helping to make it another great contemporary issue in the United States. But these and other factors brought new elements of controversy. Although public support for population programs remained high for some years, the controversial elements eventually caused it to crest and begin to wane.

The environmental movement was particularly potent in its effect on the population field. It had been simmering for some time, at least since the publication of Rachel Carson's book *The Silent Spring* in 1962. But it suddenly exploded into the national consciousness at the turn of the decade. "Earth Day" in the spring of 1970 was a memorable event for millions of Americans. The fervor continued to grow, and in 1972 the United Nations sponsored a conference on the environment in Stockholm that had a profound effect on attitudes around the world. It set the model for a series of annual issues designated by the UN for yearlong study and action, including UN Population Year in 1974.

The environmental movement had a much more radical and apocalyptic tone to it than the century-old conservation movement, which now seemed stodgy and old-fashioned by comparison. The new look was typified by the militancy of the Sierra Club and by the appearance of dozens of new ecological organizations. A vast literature appeared on the adverse results accompanying the drive for economic growth—deforestation, erosion, desertification, pesticides, air and water pollution—casting doubts on what formerly had been seen as the answer to problems of poverty, hunger, and increasing human numbers. In the minds of many, the very processes of growth and progress based on scientific and technological innovation were spawning a vast range of new problems that threatened the ecological balance of the planet and the survival of mankind.

In this climate, the Malthusian link between resources and population growth was forged anew. Rockefeller Foundation scientist Norman Borlaug won the Nobel Prize in 1970 for his work on "the green revolution," but in his acceptance speech he stressed population as the underlying problem. Prominent among the books of the time that gave an apocalyptic tone to the resources-population link were Barry Commoner's *Science and Survival* (1967); William and Paul Paddock's *Famine—1975!* (1967); Richard Falk's *This Endangered Planet* (1971); and Paul Ehrlich's *The Population Bomb* (1968).

Among the many opinion leaders who became vocal supporters of population control measures during this period was Robert McNamara, president of the International Bank for Reconstruction and Development (the "World Bank"), former president of the Ford Motor Company, and Defense Secretary in the Kennedy and Johnson administrations. In a speech at the University of Notre Dame in the spring of 1969, McNamara called for "humane and massive" reduction in the rate of world population growth.[3] McNamara continued to be outspoken on the subject, and it was his suggestion to JDR that resulted in two high-level conferences on population sponsored by the Rockefeller Foundation in April 1970 and June 1971 at its conference center, the Villa Serbelloni in Bellagio, Italy. McNamara wanted an emphasis on action, envisioning a conference of leaders who were responsible for action programs rather than experts who studied the issues. As a result, most of the attendees who joined McNamara and JDR in Bellagio were heads of specialized UN agencies or leading practitioners from a dozen or more countries. But, perhaps inevitably, the conferences still were organized around papers presented by various experts.[4]

The great surge of opinion toward action in the population field was bound to have an effect within the United Nations. As we have seen, the population issue had been kept alive in the UN ever since Julian Huxley first raised his voice in 1946 and Frank Notestein began his demographic studies under UN auspices. However, two factors had always limited UN attention to rhetoric and research. One was the opposition of the Communist bloc and most Catholic countries. The second was competition among a number of UN specialized agencies for control of population programs and funding. By the late 1960s, the climate of opinion within the UN was changing, not only because of the growing prominence of the population problem, but also because many Asian and African nations had joined the Western countries that long had supported UN involvement. The pioneering work of JDR and the Population Council in the lesser-developed countries and his "World Leaders Statement" undoubtedly were factors in this regard. And the study of the UN's role in population by the United Nations Association (UNA), which JDR had agreed to chair, came along at just the right moment.

The president of the UNA was Porter McKeever, a former journalist in Washington, D.C., who had joined Adlai Stevenson's campaign staff in 1952 and then had worked for the Ford Foundation and the Committee for Economic Development before joining UNA when it was created in a merger of several organizations in the early 1960s. Some years after the UNA population study McKeever was to join JDR's staff as an associate when Ed Young and Datus Smith retired, but at the time of the study he barely knew JDR. McKeever recalls how delighted he was to land JDR for the chairmanship "because of his international reputation in the population field."

One reason that McKeever and his staff director, Elmore Jackson, recruited a "foreigner," a young Englishman named Stanley Johnson, to head the staff for the study was so that it would not seem to be entirely an American effort. However, JDR's colleagues on the panel were all Americans, including several men with whom he had become closely associated in population work—George Woods, former head of the World Bank; David Bell, former U.S. AID director and now vice president of the Ford Foundation (which funded the study); and Richard Gardner, professor of international law at Columbia. Also a member was John Hannah, Nixon's AID director—one of the implied enticements for the UN in accepting the recommendations of the study was the likelihood of a substantial contribution from AID, whose funds earmarked for population activities had been growing each year.

According to McKeever, however, the key factor was the timing. The rivalry among the specialized agencies had forestalled action, and pressure was building for some sort of compromise solution that would allow the UN to move forward. "We knew the UN was ready," McKeever commented. He added: "Never have I seen such a direct line between the recommendations of a private body and acceptance by a public body, especially an international one."[5]

The report, delivered May 25, 1969, had gracious words for all of the UN specialized agencies, but set as its main task the solution to the organizational dilemma of the UN. It called for a "radical upgrading in the priority accorded to population activities" and proposed that "a high-level Commissioner for Population should be appointed within the United

Nations Development Program and a high-level staff be recruited to handle the resources of the Population Fund." The Population Trust Fund had been created in 1967, but thus far had received less than $2 million in contributions from member countries. The UNA report suggested that an important reason for this was the inadequate way in which the UN was organized for population activities. It specified that the commissioner should have "the central role" in planning for UN assistance in the population field, should be responsible for allocating funds, and should be the UN's representative in all forums dealing with population issues. The report also called for rapid expansion of the Population Trust Fund to $100 million within three years.[6]

The report was widely publicized, and was well received by UN Secretary General U Thant and Paul G. Hoffman, administrator of the UN Development Program (UNDP). As McKeever noted, action was swift— in a matter of weeks the Population Trust Fund was transferred to the UNDP. By November 1969, the reorganization was completed with the creation of the United Nations Fund for Population Activities (UNFPA) within UNDP. Hoffman recruited Rafael Salas, a former Filipino cabinet minister, to head UNFPA, with the title of "executive director" rather than "commissioner" as the UNA report had proposed.

UNFPA absorbed the former Population Trust Fund and quickly became the center within the UN for population activities. An advisory board was created, and JDR took a seat on it along with such close associates in supporting population programs as Alberto Lleras Camargo of Colombia, Lord Caradon of the United Kingdom, and B. R. Sen of India. For its first full year of operation, UNFPA set a goal of $15 million in contributions from member states. Using an old Rockefeller technique, USAID made a matching grant of half the total. Within two years, the annual funding reached $44.6 million, of which the largest single category of expenditure ($20.7 million) was for technical assistance in family planning programs.[7] Although advocates would always like to see more happening, the UNFPA in the intervening years clearly became an important force on the international scene in promoting population activities. In 1978 its annual funding passed the $100 million mark, still based on the pattern of USAID contributing half of the total. But the balance was made up by contributions from more than half of the UN's member states.

JDR's involvement with the UN was a positive achievement during the fourteen-month interval between the submission of the Rockefeller-Cohen report to President Johnson and JDR's appointment as chairman of the new commission by President Nixon. Other developments during this period were much more controversial. In particular, the issue of a woman's right to a safe and legal abortion became a searing political question for the first time, foreshadowing the inflammatory national political debate that would explode within a few years. With concern about high levels of population growth steadily gaining in public recognition, it was perhaps inevitable that abortion would surface as an issue sooner or later.

During the late nineteenth century, legislatures in every American state had outlawed abortion. The Roman Catholic Church, many Protestant denominations, and Orthodox Jews adamantly opposed abortion except under the most restricted circumstances.[8] Although abortion was illegal, it had not been a prominent subject of public debate. This did not prevent many observers from perceiving the existence of a serious social problem. For many years illegal abortions had been performed at the rate of scores of thousands annually although, as is the case with most illegal activity, no one could know the exact number. Abortions performed by unqualified persons often resulted in serious infections, permanent injury, and death. Occasionally an "abortion mill" would be exposed and a doctor would be prosecuted. But in the main the issue lay dormant until the 1960s, when pressure from a number of quarters mounted for the reform or elimination of what many considered overly restrictive and intrusive laws.

This was strongly fueled by sentiments and values prominent within both the feminist and youth movements of the time. As a rule, abortion was not openly and specifically advocated as a generalized means of birth control—other motivations were cited. For feminists, restrictive abortion laws were more evidence of a male-dominated society; they insisted that a woman has a basic right to decide what happens to her own body. Many others regarded abortion law liberalization as a matter of social justice— wealthy women could fly to Denmark to have an abortion performed, or to the United Kingdom, which in 1968 liberalized its abortion law, but a low-income woman wanting an abortion had to face the moral dilemma and health risks involved in seeking illegal means.

Did JDR believe in abortion as a means of birth control? Opinions differed among those who worked for him on population matters. Ray Lamontagne thought that JDR did but was wise enough to know that to say so in public would have been self-defeating. Privately, JDR pointed to the example of Japan. Postwar concern about excessive population growth in Japan abated when it became apparent that the Japanese were successful in limiting growth, chiefly because of legalized abortion. The same was true in a number of Communist bloc countries.

A different view was expressed by David Lelewer, Lamontagne's successor as JDR's associate in the population field. He thought that JDR, having become imbued with many of the values associated with the feminist and youth movements, was sincere in stating that abortion was an unfortunate choice, but one that rightfully belonged to the pregnant woman herself in consultation with her doctor. This, at any rate, was the position JDR consistently upheld from the first time that he addressed the issue in public, as the keynote speaker at an international conference sponsored by the Association for the Study of Abortion in November 1968 at the Homestead in Hot Springs, Virginia. He took a course parallel to his father's view in the early 1930s that the abuses that stemmed from prohibiting drinking were a greater evil than drinking itself:

. . . it seems to me that abortion must be considered the lesser evil. It is morally justified by the greater evils that in all too many cases flow from the absence of abortion—the unwanted child, the unwanting mother, the medical risks of nonprofessional practices, disrespect for the law. The damage done to parents, children, and society by these greater evils cannot be effectively measured by objective criteria, but it is urgent and real and, in many societies, critical. Surely arbitrary laws cannot be expected to solve such a problem; in fact, they have helped create it.

In this passage, JDR first touched on a theme that was to be important to him in respect to the population problem in general—the theme of "the unwanted child." This was the most "serious" problem of all, he held in his 1968 speech: "We all want to see children born into this world with every reasonable chance of living a life of dignity and self-fulfillment. I believe it is morally indefensible to perpetuate conditions that handicap children from the moment they are born." He repeatedly used this theme as an argument in favor of more widespread adoption of family planning methods. And in the 1968 speech, he drew the obvious conclusion that to the extent family planning was adopted the incidence of abortion would go down.

What should be done about abortion? At that time, almost no one envisioned that the Supreme Court one day (and relatively soon) would eliminate abortion prohibition laws across the country in one stroke (in *Roe* v. *Wade*, 1973). In 1968 JDR made the conventional argument for efforts on a state-by-state basis to modify abortion laws, based on a "clear, unambiguous, and liberal" mental health provision such as the one contained in the British law enacted earlier that year. But he also expressed the opinion that the "elimination of abortion laws altogether . . . will inevitably be the long-range answer." This, he said, "would give each individual freedom of choice. It would force no person to violate his own moral code. And it would give us a true basis for eliminating the social evils I have discussed."

In other ways, JDR supported abortion law reform. He pressed the

Population Council to become involved, but was understanding when Notestein and Berelson resisted doing anything beyond sponsoring research. By absorbing the old Committee on Maternal Health in the early 1960s, the Council brought to its staff Dr. Christopher Tietze, who had concentrated his studies on abortion. Since the formation of the Association for the Study of Abortion (ASA) in 1966, JDR contributed $15,000 a year in support, matched by his sister, Abby. ASA was the leading organization in abortion research, publications, and reform efforts at the state level, and was headed by two eminent obstetricians, Dr. Louis Hellman as chairman and Dr. Robert Hall as president.[9] JDR also contributed financially to other organizations supporting abortion law reform, including the American Civil Liberties Union and the American Law Institute.

As was true in so many areas of social legislation, the first real breakthrough came in New York State where Governor Nelson Rockefeller shared his brother's views on abortion. The existing law prohibited abortion under all circumstances except when the mother's life was endangered. Numerous bills had been introduced to liberalize this nineteenth-century statute, and sufficient political momentum finally developed with passage of the Cook-Lichter bill by the State Senate on January 7, 1970. In effect, it removed abortion from the criminal code and placed it under the public health code, requiring only that an abortion be performed by a licensed physician within the first twenty-four weeks of pregnancy—in other words, abortion on demand.

A wild and tumultuous period ensued with intense lobbying on both sides as the State Assembly considered the bill—all this at the very time that the Population Commission legislation was being passed in Washington and President Nixon was trying to decide on his choice for chairman. In New York State, the Catholic Church became involved in the effort to defeat the repeal with a pastoral letter from Cardinal Cooke read from the pulpits of hundreds of churches and pressure on individual legislators by members of the incipient "right to life" movement, as it eventually would be called. On the other side, feminist groups also worked diligently, presenting legislators with coat hangers symbolizing the perils of illegal abortion. Finally, on April 10, a tie in the Assembly was averted and the bill passed 76 votes to 74 when Assemblyman George Michaels of Auburn, New York, changed his vote at the last minute. In May Governor Rockefeller signed the bill into law.[10]

Those associated with JDR in population work assumed that delivery of the Rockefeller-Cohen report to President Johnson in January 1969 marked the end of the trail as far as a major domestic study of population was concerned. To many, President Nixon seemed much too conservative, not to say rightist, to be interested in any such endeavor. Even JDR lamented, in his diary, that not only was his "pretty good" report handicapped by coming at the end of an administration, but that "new administrations are not too prone to pick up reports of previous administrations and recommendations from predecessors, particularly when there is a change of party involved."

However, JDR was not one to be easily discouraged—he was determined to press the new administration anyway. This despite the fact that he was, as usual, extraordinarily busy. He was beginning to start up his youth activities and was engaged in his first unsuccessful attempts to write the book about philanthropy. He was deeply involved in the defense of philanthropy—activating the Peterson Commission, attempting to whip up a constituency, and preparing for the tax reform hearings. Lincoln Center was going through its most serious leadership and financial crisis, culminating in the exit of William Schuman as president, and there were significant changes involving both the Asia Society and the Japan Society. And many of the population activities just described were consuming JDR's time, particularly the UNA study.

In addition, JDR still lacked an associate for population affairs to replace Ray Lamontagne. As noted, the departure of Lamontagne the previous May had been difficult for JDR, more akin to losing a son that a staff aide. Perhaps because of this, the efforts of Lamontagne and others to find a replacement had not succeeded. For this reason, the planning of a demarche on the new administration fell to Barney Berelson. Though dubious about prospects, Berelson dutifully took on the assignment. He worked with JDR to produce a number of "talking points" and, based on them, drafted a letter, signed by JDR to thirty-five key appointees in the new administration, transmitting a copy of the Rockefeller-Cohen report. The basic argument was that all that had transpired at high levels in previous administrations had merely served to set the stage and that the new administration now had the opportunity to make the "transition from concern to action," as the formal title of the Rockefeller-Cohen report suggested. The letter singled out key recommendations of that report—a Presidential commission, a federally funded Population Institute, and the appointment of a special assistant to the President on population.

To everyone's surprise, the Nixon administration focused very quickly on the population problem, so quickly that the JDR letter was never sent out, although its specific points were later pressed. What JDR and his advisers were learning, along with everyone else, was that the Nixon administration was taking an unexpectedly liberal tack during its early months in office. It was as if Nixon was disposed to be magnanimous, having reached the political pinnacle after years of toiling in the wilderness, and having observed the damage done to the Democratic Party by all of the social and protest movements of the time—antiwar, youth, feminist, environmental, urban. He was not about to court or attempt to coopt all of these movements, but he also would not go out of his way to antagonize them. There were, in fact, two areas—urban affairs and population—where he felt comfortable adopting, at least for the time being, a somewhat progressive approach.

One prominent sign of this tack was Nixon's appointment of a liberal Catholic intellectual, Daniel Patrick Moynihan, as his urban affairs assistant, a post ultimately transformed into the Domestic Council, which became a White House fixture (as the "domestic" counterpart to the National Security Council). So clearly was Moyhihan identified as a liberal Democrat, having previously worked for Governor Harriman of New York and in several posts in the Kennedy and Johnson administrations, that Democrats were prone to see him as something of a traitor for joining the Nixon administration. But Moynihan was decidedly his own man, and no stranger to controversy, having come to public prominence when he earned the opprobrium of civil rights leaders as a result of his famous report *The Negro Family: The Case for National Action*, written in 1965 when he was Assistant Secretary of Labor.[11] A rumpled, pixieish figure, Moynihan was known for his brilliant, analytical mind and his eloquence, both in writing and speaking, the latter despite a slight speech impediment.

Moynihan's general assignment was to develop domestic legislative proposals and programs for the new administration. In February, less than a month after taking office, the President publicly assigned Moynihan to develop a program in the area of population growth and family planning in association with HEW Secretary Robert Finch.[12] Through other channels, JDR and his advisers learned that Finch was strongly in favor of action in the population field. His Assistant Secretary for Health, Roger Egeberg, became an outspoken advocate. Another good channel for JDR was Dr. Lee A. DuBridge, the new science adviser to the President and a Rockefeller Foundation trustee.

On March 6 JDR went to Washington for lunch at the White House mess with DuBridge and Moynihan, and agreed to their suggestion that he draft a memorandum to the President laying out specifically what he had in mind. This memorandum, dated March 26, became the blueprint for the Commission in almost every respect except the emphasis on the future to the year 2000. JDR made the case for the urgency of the population problem and for the now-familiar phrase "transition from concern to action." He discussed the structure of the Commission, offered ten areas of inquiry, and made the first tentative suggestion of nineteen names for a twenty-member Commission (the twentieth presumably would be JDR himself as chairman). Although a conventional list of public figures and experts, most of them well-known to JDR, it was also a somewhat impolitic list in that it included a number of known Democrats or persons prominent in previous Democratic administrations, such as David Bell, Patricia Harris, Douglas Dillon, Richard Gardner, David Lilienthal, and Bill Moyers. It was an interesting list from another point of view. In his memo, JDR stated that members "should be chosen for their interest, knowledge, stature and judgement rather than for their representativeness." He added somewhat weakly: "However, the representative factor is recognized as important." JDR was still absorbing some of the "new values" he was to write about in his book—more than a year later, the "representative factor" was to be very important to him as he struggled to get names for Commission membership cleared through White House political screening.[13]

A sense of momentum grew after Nixon stressed family planning in his foreign aid message in May, and numerous bills for population programs were introduced in Congress with broad bipartisan support, including such prominent Republicans as Senator Robert Packwood of Oregon and Representative George Bush of Texas. In June there were newspaper reports of debates within the White House on population policy,[14] and finally on July 18 came the President's population message—eight legal-sized, single-spaced pages of closely reasoned prose showing the Moynihan imprint. The first part outlined the worldwide nature of the problem and called for action by all relevant parties, including the UN. In this connection, the President said: "I am most impressed by the scope and thrust of the recent report of the Panel of the United Nations Association, chaired by John D. Rockefeller III." The heart of the statement focused on the need for population programs in the United States as well, and here Moynihan's touch was most visible in an extended discussion of the effects of population growth and migration on the urban problem. It was this interest of Moynihan's that led to the forward look to the year 2000. Then the statement called for Congress to create the "Commission on Population Growth and the American Future," with the proposed design following JDR's prescriptions in almost every detail.

Surprisingly, the President concluded his statement by instructing a wide range of government agencies to undertake research and plan action programs in population on a scale that one would imagine might have resulted from the recommendations of a commission instead of preceding its creation. The President stated his commitment emphatically: "It is my view that no American woman should be denied access to family planning assistance because of her economic condition." And he set as "a national goal" the provision of that assistance.

Anticipating that he would be in for a grueling two-year assignment once the Commission was created, JDR realized that he had to solve the problem of finding a new associate to replace Ray Lamontagne. He had interviewed several candidates, but none had worked out. Datus Smith broke the impasse by suggesting that the White House Fellows program might be a good source of talent. There is stiff competition for participation in this program, which gives promising young men and women a year of high-level exposure as staff aides in government agencies. The man who emerged from this talent pool as JDR's new associate was David Lelewer, a twenty-nine-year-old graduate of Amherst and the Stanford Law School, coming on board in September 1969, fully sixteen months after Lamontagne had departed. Lelewer had no specific experience in population, but that was not a prerequisite—neither had Lamontagne. There were plenty of experts available in the Population Council and elsewhere. What JDR needed was someone who could learn fast and had all the qualities of a good staff aide. Lelewer had the additional advantage of having served his fellowship in HEW, overlapping two administrations, where he was fully aware of the Rockefeller-Cohen effort and the drive to create a new commission in the Nixon administration.

As the bills were introduced in Congress in response to the President's request, the sharp edges of controversy began to multiply, a perhaps inevitable result of the tremendous buildup of attention focused on the population problem. In addition to controversies engendered by the abortion question and the sometimes radical fringes of the environmental movement, statements increasingly were made directly on population matters, reflecting the "scare tactics" that Osborn, Notestein, and JDR had always been careful to avoid. For example, a group of scientists meeting at the John Muir Institute for Environmental Studies called for *compulsory* birth control, holding that "the Nixon Administration's policy of voluntary birth control" would not work. Professor Kingsley Davis of the University of California said that family planning programs were "a hopelessly futile" means of controlling population growth, and he talked of means of restructuring the family as an approach. The author of *The Population Bomb*, Paul Ehrlich, suggested that the United States might have to resort to adding temporary sterility drugs to food shipped to foreign countries or to be placed in their water supplies with antidote chemicals distributed, per-

haps by lottery. Alternatively, he suggested that the United States halt
economic aid to countries that did not try to limit their populations. The
possibility of adopting "triage" as a national policy in the face of widespread
famines abroad was discussed. Perhaps not surprisingly, given the tenor
of these statements, the fear began to be voiced by some black leaders
that the motivation behind birth control was black genocide.[15]

For a time, the Nixon administration seemed to ignore the dissonant
voices and the potential for controversy. The President strongly supported
population programs in an address to the UN in September, and Roger
Egeberg announced that HEW would soon appoint a deputy assistant secretary for population and establish a Population Institute within the
National Institutes of Health.[16] But when the abortion law controversy
burst in New York State over the winter, there were signs that the White
House was growing cautious.

One such sign was sudden doubt about who would be named chairman
of the new Commission. It had always been an unspoken assumption that
JDR would be the choice. Given that he was the most prominent layman
in the field, a prime mover in creating the Commission, and a prominent
Republican on good terms with the President, it seemed inconceivable
that anyone else would be tapped for the role. Early in 1970, when it was
a certainty that the legislation would pass, Moynihan finally raised the
matter. Stressing that he was not yet speaking for the President, he asked
JDR the classic conditional question posed to every potential candidate for
a Presidential appointment: "*Would* you accept *if* the post is offered?"

JDR responded affirmatively, but set the condition that he wanted to
choose the other members. He now saw matters differently than when he
had submitted his memo of the previous March. He believed the effort
would be more productive if the Commission operated on as open a basis
as possible, including public hearings and possibly a filmed or televised
version of the final report in addition to the standard written one. To this
end, he felt that the membership should be broadly representative, including women, minority group members, and young people in addition to
some stalwarts in the population field. To the extent that the report could
be the product of an open and democratic process, JDR now was convinced, it would be more valid and meaningful.

After that conversation, there was silence for a considerable time from
the White House. JDR soon learned that others were being considered
for the chairmanship. It was hard to say if the cause was JDR's condition
on choosing the members or whether he was now seen as too prominent
or too liberal in a field suddenly riddled with controversy. At any rate,

JDR decided to press the matter. Among others, he spoke with his son's father-in-law, Senator Charles Percy of Illinois, who lined up Senator John Sherman Cooper of Kentucky to speak to the White House on JDR's behalf.[17]

Before this could have any effect, however, the decision was made and JDR was invited to Washington to have lunch with Moynihan on March 13. Moynihan informed him that the President wanted to appoint JDR as chairman. In JDR's handwritten notes on the meeting and in his diary entry, some further signs of caution from the White House side came through. The diary entry reads:

Mr. Moynihan mentioned that recently the President had been visited by a representative of the Sierra Club and that he had spoken about the new slogan in the population field 'Zero Population Growth.' This appears to be disturbing to the President, feeling he does not want to be in a position of advocating such a specific mandate to parents. I said that as far as I was concerned I had no brief for the phrase if it was offensive from the President's point of view.

However, JDR showed that he was no mean semanticist by immediately stating his firm belief that "population stabilization" had to be the goal, both for the world at large and the United States "if [we were to] move forward with economic development and obtain quality in life." (The two terms must be taken to mean approximately the same thing, although "stabilization" has a less contentious ring to it than "zero population growth" [ZPG, as the slogan came to be known]. The demographic reality is that once the entire population begins to have children only at the replacement level it would still take many decades to reach a zero growth rate—"stabilization"—because of the very large numbers of people already born who have yet to form households.)

Moynihan said that "population stabilization" was an acceptable term to the President, that in fact he had already used it in his population message of the previous July against "the advice of those close to him, but found himself supported by public reaction." However, Moynihan stressed that the President wanted any such goal to come as a result of careful study of the facts, and that planning for additional millions "was much on the President's mind." Moynihan used the figure of 60 million as the built-in population growth before stabilization could be attained.

JDR responded by saying that he had never been one to favor "scare" statements on population so that the "factual approach" satisfied him—the "case for population stabilization" should flow "naturally" from the facts and figures. But he said again that the "main thing" he wanted to be sure of was that the "President really believed in the need for population stabilization in the U.S." Moynihan said that he did, "but a bit of reinforcing would be all to the good."

Toward the end of the meeting JDR asked if the White House expected the Commission to recommend "a national policy on population." Moynihan said he thought the Commission offered a unique opportunity to do so, and that JDR should understand that the responsibility of the Commission was not so much to the President as it was a matter of carrying out the mandate of Congress as specified in the bill. He added that he had just wanted "to pass on certain thoughts that were on the President's mind." By the same token, the bill gave the President the power to appoint members of the Commission. Moynihan said he and JDR would work together to propose nominees, but they would have to be cleared by the White House.

At the March 16 ceremony, President Nixon had JDR at his side as he made his statement. JDR wrote: "He did it all very graciously and simply without any notes at all." After the ceremony, Nixon invited JDR into the Oval Office for a brief talk:

He seems proud of having created the Commission but somewhat concerned as to sensitivities which still surround the subject. I reassured him that as to the Catholic Church, I really did not believe there need be any worries in this direction. He was warm and friendly and seemed appreciative of my having taken on the job. I told him that I was grateful to have the opportunity to serve as Chairman because of my belief as to the importance of what the Commission could do and that also I was gratified by his confidence in me.

In the weeks that followed, JDR found himself in unexpectedly drawn-out negotiations with Moynihan over selecting the other members of the Commission. To assist him, JDR had David Lelewer and Richard W. Barrett, who had become a consultant to JDR's "youth program." Barrett was temporarily diverted to the Commission problem because of his long experience in Washington affairs. Barrett told JDR that he had never before known of a commission in which the chairman was appointed before the other members and had a hand in selecting them. It turned out that this gave JDR no advantage. His diary note of April 2 reflects some of the frustration he felt:

With David Lelewer and Richard Barrett had a long session at the White House with Moynihan concerning problems relating to the Commission on Population. Particularly we concentrated on possible members. What is disturbing to me is that we cannot just consider those who would be the best members for the

Commission but have to consider so many political factors. It really comes down to quite a bit of 'horse trading' with the White House holding the reins as the bill provides that the President shall appoint the members of the Commission. Moynihan is really very decent about it but is under considerable pressure from the political elements of the White House.

Barrett's notes provide some amusing sidelights on the JDR-Moynihan relationship, an unusual one between two very different men who came to admire and respect each other.[18]

Moynihan had just survived another bit of personal controversy when his famous "benign neglect" memo to the President was leaked to the press.[19] Unfazed by this—and unawed by anyone—Moynihan was a relaxed figure during the negotiations, beaming goodwill from behind his desk, his trademark the ubiquitous bow tie and shirt with frayed, buttoned-down collar, sometimes unbuttoned and askew. From the outset he referred to JDR as "John." In contrast, JDR was old-fashioned both in dress (though impeccable) and manner, always reticent about using first names, but before long he was calling Moynihan "Pat."

It soon became apparent that Moynihan had to clear nominees with such White House figures as Robert Haldeman, John Ehrlichman, Charles Colson, and Maurice Stans. When JDR expressed frustration over this, Moynihan spread his hands and responded with an obvious reference to political affiliation: "John, why are we arguing? They're *your* people, not mine. Your brother *fired* me!"[20]

JDR could not understand how anyone could be against some of the people he proposed, and he wanted to submit their names again after they were rejected. Moynihan said: "If you want me to, I'll go back. But it won't do any good." When JDR kept pressing for the president of one of the prestigious women's colleges in the Northeast, Moynihan responded: "John, you don't know how bad these people are And you keep pushing for the president of a college they can't get their daughters into."

Stans in particular was backing some Republican campaign contributors for slots on the Commission. One day when JDR expressed unhappiness at this, Moynihan happened to glance through the open door of his office to see Stans coming down the stairs. "There's Maury now," he said. "You want me to call Maury in? He'll explain it to you."

After one grueling session with Moynihan, Barrett recalls walking down the White House drive with JDR, who shook his head and said with a small smile: "I'll have to get that fellow some new shirts."

Overall, Barrett's view is that JDR more than held his own despite his political naiveté. JDR was particularly upset by what he regarded as White

House "blinders" toward certain types of nominees—young people, minority group members, and women. But he kept boring in. According to Barrett, JDR came to enjoy the give-and-take. "You could see his eyes twinkling. But he was a hard negotiator. He kept up with Moynihan, and nothing got past him."

In the end, JDR's persistence and hard work by Lelewer (who spent weeks scouting nominees and occupying a desk in Moynihan's office) had good results. Although, as JDR commented in his diary, few of the members were known nationally and many of his nominees were rejected, there also were no political appointees. The final group included five women (several of them housewives), four minority group members, three young people, three medical doctors, three academics, and a union representative. JDR also got three of his stalwarts on the Commission—George Woods, David Bell, and Barney Berelson. The two senators chosen for the Commission, Joseph Tydings of Maryland (later replaced by Senator Cranston of California) and Bob Packwood of Oregon, were progressive thinkers on population matters. The same was true of Congressman James Scheuer of New York (who succeeded Congressman John Blatnik on the Commission). The fourth congressional member was Representative John Erlenborn of Illinois, a conservative Republican, but he turned out to be the hardest worker of the congressional members and earned JDR's respect despite their differences on several key issues.

Locating an executive director also was not an easy matter. JDR approached three senior men—a former director of the Bureau of the Budget and two heads of population institutes at leading universities—but all turned him down. They advised him to seek a younger person who could commit two years to such an all-consuming task, and JDR finally found his man in Charles C. Westoff, a highly regarded demographer who was associate director of the Office of Population Research at Princeton under Ansley J. Coale (Notestein's successor). JDR was attracted to Westoff because much of his research and publication centered on the theme of "the unwanted child." But Westoff was not easy to get either—his problem was mainly a financial one. He felt he would have to maintain two households and bear other extraordinary expenses. The legislation limited the executive director's salary to the top Civil Service grade (GS–18). JDR was prepared to provide a supplement, but this was not permissible under federal regulations. So JDR and Westoff came to what Westoff terms "the arrangement"—JDR paid two-thirds of Westoff's salary (the other third was paid by Princeton University) and all of his expenses. In effect, JDR and Princeton contributed Westoff's services to the federal government.[21]

All of this recruiting activity took so long that the press began to wonder what had happened to the Population Commission.[22] But the first meeting of the Commission finally occurred on June 15, a daylong session at the Madison Hotel in Washington with Moynihan appearing at lunch to speak to the group. JDR commented in his diary:

What pleased me most was that there was good general participation by all of the members, some of them obviously feeling strongly about the points of view expressed. I was also glad that there was considerable divergence in the points of view which I think is healthy, although the dominant note certainly was that the U.S.'s population growth must be curtailed. . . . Am encouraged.

At this meeting, JDR spotted the person he thought would make a good vice chairman, Grace Olivarez, a forty-one-year-old woman who had just graduated from Fordham Law School: "She is Mexican-American and quite a person." He spoke to Moynihan and several members about her. At a subsequent meeting, the Commission elected Olivarez and Dr. Christian N. Ramsey, Jr., as co–vice chairmen.[23]

In contrast to the events leading up to its creation and the fireworks attending publication of its report, the work of the Commission over its two-year life was not much in the public eye.[24] Administratively, the Commission was quickly organized, with office space located in Washington and some thirty-five persons recruited to its staff, plus a host of consultants. More than a hundred research papers were commissioned on a wide range of subjects. At first the Commission itself held two-day meetings on a bimonthly basis, but the frequency of meetings increased as time passed. In the final months, a series of three-day meetings occurred.

True to JDR's desire to have as open a process as possible, five public hearings were held over a six-month period in 1971, in Washington, New York, Chicago, Little Rock, and Los Angeles. Every conceivable point of view was voiced by more than a hundred witnesses in these hearings, but only rarely did matters get contentious, as in Chicago when the Reverend Jesse Jackson alleged that "black genocide" might be the motivation behind population control efforts. JDR handled this calmly, however, and commented in his diary that Jackson "was a strong individual who presented the black point of view effectively."

Westoff recalls a contrast between JDR being "overly permissive" as chairman, but "relentless" in dealing with the staff, wanting to be kept informed on every development that might possibly lead to a recommendation and reviewing drafts with an eye to "making them understandable to everyone." The performance of the members varied widely. JDR was particularly unhappy with the fact that the congressional members, except Erlenborn, rarely attended the meetings. According to Westoff, JDR was "infinitely patient" with the most difficult of the members, a Stanford law student (one of the three young members) whose ideas ranged far afield from the subject at hand and who "seemed to want to dismantle the entire Federal Govenment." The most effective members, Westoff said, were Berelson and Bell, who were "great synthesizers," especially Berelson, who was a major strength in bringing "coherence and integrity" to the final report.

JDR had his "pet ideas," Westoff commented, including a desire to promote sex education and to restrict immigration. On the latter, Westoff termed JDR's views "simplistic." It is apparent, however, that JDR continued to act in a characteristic way as chairman—that is, he did not attempt to bulldoze his ideas through the Commission. The final report contained a chapter on immigration, but the brevity of treatment made it a side issue to the main business of the Commission.[25] The chapter on education included a discussion of sex education and a strong recommendation favoring "responsible" sex education in the schools. JDR never delved further into the complexities of immigration, but promoting sex education became a major interest for him in the years following the Commission's report.

As the Commission neared the deadline date for its report, the pressure of work increased tremendously. This might be judged by the final product—a report running to 186 oversized pages, organized into sixteen chapters and setting forth seventy-one recommendations. The report was also published in book form, along with seven volumes of research papers.[26] Additionally, JDR, Lelewer, and several Commission and staff members had been working for a year to find financial support for film and television versions of the final report, negotiating with HEW and soliciting funds from corporations and foundations. Toward this end, a nonprofit corporation, Population Education, Inc., was created in Washington in December 1971 as a subsidiary of the Commission. Its incorporators included the two cochairmen of the Commission, its general counsel, Lelewer, and Commission member Marilyn Chandler (wife of the publisher of the *Los Angeles Times*).

True to its mandate, the report covered an enormous range, with research, discussion, and recommendations devoted to such subjects as population distribution, migration, resources and the environment, effects on the economy and government, social aspects of population growth, human reproduction, numerous issues related to the status of women and children, population statistics and research, and policy and organizational changes. It supported the Equal Rights Amendment and called for a population office in the White House, a joint congressional committee on population, a new federal department of community development, and a national institute of population sciences.

But the core of the Commission's work dealt with population growth and the themes of "population stablization" and "the unwanted child." The Commission's demographic research made the case dramatically. If American couples limit their child-bearing to two children on the average, the population of the United States would be 300 million in the year 2015, would rise to 350 million in 2070, and be relatively stable thereafter. On the other hand, if the average is three children per family, the population would reach 400 million in 2013 and rise to nearly one billion in 2070. The report challenged the traditional notion that population growth is inherently desirable. Its basic message was that the nation has nothing to gain and everything to lose from the effects of the two-thirds billion increase in population that would result over the next century from the three-child average.[27]

Among the seventy-one recommendations were two that were to embroil the Commission in controversy, one on contraceptive information and services for teenagers and the other on abortion. Recognizing the alarming rise in pregnancies among teenagers and legal impediments to providing services to them, the Commission recommended

. . . that states adopt affirmative legislation which will permit minors to receive contraceptive and prophylactic information and services in appropriate settings sensitive to their needs and concerns.

On abortion, the Commission urged "creating a clear and positive framework for the practice of abortion on request. . . ."

with the admonition that abortion not be considered a primary means of fertility control, the Commission recommends that present state laws restricting abortion be liberalized along the lines of the New York State statute, such abortions to be performed on request by duly licensed physicians under conditions of medical safety.

In making such recommendations in the spring of 1972, a Presidential election year, the Commission was up against a vastly changed climate of opinion within the Nixon White House. Gone were the liberal impulses of the early months of the Nixon administration, and gone also was Pat Moynihan, packed off as a member of the U.S. delegation to the United Nations and then as U.S. ambassador to India. In his place was John Ehrlichman, presiding over what was now named the Domestic Council. Long-haired youth, feminist leaders, and liberals of all kinds were now the "enemy." For more than a year Vice President Spiro Agnew had been engaged in his vendetta with the mass media and the "nattering nabobs of negativism." President Nixon had implemented a wage and price freeze. He had successfully politicized the bureaucracy by placing his political operatives in positions traditionally held by career civil servants. He held the upper hand in his running battle with the Congress on a whole series of issues. He was flushed with the triumph of his famous opening to Communist China, and was successfully riding out protests over escalation of the Vietnam War. The changed attitude toward the urban problem was clear in the freeze that Nixon placed on government programs designed to assist low-income urban housing.

In all of this, Nixon was garnering political strength from a shift of opinion to the conservative side, as exemplified in the frequent references he and Agnew made to the "silent majority." His strength derived not only from the traditional areas of Republican sentiment, but also groups that normally voted Democratic, such as blue-collar workers and the Roman Catholic ethnic minorities. It was a time when political code words had unusually great power, even when the emotions they appealed to were vague and inchoate. One such theme often used by the Nixon administration was the "family" or "family values"—branding many social phenomena of the time as threats to the sanctity of the American family. In many people this touched nerves rubbed raw by fear of drugs and crime, dislike of the excesses of the youth and feminist movements, and perceptions of increased permissiveness and sexual promiscuity.

In particular, the abortion issue was white-hot, making the lives of politicians miserable. In all of 1972 there was scarcely a day in which the abortion issue was not reflected in the pages of the nation's newspapers, as reform efforts were pressed in many states along the lines of the 1970 New York statute and opposition to these efforts grew. President Nixon had already signaled his own view by blocking the practice of abortion in military hospitals. New York was becoming a caldron again as the state legislature moved ahead on a bill to repeal the 1970 law even though Governor Nelson Rockefeller said he would veto it.

In this climate, why did the Commission persist in making the two controversial recommendations? Especially in the case of abortion, the issue could have been sidestepped if, as the recommendation stated, abortion should not be considered "as a primary means of fertility control." General William Draper had made a personal appeal to JDR to do exactly that, according to David Lelewer.[28] More than anyone else, JDR was aware that President Nixon had become skittish about population issues as early as the time when the Commission was formed and JDR appointed chairman. It was then that JDR had told the President of his belief that he need not worry about the sensitivities of the Catholic Church.

In its interim report early in 1971, the Commission said it was considering such subjects as "family planning services and education, contraceptive technology, abortion and adoption," all of which posed "moral and ethical complexities."[29] Almost a year later, as the final report was taking shape, JDR met with an Ehrlichman assistant, Ray Waldman, and perceived that he "was somehow unhappy with us."

I asked him what was disturbing him. He referred to our chapter on the family which he indicated he had been informed about by a member of the Commission. He even suggested that the President might feel he had to make a statement in regard to this chapter because of what we said. This obviously concerned me greatly as it would be tragic for us to treat a key element in the population picture, such as the family, in a way that caused the President concern to the point of making a public statement.

It is clear from later diary entries that great care was taken in rewording the recommendations and the discussion of them in the final report. No chapter on "the family" appeared in the report; the two controversial recommendations were placed in a chapter entitled "Human Reproduction." Conceivably, JDR could have gone much further, using his considerable personal prestige and influence as chairman to persuade the Commission to eliminate one or both of the offending recommendations. David Lelewer's view is that JDR had no choice, that any such action would have been entirely inconsistent with his beliefs, principles, the open way in which he had tried to run the Commission, and the fact that the majority approved of both recommendations. The Commissioners were able to file dissenting statements, and these were published in the report—three against providing contraceptive advice and services to teenagers and five against the abortion recommendations.[30]

The report was made public in three sections in order to maximize publicity. JDR presided in all three press conferences—on March 10, 16, and 23—and, according to Lelewer, was "highly effective" in presenting the report and responding to questions. Press coverage and reactions to each section of the report were predominantly favorable. But there was silence from the White House.

Everyone expected some White House reaction, and those associated with the Commission were hoping it would be a positive one. In a meeting with Ehrlichman right after the final section of the report was made public, JDR said that as he understood it abortion was the only question where the President was in opposition to the report. He stressed that this "was

only one small fraction of our total effort, although an important one."
Ehrlichman, however, could give no assurances as to when or how the
President might comment on the report. As weeks passed, JDR grew
increasingly concerned and wrote several letters to the White House. The
result was that JDR and the two vice chairmen of the Commission met
with the President in the Oval Office on May 5:

He was warm and friendly and on my initiative we discussed particularly a follow-
up Citizens' Committee. He seemed to react favorably to this particularly so when
I mentioned Patrick Moynihan might have a leadership role in the Committee.
When I said we would hope to come back and see him again towards the end of
the year, he said: "That's a bargain."

JDR continued: "It was only after we left the President that we saw
the release which he put out on our report." That same morning the White
House had issued a press release with the President's comments on the
report:

I consider abortion an unacceptable form of population control. In my judgment,
unrestricted abortion policies would demean human life. I also want to make it
clear that I do not support the unrestricted distribution of family-planning services
and devices to minors.
    Such measures would do nothing to preserve and strengthen close family
relationships. . . . I have a basic faith that the American people themselves will
make sound judgments regarding family size and freqency of births.

This got the headlines, and Presidential commentary on the rest of the
report was submerged. JDR noted in his diary that the President's statement also complimented the Commission and said that its work should be
"of great value in assisting governments at all levels to formulate policy."
JDR glumly added: "This was good but somewhat buried in the total
statement."
    The next day the President's views were underscored when a letter he
had written to Terence Cardinal Cooke of New York was made public.
The letter said that the Cardinal's leadership in the effort to repeal the
liberalized New York abortion law had won the President's "admiration,
sympathy and support."[31] The letter continued:

The unrestricted abortion policies now recommended by some Americans and
the liberalized abortion policies in effect in some sections of this country seem
to me impossible to reconcile with either our religious traditions or our Western
heritage. . . . Yet, in this great and good country of ours in recent years, the

right to life of literally hundreds of thousands of unborn children has been destroyed—legally—but in my judgment without anything approaching adequate justification.

JDR saw the Presidential statements of May 5 and 6 as an effort to kill the impact of the report. A *New York Times* editorial of May 11, using some of Nixon's own words, summarized JDR's feelings exactly: "A report that addresses 'one of the most serious challenges to human destiny in the last third of this century' surely deserves a more reasoned and positive response from the Chief Executive who ordered it." David Lelewer says JDR was chagrined and bitterly disappointed by the President's actions, particularly his misleading geniality at the very moment that a release was being issued criticizing two recommendations and failing to say anything positive in specific terms about the great bulk of the Commission's work. JDR believed that if the President had discussed the report with him frankly there would have been a chance to clear up some misinterpretations in the President's statement (the report also was against abortion as a means of population control and it did not recommend "unrestricted" distribution of contraceptive services to minors).

Lelewer believes that "fifty percent of the effectiveness of the report was wiped out by the White House treating it as a political document." The impact of such a body of work, of course, cannot be measured in any exact terms, but Westoff takes an optimistic view, believing that Nixon's comments made little difference and that the Commission's work "had good educational results and the desired political impact overseas." Positive steps had already occurred as part of the general movement toward more activity in the population field, such as Nixon's wide-ranging instructions to the bureaucracy to support family planning activities, which were issued even before the Commission was formed. as well as the passage of the Family Planning Services and Population Research bill (Public Law 91–572) in 1970, which provided solid federal support and funding. Less than a year after the Commission issued its report came the Supreme Court decision (*Roe* v. *Wade*) that legalized abortion everywhere in the United States at one stroke. In her detailed book on the subject, Phyllis Piotrow observed that the national debate "deliberately stimulated" by President Nixon "seems more likely to promote than retard the commission's objectives."[32]

Characteristically undaunted, JDR moved ahead to promote public awareness of the Commission's work through Population Education, Inc. and a second nonprofit organization that was created, the Citizens Commission on Population Growth and the American Future (including a televised version of the report). With this done, it seemed for a time that JDR's contributions to the population field had peaked with his service on the Commission. But soon there were important new tasks for him to undertake.

26

♥

NEW CHALLENGES IN
POPULATION

UNEXPECTEDLY, the population field claimed a major share of JDR's time during the period when he was branching into new activities and focusing on the final disposition of his long-standing obligations. After the grueling assignment from 1970 to 1972 as chairman of the Population Commission, it seemed as if JDR had gone about as far as anyone could reasonably expect in accomplishing his goals in population and would now be in for a period of diminishing activity. This would be in line with what he was trying to do in his other commitments. In fact, it seemed a more certain course with population than in any other field of his interest.

The accomplishments, after all, had been impressive. The Population Council was a thriving organization with a worldwide reputation for excellence and leadership. Spurred by the World Leaders Statement and the UNA report, the United Nations had moved beyond research to become a major factor in population work, symbolized by the designation of 1974 as UN World Population Year. Family planning programs were in place in scores of countries around the world where none had existed less than two decades earlier. There had been dramatic growth in every aspect of the population field, including funding, the volume of biomedical and demographic research, and the numbers of trained personnel. In less than a decade, the United States had been converted from a reticent country on population matters to by far the major proponent on the world scene, and even had had the courage to examine its own population problems. Even the abortion issue seemed settled by the Supreme Court decision of 1973.

Given all of this, the argument was heard in JDR's staff meetings that perhaps he should begin to withdraw or divert to other activities the energy and resources he was committing to population, on the grounds that his influence had been towering in the beginning, but gradually had become marginal to the extent that the field had taken off.[1] The reasoning was that he had largely accomplished his goals, the Population Commission was a fitting culmination despite the Nixon coolness, and the work now could be left to others. JDR seemed to agree. Before 1972 was over, he told Barney Berelson that he was anxious to retire as chairman of the Population Council. Berelson was not happy to hear this, but agreed to begin thinking about candidates to succeed JDR.

But circumstances were not to permit it. Instead of a quiet period, there were new challenges to face, to the point that the next few years were to become the most active and intense period in JDR's career in the population field. There was a sudden and radical change in the political and economic environment as it affected population on the world scene. JDR was to make a dramatic appearance at the World Population Conference in Bucharest in 1974 in a hostile atmosphere. There was a leadership crisis at the Population Council, suddenly bringing the Council close to disintegration, and a serious rift occurred between JDR and the professional leadership of the Council as he tried to change the organization in line with the changing world situation. Instead of being resolved by *Roe v. Wade*, abortion became an increasingly bitter issue, and the White House increasingly sought to distance itself from its former high level of support for population activities.

At first there were only the obvious tasks in following through on the Population Commission report. Dave Lelewer already had had his peak experience in the field in his work in support of JDR as chairman of the Commission, and was anxious to move elsewhere to get on with the rest of his life and career. But he was committed to staying long enough to help see that the follow-through activities were well-launched through the two organizations that had been created for that purpose, the Citizens' Commission and Population Education, Inc. These included a variety of efforts to disseminate and publicize the report and the production of a ninety-minute program based on it that was aired on public television with Hugh Downs as host.[2]

The first sign of an impending managerial crisis at the Population Council occurred in May 1973 when Barney Barelson notified JDR that he would have to retire as president soon. Berelson had a heart condition and had suffered two recent setbacks. He set the Council board meeting of June 1974 as his deadline for leaving his post. JDR wrote:

However, he wants very much to stay on playing an important role but being relieved of the overall administrative responsibilities. In fact, he is at his best when he is handling special projects. Did not argue with him as we have been discussing our respective future roles in the Council for some time and realize that his conclusion is based on the most serious consideration, having in mind what is best for him as well as the Council. The problem of course will be finding a worthy successor.

At the next meeting of the board, a search committee of the board was established, chaired by Mary I. ("Polly") Bunting, former president of Radcliffe College.

Meanwhile, Lelewer had resigned, and JDR had moved quickly to find a new associate. Among the candidates he saw, Joan Dunlop soon emerged as the most attractive. Born in England, she had been working in the United States as assistant director of the Fund for the City of New York. Although sensitive about a lack of higher degrees, Dunlop was in fact a brilliant and highly articulate person, an ardent feminist with strong liberal views. Her father, Sir Maurice Banks, was a leading British businessman.[3]

JDR's old-fashioned side gave him some pause. His population aide tended to travel with him more than anyone else, and he wondered aloud in a staff meeting about the propriety of his traveling so often with a female aide. He seemed only to want reassurance, however, and the staff quickly supplied it, pointing out that such concerns were definitely a thing of the past. JDR also demurred briefly over the fact that Dunlop had no experience in the population field as such, but then recalled that he had never made that a prerequisite before. The decision made, Dunlop was welcomed on board early in 1973 by JDR and his staff.

Unknown to Berelson and Dunlop at the time, of course, and certainly not intended by either one, they were to find themselves at the opposite extremes in a struggle over the policy that JDR and the Population Council would follow in the years immediately ahead.

In mid-1972, very soon after the work of the Population Commission was finished, Berelson had begun concerning himself about what should be done to prepare for the World Population Year in 1974. His idea, as JDR described it, was that

the Population Council take the initiative in the establishment of an international commission for the study of the worldwide population problem. His thought was that the approach be modeled after our Washington Commission and that most of the basic work would be done by professionals with an overall group being appointed to meet a few times for consideration and final action. His thought is that because of the existing material that the job would not be really as difficult as our Commission's effort.

Berelson intended that the task would be completed in time for the World Population Conference in August 1974. JDR wrote that he was "intrigued" with the idea, but added: "I personally am inclined to feel that maybe the creation of the Commission should flow from that meeting." A series of meetings occurred over the next six months to discuss the idea, JDR and Berelson consulting with Lord Caradon of the United Kingdom, Philippe de Seynes and Rafael Salas of the UN, Antonio Carillo Flores, a Mexican who had been appointed Secretary General of the World Population Conference, and Maurice Strong, a Canadian who had played the same role for the 1972 UN Environmental Conference in Stockholm. The discussions ranged over whether a report should contain specific recommendations or background information, and whether it should be scholarly or popular in style.

Sensing that time was passing him by before he could achieve any consensus or focus, Berelson shifted to the idea of what he called a "Population Manifesto," a document that would set forth convictions and policy regarding population growth. His idea was that the support of the fifteen most populous nations in the world be sought for this. Berelson recognized that the Soviet Union and the People's Republic of China, at the least, would not agree, but he still felt that the effort should be made. Berelson's hundred-page first draft of a possible "manifesto" touched off another round of discussions. JDR's staff felt the document was too long and erudite, and various shorter drafts were attempted. For a time, JDR favored trying another World Leaders Statement, but Caradon advised against this on the grounds that it would be difficult to do better than the last time. The idea was discussed of seeking signatories from leading citizens rather than heads of state.

Finally, at a meeting of JDR, Berelson, and Dunlop in September 1973, it was agreed to drop the effort. JDR wrote that he was "not too excited about what Barney has put together" and JDR's thought of another World Leaders Statement did "not appeal too much to Barney at this point."

However, Berelson's drafting efforts were of value to him in working with the UN people who were planning the 1974 Population Conference. They had decided to create a "Draft World Plan of Action" to be considered at the conference, and Berelson, who by this time had built a towering reputation as a thinker and scholar in the population field, was the chief resource to them in preparing it.

Meanwhile, as Joan Dunlop was completing her first year as JDR's population aide, it was clear that something new was happening. She was developing major activities that were peripheral to the interests of the

Population Council, but not to JDR. This was an element in a divergence between JDR and the professional leadership of the Council that was to develop into a serious breach over the next several years.

As discussed earlier, the relationship between this prominent lay leader and the great professional organization he had created was always sensitive to a degree, and required some tact, intelligence, and forbearance on both sides. Each benefited—JDR's prominence was due in considerable measure to the success of the Council, and it in turn profited greatly from his stature and support. It would not be correct to say that the Council controlled JDR—he was too much of an independent spokesman in his own right. But it was very important to such professionals as Frank Notestein and Barney Berelson to keep JDR generally in their orbit and prevent him from going off too far on tangents. It will be recalled that Berelson originally conceived of the idea of the World Leaders Statement as a means of keeping JDR busy in a way that would be broadly supportive of the Council's interests. JDR had been the prime initiator of the Population Commission, but the Council was an important resource and Berelson played a crucial role in the effort. Again, the process was mutually supportive rather than divergent. JDR's previous population aides, Lamontagne and Lelewer, worked assiduously to keep the relationship a smooth one, and in this sense they were as valuable to the Council as they were to JDR. Both also had other interests. Lamontagne at one time or another worked on almost everything that was going on in JDR's office, and Lelewer spent a share of his time in JDR's youth activities.

With Dunlop it was different. As her two predecessors had before her, she became secretary to the Board of the Population Council and engaged in normal liaison work. But she was engaged *only* in population-related activities, and some of them, from Berelson's point of view, amounted to JDR and Dunlop following their own agenda, something he increasingly came to regard as deviant and threatening.

There were three major activities on that agenda. One of them Dunlop developed herself, brought to JDR's attention, and found him to be an enthusiastic advocate. The subject came to be known generically as "the role and status of women in development." In part, its discovery was a reflex of the American feminist movement—a concern for the plight of the great majority of women in the world, primarily in developing societies, who were bound by centuries of tradition to a subordinate status. As the analysis ran, if tradition or custom or religion keeps women in a situation where the only way they can succeed in life is to bear children, then they will continue to bear children and population will increase. The related theme of women's rights is obvious. And there is also a related development theme: to the extent that opportunities for training and education and careers become open to women, the human resources for the development process will increase.

Among proponents of this point of view, one realization that introduced almost a note of anger was the fact that students of the development process had previously ignored the subject. It was, in fact, a new concept, an undeveloped field, and there was a need not only to raise consciousness about it, but to generate research.

Dunlop found an ally who thought alike in Adrienne Germain of the Ford Foundation. Sondra Zeidenstein, wife of the Ford Foundation representative in Bangladesh, had written several papers on the role and status of women in developing societies. Abe Weisblat of the Agriculture Development Council began to develop research and seminars on the subject. Another ally was Steve Salyer, one of the youth members of the Population Commission, who became a consultant to JDR and Dunlop. Also, Gerald Barney of the Rockefeller Brothers Fund took an interest in the subject. But Dunlop initially found no response from the Population Council.

The second major activity Dunlop worked on was all JDR's—sex education, a subject he had been concerned about for years, from his interest in "new values," his *Look* magazine article, and his support of Mary Calderone and SIECUS, to his attempt to make it a major topic for the Population Commission. JDR did not drop his support of SIECUS, but he was looking for something more. SIECUS had its limitations, both in its orthodox informational approach and in the fact that it had become wounded by years of constant right-wing attacks. JDR and Dunlop agreed that a new and different approach was needed. After investigating the subject for some six months, including a visit to the Masters and Johnson clinic, Dunlop brought in Elizabeth Roberts as a consultant in January 1974, and they proceeded to develop a plan that JDR approved.

The result was the "Project on Human Sexual Development," with Roberts as executive director. Its nonprofit corporate home was Population Education, Inc., which had no other function once the effort involving the televised version of the Population Commission's report ended. As is often the case with such new programs, an academic base was sought and found in the Harvard School of Education, whose dean, Paul Ylvisaker, had been a member of JDR's "youth task force." Roberts, a Ph.D. candidate in philosophy at Marquette University, formerly had been head of the Children's Television Unit of the Federal Communications Commission.

A high-level advisory group was formed, including Joan Ganz Cooney of the famed Children's Television Workshop (creator of "Sesame Street"), Stephen Hess of the Brookings Institution, Stephen Hirsch of the National

Institute of Mental Health, Jerry Rossow of Exxon (whose productivity project JDR had supported), Homer Wadsworth, director of the Greater Cleveland Foundation, and John Gagnon, sociology professor at the Stony Brook campus of the State University of New York. It was Gagnon whose research and writings provided the intellectual base for the approach—the view that the main determinants of human sexual behavior are more a product of the social environment than biological considerations, as in the Freudian approach. In Roberts's words, the purpose was to "define goals and mechanisms . . . that would provide a framework of fresh thinking and focused discussion in the areas of sexuality and sex education."

The overall effort broke down into three areas: a continuing research and publication program known as the "Special Studies Series," a program of research and workshop discussions with television executives on the effects of television on the relationship between gender roles and sexual behavior and development, and the "Cleveland Pilot Program," billed as a "major empirical study of sexual learning in the home and ways that community resources do and could affect the process." In its level of research, the last project was reminiscent of the Kinsey studies, though focused on one community. It was supported by the Greater Cleveland Foundation and the Carnegie Corporation, as well as JDR. Over a period of four years, JDR's contributions in support of the Project on Human Sexual Development approximated $760,000.[4]

If Dunlop was the initiator on the subject of the role of women and JDR on sex education, the third major activity, involving abortion, was the result of a situation no one could have foreseen. It resulted from the 1973 *Roe* v. *Wade* decision of the Supreme Court, which legalized abortion, and the firestorm of criticism that followed, spearheaded by certain religious groups and the "right-to-life" movement. From the moment the latter developed, JDR and Dunlop spent many hours in meetings over a period of years trying to figure out ways to influence public opinion in favor of the Supreme Court decision and the so-called pro-choice position.

The tension between Dunlop and Berelson first began to surface during the work to prepare for the World Population Conference, scheduled to be held in Bucharest during the final two weeks of August 1974. This was to be the first such conference involving official government delegations, in contrast to the two previous UN population conferences, in Rome in 1954 and Belgrade in 1965, which had been nongovernmental in character. Initially it had been proposed that the 1974 conference be held in New York, but so prominent had the United States become in promoting population activities that resistance developed within the UN to an "American-staged conference," and the venue was shifted to Romania. The U.S. Agency for International Development (AID) was spending more on foreign assistance for population than the UN and all the other donor countries of the world put together. Its support of the UN Fund for Population Activities (UNFPA) was at the level of 50 percent, contrasted to overall American support of the UN of 25 percent.

As the chairman of the recently concluded Population Commission, JDR was an obvious choice to head the U.S. delegation to Bucharest, were it not for the divergence that had developed between his views and those of the Nixon administration. JDR's staff counseled him to avoid governmental status on the grounds that his ability to speak his views would be constrained by official policy. Instead, he was advised to attend the conference as a private citizen. It happened that the plan for Bucharest called for a "Population Tribune" to hold sessions concurrently with those of the official conference. The Tribune was intended as an outlet for all of the nongovernmental organizations (NGOs) in the population field. Chairing one session of the Tribune was Carmen Miro, a highly regarded scholar in population, a Panamanian who headed the UN-supported International Review Group of Social Science Research on Population and Development (CELADE) in Mexico City. An invitation soon came from Miro to JDR to be one of five speakers in a "distinguished lecture series" as a feature in the program of the Tribune. His assigned topic was "Population Growth: A View from the Developed World." At first JDR was concerned that this might be too limiting, but then it was realized that no matter what he said JDR inescapably was a representative of the developed world, and, in fact, could say anything he wished.

In the spirit of the times, there were other events scheduled for Bucharest: an International Youth Population Conference and an "Encounter for Journalists," both to precede the conference proper. Through the Pathfinder Fund, JDR contributed $10,000 to the Youth Conference and $12,000 to the meeting of journalists.

In due course, the official U.S. delegation was announced. Chairing it was HEW Secretary Caspar Weinberger, and the vice chairman was Russell Peterson, chairman of the Council on Environmental Quality. The other three members were Philander Claxton of the State Department, General William Draper, and Patricia Hutar, U.S. representative on the UN Commission on the Status of Women.

Dunlop took the initiative in working on JDR's speech, using Adrienne Germain, Steve Salyer, and Gerald Barney as consultants. Berelson began reacting to drafts and submitting his own versions. The work continued intermittently for several months with Dunlop's group dividing the labor—she doing a section on the role of women, Salver on the development process, and Barney on economic growth. As time passed, JDR began to be concerned about the lack of an overall framework and the problem of stitching the sections together. Also a concern was the rising tension between Berelson and the Dunlop group, Berelson wanting a speech that followed the approach of the Draft World Plan of Action, straightforwardly supporting direct work on birth rates, while the Dunlop group wanted to put population activities within the context of the overall development process.

The background of this growing dispute was the changing world environment of opinion regarding population, something the Dunlop group was more attuned to than Berelson. The mood in the Third World had become much more akin to the strident anti-Western tone of the 1950s and the time of the Bandung Conference than to the decade of the 1960s when there was widespread receptivity for foreign assistance programs, including, as we have seen, the remarkable growth of family planning activities. The new mood was marked by a high level of hostility toward the United States in particular, something that would be confirmed by any American who, from the early 1970s on, served as a delegate to almost any of the hundreds of international conferences held each year. All through this period, the role of the American delegates often was reduced to enduring a steady stream of verbal abuse.

In part, the new mood was a reaction to American involvement in the Vietnam War, but perhaps even more important was a new level of anger over what leaders in many developing societies regarded as an inequitable distribution of wealth and income among nations. For a time, pride was taken in the Third World in the formation of the Organization of Petroleum Exporting Countries (OPEC) and its successful oil embargo, seemingly a more effective means of fighting back against Western economic domination than verbal abuse—although, of course, it turned out that it was the energy-poor developing societies that were hardest hit. The new mood, sometimes styled as "North versus South," had been building for some time. It was evident at the 1972 Environmental Conference, and became explicit at the Sixth Special Session of the UN General Assembly in 1974, which adopted a "Declaration of the Establishment of a New International Economic Order" and called on all UN activities, including the World Population Conference, to contribute to it. This raised the danger that the Bucharest conference would become sharply politicized, given the fact that the United States, with some 6 to 7 percent of the world's population, was consuming 30 percent of its resources, and yet had become the leading actor on the world scene in telling developing societies to limit their populations.

Although some observers of the Bucharest conference were surprised at the extent to which political factors dominated,[5] there were enough intimations of it to condition the thinking of those helping JDR prepare his speech. But the directions taken by the Dunlop group did not stem so much from a desire to cater to that new mood as they did from a conviction that the question of economic growth had to be addressed, that family planning had to be placed solidly in a development context, and that the role of women was an important new consideration. Moreover, to the extent that the development context was stressed, the rationale for including the subject of the role of women was strengthened. Berelson held no brief for that topic, and stuck to his advocacy of straightforward support of the Draft World Plan of Action, which gave more emphasis to "affecting demographic variables" (family planning) in its key Paragraph 27 than to the development context.

The effort was still stalemated by June, but had reached the point where the speechwriting "doctor" was needed to work on the final draft with JDR. As always, the result was what JDR wanted, and it was more partial to the Dunlop group's views than Berelson's. There was a final session with Berelson as JDR described in his diary:

Had another long session in regard to the Bucharest talk with our group and Barney Berelson present. He started out expressing real unhappiness about it but, when we pressed him in discussion about my five principal points, it did not seem to me we were really too far apart. In any event the discussion was helpful and will, I think, lead to some rewriting by Jack Harr of the first half of the talk.

Accompanying JDR on the trip to Bucharest were his wife, Blanchette, and Porter McKeever. Also in Bucharest were Joan Dunlop, Gerald Barney, Steven Salyer, and Adrienne Germain. Wade Greene, former social sciences editor of the *Saturday Review*, was recruited as a free-lance writer with the thought that a magazine article might result from the experience.[6] JDR wrote in his diary that he hoped to make the trip in every respect as a private citizen, but that was dashed when the Tarom (Romanian) Airlines flight landed at Bucharest. The plane was loaded with Romanians returning home from Brussels, carrying goods and filling the aisles. The Rockefellers were paged on the intercom. McKeever told a stewardess that they did not want to be identified, but was told in return that no one would be allowed to leave the aircraft until the Rockefellers alighted for an official reception. Having no choice, they acquiesced. Next they found

themselves, "unfortunately," JDR wrote, in the Imperial Suite of the Inter-
continental Hotel "which, as always is the case, was not exactly to our
taste, primarily because of size." A measure of the climate of the conference was the prevalence of rumors that JDR would be assassinated, with
the result that Romanian plainclothesmen were amply in evidence wherever he went in Bucharest, to many official receptions and an audience
with President Nicolae Ceauşescu.

The tone of the conference immediately became militantly anti-Western. The preceding youth meeting had been chaotic and radical. A poll
of the official delegations revealed that twenty-one nations thought their
population growth rate was too low, eight (including the United States)
were "satisfied," and forty-two were candid enough to admit that their
population growth was "excessive." The Draft World Plan of Action was
being roundly attacked in plenary sessions. The debate was polarized, as
JDR described it, between

those who believe family planning should be the focus of national effort and those
who feel that if sound development efforts are undertaken, family planning no
longer needs to be a source of concern. My thinking lies between, the emphasis
being on merging the two, with family planning always a big element.

The Algerian and Argentine delegations led the drive to convert the
conference to a plea for the "New International Economic Order." The
most militant delegation came from the People's Republic of China, which
said that the purpose of the conference was "to carry on and develop
the militant spirit of combating the imperialism and hegemonism of the
superpowers" instead of finding means to reduce birth rates. Despite tension with Red China, the Soviet Union and its satellites also supported
the African and Latin American delegations. An unlikely ally was the Vatican, whose delegation head said: "The egoism of the rich plays a greater
part in the formidable social inequality of today than the fertility of the
poor." The dilemma confronting the American delegation was described
by the AUFS observer in Bucharest:

America's promotion of global control of population growth, given a studied unwill-
ingness of United States diplomats to admit that their nation is by far the greatest
per capita consumer of world resources, and in light of the decidedly smug American presentation at Bucharest, smacked of hypocrisy to many delegates. In the
extreme view, America was championing population control as a means for maintaining a world where Americans could continue their high consumption patterns.
At the same time, it was alleged that the United States was attempting to divert
the attention of leaders in the developing nations from such things as economic

development, increasing industrial and agricultural productivity, and international monetary and trade structures that are presently advantageous to the United States.[7]

It was only a few days before the end of the two-week conference when JDR made his appearance on the speaker's rostrum of the Tribune at the Faculty of Law building of the University of Bucharest before a capacity audience of more than three hundred. There had been quite a buildup of interest in what this American capitalist would say, a man who seemed the personification of Western wealth and privilege to many attendees. The atmosphere was "decidedly hostile," recalls Porter McKeever, not unlike the tense weekend when JDR spoke to the students at Hampshire College. And, as on that occasion, McKeever said, JDR "charmed and disarmed them" by the time he had finished.

JDR started off on a personal note, saying it would be "presumptuous" for him to try to speak for the developed countries, that he could only speak "as a citizen of one such country who is deeply interested in population." He recalled that his interest had begun forty years earlier, in 1934, when he had written a letter to his father saying that population was the field in which he wanted to "concentrate my own giving." He reviewed the growth of the field from the time when it could scarcely be discussed all the way to the convening of a great world conference. He touched on his own involvement—launching the Population Council, the World Leaders Statement, the U.S. Population Commission. In all that time, he said, there were only "two convictions on which I have never altered my view." One, as he wrote in 1934 to his father, "is that the population problem is 'fundamental and underlying,' absolutely critical to the well-being and future of the human race." The other "is that our objective is the enrichment of human life, not its restriction." JDR drove the point home: "There is only one reason for concerning ourselves about population—to improve the quality of people's lives, to help make it possible for individuals everywhere to develop their full potential."

Then came the crux of the speech—JDR's admission that he had changed his mind in certain respects as he, like many others, learned "how difficult and complex" the population field really is. He then made it clear where he was heading. He said he had long concentrated on the family planning approach, but that "the evidence has been mounting, particularly in the past decade, to indicate that family planning alone is not enough." JDR stated emphatically that he was not being "negative about family planning." Rather, he said:

I now strongly believe that the only viable course is to place population policy solidly within the context of general economic and social development in such manner that it will be accepted at the highest levels of government and adequately supported. This approach recognizes that rapid population growth is only one among many problems facing most countries, that it is a multiplier and intensifier of other problems rather than the cause of them. It recognizes that reducing population is not an alternative to development, but an essential part of it for most countries. And, it recognizes that motivation for family planning is best stimulated by hope that living conditions and opportunities in general will improve.

The balance of the speech was devoted to a reasoned discussion of the nature and moral purpose of "modern" development, as contrasted to the Western experience of the industrial revolution, which JDR argued was not relevant to the developing societies of today. He said the first task of the developed countries was clear: "to stabilize their own populations and moderate their levels of consumption in a sensible and orderly way." He added:

At the same time, I strongly believe that the developed nations must strive to understand the new and different characteristics of modern development, become more sensitive to the fact that each nation must solve its development and fertility problems in its own way, and stand ready to assist substantially in that process.

In defining "modern development," JDR called for "new and urgent attention to the role of women as a vital characteristic." He said: "In my opinion, if we are to make genuine progress in economic and social development, if we are to make progress in achieving population goals, women increasingly must have greater freedom of choice in determining their roles in society." In the light of all that he had said, JDR called for a "deep and probing reappraisal of all that has been done in the population field, all that has been learned, so that the years ahead may yield the results mankind so desperately wants."

Although there were some hostile comments in the question-and-answer period that followed, JDR's speech was a resounding success. It was the talk of the conference for several days and was billed prominently in the daily conference newspaper. It is not likely that it had any effect on the official proceedings, although the long-term view of observers is that the Draft World Plan of Action, despite all the rhetoric, political extremism, and amending, survived rather well. The approach JDR advocated, comprehensive and moderate in tone, prevailed rather than either extreme. At the end of the conference, Secretary Weinberger said that the view of the American delegation was that both family planning and development were important: "We think the draft Plan of Action represents both in a sensible balance."[8]

Reminiscing years after the speech was made, Charles Westoff, head of the Office of Population Research at Princeton and executive director of the U.S. Population Commission, called it "a political tour de force."[9] But if the speech was approved by many and had been a success in Bucharest, it was decidedly unpopular among the professional leaders of the Population Council. Notestein, now retired but still a board member, termed it "a disaster," too much in the "crisis mentality" that JDR had always shunned before. Berelson had muted his criticisms only because he feared they were becoming counterproductive, but he was bitter about the speech. Dunlop knew this. Just before the Bucharest conference she sent a copy of JDR's draft to Population Council board member Polly Bunting, and wrote: "I'm afraid Barney is very unhappy with this. He has as much as said that JDR has no right to deliver it without policy discussion at the Council board level. Perhaps it might provoke that and maybe that would be a contribution."[10]

It is not easy to understand these sentiments from a content analysis of the speech itself. Berelson and Notestein certainly would not have disagreed that population policy must be intimately associated with the development process. Rather, Berelson seems to have been offended by the shift in emphasis in JDR's speech, by the inclusion of the role of women, and by the fact that JDR came close to saying that the concentration on family planning had been a mistake. But the intensity of discontent can only be explained by emotional factors, not rational ones. Berelson was offended most of all by having been edged out as counselor to JDR by Dunlop and her group, and that led him to bitter expressions of resentment. "John's understanding of population was not nearly as sophisticated and soundly based as the professionals in the field," Berelson said. "He tended to be inhibited by his experts, so the only way he could shift gears was to get new advisers. He got tired of the old ones. He needed change. It just happened that Joan Dunlop was his latest adviser."

Notestein was even more vocal on the subject. He found it difficult to refer to Dunlop in any other way except as "that woman." He said: "She violated the liaison role with the Population Council developed by McLean, Lamontagne, and Lelewer. These men represented John to the Council, but also represented the views of the Council officers to John. She turned this into a one-way street, trying to impose her views and those of John which had been developed in isolation." To Berelson and Notestein, Dunlop's approach smacked of "radical chic," and worse, she was getting her advice from nonprofessionals. To them, Adrienne Germain was a radical feminist, Steve Salyer was a fuzzy-cheeked youth, and Gerald Barney was an unknown.[11]

Berelson and Notestein believed that JDR had become the captive of Dunlop and her youthful group of advisers, but no one else who worked in JDR's office would agree with that. Her style was to be more aggressive and closely held than had been the norm in JDR's office, but this was the product of intensity and strong beliefs. By no means did she always have her way with JDR. Frequently she expressed frustration at her inability to get him to agree or move ahead on something. At the same time, she could be conservative in moving ahead, too. The idea grew up that JDR should make a major policy speech on the role of women in development. In JDR's staff meetings, Bill Ruder had appointed himself as the keeper of the agenda and conscience of the group. Frequently he would ask what had happened to the "role of women" speech. Dunlop would respond that more had to be learned about the subject. For example, she made a lengthy field trip to Bangladesh and attended the UN Conference on the Status of Women in Mexico City in 1975. Over a period of two years Ruder kept bringing up the "role of women" speech (as well as other projects that were unfulfilled). Finally, Robert McNamara of the World Bank made a speech on the subject and JDR was preempted.

The growing rift between JDR's office and the Council was caused by changing conditions and what JDR felt he had to do to respond to them, not through any devious plot of Joan Dunlop's. In the year leading up to the Bucharest conference, JDR had become convinced that both he and the Population Council needed to adapt to new circumstances. Berelson resisted that and retreated into his professionalism in a way that bordered on arrogance. In contrast, Dunlop was an effective agent, not so much in imposing her views on JDR but in achieving changes that he wanted.

This become even more clear in the leadership crisis that beset the Council. Berelson's discontent became dysfunctional in the months following Bucharest. His glumness permeated the thinking of the senior people at the Council—W. Parker Mauldin, director of the demographic division; Sheldon Segal, director of the biomedical division; Clifford Pease, director of the technical assistance division; and Paul Demeny, the brilliant Hungarian-born demographer whom Berelson had lured to the Council from the East-West Center in Hawaii. Dunlop said these men now felt JDR had "sold them out" at Bucharest. JDR was concerned enough to meet with the four men and explain his approach and his intentions. He did this so well that Dunlop began to fear that he was "backtracking" on the position he had taken at Bucharest.[12]

By this time it had become clear that the Council was in trouble. The staff was demoralized, and there was a general feeling of drift. Sensing this, some of the major donors to the Council began to cut back on their annual contributions. The Council's annual rate of expenditures began a slow slide, from a high of $17.7 million in 1972 to a low of $11 million in 1976. One reason was that as major projects were concluded not enough new ones were in the pipeline to replace them, but this was a management failure, in itself a sign of malaise within the organization. The main problem was the lack of a firm hand at the top. It will be recalled that for reasons of health Berelson had notified the board in May 1973 that he wanted to leave his post as president no later than June 1974. In the fall of the latter year he was still serving, but his leadership had slipped, a combination of ill health, the fact that it was known he would be leaving, consequent uncertainty about the future, Berelson's reluctance to sponsor change efforts, and his frustration over the rift with JDR's office.

The Bunting committee had gone to work energetically in 1973 to find a replacement for Berelson. Consideration had been given to the ranking officers of the Council—Mauldin, Segal, Pease, Demeny—but the prevailing view was that to elevate one of these men would be to give too much ascendancy to the specialized division he had come from. Many other candidates were considered, with the committee vacillating over whether it wanted a generalist or a professional in the population field. Finally the committee thought it had its solution in going for the biggest "star" it could find in the person of David Hopper, director of the International Development Research Centre since its inception in 1970. Hopper had established an impressive reputation by building the IDRC, the Canadian government research and grant-giving organization, into a respected force in the international development assistance field.

The committee placed Hopper at the top of their list. Although his Ph.D. was in agricultural economics at Cornell, Hopper was interested in the development assistance field broadly, and the IDRC was an important factor in the population field. Hopper had been a member of the Population Council board since 1971. Notestein and Berelson could not question Hopper's credentials, and Dunlop was for him. On February 24, 1974, JDR flew up to Ottawa to spend the day with Hopper and his wife. JDR was impressed by Hopper's "knowledge and his imaginative and really far-reaching approach," but, ironically, he was concerned that Hopper's development interests were so broad that they "might unduly pull him away from population issues." He also found Hopper appearing to set conditions that could not be met. Hopper thought the Population Council should have an endowment of $100 million. In his diary JDR wryly commented: "I agreed as to the desirability but questioned the feasibility."

Hopper also said he would want his wife to work with him as an officer of the Council, and he talked about salary needs in a way that gave JDR some concern. "He pressed this last very hard " JDR wrote.

A sort of stalemate ensued with other candidates being reviewed and Hopper still in the background if a way could be found for the Council to afford him. In a memorandum to JDR on May 30, Dunlop began to enter the picture with a viewpoint that in time would further raise the hackles of Notestein and Berelson. She wrote that 'good candidates were not emerging," and that the composition of the search committee should be broadened: "We need to broaden the context, contacts, and imagination of the Committee to go beyond the academic world."

Nothing happened for a time as the Bucharest conference occupied everyone's attention, but soon after it JDR was sufficiently concerned about the sense of drift to call a special meeting of the Council's board on October 7, 1974. He had talked to Berelson beforehand to persuade him to step aside and let Parker Mauldin take over as acting president while the search for a permanent president continued. This was ratified at the meeting, with Berelson becoming president emeritus and senior fellow of the Council and Paul Demeny succeeding Mauldin as director of the Demographic Division. JDR's other ploy was approved, also—the appointing of a "program review committee" with David Hopper as chairman. In his diary, JDR made it clear what he was after:

I initiated the meeting as a post-Bucharest move to assure that the Council maintains its leadership position in the population field. . . . Under Hopper's leadership, believe that the review committee will do an imaginative and effective job. Also, am hopeful that as a result of the review efforts, we may end up with a new president.

However, the results were not what JDR hoped for. First, of course, the search committee went into hibernation—there was no point proposing candidates until the Hopper report was delivered. In fact, Polly Bunting was a member of Hopper's committee. Then when the report was presented at the Council's June 1975 meeting it contained a surprise. Instead of enticing Hopper to want to take the presidency of the Council, his inquiry made him all the more concerned about the malaise of the organization and its inability to find a focus in the post-Bucharest atmosphere. His prescription was a radical one—splitting the Council into three specialized organizations based on the three existing divisions (biomedical, demographic, and technical assistance). This was discussed soberly for two days and then was referred to the officers of the Council for comment. In a report to the executive committee in September, the four division directors unanimously stated their opinion that the Council should remain as a single entity.[13]

JDR was growing increasingly concerned over all the confusion following Bucharest and wrote in his diary about the need for "basic and in-depth study and thought" on the directions that should be taken in the population field and on the Council's role: "This kind of approach is certainly what was in mind when the Council was created, and I think people are looking to it for guidance and leadership." But that clearly could not happen until a new president was found. It was now more than two years since Berelson had signified his intention to resign, and the Council was still essentially leaderless, although JDR expressed in his diary his admiration for the way that Mauldin was handling himself "in a very difficult situation."

In an effort to get some motion, JDR had decided on another tack in the search for a president. As the conclusion of the June 1975 meeting when the Hopper report was reviewed, JDR told the trustees that every-one now should take responsibility in seeking candidates for the presidency and that the effort should be coordinated through Joan Dunlop. At the end of June he met with Dunlop and they agreed "that she must now concentrate on an all-out basis on the finding of a new president."

Dunlop began canvassing the prospects. Parker Mauldin suggested a name to her—George Zeidenstein, head of the Ford Foundation program in Bangladesh. This caused Dunlop to take a close look at the Ford residents abroad and to invite several to New York for interviews. Zeidenstein had very little knowledge of what had been going on in the Council when he met with JDR and Dunlop in August 1975, but he said all the right things. This came from conviction, not homework. He believed that popu-lation should be viewed as a sector of development, and he had made the first grants at the Ford Foundation for research on the role and status of women in developing societies. There was another reason why JDR was impressed with Zeidenstein—he was an uncommonly dedicated man. A graduate of the Harvard Law School, Zeidenstein had a promising legal career in New York City when he took time out in the summer of 1964 to go to the South as a volunteer lawyer in voter registration. That changed his life—he decided he could not spend his days in private law practice. He joined the Peace Corps and became country representative in Nepal until 1969. Then he went with the Ford Foundation, serving as deputy director of the Asia and Pacific Division in New York until 1972, when he took his post in Bangladesh, following the partition of Pakistan.

There followed some checking of references, and then JDR and Dunlop knew they had their man. JDR made it his business to brief the top staff members of the Council and found them generally "wary" because so few knew Zeidenstein. A special meeting of the board was called on October 22, and JDR and Dunlop proposed Zeidenstein for the presidency. This provoked a stormy discussion. As JDR described it: "Frank Notestein led off, indicating that he felt the appointment would be disastrous for the future of the Council. His concern is the lack of credentials and the lack of proven record relating to population." Others voiced opposition, including Berelson, Detlev Bronk, Don McLean, who had returned to the board in 1974 as chairman of the executive committee, and Sissela Bok, professor of ethics at Radcliffe College and wife of the president of Harvard. JDR wrote: "Mrs. Bok could not believe [Zeidenstein] had never published anything." Several other academics expressed the same concern, but Dr. Robert Ebert, dean of the Harvard Medical School, supported Zeidenstein. Aside from JDR, he had been the only board member to have an opportunity to interview the candidate before he returned to his post in Bangladesh. JDR described how he and Dunlop responded to the negative view:

We made our case, so to speak, primarily in terms of the man and what he had to offer, believing that it was what the Population Council needs now. We said that we felt that the fact that he was somewhat "offbeat," that his record did not fit into any category, maybe were factors of strength in terms of our needs at this time rather than the reverse. We said, too, that we recognized that there were gaps in his experience but that they were more than offset by the nature of his work over the years and his personal qualities.

The vote was taken with eleven trustees supporting the nominee, Berelson and Notestein opposing, and Detlev Bronk and Sissela Bok abstaining. Soon after the meeting, Notestein resigned from the board. JDR came to the conclusion that Berelson should resign, too, feeling that his presence would prove difficult for the new president. JDR discussed this at lunch with Berelson a few weeks later, and Berelson said he could understand the point since he was the past president, he was well established in the field, and Zeidenstein could not fail to learn that Berelson had voted against him. But Berelson added that he thought he should work out the relationship with Zeidenstein personally and that he had no thought of resigning now.

At the end of the year JDR met with Berelson to discuss the situation again. JDR said that in his experience it "was customary for the retiring president to withdraw from the scene as his successor took over. I said my understanding was that this meant physical presence as well as Board membership." In response, Berelson handed JDR a one-sentence letter of resignation from the board effective January 1, 1976, and then asked if

JDR wanted him to resign from the staff as well. JDR did not answer directly, merely saying that the situation was complicated, and Berelson said bitterly that he did not need JDR to tell him what he should do, that he was sensitive to the situation and would work it out with Zeidenstein. He added that if he resigned it probably would be more hurtful to the Council than him. JDR described how they parted:

When he left he obviously went away very unhappy, especially in relation to me. When at one point in the discussion I mentioned I felt sad that our personal relationship might be hurt, he indicated that it already had been. Obviously, too, he felt very strongly in relation to Joan Dunlop, believing, I gathered, that her influence had appreciably affected my decision in connection with the appointment of Zeidenstein. We agreed as he left that there was nothing further that could usefully be said in this conversation. . . . The whole situation makes me really sad.

Zeidenstein arrived from Bangladesh to take over as president on February 1, 1976, soon learning the full dimensions of what he had to do—overcome doubts and resentments, rebuild morale, raise money, and redefine the mission of the Council. He met with Berelson and urged him to stay on as senior fellow. JDR showed some signs of vacillating, as he sometimes did when he staked out a position and then was not sure how it was going to work out. As he had in the case of Hopper, he began to worry that Zeidenstein was too broadly concerned with development: "In a way he seems to think of the population problem as relating almost entirely to poverty."

This and other concerns were soon put to rest by Zeidenstein's performance. He went to work to produce a master plan entitled "Future Directions of the Population Council," which he presented for review to the board in June 1976. He stressed that "a concern for human welfare must underlie all of the Council's programmatic efforts," and he placed those efforts solidly within the context of development:

The Council has had a specialized concern with population, and "population" still describes something that is a major cause and consequence of development although its boundaries appear less distinct today than they did a few years ago. Population as a discrete element in understanding and influencing the development process should remain as the organizing focus of our work.

But there is an urgent need for new concepts and approaches in our field. More and more we see how intertwined the different threads of development are. . . .

Zeidenstein wrote about the two basic functions of the Council—scientific inquiry to develop new knowledge and services to foster utilization of knowledge—in a way that appeared to give slight emphasis to the former.

The result was something that would have surprised the trustees who objected to his appointment because he lacked scientific credentials and had never published—the Council was to become more of a research organization than ever before. In line with this, Zeidenstein said the Council should "with modesty" seek the "role of intellectual leader, synthesist, and catalyst in the population field." Organizationally, his prescription for achieving this was to reject the idea of splintering the Council, and instead to create two research centers within it, one for biomedical research and the other for "policy research." The latter would replace the demographic division—it would still do demographic studies, but would also broaden its focus to study development processes, interrelationships, and such selected topics as the roles and status of women.

Zeidenstein also called for both the board and staff of the Council to become "substantially more international" and for its decision-making to become "more decentralized." He cited "the immense and critical task" of broadening and increasing its financial base, and called for increased board involvement.

The board approved the document, and the effects soon began to be noticed. The two centers were created, with Paul Demeny placed in charge of the Center for Policy Research. Zeidenstein began to display skills that might not have been anticipated from his background—the skills of the manager. The internal personnel and budgeting processes of the Council were streamlined. An aggressive fund-raising campaign was launched, as well as efforts to find board and staff candidates from other countries. The Council's journal, *Population and Development Review*, improved steadily to become recognized as one of the premier scholarly journals in any field, and population clearly remained as "the organizing focus." Zeidenstein provided the much-needed firm hand at the top, but in a way that gave staff members room to grow and develop, with the result that morale improved steadily.

Within a year after Zeidenstein took over, JDR felt secure enough to proceed with what he had first tried to do five years earlier—resign as chairman. He and Zeidenstein agreed on their candidate for successor, Dean Ebert of the Harvard Medical School. Ebert became vice chairman at the June 1977 meeting, and succeeded JDR at the December meeting. JDR remained on the board as trustee and chairman emeritus. Also at the meeting, Zeidenstein's plan was ratified for launching a $25 million capital fund-raising campaign, in addition to regular fund-raising for annual expenditures. JDR was dubious that this goal could be attained, but he went along.

JDR met with Berelson several times, including what he referred to in his diary as a "reconciliation lunch." He had reason to be glad that had happened when word came in the spring of 1977 that Berelson had suffered a major setback in his heart condition. Berelson remained as a senior fellow, but had now become homebound.

Zeidenstein had known Berelson casually in previous years as a hearty and gregarious man, but found him to be decidedly cool in their relationship after Zeidenstein took over. In contrast, Notestein, who could be very austere and cold when he chose to, warmed up considerably for one who had feared in 1975 that the Council was "in mortal jeopardy." His final judgment was that he had come to respect Zeidenstein, that the scholarly base of the Council had been maintained and strengthened, and that the changed directions that the Council had taken in the difficult period of the mid- and late 1970s had been the right ones after all. Indeed, it appeared to be so. By 1983, for example, Zeidenstein had brought the annual expenditures back up to the peak level of $17.6 million, and the capital fund stood at $24.1 million, very near the goal JDR had feared never would be reached. Eight of the twenty trustees were from countries other than the United States. There was a similar ratio on the staff and the morale was high. The Council clearly had stabilized and become the acknowledged leader in its field once again.

27

¤

SUCCESS IN ASIA

MEASURING the success of JDR's many programs and activities is difficult
to do by any objective standards. But his two-week visit to Japan and
South Korea in January 1976 yielded impressive subjective evidence of the
success of his efforts in Asia.

Japan, as always, was a special case, the only country where JDR's
representations, both ceremonial and substantive, continued to be at the
highest levels. In Tokyo, JDR and Blanchette had luncheon with the
emperor and his family. It was a rare distinction, the first time that foreigners were invited to dine privately with the emperor.[1]

The Rockefellers attended and hosted other ceremonial occasions, and
went shopping for art with Dr. Sherman Lee, who happened to be in
Japan at the same time. JDR had meetings with the prime minister, the
foreign minister, the minister of education, and leaders of the Keidanren
(Federation of Economic Organizations). The Rockefellers relaxed for an
evening in the home of their old friends, the Takakichi Asos, and were
treated to a presentation of their hosts' latest acquisitions of Chinese, Japanese, and Korean ceramics, borne into the living room by a series of
attendants.[2]

The trip took place because JDR had committed himself to attend a
dinner celebrating the opening of a new wing of the International House.
He had donated $150,000 to help build the new wing, the only monetary
contribution he ever made to the I-House. In his remarks that evening,
JDR warmly praised the leadership given to I-House by his old friend,
Shige Matsumoto, and he stressed the importance of the cultural dimension in international relations as a corrective to the heavy emphasis on the
political and economic. Tactfully, he had pressed this theme in his private
meetings with Japanese leaders as well as his two other favorite ideas—
that the Japanese should develop a tradition of philanthropy and give more

443

assistance to the countries of Southeast Asia. Subsequent developments suggest that JDR's representations ultimately had a measure of success.[3]

In response to a request, JDR agreed to engage in an unscripted dialogue with Matsumoto for the benefit of the Japanese press. Surrounded by reporters, the two men sat in comfortable chairs in the Okura Hotel and chatted about their long friendship, postwar Japanese-American relations, and the unique value of the I-House. In response to gentle inquiries from Matsumoto, JDR talked about themes from his book, *The Second American Revolution*—new values, the role of the moderates in social change, democracy, the importance of a giving society. In the course of this, JDR managed to touch publicly on the three themes he had discussed privately with Japanese leaders. The dialogue was serialized in fifteen installments in *Mainichi Shinbun*, both Japanese and English editions.[4]

Almost everything about the chilly midwinter visit to Seoul and environs was in sharp contrast to Japan—but here the evidence of success was even more impressive, more typical of what was happening as a result of JDR's programs in many Asian countries around the eastern and southern rim of the great land mass.

JDR's decision to visit South Korea was an afterthought, an appendage to the trip he had committed himself to make to Japan. He had not been in Korea for more than a decade. He simply wanted to see what was going on in a country that had earned a reputation as a leader in both economic development and population control. As noted before, JDR had long since learned to avoid official contacts and briefings in his Asian travels unless they served some specific purpose of his own (always excepting the unique case of Japan), but in South Korea he had another reason for keeping his visit as informal as possible. President Park had been cracking down on any visible opposition and taking steps to strengthen his centralized control, much in the image of Syngman Rhee. JDR did not want to be "used" by the regime or to have any contacts that might be construed as suggesting approval of Park. There was no way to keep his visit a secret, but JDR told his staff that he wanted it to be "low-key."[5]

Despite all precautions, JDR's reception in Seoul, informal as it was, had the characteristics of one that might be accorded to a national hero returning home. What happened was an outpouring of warmth and affection for him from scores of highly placed Koreans who had benefited at one time or another in their lives from the fellowships and other programs of the Population Council, the Agricultural Development Council, the JDR 3rd Fund, various other Rockefeller institutions, and the Magsaysay Awards. Most of these Koreans had never met JDR or even seen him. Suddenly the personification of something that had made a marked

difference in their lives was in their midst; they simply seemed to want
to be in his presence, to honor him and somehow let him know what he
had meant to them.

What was striking about this reception, aside from its emotional content, was the clear evidence it presented of the value of investing in people, as JDR had been doing in various ways for several decades. The
Korean grantees represented cadres of trained people and leaders in all of
the fields of health, education, agriculture, development, and the arts,
both in government and the private sector. All of this and more added up
to a general reputation for JDR as a Korean benefactor, and the aggressive
Korean press hounded him wherever he went, eager reporters camping at
the door of his Chosen Hotel suite.

Delegations of former grantees in the various fields kept calling at the
hotel. JDR could not avoid a luncheon in his honor given by several dozen
Population Council grantees. On a quiet Sunday morning, he slipped away
for a visit to the Korean National Museum, a treasure house of Korean
art. Normally closed at that time, the museum was opened for his visit.
Waiting to greet him were the museum's director and two curators, all
former JDR 3rd Fund grantees.

JDR visited the Korean National Theater where the talented director,
Duk Hyung Yoo, had been a JDR 3rd Fund grantee. Like many buildings
in Seoul, the theater was unheated because of the great increase in energy
costs following the 1973 oil crisis. JDR sat in his overcoat and watched a
special presentation of vignettes of plays, both traditional and modern,
which had been produced with the aid of a JDR 3rd Fund grant, and then
he was the focal point of a roundtable discussion for several hours with a
dozen young artists who had benefited from JDR 3rd Fund grants.

The closest JDR came to an official contact was a field trip he made
with Jin Hwan Park, a special assistant to President Park, visiting villages,
agricultural stations, and a training school for the "New Village Movement." But this came about not for reason of the able and ebullient Jin
Hwan Park's official connection, but because he, too, was a former ADC
grantee.

One of JDR's missions in Korea was to learn what he could about one
of his current interests, the roles and status of women in developing countries. He was curious to learn how women were faring in a country
regarded as one of the most successful in Asia in economic development.
He pursued this interest wherever he could, in his discussion with the
young artists, talking to a young woman (one of the curators) at the
Museum, in a private meeting with half a dozen faculty members at Ewha
Women's University, at dinner for a mixed group at the home of the

Population Council resident, and in encounters with a courageous feminine leader, Dr. Tai Young Lee, a Magsaysay Award winner who was being harassed by the Park regime. The only women lawyer in South Korea, Dr. Lee ran the Legal Aid Center for Family Relations, where her clients mainly were women in need of help. Aware that Koreans disliked by the regime could be picked up for questioning or worse if they talked to foreigners, JDR was circumspect in contacting Dr. Lee. But she wanted to see him and came to his hotel, where her young aide turned the radio up full volume to mask the conversation against bugging by the Korean CIA. At Dr. Lee's request, JDR later made a public visit to her legal aid center.[6]

JDR was not surprised to learn that, despite some outward signs of progress, women remained decidedly bound by tradition in Korea and subordinate in status. He made the subject a prominent one in an afternoon he spent with a group of young Ph.D.s at the Korean Development Institute, a quasi-governmental "think tank." These men, some of them the beneficiaries of Rockefeller grants, could hold their own in intellectual debate with anyone, but JDR gave them something to think about. There were some signs of irritation and resistance as he kept bringing the discussion away from what the developers wanted to talk about to his concern about the status of women in South Korea. Gradually they began to listen as JDR presented a cogent three-point argument. He stressed human rights, the check to population growth that would result from involving women more in the economic mainstream, and the drag on South Korean development resulting from the failure to make the best use of half its human resources. By the time the session was over, the young men were exchanging glances and conceding that their elderly visitor had a good case.

The spontaneous testimonial to JDR that occurred during his week in Korea may have been so emotional because he had not been there in such a long time, whereas he had traveled more frequently to the other Asian countries where his programs were operating. The same phenomenon existed in all of those countries—broad networks of grantees representing a new wave of competence and leadership in half a dozen important fields. Porter McKeever was amazed by the extent of this when he accompanied JDR to Malaysia and Indonesia in late 1976. McKeever noted the unusual degree to which JDR's fellowship programs were successful in terms of the grantees pursuing their careers in their home countries instead of migrating to the United States. On that trip, the last one he was to make to Asia, JDR pressed the issue of the roles of women as vigorously as he had ten months earlier in South Korea.[7]

The very success of JDR's activities in Asia began to create a curious sort of vacuum for him by the late 1960s. All of the organizations and programs he had helped to create in Asia were humming along smoothly without any particular need for time and attention from him. A sign of this was that his trips to Asia gradually became less frequent. There was not much of a specific nature that demanded his presence in the field.

JDR did take an early interest in mainland China. Although this did not yield any programmatic follow-through for him, it was an important antecedent to President Nixon's famous trip to China in 1972 and the pronounced change in the climate of U.S.–China relations. In 1966 JDR pressed his staff for ideas about how he might contribute to a "search for solutions to the China problem." A great deal of exploratory work by Ray Lamontagne and James Hyde of the RBF followed, resulting in a focus on the National Committee on United States–China Relations, which had just been formed by two noted Far Eastern scholars, A. Doak Barnett of Columbia and Robert Scalapino of the University of California. This nascent organization was about to die on the vine—there were even rumors that Governor Ronald Reagan of California was going to remove Scalapino from the Berkeley faculty because of his interest in China. JDR stepped in and made the first financial contribution to the Committee and lent it his name, becoming, as Datus Smith later observed, the "godfather" of the organization. Financial support from the RBF, the Carnegie Corporation, and the Ford Foundation followed.[8]

In March 1969, the Committee held a major two-day conference in New York. In introducing the dinner speaker, Senator Edward Kennedy, JDR forcefully stated his "longtime conviction" of the need to find "a reasonable *modus vivendi* with the world's most populous nation." He said that

our thinking about that great country has been dominated by fear, so much so that in the recent past many regarded it as virtually treasonable to even raise the question of rethinking China policy. . . . This sort of rigidity has no place in a democracy. . . . I believe that the time for re-examination of our policies is now. . . . I fervently hope that we have passed through the shadows of fear and are ready to think constructively about the future.

The Nixon opening to China came as a startling surprise in the popular mind; almost unnoticed in the historical record is the important preconditioning that occurred in the many activities of the National Committee, particularly in enlisting public support for a new approach to China among a wide spectrum of responsible leaders in business, academia, government, and the media.

Given this involvement, it would seem natural that JDR might visit China and perhaps develop activities there, particularly in view of his prominence in the population field. This was occasionally discussed in his staff meetings, but the right opportunity and time never seemed to come, and, as noted, he began branching out in other areas in the 1970s.

Other ideas for Asian activities also resulted in little or no actual involvement. JDR flirted for a long time with the idea of stimulating major efforts to preserve and restore the great temple complexes at Borobudur in Indonesia and Pagan in Burma. There were sporadic discussions over the years, but the rigid isolationism of Burma for so many years precluded any project there. A serious effort finally got going on behalf of Borobudur, but by the time it occurred JDR had just about lost interest. It took some persuading by Porter McKeever and Phillips Talbot to get JDR to make a $20,000 gift in October 1974 to the U.S. Committee for Borobudur. He was the largest individual contributor—most of the $1,275,000 raised in the United States was given by some sixty corporations as part of an international fund-raising drive.

On the theory that the reason for the seeming shortage of things for JDR to do in Asia might be a lack of focus—since so many of his programs there were area-wide—he and his staff talked for a while about the possibility of his "adopting" another country as he had Japan. The favorite candidate was Indonesia, and various program ideas were considered. Although JDR encouraged these discussions from time to time, he seemed halfhearted, as if he realized that he had passed such involvements by. In truth, as he liked to put it, his "plate was full," with the new activities he had undertaken at home and the high priority he placed on making sure that the organizations he had long been committed to would complete their missions or be in fit condition to survive him.

As far as Asia was concerned, this meant that the action for him was not so much in the field as it was in New York City, where there were policy and managerial issues to be resolved for three organizations: the ADC, the Japan Society, and the Asia Society.

The problem of the ADC was an unusual one—it functioned so smoothly, effectively, and quietly that JDR and his staff scarcely knew it was there. But by 1970 the question of the future of the organization rose inexorably to the surface.

The success of the ADC was engineered by the extraordinary triumvirate of its president, Art Mosher; its vice president, Clif Wharton; and Abe Weisblat, director of the ADC's Research and Training Network. Par-

ticularly important was Mosher's uncommon combination of professionalism (as an agricultural economist), commitment (with a touch of his
missionary background), and a sensitive and flexible management style. In
part, the ADC was a professional organization and overseas assistance
agency of agricultural economists, as evidenced by the presence on its
board at various times of men from some of the leading universities in that
field—Cornell, Minnesota, Chicago, Stanford, and Louisiana State. Over
the years its careful mix of fellowships, research, publications, conferences,
seminars, field representatives in key countries, and small grants wherever
they could do the most good had proved marvelously effective. The ADC's
"social science" approach to agriculture (as distinct from the Rockefeller
Foundation's "biological" approach) enabled it to use its footing in agricultural economics in an eclectic way, constantly exploring new problems and
needs related to the human dimension. An important force was the wide-
ranging mind of Abe Weisblat. He, for example, was one of the first to
consistently explore the issue of the role of women in developing societies.

In 1970 Clif Wharton was lost to the ADC. So marked for success was
he that he was turning down job offers practically every week. Finally
one came along that he couldn't refuse—the presidency of Michigan State
University. By that time, Mosher had already begun to raise the question
of the future of the organization with his chairman, JDR.

It will be recalled that in 1953, when JDR created the Council on
Economic and Cultural Affairs (CECA, the predecessor to the ADC), he
had stated that he intended long-term support of the agricultural program,
on the order of ten to fifteen years. This was not put in the form of a
legally binding commitment; it was a statement of intent, and the exact
duration was left vague. When the reorganization occurred in 1963, with
the JDR 3rd Fund created to take over cultural activities and the name of
CECA changed to ADC, JDR reaffirmed this commitment to Mosher.
Now, in late 1969, Mosher reminded JDR that the fifteen years were about
up, and therefore the future of the ADC had to be considered.

There was no crisis. The only consistent contributors to the ADC of
real significance had been JDR and the RBF—Rockefeller Foundation support had never developed because of the early history of ideological differences between the RF agriculture program and ADC.[9] JDR contributed
$350,000 and the RBF $300,000 per year. Due to Mosher's careful management, the ADC's reserve fund had risen to nearly $5 million, and income
from this completed the revenue sources for the annual budget.

At JDR's request, Mosher laid out the options in a long letter. He
began by saying that JDR "had already substantially discharged the responsibility you took when you established the Council." He continued:

Even if you were to give the Council no further support, and its activities were to be discontinued after the present Reserve Funds were exhausted, an enormous contribution would have been made in Asia and the effect of the contribution would continue throughout the continuing careers of Asians whose competence has been increased by Council activities.

He then made the case for continuation, arguing that in another ten years the work of the ADC could double the number of trained Asians, help a number of Asian universities "carry on high quality post-graduate training in their home countries," and "help solve" a range of "economic and human problems now confronting rural Asia." He warned that doing this would require a gradual increase in annual expenditures, but said that for the first time a serious effort was being made to secure funding from other sources.[10]

Within a few months, JDR wrote to Mosher saying that he intended to continue his financial support of the ADC for at least five years.[11] JDR continued to be impressed. After one ADC board meeting, he wrote in his diary: "It is really a first rate group and do feel that the Council is making a real contribution in Asia, although it is on a quiet, behind the scenes basis." Later he wrote with pleasure about the strong endorsement of Ford Foundation executives, one of whom praised the "quality of personnel" of the ADC in Asia.

Yet the question of the ADC's future abruptly rose again in 1972 when Mosher informed JDR that he wanted to retire three years early. At first feeling that he was being let down, JDR soon realized that Mosher was genuine in believing that a younger person should take the helm of the ADC to see it through the next phase. Moreover, Mosher had succeeded in bringing in new funding sources—the Ford Foundation, the Agency for International Development, and the International Development Research Centre (of Canada). Within a few years, these three would provide more than $1 million in funding per year.

Still, the loss of Mosher seemed for a time like a mortal blow to the ADC. Matters came to a head at a meeting at the University Club one evening in May 1972 between JDR and a special committee representing the ADC. JDR found the group to be enthusiastic for continuing, buoyed by the new funding sources and the task agenda Mosher had set up. It was agreed to accept Mosher's resignation and begin a search for a new president. Mosher would retain an affiliation with the ADC, either in a field post or a consultancy, if the new president agreed. New members would be added to the board. JDR renewed his commitment of financial support for five more years. It was agreed that the ADC should stay in existence for at least five to ten years, but that a review would take place five years later, in 1977.[12]

Subsequently, Vernon Ruttan was recruited to replace Mosher as president. An ADC board member, Ruttan had been a Rockefeller Foundation economist and a member of the Council of Economic Advisers in Washington. Since 1965, he had been director of the prestigious Economic Development Center at the University of Minnesota. New board members were added: Clif Wharton; John Lewis, dean of the Woodrow Wilson School at Princeton; Nyle C. Brady, director general of the International Rice Research Institute in the Philippines; T. Scarlett Epstein of the University of Sussex in England.

The energy crisis of 1973 and the resulting recession and inflationary spiral nearly wrecked the ADC's reserve fund. Not only did the portfolio shrink in value, but the organization also had to draw down capital to cover operating expenses.[13] But the new funding sources all came through, compensating for the loss and the gradual stepping down of the RBF support to $100,000 per year. The annual JDR and Ford grants helped the ADC avoid excessive dependency on government funding. But a measure of the esteem with which the ADC was held was that $250,000 of the annual AID funding was unrestricted. At Ruttan's suggestion, the ADC headquarters were moved from New York to Singapore to cut down on administrative and travel costs. By the mid-1970s, the ADC was operating on annual expenditures of approximately $2 million, nearly double the level of a decade earlier.

Satisfied that matters were under control, JDR felt he could now relinquish the chairmanship of the ADC, as he was trying to do in all of his organizations. In 1974, JDR's old associate Don McLean, who had attended the birth of CECA/ADC in 1953, was brought onto the board and became the new chairman.

An important reason for the effectiveness of the ADC and of JDR as a philanthropist was well stated by Mosher in a "farewell" letter to JDR:

You may not know that when Don McLean first approached me about joining CECA as executive director I turned him down. When he asked why, I said it was because I did not believe a philanthropist who had established a technical organization could give its administrative head a sufficient voice in policy and program determination to develop and maintain a technically effective program over a sufficiently long period of time to do a good job.

Don's reply was: "You don't know John Rockefeller. He is unique as a philanthropist. He is interested in this program. He wants to participate personally. But he will not dominate it. He wants the Council to be a truly public organization with a strong Board of Trustees of which he will be only one member. He will exercise his own judgment in that capacity, but he will not issue orders or interfere in day-to-day operations."

I believed him, and he has been proved right.[14]

What Mosher was too polite to tell JDR then or at any time was that his initial skepticism had been engendered by his experience with Nelson Rockefeller's Latin American assistance efforts, IBEC and AIA. He thought both of these organizations had enormous potential, but Nelson would not let them alone long enough to develop a consistent program. "He would come up with a new idea and the organizations would gear up to implement it. When they hadn't transformed the world within six months, he would become restless, think of another new idea, and the organizations would drop what they had been doing and rush off in the new direction."

For the same reason, Mosher had always been wary of government support, avoiding it for a long time and seeking it only when he felt confident that the reputation of the ADC and its private support were established enough to prevent overdependency. As far as he was concerned, the patient persistence of JDR, both as a participant and a contributor, was the only right and effective approach for the support of an overseas assistance program.[15]

In the words of Edwin O. Reischauer, the events of the late 1960s "consituted a sea change in the organization and program of the Japan Society."[16] After fifteen years of service, Douglas Overton left his post as executive director. JDR announced that he wished to resign as president, although he would remain active for the time being as chairman. The plan was to recruit a paid professional or a distinguished volunteer as president. The decision to build a new Japan House was taken, and a fund-raising committee was set up under trustee James Voss of Caltex.

And, in 1967, a special program committee of the board, chaired by Charles E. Allen, issued a report calling for the Society to become active in the public affairs and economics fields and to substantially increase and improve its many cultural activities. The report also urged the Society to professionalize its management with new budgeting techniques and personnel practices, and by adding more full-time staff.

All seemed in readiness for gearing up the Japan Society in line with the booming Japanese economy and the vast increase in trade and travel between Japan and the United States. Instead, the Society had a serious managerial crisis. The new executive director, James L. Stewart, who had been the Tokyo representative of the Asia Foundation, found the new role not to his liking. He had no prior experience in New York and little in running an organization like the Japan Society. In less than a year, he departed to return to the Asia Foundation. A search for a replacement who combined a knowledge of Japan with administrative ability yielded no results. A solution to the problem then emerged in the person of Isaac Shapiro, a quiet and thoughtful young lawyer who happened to be bilingual in Japanese and English, as well as fluent in Russian and French.

Shapiro's family background was fascinating. His mother's family had fled Russia during the pogroms in 1905, and her father became a successful banker in China. Shapiro's father, a cellist and conductor, fled Russia in 1918 after the Bolshevik Revolution. He met the banker's daughter at a conservatory in Berlin where he taught and she was studying piano. They married and then lived successively in Berlin, Palestine, and China, before settling in Tokyo in 1931, a congenial environment because of the Japanese love of music. "Ike" Shapiro, one of the five brothers, was born in Tokyo in 1931 and lived and went to school there until the end of World War II. A colonel in the American occupying army took a liking to the younger man and suggested that he go to school in the United States. Ike was a stateless person with no passport, and the U.S. consular official who figured out a solution, a visa attached to an official-looking sheet of paper, was none other than Douglas Overton.

Shapiro moved to the United States, became a citizen, graduated from Columbia Law School, and became a member of the Milbank, Tweed law firm. A lawyer with a prestigious firm who was bilingual in Japanese and English seemed destined to become associated with the Japan Society. JDR first learned of Shapiro and his unusual combination of talents from his secretary, whose husband was also a member of the Milbank firm. When Ike appeared at the Japan Society, he was welcomed by Doug Overton. In 1963 Ike became a trustee and the secretary of the Society. Despite this involvement, he recalls, he barely knew JDR, having never exchanged more than a few words, until the managerial crisis occurred in 1967.[17] But in the interregnum following Stewart's resignation, Shapiro became active in helping to administer the Society, a role that was to grow steadily. Over the next decade, until he left in 1977 to open a Tokyo office for his law firm, he was to be a major force in guiding the expansion of the Society, all of his service rendered *pro bono*.

In 1969, Shapiro became chief executive of the Society on a part-time basis, by arrangement with his law firm, with staff member Daniel Meloy serving as his deputy. In 1970 Shapiro became president as JDR moved up to the chairmanship, which had been vacant since John Foster Dulles resigned in 1953. A Japan specialist on four-year leave from the U.S. Foreign Service, Rodney Armstrong, was hired as executive director.

In 1971 the new Japan House was dedicated and opened to the public, its location at 333 East 47th Street an excellent one near the United Nations and other international institutions. Designed by Junzo Yoshimura of Tokyo, the four-story building was the first in the United States in the modern Japanese style. The cost, $4.75 million, was three times what had been originally envisioned. Nearly one-third was provided by the Japanese government and the Keidanren. JDR contributed a third in the form of the land, and the remainder came from the general fund-raising drive conducted by James Voss.

Praised by architectural critics, Japan House became an instant success in the week of festivities that attended its opening in September 1973. Among those present were Prince and Princess Hitachi, the Japanese ambassador to the United States, and the president of the Keidanren.

When Armstrong left at the end of 1973, the executive committee of the Society decided that it was no longer necessary to require that the executive director be a Japanologist. There was plenty of expertise available—in JDR's experience, Shapiro's presence, and the intimate knowledge of Japan among many trustees and staff members. Over time, four former U.S. ambassadors to Japan—Reischauer, Robert Ingersoll, James Hodgson, and Mike Mansfield—became active in Japan Society affairs. Accordingly, a professional administrator, David McEachron, formerly vice president of the Council on Foreign Relations, became the new executive director. Under the leadership of JDR, Shapiro, and McEachron, the Japan Society truly entered its "take-off" stage to become a full-fledged success in every respect. From the early 1960s when knowledge of Japan by Americans was primitive (with the reverse true as well), when the operating budget of the Japan Society was little more than $100,000 a year and its activities limited to the cultural field, when it was critically dependent on JDR for financial support and his name and prominence, it had become a unique and major resource for understanding and intercourse between the two countries, by far the most successful organization of its kind. By the late 1970s, its operating budget had grown to more than $3 million per year, its staff from a handful to more than forty full-time employees.[18] Its annual dinner has become a forum for major policy addresses by Japanese and U.S. statesmen.

The highlight of this period of successful expansion was the visit to Japan House by Emperor Hirohito and Empress Nagako in October 1975, during the first visit to the United States by a Japanese emperor (save for Hirohito's stop at the Anchorage airport en route to Europe in 1971). All arrangements had to be coordinated with three formidable bureaucracies—the Imperial Household Agency, the Agency for Cultural Affairs, and the

Foreign Ministry of Japan, as well as the ambassador in Washington and the consul general in New York. JDR had invited the royal couple to lunch at Fieldwood Farm and they accepted, the first time they would dine at a private residence. The emperor and empress began their fifteen-day visit by spending two days at Colonial Williamsburg and then three days in Washington, where the Rockefellers were among those attending President Ford's state dinner for the distinguished guests

Then came the luncheon at Fieldwood Farm on Sunday, October 5. The security arrangements and bureaucratic infighting for control of the visit of Fieldwood Farm had been going on for a week, with the Japanese consul general in New York wielding a heavy hand in competition with the Imperial Household Agency. JDR commented in his diary: "It really has been quite fantastic. However, we all survived." The Japanese were not the only ones who were being possessive: so was JDR. Brother Nelson also wanted to attend the luncheon, but as far as JDR was concerned, this was *his* emperor, and he was not about to be upstaged. The problem was that by this time Nelson was Vice President of the United States, and protocol would have required that he be given the place of honor among the Americans present. The matter was finally solved by agreeing that the royal couple would first make a brief stop to see Nelson at his new Japanese house adjacent to Kykuit on the Pocantico estate, and then proceed to Fieldwood Farm. JDR was chafing, feeling that Nelson was holding up the royal couple too long, but they arrived at Fieldwood Farm just before noon, only a few minutes late.

Brother David was among the luncheon guests, but this did not present any protocol problem for JDR. He and David had been granting each other access to eminent foreign guests for years. JDR graciously managed to arrange things so that David had a few minutes of private conversation with the emperor before lunch.

JDR's idea was that the emperor and empress for once should have a relaxed and informal occasion, something very difficult to achieve under the circumstances. "Both Their Majesties are really warm and friendly people," he wrote, "given a chance to break away even a little bit from the terribly strict protocol in which they are enmeshed." The thirty-two guests, most of them Japanese, were arranged at four tables. Blanchette sat next to the emperor and JDR next to the empress, the two couples across from each other. Afterwards, JDR wrote "that it really went very nicely in the sense that it was informal, friendly, and relaxed."[19] After lunch the royal couple went to a football game at Shea Stadium, something the emperor wanted to do because President Ford had spoken to him about football. One suspects that he was mystified by what he saw.

The next day JDR attended Mayor Beame's luncheon for the emperor, and then he and Blanchette acted as host and hostess for the royal visit to the Japan Society. In JDR's words, "it had dignity and went well, and in a way was a symbolic recognition of the importance of the Society and its work."

JDR certainly had every reason to be pleased at the way the Japan Society had evolved. From the beginnings of Rockefeller philanthropy nearly a century earlier, the ever-present problem had been how to detach an organization the Rockefellers created or supported from never-ending dependency on them. JDR struggled to do this in many cases. Sometimes the only answer was to wrench himself away and let the organization sink or swim. This is what he had done in the case of Lincoln Center, for example. The Japan Society was different. Although there had been a few financial crises during the rapid expansion of the Society in the 1970s, it now clearly was a thriving success, free from dependency on him. He was no longer a financial contributor. In short, all the pain was gone from his role as chairman and only the pleasure remained—the ability to stay involved and reap the honorific rewards of more than a quarter century of devoted service.

But the end was coming for JDR. At his own suggestion, the board some years earlier had adopted a provision requiring trustees to retire at age seventy. This was now at hand for JDR. Meanwhile, Shapiro announced that he would be leaving to take up residence in Tokyo on behalf of his law firm. The loss of JDR and Shapiro at the same time was mitigated by McEachron's success as executive director and the immediate recruitment of Andrew N. Overby to succeed Shapiro as president. Overby held a special place of honor among the Japanese for having put together the first postwar loan to Japan (at the First Boston Corporation) when other banking institutions had declined.

The more difficult problem, however, was how to replace JDR as chairman, and Shapiro and Overby went to work on this. They tried hard, but could not come up with an idea for an adequate replacement. One day at lunch, they looked at each other and agreed that there was an obvious answer. The board should pass a special resolution waiving the retirement clause in JDR's case, and he should be importuned to remain. This happened, and after wrestling with his concience a bit, JDR accepted. "I think he was really pleased," said Shapiro.

The Asia Society had a much rockier path—only through a combination of working on managerial and policy problems, trying his best to wean the organization away from its ongoing dependency on him, and making a truly major "once and for all" commitment to it was JDR able to put the Society finally on a course leading toward stability.

The major potential problems had been discussed when the Asia Society was created in 1956, and they all came true. One was succinctly expressed by Datus Smith: "In a sense, there isn't any Asia. There are only Asian countries."[20]

An organization dealing with a continent, or to be more exact, part of a continent, was bound to have difficulties finding a focus. As we have seen, the way to finesse this problem was thought to be the formation of "country councils"—a "council" being a grouping of Society members with a particular interest in a particular Asian country. The effectiveness of these councils fluctuated over the years. The smaller ones—the Sri Lanka and Nepal councils, for example—tended to be the more successful. The Society provided only minimal funding to them and only rarely was a paid staff member assigned to any of them. They were operated by volunteers, some of them outstanding individuals, but with obvious limitations on sustained involvement. Frequently there were rivalries and jealousies, so that the councils sometimes seemed to be more trouble than they were worth.

The Indians were unhappy over the lack of a major organization devoted to their country in the United States, and there were subtle pressures on JDR from time to time, some from the highest levels of the Indian government, as if to suggest that the man who had created the Asia Society and resuscitated the Japan Society could at least do something about an India Society. But this was too much to contemplate, even for JDR—there could be no end to that process.

Another problem was the base of support. Don McLean had warned that if the Asia Society were not a scholarly organization it could not expect significant foundation support, and that there was not enough trade to expect significant corporate support. He was right on both counts, at least until the program of the Society and conditions in Asia began to change.

A third problem was that the Society was explicitly styled as a cultural organization from the beginning. In part, this stemmed from the desire to avoid anything that might suggest that the Asia Society was a reincarnation of the Institute for Pacific Relations. But more important was the fact that a cultural organization was exactly what JDR had in mind. His model was the Japan Society as it functioned in the 1950s. We have seen how JDR developed a distaste for Cold War rhetoric and political confrontation and developed his theme of the importance of the cultural dimension in international relations—coming directly out of his role in the Dulles peace mission to Japan and manifested so clearly in so many of his activities.

There certainly was value in his emphasis on the cultural, which is so easily lost sight of and submerged by the current excitement of political and economic issues. He was trying to correct an imbalance, but by limiting the Japan Society and the Asia Society to the cultural, he was overcorrecting. In time JDR realized that the proper course for organizations such as these would be a more balanced consideration of all three dimensions.

As would be the case with the Japan Society, broadening the Asia Society required a change of leadership. The experience and interests of the original executive director, Paul Sherbert, were limited to the cultural sphere. In late 1964, he was eased out and given a staff role with the India Council of the Society, making room for Kenneth T. Young, Jr., who came in as president of the Society. In making this switch, it gradually became apparent that JDR had gone from one extreme to the other.

From an old Maine family, Ken Young pursued a career in foreign policy in the Far East, first with the Department of Defense and then the U.S. Foreign Service. He also had standing as a scholar, having earned degrees from Harvard and the Sorbonne and published numerous articles and several books on foreign affairs, the most noted one drawing on his experience as an adviser to the UN team negotiating the end to the Korean War.[21] JDR came to know and admire Young when the latter served as an adviser to the Dulles mission to Japan in 1951. Young was a personable and articulate man, given to strong opinions—he was an early "hawk" on Vietnam, for example. By the late 1950s he had risen to the position of director of the Office of Southeast Asian Affairs in State, but then resigned to take a vice presidency with Socony Vacuum. In 1961 he was tapped by the Kennedy administration to become a U.S. ambassador. According to David Halberstam, Young was to be posted to Vietnam, which is what he wanted, but through a clerical error he was nominated and confirmed as ambassador to Thailand.[22] In June 1963 Young contracted infectious hepatitis and had to be airlifted home. After recuperating, he was hired by JDR in January 1964 as one of his associates in Room 5600. It appears that JDR had in mind moving him into the Asia Society as soon as feasible.

Like many political officers in the Foreign Service of the time, Young had little interest in administration. His main contribution to the Asia Society turned out to be a negative one in the sense that it diverted the Society from developing in a balanced way and created an overdependency on government funding. In 1966 Young negotiated with the Agency for International Development an arrangement for the Asia Society to take

over the administration of a new program to involve scholars in research
and consultation to provide information and policy advice for AID in
improving its technical assistance efforts in Southeast Asia. The program
was called the Southeast Asia Development Advisory Group (SEADAG).

Because SEADAG came into existence at a time when protests against
the Vietnam War were steadily building, the view has grown up that it
was a sinister operation designed to "coopt" academics and use them "as
a cover for covert operations in Southeast Asia." This view is set forth in
the Collier and Horowitz book on the Rockefellers, which further depicts
JDR as a tool of the State Department in hiring Young and allowing the
Asia Society to manage SEADAG.[23] All of this is erroneous. There is no
evidence to support the idea that SEADAG was ever anything other than
what it purported to be. Given the tenor of the times, it is not surprising
that some of the 140 scholars from various universities who participated in
SEADAG projects and panels decided to drop out because they disagreed
with U.S. policy on Vietnam. However, instead of military affairs and
counterinsurgency, SEADAG's concerns were with more orthodox AID
development interests such as population, agriculture, and water resources
as they were manifested throughout the region, not just in Vietnam.[24]

The real problem of SEADAG was that AID, a government bureaucracy beset with its annual appropriations battle and considerable personnel turnover, simply was in no position to make effective use of a stream
of insights and policy advice coming from a broad network of independent
scholars. It was a classic case of a seemingly good idea having little utility
in practice, which remained true even though AID funding for SEADAG
increased after the Nixon administration took over in 1969. From a level
of about $200,000 per year, SEADAG funding to the Asia Society increased
to approximately $650,000 per year in the early 1970s, and then declined
as the program was phased out.

For the Asia Society, SEADAG turned out to be a problem of another
kind in that it constituted a diversion from development of the Society
that would have lasting value. Young tended to spend his time on SEA-
DAG and his book on negotiating with the Communists instead of fund-
raising and program development. When there was a budget crunch,
Young would look to Rockefeller sources for more funding, and when that
was not forthcoming he would cut the regular program. JDR, of course,
was hoping for broader development of the Society to lessen dependence
on him. He had always been responsible for by far the largest share of the
Society's non-SEADAG funding through his personal contributions and by
lining up support from the Rockefeller Brothers Fund and his friend Mrs.

Lila Acheson Wallace, the wife of the founder of *Reader's Digest*. Her High Winds Foundation provided $200,000 a year in support over a five-year period, gradually scaled down to $100,000 in the 1970s.

When Datus Smith joined JDR's staff in 1967, it soon became clear to him that Young would have to go if the Asia Society were to develop in the manner intended. JDR did not disagree, but he was reluctant to release a high-status individual unless he was sure that he had the right replacement—he could not afford to make another mistake. The right man soon became available in the person of Phillips Talbot, who resigned as U.S. ambassador to Greece at the end of the Johnson administration. JDR had known and admired Talbot for many years, and had tried several times to enlist him in one or another of his programs. It will be recalled that Talbot was high on JDR's list to succeed Dean Rusk as president of the Rockefeller Foundation when Rusk resigned to become Kennedy's Secretary of State at the end of 1960, but Talbot followed Rusk into the State Department as Assistant Secretary for Near East and South Asian Affairs.

Recruiting Talbot was not merely a matter of JDR finding another State Department person—Talbot's reputation had been made in the private sector long before he joined the Kennedy administration. Originally a journalist for the *Chicago Daily News*, Talbot became a foreign correspondent in India and Pakistan before naval service in World War II and earning his Ph.D. at the University of Chicago where he taught for several years. In 1951 he became executive director of the American Universities Field Staff. JDR was a financial donor to AUFS primarily because of Talbot, and Talbot was an occasional adviser to JDR on his Asian programs, serving for example as a member of the group JDR assembled to consider creating the Asia Society in 1956.

Before accepting the Asia Society post, Talbot visited Southeast Asia, studied the Society's operations, and wrote a letter to JDR outlining his views. They were everything JDR wanted to hear in terms of balanced development—building the Asia Society as a major resource in cultural, economic, and public affairs, and as a meeting place and forum for scholars and leaders the United States and Asian countries. What JDR did not want to hear was Talbot's view that the initial period of growth would require increased support from Rockefeller sources. JDR demurred at this, and affirmed only that he would maintain his personal support at $200,000 per year. Because Talbot felt that the seeds were there and the potential was strong, he decided to accept the challenge anyway.[25]

He took over at the end of 1969 as Young was eased out, first on a consultancy and then as a research associate with the Council on Foreign

Relations. In 1972, while in Washington as a consultant to the Department of State, Young died of a heart attack.

The SEADAG imbalance should not obscure the fact that the Asia Society had developed a variety of programs—in such areas as the performing arts, the Asia House Gallery, Asian literature, education, and public affairs seminars, in addition to the country councils and SEADAG. Although there were frequent budget crises and deficits, these activities had grown to the point that the space available in the Asia House, the seven-story glass-fronted building on 64th Street, was inadequate even by the time of Sherbert's departure. JDR bought the brownstone next door as an annex, but even this and the departure of the Japan Society did not create enough room. SEADAG and some other offices had to be quartered in outside space. This stimulated sporadic discussions of ideas for still another new Asia House.

Moreover, the Society had its strong points. It was kept together administratively by the reliable hand of Executive Vice President Lionel Landry, who continue to serve under Talbot, and the Asia House Gallery was an outstanding success under the direction of Gordon Washburn. In a retrospective on Washburn's career, the *New York Times* cited "landmark shows" and "excellence," and referred to Washburn as

the distinguished director of the Asia House Gallery in New York, which under his leadership attained international recognition for the quality of its Oriental art exhibitions. Fully understanding the needs of the art-going public, he was able to attract wide audiences to often recondite exhibitions without compromising on scholarship or esthetic content. He produced installations that held the eye and catalogues that threw new light on Asian art history.[26]

In terms of personal stature, experience, and policy direction. Talbot was just what the Asia Society needed as an executive head The difference became apparent very soon, with improved staff morale, new program development, and, to JDR's vast relief, new funding sources, including the Mellon and Ford Foundations and gradually increasing corporate and individual memberships. From a level of approximately $1 million per year in the late 1960s, the Society's annual budget topped $2 million by 1972, yet the percentage contributed by JDR gradually declined to a level of about 15 percent. New board members were added, including Arthur Taylor of CBS, Asian scholar Howard Wriggins of Columbia, realtor Frederick Rose, and Gesualdo Costanza, vice chairman of Citibank. Costanza in particular was a strong force in fund-raising for the Society in the 1970s.

Talbot made a number of moves in the public affairs area, including opening a Washington office under Robert Barnett and instituting an annual series of high-level private conferences. The model was the Bilderberg Conferences in which businessmen, scholars, and government leaders from a number of countries meet in seclusion to probe themes of common interest. Talbot's specific idea was that attendees should come one-third each from the United States, Japan, and the countries of Northeast Asia. The trial run was held at Colonial Williamsburg in the fall of 1971 and was judged to be successful enough to continue. Because of this beginning, the series became known as the Williamsburg Conferences. The venue was changed to a different country each fall and the mix of attendees broadened to include all of the countries of the Pacific Basin. The Williamsburg VI conference in Penang, Malaysia, in the fall of 1976 was the occasion for JDR's last trip to Asia.

The Williamsburg Conferences provided the model for the much better known Trilateral Commission, which was founded by David Rockefeller to bring together leaders from the United States, Japan, and Western Europe. He got the idea when attending a Williamsburg Conference after he was rebuffed in proposing to the steering committee of the Bilderberg Conferences that Japanese leaders be included because of Japan's growing importance in world affairs. Despite its great usefulness and impressive record, the Trilateral Commission became the object of a strange outpouring of both left-wing and right-wing attacks and conspiracy theories, as either a Communist or a capitalist cabal. These groups seemed never to have discovered the Williamsburg Conferences.[27]

The value of such conferences is hard to gauge, but the attendees of the Williamsburg series were generally enthusiastic over the opportunity for a frank interchange of views and the flow of substantive ideas. Clearly, the series enhanced the stature of the Asia Society, as well as attracting new funding sources.

In the view of Datus Smith, JDR might very well have given up on the Asia Society had it not been for the transformation wrought by Phillips Talbot. But the prospect now was very different. The Society was on the right path and in the right hands. There was a very long way to go before it could be judged as secure and successful, but for the first time JDR could feel that the prospects for that were definitely there. He could contemplate giving up the chairmanship and retiring from the board. There remained only the question that JDR was considering in the case of every one of his important interests: what should he do, within reasonable limitations, so that he could genuinely feel that he had fully discharged his commitment?

28

✣

FINAL DISPOSITION

THERE WERE three ways for JDR to arrange for the final disposition of his resources and his many interests. One was to fulfill commitments during his lifetime out of current income. We have seen a number of cases during the 1970s in which JDR worked on program and financial matters for various organizations he had sponsored, found the right time to exit as chairman or president, and helped groom his successors.

The second way was collaboration with his brothers—there were major family issues that could only be worked out in concert with them. This process was to occur at a time of difficult transition for the Rockefeller family, and it was to have a good measure of drama and conflict as we shall see in succeeding chapters.

Finally, there was JDR's last will and testament. Whatever he could not resolve in his lifetime, he still had an opportunity to address through his estate. As he grew older he paid more and more attention to his will, meeting at least once a year with his legal advisers for an intensive review and update.

As it turned out, there was only one of JDR's long-standing commitments to figure prominently in his will—the Asia Society.

There was certainly nothing unusual about the amount of time and care that JDR devoted to his will, considering that he was a wealthy man who was approaching old age. He did not have a morbid preoccupation with death, or any sense that his death was imminent. He was, in fact, a healthy man who could expect to live to quite advanced years. The hereditary indications were good—his grandfather lived almost a full century, his father to age eighty-six.

Like them, JDR was a temperate man with no bad habits. He had the lean, spare physique of his grandfather. He ate and slept well, always rose early, got good medical care, and exercised in moderation. His chronic afflictions were irritating, but in no sense life-threatening—poor teeth, his mysterious bouts with laryngitis, and his thickened, somewhat deformed ankle. There was a lot that could be done about the teeth—he was forever keeping dental appointments and having root canals done. But he learned early in life that there was nothing he could do about laryngitis except patiently endure it until it went away. There was no medical cure. The ankle did not unduly restrict him throughout most of his life. He was, for example, an inveterate walker. But in the early 1970s the ankle became arthritic and he reinjured it working in his garden. By 1975 it limited his ability to walk any appreciable distance or climb long flights of stairs,[1] and he began to give serious consideration to finding out if there was any medical solution.

Prior to 1978, JDR had only one serious accident, which resulted in his landing in the same hospital as his son, Jay, at the same time under the care of the same doctor, but for different reasons. For years Jay had paid the penalty often associated with the young person who grows rapidly to a great height—excruciating back pain. There were often stretches when he had to be flat on his back for weeks. This chronic problem became so debilitating that in 1970 he finally decided on the treatment of last resort, an operation. He entered Columbia Presbyterian Hospital in New York for a laminectomy and spinal fusion, under the care of Dr. Frank Stinch-field, an eminent orthopedic surgeon. On the weekend after Jay's operation JDR decided to go for a ride on the Pocantico estate trails. His diary tells what happened:

On Saturday morning [August 29th] was riding a new horse which we had on approval. Was trotting slowly along the old aqueduct when something frightened the horse and it wheeled, throwing me off. When I got up off the ground, I realized that something more than routine had happened to me. However, I was able to catch the horse.

At this point I noticed a little way down the trail a boy sitting on a motor scooter. When he saw that I was aware of his presence he went off in spite of my waving to him. But a few minutes later he returned and this time I persuaded him that I was in trouble and needed his help. I said that I had hurt my back and was unable to remount the horse and would he therefore go to Fieldwood Farm and get someone to pick me up in a car.

In the meantime I sat down and waited for what must have been three-quarters of an hour and was surprised that no riders came by. In due course [farm manager] Pete West came back with the boy in his car. He picked me up and the boy very kindly agreed to lead the horse back to our barn.

JDR's regular doctor was on vacation, so Blanchette got the idea of calling Jay "to get his team to help out." The result was that JDR was

Kykuit (Dutch for "lookout"), the residence Junior built for his parents on the Rock-efeller Estate at Pocantico in Westchester County. It was later occupied by Junior and then by Nelson. Disposition of the estate was one of the most difficult issues the Rockefeller brothers tried to resolve in the 1970s.

Three of the Rockefeller brothers, David, Winthrop, and Nelson, enjoyed getting together at the dedication of Greenacre Park, a "vest pocket" park in Manhattan developed by their sister, Babs, in 1971.

John Gardner, John D. Rockefeller 3rd, and Amyas Ames in front of the bronze plaque dedicated at a Lincoln Center ceremony honoring JDR on his retirement from the Lincoln Center board in 1972

Three Asia Society board members, (*from left*) Datus C. Smith, George Ball, and Porter McKeever, at a Society dinner in 1977. Smith and McKeever, both office associates of JDR, helped make his hopes for the Society a reality after his death.

Donal C. O'Brien, Jr., chief family counsel, who functioned as a neutral arbiter in helping the Rockefeller brothers cope with difficult family issues in the 1970s, is shown with his wife, Katie, on a hunting trip in Scotland.

The brilliant social scientist Bernard Berelson continued the success of the Population Council when he succeeded Frank Notestein as president in 1968.

Clifton R. Wharton, Jr., vice president of the Agricultural Development Council and, later, president of the State University of New York and chairman of the Rockefeller Foundation

J. Richardson Dilworth, head of the Rockefeller family office for twenty-five years. (Arthur Lavine)

Dana Creel, president of the Rockefeller Brothers Fund for twenty-five years, who capped his career in the work of the Creel Committee

Elizabeth McCormack, senior philanthropic adviser to Rockefeller family members and member of the Creel Committee of the Rockefeller Brothers Fund

Submitting the report of the Commission on Population Growth and the American Future. Commission chairman JDR with his co-vice chairmen, Grace Olivarez and Dr. Christian Ramsey, meet in the Oval Office with President Richard M. Nixon, May 1972.

JDR's closest friend in Japan, Shigeharu Matsumoto, joins him in meeting with Prime Minister Sato Tanaka (*right*) in Tokyo, November 1972.

JDR and Blanchette survey a new display of some of their Asian art in his reception area in Room 5600.

The youngest daughter of JDR and Blanchette, Alida, worked for her brother Jay's first campaign for the governorship of West Virginia in 1972.

JDR and Blanchette in his office in Room 5600 in 1974. *(Elizabeth Gee)*

Discussing the Bicentennial of the American Revolution, JDR and adviser William Ruder met with President Gerald Ford at the White House, January 20, 1975.

JDR enjoyed a humorous moment at a Foreign Policy Association luncheon in June 1976, sitting between Theodore Sorenson (*left*) and Cyrus Vance, chairman of the Rockefeller Foundation and soon to be secretary of state.

The RCA Building in Rockefeller Center at night. The "crown jewel" of the Rockefeller fortune, the Center was another subject of debate within the family. The sale to a Japanese corporation in 1989 of a majority interest in the company that controlled the Center caused a considerable stir.

The third generation, at Pocantico in the mid-1970s. *From left:* JDR, Laurance, Babs, Nelson, and David. A portrait of their mother, Abby Aldrich Rockefeller, hangs above them, next to a portrait of a youthful Nelson. *(Globe Photos, Inc.)*

Senator John D. Rockefeller IV of West Virginia and Sharon Percy Rockefeller, with
their children, 1990: (*from left*) John D. Rockefeller V, Valerie, Justin, and Charles.
(*David Burnett*)

taken to Columbia Hospital in an ambulance and X-rayed. Dr. Stinchfield told him

that the primary damage consisted of a fracture of one vertebra, but in such a fashion that it should completely mend and that no operation would be required. Also he said that there was a crack in the pelvic region but that this in itself was relatively minor.

And so I was wheeled up to the tenth floor where Jay was already ensconced. . . . During the next few days Jay would come to visit me as he was beginning to walk and was encouraged to move around. This of course was terribly nice for us but rather an amazing situation to have us both in the same hospital at the same time. . . . However, he went through a great deal more than I did.

Dr. Stinchfield said that when he first started practice a patient with JDR's injuries would have stayed in the hospital for three months, but JDR was home after only two weeks. Jay was already there for his recuperation, with his wife, Sharon, and baby (John, born 1969). Alida, Hope, and Sandra also came to Fieldwood Farm for Alida's twenty-first birthday, September 13. JDR wrote: "So we really had a family house party lasting nearly a week. This was terribly nice in itself as it is not often the children are together in such leisurely fashion—particularly insofar as Jay is concerned."

For the first week at home JDR was confined to his bedroom and conducted some business there, including a brothers' meeting with Nelson, Laurance, and David. Then he began getting about on crutches. Not until October 1 did JDR reappear in his office, and for a while came in only a few hours a day.

In casual conversation with his associates, JDR joked more than once about the record of longevity in his family. He clearly expected to live many more years. Yet the fact that he was thinking about the phenomenon of death was indicated by the interest he developed in euthanasia about the time he was turning seventy years of age in 1976.

This seemed to have been stirred by both rational and emotional factors. JDR had been deeply touched by the double suicide of his friend and Rockefeller Foundation trustee, Henry P. ("Pit") Van Dusen and his wife. She had been terminally ill and Van Dusen was in very poor health. They chose to die together, and the fact that an eminent theologian could make this choice convinced JDR that the "death with dignity" concept was something worth thinking about. In a conversation once with Jack Harr, JDR shuddered at the thought of a man he knew who had been terribly afflicted with strokes and yet insisted on being wheeled into board meetings although he was almost totally helpless. The implication was clear that JDR would have preferred death over ending up in such a condition himself.

On the rational side, JDR thought that it was quite appropriate for someone like himself who had long been concerned about "the beginning of life" to now be concerned with "the end of life." He was taken with the apposition of these phrases and thought this might be the theme for a speech or an article some day. Bill Ruder and Jack Harr both suggested to him that it was probably inadvisable to give public voice to the apposition he liked so much. At the time JDR was being outspoken in support of the Supreme Court's *Roe* v. *Wade* ruling on abortion as the controversy on that subject raged. JDR could needlessly open himself up to critics by saying that he was approving abortion and euthanasia in the same breath. Better to keep the two subjects widely separated.

Euthanasia was indeed a controversial subject. It was coming more to the public consciousness because of advanced medical technology that could keep alive an individual who was terminally ill with no chance of improving. Incidents of "pulling the plug" on life-sustaining equipment were constantly appearing in the news. JDR began quietly exploring the subject, talking it over with medical men and finding that many of them were sympathetic to the idea of allowing an individual (or responsible family members) to choose a peaceful death rather than an agonizing one or life in a paralyzed or comatose state, but were constrained by the absence of laws that would allow it.

JDR assigned Jack Harr and Peter Johnson to research the subject, and they investigated organizations and tracked the progress of "death with dignity" legistation in a number of states. There were two responsible organizations in the field. They were separate, but related, with interlocking boards. The larger one was the Euthanasia Education Council. JDR met several times with its chairman, Katherine Mali, and with the executive director, A. J. Levinson, the daughter of Dr. John Rock, the noted gynecologist who had been both a Catholic and codeveloper of the birth control pill. The other organization, the Society for the Right to Die, had been set up specifically to lobby for "death with dignity" legislation in various states, and as such was not tax-exempt. In 1977 and 1978 JDR and Blanchette each made gifts of $3,000 to the Society, the maximum personal gift allowable at the time without incurring gift taxes. This was not inconsiderable given that the Society operated on a budget of less that $20,000 a year. It was pretty much a one-man show, the work of dedicated lawyer Sidney Rosoff.

JDR executed a "living will," a concept that was being promulgated by the Euthanasia Education Council.[2] This is a statement by an individual directing that "heroic" life-sustaining procedures be withdrawn in the event of a comatose and terminal condition as certified by two doctors. The idea behind the statement, which is not legally binding, is to make the intent known before the individual might become incompetent to do so. In 1977 JDR made a $40,000 grant to the Euthanasia Education Council, one-third to go to the Society for the Right to Die (under new tax regulations that allowed this) and the remainder to be used for planning an international conference on euthanasia in the United States. JDR was considering whether or not to be the keynote speaker at the planned conference. In a discussion about the wisdom of identifying himself publicly with euthanasia, JDR quipped that there was no problem because he was already known for his support of "youth in Asia."

But his own sudden and unexpected death was to occur before he had to make the decision whether or not to speak at the conference.

JDR's periodic revisions of his will were not fraught with melodrama of the kind one associates with bad novels or movies, with the prospective heirs waiting in a state of suspense for the family lawyer to open and read the document. The basic pattern of JDR's will was long set because of the facts of his wealth, the pertinent tax laws, and his serious and sober nature. And major decisions about certain bequests were much discussed with the recipients before being entered into JDR's will. If there was ever a wealthy man whose will was not likely to contain any big surprises or eccentricities, it was JDR. The need for periodic revising was occasioned only by changes in the tax laws and the evolving nature and complexity of some of his bequests.

For one thing, JDR could not really disinherit anyone even if he had wanted to. His wife and children all enjoyed substantial income from trusts created in the 1940s and 1950s. The bulk of family wealth was in the 1934 Trusts. As noted earlier, the nature of these trusts allowed the third generation of Rockefellers to enjoy the income throughout their lifetimes. It was this that enabled JDR to function as a philanthropist well beyond what his own personal holdings would have allowed. And in turn the trust income gave the Rockefeller brothers the appearance of being wealthier than they actually were in their own right. They had the *income*, but not the *principal*. Of course, it was possible for them to invade the principal for specific purposes if their trust committees agreed, but JDR did this the least of any of the brothers. Upon their deaths, the principal and income from the 1934 Trusts would be apportioned equally among their children. Not until the fifth generation would the principal actually be inherited in the usual sense.

By the mid-1970s, JDR's personal net worth (not counting his 1934 Trust) exceeded $100 million, a quite handsome fortune. But almost half of this was in the form of the current appraised value of possessions, rather than in cash and securities—his Oriental and American art collections, other art and personal possessions, and real estate. The Oriental art was valued at approximately $21 million and the American art at $14 million. The real estate included JDR's share of the Pocantico estate, certain small parcels, and the family residences—One Beekman, Fieldwood Farm, Mill-stream Cottage in Maine, and Bassett Hall at Colonial Williamsburg.

How much the tax laws dictate the strategy of estate planning can be seen immediately. The marital deduction clause allowed up to one-half of an estate to be willed free of taxes to a spouse. Clearly, the first step for JDR was to provide that Blanchette would be the inheritor of one half of his estate. In this tax-free category, he assigned the real estate he surmised she might want to retain, namely the four family residences. However, he provided that she could disclaim Millstream Cottage and Bassett Hall if she wished.

The next step was to put into the other half, the taxable portion, any bequests to charity that JDR might want to make, because they would be deductible and reduce the amount that would actually be taxed in the final reckoning. There was an incentive to apportion most or nearly all of this half of his estate to charitable recipients inasmuch as the maximum federal estate tax rate was 70 percent and the maximum New York rate was 12 percent. Accordingly, JDR put on this side of the ledger his one-fourth share of ownership of Kykuit and the Pocantico estate. The understanding he had with his brothers was that these holdings would eventually go for public purposes to a government or tax-exempt private organization, so the value would be deducted from the taxable portion of JDR's estate.[3] Here also JDR placed deductible bequests to a number of the organizations he had supported during his lifetime. Because in the main he intended to discharge his obligations to these organizations out of current income while still alive, these bequests were in the nature of farewell gestures. They included $100,000 each to the Japan Society, the Agricultural Development Council, the Asia Society, Riverside Church, and Phelps Memorial Hospital, $250,000 to the Loomis-Chaffee School, and $500,000 each to the Population Council, Lincoln Center, and Princeton University. Also, any pledges that JDR made to charitable recipients that remained unfulfilled at the time of his death would have to be honored by his executors. He specified that these be paid out of the taxable portion of his estate so that they, too, would be deducted.

This left the two big question marks, the Oriental and American art collections, the type of possessions for which the estate tax laws might well be regarded as confiscatory. For one thing, federal estate tax law did not allow the deduction of state estate taxes as it does in the case of income tax. Thus, the effective tax rate would begin at 82 percent of the assessed value of the art objects. However, for a variety of technical reasons, the actual tax on the art would be a factor ranging from two to two-and-a-half times the assessed value. In other words, if a painting valued at $100,000 were willed to a non–tax exempt recipient the estate would have to pay a very hefty tax, perhaps as much as $250,000. JDR's choices were to put one or both of the collections in the marital deduction side of the estate, to give them to tax-exempt organizations, or so arrange his estate as to pay the huge tax if he willed the art to his children or any other non–tax-exempt recipient. Because the collections were so substantial and expensive to manage personally, it seemed that JDR had only one real choice. Aside from providing for his heirs to select several pieces that might be of particular interest to them, JDR's decision was to will them to tax-exempt organizations through which they could be made available for the enjoyment of the public.

In 1974 JDR completed a major revision of his will in the pattern described above. He named three executors—his son, Jay; the family's senior manager and financial adviser, J. Richardson Dilworth; and senior counsel Donal C. O'Brien, Jr. JDR specified the JDR 3rd Fund as the recipient of the "residual estate"—any assets remaining after the marital deduction, charitable bequests, debts, and taxes had been paid. He also indicated that he would like the trustees of the Fund to support his principal charitable interests, especially the Population Council and the Asia Society. And, finally, JDR began to implement his decision regarding the two art collections.

JDR's solution for the Asia Society involved two important and related steps, one he had been contemplating for a number of years and the other a need that had become manifest for the Society. The first was to donate his Asian art collection to the Society, and the second was to make a substantial contribution toward a new Asia House, one that would fully meet all of the Society's needs, including housing the JDR 3rd collection. Both of these moves were to prove to be extremely complicated.

It seems that almost as soon as JDR became a serious collector of Asian art, he began thinking about the ultimate disposition of the collection. He intimated enough to get his associates thinking about the subject as well. Early on, the Metropolitan Museum of Art in New York City made a bid to get the collection, but JDR was a long way from making up his mind. In 1966 Datus Smith and Ed Young coauthored a proposal that was intended to solve a number of problems at one swoop. Their idea was that JDR fund a new building that would house all the international organizations he had created—the Asia Society, the Japan Society, the Population Council, the ADC, and JDR 3rd Fund. There would be a gallery and a major arts program with the JDR 3rd collection as its centerpiece. This was too ambitious, however, and the Japan Society soon went in its own direction with JDR's blessing and support.

JDR kept considering the disposition of the art collection, however, in his usual meticulous fashion. There were Blanchette's wishes to consider, but she was prepared to defer to his judgment—he had financed the collections and they had become his passions, especially in the case of the Asian collection, while she had hers in the Museum of Modern Art. He consulted Sherman Lee who laid the options out for him. One was a major museum such as the Metropolitan, another was a small museum such as the Asia House Gallery, and the third was to break up the collection, giving "discrete units" to a number of museums to supplement their collections. Lee's own opinion was that the collection "would be swallowed up" in a large museum, but that breaking it up in gifts to a number of such museums would be preferable to relegating it to a small museum. "A great deal more would be accomplished," Lee said, "even though the collection would lose its physical identity."[4] Gordon Washburn, who was due to retire as director of the Asia House Gallery in 1974, was also against the collection going to the Asia Society at first. He said the gallery was too small and the future of the Asia Society too much in doubt to take responsibility for such an important collection.

JDR's "Asia hands"—Datus Smith, Phil Talbot, and Porter McKeever—all were very much in favor of the collection going to the Asia Society under the right circumstances. An opinion was sought from another art expert, Lawrence Sickman, director of the Nelson Gallery in Kansas City, who praised the collection highly and opined that the Asia Society would be a good choice to receive it. Datus Smith did a study of small museums, both to show their value and to cast some light on the ancillary needs involved in donating a collection, such as gallery space, staff, educational components, museum fittings, care and preservation of the collection, and so on.

The whole matter was discussed enough around the turn of the decade to create an air of expectation among those concerned with the Asia Society. JDR continued to think through the personal considerations. The collection was still growing, and he was clear about wanting to continue to enjoy it, stay involved with it, and draw on it for exhibition in his homes and office, so that the collection, or the bulk of it at least, would have to come as a bequest rather than being transferred during his lifetime. He also wanted each of his children to be able to select one or two pieces for their personal enjoyment.

At the January 1973 board meeting of the Asia Society JDR was asked about his current thinking in regard to the art collection. He responded by saying that he had been studying many of the questions involved in donating the collection to the Asia Society, and had resolved some of them in his own mind, but that others remained. As he summarized his views in his diary: "Said that my disposition was to make the transfer but there were problems as well as financial commitments involved which I would have to look into carefully."

JDR recognized that it would not be fair to ask the Asia Society or other donors to pay for the maintenance, housing, and exhibiting of his collection. For the Society to have a permanent collection and to continue its general exhibition program would require gallery space at least twice the existing size, plus all the attendant costs. Out of this realization grew the linkage between JDR donating his art collection and JDR underwriting a substantial portion of the costs for a new Asia House. At a luncheon meeting in June, JDR said enough about this to ease Gordon Washburn's concerns.

In October a special day-and-a-half meeting of the Asia Society trustees was held at Fieldwood Farm. The purpose, as JDR put it, "was to have a give and take discussion in regard to my offer to turn over my Oriental art collection to the Society." A measure of the interest in the subject was that twenty-four of the twenty-eight trustees were present. JDR wrote:

Many questions are obviously at issue, such as the quality of the collection, the desirability of having a relatively small collection of Oriental art stand by itself in New York City, the future stability of the Asia Society with particular reference to funding and the finding of a Chairman of the Board to succeed me.

During the morning (Friday), I spoke frankly about my collection and my thoughts in regard to turning it over and then answered questions.

After lunch, JDR excused himself from the meeting "so that the Trustees could speak frankly." Later that afternoon, "I was called back and told that the Trustees felt that the acceptance of my offer was in the best interests of the Asia Society."

The discussion continued through the Saturday morning session, with four committees being set up to work on "different aspects of the question." JDR summarized the mood of the meeting:

The general feeling seemed to be that the meeting not only had brought the trustees closer together . . . but had lifted their spirits and given them greater determination than ever before to see that the Society moved forward and was assured of greater stability. This decision as to my collection is obviously a major one as far as I am concerned. I really felt pleased about it.

Events followed quickly after this meeting. George Ball, senior partner of Lehman Brothers, was elected chairman to succeed JDR at the January 1974 trustees meeting. Ball had gained recognition as a "dove" on the Vietnam War who was tolerated in the Johnson administration as Under Secretary of State. JDR was pleased, regarding Ball as "strong, able and knowledgeable about Asia."

Preliminary estimates for a new Asia House and Gallery were developed. On January 31, JDR wrote a long letter to Ball in which he affirmed his decision to give the collection to the Asia Society: ". . . it is my thought to maintain ownership of the bulk of the collection for the years immediately ahead having in mind the gradual transfer of pieces to Society ownership once the permanent gallery is completed some three years hence, but with the clear understanding that the transfer of the balance of the collection would be provided for by my will."

JDR also addressed the financial question:

I have assured the Trustees that such transfer would not result in a financial burden to the Society. This, of course, includes the construction of adequate housing for the collection, its maintenance, the matter of a limited amount for future acquisitions of highest quality and some degree of programming relating to the meaningful and effective use of the collection by the Society. . . . I do want to say that I am fully aware of the ongoing costs of setting up such a collection on a permanent basis and would expect to meet the situation as it develops, with final provision covered by my Will.

On February 6, 1974, a press conference was held at the Asia Society to announce the gift. Copies of JDR's letter to Ball were distributed, as well as a description of the collection written by Sherman Lee. "There were about forty newspaper people present," JDR wrote, "which was surprising although gratifying." In his remarks, JDR touched obliquely on the ending of the Vietnam War and the beginning of a new era in U.S.–Asian relationships: "After being involved in three land wars in Asia in one generation, we Americans must seek to develop understanding and cooperation with the two-thirds of humanity who live in Asia."[5]

Coverage was extensive, with various art critics using such terms as "first-rate," "supreme quality," and "awesome" to describe the collection.[6] It ultimately numbered 260 pieces with a valuation of close to $21 million, though worth several times that in the open market in the judgment of Sherman Lee.

The first step after the public announcement of JDR's commitment, of course, was to find an appropriate site in Manhattan for the new Asia House. JDR's three "Asia hands" were all intimately involved in the search—Phillips Talbot as the president of the Society, Porter McKeever as JDR's associate for Asian affairs, and the retired Datus Smith, an Asia Society trustee, as chairman of the search committee. But the search turned out to be a prolonged and frustrating operation, to the point that JDR began referring to it in his diary as "fantastic" and "amazing."

In his letter of commitment to George Ball, JDR had written confidently of the new Asia House and Gallery being ready in three years. It was to take four years before a site was finally nailed down and construction could begin. The fact that the search for a site was so drawn out began to have important implications for JDR's commitment and his estate.

At first everything seemed to move briskly. The searchers found an excellent site very close to home—the Central Presbyterian Church, separated from the existing Asia House only by a twelve-and-one-half-foot-wide "manse" at 64th Street and Park Avenue. Negotiations took place, the congregation voted in favor, and the Asia Society thought it had a deal. Meanwhile, a parallel search had been going on for an architect, with thirty-seven firms being considered. The choice was narrowed down to four, including I. M. Pei and Edward Larrabee Barnes. Finally, Pei was awarded an initial contract to submit design ideas. The preliminary estimate for acquiring the church site and constructing the new building was $11 million.[7]

In an optimistic mood, JDR wrote another letter to Ball almost exactly one year after the initial letter of commitment:

It occurs to me, now that we have acquired the property for our new building, that it would be helpful if I were to write to you more specifically concerning my thoughts as to the financing of the building. . . . I am glad to pledge to pay half the cost of the land and the building which is now estimated at approximately eleven million dollars. . . . It is terribly gratifying that we can now really move ahead with the building plans. . . . With you and Phil Talbot at the helm and with the support of the able group of trustees and staff, I look forward to the future of the Society with confidence and excitement.[8]

This pledge was to be the subject of controversy later on. Was JDR pledging to pay half the cost no matter what it turned out to be, or was he pledging half of the current estimate of $11 million—$5.5 million? The ensuing circumstances were such that JDR did not have reason to clarify this before his sudden death intervened. Hence, as we shall see in the Epilogue, the question became a difficult one for his executors.

The first problem causing delay occurred very quickly after JDR's letter was written. The vote in favor of the sale had been close, and a dissident group in the congregation filed suit to block the transaction. Ironically, the church building had a number of historical associations with the Rockefeller family. It was one of the lineal descendants of the original Fifth Avenue Baptist Church that Senior and his family attended when they moved to New York and where Junior had taught Sunday school in the early years of the century. The family continued to attend the church after it moved uptown to the 64th and Park site. This is where Blanchette remembers first seeing the Rockefeller boys with their heads "bobbing up and down" in one of the front pews. Several of the younger boys were baptized there. Harry Emerson Fosdick was the chief minister, and Junior bought the small "manse" next door as a gift for Fosdick and the church (it was not actually a manse in the Presbyterian sense because it was not the residence for the minister). When Junior built Riverside Church, the Baptist congregation and Fosdick moved there and the church was sold to the Presbyterians. Now it seemed to be entering Rockefeller family history once more.

It took nearly a full year before Judge Hilda G. Schwartz of the New York State Supreme Court ruled against the sale as proposed on a number of technical grounds. A few months later the dissident group took control of the church board. Nevertheless, the Asia Society continued the negotiations in an effort to forge a new arrangement satisfactory to both sides. The site was attractive because the location was familiar to the Asia Society's public, it would make for an easy move, and the old Asia House could continue to be used during the transition into the new quarters right next door.

Meanwhile, the search committee prudently considered other sites throughout 1976. Of the ten that seemed promising, four were seriously pursued, but all turned out to have intractable problems. The Carnegie Endowment for International Peace wanted to sell its office building and move to new headquarters in Washington. The location, in the "international section" of Manhattan very near the United Nations, was attractive. But the extensive renovation of an old building that would have been required for the Asia Society to meet its needs (while renting the remainder of the building to other tenants) turned out to be too expensive. The

Hartley Dodge property north of the Pierre Hotel on Fifth Avenue also was expensive and the neighborhood was regarded as too "chic" by some Asia Society trustees.

One of the two structures on another site at 70th and Park Avenue had been the former home of a prominent New York family in the textile business, the Millikens. The site was now owned by four parties, and negotiations looked promising. However, the building plan required ten feet of the adjoining property occupied by the Visting Nurses Association, and negotiations with the VNA were stalled.

For a time the searchers were excited about a CBS property across 53rd Street from the Museum of Modern Art. The possibility existed that CBS might be charity-minded and make some important concessions. CBS chairman William Paley seemed enthusiastic about having the Asia Society next to his corporate headquarters. However, no concessions were forthcoming, and the plan proposed by CBS called for an office tower with the Society occupying a portion. Its share of the structure would have cost an estimated $16.8 million.

While all of this was going on, JDR continued to consider his financial obligations to the Society. From his diary entries it is clear that JDR planned to endow a substantial portion of a "Building Maintenance Fund" of $4 million to cover his share of the extra costs associated with managing an enlarged gallery and his collection. He also discussed with Dick Dilworth and Don O'Brien his intention to use assets from his 1934 Trust in order to provide the funds needed to honor his commitment to pay for half of the new building. His advisers told him there would be no problem and that he should make the proposal to the trust committee at the appropriate time.

There was also an architectural change. Pei's first design was regarded as too radical. The next two designs included an atrium that some of the decision-makers, including JDR, did not want. JDR also did not want a separate entrance for the gallery, believing that the gallery should be fully integrated with the Asia Society itself. Finally, it was decided to try another architect, and Pei, according to Datus Smith, "was very big about it." The next choice was Barnes, whom Blanchette liked very much. He was a trustee of the Museum of Modern Art and had once made a thoughtful gesture toward the Rockefellers. He was the architect for the IBM International Building constructed on Rockwood Hall property along the Hudson River, which IBM had purchased from Laurance Rockefeller. Barnes came unasked up to Fieldwood Farm to make sure that his design would not interfere with the view of the river. His design for the new Asia House was judged to be architecturally distinguished, and was approved unanimously by the trustees. It called for an eight-story building of red Indian sandstone with a small gallery on the ground floor for temporary exhibits and a large gallery on the mezzanine for objects from the Rockefeller permanent collection. The plan also included a bookstore, a 258-seat auditorium, all of the office space needed by the Society, and a floor and a half that could be leased.

Conscious that the passing of time was inexorably increasing the costs of the project, the search committee finally decided that the Milliken property at 70th and Park was the best choice. The last attempt with the Central Presbyterian Church involved an idea for a new building that would serve the needs of both the church and the Asia Society, but this proved unworkable. In February 1977 the search committee made an offer of $2.2 million for the Milliken property, free of tenants, and resolved to continue negotiations for all or a portion of the VNA property to the east and north. This last came to no avail, and Barnes solved the problem by making modifications in his design and turning the building on its axis. As JDR noted in his diary, the result was 15 percent less space than originally planned, but this still left three times the interior space of the existing Asia House. Finally, on December 13, 1977, a quorum of the Asia Society trustees met in the boardroom of Room 5600 and approved the terms of the contract, which was then signed by JDR and Talbot, almost four years from the time that JDR had made his offer of art and pledge of financial support.

Earlier that same year, Porter McKeever analyzed the increased costs and the funding prospects for the new Asia House. It showed that the total cost was now estimated at $15,375,000. Deducting JDR's pledge (reckoned at the time to be $5.5 million) and the appraised value of the existing Asia House ($1.3 million) left a balance of $8,575,000 to be raised. The plan was to raise $2 million from corporations, $500,000 from foundations, $2 million from "Asian sources," and $4 million from individuals. Gesualdo Costanzo of Citibank would be relied upon for corporate fundraising, and Talbot would work on foundations. The personal representations of JDR were regarded as crucial in the other two categories. During his Asian trip in the late fall of 1976, JDR initiated discussions with the Keidanren in Tokyo for a $1 million gift. The most likely other prospects were thought to be South Korea and Iran. McKeever appended a list of individuals to be solicited, and told JDR that "in many cases your name appears as the major, and sometimes only, point of contact. Whether the list is right or wrong in individual cases, it clearly suggests a heavy reliance on you in the fund-raising effort." McKeever noted that $1,350,000 of the

total had already been pledged, including a $1 million gift made anony-
mously by JDR's friend Lila Acheson Wallace.[9]

Now that the site was assured, an estimated three years would still be
required for the tenants to depart, the existing structures to be razed, and
the new Asia House built. The fund-raising would have to proceed in earnest,
but there was a good deal of time in which to accomplish the goal.

In the spring of 1978 JDR entered the hospital for major ankle surgery.
It was thought that there would be plenty of time after he had fully recu-
perated for him to come back actively into the fund-raising efforts and give
attention to the exact nature of his own financial contributions. But then,
on July 10, his sudden death occurred.

Without its founder, leader, and major supporter, the next few years
were difficult ones for the Asia Society. How it managed to overcome the
problems and get its new quarters built and dedicated on April 14, 1981,
is another story—a story of dedication on the part of many people.[10]

JDR's intentions for the disposition of his Oriental art collection were
known for so long that it seemed as if it had always been destined to go
to the Asia Society. It was different for the American art collection. There
was no Rockefeller institution that provided as natural a home for the
American art. In fact, had it not been for the onerous estate tax laws,
JDR might well have divided the American collection among his wife and
children.

However, as early as 1970 it appears that JDR had a notion that grew
into a surprising decision. It was not to become firm or known publicly
for quite some time. The decision evolved gradually, given JDR's meticulous nature and all of the investigating, reconsidering, and consulting with
lawyers and advisers that was an inevitable part of the process. But JDR
was to be just as persistent in sticking to his original inclination as he was
in the case of the Oriental collection.

In June 1970 JDR made a three-day trip to the San Francisco Bay area
that seemed to have no other purpose than to visit art museums. He went
to the Oakland Museum, the Stanford University Museum, and then to
the Legion of Honor Museum in San Francisco where his cousin, Mrs.
Mary Homans, was a trustee. She introduced him to the director, Ian
White, who was also director of the M. H. de Young Memorial Museum.
White took JDR and Mrs. Homans on a tour of both facilities. He
explained that the two institutions were heading for a merger and that an
early step had been his appointment as director of both.

In December of the same year JDR was back in San Francisco for another brief visit. As he explained in his diary, he had lunch at the Mark Hopkins Hotel with Ian White "to talk with him more specifically about the future of my collection of American art."

Said that I was considering several alternative proposals as to its ultimate disposition among which were his two museums. Told him about the collection and said I would appreciate it if he would give thought as to whether it really would be in the interest of his institutions if I should finally decide to give the collection to them. Asked him whether they really would feel it desirable to place a major emphasis on American art or would it throw their total collections out of balance. We had a good talk and I liked Mr. White on this second meeting. Asked him to treat our conversation in the strictest of confidence and also stressed that there should be no misunderstanding as to the fact that neither of us was committing himself to anything.

Over the next year JDR held several conversations about the American art with Blanchette and with their adviser, Dr. Edgar P. Richardson. JDR told Richardson it was likely that the collection would go to a museum eventually, and for that reason perhaps "we should be more amenable to acquiring larger pictures although still not beyond what could be reasonably shown in our homes or the office." Later JDR told Richardson he was thinking of choosing between the San Francisco museums and the National Gallery in Washington. Richardson "felt both places would be desirable" and seemed not to have a strong opinion one way or the other. JDR was developing one, however. "I must say, I am leaning particularly towards the West Coast, as I think it would be a more exciting decision."

It turned out that what excited JDR so much about San Francisco was the opportunity to place a major collection in a region of the country where there had been no significant emphasis on the collecting and displaying of American paintings—the region being not just the San Francisco area, but the entire United States west of the Mississippi River. People in the eastern portion of the country were "terribly fortunate," JDR wrote, given the great museums and collections there, especially in New York and Washington. But the West was seriously behind.

For the San Francisco area at least, JDR had confirmed this on his first 1970 visit, noting that the Oakland and Stanford museums had nothing in the American field, while the Legion of Honor and de Young had "some material." Actually, they had more than JDR at first realized, and this was important because his collection alone could not make a sufficient difference. The recipient museum had to have made a good start toward an American collection and should demonstrate a commitment to becoming a major factor in that field.

There was nothing wrong with Ian White's hearing, and the San Francisco museums indeed began to take steps that would merit JDR's confidence. First was a major addition of space for an American gallery. Then the museums continued their own acquisitions in the American field and extended them to furniture and the decorative arts. Edgar Richardson commented on this last to JDR with approval. He said the museums' American collections were not as good as their chairman "makes them appear," but they were still "the best on the Pacific coast." Richardson said: "The addition of your pictures would move them at once into the front rank, in richness and depth."[11]

White and his chief curator, Lanier Graham, had another good idea in 1972—a major exhibition drawn from the Rockefeller collection to take place in San Francisco in 1976 as a Bicentennial project. It took JDR and Blanchette awhile to agree to this. Their collection had never been exhibited in this way before. But it would be a good test of how it would stack up as a museum collection. The project was well organized in association with the Whitney Museum in New York and the Smithsonian, which arranged a companion exhibit of photographs and documents reflecting the lives of twenty-two of the painters represented. E. P. Richardson selected 106 works for the exhibition and wrote the handsome catalogue, which White described as a "significant departure from a traditional exhibition catalogue in that it combines impeccable scholarship and warmly human narrative."[12] Funding for the project was provided by the Alcoa Foundation and the National Endowment for the Arts.

JDR and Blanchette were on hand for the opening of the exhibition at the de Young Museum in April 1976, and were joined by Alida. There were numerous social and ceremonial events, and the Rockefellers had a preview of the exhibit. Hours before the exhibit was opened to the public, JDR went around the gallery one more time for an understandable bit of proprietary fussing, but nothing of significance was changed. He wrote:

We were very pleased with the way that the paintings were exhibited. Had been concerned that since the collection had been put together in terms of our home that it might not lend itself to the galleries of a big museum. We were also concerned by the fact that we had a number of really small paintings. However, all of this was handled by imaginative breaking up of the collection into smaller units.

The exhibition was an outstanding success during its three-and-a-half-month stay in San Francisco, as it was during its three-week appearance in the fall at the Whitney in New York. JDR thought the Whitney showing had "more appeal" than the San Francisco one: "Was amazed that the 100-odd paintings . . . seemed to fill the second floor as well as they did."

The experience pointed up one advantage of his intention to give his collection to a major museum that had its own network of financial support from public and private sources in its region. The point had been made by Sherman Lee when he laid out the options for JDR's Asian collection—a large museum, a small museum, or breaking the collection up among a number of museums. The disadvantage of a small museum was that the donor almost certainly would incur substantial additional costs to insure the viability of the museum and the collection. That certainly had been the case with the Asia Society, although there were special reasons for going ahead. But JDR could not afford to do that again. In the case of a large museum, the gift of the art normally would be enough with no further expectations levied on the donor.

In a long letter written in 1977, Walter Newman, president of the trustees of what was now known as "The Fine Arts Museums of San Francisco," touched on this and other advantages of locating the collection in his "dearly beloved city." He spelled out the nature of the museums' commitment to American art and the JDR collection, and explained its "deaccessioning" policy in response to a question JDR had raised. Items from the collection would be sold only after careful due process and only for the purpose of enriching the overall collection with new acquisitions.[13]

This letter was an attempt to nudge JDR a bit further on the way to a commitment. The possibility he had revealed to Ian White in 1970 had now existed for seven years, and there was some discernible anxiety on the West Coast over the lack of a firm decision. White and Newman gently conveyed to JDR that his intentions had an important bearing on the ability of the museums to plan for the future. JDR noted in his diary that this position was "not unreasonable," and over the balance of the year he concluded discussions with his lawyers, amended his will, and conveyed his decision to Newman in January 1978. In a long letter JDR reviewed the background and described elements of his thinking, including his desire to stay involved with the collection throughout his lifetime and to allow his heirs to choose objects from it to a level of not more than 15 percent. The key sentence in the letter said:

Although I will retain ownership of the collection, together with complete freedom to dispose of it during my life and at my death, I hereby declare my every intention to donate the collection to The Fine Arts Museums of San Francisco.[14]

It was a strong statement of intent, but still not a total commitment or an irrevocable one. But it seemed as if it were so in the press conference that occurred in San Francisco on January 19. JDR was there and heard warm sentiments and high praise from Newman, White, Mayor George

Moscone, and Diane Feinstein, president of the San Francisco Board of Supervisors. In his response JDR commented on why he had chosen San Francisco and why he had acted now. Although in passing he mentioned that he was not making "a final commitment," he later added: "I might just say that the provision of the collection to come to the Museums is in my will at the present time," something his listeners doubtless were vastly relieved to hear. Only six months later JDR was dead.

Once again there was some perhaps understandable anxiety on the West Coast. Had JDR really put the bequest in his will? Or if he had done so, had he changed it since? Everything was as JDR said it was. The bulk of the collection was willed to the San Francisco museums, after allowance for Blanchette and the four children to select a limited number of works for their personal possession. In a survey of the collection the San Francisco museums listed twenty-six works as "masterpieces of American art" and another seventy-two as "excellent pictures of special significance to San Francisco." Another sixty-eight were noted as ones that would "fill gaps in our collection." Seven were listed as "more suitable for a private collection" and nine as "redundant for San Francisco." Of the total of 182 works, 151 were eventually given to the San Francisco museums.[15]

29

✠

FAMILY ISSUES

BY THE MID-1970S the Rockefeller brothers found themselves forced to deal with a series of difficult family issues that had been simmering for some time. What would be the role in family affairs to be played by the fourth generation—the daughters and sons of the brothers and their sister, Babs, known within the family as "the Cousins"? What would be the historical legacy of the family? What would be the future of various family institutions and holdings, in particular the Rockefeller Brothers Fund and the Pocantico estate? And how would the brothers arrange for the final disposition of their major interests?

The pressure to seek answers was intensified by several deaths in the family, by the aging of the brothers, and by the maturing of the fourth generation. Of the twenty-three Cousins living in 1976, seventeen were already over thirty years of age.

Early in the decade, there seemed to be no reason why such family issues could not be taken in stride and dealt with amicably. After all, death, aging, and maturing are all natural processes. The Rockefellers seemed well-prepared to manage the effects of such processes because of their strong sense of family unity—and by having considerably more than blood kinship to bind them together, in the many trusts and institutions and holdings that John D. Rockefeller, Jr., had created in his effort to position family wealth to function beneficially for future generations.

But other factors intervened to add to the pressure and put the carefully built structure of family unity under severe strain. It threatened to break apart completely as the brothers found themselves in conflict to an extent they had never known before.

One source of this added pressure was a series of events that caused a financial squeeze of a kind the family had not experienced since the Depression. More important were two events that brought to the surface deep divisions and tensions within the family, endangering the effort to settle issues and pitting generation against generation and brother against brother.

The first, early in 1976, was the publishing of a book, *The Rockefellers: An American Dynasty*, by Peter Collier and David Horowitz, two West Coast authors who were radical Marxists at that stage of their careers.[1] In all the vast literature on the Rockefellers, there are many critical books, but only this one may reasonably be compared in its impact with Ida Tarbell's great work, *History of the Standard Oil Company*. With this and the fact that both books were best-sellers, the similarities end. Tarbell attacked an institution and helped bring about important change, whereas Collier and Horowitz attacked individuals—the members of a family at a difficult transitional point in their lives—thereby changing nothing of public significance, but only embittering relations within the family. For this reason, Tarbell's work has enduring historical importance and the Collier and Horowitz book does not. But for the same reason, its impact on the family was more personal and devastating.

The authors achieved this by operating under false pretenses and by the device of cultivating some members of the fourth generation, who were their contemporaries in age and to some extent shared their political outlook. Interviews with these Cousins yielded highly critical comments about their parents, making the book lively and readable and giving it the cachet of tearing the veil off the innermost feelings and secrets of a famous family.

The timing was ideal for the authors' purpose. Youthful rebelliousness was a national cultural phenomenon of the time. The "generation gap" is a familiar occurrence in every family, but for the Rockefellers it was made especially sensitive by the peculiar circumstances of the family and by frustration over the slow pace of addressing the transition from the third to the fourth generation. These factors made some of the Cousins vulnerable to exploitation. Having found that the technique worked so well, Collier and Horowitz used it again for their next best-seller, this time with the Kennedy family as the target.[2]

The second event that worsened family relations was the behavior of Nelson Rockefeller when he returned to New York City in early 1977 after his term as Vice President of the United States ended. Two years earlier, Nelson's grueling confirmation hearings had made public a great deal about family wealth and connections, and probably served to hasten the realization that important issues had to be settled.

When he returned to the family fold after fifteen years as governor of New York and his stint as Vice President, the aging political warrior finally knew with certainty that his dream of becoming President of the United

States was over. This made his transition from the ocean of national and world politics to the pond of family affairs a jarring one. He brought with him his restless energy, his coterie of aides, his habit of command. His most recent biographer, Joseph Persico, who had been Nelson's chief speechwriter for eleven years, characterized him during this period as "irascible and imperious."[3] In an interview, his brother David summarized Nelson's behavior after his return in one word: "appalling."[4]

Nelson focused his habitual quest for power on family matters. He seemed to have no doubt that he would take over everything and settle all questions. But he met unexpected opposition—from the fourth generation and from his older brother John.

The financial squeeze of the 1970s began, for the wealthy, with the Tax Reform Act of 1969, through the elimination of the "unlimited charitable deduction" and the beginning of the end of the ability to deduct the appreciated value of securities or other assets given to charity. The "unlimited" allowed qualified taxpayers to end up paying no tax at all on current income or relatively small amounts. Taxpayers qualified if their combined income taxes and charitable contributions equalled or exceeded 90 percent of their net taxable income for eight of the ten preceding years. In almost all cases, this was achieved by gifts of appreciated securities or other appreciated assets—it doubtless would be very difficult to find any taxpayers who actually gave away 90 percent or more of current income. The "unlimited" was especially congenial to holders of "old" money like the Rockefellers. For example, the book value of an oil stock, established many decades ago, might have appreciated ten or twenty times or more in market value. Giving such stock to charity enabled the donor to take the entire market value as a deduction, not the much smaller book value, thus "sheltering" an equal amount of current income. The effect was almost as good as if the sale of the stock on the market were tax-free to the owner. The 1969 Act had several complicated formulas that served to reduce the amount of appreciated value that could be deducted (this was the beginning of change that culminated in 1986 by allowing only the original acquisition value to be deducted).

While the 1969 Act raised the percentage of income that could be deducted for charitable gifts from 30 to 50 percent for *all* taxpayers, it also scaled down over a five-year period the deductions allowed for those who had qualified for the "unlimited"—from the former maximum of 90 percent down to the new 50 percent level for everyone. The effect can be seen in comparing JDR's tax returns before this change and four years later. In

1968 JDR paid only $403,000 in federal income taxes on a total income of
$8.5 million, a rate of less than 5 percent, while making charitable contri-
butions worth $5.3 million. In 1972, the charitable contributions had
dropped almost $2 million, while income tax increased more than three
times, to $1.3 million on a taxable income of $7.6 million (more than 17
percent).

In the years after 1972 until his death, JDR settled down to a pattern
of making charitable contributions up to the allowable 50 percent of income
each year, while his federal taxes ranged from 20 to 22 percent.

These were also the years of recession and severe inflation, fueled by
the Vietnam War and the Arab oil embargo. The decline in value of assets
could be devastating in some cases, as in the example noted earlier when
the $5 million reserve fund of the Agricultural Development Council was
almost wiped out. The Rockefeller Brothers Fund portfolio declined nearly
35 percent in value from 1972 to 1974.

In addition to the disastrous performance of the stock market, the New
York City real estate market plummeted, contributing to the city's full-
fledged financial crisis of the mid-1970s. Considering all the economic
pressures of the time, JDR performed remarkably well, continuing to contribute an enormous sum to charity each year despite paying up to four
times the taxes he had paid only a few years earlier. But, even in his case,
the squeeze was on. His income increased an average of only 1.4 percent
per year from 1968 to 1976, but in real terms, despite its impressive size,
the income lagged well behind the average rate of inflation of 8 percent.
And at the same time that JDR's capacity to give was reduced, the
expenses of all the organizations he was supporting were rising due to
inflation. In the next few years, the rate of inflation kept on rising in the
phenomenon that came to be known as "stagflation."

All of the brothers were in the same bind, with income no longer
adequate to their commitments in philanthropy and business and their
expenses for the family office, their own personal staffs, and the Pocantico
estate. Nelson was particularly hard hit in that his income during this
period was only about half that of JDR's while his expense base was larger.

Ever since the death of their father in 1960, a continuing source of financial
concern for the brothers was the heavy and growing cost of maintaining
the family office—Room 5600—with its several hundred employees. As
long as he was alive, Junior paid the bulk of the costs. His widow, Martha
Baird Rockefeller, generously continued to pay a major share of the office
expenses, able to do so by virtue of having inherited some $56 million

from her husband's estate under the marital deduction clause. (As noted, the major beneficiary from Junior's estate was the Rockefeller Brothers Fund, which received $72 million.) When Martha died of a coronary occlusion in January 1971, at the age of seventy-five, the brothers suddenly were faced with much larger office expenses just at the time when their own finances were being squeezed.

One of the brothers experienced an even greater financial loss with Martha's death. As noted earlier, Nelson had charmed "Aunt Martha" to the point that she had become the largest single financial supporter of his political campaigns, a source that was now lost to him. In other respects, Martha had faithfully used her inherited wealth in contributing financially to Rockefeller family interests, such as Colonial Williamsburg and Riverside Church. She also willed $13.4 million to the Rockefeller Family Fund, the small foundation that had been created by the Cousins. As a former concert pianist, her other great interest was music; she was a generous contributor to causes in this field, including a $10 million bequest to Lincoln Center. She had been named a trustee of the Rockefeller Brothers Fund in 1960, and willed her residual estate, after expenses and taxes, to the Fund.

As respected as "Aunt Martha" had become within the Rockefeller family, the death of Winthrop in February 1973 had a much greater emotional impact. For one thing, he died prematurely, at age sixty, a victim of cancer. More important, he was one of their own, the first of the five brothers to go, and the survivors could feel the cold hand of mortality on their shoulders. As we have seen, Winthrop had been something of an outsider in family matters, having removed himself to Arkansas after his troubled youth and difficult first marriage. But there he had redeemed himself by becoming a reform-oriented governor of a backward state in his two terms, as well as a major philanthropic benefactor of the state. As a result, he was much-honored and mourned in Arkansas.

Probably more than any other event, Winthrop's death served to focus the attention of his brothers on family issues that had to be settled. This effect was more symbolic than real; his passing did not complicate the issues. Even before his illness became known, Winthrop had asked his four brothers to buy out his share of the Pocantico estate, and they had complied. And Winthrop's share of family office expenses was comparatively small, since he had his own establishment in Arkansas.

A memorial service was held ten days after Winthrop's death in the large structure he had built at Winrock Farms to house his collection of antique cars. Some thirty-five family members braved the gray, drizzly weather to come to Arkansas for the service and more than 2,000 people

in all attended, including such notables as Vice President Spiro Agnew
and Dale Bumpers, the attractive young Democrat who had defeated
Winthrop in his attempt at a third term as governor of Arkansas.

One might assume that the main eulogy would have been delivered by
JDR as the senior member of the family present and the one who had
paid the most attention to Winthrop in the later years. He, for example,
was the only brother who had attended Win's two inaugurations as governor. But Nelson was the speaker, as "the head of the family" in the words
of his biographer, Joseph Persico, who also gives an amusing account of
the extensive research required to give Nelson more than superficial familiarity with his late brother and of the difficulties Nelson had with the
wording of the speech.[5] JDR was so accustomed to Nelson moving in to
take charge that he apparently made no protest, perhaps content with the
fact that Winthrop had asked him to be the inaugural speaker in the
Governor Winthrop Rockefeller Distinguished Lecture Series at the University of Arkansas.[6] JDR's laconic comment in his diary about Nelson's
eulogy was that he "spoke considerably longer than the rest."

The implicit rivalry between these two older brothers had been submerged because of JDR's tendency to defer to Nelson; that was soon to
cease. The incident also presaged JDR's own memorial service five and a
half years later when Nelson assumed he would be the principal eulogist
and was rebuffed.

A third death in the family occurred in May 1976. The brothers' older
sister, Babs, died of lung cancer. A fiercely independent person who had
engaged in a nearly lifelong feud with her father, Babs was even more of
an outsider than Winthrop. She had not been a participant in the Pocantico
estate, nor, until very late in life, in Rockefeller Center. The brothers
periodically tried to involve her in family affairs with limited success,
although she had taken a seat on the board of the Rockefeller Brothers
Fund in 1954. And, after Martha's death, the brothers asked Babs to take
a full share in paying the costs of the family office and she complied.

During the late 1960s and early 1970s, JDR developed two new personal
interests. One was in history, both history in general and family history
in particular. And he began exhibiting great interest in and concern for
the welfare and future of the fourth generation, the Cousins. The probable
stimuli were his own growing age, his involvement in the Bicentennial,
and his long-standing interest in young people, manifested so markedly in
his "youth project."

Up to this time he had not paid much attention to the family archives, but he soon became the leader in the effort to establish the Rockefeller Archive Center. His father had taken the first step in the mid-1950s when he became aware of the tremendous accumulation of documents, books, photographs, film, and other records that had occurred over the sixty or so years of his active career—not only his own papers, but also those of his father, other family members, and the many organizations the Rockefellers had created. Storage space was overflowing and valuable historical records were in danger of being lost or damaged.

Junior hired Joseph Ernst, a professional historian who had done his graduate work at Columbia University, to start the process of bringing order to the mountains of material. Space was taken on the mezzanine floor of the RCA Building for a family archive, although no sign on the door denoted it as such. Within a few years Ernst developed systems for sorting the material, classifying it, and scheduling availability of certain portions to inquiring scholars.

When it became clear that large portions of the material pertained to the Rockefeller Foundation and Rockefeller University (originally the Rockefeller Institute for Medical Research), the idea grew of creating a greater institution—an archive "center" instead of only a "family" archive. Both the Foundation and the university had large additional accumulations of material that could be included; other institutions that had records to preserve, such as the Rockefeller Brothers Fund, could also participate. This idea became a frequent subject at the periodic "brothers' meetings," with reports on the progress of negotiations among the institutions and discussion of questions of organization, management, site, and funding.

During these early stages, Nelson was the brother who most actively pressed the plan for developing the Center. When the idea of building it on or near the Manhattan campus of Rockefeller University became impractical, mainly for reasons of cost, it was Nelson who proposed that it be located somewhere on or near the Pocantico estate. About this time his ardor for the project cooled when it became clear that there would be little or no monetary advantage for him because of changes in the tax laws regarding deductions for the donation of papers and a more rigid definition of what constituted "self-dealing."

JDR then became the champion for the project among the brothers. The additional incentive for him was the realization that all of the repositories would be related to philanthropy so that the Archive Center would, as he commented to his staff, become "a center for the study of the third sector" in addition to the basic function of organizing and preserving important historical records and making them available to scholars.

An attractive possibility for a location emerged after the death in 1971

of Martha Baird Rockefeller. It was a house called Hillcrest that she had
built on acreage at the northern edge of the Pocantico estate, after having
given up on the idea of maintaining Kykuit as a residence for herself. It
will be recalled that the brothers had purchased Pocantico from their
father, but that he had maintained a life interest in Kykuit, the mansion
at the center of the parklike core of the estate. When Junior died in 1960,
this interest extended to his widow, but she was happy to waive her rights
so that Nelson could make Kykuit his home address as the governor of
New York State.[7]

Martha's primary residence was the vast Park Avenue triplex apartment
that she had inherited from her husband, but she still felt she needed a
"country place" and so began construction of Hillcrest, with a design by
Mott B. Schmidt that was more congenial to her tastes than Kykuit. She
turned over Kykuit to Nelson in 1962 and finished Hillcrest the following
year, but, as matters turned out, she never stayed overnight in her attractive French Provincial country home. It passed to the Rockefeller Brothers
Fund as part of her residual estate.

A study in 1972 indicated that Hillcrest was ideal for the administrative
and scholarly functions of an archive center with almost no alterations,
and that it was feasible to build the temperature-controlled storage vaults
underground. The plan called for the Center to be constituted as part of
Rockefeller University and to function under a governing council composed
of delegates from all of the participating institutions. The university, under
the chairmanship of David Rockefeller, accepted the plan, but wanted
more acreage in the event that it wished to expand what in effect would
become a branch campus.

Although Hillcrest was accepted by the brothers on the grounds that
it required the least capital expenditure of all the sites reviewed, JDR kept
insisting that an endowment fund of at least $5 million was needed. The
retired family counsel, John Lockwood, had done much of the research
and planning for the Archive Center, and he had estimated the endowment
need at from $5 million to $10 million. The brothers had assumed that the
Rockefeller Brothers Fund would provide all or most of what might be
needed from the proceeds of Martha's estate, but the staff of the Fund
was sounding very cautious on this score. JDR opined that each of the
brothers should make a contribution in the interim, something Nelson,
Laurance, and David did not want to hear, feeling themselves hard-pressed
financially.

JDR also said that no action should be taken until all constituents had
committed themselves to the project. For a time, the Rockefeller
Foundation seemed to be dragging its feet, but when the Foundation

finally agreed to join, the project moved ahead with the donation to the university by the Brothers Fund of Hillcrest, the surrounding twenty-four acres of land, $1.5 million for building the vaults, and $3 million for an endowment fund.

The Rockefeller Archive Center was formally initiated as a division of the university on January 15, 1974. The antique wood paneling and furnishings of Junior's old office were brought out of storage and installed in one of the ground-floor rooms of Hillcrest with almost the exact dimensions of the space in Room 5600 where Junior had held sway. The initial repository of records from the founding institutions totaled about 7,000 cubic feet, with plenty of room for growth in the eleven underground vaults with their combined capacity of 34,000 cubic feet.

JDR kept pressing for the full endowment fund. In 1977 he saw an opportunity for a *quid pro quo* when the brothers were trying to forge another of their many agreements on the disposition of the Pocantico estate. He attached to this discussion a proposal that each of the four brothers contribute $500,000 to make up the difference and bring the endowment for the Archive Center up to $5 million. JDR contributed $505,000 outright to Rockefeller University for the Archives Center and David pledged $500,000; Nelson and Laurance declined to participate, but they joined the others in supporting two further grants from the Brothers Fund totaling $1.25 million, which put the endowment fund past JDR's goal of $5 million.[8]

On three levels, creation of the Archive Center was an important accomplishment for JDR. For the family itself, he now knew that its historical legacy would be dealt with in a professional and systematic way, and he believed this could not help but be significant for the Cousins and future generations. For the study of history in general, an important institution had been created in a neglected field. On this, for example, Professor Stanley Katz, president of the American Council of Learned Societies, said the creation of the Archive Center was "an important breakthrough." He said: "Until then, it was virtually impossible to get access to the records of even one major foundation."[9] Finally, as the leading champion of philanthropy in American society, JDR hoped that the Center would become a force in the understanding and support of his cherished "third sector" in an active program of research, conferences, and publications.

30

☙

THE CENTER AND
THE ESTATE

FOR SOME TIME the brothers had been grappling with issues having to
do with Rockefeller Center, by now the main respository of family wealth.
The most difficult issues were rooted in the fact that Columbia University
owned most of the land on which the Center stood, while the Brothers
and then the 1934 Trusts owned the buildirgs and the management corporation—Rockefeller Center, Inc. (RCI).[1]

This fundamental fact severely restricted the maneuverability of the
brothers in respect to the Center. For example, a huge amount of cash
had to be held in escrow to guarantee lease payments to the University.
Dividends could not be declared until all debt was paid. The family could
sell shares beyond 20 percent only to family members. Thus the marketability of the Center was strictly curtailed.

Some of these restrictions were eased or eliminated in successive lease
renegotiations with Columbia and by the passing of time. But the basic
one remained—Columbia adamantly refused to consider selling the land
to RCI.

Further, the brothers faced a dangerous situation for their estates in
personally owning large blocs of stock in RCI. The estate tax consequences
would be devastating. For this reason, the brothers sold their stock (in
actions taken in 1955, 1963, and 1967) to their 1934 Trusts, the university
agreeing that this represented "family."

It will be recalled that creation of these trusts was Junior's basic and
cautious way of providing wealth not only for his wife and six children,
but for the next several generations as well. His wife and children would
receive the income from the trusts during their lifetimes (with the brothers
also allowed to invade principal with the agreement of their trust committees). These were so-called generation-skipping trusts, meaning that upon

491

the death of one of the beneficiaries the income would be divided equally among his or her children (the Cousins' generation), with the principal being paid out and the trust ceasing to exist only when members of the fifth generation inherited their parents' share.

The five brothers had done very well up to the 1970s. Their father had sold his stock in Rockefeller Center to them in 1948 for a total of $2,210,000. In 1952 Junior made a gift to the Rockefeller Brothers Fund of the sum owed to him by Rockefeller Center, some $57.5 million. In selling their stock to their trusts the brothers together netted $61,376,000, after deducting taxes and their purchase price. Interestingly, the total of these transactions (plus several other minor ones) came within $1 million of Junior's estimated total investment in Rockefeller Center ($122,653,000).

In sum, Junior's investment had been recouped, the brothers received assets with a substantial value, and the value of their joint philanthropic instrument (the RBF) was significantly enhanced; and the brothers each enjoyed a potential tax write-off equivalent to one-fifth of the loss on the book value of Junior's RCI stock, approximately $10 million. And, the family still owned RCI through the 1934 Trusts.

But problems remained. RCI finally finished paying off the debt (Junior's gift to the RBF) in 1969 and thus was free to pay dividends. But the Center had started to show a profit only in 1964, and for a long time it was a relatively meager annual profit. For example, the profit of $1.66 million in 1967 represented little more than a 1 percent return on the then value of RCI stock of $108 million. RCI did not start paying dividends regularly until 1976 (one "technical" dividend of $281,000 had been paid by agreement with Columbia in 1960).

In order to purchase the RCI stock, the Trust Committees of course had to sell off other assets. Because RCI was not paying out, this meant that the income from the trusts was correspondingly lessened, a fact that contributed considerably to the financial squeeze the brothers were feeling in the 1970s. Several other steps taken early in the decade intensified this pressure, though they were to have long-term benefits for the family.

The first was a renegotiation of the lease with Columbia that was protracted and acrimonious, taking a year to consummate in 1972–73. For the tenth time since 1928, Columbia refused to sell the land. But it did agree to eliminate the escrow requirement and reduce the percentage of stock required to be held by the family from 80 percent to 20 percent. The lease payments were increased and the lease extended to the year 2069, and RCI agreed to a onetime payment of $4 million to the university to compensate for lower revenues in the preceding years.

The big concession on stock ownership marked a watershed change for RCI. Much more of the stock was now marketable and so RCI moved to become a conglomerate by expanding and diversifying, with investments other than the Center itself in the construction, real estate, packaging, and communication fields.

This, however, coincided with the sharp decline in the New York real estate market and the period of "stagflation" that followed. RCI needed capital, and at this point the best way to get it was from the family. The method used was for the trusts of John, Laurance, and David to each purchase $6,666,666 worth of a new issue of cumulative convertible preferred stock to be issued by RCI. Nelson's trust did not participate. The reason was that his trust already owned considerably more RCI stock than the others. In the 1955 purchase Nelson had asked his brothers to permit him to buy a larger share of stock than they. Nelson then was the chief executive officer of Rockefeller Center and apparently felt bullish on its future. The result, however, was that Nelson was suffering more than his brothers by the inability of RCI to pay dividends. To make up the balance of RCI's new capital needs, the brothers also persuaded their sister, Babs, to allow her trust to purchase $10 million of the new issue, the first time that her trust owned shares in Rockefeller Center.[2]

By this action, RCI raised $30 million in capital for its diversification program and the three participating brothers saw their trust income declining as a result. Now nearly half of the value of the various 1934 Trusts was in the form of RCI stock.

These measures had the effect of turning JDR 3rd into something of a nag on the subject of RCI's performance. As his diary shows, he frequently buttonholed Dick Dilworth, the family's senior manager and chairman of RCI. Dilworth kept reassuring JDR that the policy of expansion rather than payout was best for RCI and for the family in the long run. JDR kept fretting about his curtailed income, raising questions about the policies and the competence of RCI management. In the diary entries he comes through as bemused by what was happening and Dilworth as bland and reassuring.

The attempt to forge a mutually agreeable plan for the future of the other major physical property owned by the Rockefeller brothers, the Pocantico estate, proved to be an extremely complicated and at times contentious issue for them.

The estate is an extraordinarily lovely enclave of rolling hills, woodlands, and outcroppings of rock located between the Hudson River and the Saw Mill River Parkway, slightly to the north and east of Tarrytown in Westchester County. From various points of high ground, the views of the Hudson River and the Palisades to the west are breathtaking. Some idea of Pocantico's size may be gained from the fact that at its peak, nearly 3,500 acres, it was almost four times the size of Manhattan's Central Park.

John D. Rockefeller began assembling land in the area in the last decade of the nineteenth century when he was struck by its beauty during a visit to the estate of his brother William, Rockwood Hall, which fronted on the Hudson River. For years Senior kept acquiring land, including the purchase of Rockwood Hall, in what was then a very sparsely settled area of farms and villages.

For a few years the senior Rockefeller and his only son were content to make use of dwellings that happened to exist on some of the acquired acreage for their limited residence of occasional weekends and summer months. But when the house his parents used burned down in 1902, Junior embarked on the building of a country mansion for them in the Georgian style, situated on a hill called Kykuit (Dutch for "lookout"), with a commanding view in all directions. Though not immense, Kykuit is certainly a stately country mansion because of additions over the years to the relatively modest original structure. These include an additional floor and mansard roof, new wings and underground grottos and passages, and a beautiful variety of gardens cascading down from the crest on all sides.

Some other houses and working farms were maintained on the estate, and new structures were built. The most notable structures are the "Orangerie" (patterned after the original in Versailles) to house citrus and other plants, a huge brick "Coach Barn" for carriages, stables, and tack rooms, and a rambling "Playhouse" built by Junior in the French Norman style half a mile across a nine-hole golf course from Kykuit.

These buildings are all located in the manicured core of the estate, an area of 249.5 acres that came to be known as "the Park," in contrast to "the open spaces," the balance of the estate, which for the most part was left in its natural condition except for riding trails. Portions at times were opened to the public.[3]

Several public roads bisect portions of the estate, but a passerby would assume it to be a forest preserve rather than an enclave of the wealthy. The village of Pocantico Hills on Bedford Road, where the main entrance is located, is surrounded by the estate. It has something of the character of a company town with many houses owned by the Rockefellers and others by employees, although there are also independent householders.

Transferring ownership of such a magnificent property from one generation to the next became increasingly complicated as time passed. In 1925, when Junior took over ownership from his father, there was no problem because income, estate, and gift taxes were not significant factors. By the 1950s, however, Junior reluctantly had to listen to the advice that because of estate taxes his personal ownership of the property would pose an immense financial problem for his heirs. The only solution, he was told, was to *sell* the Pocantico estate to his sons while still living.

His way of accomplishing this was to create a corporation called Hills Realty in 1952 and to give it the estate in return for 1,000 shares of stock. He then sold one-fifth of the stock to each of his five sons for $152,059, or a total of $760,295, subject to his life tenancy. He indeed remained the dominating factor, continuing to live in Kykuit and paying for annual maintenance of the entire Pocantico estate, approximately $1 million a year.

The price certainly seems an incredible bargain, yet that was Pocantico's appraised value at the time and the transaction passed muster with the Internal Revenue Service. One reason for the low valuation was that the marketability of the property was virtually nil, given the limiting factors of Junior's life tenancy and a formal agreement by the brothers that all had to agree to any sale.

The brothers did agree to an important change in 1954. Winthrop had relocated to Arkansas to expedite his divorce from Bobo. His four brothers thereupon agreed to buy the Park from Hills (for $311,298), compensating Winthrop for his one-fifth share in the process. This left the open spaces still in Hills, with all five brothers sharing the stock equally. The main reason seems to have been that Winthrop would not be using Pocantico or maintaining a house there, but the brothers might also have been concerned that his share of the Park might become entangled in the divorce settlement. The four brothers divided the Park unequally among themselves, reflecting their anticipated degree of use. JDR took only 7.75 percent, David 23 percent, Laurance 30.75 percent, and Nelson 38 percent.

One reason for this pattern was that the country homes of John and David were both on the edge of the estate, John having Fieldwood Farm on land given to him by his father and David having acquired Hudson Pines from Babs in 1946 after her divorce from David Milton. In contrast, the residences of Laurance and Nelson were both close to the center of the estate. Although Laurance had been given the Rockwood Hall property by his father, he used the Kent House for his country place. Nelson had the Hunting Lodge and stayed in the Hawes House whenever he visited Pocantico. Nelson's large share may also have come about because he envisioned himself living in Kykuit after his father was gone.

As we have seen, this indeed happened when, after Junior's death in

1960, his widow, Martha, built Hillcrest as her country place and turned Kykuit over to Nelson despite her inherited option of life tenancy. From 1960 on, the five brothers shared equally in maintenace costs for the open spaces, but the four custodians of the Park prorated those costs according to their percentage of ownership.

Within a decade the brothers perforce had to begin thinking about the problems posed for *their* heirs by personal ownership of portions of the Pocantico estate. Junior's solution of selling the estate to his heirs was not practical for the brothers. He could deal with his five sons in a reasonably coherent way as a group, but the numerical increase of the family made this impossible for the brothers in their turn. So varied were the twenty-three Cousins in age, location, interests, and financial situation that there never was a possibility of them functioning effectively as owners or managers of the Pocantico estate.

This by no means meant that the Cousins were dismissed from consideration. The brothers continued to seek some means by which the Cousins could participate in the future of Pocantico. There was a standing offer for them to acquire some acreage to build their own country homes, but few took advantage of this and only one, Nelson's eldest son, Rodman, built his primary residence there. Of particular interest was the Playhouse— visiting Cousins and those living in the New York area frequently made use of its amenities. This huge, somewhat gloomy structure includes a basketball court, an indoor tennis court, a tiled indoor pool (as well as an outdoor pool), squash courts, bowling alleys, billiard rooms, exercise rooms, card rooms and lounges, dining facilities, and the great baronial hall mentioned earlier where Junior and Abby hung the wartime oil portraits of their five sons and Babs. During one of the later efforts to plan for the disposition of Pocantico, the Cousins were polled to see if they would be interested in acquiring the Playhouse, at least for lifetime use, but the majority voted in the negative, presumably for reasons of cost and inability to make enough use of it.

With the Cousins providing no solution to the problem for the brothers of getting Pocantico out of their estates, they began in 1967 to study the device that had worked so well for them in the case of Rockefeller Center—selling the Pocantico estate to their 1934 Trusts. JDR for one was very uneasy about this idea. Although the study continued for a long time, the idea was eventually abandoned. Under the new laws, the tax implications were not entirely clear. Morever, it did not make much sense for the trusts to sell off income-producing assets to acquire something that in large measure did not produce income and cost money to maintain. Further, the long-term effect still would have been "balkanization" of

Pocantico because the trusts in due course would pass to the Cousins and through them to their children. And a large number of owners would not auger well for effective management and planning—the brothers were having a difficult enough time with their limited number.

Beginning in the late 1960s, the brothers embarked on a long-term effort to plan effective disposition with the aid of a series of land-use planners and real estate appraisers on contract—such names as Sasaki, Vollmer, Aldrich, Rouse, Goldstone, and Yates appear and reappear frequently in the voluminous record. Central to this effort was the permanent staff, especially Donal O'Brien, who had succeeded John Lockwood as chief counsel for the family. So demanding was this assignment over such a long period that the brothers eventually began to worry about the stress on O'Brien and the effect on his health. O'Brien frequently was the man in the middle, trying to mediate among the conflicting views of the brothers and trying to move the process from one complicated series of discussions and negotiations to the next. Even when the brothers seemed to agree on something it was a herculean (and often fruitless) task to try to pin the agreement down and move on.

Although there were some aberrations and variations, the outside planners tended to share a vision of beneficial effects for everyone in the proper disposition of the Pocantico estate. They might have felt the way that Frederick Law Olmsted and Calvert Vaux did in 1856 in contemplating the planning of Central Park on acreage that New York City had purchased (for $5.5 million), a vision of a wondrous gift for the public in the use of land that otherwise surely would have gone the way of random commercial and residential development. For their own purposes, to be sure, the Rockefellers nevertheless had succeeded in protecting a marvelous sector, rich in natural beauty and history, from the rapid development of Westchester County.

The idea of converting most of the estate into a public park and preserve rapidly became the dominant vision of both the brothers and the planners. Soon the companion idea emerged of the Park becoming a national historic site, preserved, managed, and open to the public much in the manner of Colonial Williamsburg. To the extent that land went for these purposes to nonprofit uses, there would be no estate or tax problem. But there would be very heavy expenses for making these uses possible, all the costs of conversion, maintenance, and management, a responsibility for the donors, just as JDR could not simply give his Asian art collection to the Asia Society, but also had to provide funds for its ongoing maintenance and support. For this reason, various plans considered by the brothers also identified sections of the open spaces that might be especially well suited for limited commercial and residential development. Sale for such purposes would yield revenues that could be applied to the expense of making public usage possible.

The first comprehensive presentation of this multi-use disposition of the estate was done by Hideo Sasaki in 1972; the "Sasaki plan" remained the basic concept through all of the studies and variations that followed.

In addition to holding Pocantico land, Hills Realty had become a convenient entity for the brothers in making other real estate investments over the years. As a result, Hills at various points owned such properties as the Carlyle Hotel in New York City; a shopping center in Moorestown, New Jersey; the building housing the Parke-Bernet auction house in New York; and an industrial center in Edison, New Jersey. It also owned a number of houses in the village of Pocantico Hills and the open spaces with limited areas suitable for residential, commercial, or industrial development. The market value of the outside properties was estimated at $20 million.

In 1970 Winthrop asked his brothers to buy out his share of Hills Realty. In taking this up, the four brothers also heeded the advice of O'Brien to equalize their holdings in the Park. By 1972 the new arrangements were completed. Win sold his share of Hills for $4 million, Hills Realty was dissolved, and JDR and David completed transactions with Laurance and Nelson to bring each brother's interest in the Park to 25 percent. The result was that the four now owned the entire Pocantico estate as "tenants in common," as distinct from certain properties each already held individually (such as Fieldwood Farm in the case of JDR). An added motivation for the Park equalization was to help Nelson financially. The memoranda of the time make references to "Nelson's substantial commitments" and the need to help Nelson "find a solution to his own financial problems," occasioned in part by his former 38 percent ownership of the Park.

O'Brien also urged that the Pocantico estate be treated in a like manner in the wills of each of the brothers. One problem was deciding on which nonprofit entity was best suited to receive Pocantico and adapt it to the park and historical purposes intended. At various times, New York State, Westchester County, the Taconic Park Commission, the National Park Service, the National Trust for Historic Preservation, and Sleepy Hollow Restorations figured in the discussions. Pending a final decision, O'Brien sought to finesse the estate tax problem by urging each brother to express the basic intent in his will of passing his one-fourth share to a nonprofit entity for public use and naming several such agencies, but not a specific recipient (always with the option of lifetime use by the brother and his wife). In the event of the death of one of the brothers, this would put his share on hold and empower his executors to continue negotiations to find an agreed-upon solution with the surviving brothers.

The big stumbling block was money. By the mid-1970s, the best estimate was that it would take $45 million to put the open spaces and the Park into operation for public purposes and endow them for continued operation. For several more years, O'Brien and various consultants labored to produce a bewildering variety of plans and proposals for consideration by the brothers. These offered different combinations of recipients and differing patterns and options for funding. By 1977 there seemed to be general agreement that the only viable financial plan would embody three elements: some $10 million raised from the sale of outside properties that the brothers agreed to sell; a contribution of $5 million provided by each of the brothers in their wills, for a total of $20 million; and the final $15 million to come from some public source or a foundation, with the Rockefeller Brothers Fund always the target of last resort.

By this time Nelson had returned from Washington and friction between him and JDR was getting in the way of a solution. JDR voiced his doubts about making the Park into a historic restoration, an idea that was dear to Nelson's heart. As early as 1966 he had referred to it as a potential "national shrine." There were probably several reasons for JDR's position. One was a genuine streak of modesty about extolling the family's historical legacy, feeling that that was for others to do. One can see a similarity in his reticence about doing an autobiography or having a biography of himself done. He believed the Archives Center was the real historical site for the family, an entirely legitimate one, and it irked him that he had to keep pushing to make the Center a reality while Laurance and Nelson seemed to him to be dragging their feet.

He also found Nelson's proximity and magisterial presence in Kykuit a frequent irritation. There was some symbolism here, even though JDR had never wanted to live in Kykuit himself. From the house where the patriarchs of the two preceding generations had lived, Nelson could be imagined proclaiming: "You see—I'm *really* the head of the family!" What is more, he acted like it. A prodigious collector of art, especially modern art, Nelson had taken to placing outdoor sculpture around Kykuit, spilling out beyond what JDR considered the proper limits. And Nelson frequently used estate employees to move these pieces around. All of this infuriated JDR, who paid one-fourth the salary of these employees and had helped ease Nelson's financial plight in the equalization agreement. He complained about the sculpture frequently in brothers' meetings, and every so often Nelson would resent this enough to say that he would sell his pieces, or he would propose some aberrant scheme such as letting the entire estate go to commercial and residential uses.

For a time JDR was inclined to the idea that the entire Pocantico estate should simply be a public park without any special effort at historical restoration, even though Kykuit and its immediate surroundings were declared a National Historic Landmark in 1976. Pending agreement he withheld support of the idea of each brother making provision in his will for a $5 million contribution. To try to persuade him, O'Brien commissioned Harmon Goldstone and aides to do a survey of national historic sites. After almost a year they came back with an impressive report, including analysis of more than twenty comparable sites. JDR's saving grace always was that he was open-minded when things were done properly and carefully. He listened and read and proclaimed that he now would accept the plan.

His change of attitude may also have been encouraged by the enthusiasm of various nonprofit agencies. For a time, the likely combination seemed to be the Taconic Park Commission (an agency of New York State), with Sleepy Hollow managing the historic site. Then Carlisle Humelsine, chairman of the National Trust for Historic Preservation (and former president of Colonial Williamsburg) breezed through the property and proclaimed that all of it, open spaces *and* the Park, should be a historic site, the one integrally linked with the other. He had the encouraging idea that ample funds might be available in the billions of dollars that would be assigned to historic preservation by federal legislation dealing with revenue from offshore oil drilling leases.

By 1978 the National Park Service, in combination with Sleepy Hollow, had become the prime contender. There had been some reluctance to deal with a federal agency while Nelson was still Vice President, but that inhibition was gone and Park Service representatives were enthusiastic about a concept they called Four Centuries. Sleepy Hollow Restorations, Inc., is the small gem that Junior had created to manage three historic sites on the Hudson River, Washington Irving's home (Sunnyside), and two colonial estates, Van Cortlandt and Philipse manors. These properties represented the seventeenth and eighteenth centuries in the region, while Rockefeller Park would represent the nineteenth and twentieth—four centuries. The Sleepy Hollow organization had always been a sentimental and professional favorite in the discussions, but because the new tax laws presented "self-dealing" problems for the brothers in dealing directly with a family-related institution, no matter how pure, public, and nonprofit it might be, it could enter the picture only as a subsidiary institution to one of the other contenders.[4]

Because the Park Service also offered hope for public funds to make up the balance of the endowment needed, the Four Centuries concept carried the day and appeared to be the agreed-upon plan as of mid-1978. And then sudden death intervened. JDR made the right provision in his will for the recipients by following the O'Brien formula, but did not get around to providing for the $5 million contribution by the time he died in an automobile accident on July 10, 1978. When Nelson died of a heart attack six months later, he hadn't provided for the $5 million either, but he did complicate the planning process by willing his interest in Pocantico to a specific recipient—the National Trust for Historic Preservation.[5]

Now Laurance, David, and JDR's executors were much more limited in their range of choices. The National Trust joined them as a fourth owner, having no money to offer, but possibly willing to sell its share to the others. For Don O'Brien, it was back to the drawing board for more tedious years of labor.[6]

31

🐝

BROTHERS AND
COUSINS

THE CLASH of opinions among the Rockefeller brothers over the Archive Center, Rockefeller Center, and the Pocantico estate was but the merest prelude to the fireworks attending two other issues—control of the family office and the future of the Rockefeller Brothers Fund. These were the most volatile for two reasons: they were the main targets in Nelson's drive to regain the reins of power, and both were directly affected by the gap that yawned between the third and fourth generations of Rockefellers.

The question of the role in Rockefeller family affairs to be played by the members of the fourth generation—the Cousins—began to be discussed early in the 1960s. It was sporadically raised in the following years, but no one could come up with a clear picture of what could or should happen.

The transitions that had occurred in the preceding generations offered little or no guidance. As the only son of John D. Rockefeller, Junior had entered his father's office fresh from college in 1897 to find that the old man had retired, with the result that Junior was left pretty much to find his own way under the tutelage of Frederick Gates. More than thirty years later, as the chief figure in a much-expanded family office and network of Rockefeller organizations and interests, Junior had to face the question of how his five sons might relate to family affairs in the launching of their own careers. There was only one ceremonial beginning—the press conference in 1929 on JDR 3rd's first day of work in the family office. In response to a reporter's question about how he was preparing for the entry of all five of his sons into their adult careers, Junior said: "As a matter of fact, we don't know the right way to start a Rockefeller in business. When we get to the fifth son, we'll have a technique developed, I hope."[1]

It was not to be. No "technique" was ever developed. JDR's role had been largely ordained, but the other brothers forged their careers on the basis of their interests and the available opportunities, though all five, as we have seen, were bound together to a considerable extent by the family heritage and institutions, including the instrument they had jointly developed, the Rockefeller Brothers Fund.

In the case of the Cousins, their sheer number and diversity defied any neat and logical transition into family affairs. In 1976, the twenty-three Cousins ranged in age from Babs's eldest daughter, Abby O'Neill, forty-eight, to nine-year-old Mark Fitler Rockefeller, the younger of Nelson's two sons by his second wife, Happy. There were nearly fifty members of the *fifth* generation on hand, some of them well past twenty years of age, and the sixth generation was due to make its appearance shortly.

The Cousins lived all over the country, most of them somewhere other than New York. Their knowledge of family history and affairs was sketchy, not inculcated in any systematic way, but only in bits and pieces within the particular circumstances of each Cousin's family. There was no single family patriarch to indoctrinate them as Junior had attempted with his six children.

Yet the Rockefeller mystique was present in the lives of each of them, along with the attendant problems of growing up with such a famous name and the image of great wealth. David Rockefeller, Jr., the oldest of David's six children, refers to this as "the beautiful woman syndrome"—is a person evaluated according to external characteristics such as beauty or wealth or for inner worth as a human being?[2] Almost all of the women among the Cousins, who outnumber males almost two to one, lost the Rockefeller name through marriage. Most of those marriages ended in divorce, and the tendency among the divorcees has been to retain their former husband's surname or adopt a family name.

As Rockefellers, the Cousins were somewhat sequestered in their early years, attending elite private schools and often spending vacation periods in the family enclaves at Pocantico or Seal Harbor. For their parents, this was entirely normal, given the never-absent fear of a Lindbergh-style kidnapping or other violent act visited upon one of their children. For the Cousins, however, the protective atmosphere became an element in the spirit of rebelliousness that many of them developed as the years passed.

In other respects, the upbringing of the Cousins was much more lax and open than that of their fathers. For example, pressure to attend church and keep account books faded out early and the children were much more exposed to "pop" culture than their parents had been.

Most of the Cousins had basic financial security for life by virtue of the 1952 Trusts their grandfather had created, although some of them may not even have been aware until they turned thirty years of age that these trusts existed. Each brother had control of setting conditions for payout from the trusts until that time, and the brothers apparently handled this in different ways. Since Junior had established the trusts when most of his grandchildren were quite young, the trusts grew over the years to have significant value, probably as much as $10 million each. The only three grandchildren living in 1952 for whom Junior did not create trusts were Babs's two daughters and Winthrop's only son.[3]

Ironically, it was these same three grandchildren who were the first of the Cousins to benefit from the larger source of wealth, the 1934 Trusts, because of the deaths of Babs and Winthrop. Babs's trust was divided into two equal parts with the income going to her daughters, Abby and Marilyn, while Winthrop Paul was Winthrop's only heir.

As the members of the fourth generation became adults they began to avail themselves of the wonderful convenience of Room 5600 services— everything from having tax returns done to help in buying a new car. Many of them gradually became dissatisfied with the relationship, however, feeling somewhat impotent with no voice or power and beginning to resent what they regarded as paternalistic treatment. It was not an easy relationship for the office employees, either; they naturally were beholden to the brothers, but they also had a stake in seeing the office valued and maintained by the Cousins in the future. The problem was that no one knew with any certainty just what the ground rules were, even though several efforts had been made to plan for the coming of age of the Cousins and their integration into the family office.[4]

One answer was for the Cousins themselves to get organized in order to press their interests with the family and the office more effectively; this they proceeded to do late in the 1960s. In effect, they formed an association, electing their own officers and meeting twice a year, in June and at Christmas. Spouses were also included. In 1967 the Rockefeller Family Fund (RFF) was created as a counterpart of the Cousins' generation to the Rockefeller Brothers Fund (RBF). The small initial capitalization came from the brothers and David Rockefeller was the first chairman, with JDR and Laurance also serving on the board. The idea was for the Cousins to take it over gradually by beginning to contribute to it and serving on the board. By 1972 a dozen Cousins were on the board, David Jr. had succeeded his father as chairman, and the RFF now had significant resources with the $13.4 million bequest from Martha's estate. But the three brothers were still board members.

On balance, the political orientation of the Cousins was decidedly left of center in the late 1960s and the 1970s. These, of course, were the times of Vietnam War protest, the youth and sex revolutions, and burgeoning "movements" for civil rights, women's rights, and the environment. Most of the young Rockefellers, especially the women, were heavily involved, spurred by a different mix within each of them of the spirit and camaraderie of the times, intellectual conviction, and rebellion against the family name and elements of its legacy. Many of the Cousins were going through a prolonged identity crisis, acutely sensitive to the fact that their fathers were widely seen as the very epitome of the capitalist establishment. Their protests and probings directed to the staff in Room 5600 often dealt with the stock in their trusts of companies that did business in South Africa or had arms contracts or appeared to discriminate against women and minorities in their hiring and promotion policies.

The political gradations of the Cousins resist easy classification, ranging fully across the political spectrum from the staunch Republicanism of Nelson's eldest son, Rodman, to the professed Marxism of David's daughter, Abby, who was a vocal critic of everything she thought the family represented. Her sister Peggy and Laurance's daughter Marion were also to the left, the latter almost as a personification of the counterculture. Abby and Marion were among those who proclaimed that they did not want their inherited wealth, only to be told by Room 5600 that the trusts existed and nothing could be done about it—but both made good use of their money in supporting causes they favored.

Nelson's son Steven was on the left side of the spectrum as well, but his views seemed the product of introspection, more personal and philosophical. He had lived through a difficult first marriage and had become a theologian and then a faculty member of Middlebury College in Vermont. JDR's youngest daughter, Alida, was a student at Stanford at the height of the war protest and youth movement, and was heavily influenced by radical groups on the campus. This left her a confirmed liberal, but she resisted the extremes of behavior.

Others were mainstream liberals or centrists, such as Jay, David Jr., Larry, and Neva, while others were more concerned about developing their careers than with politics—Lucy as a psychiatrist, Hope as a journalist, Richard in medical school, Laura in history with an interest in family counseling.

Not surprisingly, JDR took a particularly avid interest in the Cousins, his natural avuncularity blossoming as he sought out various nieces and nephews for lunch dates when they happened to be in New York, corresponded with them, learned from them, and counseled them from time to time. This increased during the years that he was involved in his youth project and working on his book. He was not argumentative but supportive and keenly interested in their views even when he did not fully agree with them.

Some thought this went too far at times, as when Blanchette wryly commented that her husband had as much business counseling David Jr. away from the law and into his first love, music, as brother David might have had were he to counsel Jay to become a collector of beetles.[5] Aside from David Jr. and his own son, Jay, JDR had the most marked affinity for Steven. He appreciated Steven's keen intellect and philosophical bent; they were allies in opposing the sale of the Pocantico estate to the 1934 Trusts.

In these relationships, JDR might have been keeping an eye out for the individual who might emerge as the leader of the Cousins' generation in family matters and councils. The brothers were agreed that Jay was the ideal candidate for this, but he was devoted to his political career in West Virginia and was not available. For a time Steven indeed was the most articulate spokesman for the Cousins, but he was not interested in more than that. In truth, no one could represent the widely varying interests and views of all the Cousins in any unified way, but David Jr., a graduate of the Harvard Law School, gradually emerged to fill a sort of vacuum. Bearded, friendly, articulate, and possessed of a fine baritone voice, he had become assistant manager of the Boston Symphony and enjoyed working with and participating in choral groups. Deeply interested in philanthropy, David Jr. in 1984 took an office in Room 5600, traveling from Cambridge three days a week as director of human resources in the family office.[6]

At first the semiannual meetings of the Cousins were largely social affairs, with some strong friendships developing across family lines. But by 1972 the group had become more organized and feistier. Sharon Percy Rockefeller was elected chairman at the June meeting. Discussion groups were organized and the issues debated, with innermost feelings being revealed. The Cousins were being asked to chip in and help support the family office, but most of them felt that they had been given too little responsibility and had too little influence in Room 5600 to do that. After the sessions, Larry wrote to the brothers to express some of the concerns. They discussed his letter briefly in a brothers' meeting and agreed to meet with Larry. The suggestion was made that perhaps he should be elected to the board of the Rockefeller Brothers Fund.

If JDR was the brother most sympathetic to the Cousins, Nelson was at the opposite end of the spectrum, and he gradually became the brother most disliked by members of the fourth generation. His ebullience and heartiness made him hard to dislike in person, even if one saw his personality as a facade. But his public persona became anathema to most of the Cousins.

Nelson unquestionably was a brilliant man in some ways, often capable of being visionary, and a skilled political tactician. But by the 1970s most of the Cousins—and many other people—were reacting negatively to his unquenchable thirst for power, his image as a consummate Cold Warrior, his increasingly conservative views and actions.

Joseph Persico has pointed up the irony of Nelson continuing to be regarded by the right wing of the Republican Party as "too liberal" even as he moved to the right himself and became a loyalist, as for example in stumping actively for President Nixon's reelection in 1972.[7] So staunch had Nelson been on such issues as law and order and support of Nixon's hard-line Vietnam policy that he had been rewarded with the honor of placing the incumbent President's name in nomination at the 1972 convention.

Nelson had earned the liberal label early in his public career, and it had been strengthened in the 1960s by his opposing the favorites of the right wing, Nixon and Goldwater; indeed, much of his politics was congruent with that image. He was always a man of big ideas, which inevitably were followed by big spending and big taxes. He had been consistent in supporting freedom of choice in the abortion issue. But he became caustic about welfare "drones" and student protesters, jeering back at hecklers during his speeches. By such actions as the bloody quelling of the Attica prison revolt and pushing through an antidrug program so extreme that it proved unworkable, he increasingly came to seem like one of the right-wingers who continued to reject him.

Nelson's friendship with his old opponent, Richard Nixon, was useful to him in elevating his state commission to national status as the Commission on Critical Choices for Americans, though no federal funding resulted. Nelson raised $6.5 million for the effort in the private sector (including $1 million each from himself and brother Laurance) and named thirty-seven "leading Americans" to the commission, plus himself as chairman. Included were such luminaries as Edward H. Teller, Daniel Moynihan, Nobelist Norman Borlaug, Walt W. Rostow, Bill Paley of CBS, Lane Kirkland of the AFL-CIO, and the majority leaders of the House of Representatives, Tip O'Neill and Gerald Ford. Nearly one hundred staff members and consultants were put to work developing research, ideas, and position papers on a wide range of subjects divided into three broad areas of inquiry. The topics that Nelson was most drawn to himself were energy policy and international security. Altogether, the effort was at least as visionary as "Prospects for America," the Rockefeller Brothers Fund Panel Report that Nelson had masterminded in the late 1950s, elements of which had appeared in both the Democratic and Republican Party platforms of 1960.

In defeating Arthur Goldberg in 1970 and winning his fourth four-year term as governor of New York, Nelson set a modern record for longevity in office. He had played the role of governor with enormous zest, but he had never taken his eyes off the greatest prize in American politics. There is no question that his resignation in December 1973 in order to plunge into the work of his new commission was a strategy designed to give himself one last shot at the Presidency. He had freed himself from the toils of state politics and administration and taken a new platform to stay in the public eye by examining the great issues of the time. The strategy assumed the obvious—that the newly reelected Richard Nixon would complete his second term, leaving the field open for the Republican nomination in 1976 by virtue of the fact that the law would prevent him from seeking a third term. Although Nelson would turn sixty-eight that year, he discounted the age factor, feeling as energetic as ever. Moreover, he apparently was in favor with Nixon and his people, while the only real rival he could see, Ronald Reagan, was heartily disliked by the Nixonites. Vice President Spiro Agnew, the man Nelson had stranded by his abrupt withdrawal from the 1968 race, should prove to be no competition.

However, by the time Nelson received federal status for his commission and was planning his resignation, Agnew was gone, having resigned the Vice Presidency under the cloud of accepting improper payments dating back to his days as governor of Maryland. There was a brief flurry of hope that the mantle might fall on Nelson as Nixon's successor much sooner than expected, but the President chose Gerald Ford for the vacancy instead. Now the success of Nelson's strategy depended on Nixon weathering the storm of Watergate. Nelson thought it possible that Vice President Ford would not seek the nomination in 1976; if he did, Nelson liked his chances of defeating both Ford and Reagan. Nelson went ahead with his strategy. Unlike his brother John, he carefully refrained from saying anything critical about the Watergate cover-up.

With Nixon's resignation in August 1974, Gerald Ford became President and the Vice Presidency was open again. Just as Nelson was about to leave Kykuit with his wife and two youngest sons for a summer vacation at Seal Harbor, phone calls came in from press secretary Hugh Morrow and former Defense Secretary Melvin Laird. Apparently Nelson's friend Gerald Ford, still a member of his Commission on Critical Choices for Americans, wanted Nelson as his Vice President. This was confirmed when Ford himself got Nelson on the telephone at Seal Harbor. It was Nelson's third offer of the Vice Presidency. The man who had said many times that he was not built to be "number two," that he was not "standby equipment," thought it over for a few days. Under the new conditions, however, this clearly was his last chance—to be a heartbeat away from the Presidency, to be in the prime position should Ford elect not to run in 1976. Nelson accepted, setting the stage for the drama of his confirmation hearings.

Aside from Laurance, most members of the Rockefeller family greeted these developments with a sense of foreboding. The hearings threatened the veil of privacy the Rockefellers had steadfastly maintained for the better part of a century over their personal lives, connections, and wealth. Most of the Cousins, having worked hard in a variety of ways to escape the glare of publicity attending their name, family background, and presumed wealth, now were to find these and other matters subjected to intense public scrutiny. On the one hand, it could be argued that very few men in the history of the Republic were as well prepared by experience to assume the second highest office in the land. On the other hand, one could scarcely think of any controversial issue of the kind that governments and politicians deal with that Nelson Rockefeller had not been involved in, one way or another, in his thirty-two years in public life, especially during the most recent fifteen years as governor of New York. Those who had opposed him on any of those issues would be eager to denounce him in testimony before congressional committees.

The fact that Nelson knew all of this as well as anyone, and yet had decided to go ahead, fortified the image the Cousins had of him as a power-seeker at any cost.

In late September 1974, Nelson appeared before the Senate Rules Committee, ushered in by a phalanx of advisers and lawyers and exuding confidence and goodwill. He led off by reading a seventy-two-page statement on family history and his career, and followed this by a much-awaited description of his financial holdings. This of course, was the subject that fascinated both the senators and the public at large. The curiosity was well stated by columnist William Shannon in the August 25 *New York Times*: "Not since Lady Godiva rode naked through the streets of Coventry have the inhabitants of any town itched to see something usually hidden as people here now desire to see the extent of the Rockefeller fortune."

All were bound for disappointment on two counts. First, Nelson's discussion of the *family* fortune (as distinct from his own) was limited to pointing out that his father had received $465 million from *his* father and had used $100 million to create a series of trusts for family members (the 1934 Trusts). Nelson's trust was worth $116 million. Second, Nelson itemized his own net worth as only $62 million, nearly three-fourths of it accounted for by his huge art collection ($33 million) and real estate ($11 million). This is a handsome fortune by most standards, but did not come close to measuring up to the Rockefeller image in the public mind, even when the senators and the press added the two figures for a total in excess of $178 million, not understanding, as usual, the nature of the trust. Nelson was the lifetime beneficiary of the income from his 1934 Trust, but as for the principal the trustees had a fiduciary responsibility to the next two generations. Under the terms of the trust, Nelson could invade principal, but only with the approval of the trust committee. Yet his trust was only about half as valuable as his brother John's (a comparison not available to the congressional committees). Clearly, he had invaded principal a great deal more than JDR had over the years, and yet he did not have much in the way of economically productive investments to show for it. One can only assume that the trust committee had given him a great deal of latitude in taking assets from the trust for his own personal use.

In the hearings, the Republicans lobbed a few softballs and the Democrats tried some pointed questions, particularly Senator Robert Byrd of West Virginia, who tried to probe beyond Nelson's net worth to the larger question of Rockefeller power as derived from institutions, director-ships, and stock holdings in major companies by all members of the family and senior staff. Nelson handled everything with ease and went off for a brief vacation at Seal Harbor when the hearings adjourned. Meanwhile, scores of FBI and IRS agents and others were hard at work examining every aspect of his life and career. By the time Nelson reappeared, some storm clouds had gathered.

Rumors and leaks to the press concerned such subjects as back taxes owed, the huge sums that Nelson had spent on his political campaigns, a covert operation involving his brother Laurance to finance a book critical of Nelson's most recent political opponent, Arthur Goldberg, and large personal gifts Nelson had bestowed upon associates and friends, some of them holding public office at the time the gifts were made.

The Senate hearings were not resumed until November 13 to allow for the election. During this recess the news of the breast surgery undergone by Nelson's wife, Happy, brought a wave of sympathy as had occurred earlier for President and Mrs. Ford when Betty Ford had experienced the same trauma. But the derogatory information that had piled up made the completion of the Senate hearings a much more grueling experience for the nominee than the earlier three days of testimony. Most embarrassing was the affair of the Goldberg biography written by right-wing columnist Victor Lasky, funded by $60,000 Laurance had provided through several intermediaries. For a while Nelson seemed to be professing surprise at this, leaving Laurance to take the blame, but his memory cleared up by the time of the hearings and he took full responsibility.

Nelson produced a long list of associates to whom he had made cash gifts or loans that were later forgiven. The most eye-catching name was that of Henry Kissinger, who had received $50,000, but others received larger amounts: Dr. William J. Ronan, head of New York City's Metropolitan Transit Authority, $625,000; Alton G. Marshall, secretary to the governor, $306,687; Edward Logue, chairman of the Urban Development Corporation, $250,000; Hugh Morrow, press secretary, $135,000; Henry Diamond, New York State Commissioner of Environmental Conservation, $100,000.

There were outcries about this and accusations of bribery, but in the end it all came down to a rich man showering his closest and most loyal associates with rewards. Ronan, for example, had been associated with Nelson since serving as staff director of the commission studying the state constitution in 1957, which had provided one of the springboards that helped make Nelson the governor of New York State. Known widely for both competence and supreme self-assurance, Ronan had always been available to Nelson for special assignments. Persico records that when a reporter asked Ronan how he had responded to such munificent gifts, Ronan "gave a complacent grin and answered that he had said, 'Thank you.' "[8]

Alternating between jaunty confidence and stonewalling techniques, Nelson seemed to wear out his inquisitors and so managed to survive the hearings. No true malfeasance had been uncovered. But Nelson's reputation had been tarnished to a degree, and by extension that of his family, causing no small amount of agitation among his brothers and the Cousins. Part of the concern was that Nelson was not truly representative of the family and its traditions because of the special circumstances of his flamboyant personality and dedication to a political career. For example, his list of charitable giving over the previous seventeen years totaled only $24.7 million, and was regarded by some observers as deflating the vaunted reputation of Rockefeller philanthropy. By this time JDR 3rd's giving had exceeded $100 million, and David and Laurance would soon pass this level as well.

Now Nelson had to appear before the House Judiciary Committee, which only eight weeks earlier had voted impeachment articles against Richard Nixon. Here the pressure was intense for full disclosure of the specific worth and holdings of each member of the family. Persico reports that Nelson contemplated withdrawing before he would agree to that:

"Some of our children have gotten more than others," he said. "We can't let that out. It would destroy the family." Two of his aides, Robert Douglass and James Cannon, came up with a compromise that they sold to Jack Brooks, a tough Democrat from Texas on the committee, but one who admired Nelson and wanted to see the hearings handled with dispatch. The idea was that all information wanted by the committee on family wealth and connections would be supplied in the aggregate, not broken down for any individual except Nelson.[9]

The committee accepted this proposal, even as newspaper articles and academic papers were submitted alleging that a vast and dangerous concentration of wealth and economic control was managed in the family office for the benefit of the Rockefellers. The implication was that a key figure in such an economic network serving as Vice President of the United States would be able to exert undue influence and would be unable to avoid serious conflicts of interest.[10] These charges were very much in line with the enduring populist strain in American politics, which regards great wealth with deep and abiding suspicion.

This set the stage for the appearance before the committee of the doyen of Room 5600, chief manager and financial adviser J. Richardson Dilworth. Armed with a series of charts, he gave the members an unprecedented public accounting of the combined financial assets of eighty-four Rockefeller family members. The total valuation was $1.3 billion. As in the case of Nelson's own holdings, this was much less than the members and the press expected, and it tended to deflate the opposition. Under intensive questioning, Dilworth deftly managed to refute other charges, showing for example how small was the percentage of stock held by the family in major corporations, usually only a fraction of 1 percent. Although Dilworth provided a great deal of information, his was an excellent performance from the point of view of the family for the details and inside information that he was not forced to reveal.

During the hearings the news came that Happy would have to undergo surgery a second time. She refused until the hearings were over, saying that she wanted to be at her husband's side. When he learned this, Chairman Peter Rodino expedited the process by taking the unusual step of holding day and night sessions. In nine days of testimony, Nelson had to deal with all of the same issues and charges that had surfaced in the Senate hearings, including strident opposition from the far left and right. In the end, however, no one was willing to take the position that an individual should be denied high office solely on the basis of personal wealth. The nomination went to the floor and on December 19, four months from the date that President Ford had chosen him, Nelson was confirmed as Vice President of the United States.

Historically, the Vice Presidency is a notoriously empty job, the most famous characterization of it having been supplied by FDR's first Vice President, John Nance Garner, as "not worth a bucket of warm spit." Nelson had the usual promises that his would be a "working" Vice Presidency, with important assignments to be given to him by the President. Given Gerald Ford's image as an amiable though not terribly bright person, Nelson and his staff might well have had great expectations. His first love, foreign affairs, was firmly in the grip of Secretary of State Henry Kissinger, a man who had become a power unto himself. Though he was Nelson's former employee and longtime friend, Kissinger now was answerable directly to the President. So Nelson turned in the other direction and managed to have his man, James Cannon, named as head of the Domestic Council in the White House. This turned out to be awkward for Cannon and unrewarding for Nelson because Cannon's line of responsibility, just as in the case of Kissinger, now ran not to Nelson but to the President.

Nelson managed to keep busy for a time by probing into important subjects, the most noteworthy being his study of the CIA, as well as commissions dealing with productivity, water quality, the right to privacy, and federal compensation. But Ford was much more in control of the Presidency than popularly imagined, and Nelson gradually was reduced to the classic limitations of his job, mainly standing in for the President on the less important public occasions at home and funerals abroad. To Nelson's credit, he accepted this without any public complaint.

The blow came on November 3, 1975, less than a year after Nelson had taken office. Not only was Ford going to run for election in 1976, he was also dropping Nelson from the ticket The wisdom among his advisers was that Nelson, at sixty-seven, was too old and he was still a liability with the right wing of the party. As is usual in such matters, the President told the public that Nelson had decided to withdraw from consideration; Persico confirms that the President had called Nelson at home to give him the bad news.[11] There was immediate press speculation that Nelson might compete with Ford for the nomination, but there is no evidence that he contemplated a move that would have linked him forever in history with Harold Stassen. Whatever happened to Gerald Ford in the 1976 election, Nelson still had more than a year to go before he would return to private life. But before that time there came another personal blow.

*   *   *

Joseph Ernst, director of the Rockefeller Archive Center, will never forget the day early in 1976 when he was abruptly summoned to Nelson Rockefeller's New York City office. Ernst had an idea of the reason and he entered the office with some trepidation to find the Vice President seated at his desk with a book open before him.

Nelson fixed Ernst with a baleful glare. "What I want to know," he rasped, "who is the dumb son of a bitch who let these goddamned Commies in?"

The book was the just-published *The Rockefellers: An American Dynasty,* by Peter Collier and David Horowitz, more than 700 pages of almost unrelenting attack on four generations of the Rockefeller family, written with a decidedly Marxist cast to it. Nelson's question was occasioned by the fact that the authors had been given entry into the family archives. Who had allowed this?

Ernst gulped and said, "It was your brother Laurance, sir."

It was true. Ernst had allowed Collier into the archives because Laurance had approved the request. At this time, most of the family papers were still located in the mezzanine space in the RCA Building; years of review and processing were required to progressively clear sections of the records to eventually be transported to Pocantico for permanent housing. Writers were given access to cleared portions of the records when they had a bona fide research project reviewed and approved by Ernst or when a family member gave permission. More than ninety scholars had been granted access before Peter Collier's letter to Joe Ernst came in saying that he wanted to do research in the archives on the subject of how Junior had "passed the torch of social responsibility to his children and grandchildren." Because Collier mentioned that he had been referred by Marion Weber, Laurance's daughter, Ernst passed the letter up the chain to O'Brien to Dilworth to Laurance, and it came back approved.

Clearly, the writers were not being very forthcoming about their project. For one thing, they approached the family office separately, and it was a long time before anyone became aware that they were in fact collaborating. Collier came in to do the research, spending about five days in the archives in the spring of 1973. Later, David Horowitz told George Taylor, the family's public relations man, that he was doing a book on the Rockefeller Foundation. Horowitz got an interview with Dick Dilworth and said that the project was a book on "modern American philanthropy." The authors were particularly avid in seeking out various Cousins for interviews, and one Cousin would pass them along to another as "people who could be trusted," according to Taylor.[12] JDR agreed to see Horowitz for a ninety-minute interview, commenting in his diary: "Alida had strongly urged that I see him. He claims to be writing a book in regard to our family or maybe it is philanthropy more broadly . . . I was concerned that he did not really know his objective."

Soon after this interview, David Rockefeller somehow got wind of the fact that Collier and Horowitz were working together and that they were coeditors of the New Left publication *Ramparts*. His warning stopped further interviews in Room 5600, but the authors by this time had enough and still had access to some of the Cousins.

The book is well written and highly readable, despite its bulk; this plus its aggressive purpose, its radical-chic tone of exposé, and public curiosity about the Rockefellers combined to make it a best-seller. With only one exception, reviewers adored it, failing to note the copious factual errors, transparent bias, and deterministic thesis. The book's sheer bulk, the perfect timing of its publication, and the appearance of meticulous research all combined to project an almost inescapable impression that this was *the* definitive book on the Rockefellers.[13]

For a time Joe Ernst entertained himself by carefully noting factual errors, having logged an average of more than two per page by the time he gave up in disgust only halfway through the book. This much is understandable, given the vastness of the subject and the fact that the authors only used the archives for a total of two weeks.[14] The many instances of bias are much less palatable; in combing the book it is difficult to find examples of anything any of the Rockefellers did that might generally be regarded as praiseworthy without the authors adopting a snide tone or pejorative twist.

Junior emerges as the villain of the piece, characterized by the authors as "an odd little man, filled with contradictions" and the "author of a myth regarding the Rockefeller family." Resurrecting the old thesis that the sole explanation for Rockefeller philanthrophy is guilt, the authors elaborate the myth as follows:

At the core of Mr. Junior's dynastic project was a shrewd piece of moral calculation. Through his philanthropic efforts, the taint in the family fortune would be expunged, the blot on the name scoured away. Beginning with an obsessive need to believe his father pure, Junior's life gradually developed into a prolonged exercise in self-justification. The family became the vehicle of his quest to prove that the money, of which he was now the custodian, was not only fairly gotten, but well-deserved. . . . The concept of stewardship implied in Senior's claim that God had given him his money was refined by Junior into a comprehensive morality whose terms his heirs would come to understand quite well: power, like money, was an obligation; like money, it was a necessary part of the legacy.

In short, the Rockefellers were predestined and driven by Junior's "myth" and the conditions of wealth to continue attempting to mold

American society to their liking and benefit. All five brothers failed misera-
bly, in the authors' estimation:

JDR's foundering in the role of heir apparent would become obvious when he tried
to grow beyond it, beyond the task of being his father's representative. The meaning of Laurance's inability to step decisively from the background and of Winthrop's
self-destructiveness would become clear toward the end of their lives. The message
of David's stately rise at the Chase was that finally Junior's institutions supplied
the energy for the Rockefeller aura, not the other way around. And Nelson's
ambition, like some devouring metabolic disorder, finally turned upon the traditions at the very marrow of the family's morality, consuming them indiscriminately
along with everything else.

Characterizing "the Rockefeller saga" as "an extravagant mummery on
the theme of the vanity of human wishes," Collier and Horowitz conclude
with a statement that could have come straight from the pages of *Ramparts*:

For more than a hundred years, the Rockefellers have molded their ambition to
the imperial course of the nation itself. Now their decline comes into view at the
time the American Century too is ending, over fifty years before its term. Far
from what Junior envisioned, in neither fact is there cause for much regret.

It was the extensive interviews with many of the Cousins that gave the
book its special appeal. The image projected in the book is one of a somewhat confused and long-silent fourth generation finally having an opportunity to talk back. The authors' favorites were three Cousins well on the
left side of the spectrum—Laurance's daughter Marion, David's daughter
Abby, and Nelson's son Steven. Abby alone is given seventeen pages and
Steven fifteen. Marion is quoted extensively, as are many of the other
Cousins. Clearly, one of the authors' purposes was to support their negative portrayals of the brothers with critical comments from their children.
They succeed to a considerable degree; their timing was excellent given
the generally exacerbated generation gap in the nation at large and the
generational strains within this particular family.

Yet, in reading the quotations, one is struck by the absence of anything
that could truly be called scandalous or malicious. There are criticisms to
be sure, yet in the main the Cousins are speaking candidly as they might
to a peer, not to their parents. Indeed, the relationship that Collier and
Horowitz established with many of the Cousins was a peer relationship—
the authors were comparable in age and were seen as sympathetic and
objective. Given this, one of the least palatable notes in the book is that
Collier and Horowitz, having used the Cousins for their purposes, then
wrote them off: "The Cousins' attempt to recapture a personal identity

from the family is too tentative and stumbling, and finally too mundane, to be seen as a heroic enterprise."[15]

It comes as no surprise to most parents to realize that their children will talk much more candidly to their peers than they will to the older generation. This much the brothers could understand. But to have this happen in public and to be used in the final section of a book to drive home negative portraits of them, their father, and their family as a whole caused something of a firestorm among the ranks of the brothers.

JDR 3rd was the least affected. Three of his four children were interviewed, but Collier and Horowitz got very little of a critical nature from them. The main targets in the book were Junior and Nelson, followed closely by David and Laurance. It was as if Collier and Horowitz were not quite sure what to make of the liberal tone of JDR's book, *The Second American Revolution*, and his obviously genuine interest in young people and the "youth revolution." In the end, they decided he just wasn't very interesting, taking their cue from the hatchet job turned in by Geoffrey Hellman in the 1972 *New Yorker* profile, the easy route of dismissing JDR as ineffectual and bumbling, easily swept aside by his more aggressive brothers. How little they understood him is revealed by their final word that his "foundering" became obvious only when he tried to go beyond the role of heir apparent, "beyond the task of being his father's representative." Of course, precisely the opposite is true; JDR was foundering *in* that role and achieved his notable successes *only* when he freed himself and went beyond it.

JDR had heard all of this before and was quite able to take it in stride. Moreover, his interest in young people and in the social movements sweeping the country had taught him something not easy to learn for a man of his age and generation, that there was something to be said for the "new value" of "letting it all hang out," of being open about one's feelings and dealing with them rather than suppressing them. He had already heard much of what the Cousins had to say to Collier and Horowitz in his own many luncheon meetings and discussions with various Cousins over a period of years. His conversations with Alida, in which she expressed the many antiestablishment charges and points of view she had been hearing at Stanford, amounted to a dress rehearsal for JDR. In these conversations, he did a great deal more listening and questioning than arguing.

All of this equipped JDR to attempt the role of peacemaker between the generations, a formidable task indeed. He was well aware of the bitterness and anger that seized his three brothers at what they regarded as not merely the breaking of a family norm by the Cousins, but as betrayal.

Nearly a year after the Collier and Horowitz book was published, JDR noted in his diary after a meeting with Nelson that his brother still regarded the Cousins as "disloyal, ungrateful, and irresponsible."

JDR was also sensitive to the fact that the Cousins, just as in the case of Jerry Swift and the *New Yorker* profile, would not want to be put in the position of having to apologize, to the extent that they might regret their role in the Collier and Horowitz portrayal. To the contrary, he regarded much of what they had said as valid expressions of real feelings, and he hoped that getting it all out on the table might in the end have some salutary effect. He pressed this point of view with his brothers and took the position that it was up to them to take significant steps toward a rapprochement.

As he moved back and forth between the Cousins and his brothers, he was motivated also by the realization that the two most difficult intergenerational issues were yet to be faced—the governance of the family office and the future of the Rockefeller Brothers Fund.

32

♚

CONFRONTATION

PLANNING for the future of the Rockefeller Brothers Fund (RBF) began in 1973 as a highly rational exercise by the brothers and the senior RBF staff, but degenerated over the next few years to an open and bitter confrontation, with the positions taken by Nelson and JDR at the opposite poles. The conflict reached its peak in 1977 and early 1978 to the point that it nearly tore the family apart.

Similarly, the attempt to bring the Cousins into shared governance of the family office was marked by confrontation between Nelson and the Cousins that was overshadowed in dramatic intensity only by the RBF issue.

The RBF evolved over the years in several distinct phases to the point that it was serving three different purposes. By the beginning of the 1970s, two of these purposes governed the policy by the Fund in almost equal measure. The conflict arose over the question of which one should be the controlling purpose for current decision-making and for the future of the Fund. The dispute was not a question of right or wrong, of legality or morality; each of the purposes could be justified. If all four brothers had the same point of view or could be persuaded to accept one position or the other or could agree to let both purposes continue to coexist, there obviously would have been no conflict. But in fact, opinion was sharply divided and the attempt to resolve this difference was exacerbated by matters of personality, style, motive, and the generational conflict that was already at work within the family.

To understand the issues and the conflict, it is necessary to see how the RBF evolved over the years.

The five Rockefeller brothers created it in 1940 as a means of handling in an organized and collective way what they regarded as their "citizenship" giving—meaning the more routine charitable gifts that leading individuals might be expected to make. Each of the brothers contributed annually to the Fund, and the gifts were administered by Arthur Packard, the staff member in the family office in charge of philanthropy. He was assisted by Dana Creel, a young man from Georgia who had graduated from Emory University and the Harvard Business School.

It was a useful device for the brothers—they could refer certain kinds of requests to the Fund and be free each to pursue his own special interests through other channels. Pleased by this evidence that his sons were taking seriously all of his teachings about the importance of giving, Junior in 1952 made the first of two major gifts to the RBF—the notes for the amount that Rockefeller Center owed to him, some $57.7 million. This enabled the Fund to quintuple its annual giving. Most of the increase went for a new function—support of philanthropic interests the brothers had developed individually, in contrast to the joint "citizenship" function. A sign of this expansion of interests was the addition to the board of the first two nonfamily trustees, Detlev Bronk of Rockefeller University and the architect Wally Harrison, both closely associated with the family.

Over the years a rough parity evolved in the grants going to the varied interests of the brothers. While these projects were identified with one or another of them, they tended to fall into certain broad categories—international relations, interracial and interfaith progress, conservation, population, the arts, and projects of special interest to their home city of New York.[1]

Dana Creel had become staff director of the Fund in 1950 after the resignation of Arthur Packard, due to poor health. Creel proceeded to develop these new categories in consultation with the brothers, gradually adding staff members in several of the fields. JDR had served as president of the RBF from the beginning, but, overburdened with other assignments, he stepped aside in favor of Nelson when the latter returned to private life at the end of 1955 after public service in Washington. Nelson added the "special panel reports" staff to the RBF, with Nancy Hanks as executive secretary, and used this as the base for his major "Prospects for America" project, with Henry Kissinger brought in as project director. When Nelson resigned to enter the gubernatorial race in New York in 1958, Laurance took over the presidency of the Fund.

By this time the Fund had started to take on a third role, that of an innovative foundation above and beyond its other two purposes. This resulted from the growth of both endowment and staff. A review of operations at the end of the decade estimated that 15 percent of the grants were devoted to the "citizenship" function, 70 percent to the special interests of the brothers, and 15 percent to "innovative undertakings."

Following the death of Junior in 1960, the RBF received its second major infusion of capital, some $72 million, from his estate. This enabled annual grant-making to move up toward $10 million, placing the RBF in the ranks of the major American foundations. With its portfolio growing in value, heading toward $200 million in market value by the end of the 1960s, it had become the twelfth largest foundation. The staff grew in size and expertise, and another outside director was added. Reflecting the growth in staff, Dana Creel was elevated to the position of president and Laurance moved to the newly created post of chairman. These developments, plus the domestic turmoil late in the decade, had the effect of increasing the percentage of effort devoted to the third purpose, the "innovative" role, while "citizenship" giving declined to a smaller proportion of the total.

The Tax Reform Act of 1969, with its many provisions affecting philanthropy, especially the strictures against "self-dealing," was to have a substantial impact on the operation of the RBF. Although the Act did not specifically address the question of who should or could control private foundations, its intent lent weight to the view that the family should participate less in the goverance of the Fund's affairs. The brothers, for example, soon ceased the practice of making annual contributions to the Fund because the deductibility of these gifts was now questionable.

As we have seen, JDR had been deeply involved in trying to influence the way in which philanthropy was treated in the tax reform process, in his personal leadership and lobbying and in bringing the Filer Commission into existence. He therefore strongly believed that everything should be done to live up fully to the spirit of the Act, not merely the letter of the law. Under his prodding, for example, management of the RBF's portfolio was shifted out of the family office to the firm of Brown Brothers Harriman. A finance committee was constituted under the chairmanship of a new trustee, the retired chairman of the Federal Reserve, William McChesney Martin. Joining Martin on the committee were nontrustee experts in finance, such as former Treasury Secretary Henry Fowler and Felix Rohatyn of Lazard Frères, who later headed the effort to pull New York City out of its financial peril. Family members no longer managed the financial affairs of the RBF.

JDR began to be regarded by his brothers as the self-appointed "conscience" of the RBF in federal tax law matters in a way that seemed to them overly zealous, even uncooperative. For example, he kept pressing for the RBF to move out of Rockefeller Center and rent office space elsewhere, even though the 1969 Act allowed ten years for compliance on such matters. His view was that anything having to do with the Rockefellers should lead the way in compliance rather than come in late in a way that might appear to be reluctant. This simon-pure attitude became increasingly irritating to his brothers.

The influence of the 1969 Act and the much-enlarged endowment both served to encourage the trend toward professionalization of the RBF's operations in the early 1970s. Among the new staff members brought to the Fund, a key addition in 1970 was William M. Dietel, formerly headmaster of the Emma Willard School in Troy, New York. Dietel soon became the heir apparent to Dana Creel, who was due to retire as president of the Fund in 1975. Another staff member, a highly regarded young lawyer named Robert W. Scrivner, took over administration of the Rockefeller Family Fund, with the RFF reimbursing the RBF for this and other maintenance services.

The existence of a relatively large professional staff worked a gradual influence in the direction of the third function of the RBF, that of an innovative foundation above and beyond the interests of particular brothers and their joint "citizenship" giving. These skilled and motivated staff people naturally were drawn to such tasks as thinking through objectives, analyzing proposals, developing alternatives, and exploring new areas within their fields of competence. A staff review in 1971 commented that too much of the citizenship giving was "palliative rather than remedial," and that "the third category of giving—the pioneering or innovative kind— was not being as creative as it should be."[2]

In effect, the staff was proposing a degree of consolidation of categories and programs to give the Fund "greater unity and impact." This could be done by making the citizenship giving more selective and reducing it still further by eliminating support of "static" organizations and favoring those that fit within the Fund's major program areas and objectives. A similar proposal was made in regard to grants to recipients of special interest to the individual brothers (somewhat delicately referred to as "trustee leadership") and historical interest to the family, making the point that "the more they are limited to program objectives, the greater will be the unity and impact of the Fund's program, just as in the case of citizenship giving." The recommendation here was that the trustees consider reducing Fund support for projects in which they were personally interested, but that otherwise would not come within the Fund's program. The staff expressed the conviction that many grants would still be made that reflected the interests of the brothers, but that the approach would change toward measuring these against the agreed-upon program areas of the Fund as a whole.

These recommendations were accepted in principle by the board, along with consolidation of the program into three broad areas: New York City, national, and international, with the national program devoted to four themes: economic opportunity and development, equal rights, environmental integrity, and civic and cultural values. An examination of any of the annual reports of the RBF in the 1970s reveals scores of grants to a wide range of organizations within these fields.

Under the leadership of Creel and Dietel, and with solid support from the brothers, the RBF compiled an especially noteworthy record in support of the needs and aspirations of blacks in American society, in particular Afro-American cultural organizations, rural assistance, and activist civil rights organizations. In his book *The Big Foundations*, Waldemar Nielsen uses the "race question" as a barometer of innovation among foundations and willingness to address "the great issues of social change." He lists the RBF as one of only four foundations showing "a high degree of interest in and an activist approach to the problems of blacks."⁵ He adds:

But the published list of the [RBF's] many grants is only a partial indication of the fund's readiness to respond to crises in the black community. Some of the most eminent leaders in the civil rights struggle have recounted in private conversations how the officers and trustees of the fund have repeatedly provided personal assistance to them and generated other financial contributions when emergencies arose.

A further indication of the trend in the RBF away from the handling of philanthropic giving to the interests of family members came with the recruitment of Elizabeth J. McCormack in 1973 when she resigned as president of Manhattanville College. McCormack at first served as an assistant to Dietel and worked on educational matters, but she was slated to head up a revived philanthropic staff function in the family office. This was to be split off from the RBF within the ten-year grace period afforded by the Tax Reform Act of 1969. By the end of 1976 McCormack and her staff had moved to the fifty-sixth floor, where she served as a philanthropic adviser to several of the brothers and to a growing number of the Cousins.

Even as "citizenship" giving was being resolved, there was recognition of the fact that the Fund had an obligation to deal in some special way with other organizations that historically had been dependent on RBF and other support from members of the Rockefeller family. Some had been supported for decades and others in more recent times were identified with the special interest of one or another of the brothers. The concern was that some might not fit within a strict interpretation of the RBF's new program areas, while the support of others was largely based on tradition and annual maintenance rather than on innovative qualities.

The death of Winthrop in 1973 gave his surviving four brothers good reason to begin to think about the future of organizations they cared deeply about. Each of them had his own strong personal interest in certain organizations. They all realized that after their own deaths they could not expect any of the Cousins to carry on that interest to the same degree. For example, in the case of JDR's most passionate interest, the Population Council, he had hoped that one of his children would follow in his footsteps. Since this was not possible for Jay or Sandra, he looked to Hope as a candidate. But while Hope, like her mother, certainly appreciated the importance of the population field at an intellectual level, she simply did not have the same intense personal concern that her father had; she had her own interests.

Recognizing this concern on the part of the brothers and the need to rationalize family support, Dana Creel in late 1973 wrote to Laurance, the chairman of the RBF, proposing that the organizations be identified and that a systematic review process begin to reach an equitable end to the special relationships.

Right at the outset, a difference of opinion among the brothers surfaced. JDR's diary records that at a brothers' meeting at the Playhouse on December 23, the Creel memo was discussed. Nelson and Laurance warned against "going too far in abandoning some of the organizations we have traditionally supported." They expressed the view that the RBF had gotten too far away from this in supporting projects the staff had developed. JDR's response was that the staff was excellent and that the best of them would not long stay with an organization in which their initiative was stifled. The brothers left the subject with the agreement that they would meet soon with Creel and Dietel to discuss the situation.

A number of meetings occurred in 1974, spurred by the fact that the organizations to be considered had been hit hard by the recession and some were appealing to the RBF for increased help. Over a period of months, the Creel idea took root and some procedures and ground rules were established. The goal was to work toward a clean slate in the sense that, after intensive reviews in consultation with the trustees and officers of the organizations, the RBF would make grants to meet genuine needs and discharge any historical obligation to the organizations held by individual brothers and the RBF as an institution. Once this was done, the organizations would have no special standing with the RBF and future grant requests would be treated in the same manner as those coming from other organizations and programs. The careful process and the likelihood that the grants would be significant ones apparently eased the concern that Nelson and Laurance had expressed earlier of "abandoning" the organizations. At a brothers' meeting, the possibility was discussed that the total of capital grants could be "up to one-half" of the Fund's endowment, which was the cause of a later misunderstanding between JDR and his brothers.

In 1975 the process began in earnest with the establishment of the three-member "Creel Committee." As the name suggests, Creel was the chairman; Dietel and McCormack were the other two members. Initially there were twenty-five organizations on the list, but several were in a gray area or so minor that it came to be referred to most often as the "22+ list."[4] Assignments were made to RBF staff members to engage in reviews of organizations in their areas of professional expertise. These were meant to be intensive studies and analyses of real needs of the kind that a management consulting firm might make.

Most of the organizations of the Creel list were there because their support from the RBF stemmed from active and continuing association with one or more of the four brothers. The exceptions to this general rule were organizations of long-standing historical association with the family, dating back to Junior's day and even to Senior's, but in which the brothers no longer maintained active involvement. This group included the Riverside Church, Colonial Williamsburg, Spelman College in Atlanta, the Metropolitan Opera, and the original International House at Columbia University.

Two of the organizations were unique in that they were identified with all of the brothers, but more with JDR than any other—the Rockefeller Archive Center and the Ramon Magsaysay Foundation in Manila.

As a full-time philanthropist, JDR had more ties than any of the others: five of the many organizations he had built were on the Creel list because they had enjoyed prior support from the RBF. These were the Population Council, the Agricultural Development Council, Lincoln Center for the Performing Arts, the Asia Society, and the Japan Society.

The Museum of Modern Art occupied a prominent place on the list because of its many connections with the Rockefeller family. Nelson and David were both strongly identified with it; their mother had been one of the founders and JDR's wife, Blanchette, currently was its chairman. Nelson's only other direct interest on the Creel list was the Metropolitan Museum of Art, for the wing on primitive art dedicated to Michael C. Rockefeller, Nelson's son who had been lost off the coast of New Guinea.

Laurance had his conservation interests—the Jackson Hole Preserve, the American Conservation Association, and the New York Zoological Society. He was also very deeply committed to the Memorial Sloan-Kettering Cancer Center, which was built on land donated by Junior in 1935. Laurance had become chairman after the Sloan-Kettering Institute, founded in 1945, merged with Memorial Hospital in 1960 to create one of the world's preeminent cancer research facilities and teaching hospitals.

David had strong ties to two organizations on the list. His consistent interest in Latin American had involved him in the founding of the Center of Inter-American Relations in the mid-1960s as a forum for the discussion of hemispheric issues. He also had assumed his father's responsibility in the mid-1940s for Rockefeller University, serving as a trustee and then as chairman from 1950 to 1975. Junior had been the prime force in building this institution with his father's money early in the century, when it was known as the Rockefeller Institute for Medical Research. It had become one of the premier biomedical research institutions in the world, numbering sixteen Nobel laureates on its faculty at one time or another, so that its funding needs were virtually open-ended.

As the Creel Committee worked through 1975 and much of 1976, some preliminary judgments began to be made on the basis of the studies of various organizations that were produced. Word of the process had seeped out and some of the organizations began to lobby for their share of what inevitably would be scarce goods. How scarce was not known since no exact target figure had been set. JDR's understanding was that the ultimate total would be whatever sum the careful analytical process produced. But he became aware that his brothers had taken the earlier discussion about spending half of the endowment literally, noting in his diary his concern that he had heard the figure of $75 million being mentioned as a total for Creel Committee grants. This would be close to half of the RBF's endowment, the market value of which, in 1974, had fallen for the first time below the book value of $151.8 million because of the effects of the recession.[5] One reason for the position of David and Laurance was that they were thinking in terms of truly major grants for their primary interests (Rockefeller University and Memorial Sloan-Kettering), on the order of $10 million to $15 million or more.

Nelson obviously was preoccupied as Vice President during this period, but managed to stay in touch with developments through occasional attendance at brothers' meetings. He had returned briefly to the RBF board after resigning as governor, but left again after becoming Vice President without having attended any meetings. He was replaced by his wife, Happy. Other family members on the board were Laurance David as vice chairman, JDR, two of David's children (Neva Kaiser and David Jr.), JDR's daughter Hope, and Abby O'Neill, Babs's eldest daughter. The nonfamily members included Creel and Dietel, William McChesney Martin, John Gardner, Gerald Edelman, and Richard Cooper.

From the time the Creel Committee began its work in 1975 until Nelson's return from Washington in 1977, it can be said that the RBF was operating on two levels. Overtly, the atmosphere was businesslike, with a series of proposals emerging from the work of the Creel Committee to be acted upon by the board in late 1976 and early 1977, aided by the fact that the endowment was beginning to recover from the recession (with the market value up to $204.7 million by the end of 1976). At the same time, there were signs of friction among the brothers as the positions of JDR and Nelson began to harden in opposition to each other. Laurance generally appeared to side with Nelson, while David was the man in the middle, trying to stay neutral and mediate among the others. Not until Nelson appeared personally on the scene in 1977 did the struggle become disruptive.

On the business side, four capital grants proposals from the Creel Committee were ratified by the RBF board by the end of 1976: $750,000 to the Riverside Church, $250,000 to the Metropolitan Museum of Art, $1.5 million to the Asia Society, and the establishment of a $1 million trust fund for the Magsaysay Foundation in Manila (to enable it to increase its annual awards from $10,000 to $20,000 each). In early 1977, the board agreed to three more capital grants: $1.5 million to the Japan Society for "future building and program needs," $1.5 million to the Metropolitan Opera to help it emerge from a fiscal crisis, and $2 million for the Rockefeller Archive Center. Although the last grant went to Rockefeller University, it was earmarked for the Archive Center, and thus in no way affected David's strong interest in a major unrestricted grant for the university, which was to be considered later.

With this first series of capital grants, the RBF by early 1977 had made considerable progress toward discharging its "historic obligation" to family-related organizations. The current needs and future directions of eight organizations, more than a third of the Creel Committee total, had been considered and funds totaling $9.5 million had been distributed or committed to them from the RBF endowment. All of this had been done with relative ease, very much in the spirit in which the Creel Committee had been created. It thus might have seemed to augur well for the rest of the Creel agenda. But this was illusory—the RBF in fact had dealt with the easy proposals first. The big-ticket and somewhat controversial items were yet to come. The return of Nelson and the growing tension among the brothers brought the Creel process to a virtual halt by the spring of 1977.

The first sign that the difference of opinion among the brothers, which had arisen at the beginning of the Creel process, was still present and might in time prove disruptive occurred at the March 1975 board meeting of the RBF. JDR was concerned that two items on the docket did not fit in with what he felt the Fund's policies should be or within the intent of the Tax Reform Act of 1969. As he recorded in his diary, at issue were two "family-related" proposed grants to the "Historical Society of Providence, Rhode Island (for renovation and maintenance of the Aldrich family home), and the Michael Rockefeller Wing at the Metropolitan Museum." Pointing out that philanthropy was still subject to criticism in Washington, he emphasized the importance of "there not being any gray areas in our own procedures." While on the subject, JDR made two other criticisms. He said he thought that trustees should leave the room when projects in which they have an interest are presented, a practice followed on every other board that he served on. And he criticized "the lack of change in the nominating committee" of the Fund, saying that "greater trustee participation generally would be useful and desirable."

Apparently, David, as chairman of the nominating committee, took offense at the last point. JDR confided to this diary that he had "some regrets" on this score, but added: "I realized that what I had to say would not be greeted with acclaim but said it anyway, feeling that in the long run it would be recognized as sound and right."

Nelson was spending the following weekend at Kykuit, as he often did while Vice President, and he and David called for a brothers' meeting to discuss JDR's complaints. They said his position was tantamount to undermining family leadership of the Fund. JDR responded that he was only advocating standard procedures on nonprofit boards, such as those followed by the Rockefeller Foundation, and that he saw no way that they would adversely affect the brothers' leadership in the RBF. JDR recorded in his diary that "there was strong and unanimous opposition to the position I had taken and the discussion didn't change the feeling." His brothers said that such matters should be decided among themselves, "hence the implication was that I should cease and desist." JDR said that if this had been the practice earlier "in relation to my strong proddings in regard to RBF investment policy, no changes would have been made, changes which Nelson has recognized without reservation were of real value in terms of his testimony when being questioned as a candidate for the Vice Presidency."

In subsequent diary entries, JDR noted his concern several times that questions such as he had raised kept getting deferred. In 1976 he found new cause for concern when he heard that Laurance and David now thought that $100 million of the RBF's endowment should be earmarked for the "22+" organizations. This target figure was in line with the early discussion among the brothers that Creel Committee grants could total "'up to" one-half of the market value of the RBF's endowment, which, by mid-1976, was moving back up toward the $200 million level. David and Laurance tended to see this as an agreement, and therefore regarded the expenditure of one-half the resources in capital grants to the Creel organizations as a goal to be achieved; for JDR, the goal now was to avoid setting any target figure and to come in eventually at considerably less than one-half. He now resolved to try to lay this to rest.

Before the June 1976 session of the board, JDR met with Creel, Dietel, and McCormack to discuss this issue. By this time, Creel had retired as president of the RBF, to be succeeded by Dietel, but had been named a vice chairman of the board and was staying on to complete the work of his committee.[6]

JDR told the three that he personally "was all for the idea" of terminating the special relationships with the "22 + ' organizations "on some kind of thoughtful and positive basis, maybe over a period of years." But he expressed the strong view that "the decisions to be reached in regard to each organization must be much broader than just an infusion of a substantial amount of money." He thought the idea of setting a large target figure in advance militated against a thoughtful process. Further, he was concerned that the Fund's capital might "be dissipated to a point where a staff morale question will be created and where the Fund will no longer be able to be a major factor for the Cousins in the same way it has been for my generation."

He was not likely to find any disagreement from the three staff people, but he was pleased at the board meeting to find his point of view accepted after Laurance and David had talked about the idea of a target figure. JDR wrote: "All agreed, I believe, that the [Creel] concept is sound. Most [board members] had reservations about appropriating any money for the purpose until the research efforts had proceeded further."

Trying to leave nothing to chance, JDR pressed for a clear statement of the Creel Committee process at the October 1976 board meeting. The minutes of the meeting contain the following passage:

In the course of the discussion, it was re-emphasized, and agreed, that the purpose of the Creel Committee is to consider the nature of any special commitments that the corporation may have to the twenty-five organizations it is reviewing, and that action taken pursuant to a recommendation of the Creel Committee . . . is intended to discharge any such commitment. . . . It was also agreed that while contributions thereafter to such an organization are not necessarily to be precluded, any such contributions are to be made solely on the merits of the request and within the guidelines of the Fund's programs, and not out of regard to considerations bearing on a historical or special relationship. . . .

If this was a victory for JDR, it was more apparent than real. While the board, at his urging, had declined to set a target figure, this action in no way constrained Laurance and David in seeking major grants for their primary interests. In fact, by the time the first round of eight Creel grants had been acted upon, JDR registered his alarm in his diary over hearing much larger figures being discussed for Rockefeller University and Memorial Sloan-Kettering—on the order of $20–$30 million instead of the $10–$15 million he had heard a year earlier. And there were other organizations still on the list that were candidates for very substantial grants. As the leading spokesman for philanthropy as a social force in the United States, JDR was less concerned about securing large Creel grants for his organizations than he was about preserving what he regarded as the integrity of the RBF as an independent foundation and its value as a philanthropic instrument for the next generation of Rockefellers. This put him in disagreement with Laurance and David, both of whom believed that spending half of the RBF's endowment was necessary to achieving the purposes of the Creel exercise and would not destroy the Fund.

This was the situation when Nelson returned to reclaim his RBF seat from Happy in January 1977, his term as Vice President having ended. He had been bruised by being dropped from the ticket by President Ford and by his sense of betrayal over the comments of the fourth generation in the Collier and Horowitz book. But he was as energetic as ever. Persico captures his mood as he returned to New York:

Retreat and deceleration were alien to everything he had ever been or done. Thus, for every withdrawal from an old pursuit, he began a new one, as though resisting a tide pulling him toward some inevitable and dreaded end. He withdrew from politics with a suddenness and thoroughness that left the Republican Party initially disbelieving, until old comrades tried to get a contribution or an appearance out of him. This part of Nelson Rockefeller was certifiably dead. He never made another speech of consequence or gave a dime to anyone's campaign.[7]

Still strapped for cash, Nelson sold some of his real estate and launched into the publishing of art books based on his collections. He worked on a plan to manufacture and sell reproductions of some of his art pieces, an idea that some family members and purists in the art field found appalling. He developed a grandiose scheme for directing the huge petroleum profits of the OPEC nations into the "right" investments, meaning mainly in the United States, but this came to naught. He announced his intention to move out of Kykuit to the nearby Japanese House so that the burden of maintaining the mansion would be shared by all four brothers instead of resting mainly on him. But, above all, his sights were aimed at taking over the family office and the RBF, which he thought had suffered in his absence and needed redirecting.

Altogether, Nelson seemed to project the view that it was time to stop fooling around, that he was back now and soon would set everything straight. As subsequent events made clear, this meant that Nelson's goal was to centralize power and decision-making in the hands of his generation and to establish his primacy among the brothers. In effect, he was intent on a return to the autocratic rule over family affairs that his father had exercised, in place of the loose, inclusive system that had grown up, with its emphasis on compromise and accommodation of everyone's views and interests.

Even though it would take a while before the formalities could occur to put Nelson back on the RBF board in place of Happy, this was really a technicality. He got right to work, telling his brothers that he was undertaking his own study of the RBF. Meanwhile he planned to take charge of the family office, raising the question several times in brothers' meetings.

JDR was satisfied with the way that management of the family office had been evolving. Harper Woodward had been working for several years on closer integration of the Cousins into family affairs, interviewing each of them and making recommendations from time to time. Beginning in the late 1960s, the Cousins were being charged individually for specific services rendered by Room 5600. The Cousins' association had a subcommittee on the subject of the family office, and the members had been placed on the Board of Managers, "the official body for office matters," in JDR's words. Other members included the four brothers and Dick Dilworth as the executive head of the office. Several times in his diary JDR noted his pleasure over the growing presence of the Cousins in family affairs.

This evolutionary process was jolted in the late spring of 1977 by Nelson's power thrust. He proposed that the family office be legally incorporated, that the titles of chairman and chief executive officer be created, and that he take over these roles and powers with Dilworth reporting directly to him. His brothers demurred and in the end Nelson agreed that the CEO portion of the title be dropped. Nelson's desire to be chairman was conveyed to the Cousins who had convened at Pocantico the weekend of June 18–19 for their semiannual meeting. Nelson proposed that the executive committee of the Cousins' association meet with the brothers on Sunday morning to discuss the family office. As JDR reported, the Cousins attending included "Stevie as chairman, Jay, Sharon, Peggy, David Jr., Roddy, Mitzi, and three or four newer members including Alida."

The Cousins put forth some of their views about the office and then said that they had unanimously voted to elect Laurance as chairman. Because they knew Nelson wanted the title, "his rejection for the position was a deliberate choice by the Cousins," JDR wrote. Nelson was furious and said he was entitled to an explanation. JDR reported:

There followed a very forthright discussion with the Cousins one after another expressing their very strong reservations as to the way Nelson had handled himself in relation to the office, the RBF, and the family since his return from Washington. *Nelson was obviously considerably taken aback* but very much on the defensive— or should I say offensive?[8]

For the gentlemanly JDR, to term something a "very forthright" discussion and to make even the slightest sarcastic crack, as he did at the end of this comment, was strong language indeed. The discussion, in fact, was acrimonious and infuriating to Nelson, who was not used to being criticized in person, especially by young people, including two of his own children.

Now it was JDR's turn to be put on the spot. The brothers retired to a brothers' meeting to talk about how to handle this rebellion. They had the power since votes were weighted according to the amount one contributed to the annual costs of maintaining the office, and the four brothers together accounted for well over 90 percent of the budget. In short, they were analogous to the Security Council of the UN and the Cousins to the weaker General Assembly. Moreover, the brothers had a long-standing tradition of making decisions by discussion among themselves without resorting to voting, not only in regard to family matters and the office but also on the RBF board.

JDR's strong inclination this time was to break the tradition and vote with the Cousins. His three brothers worked on him for an hour and a half before he agreed to stick with them. His vote for the Cousins would have been a gesture, because Nelson still would have become chairman according to the weighted voting procedure. And had this not been the case, Laurance very well might have refused to take the chairmanship. A deal was struck. David would report to the Cousins that the four brothers supported Nelson, but also that the brothers accepted the recommendation that voting in the future would be on a nonweighted basis. JDR had a final word on the episode in his diary.

I went home with a heavy heart as to whether I had done the right thing but very proud of the Cousins for the way they had stood up to the brothers. The question of the deep-seated feeling in regard to Nelson was terribly important to get out into the open. I honestly felt that *as of today the Cousins had, as a group, come of age*.

The next morning JDR met in Room 5600 with Nelson for an hour and a half to talk about what had happened. JDR wrote that Nelson "could not believe that he was really the person the Cousins were speaking so forthrightly about. He just could not see that there were grounds for their accusations." JDR, knowing that he would have been devastated if the

Cousins had been so outspokenly critical of him, wrote in some wonderment that Nelson did not seem at all depressed. JDR attributed this to the politician's experience of meeting major setbacks and still having to function in public life. Nelson did say, according to JDR, that perhaps his performance as chairman of the office board "would give him the chance to make good with the Cousins." Then JDR went down to the promenade restaurant next to the Rockefeller Center skating rink to have lunch with Steven. They agreed that what had happened was important, but "we shared concern as to *how much his father would or could change his ways* even after such a clear message being transmitted to him."

JDR and Steven, of course, were correct. Nelson did not change his ways, but intensified his power drive. The Cousins were not the only ones who were critical. We have already noted how David, in an interview years later, characterized Nelson's behavior as "appalling," and how Joseph Persico described him as "irascible and imperious" during this period. Neva said that Nelson "was destructive. He came back to destroy. *Après moi le déluge.*" Like Neva, John Gardner was a witness to the struggle as an RBF board member. He said Nelson's guiding star was "power," while JDR's was "principle." Alida said that her father's qualities that made him a "square" to his brothers made him "a hero to the Cousins." Even Dana Creel, classically the man in the middle and always a judicious and tactful person, said years later that JDR's motive was "the public interest" and Nelson's was "self-interest."[9]

JDR thought that Nelson would want to become "chairman and chief executive officer" of the RBF as well as the family office. It would be hard to resist him since he had been head of the Fund only briefly in the mid-1950s before his election as governor. Laurance had succeeded him and still held the post eighteen years later. In JDR's mind it was time for a change, but his candidate was David, who told JDR he was amenable, but only if Laurance was ready to step down and all the brothers wanted David.

Nelson kept deferring such matters while his study of the RBF was proceeding, but in several brothers' meetings in the late spring of 1977 the opposing positions began to harden. After each meeting Nelson would write a "memo for the record," which JDR said was a new concept to him, especially when the memos attempted to codify agreements he did not recall being reached, in some cases not even discussed. So he began to return in kind with memos correcting Nelson's memos.[10]

Nelson wanted all Creel Committee recommendations to be submitted "informally" to the brothers before being sent to the board. Then he wanted the brothers to be "ex officio" members of the Creel Committee and proposed that any brother who desired could serve on any committee he wished. He also wanted the chairman to set the agenda for the meetings rather than the traditional way of relying on consultations with the president and a docket prepared by staff.

There was sharp disagreement over filling vacancies on the board. As chairman of the nominating committee, David said he had in mind proposing JDR's daughter Hope Spencer for reelection to the board. Nelson said this was unacceptable to him, that future trustees should be selected on the basis of their agreement with the brothers' philosophy and general purpose of the Fund. He added that as a board member Hope meant a vote in John's pocket. JDR did not record his response to this allegation, but one can imagine his resentment, knowing as he did that Hope was an independent-minded person who would not kowtow to anyone.

On another occasion, Nelson put forward for the board vacancies the names of Henry Kissinger and Nancy Hanks, two individuals with whom he had been associated for several decades. JDR did not return the charge that this meant votes in Nelson's pocket, but merely said he could not support any vote by the brothers conveyed to the board in a manner that suggested the matter had already been decided.

On still another occasion David suggested JDR to succeed him as chairman of the nominating committee. Nelson said this was not acceptable to him, adding that until John was prepared to accept the brothers' leadership and guidance to the Fund and vote with his brothers, he should not hold any chairmanship.

This got down to the crux of the matter. Nelson wanted the RBF to operate the way it had in the 1950s, meaning primarily as a vehicle for funding causes to which the brothers, individually or collectively, were devoted. Nelson professed to be shocked in returning to RBF affairs after a long absence to find out how far the Fund had strayed from what he regarded as its proper mission. It was his duty to straighten this out.

If somewhat self-centered, Nelson's position was not an unreasonable one, and it was certainly legal. JDR felt just as strongly that time had passed this point of view by. He termed it "retrogressive." In one of his memos to his brothers, he said he had "no objection" to the Fund supporting "projects in which brothers have an ongoing personal and financial relationship where the projects come within the RBF program." He added: "The RBF today is a national foundation with a responsible Board of Directors. Decisions as to policy and program must be made by the Board with all the facts on the table and with frank and free discussion."

JDR had a high-minded concept of the fiduciary role of a trustee and an officer of a nonprofit organization, one that John Gardner independently praised as the model that all should follow. JDR had cultivated this concept over nearly a lifetime. As chairman of the Rockefeller Foundation, he could influence broadly the directions the foundation might take, as we have seen, but in a scrupulously open and evenhanded way. If a proposal came up in which he had any personal interest, he would leave the room. On several occasions when JDR brought up the analogy of the Rockefeller Foundation, he was met with the retort from Nelson, "Yes, you gave the foundation away!" Laurance and David did not disagree. JDR did not record whether he ever pointed out that he was following his father's example. If anyone gave the Rockefeller Foundation away, it was Junior, who as chairman before JDR had rigorously insisted on having independent-minded trustees and no personal interference.[11]

The importance JDR placed on bringing the Cousins in as full-fledged partners in the RBF might seem somewhat contradictory to his position against too much family influence. But he kept insisting that he had no problem with brothers or Cousins pressing for projects that deeply interested them so long as this was done with a strong role for the staff, full and open discussion with all trustees, and within agreed-upon program areas.

His repeated emphasis on bringing the Cousins into full partnership was anathema to Nelson. In responding to one of Nelson's memos urging that the brothers' interests have priority, JDR wrote back: "I believe the time has passed for such a statement. If 'cousins' were substituted for 'brothers,' I would feel more responsive." This was also the reason, as Elizabeth McCormack expressed it, that JDR did not want "to give away half of the store" in Creel Committee grants.

In the power struggle that now was clearly going on, JDR recognized that the odds were against him. In a brothers' meeting just before the annual RBF meeting in June 1977, Nelson and JDR each argued their widely separated points of view once again. JDR commented in his diary:

Obviously in this situation *the chairmanship is important*. To me there is no question that the Board generally would like to see David as chairman but is inclined to feel it would be too difficult to tactfully dislodge brother Laurance. Obviously, too, Nelson wants Laurance to continue on because of their close relationship and Nelson's dominant role.

JDR let his brothers know that he would not join in any decision that would be conveyed to the RBF board as representing the wishes of all the brothers, saying that this would make it impossible for other board members to "act with any degree of freedom or independence." He then reflected on one of the reasons for the growing conflict with his brothers:

I think a basic problem is that Nelson particularly but David also are so used to power and control that it puts them on a somewhat different wavelength from me. I have always operated on a basis of getting good people together, working with them and giving them considerable responsibility. Their approach is more to bring in good people and then control what they do. Laurance is of course completely in Nelson's hands so the odds were somewhat against me.

Perhaps understandably, JDR's assessment of Laurance and David seems a bit overstated in this entry. Laurance and Nelson had been exceptionally close as brothers ever since their early childhood, so it was natural that Laurance would always give Nelson the benefit of any doubt and tend to side with him. But he was also capable of independent action, and indeed in later diary entries JDR noted that Laurance was becoming restive over Nelson's behavior and that David was trying hard to play a moderating role.

The gulf between the positions of JDR and Nelson was real and apparent to everyone, but JDR does not seem to have understood that he had managed to alienate Laurance and David to a degree as well. They both might well have regarded JDR's struggle to hold down the Creel expenditures as a possible threat to their strong desire to see their two major interests receive grants of the magnitude that they thought essential. And Laurance must have been irritated by JDR's open desire to see him vacate the chairmanship.

In an interview years later, David also spoke of the difference in styles between himself and Nelson on the one hand and JDR on the other. He and Nelson had had many years of executive experience, but to David this was not so much a matter of "control" as it was of handling the business at hand with efficiency and dispatch.

David did not disagree with JDR's long-term goals for the future of the RBF, but thought that he was pursuing them in an unnecessarily irksome way. He believed that the Creel process, if properly handled, would take care of the important concerns of the brothers. David's goal was to let this process play its way out without an irreconcilable split occurring among the brothers. He and Laurance both believed that spending half of the endowment would not deal a mortal blow to the Fund.

If JDR was depressed by the brothers' meeting, he was due to feel even more so by events in the next few weeks. In June 1977, Nelson made his first appearance at an RBF board meeting in twenty years. The nominating committee recommended Nelson's son Steven for the board, which JDR liked. But the committee also recommended Kissinger and Hanks, as well as Richard Parsons for associate counsel of the RBF. Parsons's most recent assignment had been as special counsel to Nelson. JDR

raised questions about Parsons (but was relieved to learn months later from
Bill Dietel that Parsons was "okay," that he was performing in an evenhanded way). [12]

The most disturbing item pressed by Nelson was for a $3 million grant
to a brand-new institution, the New York College of Osteopathic Medicine,
which, JDR wrote, was "started on a shoestring under the leadership of
Dr. W. Kenneth Riland who has meant so much to Nelson healthwise
these past many years." This was clearly an overt attempt by Nelson to
ram home his view that the RBF existed primarily to serve the interests
of the brothers. The proposal came as a surprise, it did not fit remotely
into any RBF program area, and its insertion at that particular time was
bizarre, given the preoccupation of the RBF with the Creel Committee
agenda. The sole justification was that Nelson wanted it.

Pointing out that osteopaths emphasize treatment "by manipulating the
musculoskeletal system," Persico characterized the Nelson-Dr. Riland relationship as follows:

Nelson literally placed himself in the hands of the same physician for nearly forty
years. . . . He usually saw Riland twice a week, and Kenny was not only his
physician, but one of his few intimates. He was, as well, a great favorite among
the Rockefeller circle for down-to-earth sense and ready humor. The doctor and
his portable treatment table became a fixture of the Rockefeller road show, as
much as advance men and reporters. It was always with a certain uneasiness that
I entered the Governor's suite in some out-of-town hotel where Riland would be
thumping, bending, and wrenching his patient with alarming gusto. [13]

The Riland proposal was not greeted warmly around the table, so Nelson asked that it be held over until a study could be done to present more
evidence of its significance. JDR wrote: "This was accepted as a courtesy
to him."[14]

JDR was due for an even greater shock within a few weeks. John
Gardner telephoned to say that he had sent his resignation from the RBF
board to chairman Laurance Rockefeller. JDR was "terribly disturbed" to
hear this. Gardner said it was difficult for him to work with a group where
he was "not respected or trusted." JDR wrote his diary account with a
sense of having been betrayed. "He had assured me on more than one
occasion that I could count on his support as long as I needed it." He
added that it was hard to see how Gardner "would shrink from conflict
within the RBF when he believed so keenly in the cause for which he
and I have been working." In this last comment, JDR was placing the
RBF struggle in the larger context of his concern for the welfare of the
"third sector" generally, in which he and Gardner were staunch allies,

though Gardner preferred calling it "the independent sector." JDR was hurt by Gardner's resignation not only for losing a valued trustee, but also because Gardner had not consulted with him in advance. He seemed to have forgotten recording in his diary a year earlier that Gardner had told him that he was resigning from all of his trusteeships except Stanford University and the RBF, and could give those two only another year. In fact, just two months before resigning from the RBF, Gardner had left Common Cause, which he had created and headed for six years.[15]

That same afternoon, as if to add injury to insult, JDR kept a dentist's appointment to have four of his lower teeth removed and replaced by a temporary bridge. Ever the optimist and capable of bouncing back, he told his diary: "It went amazingly well."

Yet, with the loss of Gardner, he faced a changed situation on the board. Those who were rooting for his point of view, RBF staff members and Cousins, had been wondering, sometimes aloud, why he did not press matters to a vote. "He has the votes," they would say. But JDR did not want to be the one to break the long-standing convention among the brothers against deciding matters by voting. He might well have feared that to do so would result in such a deep and open schism that it could never be repaired. He strongly believed that his position was the right one for the long term, and that he could gradually get others to see this by persuasion. And so his diary shows many instances of meeting with Nelson and writing to him, almost always reflecting an effort to be moderate and persuasive.

Also, as time passed, it was not at all clear that JDR did have the votes, were things to come to this pass. If only the brothers were to vote, JDR would lose three to one, or at best two to one, with David abstaining. With Gardner gone, JDR's only certain ally among the "outside" directors on the board was William McChesney Martin. Gerald Edelman, vice chancellor of Rockefeller University, was independent, having spoken against the osteopathy proposal, for example, but he had to be mindful of the presence on the RBF board of the chairman and another trustee of his university board. Richard Cooper was leaving the RBF board to take a State Department assignment, but his replacement was scheduled to be James H. Evans, chairman of Union Pacific, a close friend of Laurance's. And JDR certainly would have doubted that Kissinger and Hanks would side with him on some sort of showdown, as much as he respected both of them.

So JDR kept on with his own brand of genteel lobbying, meeting several times with Nancy Hanks, for example, to assure himself that she would be open-minded on the issues.

Tempers flared at the fall 1977 meeting of the board, during a discussion of the report of the Planning and Review Committee, of which Nelson was chairman. One section was entitled "internal operating guidelines and procedures." JDR reported in his diary that "some felt that the way it was worded indicated a lack of trust between the staff and the trustee officers." Bill Dietel was one of those who commented on this, only to find himself being angrily denounced by Laurance. Humiliated, Dietel left the room, trying to decide whether he would resign immediately or wait until he calmed down a bit. An executive session was immediately called, at which, JDR reported, "a strong *resolution of confidence in Bill Dietel* as Chief Executive Officer was passed." This was tantamount to an apology by Laurance, so the general session was resumed and Dietel returned.

Toward year's end, signs began to appear that the brothers were wearying of the tension. At a brothers' meeting at Nelson's Manhattan apartment in November, Nelson seemed expansive on the subject of the Pocantico estate. He said, JDR reported, that "he had completely changed his approach: that for a long time he had had a dream of the Kykuit area being a beautiful and significant historic site open to the public; that he felt he had aroused opposition and feeling within the family because of his having pressed his ideas; and that now he was going to relax and try and go along with what others wanted." However, JDR added, it also came out that Nelson was planning to change his will to leave only the Kykuit or "Park" area for public purposes, "with the much larger woodland area going to Happy." Nelson also said he was talking to the Marriott Hotels people about a hotel and conference center on the portion of the estate that he personally owned. For JDR the only good news was that Nelson said he was planning to sell some of his modern sculpture in the Kykuit area.

JDR, David, and Nelson stayed on for dinner together after Laurance had to leave. When the subject of the RBF came up, David spoke candidly to Nelson, perhaps encouraged by Nelson's calm recitation on the Pocantico subject. As JDR reported in his diary: "David pointed out to Nelson that he did not think that he fully appreciated the unfavorable impression he is making. . . . He stressed his overbearing manner as a strong individual who has held high public office."

In subsequent meetings JDR kept trying to reason with Nelson. In early December, at his request, he had lunch with Nelson at "the old family home [13 West 54th] which [Nelson] bought many years ago and maintains really as an informal club." It was the house where JDR had been born in 1906 and Nelson was to die of a massive heart attack in January 1979.

We had, I felt, a useful and frank talk, and I came to understand better his objectives although I almost completely disagree with him. To me, in a way he is trying to move the situation back twenty years as far as the RBF is concerned. It is all sad and discouraging, but certainly the family and the office will come through. The main question is as to what will be left of the RBF in terms of funds and staff if he prevails.

In January 1978 JDR had one of his rare luncheons with Laurance, at the latter's suggestion. He found Laurance "in a relaxed mood and, as he often does, [he] tends to philosophize. Was interested as to the rather critical comments he made concerning some of brother Nelson's actions of recent months, particularly in connection with his handling of people." Laurance seemed to be realizing, as David's daughter Neva commented in a later interview, that even he could be "squeezed and used by Nelson."

JDR even contemplated resigning from the RBF board after conversations with several of his advisers, who were concerned about the strain he was under. The prevailing view was that he would lose the struggle to limit capital distributions from the Fund to the Creel organizations, unless he pressed the issue to a vote. If he kept up the fight without recourse to a vote, the only result might be that the organizations he cared about would come up short. The only other option would be to divorce himself from the Fund in order not to be associated with actions with which he was not in sympathy.

The RBF had set the retirement age of sixty-five, but the three trustees over this age—JDR, Nelson, and William McChesney Martin—were all covered by a "grandfather" clause. JDR would turn seventy-two years of age in March 1978. It might be a good time to retire. He discussed this with David Jr., who said he saw no reason for JDR to retire unless it was out of concern for his health.

After having been stalled for months, the Creel Committee was ready by late 1977 to begin advancing some of the larger proposals for decision. The first of these to come up was for the Museum of Modern Art, which needed all the financial help it could get because of the plan to build the Museum Towers apartment building in the air space above the museum. The board approved a grant of $10 million to MOMA, accompanied by intense debate over a move to exempt the museum from the understanding that this was a terminal grant. JDR was opposed to this on the grounds that it violated the Creel Committee rules, and the issue was left hanging. This episode heightened JDR's fear that huge inroads on the RBF endowment would leave the Fund an empty shell. He was aware that in 1978 David would be looking for a $30 million commitment to Rockefeller

University and that Laurance wanted $20 million for Memorial Sloan-Kettering.

The result of this concern was that JDR resolved to stay on the board to continue trying to hold down the level of capital giving and to see David succeed Laurance as chairman.[16] The market value of the RBF's endowment had already declined from $204.7 million in 1976 to $178.2 million at the beginning of 1978. JDR began meeting with Dana Creel to encourage him to speak out candidly with his own opinions on each of the proposals. Creel told JDR that the total of current proposals would take capital distributions "way beyond the $100 million mark." He wanted to ask the board to rethink the ceiling. JDR said that this "would be unsatisfactory in every way" and told Creel he hoped he would simply report developments to the board and say that his committee would continue working on each item on its own terms. Otherwise, JDR said, the negotiations would become a "power play" that would be very different "from Creel Committee members using their best judgment for each item with no total limit established."

In March, Creel told JDR that he had followed his advice and now thought that the total could be held to $85 million. He said that some items could be acted upon within a few months, but others would not be ready until the end of 1978. In the RBF board meeting in March Creel defended the $85 million figure, and JDR wrote that he was "pleased that brother Laurance, as Chairman, supported it."

In April, JDR commented that Creel "was handling a tough problem as effectively as possible" and was "courageously putting forward his own and his Committee's views." There had been talk of relieving Creel, who had a heart condition, but he had asked to stay on through 1978, when the bulk of his work would be done.

These developments were encouraging to JDR. He now thought it possible that with careful follow-through an end was in sight in which the RBF's obligations would be discharged and the Fund would survive reasonably intact, with the right principles anchored in place for the future.

Toward the end of April, however, JDR had to remove himself from active participation in the process. The reason: an opportunity to finally resolve a health problem that he had lived with for a long time.

33

✠

JULY 1978

On the afternoon of April 18, 1978, JDR entered New York University Medical Center for surgery to reconstruct his left ankle.

It was elective surgery. The ankle rarely was painful, but it was deformed and increasingly hampered JDR's mobility. The problem began when he sprained the ankle three times while playing on the tennis team in prep school in 1924 and 1925. Several more sprains later in his adult life made the ankle somewhat misshapen. Still, it seemed a minor problem in that it did not unduly restrict JDR in the exercise he enjoyed—horseback riding, golf, gardening, chopping wood, swimming, and, above all, walking. For decades, he habitually walked the eight long crosstown blocks from his Beekman Place apartment to work at Rockefeller Center.

By the early 1970s, however, an arthritic condition had set in and the ankle joint lost much of its function. Then JDR sprained it one more time while puttering in the garden one weekend at Fieldwood Farm. After that, he found he could no longer walk any appreciable distance without real difficulty.

From his doctor, JDR learned of a relatively new operation to reconstruct damaged ankles. The top man in this specialty was Dr. Theodore Waugh, an orthopedic surgeon who practiced in Orange, California, a suburb of Los Angeles. JDR went to see Dr. Waugh in August 1977. After examining the ankle, Dr. Waugh told JDR that he was definitely a candidate for the operation, but there was no emergency and he could afford to wait a year or two. He said he had performed the operation 265 times with more than a 90 percent success rate, and that orthopedic surgeons in general now were permitted to perform it. The time required for recuperation was approximately six weeks, including two weeks in the hospital. If the operation was not successful, one could resort to fusion, which eliminated pain but immobilized the joint.

Several months later, when JDR learned that Dr. Waugh was transfer-

ring his practice to New York City, he resolved to arrange his life to allow
for the needed six weeks, reasoning that if he was going to have the
operation eventually, sooner was better than later. The surgery was performed on the morning of April 20, and the prognosis was good.

However, on the second night after the surgery, JDR nearly ruined
his ankle and the work of the surgeon for good. He took two Percodan
tablets, a sleeping pill, and two aspirins, but woke up at 1:30 A.M. wanting
to go to the bathroom. Groggy, he grappled with the guard rail and fell
to the floor, tearing loose the intravenous feeding tube and the suction
tube from the wound. Undaunted, he crawled to the bathroom and back,
leaving a trail of blood on the floor, and managed to get back in bed,
conscious only that he had sprained his wrist badly. Then he rang for the
nurse. A panicky team materialized in a hurry to reconnect him. X-rays
were taken showing that the wrist was not fractured and that by some
miracle the reconstructed ankle had not been affected. A splint was put
on the wrist. JDR wrote in his diary:

My adventure caused quite a stir in the hospital partly I guess because of concern
that such an experience could occur at all. I myself could not help but be somewhat
amused by it. However I was certainly terribly fortunate that nothing really bad
had occurred to adversely affect the ankle operation or cause other damage such
as landing on my head. In any event it served as a conversation piece for several
days.

JDR was in the hospital for seventeen days. He then spent weekdays
at his Manhattan apartment and weekends at Fieldwood Farm, having
physical therapy sessions, increasingly exercising the ankle by walking
somewhat flat-footed, and keeping it elevated the rest of the time. Not
until June 5 did he reappear in his office, rarely spending more than half
a day for the next several weeks. Dr. Waugh pronounced the operation a
success, but JDR continued to be bothered by the fact that the ankle
remained swollen. Waugh told him that this was natural and would be a
factor for as much as six months.

During his convalescence JDR had a steady stream of visitors related
to his work interests, and had at least one meeting almost every day. Back
at the office, his secretary, Joyce Tait, worked to control this traffic as
much as possible, but JDR's workaholic nature was not to be suppressed.
The junior secretary, Monica Lesko, came to see him every other day to
take dictation.

All through this period it seems that there was scarcely a single one of
the significant interests that had occupied him at some point in his career
that was not touched upon at least once. In his diary he noted his pleasure

that a family member had taken a seat on the Population Council board. This was Peggy Dulany, David's daughter, one of the many Cousins whom JDR admired so much. He met several times with George Zeidenstein and Joan Dunlop to talk about the Pop Council and his interest in the welfare of women in developing countries.

He met with Ike Shapiro on Japan Society matters, with Porter McKeever on the progress of the Asia Society, and with Amyas Ames on Lincoln Center. With Jack Harr and Peter Johnson, he met with the eminent historian Richard Morris of Columbia University to discuss the upcoming bicentennial of the U.S. Constitution. With his chief art adviser, Dr. Sherman Lee, he was able to visit several art galleries. He worked on revising his will with the lawyer Squire Bozorth. In correspondence with Patricia Harris, Secretary of Housing and Urban Development, he came to a vague agreement to meet sometime in the fall to talk about the Urban Home Ownership Corporation. He kept up to date on the effort to hold down the total of Creel Committee disbursements in meetings with Creel and Dietel, and was able to attend the June meeting of the RBF board, with his diary note revealing only minor discontent. He also attended a meeting of the Room 5600 Board of Managers, and met several times with Don O'Brien to hear encouraging new ideas for solving problems relating to the future of the Pocantico estate.

A nettlesome problem had arisen at the Rockefeller Foundation, where a number of trustees were in open rebellion against the somewhat erratic behavior of the president, Dr. John Knowles. JDR discussed this with several of the trustees and met with Knowles, not knowing, as it would turn out much later, that Knowles was terminally ill.

The stream of meetings and subjects went on: with Faye Wattleton, the new president of Planned Parenthood–World Population, who he felt was an "inspired" choice; with Joan Dunlop and Liz Roberts on his Project on Human Sexuality; with Patricia Lucas and Porter McKeever on the JDR 3rd Fund's Arts in Asia program; with Joe Ernst on a new project for the Rockefeller Archives Center; with Harr and Johnson on his interest in euthanasia, deferring the decision as to whether he would be the keynote speaker at a planned conference in the fall.

JDR was even able to resume appearing at affairs honoring distinguished foreign visitors, attending two functions for the new prime minister of India, Morarji Desai, head of the Janata Coalition that had ousted Indira Gandhi from power. At the second function, an intimate luncheon at the River Club cohosted by Nelson and David at the request of the Indian ambassador, JDR was able to have a private conversation with Desai on his favorite subject and was pleased to find that the prime minister agreed with him completely on the need for effective family planning programs in India.

All through this welter of activity and contacts, JDR focused particularly on the future of three of his interests—the Agricultural Development Council (ADC), the Rockefeller Public Service Awards program, and the welfare of "the third sector."

The ADC was on the Creel list, but had not been actively considered because JDR was scheduled to conduct an internal review first to determine if the organization should be continued. When this came up in 1977, JDR was somewhat surprised to find that all of the regulars at his staff meetings—McKeever, McCormack, Harr, Dunlop, Ruder, and Johnson—were enthusiastic about insuring the future of the ADC.

To help out, Don McLean, the retired former associate of JDR's, had been serving as interim chairman of the ADC. While convalescing from his ankle operation, JDR met with McLean a number of times and interviewed a candidate for the presidency of the ADC. To gave a major assist to revitalizing the organization, JDR's staff proposed that he take over the chairmanship temporarily. He almost agreed to do this, but then decided instead to chair the ADC's Committee on the Future, which would serve the same purpose without his taking on other duties of the ADC chairmanship. JDR then moved to have the ADC considered in the Creel Committee process. He discussed its future with Dana Creel, saying that a grant of $3 million to $4 million would put the ADC on a sound footing indefinitely. Dietel took a deep interest in the ADC, at one meeting suggesting that some kind of working relationship be forged between the ADC and the Winrock Livestock Project, of which Dietel was president.

The Rockefeller Public Service Awards program was also coming up for renewal. It will be recalled that JDR had funded a three-year test of the idea of making the awards available not only to government employees but to any Americans who performed a notable public service on their own initiative. The opinion among all those involved in the program was that the experiment had proved even more successful than hoped. JDR agreed to fund the program for another three years, but, conscious of his age, also convened a meeting on June 7 to discuss ways of insuring its future beyond the three-year extension. Aside from JDR's advisers, the group included Dean Donald Stokes of the Woodrow Wilson School at Princeton; Ingrid Reed, administrator of the program; the noted economist Robert Nathan, who chaired the selection committee for the awards; and two prominent businessmen, William Roth of San Francisco and R. Manning Brown, president of New York Life.

JDR, like his father, had always shied away from endowing programs he had created, knowing that future conditions could not be foreseen, especially in the case of programs affected by social, political, and economic trends. However, he said he did not rule out participating in finding some longer-term base for continuation of the awards program. Two major business concerns, a brokerage house and a pharmaceutical company, had expressed interest in funding the awards, but there was concern in the group that this might lead to commercialization. JDR and his staff had never interfered in the selection of award recipients, and the program had been managed with the highest integrity by the Woodrow Wilson School. Bob Nathan in particular was concerned that any "outside" funding that would require a change in the name of the program would be to lose one of its most valuable assets, the spirit of giving and service that was exemplified in both its name and its history.

While the discussion was going on, Nathan had been crunching numbers. He began to muse aloud, while still scribbling on the pad. If JDR would consider funding a longer extension of the program, say five or six years out, and provide the money up front, and if this could be matched by funds raised elsewhere without any basic change in the nature of the program, then the resulting sum would yield enough interest to more than pay for the annual cost of the awards.

JDR indicated that he would consider participating in this way. The meeting ended with a plan to meet again in the fall after Nathan had a chance to refine the numbers and, with everyone else, to think about possible sources of contributions.

Of all the planning for the future, the subject that excited JDR the most was that of advancing his ideas on "the third sector"—raising awareness of its nature and its importance as the balance wheel of American democracy, encouraging greater participation of individuals in giving and volunteering, and improving conditions for the maintenance and welfare of the private nonprofit sector through greater understanding of it among business and government leaders. He pursued these goals in a variety of ways in June and early July—meeting with Robert Ahmanson and David Jr. to hear about the disappointing lack of initiative among foundations in the Los Angeles area; lunching with Walter McNerney, Waldemar Nielsen, and Porter McKeever to consider ways to advance the Filer Commission recommendations in Washington and with the Carter administration; and interviewing candidates to assist him in writing a book on the subject.

JDR and Jack Harr had agreed to employ again the three-man process that had worked well in the writing of *The Second American Revolution*. But this time they agreed that Harr would reverse roles to be "the third man" (as Dick Barrett had been before) and to recruit a new person as the primary writer. The search had narrowed down to a brilliant young Englishman named Peter Bocock, who had been one of the "young Turks" on Prime Minister Heath's staff in London before moving to the United States to take a job with the World Bank.

Meanwhile, a pleasant diversion from the press of work was pending— the wedding on June 24 of JDR's youngest daughter, Alida, and Mark Dayton, son of Bruce Dayton, former chairman of the Dayton Hudson merchandising company headquartered in Minneapolis. Mark and Alida had met on the West Coast in 1975 and again in 1977 when they had participated in the activities of a group of young people who had in common both the fact of inherited wealth and being regarded as representing the "enemy," meaning the capitalist class, by others. These wealthy young liberals worked with Obie Benz and the Vanguard Foundation and formed their own "combination social club and support group for rich kids," as Alida expressed it. A graduate of Yale at the end of the turbulent 1960s, Mark had taught in a ghetto school in Boston and served on the staff of Senator Walter Mondale.

At the wedding dinner at Windows on the World atop the World Trade Center, JDR enjoyed sitting next to Mrs. Lee McPhail, Mark's divorced mother, who had married the president of the American League. The ceremony was planned out of doors on the lawn southwest of the main house at Fieldwood Farm. JDR wrote: "The day was absolutely perfect— temperature, humidity, sun, no wind—really ideal for a summer wedding." Once the guests had arrived, shortly after 4:00 P.M., including Vice President and Mrs. Mondale, the ceremony began. "My part," JDR wrote, "was to bring Alida down from the terrace in a wide circle so as to have an easy grade. She was calm and fine and looked very pretty in her Mexican wedding dress."

After Mark and Alida recited their vows from memory, a reception, buffet dinner, and dancing followed, all organized by Timothy Marquand, Blanchette's nephew and the son of novelist John P. Marquand. By nine-thirty the party had ended, and buses took guests back to Manhattan.

Then it was back to work for JDR, who now was spending full days in the office, but taking an occasional day off. He spent a restful Fourth of July weekend with Blanchette at Fieldwood Farm, noting that because the Fourth was on a Tuesday "many institutions including our office are giving their people a four-day holiday." But he was back at his desk in Room 5600 for the remaining three days of the work week. On Friday, July 7, he had his last business luncheon, with Jack Harr and Peter Bocock to discuss the "third sector" book. He wrote in his diary: "We were again favorably impressed with [Bocock] and agreed to go ahead. It will, I feel, be an interesting project and if we do it well, could be a major contribution."

JDR left his office at 3:00 P.M. that afternoon for the weekend at Fieldwood Farm, but not before deciding that he would stay there on Monday as well, to avoid the city heat, give his ankle a rest, and handle a considerable amount of dictation that had accumulated. He could do that as well at home as in the office—Monica Lesko had agreed to drive over from her home in Westwood, New Jersey, on Monday for the purpose.

Chauffeur Tom Kissick drove JDR to Fieldwood Farm and came back on Saturday to take JDR and Blanchette to Oyster Bay, Long Island, to attend the memorial service for Babe Paley, the late wife of CBS chairman William S. Paley. On the way home JDR learned that Blanchette wanted Kissick to take her to visit her sister in Pennsylvania on Monday and then directly back to Manhattan late in the afternoon for a meeting at the Museum of Modern Art. Kissick wanted to hire a limousine or see if another family chauffeur might be available to take JDR from Fieldwood Farm to the Manhattan apartment Monday evening. As almost always in such situations, JDR declined—he would simply take a taxi to the Tarrytown train station, the train to Grand Central, and a taxi to One Beekman Place.

On Monday, July 10, JDR and Monica finished their work shortly after 5:00 P.M. He asked her if she would drop him off at the Tarrytown train station. Concerned about long flights of stairs at both ends of the train trip, Monica suggested that she drive JDR down to the city. After some persuasion, he agreed and offered in return to guide Monica on a driving tour of the Rockefeller estate, which she had never seen.

They departed at five-thirty in Monica's 1965 Mustang convertible, turning east at the Fieldwood Farm entry gate on Sleepy Hollow Road and then northeast roughly paralleling State Route 117. They crossed Route 117 close to its junction with the Taconic Parkway and then made an acute right turn onto the Bedford Road heading south toward the village of Pocantico Hills and the main entrance to the estate two and a half miles distant. JDR liked this more circuitous route when he traveled by car to the city—it avoided Route 9 traffic through the Tarrytowns and passed through the portion of the estate that he enjoyed the most, the wooded and relatively undeveloped northern acres.

Bedford Road is an old two-lane concrete highway only twenty feet wide with no true shoulder in places where it is closely bordered by massive old trees and stone walls. It is a lovely drive through the gently rolling hills of southern Westchester County, but it can be dangerous because of its grades and curves and narrowness—a double yellow line to prohibit passing runs down its center on most of its length.

Monica made her turn onto Bedford Road just after a small red Honda had passed by heading south. She followed the Honda as they began to pass through a portion of the Rockefeller estate owned by Laurance. Monica accelerated to about forty-five miles per hour as the car ascended the slight rise known locally as Stillman Hill. As they crested the hill, the trees and brush lots gave way to open fields where Peggy, David's wife, pastured her Simmental cattle.

Coming from the other direction was a 1976 Volkswagen sedan driven by sixteen-year-old David Low. David had left his house in Briarcliff Manor in something of a huff after a dispute with his mother. He had a learner's permit that allowed him to drive only during daylight hours.

The red Honda in front of JDR and Monica braked suddenly and swerved to the right, but not in enough time to avoid being sideswiped by Low's car. That impact caused Low to lose control. He lurched to the right, overcorrected, and careened squarely into the oncoming lane, colliding head-on with the Mustang. Trapped in his car, David died within a few minutes of multiple injuries. In the driver's seat of the Mustang, Monica was unconscious and covered with blood from a deep scalp laceration and a badly damaged hand. She would survive, though she faced severe depression and years of plastic surgery to restore her hand.

In the passenger seat, JDR had no chance. He died instantly.

In Manhattan, Tom Kissick was alerted that a tragedy had happened and that he should bring Blanchette to Hudson Pines, David's Pocantico house, as soon as possible. He had not been told what the tragedy was. When he arrived at the Museum of Modern Art and entered the building he saw Blanchette leaving the reception area to take a telephone call. It was from Peggy Rockefeller, telling Blanchette of her husband's death.

All that evening, family members in the New York area gathered at Hudson Pines to share their grief. The television networks broke into their programming with a news bulletin shortly after 8:00 P.M. Jay flew up from Washington that evening. Alida and Mark Dayton arrived at Fieldwood Farm the next day and Hope came in from Arizona. Sandra could not bring herself to come and grieved alone at her home in Cambridge. Laurance came from his vacation home in Woodstock, Vermont, and Nelson was on his way back from his ranch in Venezuela.

All day Tuesday and Wednesday Blanchette and Jay consoled a steady stream of visitors who had come to console them. Blanchette visited Monica in Phelps Memorial Hospital, and offered her condolences to David Low's heartbroken mother. President Carter telephoned and spoke to Blanchette and Jay. Phone calls and telegrams came from all over the world. More than one hundred winners of the Rockefeller Public Service Awards over the years wrote to Blanchette, trying to express what her husband's vision and generosity had meant to them at critical points in their own lives. Ted Hesburgh, attending a conference in Johannesburg, South Africa, sat stunned before the television set in his hotel room, trying to comprehend the death of a man he respected so much and had worked with for so many years. Then, he took out his sacramental vessels and celebrated a solemn requiem mass in the solitude of his room.

A memorial service for JDR was set for Thursday, July 13, in the beautiful setting of Riverside Church where Junior had been eulogized eighteen years earlier. Nelson arrived at Fieldwood Farm on Wednesday, bringing the notes he had written for the eulogy he expected to deliver as the senior member of the family. Blanchette and Jay politely told him he would not be asked to speak, that Jay would deliver the principal eulogy. Jack Harr was present, having been asked by Jay to come up to tell him about his father's most recent interests. The two went downstairs to the starkly modern subterranean area that Blanchette had had built for her art collection. It was an emotional conversation, not a speechwriting session. Jay knew what he wanted to say.

The death of a man of JDR's stature inevitably brings forth assessments of his life and career: a measuring of obstacles overcome, contributions made, objectives achieved. Editorial writers could cite the evidences of his leadership, but had more difficulty expressing the essence of the man and his qualities of character, his stubborn adherence to principle and his great conscience. The *New York Times* extolled his leadership of the Rockefeller Foundation, his role in the building of Lincoln Center, his lifelong dedication to the cause of curbing excessive population growth, and concluded that the "Rockefeller inheritance and all who benefitted from it were enriched by having so conscientious a steward." The *Los Angeles Times* focused on his work in improving Asian-American relations and his advocacy of a strong "third sector" at home. The *Washington Post* perhaps came closest to the story of the man:

Between the public's relentless interest in the super-rich and the peculiar burdens that belonging to a great family can entail it cannot have been easy to be a grandson of the fabled John D. While his brothers pursed interests that often brought them into the public light, John D. III, a reserved and almost shy man, stayed on an essentially private track. Yet he had an acute sense of the larger public interest arising in good measure from his exposure to the troubles of people and peoples less fortunate than himself. Though he was himself beyond need, he had a feeling for those who are in need. "It will take the best efforts of everyone," he once said, "to avert a global disaster of poverty and chaos." Truly his death at 72 . . . leaves the nation and the world poorer.

At the memorial service, Steven Rockefeller spoke of his uncle "as a humanist in the best sense of the word" and touched on elements of his character in reading selections from John Dewey, St. Paul, a Japanese poet, a Taoist philosopher, and Socrates. Sherman Lee spoke feelingly of his friend's great love of Asian art and his commitment to making its beauty and ideas more available and explicable to Americans.

Jay had been concerned that he would not be able to get through his eulogy. But, with only a catch in his throat at the beginning, he spoke with strength and deep feeling:

He was a gentle person—dignified, modest, some said shy—but yet a man of bedrock strength and perseverance.

He spent his entire life in service to others—to his community, to his country, and to the world. But he never thought of himself as a "do-gooder." He was not self-indulgent. He was not self-satisfied. He was serious, purposeful, idealistic, realistic, totally dedicated.

I am his son, and I loved him. I speak now for my family—for my strong and loving mother, for Sandra, for Hopie, and for Alida. Perhaps I speak as well for all of you, for all of those who loved him.

I am infinitely, tenderly, and fiercely proud of him as a father, as a man, as a Rockefeller, and as an American. His sense of family, and of the special responsibility of our family, was clear, honest, courageous, unwavering.

His principles were deep and abiding, and he did not compromise them. For all his gentle nature, he was firm in his convictions, and formal, perhaps, in his ways, even old-fashioned sometimes. Yet he was extraordinarily open to new ideas and needs. He grew as a human being every day of his life.

My father never sought recognition for himself, but he would fight to the ends of the earth for what he believed in. Decade after decade, he pursued with all his being the most fundamental and difficult problems of our world:

the global problem of population growth,
the enhancement of the most basic rights of a democratic system,
the building of spirit, morale, and competence into public life,
the progress and welfare of blacks, women, and young people,

cultural exchange, strengthening the ties between Japan and the United States, in fact, all of Asia and the United States,

the improvement of the roles and status of women in the developing countries,

giving every American school child an appreciation of the arts,

improving the ability of Asian farmers to produce food,

the quality of working life and corporate responsibility,

and preserving and strengthening the unique American tradition of giving, of one's resources and one's self, for the common good.

This, in part, was his agenda. This is what he was trying to do. What did he accomplish? He would have said: not enough. By their very nature, the problems he took on did not lend themselves to neat and clear solutions. But you know, and I know, and we can say what his modesty would not let him say: that all over the world the lives of millions of people have been touched and eased and enhanced by the work he has done.

He would never cease trying. Only last Friday he was completing arrangements for a project that would have occupied him for the next two years. It was to be a new book about what he called "the third sector"—that is, the private, nonprofit sector—as distinguished from government and from business. He used to use the term philanthropy; indeed, he was widely referred to as a philanthropist, which is true enough, but he had gone way beyond that in his own thinking. He was not concerned about philanthropy as some amiable custom, as a return to a golden age, but rather about the health of the entire private nonprofit sector of our society as crucial to our nation's future.

My father was a determined and relentless optimist. He never lost faith. Let me read for you just one paragraph from his book, *The Second American Revolution*, which I think expresses his spirit. He wrote:

My belief is that it is quite possible to understand fully the gravity of our situation today and yet continue to be basically hopeful and optimistic about the future. . . . I feel this is an exciting time to be alive. Virtually everything seems to be wide open for change. I look upon this positively for to me it means that everything is wide open for improvement and progress. It means to me that each person has the opportunity to influence the course of events, in however small or large a way. I would much rather be alive during a time of challenge such as this than during a sedate and static period of history.

My father's life was long and very full. But it was cut short very suddenly. There was so much more that he wanted to do. But he endures. He endures in what he stood for, in what he did, and in the inspiration and guidance that he has given each of us.

Let me say to you, Daddy, that you helped shape a country and a world in your own quiet way—and that we know that.

You have been a loving and strong father, and we, your children, are grateful. You have set a standard for our family and for each one of us as individuals. Let me say to you that we are strong and we are ready to carry that standard forward; that we know and we accept our responsibility; and that we cherish you, now and forever.

I am crushed by your death, but I am, and we are, profoundly proud of your life.

You have blessed and touched this world in good ways that will last forever.

Daddy, rest in peace.

The service concluded with Leontyne Price singing "The Lord's Prayer" and the Reverend William Sloane Coffin offering a closing prayer and benediction.

Members of the Rockefeller family drove from Riverside Church directly to the Rockefeller Cemetery, situated on a slight rise overlooking the Hudson River near the Pocantico estate. While the family members stood in a circle clasping hands, the urn containing the ashes of John D. Rockefeller 3rd was lowered into the ground near the graves of his parents.

EPILOGUE

The fact that the deaths of JDR 3rd in July 1978 and of his brother Nelson six months later were both sudden and unexpected obviously left many issues unresolved. In the decade following their deaths, all of these issues were dealt with in one way or another, with the single exception of the ultimate disposition of the core of the Pocantico estate known as the "Park." At this writing, this last issue also appears on its way to a solution.

Nelson died of a massive heart attack late on the evening of January 26, 1979, in the townhouse at 13 West 54th Street that had been the first Manhattan residence owned by his parents early in the century and where four of his siblings had been born—Babs, JDR, Laurance, and Winthrop. Ostensibly working on one of his art books, Nelson was alone except for the company of a young female assistant, Megan Marschak. This fact was initially covered up, as well as an apparent delay of an hour in summoning emergency assistance, leading to intense concentration on the story by the media and a great deal of speculation and innuendo. Someday the full story will probably come out, but at present the exact details still are not known.

As noted several times, the greater part of the wealth of the six members of the third Rockefeller generation reposed in the 1934 Trusts created by their father. Under the conditions established in 1934, JDR 3rd's trust passed immediately after his death in equal shares to his four children and Nelson's trust likewise was immediately shared by his six children. The conditions are the same for these recipients as for their fathers—they are lifetime beneficiaries of the income from the trusts and can petition their trustees to invade principal. Only upon their deaths will the trusts be paid out (in equal shares to *their* children) and cease to exist.

JDR's personal assets (as distinct from his 1934 Trust) were probated at $111,180,000: securities valued at $46.5 million; art and other possessions at $39.8 million; real estate with an appraised value of $12.3 million; $6 million in mortgages, notes, and cash; and more than $6 million in various transfers to individuals and organizations that had been made in the last three years of his life, which, according to federal tax law, had to be added back into his estate for purposes of appraisal.

Deducted from this probated total were debts, funeral expenses, the cost of administering the estate, and payment of commitments JDR had

554

made before his death (without specifying them in his will) that were
honored by his three trustees—his son, Jay, lawyer Donal O'Brien, and
the Room 5600 staff chief, J. Richardson Dilworth. In the main these
commitments were contributions JDR had pledged to Princeton
University, the Rockefeller Public Service Awards, the JDR 3rd Fund,
the Asia Society, and the Program on Non-Profit Organizations at Yale
University.

After these deductions, the balance was divided into two equal portions
of $48.5 million each. One portion went to JDR's widow, Blanchette, con-
sisting of most of the securities and real estate; it was exempt from estate
taxes under the marital deduction clause. All of the charitable bequests
JDR made in his will went into the other, taxable portion. Aside from the
two art collections, his one-fourth share of the Pocantico estate, and the
gift of Bassett Hall to Colonial Williamsburg, these included the relatively
small bequests noted in Chapter 28, to provide a modicum of transitional
support to a number of his major philanthropic interests.

This process reduced the taxable portion of JDR's estate to $4,542,574.
On this amount, his executors paid federal estate tax of $1,860,808 and
New York State tax of $340,368. The balance, or "residual estate," of
$2,341,398 passed to the JDR 3rd Fund under the terms of his will.

In Nelson's case, both his 1934 Trust and personal estate were smaller
than JDR's, the latter being probated at some $62 million, more than half
of it accounted for by art and other possessions. His executors were
O'Brien, Dilworth, and brother Laurance. Two factors about Nelson's
estate influenced family decisions yet to be made. One stemmed from a
revision of his will that Nelson made about six weeks before his death in
which he left his share of the "outer spaces" of the Pocantico estate to his
wife, Happy, and named the National Trust for Historic Preservation as
the specific charitable recipient of his fourth of the estate's "Park" area.
This is what has delayed the final disposition of Pocantico for so long.
Second, the circumstances of Nelson's 1934 Trust added weight to the
general desire of the younger Rockefellers to find ways to tap into the
wealth tied up in Rockefeller Center. The reason was that Nelson's Trust
not only was smaller than the others and had to be divided six ways, but
it also had a larger proportion of Rockefeller Center stock than the other
1934 Trusts.

The fact that so short a time separated the deaths of the two oldest
Rockefeller brothers meant that Nelson made no discernible progress
toward his goal of taking charge of family matters. One can only speculate
as to how much he might have succeeded had he lived longer. The legacy
of JDR's ideals and principles, the opposition to Nelson among the Cous-

ins, and the growing restiveness of Laurance and David might well have curtailed his ambitions.

Summaries of developments in the past decade in regard to the three principal family issues follow:

THE ROCKEFELLER BROTHERS FUND

The culmination of the Creel Committee process vindicated both Dana Creel's last estimate to JDR that the capital grants total would be approximately $85 million, and David and Laurance in their belief that expending $100 million (half of the RBF's endowment at the time) would not be ruinous. The seeming contradiction is explained by three facts: (1) grants to eighteen organizations on the Creel agenda while JDR was still alive totaled $85,490,000; (2) in 1981 a new provision was added to the Creel total, $15 million set aside for Sleepy Hollow Restorations, Inc., for its possible participation in the ultimate disposition of the "Park" portion of the Pocantico estate (discussed below), bringing the total to $100,490,000, very close to the target figure Laurance and David had proposed; and (3) good management and the bull market of the 1980s have brought the value of the remaining endowment up to $297 million as of the end of 1989.

Aside from the Sleepy Hollow grant and the $10 million to the Museum of Modern Art, only three other Creel grantees received $10 million or more: Rockefeller University, $22.5 million; Memorial Sloan-Kettering, $17.5 million; and the Population Council, $10 million. The remaining $40,490,000 was disbursed in grants of varying size to the fourteen other organizations on the Creel list.

The sum given to the Population Council, in the main decided after JDR's death, bears some explanation. As noted, he did not play the role of advocate of "his" organizations beyond what emerged from the Creel Committee's deliberations, for reasons both of principle and of his goal of holding down the level of capital grants. The result was that grants totaling only $3,750,000 were committed to the Council before JDR's death for its general budgetary support for the years 1978–80 and toward "the policy-related aspects of the Council's program." After JDR's death, the opinion grew among his survivors, other members of the family, and his associates that he had, in fact, come up short in the Creel Committee results. For two reasons, this sentiment became focused on reopening the Creel deliberations for the benefit of the Population Council: the knowledge that population had for a long time been JDR's highest priority, and effective lobbying by the Council's leadership and Joan Dunlop, JDR's associate in population matters. The result was that the Council was reconsidered by the RBF and, through a complex formula of capital and program grants, finally received additional monies to bring its total up to $10 million.

One can only speculate as to whether JDR himself would have chosen this outcome. Unquestionably, he was most identified with the population field, but the evidence suggests that his highest priority in his later years was the "third sector." But no organization existed in this area to be placed in the Creel process. Two of JDR's organizations on the Creel list *did* come up short—the Asia Society and the Agricultural Development Council, both of which were in dire straits at the time of his death. The ADC received nothing and the Asia Society only $1.54 million (see below).

JDR's desire to see David succeed Laurance as RBF chairman came to pass in June 1980. As the "man in the middle" of the feud between JDR and Nelson, David was ideally suited to heal the wounds: he had accepted neither JDR's fear that the Creel grants would unduly damage the RBF nor Nelson's view that the Cousins had forfeited their right to leadership of the RBF. He superintended both the completion of the Creel process, which brought the RBF's endowment down to $160 million in 1983, and the rapid recovery of that endowment to a new high in the ensuing years.

JDR would be pleased, also, by the way that the Cousins have exerted leadership in the RBF, holding seven of the nineteen positions on the board and helping to give the Fund a new sense of mission as the result of the work of a program review committee established in 1981 with David Rockefeller, Jr., as chairman.

In 1987, at a celebration in Bangkok marking the twenty-fifth anniversary of the Ramon Magsaysay Award Foundation, David announced his retirement as RBF chairman, and was succeeded by his son, David, Jr. Soon after, Bill Dietel completed a twelve-year tenure as RBF president that had been filled with turmoil and change. Colin Campbell, former president of Wesleyan University, succeeded him.

The process of transition within the RBF was complete. With its historic obligations discharged, its endowment at a new high, and with new leadership and mission, the RBF no longer is a vehicle for the special interests of any individual board member, but is now totally the independent and innovative foundation that JDR envisioned.

ROCKEFELLER CENTER

As noted earlier, Rockefeller Center had become by far the largest single repository of family wealth because of the substantial purchases of stock and debentures by the 1934 Trusts and the growth in value of the

Center. But this wealth was tied up because the Center paid almost no dividends for decades, at first because of indebtedness and restrictions in the lease with Columbia University and later because of the policy of plowing earnings back into growth of the Center's overall value. This last was concentrated on diversified acquisitions in an effort to correct the overwhelming dependency of the Center on the real estate market, with Rockefeller Center, Inc. (RCI), taking on the characteristics of a holding company.

It was noted also that this gradually became an issue for some of the beneficiaries of the 1934 Trusts because their annual income from the trusts was held down by the lack of RCI dividends. With the deaths of JDR and Nelson, this pressure increased because the number of Rockefeller family members dependent on income from the 1934 Trusts now exceeded a dozen. On their behalf, the Trust Committees began pressing for a plan that would begin to yield a payout from Rockefeller Center.

Soon after retiring as chairman of the Chase Manhattan Bank, David Rockefeller in 1982 was elected chairman by the RCI board, succeeding J. Richardson Dilworth. The name of the company was changed to Rockefeller Group, Inc. (RGI), and Richard Voell was brought in as president. Under Voell's leadership, the policy of acquisition and diversification was stepped up even further, with the use of some $700 million in borrowed funds.

A dramatic change occurred in 1985 when Voell succeeded in purchasing the land under the Center from Columbia University for $411 million, thus finally bringing to a successful conclusion a long-sought goal of the Rockefellers. The clinching argument with the university's negotiators was that the university would receive a greater return in the future from the income and growth in value of the $411 million than from annual rent paid by RGI.

With the land and buildings now united in the same hands, pressure intensified for payout from RGI, but first the greatly increased debt had to be dealt with. This was accomplished later in 1985 by the successful marketing of a Real Estate Investment Trust (REIT) involving the land and the buildings wholly owned by RGI (some 71 percent, comprising all the land and buildings of the "original" Center, that part east of Sixth Avenue). Akin to a public stock offering, the REIT has the character of a mortgage in that the stock can be repurchased by the seller. The transaction yielded $1.3 billion, most of which was used to pay down the debt.

Then in November 1989 came the sale of 51 percent of RGI to the Mitsubishi Estate Corporation for $846 million.

All of this is enormously complicated and can barely be summarized here. Consider, for example, the fact that what Mitsubishi purchased was 51 percent of the 29 percent ownership of Rockefeller Center left in RGI after the marketing of the REIT, consisting of substantial RGI holdings in three buildings west of Sixth Avenue and the non–real estate holdings of RGI. The net effect, roughly, is that Mitsubishi owned 15 percent of the totality of Rockefeller Center and 14 percent remained with the Rockefellers. In two additional transactions (July 1990 and July 1991), Mitsubishi purchased another 29 percent of RGI stock, bringing its total holding to 983,234 shares. The price was $527 million, bringing the cumulative purchase price to $1,373 billion. The result is that Mitsubishi now owns 80 percent of RGI and 23.6 percent of Rockefeller Center. The 1934 Trusts continue to own 20 percent of RGI and 5.4 percent of the Center (with the remaining 71 percent held by the publicly owned REIT).

These events finally loosened the financial bonds that had held the Rockefeller family together for more than fifty years, with individual family members able to face the future in an entirely different way now that the sale of RGI stock by the 1934 Trusts has dramatically increased their income.

THE POCANTICO ESTATE

The fact that Nelson changed his will shortly before his death in ways that deviated from the plan the brothers had finally agreed upon (only a year earlier) effectively derailed that plan. Don O'Brien, the two surviving brothers, and the executors of JDR's will had to start all over again to try to overcome the obstacles that Nelson's will created.

It will be recalled that in late 1977 and early 1978, after many years of reviewing and disagreeing over a series of proposals, the four brothers had finally agreed to a new plan for the future of Pocantico that accommodated their differing points of view. This new plan, fashioned by Don O'Brien and Harmon Goldstone, most nearly resembled the original Sasaki Plan, in that it provided for "best use" of various portions of the estate. Here we need be concerned only with the two major uses: (1) converting most of the several thousand acres in the "open spaces" to a public park, maintained in its natural state, and (2) dedicating most of the 249.5 acres in the "Park" to a historic site, with the buildings and grounds maintained and staffed for public visitation. JDR's priority was the first use and Nelson's the second.

It was always understood that those outcomes would not be fully realized until after the deaths of the four brothers; in short, they would maintain life use. But to accomplish the objectives it was critical that the brothers all make the same provisions in their wills, the most important of these being the bequest of their share of the Pocantico estate to an unnamed charitable recipient. This would enable the surviving brothers and executors of any deceased brothers to continue to work together to negotiate the implementation of the plan and decide on the ultimate recipient to carry it out.

JDR followed this prescription, but Nelson did not; he jumped the gun by naming a specific charitable recipient, the National Trust for Historic Preservation, for his one-fourth of the "Park"—before any negotiations or settling of details had been done. He also left much of his art in Kykuit and outdoor sculpture to the National Trust, and willed his fourth of the "open spaces" to Happy.

The survivors began to try to untangle this by separating the major uses into two projects and pursuing resolution of "the open spaces" first. The solution was a complex transaction involving the transferring of acreage so that Laurance, David and the estates of JDR and Nelson each ended up owning specific sections of Pocantico in place of the joint and undivided ownership that had existed before. JDR's one-fourth share of the "Park" and Kykuit was traded for acreage in the "open spaces." Nelson's executors gave up the "open spaces" and received a larger portion of the "Park" in return. The two surviving brothers also ended up owning specific sections of the "open spaces" and the "Park."

JDR's estate now owned 681 acres of the "open spaces" and none of the "Park." This land, plus sixty-two acres contributed by David, was donated to New York State to be held in reserve for the eventual creation of Rockefeller State Park. The gift was announced in a public ceremony at Kykuit on December 23, 1983, attended by Governor Mario Cuomo, Blanchette, Laurance, David, and various public officials. At the same time, the JDR 3rd Fund, the residual legatee of JDR's estate, announced a gift of $3 million to New York State for maintenance of the new public preserve, and other Rockefeller family members announced their intention to add another thousand acres in the future to the 743 acres already transferred.

Thus, more than five years after JDR's death, his main hope for the future use of the Pocantico estate was realized.

It will be recalled that a major problem in the planning for Pocantico was the cost involved, especially for maintaining the "Park" as a historic site. The last estimate before JDR's death had been that $45 million would be required. To get a start on raising this, O'Brien proposed that each of the four brothers provide for a contribution of $5 million in their wills.

Both JDR and Nelson failed to do this. A new start on providing for this
cost occurred when the RBF appropriated $15 million to be held for the
possible involvement of Sleepy Hollow Restorations, Inc., which since has
changed its name to Historic Hudson Valley. In effect, this sum was put
in escrow pending the adoption of a final plan for making the "Park" into
a historic site. A provision of Babs's will added $1.5 million to this trust.
As a result of the boom years of the 1980s, this account was worth some
$37 million at the end of 1989.

This sum can be used if an appropriate solution is found to the goal of
converting the "Park" to a historic site; if not, the monies will revert to
the RBF.

The complex transactions noted above included provisions designed to
give the National Trust a basis for proposing a solution to the problem.
Nelson's estate ended up with an eighty-six-acre section of the "Park,"
an area that includes Kykuit, the Coach Barn, the Orangerie, and the
greenhouses, all of this owned by the National Trust under the provision
in Nelson's will. The agreement with the Trust gave it two years to come
up with a plan for the historic area to be submitted for the approval of
Laurance and David. If they did not approve the study, they would have
the option of purchasing the property from the Trust "at fair market value"
in order to proceed with finding another solution. The study, delivered in
1985, was not accepted by either Laurance or David, and they moved to
exercise the option to purchase the property back from the Trust. A substantial disagreement on what constitutes "fair market value" has stalled
these negotiations for years.

At this writing, a possible solution is being discussed in which the Trust
would pass the property to the RBF, which would use Kykuit for a conference and study center. Using the escrow fund, Historic Hudson Valley
would maintain the property as a historic site and conduct tours of the
buildings and grounds. This solution would at least partially realize
Nelson's dreams for the final use of the "Park."

JDR's Philanthropic Interests

Three of JDR's five organizations on the Creel Committee list were
very well treated.

The *Japan Society*, the most successful of the U.S.-based bilateral organizations, received $1.5 million. JDR's energetic revival of the Society in
1952 was his first major step in his sudden emergence as a remarkably
effective and successful philanthropist. Although the Society obviously had
benefited from the great postwar recovery of Japan and the close ties

between Japan and the United States, it was JDR's initiative, devotion, and leadership that gave it such a strong financial footing and its own building in Manhattan. It was for these reasons that the RBF terminal grant to the Japan Society was comparatively small, but it was well received by the Society's leadership as a pleasant surprise.

Lincoln Center for the Performing Arts received a $3 million terminal grant from the RBF. There are several reasons why the grant was not larger—Lincoln Center had already received a great deal of financial support from Rockefeller family sources, especially the RBF and JDR himself. And the Center had recently received $10 million from the will of Martha Baird Rockefeller. Moreover, JDR had severed his long connection with Lincoln Center, partly to begin to bring to an end a dependency on Rockefeller financial support that could not go on indefinitely.

The Population Council, with the help of the $10 million in Creel Committee support discussed above, has continued to thrive as the world's preeminent institution in its field, despite the almost complete ideological reversal in U.S. population policy engineered by recent Republican administrations under pressure from the right wing of the Republican Party. Under the leadership of George Zeidenstein and a board of trustees drawn from many countries, the Population Council is more than ever an international organization, and, by all accounts, remains a highly effective one.

The fate of three more of JDR's philanthropic contributions is worthy of note:

The Asian Cultural Council

This is the new name of the "Arts in Asia" program of the JDR 3rd Fund, which JDR initiated in 1963. He provided the sole financial support for the program, described earlier as a "small gem" in American philanthropy for the purity, economy, and cultural significance of its mission. No one could have expected it to survive JDR's death for very long when it was reconstituted as a separate organization with its new name by the trustees of the JDR 3rd Fund in 1980; they could provide only minimal funding. Surprisingly, the Asian Cultural Council has thrived. Richard Lanier remained as its director. An art historian from Tulane, Lanier faced a difficult assignment. He not only had to maintain the high standards of the program, but he also had to raise the funds needed to support it. He has succeeded admirably, attracting support from a wide range of individuals, corporations, and foundations in the United States and abroad. By the end of the 1980s Lanier had raised an endowment of $12 million and ran an operating budget of $2 million per year. Affiliation with the Rockefeller Brothers Fund at the beginning of 1991 will enable the Council to reduce its administrative overhead and devote even more of its funds to program development and fellowships.

The American Art Collection

JDR's pledge to will his American art collection to the San Francisco museums was, of course, carried out. After his death the museums began a program of renovation and expansion to accommodate the collection. In 1984 the American Galleries of the de Young Museum were reopened and rededicated after being closed for two years of preparation. On hand for the occasion were Blanchette, Jay, and Sharon. A newspaper account described "the long-overdue renovation" and the Rockefeller collection as "a wonder to behold" (*San Francisco Chronicle*, June 23, 1984). The story added: "The Rockefellers instantly transformed San Francisco into a truly major center of American art . . . in a terrific windfall for the city and the whole Far West."

The Rockefeller Public Service Awards

Only a month before his death, JDR formally pledged funds to the Woodrow Wilson School at Princeton sufficient to extend the RPSA for another three-year period, during which, by agreement with the group that met on June 7, 1978, he planned to cooperate in an effort to raise enough money to guarantee continuation of the program indefinitely.

His executors honored the three-year pledge and the program was continued during that period. But with JDR gone, efforts to raise endowment funds failed, and the RPSA finally had to be terminated. Two of JDR's associates (Harr and Johnson) and the leadership of the Woodrow Wilson School (Dean Stokes, Ingrid Reed, and Rufus Miles) agreed that finding a way to continue the RPSA would be the most fitting testimonial to JDR that could be devised. Many of his good works in various functional fields were assured of continuity, but the public service awards uniquely captured the spirit of the man. The program bore his name and its new version was central to his deep concern for the "third sector." This point of view was expressed in a fund-raising document produced by the Woodrow Wilson School entitled "The RPSA Program: A Potential Living Memorial to John D. Rockefeller 3rd." However, the top administrators of Princeton frowned on efforts to raise funds for restricted purposes, much preferring financial support for the university as a whole rather than one specific unit, especially for a program that paid no overhead. At the same time, JDR's survivors were hard-pressed to meet other demands not cov-

ered in his will, especially for the Asia Society (see below). With JDR
gone and no support coming from the university or members of the
Rockefeller family, the fund-raising effort had no chance.

Finally, there remains the fate of two of JDR's major organizations to be
recounted, one a great success story, the other considerably less so:

The Asia Society

The Creel Committee grant of $1,540,000 to the Asia Society was in
the nature of a token terminal grant, not one that seriously addressed the
real financial needs of the Society. The reason was that it was well known
that JDR intended to take care of this himself, having made some commitments in this direction in connection with his decision to will his Asian art
collection to the Society, provide funds for its maintenance, and aid in the
building of a new home for the Society in Manhattan that would be large
enough to accommodate the collection. In Chapter 28, the story was told
of JDR's plans for the Society and the unexpected delays in finding a
building site that stretched out the planning period and created a difficult
financial situation.

With JDR's death, the Society had lost is founder and leader, its best
fund-raiser, and its most generous contributor, who intended to do a great
deal to meet the new financial problems out of current income and from
his 1934 Trust in future years. It will be recalled that in 1974 the cost of
the land and the new building was estimated at $11 million. On January
15, 1975, JDR wrote to George Ball, chairman of the Society, pledging to
contribute half of the cost. He intended to pay this out of his 1934 Trust,
but, because of the delay in locating a site, the need had not yet arrived
for JDR to go to his Trust Committee for the funds he had pledged before
his death occurred. Because a written commitment existed, the problem
fell into the laps of the executors of his estate. But by this time the cost
for the land, construction, and furnishings for the new Asia House had
escalated to nearly $21 million. With the Asia Society facing a desperate
financial situation, Porter McKeever tried to make the case that perhaps
JDR's pledge should be construed as half of the amount needed, not half
of an estimate that was made in 1974. The executors rejected this, having
enough of a problem finding $5.5 million in the estate for the Asia Society,
given all of the other needs and constraints they were dealing with.

How the Asia Society overcame its financial problem makes a remarkable story. The first step was to obtain a $3.7 million loan from Citibank.
Several key board members and JDR's "Asia hands" (McKeever, Phil Tal-

bot, and Datus Smith) worked hard on fund-raising, and there was new blood as well. Succeeding the retired Phil Talbot as president in 1981 was Robert Oxnam, a scholar with a flair for management. He had done graduate work in China and Japan Studies at Yale and had taught at Trinity College. At the same time there was considerable turnover among trustees resulting, in Oxnam's judgment, in a greatly strengthened board. Although he had made a personal contribution of $50,000, George Ball did not play an active role in fund-raising. He resigned as chairman to be replaced by a Harvard-educated Texan, Roy M. Huffington, at the end of 1982. President of his own natural gas company, with primary operations in Indonesia, Huffington has been an active and successful chairman.

With considerable success, McKeever concentrated on foreign giving. The Japanese government contributed $1 million and the Keidanren $750,000. About $1 million was raised from other Asian sources, about half coming from Korean business firms. The Indian government donated the red sandstone for the interior (the exterior was done in red granite). Other sources included $2 million from U.S. corporations, $1 million from foundations, and $3 million from individuals. The $5.5 million paid from JDR's estate by his executors and the $2 million sale of the old Asia House to the Russell Sage Foundation completed the basic fund-raising.

Beyond this, there were two other significant gifts. JDR had committed himself to providing funds for an endowment with the proceeds to be used for annual support of the gallery and his collection. However, this was not binding because he had not mentioned a specific amount in his will or in correspondence. Nevertheless, the JDR 3rd Fund, as his residual beneficiary, honored this in 1981 by making a grant of $3.35 million to the Asia Society to establish an endowment for annual maintenance. In effect, this was a decision taken by JDR's immediate family—the new trustees of the JDR 3rd Fund included Blanchette and two of her daughters, Hope and Alida, as well as Elizabeth McCormack. The following year the JDR 3rd Fund made an anonymous grant to the Society, the reason being the desire to avoid overdependence on Rockefeller sources. This grant was for $2.5 million, with matching terms that resulted in raising an additional $1.5 million. In effect, Blanchette was making use of the JDR 3rd Fund as a foundation, just as her husband had done.

As a result of all these factors, the Asia Society paid off its Citibank loan in 1983, began operating on a balanced budget of approximately $5 million per year, and significantly enhanced its endowment and reserve fund. In interviews in September 1983 and January 1985, Oxnam reflected great pride in the way that all those involved had vindicated JDR's faith in the Asia Society by helping to make it the solid, ongoing success that

JDR's instincts had told him it could be. Particularly gratifying has been the critical and public acclaim of the new gallery and the "Mr. and Mrs. John D. Rockefeller 3rd Collection of Asian Art." Said Oxnam: "It is stunning to see these pieces grouped together and so beautifully displayed."

The Agricultural Development Council

The organization that was the great loser in the Creel process and the sudden death of JDR was the ADC, despite the fact that it very probably was the most successful single example of development assistance operated out of the U.S. private sector. As described in Chapter 27, the ADC, functioning largely out of the public eye, was intelligently managed, free of political biases, and operated with great quality, flexibility, and effectiveness in the transformation of Asian agriculture.

The ADC was on the Creel Committee list, but it was not actively considered because it was undergoing internal review, with JDR and its board trying to determine whether the organization had largely accomplished its mission or if new funding should be sought for continuation with a new direction. Not until late 1977 was it agreed, with strong endorsement from all of JDR's associates, that the ADC should continue, buttressing its traditional programs in agriculture with attention to the correlation between population and development and the roles and status of women in developing societies. JDR thereupon spoke to Creel and Dietel about the needs of the ADC and the prospect of a Creel Committee grant of $3–$4 million, but his death came before this progressed any further.

No formal commitments had been made by JDR, with the result that the two potential Rockefeller sources of funding for the ADC, the Creel process and the JDR 3rd Fund, were closed to it after his death. Not aware of JDR's thinking on the ADC, Blanchette and Jay put their emphasis on the Population Council in a special meeting of the RBF in November 1978 to consider reopening the Creel process. And the JDR 3rd Fund, as noted above, was overburdened in trying to take care of the Asia Society. Aware of JDR's new hopes for funding the ADC, its board made representations through Elizabeth McCormack for help from either the RBF or the JDR 3rd Fund, but at this point there was no chance.

The ADC straggled along for a few years as its financial base eroded. Finally, its great tradition and network of agricultural economists were combined with the staff of the Rockefeller Foundation's International Agricultural Development Service and both absorbed within the shell of the reconstituted Winrock International Foundation based in Arkansas. Unable to bring any significant funding to the merger, the ADC, for all practical purposes, seems to have disappeared.

*   *   *

As Jay said in his eulogy, the work of his father touched the lives of millions of people all over the world and the good effects will live long after his death. Having only a fraction of the resources available to his father, JDR was tormented for years by the fear that he would never live up to Junior's imposing standards in philanthropy. That he did so far beyond what he or anyone could have imagined in the period before 1952 when his career seemed stalled is amply attested to by the record of his life and the scope and depth of his commitments and accomplishments. Only a portion of that record is reflected in this discussion of the fate of his interests since 1978.

There is one more great effect of his work that in a sense underscores everything he stood for—his championing of the "third sector." No longer will the private nonprofit sector of American life be as underrepresented as it was in 1968 and 1969 when JDR was virtually alone in defending it in Washington. The meeting that he was scheduled to attend the day after his death on the subject of organizing the sector was not postponed because the participants knew he would have wanted it to go forward. The result of that meeting was the realization of one of JDR's goals—a new organization called The Independent Sector, representing all of the diverse interests of the private nonprofit sector and with John Gardner as its first leader. Progress has also been made toward JDR's hope that the academic world would adopt the third sector as a legitimate area of research and study, as it long ago did in the case of the business and government sectors.

JDR would have been pleased by these developments and the general growth of volunteerism, public service, and philanthropic giving that has occurred in the years since his death.

APPENDIX

The Rockefellers—Third and Fourth Generations

The six members of the third generation of Rockefellers (the children of Mr. and Mrs. John D. Rockefeller, Jr.), together with their spouses and children. Not shown are the sixty-seven members of the fifth and sixth generations.

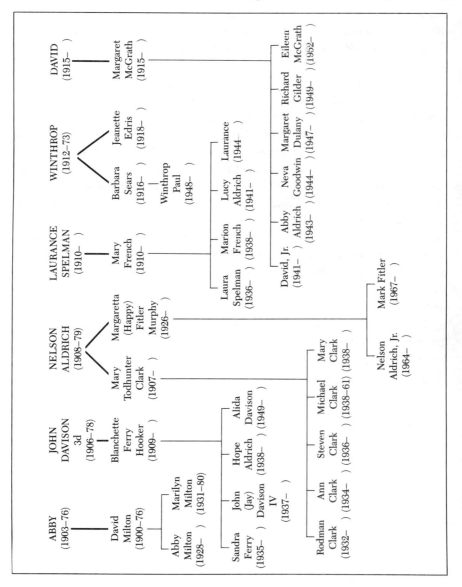

NOTES

CHAPTER 1

1. "How the Rockefellers Sold Their Name," *Manhattan, Inc.*, Vol. 7, No. 1 (January 1990). What the Mitsubishi interests actually purchased was 51 percent of the Rockefeller Group, Inc. (RGI), which owned 29 percent of the shares of the "old" Rockefeller Center (consisting of most of the properties east of Sixth Avenue). The other 71 percent of the shares were sold in a public offering in 1985. The various types of securities that constitute shares of ownership in Rockefeller Center function as a mortgage that can be converted into permanent ownership in the year 2000. RGI has other holdings, such as the Rockefeller Center Management Corporation, Rockefeller Center Telecommunications, the real estate firm of Cushman & Wakefield, and so on.

2. For the story of JDR's involvement in the peace mission, see John Ensor Harr and Peter J. Johnson, *The Rockefeller Century* (New York: Scribners, 1988), Ch. 26, "Mission to Japan."

3. *Manhattan, Inc.*, p. 49

4. "Budget and Annual Statement for John D. Rockefeller, 1915," Tax and Accounting Files, Rockefeller Family Office, New York.

5. Lee's simple but powerful idea that distinguished "public relations" from "press agentry" was that those concerned about public opinion should give as much attention to correcting their policies as they did to what the press said about them. Though the distinction is probably much honored in the breach since, there is no doubt that Lee tried to take the high road and thus is deserving of the sobriquet. See Ray Eldon Heibert, *Courtier to the Crowd* (Ames, Iowa: University of Iowa Press, 1966)

6. In the January 1990 issue of *Manhattan, Inc.*, editor Clay Felker (who has the distinction of having created *New York* magazine) has a particularly fulsome version of the myth in his full-page editorial ("The End of Dynasty") on the Mitsubishi purchase, p. 8. In recent years, even such distinguished commentators as Bill Moyers (in his PBS series on the twentieth century) and Stephen Birmingham (in his book *America's Secret Aristocracy* [Boston: Little, Brown, 1987], pp. 225–29) relate the myth as truth and thereby give Ivy Lee unwarranted credit for creating Rockefeller philanthrophy.

7. Allan Nevins, *Study in Power: John D. Rockefeller, Industrialist and Philanthropist*, Vol. I (New York: Scribners, 1953), p. 18.

8. The specific assignment was to find out the truth about the "Ludlow massacre" and advise on how best to communicate that truth. As board chairman of a company owned by his father (Colorado Fuel & Iron), John D. Jr. came in for tremendous criticism when eleven women and two children were inadvertently suffocated during a battle between striking workers and the National Guard in the hamlet of Ludlow. To try to rectify the situation, Junior retained Ivy Lee for the above purpose and W. L. Mackenzie King (later to become prime minister of Canada) as a labor adviser to try to find a fair solution and end the strike. King became Junior's closest friend, and his work led to Junior's commitment to the field of industrial relations. See Harr and Johnson (1988), Ch. 7, "Some Lessons Learned," for the fascinating story of Ludlow, the limited role of Ivy Lee, and the friendship of Junior and King.

9. As Carnegie's biographer observed, organization was "as natural a development in

the field of philanthropy as Standard Oil and United States Steel were in manufacturing."
See: Joseph Frazier Wall, *Andrew Carnegie* (New York: Oxford University Press, 1970), p.
833. For an accurate account of the origins of Rockefeller philanthropy, see Robert Bremner,
American Philanthropy (Chicago: University of Chicago Press, 1960).

10. For a full account of Junior's experience at Brown University and the influence of its
remarkable president, E. Benjamin Andrews, see Harr and Johnson, 1988, pp. 44–50. The
interesting fact is that the elder Rockefeller did not strain to indoctrinate his son, but instead
seemed confident that a good home, religious upbringing, and the example he provided
would suffice to set his son on the proper course. Junior was to be a very different kind of
father, so worried that his children would succumb to temptations that he worked hard to
indoctrinate them.

11. The Abby Aldrich Rockefeller Sculpture Garden of the Museum of Modern Art now
stands where Nos. 4 and 10 were, but No. 13 still exists, its graceful facade a bookend match
to No. 15 next door. Nos. 4 and 10 were among the Rockefeller properties given, traded,
or sold by Junior to the Museum his wife had helped to found. He disliked modern art so
that his gifts to the Museum were not overly generous and were not something Junior would
have chosen to do independently, but were made because of his wife's passionate interest.

12. Abby had the same given name as her mother, hence the nickname "Babs." John 3rd
himself chose the Arabic designation rather than the Roman; it almost always appears wrongly
in the public prints.

13. Samuel Williamson, "The Rockefeller Boys," *New York Times Magazine*, April 9,
1939.

CHAPTER 2

1. JDR's personal diaries, which were made available to the authors by Blanchette
Rockefeller, are a priceless source of information. He began writing a diary at the age of
thirteen and continued until his death. He never thought of creating anything of literary
merit, merely a record of people, time, and events for his own use. Yet there are times,
especially in the early and later years, when the entries become personal and revealing, even
eloquent.

2. The book value of Junior's stock was $55.3 million. Deducting the sale price of $2.2
million would have left him with a tax loss of $53.1 million if he had sold Rockefeller Center
to anyone but his relatives. However, the tax loss carried over to the buyers; it had no
immediate benefit for the five brothers, but the time would come when they could each use
the write-off.

3. The market value of the Pocantico estate presumably would have been much higher,
were it possible to sell it off for corporate headquarters and residential development. But
such uses were not in the minds of Junior and his sons, as indicated by the restrictive
agreement. Junior set up the transfer by creating a corporation called Hills Realty and turning
the estate over to it in return for 1,000 shares of stock with a book value of $700,000. Each
brother paid $152,059 for a one-fifth share of the estate. As noted, Junior continued to pay
the bills and run the show. The year after the sale his costs for maintenance of the estate
amounted to $1,272,639. And in 1953 he paid $150,000 to add an outdoor swimming pool
next to the Playhouse. Everything was amicable among the brothers at this stage, but more
than twenty years later, as we shall see, issues stemming from handling and disposing of the
estate became highly contentious for them.

4. Junior had made it very clear that significant gifts beyond the trusts were contingent
upon evidence of a sense of stewardship and use of funds for the benefit not of oneself but
for others. Babs gave him much less evidence than her five brothers did.

5. Laurance had started his conservation work in managing the affairs of the Jackson
Hole Preserve, a foundation his father had established in connection with the creation and
enlargement of Grand Tetons National Park. Virgin Islands National Park, consisting of 85

percent of the land area of St. John, was opened in 1956, the twenty-ninth national park, created through the contributions of Laurance and his father (through the Jackson Hole Preserve).

6. The committee's authority was based on the "negative veto" provision of the Government Reorganization Act of 1945, which Congress had passed to speed the dismantling of wartime agencies. The logic of the Act was that the Executive Branch was likely to be more efficient in reorganizing government agencies than the Legislative Branch, but that the Congress should retain the possibility of a final say in the matter. Thus a reorganization approved by the President takes effect after sixty days unless either branch of Congress takes the initiative to vote it down, hence the "negative veto."

7. Nelson went against prevailing State Department opinion on two counts, first by insisting on the inclusion of Juan Perón's Argentina in the United Nations and second, by collaborating with Senator Arthur Vandenberg in broadening the reference to "regional arrangements" in the UN Charter to include the Act of Chapultepec. Ironically, the latter was what made NATO possible later on.

8. Nelson's AIA was the model for technical assistance to underdeveloped countries that prompted Ben Hardy of the State Department to propose what became the "Point Four" idea in the President's address. Hardy had worked for Nelson in the OCIAA. The State Department higher-ups squelched the idea, but it was reinserted when the President complained to aide Clark Clifford that the speech "lacked punch."

9. Nelson's committee made its proposal in a farsighted report, "Partners in Progress," but the President created the Technical Cooperation Administration (TCA) *within* the State Department.

10. USIA has continued to exist to this day, but the FOA was brought back into the State Department within a few years and renamed the International Cooperation Administration. Then, after a few more years, the Kennedy administration created the Agency for International Development (AID) as a separate agency.

11. Dulles was so totally in command of foreign affairs in the Eisenhower administration that Nelson's efforts to be an activist in the White House were doomed to failure. In later administrations, the locus of power in foreign affairs did shift to the White House under such figures as McGeorge Bundy, Walt Rostow, Henry Kissinger, and Zbigniew Brzezinski.

12. Senior's nervous collapse came in the 1890s when he was overwhelmed by the burdens of business and philanthropy. It was his bringing the Reverend Frederick Gates in to assist him that helped pull him through. Junior's bout with depression seemed to have been even more severe, judging by the fact that he was unable to work for almost a year. In part his problem seems to have been an identity crisis—trying to decide what he would do with his life and worrying over whether he could live up to expectations.

13. JDR to Junior, March 17, 1934, RAC.

14. Junior to JDR, June 16, 1952, RAC.

15. Dulles himself was entirely favorable to JDR becoming chairman.

CHAPTER 3

1. The two best-known alarmist books were *Our Plundered Planet*, by Fairfield Osborn (Boston: Little, Brown, 1948) and *The Road to Survival*, by William Vogt (New York: Sloane, 1948).

2. A set of the documentation can be found in the Rockefeller Archive Center (noted hereafter as the "RAC"), which is located adjacent to the Pocantico estate in Westchester County, New York. Unless otherwise noted, all citations are drawn from papers in the RAC.

3. A list of those attending the Williamsburg Conference is given in *The Population Council: A Chronicle of the First Twenty-Five Years* (New York, 1978), pp. 155–56. Two

names were inadvertently omitted from the list: Warren Weaver of the Foundation and Isadore Lubin, a prominent economist then working with UNESCO and ECOSOC.

4. Official transcript, National Academy of Sciences, "Conference on Population Problems," held at Williamsburg Inn, Morning Session, June 22, 1952, pp. 42–43, RAC.

5. McLean memo to files, July 22, 1952.

6. Jamieson memo to JDR, July 31, 1952.

7. McLean to files, June 25, 1952.

8. McLean to files, September 4, 1952.

9. JDR memo of September 9, 1952. The final four points were more general and comparatively innocuous—about serving as a focal point, as a channel of contact, and taking leadership in the population field.

10. McLean to files, September 9, 1952.

11. Draft paper dated November 20, 1952, and entitled "Proposed Establishment of Population Council." The text of this paper was adopted at the first board meeting on the same date.

12. *New York Times*, April 28, 1953.

13. McLean memoranda to JDR, November 14 and December 15, 1952.

14. See Phyllis Piotrow, *World Population Crisis; The United States Response* (New York: Praeger Publishers, 1973), Ch. 2, "Scientists and Activists in the 1950s," pp. 12–19.

15. JDR to Board of Trustees of Population Council, December 23, 1953.

16. JDR to H. Rowan Gaither, Jr., March 17, 1954.

17. Joseph M. McDaniel, Jr., to Frederick Osborn, April 1, 1957.

18. David to JDR, December 22, 1954.

19. For a discussion of the sensitivity of these early missions, see: *The Population Council* (1978), pp. 45–49.

20. The demographic committee included three men who were among the pioneers in the field—Clyde Kiser, Frank Lorimer, and Pascal Whelpton—as well as the sociologists Kingsley Davis of Columbia and Philip Hauser of the University of Chicago, plus a Jesuit scholar, the Reverend William J. Gibbons of Loyola-Baltimore. The three medical advisers were Dr. George Corner of the Carnegie Institute of Washington, Dr. Alan Guttmacher of Mt. Sinai Hospital, and Dr. Howard Taylor of Columbia-Presbyterian Medical Center.

21. Quoted in James Reed, *From Private Vice to Public Morality: The Birth Control Movement and American Society Since 1830* (New York: Basic Books, 1978), p. 305. Dr. Clarence J. Gamble, an heir to the Proctor & Gamble fortune, was one of the early pioneers in promoting population programs. By the late 1940s, his National Committee on Maternal Health still existed, but had become inactive.

22. Interview with Frank Notestein, May 1979.

23. Richard Symonds and Michael Carder, *The United Nations and the Population Question* (New York: McGraw-Hill, 1973), Part III, pp. 69–112.

24. Piotrow (1973), p. 302. Osborn not only wanted to avoid provoking the Church, but he also figured that Washington was exactly the wrong place for a population conference, given the sensitivities in the lesser-developed nations.

25. Ibid., Ch. 4, "1954: The Draper Commission Spotlights the Issue," pp. 36–42.

26. Ibid., p. 45.

27. *New York Times*, December 3, 1959.

CHAPTER 4

1. For a discussion of the Bureau of Municipal Research, see Harr and Johnson (1988), pp. 112–115. On the Spelman Fund, see the same source, p. 192. It was spun off by a larger fund, the Laura Spelman Rockefeller Memorial, which had been created by John D. Rockefeller in memory of his wife.

2. Kennan graduated from Princeton in the Class of 1925. He joined the new U.S.

Foreign Service (created by the Rogers Act of 1924) and served briefly at the U.S. Consulate General in Geneva. In his memoirs he relates how he decided to resign to go to graduate school, but then discovered that the "Foreign Service School" operated by the State Department was offering three years of graduate study at European universities for officers willing to specialize in one of four difficult languages—Chinese, Japanese, Russian, and Arabic. Kennan applied to study Russian and was accepted. Instead of taking the scheduled third year at the University of Berlin, Kennan received permission to work in the "Russian section" of the U.S. Legation in Riga, Latvia. See George Kennan, *Memoirs: 1925–1950* (Boston: Little, Brown & Co., 1967), pp. 23–35.

3. McLean formed the habit of writing frequent memoranda as his complex research and negotiations progressed, some of them addressed to JDR and others for the files. Two extensive memoranda covering his consultations were dated November 11 and December 6, 1951. These and other memoranda, letters, and papers cited in this chapter may be found in various files in the RAC under such headings as "Education" and "Rockefeller Public Service Awards."

4. The most directly relevant recommendation was No. 4C under the heading of "Personnel Management." See "Status of the Hoover Report," Citizens Committee for the Hoover Report, Washington, D.C., September 1953.

5. Kennan quotation from McLean memorandum of November 27, 1951.

6. Undated paper entitled "Proposed Distinguished Service Fellowship Program," with handwritten notation by JDR: "Memo prepared by Littauer School at Harvard for D. H. McLean, Jr., at his request," RAC.

7. JDR moved promptly to start the "Intellectual Exchange Program" at the East Asian Institute of Columbia University, making a grant of $101,000 for this purpose two weeks after Conant's letter of rejection.

8. JDR to Dodds, December 27, 1951.

9. Untitled memorandum by McLean, December 2, 1952.

10. The IIA became the U.S. Information Agency in 1953 as a result of Reorganization Plan No. 8 of June 1. This was one of the series of reorganizations implemented by Nelson Rockefeller.

11. This description of the proposed curriculum was taken from a sample letter drafted by McLean and representatives of the Foreign Service Institute on December 4, 1952, bearing the headline "Draft Letter to University in Connection with the Proposed State Department Personnel Training Program." There were numerous attempts to draft a description of a course on the theory and practice of international communication; the quoted one is typical of these efforts.

12. Untitled McLean memorandum of December 12, 1952.

13. "The Nature and Objectives of the Center for International Studies: A Summary," undated paper transmitted to JDR by McLean on January 7, 1953; also, see McLean memorandum of January 9 and letters from Dean Mason to McLean on February 13 and 20.

14. JDR to Dulles, January 23 and 31, 1953; Dulles to JDR, February 2, 1953.

15. JDR to Dulles, May 4, 1953; Dulles to JDR, June 12, 1953.

16. Other members of the original committee were Elliot V. Bell of McGraw-Hill Publishing; Laird Bell, Chicago lawyer and board chairman of the University of Chicago; two Rockefeller Foundation board members and JDR friends—Dean W. I. Myers of Cornell and Thomas Parran of Pittsburgh; Anna Lord Straus, former president of the League of Women Voters; and Professor Leonard D. White of the University of Chicago. When Compton resigned in 1953, Laird Bell became chairman.

17. The Truman letter was dated February 7, 1952. In his letter of February 21 to JDR, Dodds reported reactions after his Washington rounds. He told one interesting story to the effect that the director of personnel at the Department of Agriculture had linked the RPSA idea with the early work of another organization created and supported by the Rockefellers. He cited the General Education Board for "establishing agricultural experiment stations and

extension work in the South. He credited the present far-flung agricultural organization to the Rockefellers."

18. Dodds to JDR, December 12, 1951. It seems that JDR and McLean were not aware of the earlier Kennan training experience of two years in Berlin, which was certainly critical to his career. Their model was his action of resigning to go to the Institute for Advanced Study in Princeton. "He wanted time to get out and refresh himself and decide about his future," Dodds wrote. But Kennan had already returned to the State Department late in 1951, reluctantly, Dodds reported, and the "question of saving his pension was a major consideration." After he had made the decision to return, his appointment as ambassador to Moscow came along. Kennan lasted there only a year. He was forced out by the Russians, rather than the incoming Republicans. Kennan returned from retirement one more time, to serve as ambassador to Yugoslavia during the Kennedy Administration.

19. According to McLean, JDR did not demur, but he did check with his father and brothers before agreeing to use the family name.

20. The winners were designated on the basis of the year they won the award, not when they entered or ended their training. Thus the 1952–53 winners were those chosen late in 1952. Their names were announced early in 1953 and the awards ceremony took place at a luncheon in Washington in April. In most cases, they would not start using their sabbatical year of training until September 1953.

21. Robert W. van de Velde, *The Rockefeller Public Service Awards: A Fifteen-Year Report* (Princeton, N.J.: Princeton University Press, 1967), p. 12. The original faculty secretary, Joseph McLean, left to take a cabinet post in the state government of New Jersey in 1955. He was succeeded by Stephen K. Bailey who left in 1957 to become dean of the Maxwell School at Syracuse University.

22. JDR to Dodds, December 27, 1951.

23. For a full list of the award winners and their fields of interest through the year 1966, see: Van de Velde, *op. cit.*, pp. 67–98. Of necessity, Joseph McLean pioneered many of the techniques used to handle the mechanics of the awards program—generating nominations, building dossiers on the nominees, sorting these into groups, making preliminary evaluations for the Selection Committee, and so on.

24. Junior to JDR, August 28, 1952.

25. Van de Velde, *op. cit.*, pp. 14–15.

26. Dulles finally lost patience when McCarthy's two young aides, Roy Cohn and David Schine, traveled to U.S. embassies during the summer of 1953 to ferret out "subversive" books in embassy offices and USIS libraries, and, it was rumored, to burn them. Dulles reacted violently and the strange Cohn-Schine episode came to a quick end.

27. McLean memorandum to JDR 3rd, September 1, 1953.

28. Donald McLean to Joseph McLean, September 25, 1953.

29. Shulman made this comment in his letter to Mrs. John D. Rockefeller 3rd after JDR's death in 1978. Almost all of the RPSA winners over a twenty-five-year period wrote letters to Mrs. Rockefeller trying to express what the program her husband had started had meant to them. These letters are on file in the RAC.

30. Van de Velde, *op. cit.*, p. 14.

31. JDR to Dodds, April 23, 1954.

32. President Eisenhower to Dodds, June 16, 1954.

33. JDR to Dodds, June 24, 1954; Dodds to JDR, June 29, 1954.

34. Dodds to JDR, January 12, 1955, and April 28, 1955.

35. Dodds to JDR, September 15, 1954.

36. McLean to Clark, December 14, 1956.

37. *Congressional Record*, Senate, May 1, 1958, pp. 7011–12.

38. Van de Velde, *op. cit.*, p. 22.

39. McLean to Dodds, June 2, 1958.

40. Winslow to McLean, July 9, 1958.

CHAPTER 5

1. Stacy May to JDR, memo entitled "Recommendations for Exploring Projects to Increase Domestic Food Supply to Japan," October 17, 1952.

2. Stacy May to JDR, memo entitled "Proposal for Far Eastern Research Institute," November 14, 1952.

3. The little-known General Education Board (GEB) was created by JDR's father and grandfather in 1903 primarily for the purpose of improving education for blacks in the South. Its accomplishments in this and a dozen other difficult missions make the GEB probably the most remarkable success story in the entire history of American philanthropy. Much of JDR's compassion for the disadvantaged and his instinctive grasp of the development process undoubtedly came from his association as a young man with the GEB in its latter years. For a brief account of the GEB, see Harr and Johnson (1988), pp. 70–82.

4. Wolf Ladejinsky, "Too Late to Save Asia?" *Saturday Review of Literature*, July 22, 1950, quoted in: Bryant E. Kearl and A. M. Weisblat, "Institutional Innovational Reform: The Ladejinsky Legacy," ADC Seminar Report, No. 19, April 1979, Agricultural Development Council, Inc., New York, p. 2.

Ladejinsky was one of the truly outstanding characters in Asian development during this period. He liked to joke about his conversion from a landlord to a land reformer. A White Russian and the son of a well-to-do landowner in the Ukraine, he fled at the time of the Revolution at the age of seventeen. He sold newspapers on the street corner as Rockefeller Center was being built to help put himself through Columbia.

One of the more ridiculous moments in the right-wing hysteria of the postwar years occurred when Eisenhower's Secretary of Agriculture, Ezra Taft Benson, accused Ladejinsky of being a "national security risk" in 1955 and dismissed him from the Foreign Agricultural Service. He was then hired by the Foreign Operations Administration on the strong recommendation of Colonel Edward G. Lansdale, famous for his counterinsurgency work in the Philippines and Vietnam. Ladejinsky served as land-reform adviser to Diem until 1961 and ended his career as Ford Foundation representative in India and Nepal.

5. Wolf Ladejinsky, "The Plow Outbids the Sword in Asia," *Country Gentleman*, June 1951.

6. Quoted in Symonds and Carter (1973), p. 54.

7. Colonel Edward G. Lansdale became close to Magsaysay. Lansdale's book (*In the Midst of Wars* [New York: Harper & Row, 1972]) describes the evolution of Magsaysay's career.

8. Stacy May to JDR, memo entitled "Discussion with Dean W. I. Myers of Cornell re Far Eastern Project Based on Rice Research," April 24, 1953.

9. Taken from Warren Weaver's reminiscences in the Columbia Oral History Project, 1962. Weaver said his criticisms were not of his colleagues but of "our total procedure and total approach to the problem."

10. Quotations taken from transcript of Myers's oral history tapes at Cornell University.

11. Wolf Ladejinsky, "Rural Reconstruction under the China Aid Act," *Foreign Agriculture*, August 1950, pp. 167–74.

12. JDR to J. Norman Efferson, July 31, 1953; paper by Stacy May entitled "Tentative Formulation of Project in Agricultural Economics in South and Southeast Asia," July 30, 1953.

13. Norman Efferson, paper entitled "A Suggested Program for Stimulating the Development and Expansion of Agricultural Economics Research, Teaching, and Extension in Asia," November 1953.

14. Memo by JDR to files, "Objective and Focus of My Asian Interest," November 17, 1953.

15. An example JDR gave in his November 17 memo was a short-term public health project in Mindanao that Ramon Magsaysay had spoken to him about.

16. McLean memo to JDR, April 21, 1955.

17. JDR to Board of Trustees of CECA, December 30, 1954.

18. CECA, "Three Year Report by the Director of Agricultural Economics," November 23, 1953, to December 31, 1956.

19. Rockefeller Foundation, *Program in the Agricultural Sciences, Annual Report,* New York 1960–61, pp. 293–95.

CHAPTER 6

1. Wolf Ladejinsky, letter to Ford Foundation in response to request for advice in setting up assistance programs, p. 13, in ADC collection, Vol. 11.

2. JDR to Mr. Harry Prioleau, president of Standard Vacuum, January 23, 1959.

3. The trip diaries and personal letters were made available to the authors by Mrs. John D. Rockefeller 3rd.

4. L. H. Lapham, "The Journey of an Itinerant Philanthropist," draft in RAC (ellipses in original).

5. There is one paragraph that might mislead in Lapham's otherwise excellent prose; it is the one with ellipses that refers to "numbers" and "quality." The reader might easily think that JDR was making some point on genetics, but everything about his career in the population field suggests that what he was referring to was the quality of life (not the racial stock) being impaired by overpopulation.

6. Marvin L. Stone, "The Rockefeller Who Lives on $27 a Month," *The American Weekly,* October 5, 1958.

7. Ibid. See also the *Life* magazine issue of February 2, 1959.

8. "Oral History of the Japan Society with Particular Reference to the Years 1952–1967," Douglas Overton, transcript on file at Japan Society and RAC.

CHAPTER 7

1. McLean to JDR, April 9, 1954.

2. See the agendas for November 24, 1954, and January 19, 1955, for example.

3. New York: Simon and Schuster, 1978, p. 85.

4. Ibid. Caute offers (p. 29) a generalization that seems particularly apt: "Whereas the conservatives in both parties loathed domestic radicalism and the New Deal, and merely offered token gestures of defiance toward distant Russia, Fair Deal Democrats increasingly loathed Soviet policies and offered token gestures of hostility toward domestic Communism."

5. New York: Columbia University Press, 1972, p. 5.

6. *New York Times,* April 8 and November 16, 1952.

7. See Harr and Johnson (1988) p. 408.

8. Caute (1978), p. 316; See Ch. 5 on the Institute of Pacific Relations and Ch. 15 on the purge of the "China hands."

9. Ibid., p. 317; *New York Times,* December 10, 1952.

10. December 11, 1952.

11. Nielsen (1972), pp. 84–85.

12. *New York Herald-Tribune,* August 12, 1953.

13. Caute (1978), p. 317. It was the withdrawal of the tax exemption that led to the Institute's suit against the government in 1956; in 1960 District Judge David Edelstein ruled that not a "scintilla of evidence" had been introduced by the government to support its denial of tax-exempt status for the Institute. Johns Hopkins University behaved honorably throughout Lattimore's ordeal, suspending him on full pay until the government dropped its case against him in 1955, and then restoring him to the faculty.

14. Harr and Johnson (1988), pp. 554–55.

15. Noyes kept notes of the meeting: "Notes on Conference held June 1, 1955, in Board Room of Room 5600, on initiative of JDR, 3rd." Among those unable to attend were James Michener and DeWitt Wallace of the *Reader's Digest*.

16. McLean memorandum to the files, September 14, 1955.

17. "Survey Regarding a Possible Asian-American Organization," October 12, 1955.

18. Young and Noyes memorandum to JDR, "A Possible Asian Organization," October 14, 1955.

19. JDR to Allen Dulles, September 28, 1954.

20. Jamieson memorandum to JDR, September 20, 1954.

21. *New York Times*, March 22 and 24, 1967.

22. Once again, Noyes kept "Notes on Conference held in Room 5600 at 4 P.M. November 21, 1955, to discuss the possibility of an Asian organization," December 8, 1955.

23. Grayson Kirk to JDR, June 25, 1957. The Asia Society sold its first building, at a loss, for $225,000.

24. New York: Random House, 1969, p. 390.

CHAPTER 8

1. The idea of importing Japanese goods came to JDR in a memo dated December 2, 1953, written by Douglas Overton, director of the Japan Society. He had three justifications for the project: overcoming Japan's image as a producer of "junk," allowing Americans access to the beautiful Japanese goods enumerated, and helping Japan's economy.

2. JDR thought of Hong Kong as British, not Oriental, and disliked the importing of such Hong Kong products as boats, carpeting, and expensive furniture. The height of absurdity was reached when JDR learned that one of the most profitable items was a line of women's shoes with decorative materials from India—but manufactured in Brooklyn!

3. The book was published as *Russia and America: Dangers and Prospects* (New York: Harper & Bros., 1956). The Ford Foundation funded the project and the study group was chaired by John J. McCloy.

4. See JDR to Philip Mosely, January 4, 1956. Also JDR's views were reflected in marginal notes on his copies of documents prepared for the sessions.

5. For the story of how Junior was moved to create the "I-Houses" on university campuses after hearing about the acute loneliness of foreign students, see Harr and Johnson (1988), p. 166.

6. Interview with Chadbourne Gilpatric, September 21, 1982.

7. See Rusk to Deshmukh, April 29, 1958, for example. This and other documents may be found in the RAC in an unpublished study and compilation of papers in four large notebooks done by Don McLean, after his retirement, on his activities on JDR's behalf. Referred to hereafter as "McLean Study."

8. McLean to JDR, May 25, 1959.

9. McLean to JDR, June 3, 1959.

10. McLean to Deshmukh, July 14, 1961; Rockefeller Foundation docket no. 66036 of May 20, 1966, reproduced in McLean Study.

11. McLean's views expressed in his study, Bk. IV, pp. 206–207; Gilpatric's views in interview of September 21, 1982.

12. A conventional "I-House" (one built on a university campus primarily for foreign students) was funded by the Rockefeller Foundation at Los Baños in connection with the International Rice Research Institute.

13. An erroneous version of the origins of the Maysaysay Awards is given in Peter Collier and David Horowitz, *The Rockefellers: An Amercian Dynasty* (New York: Holt, Rinehart and Winston, 1976), pp. 368–69, which exaggerates Nelson's role and projects to an unwarranted degree a political and Cold War atmosphere about the project.

14. McLean to files, March 28, 1957. "Creel" is Dana Creel, by this time the staff chief of the Rockefeller Brothers Fund.

15. The Rusk, Murray and Fahs quotes are all contained in McLean to files, April 4, 1957.

16. Sebald is quoted in a special report written by McLean ("The Ramon Magsaysay Award Foundation, 1957–1976: The Role of John D. Rockefeller 3rd") and located in Bk. IV of his study. All documents subsequently cited in this chapter may be found in the McLean Study.

17. Memo to JDR and Nelson Rockefeller from McLean, Creel, and Noyes, April 5, 1957.

18. McLean Study, pp. 10–11.

19. Again, Collier and Horowitz (1976) err in saying that it was Nelson who brought Lansdale into the planning. Ravenholt had known Lansdale in the Philippines and was aware that Lansdale and Magsaysay had been intimate friends. Far from being a sinister character, Lansdale was an unusual military man in that he saw that it was crucial to correct the underlying causes of peasant discontent instead of merely mounting a military response to insurgency. It was this deeply held point of view on Lansdale's part that led him to become an expert on counter-insurgency and in turn to be of value to the CIA in both the Philippines and Vietnam. He saw the CIA as offering a greater variety of tools than military action alone. None of this changed his somewhat romanticized concept of the soldier's role. This comes across in a submission he made for one of the categories of the Magsaysay Awards: "broadening the military outlook to include brotherly help to needful people, manful courtesy toward the civilian, while seeking to protect the nation; the soldier becomes not an armed oppressor but a dutiful son of his people." This suggested category was not included, though it certainly was congruent with Magsaysay's own beliefs. In McLean Study. April 23 draft of "terms of reference."

Given the facts about the origins of the Magsaysay Awards, the attempt of Collier and Horowitz to portray JDR (p. 369) as the "partner of the real life prototype for *The Ugly American* [Lansdale]" and as a puppet being steered in the service of "the mission of American power in Asia" by the "authority figures" in his life—Nelson and the Dulles brothers— is ludicrous, a good example of the bias that permeates this book. However, they are correct in saying that JDR "was unlike Nelson in that he was never emotionally caught up in the conflict with Communism and revolution and never became a political crusader."

20. JDR's marginal notes can be seen on drafts of terms of reference for April 23 and 25 in the McLean Study. Ladejinsky's influence can be seen in his language for the category that became "Community Leadership." Ladejinsky's draft said: "helping the man on the land to have fuller responsibility and a better life." Ladejinsky's words were not accepted, but there have been a number of winners of the Magsaysay Awards that he would approve of highly for their work on the rural scene.

21. McLean to JDR, May 13, 1957.

22. At the time he won the award, Lubis's voice was suppressed. He was under house arrest in Indonesia on political grounds and could not come to Manila for the awards ceremony.

23. H2416 submitted to the House of Representatives by Congressman Aguja of Leyte. In McLean Study.

24. Belen Abreu to JDR, February 19, 1962; McLean to Belen Abreu, April 13, 1962.

25. Phillips to McLean, October 26, 1976. Under the terms of the trust, at the end of twenty years the RBF must decide whether to cancel the trust, extend the terms, or hand over the principle to the RMAF. The $5.18 million total includes the trust fund and the $2 million mortgage.

CHAPTER 9

1. For the story of the origins, see Harr and Johnson (1988), Ch. 16, "Rockefeller Center."

2. Rudolf Bing, *5,000 Nights at the Opera* (New York: Doubleday, 1972), pp. 138–40.

3. By the mid-1950s, the New York City urban renewal program administered by Moses was under fire owing to tenant-relocation complaints, the delay in starting some projects, and allegations of political favoritism. See Robert Caro, *The Power Broker: Robert Moses and the Fall of New York* (New York: Vintage Books, 1975), pp. 962–83 and 1005–25.

4. Title I of the Federal Housing Act of 1949 gave cities the power to buy slum property (through condemnation procedures where necessary) and to resell the land at a lower "fair re-use value" to qualified developers. The difference between the city's cost of acquiring the land and its fair re-use value, known as the "land write-down," would be financed two-thirds by a federal grant and one-third by the city.

5. One reason the Met sought the company of the Philharmonic in building at Lincoln Square may well have been the realization that there was a large element of risk in moving to a slum area that had no distinguishing features among New York City neighborhoods. If both institutions went in together, the chances would be increased of turning the neighborhood around. The much larger plan that became Lincoln Center virtually guaranteed that kind of success.

6. C. D. Jackson to Junior, July 26, 1951, and April 18, 1952, Cultural Files, RAC.

7. C. D. Jackson to Junior, January 2, 1955, Cultural Files, RAC.

8. Interview with Dean Rusk, March 19, 1979. Both Rusk and Harrison knew that JDR had been searching for a suitable New York City involvement in the cultural sphere.

9. Robert E. Blum should not be confused with the Robert Blum who had transformed the Committee for a Free Asia into the Asia Foundation (*supra*, Ch. 7). Robert E. Blum was a vice president of the Abraham & Straus department store in New York. Devereaux C. Josephs, in addition to his service on the Foundation board, was well-known to JDR as a trustee for the 1934 Trusts of the Rockefeller brothers. Representing the Philharmonic were Arthur Houghton and David Keiser, who was a sugar magnate and concert pianist. In addition to Spofford, the Met's representatives were C. D. Jackson and Irving S. Olds, retired chairman of U.S. Steel. The ratio of three Met representatives to two for the Philharmonic was retained throughout.

10. Quoted in Edgar B. Young, *Lincoln Center: The Building of an Institution* (New York: New York University Press, 1980). p. 21.

11. Ibid., p. 18.

12. John D. Rockefeller 3rd, "The Evolution: Birth of a Great Center," *New York Times Magazine*, September 23, 1962.

13. Albert Christ-Janner to Dana Creel, November 8, 1951; Creel memorandum, November 5, 1951, Cultural Files, RAC; interview with Dana Creel, August 23, 1982.

14. Dana Creel to Laurance S. Rockefeller, March 6, 1953; Lawrence Elliman to Laurance S. Rockefeller, November 2, 1953, RAC.

15. Nelson had supported the ballet well before the City Center came into existence. In 1935 he was a donor to Geroge Balanchine's American Ballet, predecessor of the New York City Ballet; in 1941, as coordinator of the Office of Inter-American Affairs, he sent the ballet company on an extensive and very successful tour of South America.

16. Newbold Morris to Junior, April 14, 1943, RAC.

17. Young to JDR, March 2, 1954. The City Center's plans were based on a 1953 survey done by Kersting, Brown & Co. See: Baum to JDR, June 3, 1954, RAC.

18. Interview with Edgar B. Young, August 15. 1982. Only a draft of the document in which JDR expressed his policy ideas for the City Center can be found in the RAC. It is

dated "December" and is unsigned. Most likely it was drafted by Ed Young and edited by JDR.

19. For a brief assessment of Kirstein's career, see John Russell, "Lincoln Kirstein—A Life in Art," *New York Times Magazine*, June 20, 1982.

20. Quoted in Young (1980), p. 53.

21. This search for additional constituents is recounted in Young's Chapter 4, "Development of the Institution: 1956–1959," pp. 55–64. In addition to JDR, the trustee most directly responsible for securing new constituents was George D. Stoddard, dean of education at New York University and former president of the University of Illinois.

22. The other key persons in the formation of the Repertory Theater Association were Elia Kazan and George D. Woods, chairman of the First Boston Corporation.

23. The Board of Estimate balked at the $2.5 million price and cut it to $1.5 million, whereupon Kennedy sued. He ended up with $2.4 million. For the story of the miserly way in which he held the "loss" of $100,000 against Lincoln Center, see next chapter.

24. There was some sensitivity within the Rockefeller Foundation over the fact that such a large grant was being made to a program so strongly identified with the Foundation's chairman, but Rusk and the trustees were satisfied on the merits of the grant and the belief that it would have been made if JDR were not involved with Lincoln Center.

25. Young (1980), p. 52.

26. Ibid., p. 28.

27. Quoted in ibid., p. 55.

28. Ibid., p. 89.

29. Ibid., Ch. 7, "Ground Breaking, May 14, 1959."

CHAPTER 10

1. The violinist Isaac Stern came to see JDR to persuade him to take the chairmanship of the Save Carnegie Hall Committee. JDR considered this, but decided that it was not possible for him to head up efforts on behalf of both Lincoln Center and Carnegie Hall.

2. For detailed consideration of many of the problems discussed in this chapter, the reader is referred to Young (1980).

3. JDR to Kirstein, July 1, 1959; Kirstein To JDR, July 7, 1959, RAC. Kirstein's puzzling letter foreshadows some of his comments in his review of Edgar B. Young's book ("Lincoln Shelter," *New York Review of Books*, August 13, 1981). Kirstein dismisses Lincoln Center as a "vast real-estate caper," and criticizes Young's book, among other reasons, for assigning a "central influence" to JDR in the project. He also suggests that JDR's motive for becoming involved was "control," as in "population control." If anything, Young bent over backward, because of his long association with JDR, to underplay JDR's role. And JDR's motive for his interest and sustained effort was anything but control.

4. Edgar B. Young report to Lincoln Center board, June 25, 1959, RAC. Aside from the flawed initial estimates, there were other reasons for the big gap such as delays in land acquisition, planning uncertainties, and the (modest) inflation of the Eisenhower years. But the main reason probably was the split responsibility—each constituent was responsible for specifying what it wanted in its building and for design approval, yet not for fund-raising, which was left to Lincoln Center.

5. The long, complicated story of obtaining additional federal funds can be traced in the extensive correspondence among JDR, Moses, Wagner, and federal officials, in the RAC. For the attitudes of the "feds" toward Moses, see Caro (1975).

6. Interview with John Lockwood, October 26, 1982. At several key junctures, Nelson had had to ask favors of JDR, as in not standing in Nelson's way in taking over Rockefeller Center or in relinquishing the chairmanship of the Rockefeller Brothers Fund to make way for Nelson; see Ch. 12. On the other hand, JDR scrupulously avoided any appearance of asking Nelson for favors—until Lincoln Center.

7. Aside from funding proposals and changes in laws, JDR's list included such items as tax-exempt status, permission for multiple liquor licenses in the Center, and use of Damrosch Park as a construction base.

8. Lockwood had been involved in Lincoln Center legal matters almost from the beginning. The Center had retained his firm (Milbank, Tweed), which also represented the Rockefeller family office. Lockwood was counsel to the familiy and a longime friend of Nelson's.

9. Young (1980), pp. 132–37.

10. Young, p. 120.

11. Even this required a difficult negotiation. See Young (1980), p. 231.

12. Ibid., p. 59.

13. Ibid., pp. 241 and 307. JDR's negotiating position was weakened, of course, by the concessions already made to the Met. But the Met leaders at least never questioned that they would be occupying their building on a lease from the Center. Another point was that compared to the State Theater the Met building was extremely complex and much less suitable for a variety of attractions. Lincoln Center leaders wanted access to at least two buildings—the Philharmonic and the State Theater—to give program flexibility. The Music Theater had existed throughout the World's Fair as a constituent in the State Theater along with the New York City Ballet. Baum felt that allowing the Music Theater to continue was a great concession on his part. Although the Music Theater had a faithful and enthusiastic public, its deficit caused it to be shut down in 1970.

14. Cited in Young (1980), p. 120.

15. Ibid., pp. 280–81, presents figures from Edgar B. Young's cumulative thirteen-year report completed in 1970, RAC.

16. Ibid., p. 131. Report of the Financial Policy Committee, May 23, 1960, RAC.

17. In this regard, JDR had indifferent success. He was to remain disappointed over the extent to which board members of Lincoln Center or any of the constituent organizations contributed to Lincoln Center, with some notable exceptions. Aside from JDR, only three others gave $500,000 or more.

18. *New York Times*, May 12, 1965. Junior wrote to JDR (July 9, 1959) warmly endorsing his son's intention to give the proceeds of the trust to Lincoln Center. In an interesting discussion of his father's philanthropic views, Junior said he believed his father would have placed "the full weight of his support behind this unique and exciting enterprise" (Lincoln Center).

19. Henry Ford II to JDR, October 10, 1964; JDR to Henry Ford II, October 23, 1964.

20. Mrs. John F. Kennedy to JDR, April 23, 1962.

21. Memorandum to the files by JDR, October 19, 1961, RAC.

22. JDR to Joseph P. Kennedy, November 1, 1961; Joseph P. Kennedy to JDR, November 28, 1961.

23. Richard Whalen, *The Founding Father* (New York: New American Library, 1964).

24. JDR to Maxwell Taylor, April 20, 1966.

25. Shigeharu Matsumoto to JDR, July 31, 1962; Edwin O. Reischauer to JDR, August 6, 1962.

26. *New York Times*, July 7, 1963

27. David Rockefeller to Clarence Francis, July 18, 1960.

28. Collier and Horowitz (1976), pp. 373–74, give an erroneous version of the JDR-Getty relations, suggesting that only one meeting took place, the one in Paris in February 1958. After this Getty is said to have turned down JDR abruptly, causing him to adominish Getty in a scathing letter that concluded: "And I am sorry for your children, if you have any." There is no such exchange of letters in the Rockefeller Family Archive, which is cited as the source. The acquaintance extended in fact over ten years and was cordial, even though the two men held such different views.

29. J. Paul Getty to JDR, April 29, 1958.

30. J. Paul Getty to JDR, November 2, 1967; JDR to Getty, May 20, 1968. Getty, of

course, does come in for posthumous recognition as a philanthropist for leaving his huge fortune to fund the Getty Art Museum in Los Angeles.

31. Saarinen died in 1961. Bunshaft completed the design of the combined building, working with members of Saarinen's staff.

32. "Troubles Stalk the Beaumont," *New York Times*, January 10, 1983.

33. The unique New York philanthropic alliance between wealthy Jews and Gentiles, in which Senior and Junior had participated so actively, flagged somewhat after the 1948 creation of the State of Israel, because so much of the Jewish money available then went to the United Jewish Appeal and other fund-raising programs for Israel. The Lincoln Center leaders feared that substantial contributions would not be coming from the Jewish community, which was one reason why Wien's enthusiasm was so welcome.

CHAPTER 11

1. Interview with Frederick Osborn, June 6, 1979. One reason Notestein felt comfortable in leaving the Office of Population Research after twenty-three years was that he had a first-rate man, Ansley Coale, on hand as his successor.

2. Interview with Frank Notestein, August 18, 1982.

3. Dr. Guttmacher (Mt. Sinai Hospital) and Dr. Taylor (Columbia-Presbyterian), both eminent men in their fields, were two of the original members of the Population Council's Medical Advisory Committee. Notestein estimated that 90 to 95 percent of the financial support for research on the improved IUD during this period came from the Pop Council. For a discussion of the research effort, see *Population Council: A Chronicle of the First Twenty-five Years, 1952–1977* (New York, 1978), pp. 61–65.

4. Interview with Bernard Berelson, June 6, 1979.

5. For a recounting of JFK's tentative remarks and Eisenhower's reversal, see Piotrow (1973), pp. 72–76.

6. Most European Communist countries were successful in controlling population growth through a combination of industrialization, widely available clinical services, and a permissive attitude toward abortion. Marxist theory is directly counter to Malthus, holding that it is not the number of mouths that causes poverty but capitalist control of the means of production and the exploitation of workers, resulting in inequitable distribution.

7. See Piotrow (1973), Ch. 11, "The Gruening Hearings: 1965–68," pp. 103–11.

8. Symonds and Carder (1973), p. 182.

9. For a good discussion of the incremental efforts in State and AID during this period, see Piotrow (1973), pp. 59–69.

10. Lleras Camargo was elected a trustee of the Rockefeller Foundation at the annual meeting in December 1966.

11. For the remarkable pace of events in Washington in 1956–67, see Piotrow (1973), Ch. 12, "Famine Triggers Action: 1966"; Ch. 13 on the response by the bureaucracy, including the appointments of Claxton and Ravenholt; and Ch. 14, "Congress Legislates Priorities: 1967." The most persistent gadfly on the foreign aid bill was General William Draper. Reimert Ravenholt of AID was the brother of Al Ravenholt of Manila, with whom JDR had worked in the establishment of the Magsaysay Awards.

12. Chairman Kosygin to JDR, September 16, 1967, RAC. See also Frank Notestein's commentary on the Kosygin response in his letter to Ray Lamontagne, September 28, 1967. JDR tried to counter Kosygin's points in a letter to the chairman dated October 9, 1967.

13. *New York Times*, December 12, 1967.

14. *This Week* magazine, February 11, 1968.

15. JDR to Bill D. Moyers, June 14, 1967. By this time Moyers had left the White House and was with *Newsday* on Long Island—but he was presumed to still have influence with LBJ.

16. Lamontagne had performed very well, not only in his major involvement in the

population field, but in many of JDR's other activities as well. Much like Don McLean, he had an open and frank style that JDR prized. Therefore, his loss was a difficult one for JDR, which may in part account for the substantial gap in time before a successor was hired. See Ch. 15, "The Man at Work," for a discussion of JDR's staff and his relations with staff members.

17. JDR to President Johnson, April 30, 1968, RAC.

18. Recorded in JDR's diary under date of Thursday, May 23, 1968.

CHAPTER 12

1. The 1934 attack on JDR by RF trustee Jerome Greene was probably a contributing cause to the severe depression that afflicted JDR for a considerable time. The three senior men who successfully opposed JDR's efforts to redirect the postwar course of the RF in 1946 were a formidable trio indeed—his father's closest adviser (Fosdick), the chairman of the RF and president of the Institute for Advanced Study at Princeton (Stewart), and an RF trustee, highly successful executive as the CEO of New Jersey Bell, and author of the classic *The Functions of the Executive* (Barnard). For the story of the 1934 episode, see Harr and Johnson (1988), pp. 349–53, and for the 1946 clash, pp. 437–43.

2. This emerges from the "portraits" of the major foundations in Waldemar Nielsen's book, *The Big Foundations* (New York: Columbia University Press, 1972).

3. Ibid., table on p. 22. Since 1968 several new foundations have been created with more in assets than the RF.

4. Of course, JDR had many more close relationships with directors and officers of Carnegie and Ford. For example, Dev Josephs was president of the Carnegie Corporation for four years right after World War II. John J. McCloy left the RF board to become chairman of Ford, and JDR was also well-acquainted with his successor, Dr. Julius Stratton.

5. Nielsen (1972), p. 31 and p. 45.

6. Ibid., p. 78.

7. Ibid., p. 80.

8. Harr and Johnson (1988), pp. 435–36.

9. Nielsen (1972), p. 97 and p. 350.

10. Ibid., p. 69.

11. Rusk comments in this chapter from interview in September 1979.

12. Interview with J. George Harrar, September 1979.

13. For a discussion of the reorganization that brought programs of the GEB and LSRM into the RF, see Harr and Johnson (1988), pp. 192–96.

14. This appeared in a memorandum JDR wrote to his staff on September 6, 1966 ("Goals and Objectives re Fields of Interest"). It was a "weekend effort" in response to a request from his staff members. Henry Romney, then an information officer on the RF staff, said (interview, April 28, 1983) that the Equal Opportunity program was the one that JDR paid most attention to and pushed with Harrar and the staff.

15. Nielsen (1972), pp. 69–70.

16. Of course, the question becomes one of what happens when the leadership changes and the pressure is removed. In fact, after JDR and Harrar retired, the RF began to flounder under the next two presidents, John Knowles and Richard Lyman.

17. "The Rockefeller Foundation Five-Year Review and Projection," Williamsburg, Va., December 2–3, 1968.

18. Nielsen (1972), pp. 71–72.

CHAPTER 13

1. *New York Journal-American*, August 24–29; *Look*, March 26, 1963.

2. *New York Herald Tribune* and *New York Times*, September 11, 1957. Nelson's effort, of course, failed, and the Dodgers went off to Los Angeles.

3. For the remarkable story of how Nelson's "open skies" idea made it into the President's speech and the amusing aftermath, see Harr and Johnson (1988), pp. 548–50.

4. None of Nelson's four brothers served on the "overall" panel until Laurance succeeded Nelson as chairman in 1958.

5. The writer of the panel report on foreign policy ("Report I: The Mid-Century Challenge to U.S. Foreign Policy") was August Heckscher, director of the Twentieth Century Fund, a small New York foundation. *Prospects for America* was published by Doubleday in 1961.

6. *Newsweek*, April 28, 1958. The writer of the piece, General Editor James Cannon, later became one of Nelson's political aides.

7. The constitutional convention was not held. See Joe Alex Morris, *Nelson Rockefeller: A Biography* (New York: Harper and Bros., 1960), pp. 310–12.

8. The best guess is that Laurance was enthusiastic, but that JDR, Winthrop, and David were all cautious in varying degrees. Information on family giving to Nelson's campaigns was made public during the hearings attending his nomination as Vice President in 1974. See U.S., Congress, *Nomination of Nelson A. Rockefeller to be Vice President of the United States*, Hearings before the House Committee on the Judiciary, 93rd Cong., 2nd Sess., 1974, pp. 265–66. On the $18,000 that Lockwood proposed the brothers give (see his letter of August 5, 1958, RAC), only several $3,000 gifts went to committees directly concerned with Nelson's campaign. The rest was divided among a dozen other Republican campaign committees, both national and state, in the traditional pattern of Rockefeller campaign giving. In subsequent campaigns, most family giving went directly to Nelson.

9. Issue of September 24, 1956.

10. *Tarrytown Daily News*, November 11, 1958.

11. The description of Junior's attitudes in this section is based on interviews with several of his surviving associates who requested anonymity.

12. *New York Times*, November 5, 1958.

13. Interview with Lindsley Kimball, who had been associated with Junior in 1940 and was loaned by him to the United Services Organization (USO) during the war. There Kimball met Chester Barnard, who had been loaned to the USO by AT&T. Kimball became vice president under Barnard when the latter was president of the Rockefeller Foundation, and he was totally devoted to Junior and Barnard.

14. It is not possible to be precise about large estates such as Junior's because of differences in book value, appraised value, and market value of various assets. Some transactions take years to become final. The $72 million for the RBF is, however, a final figure.

15. Interview with Hugh Morrow, January 18, 1983.

16. Winthrop Rockefeller contributed a total of $260,528, most of it for Nelson's later campaigns after Winthrop became governor of Arkansas. Although JDR gave a smaller total than Laurance and David, his contributions were the most uniform throughout the whole period. In contrast, David gave much less than JDR until the 1970 election, when he contributed $458,000, more than three-fourths of his total giving.

17. Such views of Nelson are either hinted at or presented directly in the many books describing his political career—for example, in Morris (1960), Gervasi (1964), Collier and Horowitz (1976), and Moscow (1977). The picture is drawn most clearly in Joseph Persico, *The Imperial Rockefeller* (New York: Simon & Schuster, 1982). Despite the title and sometimes critical tone, this is not an unfriendly book, but a frank and honest one.

18. Most prominently, the "missile gap" theme in JFK's campaign was based in part on the defense panel report of *Prospects for America*.

19 Former aides of Nelson's agree that Jamieson was closer to him than anyone other than his brother Laurance and probably was the only aide who could influence him on such a matter. Of course, Junior was the most formidable influence, though not on political grounds. As long as Junior was alive, Nelson would not dream of undertaking a divorce. Blanchette Rockefeller believes that Nelson's career went irretrievably off the tracks after

Jamieson's death. Persico (1982) describes how Nelson's excess energy and virility drew him into a series of liaisons, mostly originating during his two stints in Washington. Though not "immediately fatal" to his marriage to Tod, Persico says these "marked the beginning of a protracted death of the marriage." Pp. 33–35.

20. *New York Times*, November 19, 1961.

21. One of the early plans for utilizing the Pocantico estate was to make plots of land available to Rockefeller relatives and friends. The Murphys were one of the first couples to be able to guy some acreage under this plan, which was later abandoned.

22. It may not have helped her public image much at the time if it had been known, but Happy did not "abandon" her children. The agreement gave her more than half-custody, but one stipulation was that this would be kept secret.

23. See Persico (1982), p. 43, and Collier and Horowitz (1976), p. 348. Given the legacy of Junior's strong moral view, it is not surprising that family members were shocked that Nelson was actually going ahead with the wedding. JDR and Blanchette did not refuse to attend—they were not invited. It was an awkward situation, and Nelson probably decided that the easiest course was not to invite anyone but Laurance, Mary, and Martha Baird Rockefeller.

24. "Aunt Martha's" loyalty to Nelson extended to donating $200,000 to the campaign of Nelson's candidate, George Romney, before Romney's fatal remark about being "brainwashed" in Vietnam forced him out of the race.

25. Moscow (1977), p. 265.

26. John Ward, *The Arkansas Rockefeller* (Baton Rouge: Louisiana State University Press, 1978), p. 4.

27. *Washington Star*, September 1, 1957.

28. Ward (1978), p. 17.

CHAPTER 14

1. Things were not too spare, however. Sigried and Margo were staff members ("Heavenly staff!" Blanchette recalled). Sigried was an excellent cook who had worked for Junior at Bassett Hall.

2. In this and in the following chapter, the recollections and opinions of members of JDR's family were obtained by the authors in a series of interviews from 1980 to 1982, including interviews with Jay and Sharon at the Governor's Mansion in Charleston, W. Va.; with Alida in her home in Minneapolis; with Sandra in her home in Cambridge; with Blanchette in Manhattan; and with Hope in Washington.

3. Taken from Dr. Lee's eulogy. "Words of Commemoration," delivered at Riverside Church, New York City, July 13, 1978.

4. Interview with Kershaw Burbank, April 28, 1982. Burbank was an aide to JDR briefly in Williamsburg and New York.

5. Russell Lynes, *Good Old Modern: An Intimate Portrait of the Museum of Modern Art* (New York: Atheneum, 1973), pp. 378–89.

6. Ibid.

7. Interview with Mrs. Rockefeller, January 27, 1982. See also description of the guest house in Lynes, op. cit., pp. 382–83.

8. Blanchette had a temperature-controlled office and gallery for her remaining art built in part of the basement space at Fieldwood Farm. The "guest house" eventually was sold by MOMA to a Connecticut woman who is interested in preserving examples of Johnson's architecture. The house still stands at 252 East 52nd Street.

9. JDR's interest in the "new values" is discussed in Chapters 19 and 20.

CHAPTER 15

1. Mary Ellen Chase, *Abby Aldrich Rockefeller* (New York: Macmillan, 1950).

2. Jay considered California because of its greater population size and political diversity,

its impressive media, and its position in the mainstream of America politics. In the six Presidential Elections since 1968, candidates from California, Richard M. Nixon and Ronald Reagan, have won four.

3. In his remarks, JDR complimented the Community Improvement Association for the "terrific job" it had done starting from scratch. He drew some parallels with his own efforts to get Lincoln Center going in New York, pointing out that a creative effort often takes time and that one must not become discouraged. He praised community members for taking the initiative to create something they wanted instead of waiting for the government or someone else to do it for them.

4. Interview with Jay Rockefeller, November 10, 1982.

5. Interview with Alida Rockefeller Messinger, March 17, 1983.

6. JDR 3rd, Annual Financial Statements, Room 5600 financial files.

7. JDR 3rd, Trust Files, Room 5600.

CHAPTER 16

1. *New York Times Magazine*, "A Rockefeller Enters 'Show Biz,' " September 18, 1956.

2. As demonstrated in Kirstein's review of Edgar B. Young's book on Lincoln Center ("Lincoln Shelter," *New York Review of Books*, August 13, 1981).

3. *New York Times*, September 20, 1982.

4. Abby's love of art was kindled in her childhood in the upper-class surroundings of her family home in Providence, Rhode Island. Her breadth and skill as a collector deserves more recognition than it has received, given that it flourished in three major branches of art and was carried out with much less in the way of financial resources than her husband and father were able to devote. Her sister, Lucy, was also a great collector of Asian art. Starting quite young, Abby had, by 1930, amassed one of the largest and finest collections of Japanese prints in the world, including more than 400 Hiroshige bird and flower prints. She gave nearly 700 of her Japanese prints to the Rhode Island School of Design in 1934.

5. Interview with Mrs. John D. Rockefeller 3rd, January 27, 1982, and with Sherman Lee, September 8, 1982.

6. Interview with Robert Mowry, curator, Asia Society, September 21, 1982.

7. Interview with E. P. Richardson, August 26, 1982. Only after Richardson retired from Winterthur did he begin receiving an honorarium from JDR.

8. E. P. Richardson, *American Art: A Narrative and Critical Catalogue of an Exhibition from the Collection of Mr. and Mrs. John D. Rockefeller 3rd* (San Francisco: The Fine Arts Museums, 1976), Preface.

9. The CECA paper is cited in the fifteen-year report of the JDR 3rd Fund: *The JDR 3rd Fund and Asia: 1963–1975*, p. 15.

10. Interview with Abraham M. Weisblat, August 12, 1982.

11. Interviews with Porter McCray, June 20 and July 7, 1979. McCray's career with MOMA is discussed in Lynes, op. cit. For the period of dissension and McCray's departure, see pp. 388–91.

It is interesting to note the seminal role of Nelson Rockefeller. First, he pioneered the whole idea of cultural exchanges when serving as coordinator of Inter-American Affairs, and then he was instrumental in creating the International Program of MOMA in the early 1950s. Finally, there was his strong support of the arts when he was governor of New York.

12. See the JDR 3rd Fund fifteen-year report, pp. 8–9.

13. A copy of the Heckscher report may be found in the RAC.

14. *Washington Post*, March 25, 1969; also, Hanks to JDR of same date.

15. Hanks to JDR, March 6, 1975.

CHAPTER 17

1. JDR was miffed at the White House, not McNulty, who explained that he really could not refuse. McNulty had been "borrowed" because of expertise gained in JDR's office. The purpose was to draft speeches in connection with the visit to the United States of President and Mrs. Marcos of the Philippines. Besides, JDR was not told that McNulty would stay in Washington until the three-month loan of his services was nearly over. After the Johnson administration left office, McNulty got a job with General Motors in Detroit and eventually became GM's vice president for public relations.

2. The memo is reproduced in the unpublished McLean study, Book II, "Organizing for the Future," pp. 125–28.

3. In hearings on his nomination for the Vice Presidency, Nelson in his testimony provided details of his gifts and loans over the years to a long list of individuals who had worked for him in the family office or the state of New York, or both. These ranged from relatively small sums of the order of $25,000 to the total of $550,000 in gifts and forgiven loans that Nelson gave to his close adviser, Dr. William J. Ronan. See U.S., 93rd Cong., 2nd Sess., "Nomination of Nelson A. Rockefeller to Be Vice President of the United States," Hearings before House Committee on the Judiciary, 1974, pp 36–40. For Dr. Ronan's testimony, see pp. 948–1002.

4. This was the "T Group" ("T" for "training") methodology of NTL based on the research and experiments of Kurt Lewin and others. For perhaps the best and most thorough exposition, see Leland P. Bradford, et al. (eds.), *T-Group Theory and Laboratory Method* (New York: John Wiley & Co., 1964). Argyris's seminal book was *Personality and Organization* (1957); it was followed by a dozen others.

CHAPTER 18

1. The seminal roles of Junior and his father in building modern philanthropy are described in detail in the first ten chapters of Harr and Johnson (1988).

2. The unlimited charitable deduction was first provided for by an amendment to the Revenue Act of 1924, the so-called Philadelphia nun clause. The amendment was passed specifically to eliminate the problem the income tax laws caused for a nun from the wealthy Drexel family who had taken vows of poverty and was giving away her entire income of $1,000 per day to charity. See T. Willard Hunter, *The Tax Climate for Philanthropy* (Washington, D.C.: American College Public Relations Association, 1968), p. 12.

The 1954 amendments that allowed JDR to qualify for the unlimited charitable deduction also brought a windfall to Junior, or more accurately, to various charitable causes he supported. Under the new provisions, Junior qualified for the "unlimited" for five of the years prior to 1954. The revision of his tax returns for those years diverted $21 million from the U.S. Treasury back to Junior except that the money had to go to charity, not to him personally. The money did not finally become available until 1959. Among the many gifts he made to various charities from this total was his second $5 million gift to Lincoln Center in December 1959 (see Young, 1980, pp. 130–31).

The fact that none of this caught the attention of the press makes an interesting comment on the difference in the mood of the 1950s compared to the 1960s when anything that could be interpreted as a benefit to the wealthy came in for severe criticism.

3. Nielsen (1972), p. 5.

4. *New York Times*, September 16, 1964.

5. *Treasury Department Report on Philanthropy*, House Committee on Ways and Means, 8901, February 2, 1965.

6. March 6, 1965.

7. *New York Times*, March 29, 1965.

8. The "One Per Cent Plan" group consisted of a number of business firms in Cleveland

that had joined together to pledge contributions to higher education. JDR addressed this group May 8, 1962, and spoke to the "inaugural dinner" of the Federation of Jewish Philanthropies at the Plaza Hotel in New York on October 4, 1964.

9. Nielsen (ibid., p. 14) cites lobbyists who were trying to protect the oil depletion allowance as among those who tried to divert congressional attention to the foundations.

10. Patman's comments were made in a letter to the Ways and Means Committee on May 5, 1969. It was included under date of February 18 in the committee record of the hearings.

11. Finch made his views known in a letter to Treasury Secretary David N. Kennedy. See *New York Times*, September 17, 1969.

12. Nielsen, ibid., p. 15.

13. A conformed copy of JDR's testimony is available in the philanthropic files of the RAC.

14. From the press release accompanying the report, May 10, 1970. See philanthropic files in the RAC.

CHAPTER 19

1. Interview with Dean Rusk, March 1979.

2. The associates also believed that JDR was the perfect choice for ambassador to Japan at that time. If JDR had accepted the bid, his New York office would have been radically curtailed to a standby basis, but his associates were able to view the question without a conflict with their own self-interest. Smith and Young were both nearing retirement age, and the tendency for younger associates was not to see employment with JDR as a life's work, but as an interesting experience for a few years, much as joining a new administration in Washington might be.

3. JDR liked President Ford, but he wrote that he voted for Carter "because he seemed to me to offer more promise." He did not mention the fact that Ford had dropped Nelson from the ticket for the 1976 campaign. It is quite possible that JDR voted for Democrats in previous elections, especially in 1972 when, as we shall see, he had his reasons for disliking President Nixon.

4. In their book *The American Establishment* (New York: Basic Books, 1980), Leonard and Mark Silk begin by relating the story of JDR seeking out John Oakes, editorial page editor of *The New York Times*, to express the hope that the *Times* could be more supportive of U.S. policy in Vietnam. JDR said that criticism of the Diem regime was having a bad effect on South Vietnamese morale and American efforts to contain communism. JDR had been urged to do this in a telegram from the U.S. ambassador to South Vietnam, Frederick Nolting. In his diary JDR wrote that Oakes "seemed open-minded and flexible in his approach." Later JDR expressed a similar concern at an editorial board luncheon at the *Times*. However, these episodes happened fairly early. Like many Americans, JDR's ambivalence toward the war grew as time passed.

5. Harr and Johnson (1988), pp. 3–10.

6. This draft is in the RAC, entitled "Manuscript for John D. Rockefeller 3rd by Richard Schickel, 7/1/69."

7. Smith knew that Harr had completed book-length projects, having helped him publish his third book (*The Professional Diplomat*) at the Princeton University Press where Smith had been president for many years. Although Harr's books were all in his academic field, Smith thought that his writing style would be suitable.

8. In contrast to JDR's careful involvement was his brother Nelson's "cavalier attitude toward books," as described by Joseph Persico, who served as speechwriter to Nelson. A number of books have been published with Nelson listed as author, but all were ghostwritten. In 1970 press secretary Hugh Morrow brought the manuscript of a new book, *Our Environment Can Be Saved*, to Nelson to read before it went to the publisher, but Nelson

was busy and begged off. The book was published under Nelson's name, and Persico commented: "Thus the book achieved a fairly rare distinction even for a ghosted work—not only had it not been written by the putative author, it had never been read by him." See Persico (1982), pp. 131–32.

9. Ibid., p. 50.

10. When sales of the book tapered off, JDR puchased the last several thousand copies from the publisher at author's discount in order to avoid having them "remaindered." The books were sent to public libraries.

11. The *Times* never ran a review of the book, although it did carry a feature article about JDR and the book on the day of publication ("Book by a Rockefeller Scores Materialism," by Eric Pace, February 26, 1973).

CHAPTER 20

1. JDR always referred to "the youth project" because it implied something less permanent than a "program." However, everyone used "program" or "youth task force" to refer to the total operation.

2. Minutes of JDR 3rd Fund Board Meeting, October 9, 1970, RAC.

3. The group waiting outside of the building definitely was composed of the "extremists," as JDR noted. For a few seconds the atmosphere was menacing as these people began to move in on JDR and Blanchette. It was the one time during the weekend when all of JDR's advisers were handy as they collapsed around the Rockefellers in a sort of phalanx as they moved to their car.

4. See Harr and Johnson (1988), p. 84.

5. *New York Times*, December 12; *Boston Globe*, December 7; *Time* and *Newsweek* issues of December 21, 1970.

6. There was no systematic attempt to evaluate the "dialogue" program, and the files of the youth program are of little help. One exception is a paper entitled "Louisville Dialog," written by Paul Swift, who, as a member of the youth staff, was the organizer of the "dialogues" in Louisville and Chicago. His paper, written in December 1972 and located in the RAC, projects the flavor of the Louisville experience, from its frail and difficult beginnings to the point where the youth-business group began to coalesce and take on projects in their community. Swift concluded that he did not fully understand the "pace" of the group, "but I do know that the relations formed . . . are having dramatically humanizing effects on each member."

7. Hellman's two-part profile of Nelson, appearing in the issues of April 11 and 18, was highly laudatory, focusing on Nelson's exciting role as "coordinator," and also covering his accomplishments with the Museum of Modern Art and Rockefeller Center. There was also a two-part profile of David Rockefeller in *The New Yorker* (January 9 and 16, 1965, by E. J. Kahn, Jr.), also very positive in tone. No profile was ever done on Laurance or Winthrop.

8. The passages quoted are just a few of many that project Hellman's bias. It was, of course, quite possible that some of the people associated with Lincoln Center were resentful when JDR finally detached himself. What was wrong with Hellman's article was that he left such sentiments unchallenged, failing to examine the motives of the man he was "profiling" and the healthy reasons why it made sense for JDR to end his active involvement with Lincoln Center. And no objective writer would have left unexamined the inference that JDR's primary reason for being involved with Lincoln Center was to create a "monument" to himself, so far at odds was that with the facts. If anything, JDR's staff was critical of him for subordinating himself too much.

9. The presentation of Jerry Swift's side of the story is based on discussions with him at the time of the incident and several authors' interviews with Paul and Jerry Swift in 1983 and 1984.

10. The other writer was Nicholas von Hoffman of the *Washington Post*. He telephoned the JDR youth office one morning to announce that he was preparing an "exposé" of JDR's effort to coopt young activists. He refused to come up to the fifty-sixth floor but challenged Swift to meet with him in the Promenade Lounge downstairs to dissuade him—something he admitted with characteristic flair was "impossible." So Swift and colleague Peggy Blumenthal went down to meet with Von Hoffman, who seemed intent on studying the ice skaters on the Promenade rink as Swift went through his two-step process—describing his own initial skepticism about JDR and then the man he had come to know. After some interrogation, Von Hoffman apparently began to suspect that JDR was "for real." He demanded an interview with him. Swift went upstairs to try to arrange it, and JDR agreed. Later that day when Von Hoffman called back to check, he decided JDR really *was* "for real." The only way Von Hoffman could get an "exposé" that fit his initial design would be to do a dishonest story. So he dropped the whole idea and passed up the interview. Hellman was a different case.

11. The Reid controversy centered on the writer's admission that he frequently had been inventive about the facts in order to go beyond the "strictly factual" in search of a larger truth. In a letter to the authors on November 15, 1984, Swift referrred in particular to the "composite interview"—a nonfiction technique denounced by the *New Yorker* in which the writer partially invents what the respondent is quoted as saying and links together fragments of conversation out of context. On the Reid matter, see *Wall Street Journal*, June 18, 1984; *New York Times*, June 19 and 20, July 3, 1984. The issue flared up again in 1989 in a two-part piece in the *New Yorker* by Janet Malcolm (March 6 and 13) in which she attacked the "treachery" of journalists for "betraying" their subjects. In the outcry that followed, other journalists were quick to note that neither Miss Malcolm nor the *New Yorker* had disclosed that she had been sued for precisely the same practices and in court had admitted fabricating quotations in an earlier *New Yorker* piece on the psychologist Jeffrey Masson. The suit was dismissed and appealed. See *New York Times* of March 21 and August 5, 1989, and a *Times* editorial of March 19.

12. The *New Yorker* has an enviable reputation for meticulously checking facts in its articles. Dealing with the interpretations or biases of a writer is something else, however. As far as "internal evidence" was concerned, Swift could point to something as broad as how a man who gave away most of his income every year could be portrayed as niggardly, or something as specific as Hellman's quoting of Swift to the effect that JDR couldn't call people on the telephone for fear of being hit constantly with financial requests. Anyone familiar with JDR's habits, as Swift certainly was, knew that JDR had no such inhibition, spending half his working day on the telephone, and much of his evenings and weekends as well.

13. Supported by five foundations, including the JDR 3rd Fund, Yankelovich's final youth study was published in summary form in a booklet entitled "Changing Youth Values in the Seventies." Later in 1974 the full study was published in paperback form by McGraw-Hill as *The New Morality: A Profile of American Youth in the Seventies*.

CHAPTER 21

1. The origin of the Tocqueville quotation that JDR used so many times in speeches and articles became something of a mystery at one point. JDR wanted to use the quotation again in his book, so Datus Smith decided to track down the citation, feeling a bit suspicious because the words sounded too modern. He enlisted the aid of a Princeton historian. The exact quotation could not be found in Tocqueville's writings, even though John Gardner and several other authors had used it as well, presumably getting it from JDR, whose usage dated back the longest. The mystery was finally solved when the quotation was found in a philosophy book published early in the century, which was on the bookshelf in JDR's office (since lost, it cannot be cited here). That author had paraphrased Tocqueville, and JDR had picked up the passage for his own use. Meanwhile, the Princeton scholar had agreed that the paraphrase projected the sense of Tocqueville, though not his own words. JDR still insisted

on using the quotation in his book, and even agreed reluctantly to refer to it as "attributed to Tocqueville."

2. Material on these activities dating from the 1880s is available in the RAC under the headings of "civics" and "general welfare" as well as "housing."

3. The UDC has not nearly lived up to the high hopes Nelson had for it when he asked the state legislature to create it in 1968. Under the leadership of Edward J. Logue, the UDC seemed to have great potential, but was handicapped early when voters turned down an urban development bond issue in 1969. This led Nelson to issue bonds anyway, under the "moral authority" of the state, but with no specific bonding authority, and that led to a number of problems, including court cases.

4. The original proposals to create UHO were a twenty-five-page document written by John E. Harr ("PROPOSAL: A Pilot Project to Test One Major Method in Making Home Ownership Possible in the Slum or Near-Slum Areas of Urgan Centers"), circulated to JDR's staff on January 25, 1968, and a four-page memorandum from Harr to JDR ("The Cooperative Housing Idea for New York City") on January 31, 1968.

Information for this segment on UHO was drawn from the documentary record, interviews with the principals involved, and Harr's experience as a member of the UHO board.

5. It is ironic that it was a profit-making bank that agreed to take this high risk instead of a government program specifically set up for that purpose. The Chase bank became involved only because urban affairs officer Joseph Quinn felt he was doing his job, not because of any Rockefeller connection. Apart from Laurance's act in agreeing to the UHO grant as chairman of the RBF, it is doubtful that JDR's brothers were ever more than fleetingly aware of the existence of UHO. It should be noted that UHO never defaulted on any of its Chase "seed money" loans, although payments were stretched out in some cases.

6. Section 8 was so ill-suited to actually producing affordable housing (although useful in part in shoring up existing projects) that there was speculation in one UHO board meeting that the person who designed it must have had a "Section 8" discharge from the military. The Section 221d3 program (in place when UHO came into existence) was the most flexible and workable program. Section 236 was the relevant part of the Housing and Urban Development Act of 1968, LBJ's response to the urban problem and his bid to create "a Magna Carta to liberate our cities." It was intended to produce 1,700,000 units of low-income housing over the next three years, but of course fell far short of that, the victim of electoral change and all of the appropriations, administrative, and delivery system problems that plagued "Great Society" programs. Section 236 otherwise was workable, although it introduced some rigidities such as income quotas for residents in projects. Section 8 came along after the freeze.

7. Not only is there no way to convert a tax-shelter project to a co-op before the five-year accelerated depreciation period ends, but it would even be illegal to manifest any intention of doing so before that time expires. HUD likes tax shelters because they are based on a 90 percent mortgage guarantee instead of 100 percent, the other 10 percent being the money from investors, the "tax shelter." The investors will profit no matter what happens, through the tax write-off and possible profit if the building is salable after the five-year depreciation period. Although basically similar in structure, contemporary real estate tax shelters are not comparable to the limited-dividend corporations Junior invested in during the 1920s. An allowed 6 percent profit would not be competitive in modern circumstances. Junior's motive for investing was more to help create affordable and decent housing for low-income families than for profit or tax reasons.

8. "White Paper by the Board of Directors, Urban Home Ownership Corporation," thirty-one-page undated manuscript produced in 1976, RAC.

9. JDR to Harris, February 1, 1977; Harris to JDR, May 16, 1977; JDR to Harris, May 27, 1977, RAC.

10. JDR to Moynihan, December 27, 1977; Moynihan to JDR, March 1, 1978, RAC.

11. JDR to Harris, May 4, 1978; undated paper entitled "Proposal for Participation of the

Third Sector in the Housing Field" (submitted to HUD by Board of Directors, Urban Home Ownership Corporation); Harris to JDR, June 13, 1978; Harr memorandum to JDR, June 19, 1978; JDR to Harris, June 22, 1978, RAC.

CHAPTER 22

1. *The Second American Revolution* (Harper & Row) 1973, p. 10–11, 193–194.

2. Boston, Washington, and Miami were the other three competitors. Philadelphia had an edge because of the fact that both the Centennial Exposition of 1876 and Sesquicentennial Exposition of 1926 had been held there, and also because of political clout provided by Senator Hugh Scott. The negative factors were serious funding problems, a general sentiment that major expos had gone the way of the dinosaur, and a view that an expo in 1976 would provide too much of a focal point and detract from local celebration of the Bicentennial.

3. This was an interesting organization because it was eerily suggestive of what the United States must have been like during the period of the Articles of Confederation—usually hamstrung by parochial considerations, yet with some leaders emerging who campaigned for more unity and effective action, especially Richard Gibbs of North Carolina and Clifford Clarke of Georgia.

4. The series was front-paged on August 14, 15, and 16, 1972.

5. Source material for this chapter is the documentary record of the time and interviews with many of the people involved, including Barrett, Spector, Ruder, Mahoney, and Sterling. The most thorough record of the Bicentennial may be found in the pages of *USA-200*, a twelve-page monthly newsletter initiated by Dick Barrett and Jack Harr in 1971. It was officially endorsed by the Bicentennial Council of the 13 Original States and ultimately taken over by the National Committee for the Bicentennial Era, the organization created by JDR in 1975. A bound volume of all issues of *USA-200* from 1971 to 1976 may be found in the RAC.

6. For the background of Nelson's "Critical Choices" operation, including the amusing story of how he tried to get $20 million in federal funds to finance it, see Persico (1982), Ch. 18. Two of the members of his commission were the two party leaders in the House of Representatives. Thomas "Tip" O'Neill, Jr., and Gerald Ford, the latter staying on even after he was appointed Vice President to succeed the disgraced Spiro Agnew.

7. This incident occurred almost a year after President Nixon had scuttled JDR's Population Commission report, but JDR had not taken that personally and saw no reason why he could not cooperate with the White House on some other project, particularly in this case because he was merely checking with the White House as a gesture of good faith to indicate that he was not trying to set himself up as a rival force on the Bicentennial. In this, however, he was probably being naive and underestimating the extent to which he was seen as "too liberal" for the Nixon administration's taste. In contrast, Nelson and Nixon had once been bitter rivals, but had buried the hatchet several times and were now political allies. Also, Nelson had taken a conservative tack on most issues during his latter years as governor of New York State in contrast to his earlier image as a liberal Republican. However, Persico (1982) points out that there was no real affection between Nelson and Nixon, and he describes Nelson's disappointment when Nixon selected Gerald Ford as his Vice President to replace Agnew instead of Nelson (pp. 239–42).

8. Because the ARBC was in such bad shape, the Nixon administration pressured the National Endowment for the Arts and the National Endowment for the Humanities to take up the funding slack for Bicentennial projects.

9. The evolution of the "American Issues Forum" may be traced in the *USA-200* issues of April and June 1974 and June and July 1975. At one point there was a flurry of interest in the possibility of Nelson's "Critical Choices" operation providing the calendar of issues, but this died out.

10. For details on the involvement of Ruckelshaus, see *USA-200* issues of February and May 1974.

11. Almost all of the national program ideas for the Bicentennial foundered sooner or later because of lack of funds, in contrast to regional and local ideas funded by states and communities, as amply recorded in the pages of *USA-200* over nearly a six-year period. For background on some of the projects for which JDR provided seed money, see the following issues of *USA-200*: "New Federalist Papers," May 1971; "Third Hoover Commission," September 1975; "Citizen Involvement Network," October 1974, September 1975, June 1976. The last survived the longest, but expired when it fell far short of its $7 million funding goal.

12. The five participating companies were Mobil, IBM, Coca-Cola, International Paper, and TRW.

13. For a description of the press conference, television show, the text of the Bicentennial Declaration, and list of signers, see *USA-200* of March 1975.

14. The text of the bill was printed in *USA-200* of April 1976, and a story of the hearings appeared in the May 1976 issue.

CHAPTER 23

1. Robert W. van de Velde, *The Rockefeller Public Service Awards: A Fifteen-Year Report*, Princeton University Press, 1967, p. 24.

2. At first the award was $3,500 in cash plus $6,500 available to pay the expenses of campus visits of the winners. But the high rank of the winners prevented them from sparing the time, and the expense fund was not utilized, so after a few years the award reverted to a full $10,000 in cash. In some years six awards were given, and at various times joint awards were given in several categories, with the winners splitting the award stipend.

3. For information on all award winners for the first fifteen years of the RPSA plus excerpts from speeches made at the awards banquet annually, see Van de Velde, op. cit., pp. 65–108.

4. However, the new law allowed individuals like JDR (whose contributions and federal taxes combined exceeded 90 percent in 1969 and prior years) to phase down gradually to 50 percent over a five-year period. This lessened the "shock" to JDR of being forced to give away less of his income each year (as more went to taxes). Thus from $4.9 million in 1969 his total personal giving fell to $3.8 million in 1970, to $3.5 million in 1971, and to $3.3 million in 1972. But from that point on JDR's giving began to move back up again toward the $5 million level even though he could deduct only 50 percent of his net taxable income for charitable giving. The reason for the gradual increase in giving was that his income was increasing, due to inflation and the fact that much of his income came from oil stocks, which did well throughout the time of the oil embargo and recession. However, inflation also made these post-1972 dollars worth less than before.

5. "Report of the Committee to Review the Rockefeller Public Service Awards Program," p. 12, undated typewritten manuscript located in RAC.

6. Background information on the transition from the second to the third phase of the RPSA was obtained when the authors met at the Woodrow Wilson School in October 1982 with a group of people connected with the program over the years, including Dean Stokes, Don McLean, Robert van de Velde, Robert Nathan, Rufus Miles, Ingrid Reed, Roger Jones, and others.

7. Jones had been a key person involved in the creating of the RPSA in 1952 and years later served on the Selection Committee. Robert Nathan, a noted economist with his own firm in Washington, served as Selection Committee chairman from 1973 until the termination of the program. Staats, the Comptroller General of the United States, was a former RPSA winner.

8. John E. Harr, memorandum to the files, "JDR and the Rockefeller Public Service Awards," August 28, 1978, RAC.

9. Woodrow Wilson School, Princeton University, "The RPSA Program: A Potential Living Memorial to John D. Rockefeller 3rd," December 1978 (unpublished), copy located in RAC. This document, a proposal for continuing the RPSA after JDR's death, briefly recounted the history of the program.

CHAPTER 24

1. "The Non-Spending of Non-Taxes," *Washington Post*, April 22, 1976.

2. In his article (May 23, 1976), Greene quoted Surrey and Ylvisaker. Greene's pessimistic view of the future of philanthropy did not prevent him from taking a position as Elizabeth McCormack's assistant in the Rockefeller family philanthropic office after the Filer Report.

3. After the ceremony in Ullman's office, JDR made the thoughtful gesture of paying a personal visit to Congressman Wilbur Mills, who had fallen from grace—and worse, from the chairmanship of the Ways & Means Committee—after his "Fanny Fox" episode and the revelation of his long struggle with alcoholism. Mills, who JDR noted was "largely responsible for the Filer Commission coming into being," had not attended the ceremony. JDR wrote that Mills "was his usual rather gruff self but seemed to be in good health and spirits."

4. Published as a companion piece to the report was a larger fifty-page booklet containing a summary of each of the Commission's research projects (*Guide to the Sponsored Research of the Commission on Private Philanthropy and Public Needs*).

5. By that time Simon had succeeded in obtaining grants of $100,000 a year from the Sloan Foundation and $50,000 a year from the Carnegie Corporation. JDR paid $75,000 of his pledge. The rest of his pledge was honored by his executors and paid from his estate after his death.

6. JDR's choice in previous elections is not known, although it is likely that he normally voted for the Republican candidate. As noted earlier, the 1976 election was the only case in which JDR indicated his choice in his diary.

7. The five letters cited between JDR and Eizenstat are in the RAC. The dates cover the period March 31, 1977, to May 11, 1977.

8. Authors' interviews with Smith and McKeever in August 1982.

9. Nielsen's paper, in the RAC, was dated September 26, 1977.

10. JDR was to host the second meeting, in Room 5600, but it occurred one day after his death. The meeting went ahead as planned, and was one step on the way to the eventual merger to create a new umbrella organization called the Independent Sector, with John Gardner as chairperson. Among the board members well-known to JDR at the time of the creation of the organization in 1979 were John Filer, Walter McNerney, Waldemar Nielsen, Juanita Kreps, and Kenneth Dayton as vice chairperson. In a speech at the thirtieth annual conference of the Council on Foundations, Gardner described the genesis and purpose of the Independent Sector, tracing it directly to the recommendations of the Peterson and Filer Commissions.

With JDR's death and the advent of the Independent Sector, the late-starting Committee on the Third Sector in Washington, organized by Walter McNerney at JDR's initiative as a "post-Filer" effort, never really got off the ground and was terminated. If JDR had lived, it is quite possible that the Independent Sector would have been called the Third Sector. With JDR's continued leadership, including the book he was planning to write, he might have succeeded in winning the battle of semantics. The term "third sector" had begun to crop up in usage here and there by others (see, for example, the article by management consultant Peter Drucker in the *Wall Street Journal* of October 3, 1978, "Managing the 'Third Sector' "). However, much more important than semantics is how well the Independent Sector will succeed as the overall organization long envisioned by JDR and others.

11. In a memorandum on the subject of a biography of JDR written to Blanchette Rocke-

feller after her husband's death. Dated December 13, 1978, and marked "confidential," the memo is in the RAC.

CHAPTER 25

1. Public Law 91–213, 91st Congress, S. 2701, March 16, 1970. The five areas of inquiry were stated as follows in the bill:

(1) the probable course of population growth, internal migration, and related demographic developments between now and the year 2000;

(2) the resources in the public sector of the economy that will be required to deal with the anticipated growth in population;

(3) the ways in which population growth may affect the activities of Federal, State, and local government;

(4) the impact of population growth on environmental pollution and on the depletion of natural resources; and

(5) the various means appropriate to the ethical values and principles of this society by which our Nation can achieve a population level properly suited for its environmental, natural resources, and other needs.

2. Press Release, Office of the White House Press Secretary, "Remarks of the President upon Signing the Bill on Population Growth and the American Future," the Roosevelt Room, March 16, 1970, p. 2.

3. *New York Times*, May 2, 1969.

4. Extensive files on the two conferences are available at the RAC.

5. Interview with Porter McKeever, April 28, 1983.

6. Report of the UNA-USA Panel on "World Population and the Quality of Human Development: A Challenge to the United Nations and Its System of Agencies," May 25, 1969. See also *New York Times* front-page story of that date.

7. Report to the Secretary General of the United Nations from the Review Committee of the United Nations Fund for Population Activities," New York, October 1972, p. 21. JDR was one of the seven members of this committee, which was drawn from the membership of the UNFPA Advisory Board.

8. The Roman Catholic Church opposes abortion on all grounds except ectopic pregnancy and "unnatural" pregnancy. Under the latter category, pregnancy resulting from incest is considered unnatural, but not so in the case of rape.

9. Dr. Hellman was head of obstetrics and gynecology at the State University of New York, and Dr. Hall had the same position at Columbia University.

10. A description of the events of this period regarding abortion can be found in a book by an outspoken advocate of abortion law reform, Laurence Lader (*Abortion II: The Making of a Revolution* [Boston: Beacon Press, 1973]). Abortion law reform was in progress in some seventeen states at the time that New York became the first to pass such a liberal law.

11. Moynihan's study of "the Negro family" was leaked to the press in June 1965, and some of the findings, such as the tendency for fathers to be absent, were attacked by such black leaders as Bayard Rustin, Martin Luther King, Jr., Floyd McKissisk, and Jesse Jackson.

12. *New York Times*, February 11, 1969.

13. Others on the list included the Reverend Theodore Hesburgh of Notre Dame, General William Draper, and George Woods. Only two of the people on JDR's list—Woods and David Bell—became members of the Commission.

14. *New York Times*, June 11, 1969. Piotrow (1973) provides a detailed description of the events in Washington leading up to Nixon's message in her Chapter 16, "President Nixon's Message on Population, 1969," pp. 163–70.

15. See the *New York Times* of July 4, September 22, October 5, and November 25, 1969.

16. The first of Egeberg's intentions was adopted, with Dr. Louis Hellman becoming the

first deputy assistant secretary for population within HEW despite his background of support for abortion law liberalization. However, the second idea of creating a Population Institute did not materialize.

17. A copy of Percy's letter to Cooper, dated March 10, 1965, is in the RAC. In it Percy told Cooper: "I have already sent a letter to the White House some time ago suggesting John as Chairman but because of my relationship with the family it would not be as affective [*sic*] as a word from you. . . ." On the margin of the copy, Percy wrote a note to JDR: "John Cooper said he'd be very pleased to follow up on this. Chuck."

18. Interview with Richard W. Barrett, June 8, 1983.

19. The text of the memo was printed in *The New York Times*, March 1, 1970. The "benign neglect" reference was well-intentioned, but too colorful a phrase and too easily subject to the misinterpretation of suggesting official neglect of the race problem. Actually, Moynihan was calling for less rhetoric and more progress.

20. A tongue-in-cheek remark. Moynihan was serving as one of the confidential secretaries to Governor Harriman of New York when Nelson was elected in 1958. Obviously, there was no chance that Moynihan would be carried over in such a role with a new governor of the opposing party.

21. Interview with Charles C. Westoff, June 19, 1979.

22. See, for example, Carl Rowan's column in the *Washington Post* of May 24, 1970, with the heading "What Has Become of the Population Commission?"

23. Ramsey, one of the three younger members of the Commission, was president of the Institute for the Study of Health and Society.

24. A tragedy occurred, however, when Ritchie H. Reed, one of the research directors on the staff, was murdered by unknown assailants in the men's room in the building where the Commission's offices were located. The Commission's final report was dedicated to Reed.

25. The chapter on immigration was one of the thinnest in the final report, only four pages long. The majority held that immigration should be maintained at "the present level," whereas JDR thought it should be reduced.

26. Entitled *Population and the American Future*, the report was published by the Commission in Washington, D.C., on March 27, 1972. With the same title, the paperback edition was published simultaneously in New York by Signet Books (New American Library).

27. See chapters of the Commission's report: "Population Growth" (pp. 16–24) and "Population Stabilization" (pp. 110–113).

28. As noted previously, Draper for years was one of the most vocal leaders in support of population programs, but abortion was one subject on which he was cautious.

29. "Population Growth and America's Future," Interim Report Prepared by the Commission on Population Growth and the American Future, Washington, D.C., March 16, 1971, p. 29.

30. The Commissioners who dissented on the recommendation regarding contraceptive advice and services to teenagers were Senator Cranston, Congressman Erlenborn, and Dr. Paul M. Cornely. The same three dissented on the abortion recommendation, as well as Grace Olivarez and Marilyn Chandler. Mrs. Chandler stated a preference for the American Law Institute model abortion statute.

31. The New York State Legislature subsequently did pass a repeal bill and Governor Rockefeller did veto it.

32. Piotrow (1973), p. 197.

CHAPTER 26

1. Sources for some of the material in this chapter include the involvement of one of the authors (Harr) at the time and interviews by the authors of participants in JDR's office and the Population Council.

2. Financial support for the televised version of the report came from Xerox—$50,000;

Ford Foundation—$75,000; Scaife Family Fund—$100,000; Sunnen Foundation—$50,000; Commonwealth Fund—$25,000; and the Department of Health, Education and Welfare— $87,000. The HEW money, in two separate grants, had been committed early in the process, before the coolness developed between JDR and the Nixon White House. By the time work started on the televised report, there was no chance of further HEW money. In fact, HEW refused to include the television program in its film distribution service.

The program was broadcast on PBS after JDR struck out in trying to interest one of the three commercial networks (ABC, CBS, and NBC) to air the show. He met with the CEO and news director of each of the three, and was politely told in all cases that the networks could not take a "news" program produced by an outside organization because of both long-standing practice and the "fairness" doctrine of the Federal Communications Commission then in effect. Clearly, the controversial nature of the subject was a factor as well.

3. Sir Maurice Banks retired as deputy chairman of British Petroleum in 1967. He returned as chairman of the Laird Group, 1970–75, in an attempt to straighten out the problems of British Leyland.

4. The Cleveland Pilot Program resulted in two publications: *Parents and Sexual Learning in Childhood: A Community Study*, and *Service Organizations and Sexual Learning: A Community Analysis*. For John Gagnon's theory, see his book *Sexual Conduct: The Social Sources of Human Sexuality* (Chicago: Aldine Press, 1973).

5. The political environment of the Bucharest conference and U.S. prominence in supporting population programs is discussed in Marcus F. Franda, "Reactions in America at Bucharest," American Universities Field Staff Reports, Southeast Europe Series, Vol. XXI, No. 3 (1974), pp. 1–3. See also Carmen A. Miro, "The World Population Plan of Action: A Political Instrument Whose Potential Has Not Been Realized," *Population and Development Review*, Vol. 3, No. 4 (1977), pp. 421–23.

6. Before the Bucharest conference, Steve Salyer and Adrienne Germain were married. Barney Berelson and Frank Notestein also attended the conference. Jack Harr, the associate who worked with JDR on writing projects, was unable to go to Bucharest because of a back operation, so Greene was recruited to go in his place. However, Greene did not produce the proposed magazine article.

7. Franda, op. cit., p. 1.

8. Ibid. The point of Carmen Miro's article (1977) was that the World Plan of Action, amended as it was at Bucharest, still had great potential, and indeed, it did seem to influence policy directions in some countries. A number of countries that had been vociferously opposed to birth control measures at Bucharest in 1974 have since adopted massive programs to control their population growth, the most notable one, of course, being the People's Republic of China.

The United States, on the other hand, has flip-flopped the other way. JDR would have been aghast at U.S. policy at the next UN Population Conference, at Mexico City in 1984, ten years after Bucharest. Firmly in the grip of the conservatives of the Reagan Administration, the U.S. delegation was chaired by former Senator James Buckley of New York and included Ben Wattenberg, whose views may be judged by his statement that there is no population problem (in the televised version of the Population Commission Report). According to the State Department's senior adviser on population, U.S. policy in 1984 was forged by "the right wing of the right-to-life movement, which has supporters on the White House staff." The U.S. position had become aggressively ideological, holding that "the natural mechanism for slowing population growth" is a free-market economy and that population growth itself is a "natural phenomenon." The policy also included new restrictions related to abortion. Since 1974 the United States has not allowed foreign aid funds to be used directly for abortion programs. But in 1984 it announced that funds would be denied to nongovernmental organizations and foreign countries that "actively promote abortion" even though other funds (non-U.S.) are used—this despite the fact that abortion is legal in the United

States. See *New York Times*, August 11, 1984, p. 3, and *Time* magazine, August 6, 1984, p. 25.

9. Interview with Charles Westoff, June 19, 1979.

10. Dunlop to Bunting, August 5, 1974, RAC. Notestein's and Berelson's points of view and quotations taken from interviews with Notestein (August 18, 1982) and Berelson (June 6, 1979).

11. He did not remain "unknown" for long. Barney became the director of a special interagency effort generated by the Carter White House that produced the "Global 2000" report, postulating dire effects from a continuation of present world trends, including population growth.

12. Dunlop memorandum to the files, September 27, 1974, RAC.

13. The Hopper Report and the response of the division directors ("A Report to the Executive Committee of the Population Council on Organizational Issues") may be found in the RAC.

CHAPTER 27

1. As distinct from the emperor's presence at state dinners for high-ranking foreign guests of state. Also invited to the private luncheon with the royal couple were Mr. and Mrs. Isaac Shapiro, he being the president of the Japan Society.

2. Mrs. Aso was the daughter of Japan's first postwar prime minister, Shigeru Yoshida. Accompanying the Rockefellers on the trip to Japan were the Shapiros and Mr. and Mrs. John E. Harr. JDR and the Harrs went on to Korea; Blanchette and the Shapiros returned home after the week spent in Japan.

3. See, for example, JDR's follow-up letter to Foreign Minister Kiichi Miyazawa, February 26, 1970, RAC. The text of JDR's International House address may also be found in the RAC. It will be recalled that JDR got the first Japanese gift to a foreign cause for Lincoln Center. He also got Japanese financial support for the Japan Society. After JDR's death, substantial gifts from Japanese sources came to the Asia Society and to the Asian Culutural Program of the JDR 3rd Fund. The first substantial Japanese gift to a non-Rockefeller institution was a $1 million grant from Sumitomo Metals to the Fogg Museum at Harvard. There have been many more since that time.

4. Beginning February 3, 1976.

5. The "staff" in this case consisted of Harr and the Population Council resident in South Korea, Peter Donaldson.

6. Dr. Lee won the Magsaysay Award in 1975. She had been denied her passport several times by Korean officials, but was given it in order to go to Manila to receive the award. Her husband, Y. H. Chung, was a prominent member of the opposition to President Park in the South Korean parliament. On several occasions in the years after JDR's visit, Dr. Lee and her husband were subject to house arrest.

7. Interview with Porter McKeever, April 28, 1983. Also see McKeever's extensive memoranda to the files on events during the 1976 trip to Malaysia and Indonesia. As in Korea, delegations of grantees kept turning up to see JDR, and the insights that these networks of bright, able, committed people could provide into the situation in their country were invaluble.

8. On the development of JDR's support for the Committee, see the following letters and memoranda in the RAC: James Hyde to RBF Files, November 4, 1966 (in which Hyde cites the "newspaper gossip" about Reagan removing Scalapino); Hyde to Lamontagne, November 17, 1966; Lamontagne to JDR, January 18, 1967; JDR to Scalapino, February 24, 1967; Scalapino to JDR, March 7, 1967; Datus Smith to JDR, October 16, 1969.

9. Prior to 1970, the only substantial grant to ADC other than from JDR or the RBF was a short-term one from the Ford Foundation.

In the early 1950s, Mosher had done some evaluative studies of overseas development efforts for the Ford Foundation and the National Planning Association. Among others he studied Nelson Rockefeller's AIA and IBEC programs in Latin America and the Rockefeller's Foundation's agricultural program. Although he praised the latter as one of the best overseas programs in existence, he also offered some criticism. He believed that George Harrar and Warren Weaver held this against him.

10. Mosher to JDR, September 25, 1969. The options Mosher offered to JDR ranged from doing nothing more to providing a $5 million endowment.

11. JDR to Mosher, February 2, 1970.

12. The special committee was composed of Vernon Ruttan, J. Norman Efferson, Clif Wharton, and Don McLean. At the time the committee met, Wharton and McLean were not board members of the ADC.

13. A measure of the impact of the recession on nonprofit organizations was that JDR and Mosher were counting on both the income and capital growth of the reserve fund to help cover current expenses, but neither was possible.

14. Mosher to JDR, May 31, 1973, RAC.

15. Interview with Arthur Mosher, March 31, 1983.

16. Edwin D. Reischauer, *Japan Society 1907–1982: 75 Years of Partnership Across the Pacific* (New York: Japan Society, 1982), p. 85.

17. Interview with Isaac Shapiro, July 7, 1984.

18. A more detailed account can be found in Reischauer's history of the Society, op. cit.

19. It was the Fieldwood Farm luncheon that stimulated a return invitation from the royal couple to the Rockefellers to dine at the Imperial Palace in January 1976.

20. Information in this section is drawn from a series of interviews in 1982 and 1983 with Datus Smith, Porter McKeever, and Phillips Talbot, as well as the files on the Asia Society at the RAC.

21. *Negotiating with the Chinese Communists: The United States Experience, 1953–67*, Council on Foreign Relations book published by McGraw–Hill, New York, 1968.

22. David Halberstram, *The Best and the Brightest* (New York: Random House, 1969), p. 130–31.

23. Collier and Horowitz (1976), pp. 370–71. As their sole source, the authors cite one Joe Fischer, "an Indonesion expert who had once convinced JDR 3 to help restore the Burmese temple of Pagan." JDR did not become involved with Pagan. The Collier and Horowitz picture of a "smoldering rebellion" caused by SEADAG within the Asia Society that forced the replacement of Ken Young and forced SEADAG to move "its headquarters out of Asia House" is erroneous. Young was replaced for other reasons. SEADAG was continued by his successor until the program was terminated by AID. SEADAG and other Asia Society programs were located in outside quarters for the simple reason that there was not enough room in Asia House.

24. For a candid and more balance appraisal of SEADAG, see: "Evaluation of SEADAG by the Asia Society, New York, 1970–72," report of an ad hoc committee chaired by Frank H. Golay, which can be found in the RAC. The report cites a number of reasons for the turnover in SEADAG's academic network, one of which was a form of generalized protest over the Vietnam War.

25. For the thinking of JDR and Talbot during this period and the exchange of views between them, see the following memoranda and letters in the RAC: Talbot to JDR, August 14, 1969; JDR to Dana Creel of the RBF, August 19, 1969; Talbot to JDR, September 26, 1969; JDR to Creel, September 29, 1969; Creel Notes for Conversation with JDR, October 1, 1969.

26. *New York Times*, September 25, 1985.

27. On the origins of the Trilateral Commission, see Moscow, *The Rockefeller Inheritance* (Garden City: Doubleday & Company, Inc., 1977), p. 265.

CHAPTER 28

1. This ended his days of walking to and from work. JDR's pride did not prevent him from using wheelchairs to travel long distances in airport terminals. A good example of the new limitations he was experiencing occurred during his visit to the Korean National Museum in Seoul in January 1976. Because it was a Sunday, the elevators were not working. The director of the museum had arranged for tea in his second-floor office for his distinguished guest and his two companions, Jack and Nancy Harr. The only way to get there was up an immense flight of marble stairs. JDR took one look and decided not to attempt to negotiate it. So he waited patiently on the main floor chatting with a young curator while the Harrs went upstairs for the obligatory social function of having tea with the director.

2. The name of the organization later was changed to "Concern for Dying, Inc.," getting away from the emotion-charged word "euthanasia."

3. See Chapter 30 and the Epilogue for the story of the Pocantico estate.

4. Interview with Sherman Lee, September 8, 1982.

5. *Newsweek*, February 18, 1974, p. 60.

6. See, for example, *Newsweek* of September 18, the *New York Times* and *Washington Post* of September 8, and the *London Times* of February 26, 1974.

7. The very first estimate, made in late 1973, was for a total cost of $9 million.

8. JDR to George Ball, January 15, 1975, RAC.

9. McKeever memorandum to JDR, February 14, 1977, RAC.

10. See Epilogue for a brief summary of this story.

11. Richardson to JDR, May 25, 1977.

12. In his foreword to the catalogue, which was published by the Fine Arts Museums of San Francisco.

13. Newman to JDR, March 22, 1977.

14. JDR to Newman, January 16, 1978.

15. See Epilogue for an account of the effect of JDR's gift of his American collection to the San Francisco museums.

CHAPTER 29

1. Published by Holt, Rinehart and Winston. For background information on Collier and Horowitz and their move from radical leftist leanings to the new right, see the next chapter.

2. *The Kennedys: An American Drama* (New York: Summit Books, 1984.)

3. Persico (1982), p. 299.

4. October 1982.

5. Persico (1982), pp. 159–61.

6. Supra, Ch. 22.

7. The brothers, of course, owned Kykuit, but subject to the life tenancy of Junior and Martha. After Junior's death the brothers met in Kykuit to divide up some of the furnishings and art objects, although enough was left to keep the place well-furnished.

8. For full information on the funding of the Center, see its "Five-Year Report, 1974–79," RAC.

9. *New York Times*, November 18, 1986.

CHAPTER 30

1. For the history of Rockefeller Center, see Harr and Johnson (1988), Chs. 16 and 27.

2. The stock issue and purchase took place on August 21, 1975. The stock could be converted to common stock at any time and paid a fixed dividend (in response to the desire of some family members to begin receiving income from RCI). And in the event of liquidation

of RCI, holders of the preferred stock would be entitled to payment of $100 a share plus accumulated dividends before any other security would be honored.

3. For a more complete description of the Pocantico estate, see Harr and Johnson (1988), pp. 524–29.

4. For the story of the creation of Sleepy Hollow Restorations, Inc., see Harr and Johnson (1988), p. 476–77.

5. For a full description of the National Park Service/Sleepy Hollow plan, see O'Brien's memorandum to the four brothers, 9/29/77, and an O'Brien/Goldstone summary to the brothers, 5/10/78, Room 5600 Files.

6. The discussion of the Pocantico estate issue is based in part on the voluminous documentary record of the various plans and memoranda covering a fifteen-year period, Room 5600 Files. For a report on what eventually happened to the estate, see the Epilogue.

CHAPTER 31

1. Harr and Johnson (1988), p. 301.

2. Kathleen Teltsch, "The Cousins: The Fourth Generation of Rockefellers," *New York Times Magazine*, December 12, 1984, p. 16.

3. Harr and Johnson (1988), pp. 522–23.

4. The first attempt to plot a course had been made in the 1960s in a study by Devereaux Josephs, former chairman of New York Life, friend of the brothers, and chairman of the 1934 Trusts committee. The second attempt, in the 1970s, was made by Harper Woodward, a senior financial adviser to the family. There were good ideas in both studies, but no plan could capture the evolution of the brothers/Cousins relationship.

5. Interview with Blanchette Rockefeller. David's youthful hobby of collecting and studying beetles had been pursued with such characteristic meticulousness that he was a genuine expert on the subject.

6. The salience of David Jr. among the Cousins is attested to by the fact that his is the cover picture in the case of two major articles on his generation, the one in the December 12, 1984, *New York Times Sunday Magazine* and the second in the August 4, 1988, edition of *Fortune* ("The Rockefellers: End of a Dynasty?," by Carol J. Loomis).

7. Persico (1982), pp. 207–208.

8. Ibid., p. 257.

9. Ibid., pp. 253–54.

10. See in particular the testimony of two Berkeley professors, G. William Domhoff and Charles L. Schwartz, on December 2, 1974, in U.S., House of Representatives, "Nomination of Nelson A. Rockefeller to Be Vice President of the United States," Hearings before the Committee of the Judiciary, 93rd Cong., 2nd Sess.

11. Persico (1988), p. 272.

12. Interviews with Joseph Ernst and George Taylor.

13. The negative review, which looks very good in retrospect, did not weigh much at the time because it was written by a friend of David Rockefeller, George Gilder (*Bookletter*, March 1, 1976). The brothers and the staff possibly were lulled into complacency by the thought that Alvin Moscow was producing the definitive book on the Rockefeller family. Moscow, an established author with a reputation for objectivity, had been working on his book for years (*The Rockefeller Inheritance*, published by Doubleday in 1977), but it was upstaged by the 1976 Collier and Horowitz book.

14. Other factors were that substantial portions of the records had not been processed and consequently were not open to anyone at the time Collier did his research, and possibly some haste to make sure that the Collier and Horowitz book appeared before the Moscow book. The success of the former so doomed the latter to obscurity that Moscow and his publisher allowed the book to appear without any footnotes or research references.

15. The quotations in this chapter from the Collier and Horowitz book are taken from

the Epilogue, pp. 622–26. Of special note is the fact that in the years since their book was published, Collier and Horowitz have flip-flopped politically from *Ramparts* to voting for Ronald Reagan, following the same curious path to neoconservatism taken by other former leftists such as Irving Kristol and Norman Podhoretz. This time, their book on the transformation, *Destructive Generation: Second Thoughts about the '60s* (Summit Books, 1989), was burned by the critics. In the *New York Times* (June 1, 1989), Christopher Lehmann-Haupt writes: "A reader can't help sensing that in their angry shift to the right the authors are simply indulging the same form of temper tantrums that once led them to be leftists." In a Sunday *New York Times Magazine* article, "Radical Transformations," by Sharon Churcher (July 16, 1989), the following curious passage about the early collaboration of Collier and Horowitz appears: "The two began writing what they thought would be a critical Marxist study of the Rockefellers. But once into the project, Collier and Horowitz found their research contradicting many of their assumptions about capitalists. For the first time, they say, they began to see people not as a function of their economic class, but as individuals."

CHAPTER 32

1. For a more detailed description of the origins and early operations of the RBF, see Harr and Johnson (1988), pp. 392–93 and 536–39.

2. "The Rockefeller Brothers Fund—An Overview," an eleven-page undated and unpublished document, but from internal evidence probably written by an RBF staff member for Nelson Rockefeller in 1971, RAC.

3. Nielsen (1972), pp. 350–51.

4. Minor organizations that fell between "22 +" and 25 were the Rehearsal Club of New York and Greenacre Park, a Manhattan "vest-pocket" park that Babs had created. Sleepy Hollow Restorations, Inc., was in a "gray" area and was being considered separately for an "arm's length" role in future public use of the Pocantico estate.

5. For Laurance and David, the operative words were "one-half." The $75 million figure was advanced when the endowment was about $150 million and it moved up to the $100 million level when the endowment grew to $200 million. For JDR, the operative words were "up to"—he hoped the total would be much less than one-half.

6. On Creel, see Chairman Laurance Rockefeller's statement in the RBF 1975 annual report, entitled "A Tribute to a Master Craftsman in American Philanthropy."

7. Persico (1982), p. 283.

8. In quotes from JDR's diary the italics shown are in the original.

9. With the exception of Persico, these views were expressed in interviews with the persons named.

10. The quotations and opinions in this section were taken from interviews with many of the participants, from JDR's diary, and from documents in his files. Nelson Rockefeller's papers are not yet available to scholars. The documents include a seven-page memo entitled "Outstanding Items for Consideration by the Brothers," JDR to Nelson, Laurance, and David, April 29, 1977; JDR to Nelson, August 30, 1977; JDR to Nelson, October 4, 1977 (with three pages of comments attached on Nelson's memo to JDR of August 11); and JDR to Laurance and Dietel, October 21, 1977 (with JDR's editing of RBF minutes attached). In several of these papers JDR quotes from Nelson's letters and memos.

11. For the evolution of Junior's very strong position against family influence on the Rockefeller Foundation, see Harr and Johnson (1988), pp. 144–49 and 364–67; for the story of how JDR learned this lesson the hard way, but learned it well and applied it, see pp. 435–43 and 552–55.

12. Even though he was Nelson's nominee, Parsons was no more biased than John Lockwood had been when Nelson brought him in as family counsel following their work together in World War II. When Dietel told JDR that Parsons was "okay," he expressed his regret that Parsons would be leaving soon to go into private practice.

13. Persico (1982), p. 192.

14. JDR was not happy to hear that the study would be done by Lindsley Kimball, a consultant to the RBF who had retired as a Rockefeller Foundation vice president nearly twenty-five years earlier. He had been one of the "old guard" at the Foundation who opposed JDR. Kimball's report, turned in at a special RBF meeting called by Laurance to consider the osteopathy request, said that osteopathy was an entirely legitimate branch of medicine, but that Riland's college was not yet ready to receive major grants. He proposed a small grant to help the college organize its fund-raising activities. There were a number of negative comments, but the board finally accepted Kimball's compromise.

15. Gardner, like JDR, was trying to divest himself of all his commitments so that he could devote his time to study, writing, and speaking, and to his single remaining organizational goal—to help bring into being an organization devoted to the welfare of the "independent sector."

16. JDR kept raising the issue of the chairmanship with Nelson, Laurance, and David. By this time, his reason did not seem to be so much that Laurance was his opponent, but that he had been chairman far too long and that the post should rotate more, including to nonfamily trustees or Cousins. At one point David suggested Nancy Hanks to his brothers, but no action was taken. Finally, Laurance told JDR that he would be happy to yield the reins to David, but that could not happen until David retired as chairman of the Chase Manhattan Bank (in 1981), for reasons both of time pressure on David and possible conflict of interest. JDR still thought that being chairman would take no more time than David was already putting in and that there would be no conflict of interest.

INDEX

Abortion rights, 401–3, 415, 416–19, 422, 427
Abramovitz, Max, 136, 154
Abreu, Belen, 115–16, 117, 119
Across the Board (magazine), 390
Action for Appalachian Youth, 241
Adams, Charles F., 364
Adams, Sherman, 67
"Adams Chronicles, The" (miniseries), 364
Advisory Committee on Benevolences, 91
Aetna Life & Casualty Company, 377
Agency for International Development (AID), 159, 170–71, 450, 458–59
Agnew, Spiro T., 348, 415–16, 508
Agricultural Development Council (ADC), 75, 259, 448–52, 468, 485, 545, 566
Ahmanson, Robert, 546
Aid to China Program, 65
Alcoa Foundation, 479
Aldrich, Abby, 8–9
     See also Rockefeller, Abby Aldrich
Aldrich, Nelson, 8–9
Aldrich, Winthrop, 19
Allahabad University (India), 74
Allen, Arthur M., 18
Allen, Charles E., 452
Allen, Martha Baird, 18–19
Allen, Vivian Beaumont, 132, 147
Allen, Yorke, 41
American Ballet Theater, 130
American Civil Liberties Union (ACLU), 403
American Conservation Association, 272
American Federation of Labor–Congress of Industrial Organizations (AFL-CIO), 295

American International Association for Economic and Social Development (AIA), 20–21, 282
American Issues Forum, 360
American-Korean Foundation, 90
American Law Institute, 403
American National Theater and Academy (ANTA), 132
American Red Cross, 15, 48, 133
American Revolution Bicentennial Administration (ARBA), 351, 360, 361, 362–63
American Revolution Bicentennial Commission (ARBC), 347–51, 360
American Symphony Orchestra League, 157
American Universities Field Staff, 73, 112, 256
American Youth Hostels, 307
Americas Society, 217
Ames, Amyas, 157
Amherst College, 322
Ammidon, Hoyt, 157
Andrews, T. Coleman, 95
Apollo Oil Company, 83
Argyris, Chris, 280–81
Arkansas Industrial Development Commission, 218
Armstrong, Anne, 353
Armstrong, Rodney, 453
Arts in Education program, 262, 265–66
Ashmore, Harry, 219
Asia Foundation, 91, 98–100, 102
Asia House Gallery, 102, 461, 469–76
Asian Cultural Council, 562–63
Asia Society, 101–3, 153, 214, 259, 275, 300, 328, 456–62, 468, 469–77, 544, 564–65
Aso, Takakichi, 443

605

Association for the Study of Abortion (ASA), 402–3
Avalon Corporation, 161
Avery Fisher Hall, 154
  See also Lincoln Center for the Performing Arts; Philharmonic Hall

Bahrain, 78
Bailey, Stephen K., 58
Balanchine, George, 126
Balfour, Marshall, 32–33, 34, 36
Balfour Report, 32
Ball, George, 472, 473
Bandung Conference, 79, 429
Banks, Maurice, 423
Barnard, Chester, 180, 185, 190, 207
Barnes, Edward Larrabee, 473, 475–76
Barnett, A. Doak, 447
Barnett, Robert, 462
Barney, Gerald, 426, 428–29, 430, 435
Baroni, Gino, 356
Barr, Joseph, 293
Barrett, Richard W., 312–13, 316, 317, 320–21, 323, 331, 348, 351, 352, 359, 361, 410–12
Bartley, Anne, 219
Bartley, Bruce, 219
Baum, Morton, 126, 127, 129, 130, 141, 144, 145–46
Baumol, William, 263
Bates, Robert, 33, 34, 36, 38
Beame, Abe, 456
Bell, David E., 55, 171, 182, 399, 406, 412, 414
Bell & Howell, 295
Belluschi, Pietro, 136, 154
Bentley, Elizabeth, 92
Berelson, Bernard (Barney), 162–63, 166, 167, 168, 171, 177, 403, 404, 412, 414, 422–24, 425, 428–30, 434–40
Berman, Ronald, 363
Bernstein, Leonard, 231
Bernstein, Robert, 391, 392
Best and the Brightest, The (Halberstam), 102
Bicentennial Council of the American Revolution
  history of plans for public celebration, 347–51
  JDR 3rd's involvement with, 346–47, 351–65
Bicentennial Council of the Thirteen Original States, 349
Bierstadt, Albert, 255
Big Foundations, The (Nielsen), 92, 182–84, 195, 292, 390, 523
Bilderberg Meeting, 217

Bing, Rudolph, 120, 124, 143, 146
Bingham, Barry, 188
Birth control. See Population Council
Birth control pill, 162
Black, Eugene, 161
Black P Stone Nation, 327
Blatnik, John, 412
Bleiman, Jay, 370, 371–72
Bliss, Anthony, 125, 134, 144
Bloom, Kathryn, 266, 276, 280
Blum, Robert, 98–99, 123
Blumenthal, Peggy, 325, 331
Blumenthal, W. Michael, 387
Bogolepov, Igor, 92
Bohlen, Charles, 368
Bok, Sissela, 439
Bolton, Howard, 272, 293, 376
Bonham, Robert T., 337–40
Boorstin, Daniel, 384
Borlaug, Norman, 190, 398
Borton, Hugh, 88
Boston Globe (newspaper), 324
Boudreau, Frank G., 43
Bourguiba, Habib, 164, 172, 277
Bowen, William, 263, 370
Bowles, Chester, 64, 71, 90, 99, 188
Boxer, Evelyn, 336
Boxer, Jerome, 336
Bozorth, Squire, 544
Brady, Nyle C., 451
Brearly School, 236, 237, 245, 247
Brewster, Kingman, 356, 377, 384–85
British-American Petroleum Company (BAPCO), 78
Bronk, Detlev, 33, 35, 39, 159, 214, 439
Brown, R. Manning, 545
Brown University, 6
Brundage, Avery, 252
Buck, J. Lossing, 73–74, 282
Buck, Pearl, 73
Buckley School, 247
Budenz, Louis, 92
Bullitt, William C., 47
Bumpers, Dale, 220
Bunche, Ralph, 54, 187–88
Bundy, McGeorge, 53, 168, 182, 296
Bunker, Dennis M., 255
Bunker, Ellsworth, 161
Bunshaft, Gordon, 136
Bunting, Mary I. (Polly), 423, 434, 437
Burchfield, Charles, 255
Burdick, Edward, 273
Bureau of Municipal Research (BMR), 47
Bureau of Social Hygiene, 24
Bureau of the Budget, 48, 58
Burma, 64, 71, 448
Burns, Arthur, 203

Bush, George, 406
Business Committee for the Arts, 217
Byrd, Robert, 510

Calderone, Mary, 320
Califano, Joseph A., Jr., 177
Cambodia, 99
Canfield, Cass, 159
Cannon, James, 512, 513
Caradon, Lord, 174, 176, 307, 400, 424
Carnegie, Andrew, 6, 289
Carnegie Corporation, 161, 181–83, 295, 378, 392, 447
Carnegie Endowment for International Peace, 93
Carnegie Hall, 121, 138
Carnegie Institute, 43
Carney, James A., 308, 319
Carroll, R. Lynn, 348
Carson, Rachel, 397
Carter, Jimmy, 303, 344, 386–87
Carter administration, 342, 343–44, 386–89
Case, Clifford, 94
Case, Laura Rockefeller, 214
Cater, S. Douglass, Jr., 171, 173, 177, 260
Catholic Charities, 39
Caute, David, 91–92
Ceaușescu, Nicolae, 431
Cellar, Emmanuel, 93
Center for Inter-American Relations, 217
Center for the Development of Cooperatives (CENDEVCO), 336
    See also Urban Home Ownership Corporation
Central Intelligence Agency (CIA), 96–100, 186, 292, 293
Central Presbyterian Church (New York City), 473–74
Century Association, 282
Ceylon, 63
Champion, George, 216
Chandler, Marilyn, 414
Chapman, Gilbert W., 132
Chase, Mary Ellen, 238
Chase Manhattan Bank, 19, 116, 216–17, 340
Chevalier, Maurice, 243
Chiang Mon-Lin, 116
China, 24, 62, 63, 64–65, 68, 447–48
China Institute, 90
Chorley, Kenneth, 26
Chou En-lai, 79
Chowdhury, Amithaba, 116

Christ-Janner, Albert, 125
Chrysler Corporation, 148
Church, Frederick, 253, 254
Citibank, 216
Citizen Involvement Network, 361
Citizens Advisory Committee on Environmental Quality, 215
Citizens Advisory Committee on Recreation and Natural Beauty, 215
Citizens Commission on Population Growth and the American Future, 419–20, 422
Citizens Union, 334–35
City and Suburban Homes Company, 334
City Center for Music and Drama, 123, 125, 126–28, 129–30, 139–41, 143–45
    See also Lincoln Center
City Housing Corporation, 335
Civil Service Commission, 58, 60
Clark, Joseph C., 58
Clark, Tom, 93
Clausen, A. W., 326, 352
Claxton, Philander P., Jr., 174, 175, 428
Cleveland Museum of Art, 251, 252, 253
Coale, Ansley J., 412
Coalition of National Voluntary Organizations, 391
Coggeshall, Lowell, 188
Cohen, Jerome, 63, 66
Cohen, Wilbur, 170, 174, 178, 397
Cold War, 72, 99, 158, 203, 304
Cole, Charles Woolsey, 88
Cole, Kenneth, 353
Cole, Thomas, 255
Collier, Peter, 459, 483, 514–18
Colombia, 173
Colonial Williamsburg, 12, 18, 23–24, 25–26, 32, 33, 105, 205, 207, 234–35
    Bassett Hall, 280–81
Colson, Charles, 411
Columbia Broadcasting Company (CBS), 321, 322
Columbia University, 16, 64, 87, 106, 162, 306, 307, 308, 320, 491, 492
Commager, Henry Steele, 384
Commission on Critical Choices for America, 354, 507–8
Commission on Population Growth and the American Future, 395–96, 422
    and abortion rights, 401–3, 415–19
    appointment process, 405–12
    report, 414–20

Commission on the Role of a Modern State in a Changing World, 353
Committee for a Free Asia, 98
See also Asia Foundation
Committee for the Third Sector, 391
Commoner, Barry, 398
Commonwealth Fund, 161
Communist Party, French, 55
Compton, Karl W., 34, 39, 54, 56
Conant, James B., 43, 50
Concord Academy, 245, 247
Conference Board, 389, 390
Conference on Population Problems, 33–37
Connally, John, 367, 376
Conservation Foundation, 34, 40
Cooke, Terence (Cardinal), 403, 418–19
Cook-Lichter bill (New York State), 403
Cooney, Joan Ganz, 356, 426
Cooper, Sherman, 409
Copley, John Singleton, 255
Costanza, Gesualdo, 461, 476
Council of the Americas, 217
Council on Economic and Cultural Affairs (CECA), 72–75, 88, 104, 256–58, 449
See also Agricultural Development Council
Council on Foreign Relations, 76, 87, 102, 105, 106–7, 120, 217, 304
Cousins, Norman, 87
Cox, Archibald, 359
Cox, E. Eugene, 93–94
Cranston, Alan, 412
Creel, Dana, 34, 36, 38, 113, 114, 122, 125, 126, 214, 261–63, 272, 273, 274, 293, 520–25
"Creel Committee," 525–29, 540–41
Crisp, Peter O., 272
Cronkite, Walter, 356, 360
Crotona Park East, 338

Dalrymple, Martha, 34, 36, 38, 63, 91, 114, 273
Damrosch Park, 131
Dartmouth Conference, 217
David, Stephen, 273
Davis, Kingsley, 407
Day & Zimmerman, 134
Dayton, Bruce, 325, 376, 391
Dayton, Kenneth, 391
Dayton, Mark, 391
Dean, Arthur, 96
Debevoise, Thomas, 272
De Forest, Robert, 335
de Gaulle, Charles, 150
Demeny, Paul, 435, 436, 437, 441

Democracy in America (Tocqueville), 333
Democratic Party, 241, 244, 303–4
de Murville, Couve, 150
Desai, Morarji R., 78, 544–45
Deshmukh, C. D., 108–11, 116
Dewey, Thomas, 204
de Young Memorial Museum, 477–79, 563
d'Harnoncourt, Rene, 136, 257–58
Diamond, Henry, 511
Dickey, John, 187, 203
Dies, Martin, 92
Dietel, William M., 272, 522, 545
Dillon, C. Douglas, 187, 188, 293, 295, 298, 377, 378, 387, 406
Dilworth, J. Richardson, 272, 273, 293, 376, 469, 475, 493, 512
Dobrynin, Anatoly F., 175–76
Dodds, Harold W., 49–51, 52, 53–55, 57–58, 60
Dodge, Joseph, 62–63
Dodgers, Brooklyn, 202
Donovan, Hedley, 361
Douglas, Howard, 272
Douglas, William O., 296–97
Douglass, Robert, 512
Downs, Hugh, 422
Draper, William H., 44–45, 159, 167, 416, 428
Draper Report, 167
Drye, John W., 131
Dryfoos, Orvil, 188
d'Seynes, Philippe, 173, 424
Du Bois, W. E. B., 335
DuBridge, Lee, 188, 405
Duke, Doris, 151
Dulles, Allen, 99, 113, 186
Dulles, John Foster, 4, 21, 26, 27, 53, 56, 72, 77, 80, 99, 105, 107, 304
Dunbar, Paul Laurence, 335
Dungan, Ralph, 58
Dunlop, Joan, 423, 424–26, 428–30, 434–39, 544

East Kentucky Health Services Center, 327
Ebert, Dean, 441
Edna McConnell Clark Foundation, 339
Edris, Jeanette, 218–19, 220–21, 243
Efferson, J. Norman, 69, 71–72
Egeberg, Roger, 405
Egypt, 165, 172
Ehrlich, Paul, 398, 407–8
Ehrlichman, John, 411, 415, 417–18
Eisenhower, Dwight D., 20, 21, 27, 45, 57, 60, 80, 137, 166–67, 202, 215, 301

Eizenstat, Stuart, 387–89
Elliman, Lawrence, 125
Elliot, Lloyd, 96
Ellsworth, Harris, 60
Embarcadero Center (San Francisco), 217
English Language Education Council (ELEC), 88–89
Ensminger, Douglas, 108
Environmental movement, 397–98
Epstein, T. Scarlett, 451
Equal Rights Amendment, 414
Erlenborn, John, 412, 413
Ernst, Joseph, 488, 514, 515, 544
Esso (Standard Oil of New Jersey), 16
European Recovery Program, 65
Euthanasia, 465–67, 544
Euthanasia Education Council, 466–67
Exeter, see Phillips Exeter Academy
Experiment in International Living, 236
Eyrie, the (Seal Harbor, Maine), 8, 233–34

Fahs, Burton, 113, 122
Falk, Richard, 398
Family Planning Services and Population Research bill, 419
Famine—1975! (Paddock and Paddock), 398
Far Eastern Association, 96
Faubus, Orval, 218, 219–20
Federation of Jewish Philanthropies, 293, 294
Feinstein, Diane, 481
Fernald, David, 272
Fidelity Union Trusts, 16, 247
Field, Frederick Vanderbilt, 93
Fieldwood Farm, 37, 77, 206
Filer, John H., 377–81, 390
Filer Commission on Private Philanthropy and Public Needs, 377–83
Finch, Robert, 297, 405
Fine Arts Museums of San Francisco, 480–81
Finland, 172
Fisher, Avery, 154
Five Colleges, Inc., 322–24
Fleeson, Doris, 218
Flores, Antonio Carillo, 424
Food and Agriculture Organization (FAO), 165, 167
Foote, Hugh, 174
Ford, Gerald R., 297, 303, 361, 362, 369–70, 373, 387, 455, 508–9, 513
Ford, Henry, II, 94, 148

Ford administration, 361–62
Ford Foundation, 41–42, 52, 68, 69, 74, 78, 88, 93, 94, 130, 134, 146–47, 148, 161, 164, 181–83, 186, 293, 295, 296, 311, 338, 377, 391, 392, 447, 450, 461
Fordham University, 133
Ford Motor Company, 148
Foreign Affairs (journal), 47
Foreign Assistance Act of 1967, 174
Foreign Operations Administration (FOA), 21
Foreign Policy Association, 76
Foreign Service Act of 1946, 48
Foreign Service Institute, 48, 53
Fortas, Abe, 296–97
Fortune (magazine), 321, 322
Fosdick, Harry Emerson, 39, 474
Fosdick, Raymond B., 25, 180, 185, 189, 205
Foundation Luncheon Group, 326
Fowler, Henry, 293
Francis, Clarence, 133, 134, 146, 150
Franks, Lord, 173, 188
Freer Galery of Art, 252–53
Frei, Eduardo, 173
Friday, William, 356, 362, 387
Fulbright, William, 168
Fund for the Republic, 94–95

Gagnon, John, 427
Gaither, Rowan, 41–42, 94, 182, 183
Galbraith, John Kenneth, 231
Gamble, Clarence, 159
Gandhi, Indira, 108, 172, 304
Garcia, Carlos P., 114, 115
Gardner, John, 168, 170, 175, 182, 203, 231, 293, 334, 368–69, 371, 377, 383, 391
Gardner, Richard, 399, 406
Garment, Leonard, 353, 354
Garner, John Nance, 513
Gates, Rev. Frederick T., 6, 502
General Education Board (GEB), 6, 64
General Motors, 148
Georgetown University, 169
Germain, Adrienne, 426, 428–29, 430, 434–35
Getty, J. Paul, 152–53, 290
Gibbs, Richard, 359
Gilpatric, Chadbourne, 110
Giscard d'Estaing, Valéry, 150
Giving in America: Toward a Stronger Voluntary Sector (Filer Commission Report), 381–82
Gladstone, Harmon, 500
Glen Alden Corporation, 338
Goheen, Robert F., 58, 368, 376
Goldberg, Arthur, 212

Goldwater, Barry, 212
Goodell, Charles, 244
Gordon, Kermit, 316
Goulandris, Nicholas, 151
Gould, Samuel B., 260, 263, 266
Government Employees Training Act,
    60–61, 207, 366
Governor Winthrop Rockefeller Dis-
    tinguished Lecture Series (Uni-
    versity of Arkansas), 487
Graham, Katherine, 361
Graham, Lanier, 479
Graham, Lloyd, 83
Graham, Philip, 54
Great Depression, 11, 12
*Great Fear: The Anti-Communist
    Purge Under Truman and
    Eisenhower, The* (Caute), 91–92
Greene, George H., 98
Greene, Wade, 380–81, 430
Gregg, Alan, 185, 189
Gross, Ernest A., 101
Gruening, Ernest, 168
"Guerilla Players" (University of Mas-
    sachusetts), 323–24
Guettinger, Roger, 325
Guggenheim Fellowships, 46
Guitar Player, The (Bunker), 255
Gunther, John, 167, 231
Guttmacher, Alan F., 162

Haas, Walter, 356, 376, 378
Haft, Steven, 325, 331
Hair (musical), 308, 334
Hajnal, John, 33, 34
Halberstam, David, 102, 330, 458
Haldeman, Robert, 411
Haley, Alex, 279
Hall, Robert, 403
Hamilton, George, 243
Hammarskjold, Dag, 128
Hampshire College (Amherst, Mass.),
    322–23
Hanks, Nancy, 203, 261–63, 265,
    266–67, 520
Hannah, John, 399
Hardin, Clifford, 188
Harmon, Willis, 316
Harper & Row, 313
Harper's (magazine), 81
Harr, John E., 275, 307–8, 312, 316–
    17, 321, 351, 352–53, 354, 360,
    387, 388, 391, 392, 465–67, 544,
    546–47
Harrar, J. George, 68, 69, 71, 189–97
Harriman, W. Averell, 21, 204
Harris, Ladonna, 356
Harris, Patricia, 342, 343–45, 406,
    544

Harrison, Wallace K., 121, 122, 123,
    124, 133, 134, 136, 154, 188,
    214, 257–58
Hartford, Huntington, 151
Harvard University, 49, 50, 51, 52–53,
    48, 49, 85, 86, 247, 426
Haskins, Caryl P., 43
Hassam, Childe, 255
Hays, Wayne, 95
Heald, Henry T., 125, 182
Health and Welfare Council, 39
Health Council (New York City), 39
Heath, Ron, 325, 331
Heckscher, August, 262–63
Hellman, Geoffrey T., 327–31
Hellman, Louis, 403
Henry Street Settlement, 335
Henshaw, Paul, 34
Herod, W. R., 100
Hesburgh, Theodore, 169, 188, 203,
    356, 362
Hess, Stephen, 426
Hicks, Edward, 255, 273
High Winds Foundation, 460
Hillcrest, 489, 490, 496
Hills Realty, 495, 498
Hilsman, Roger, 240
Hinman, George, 204
Hirohito (emperor of Japan), 443, 454–
    55
Hirsch, Eloise, 325, 331
Hirsch, Stephen, 426
Hiss, Alger, 93
History of the Standard Oil Company
    (Tarbell), 483
Hobby, Oveta Culp, 21
Hodgson, James, 454
Hoffman, Paul G., 93, 94, 99, 182,
    400
Holland, Kenneth, 96
Homans, Mary, 477–78
Homer, Winslow, 255
Hooker, Blanchette Ferry, 22
    See also Rockefeller, Blanchette
Hoover Commission, 48, 60
Hopper, David, 436–38
Hopper, Edward, 255, 273
Horowitz, David, 459, 483, 514–18
Houghton, Arthur A., Jr., 121, 122,
    188
Housing, urban, 334–45
Hovendon, Thomas, 255
Hubbard, Muriel McCormick, 148
Hughes, Emmett, 272–73
Huk rebellion, 67
Humanae Vitae (Pope Paul VI), 170
Humelsine, Carlisle, 348, 500
Humphrey, Hubert H., 171, 177, 367
Hunt, William Morris, 255

Hutar, Patricia, 428
Hutchins, Robert Maynard, 93, 94–95
Huxley, Julian, 31–32, 66, 398
Hyde, James, 447

Ichimada, Hisato, 83
Idemitsu, Sazo, 83
Imperial Rockefeller, The (Persico), 316
India, 64–65, 67–68, 71, 90, 165, 172
India International Centre, 108–11
Indonesia, 64, 71, 78, 79, 80–81, 90, 448
Ingersoll, Robert, 454
Institute for Advanced Study (Princeton), 48
Institute for Pacific Relations (IPR), 66–67, 91, 93–94, 95, 96, 98, 101, 102
Institute of Current World Affairs (ICWA), 238
International Basic Economy Corporation (IBEC), 21, 335, 452
International Christian University (Tokyo), 85–86, 247
International Development Advisory Board, 21
International Development Research Centre (of Canada), 450
International Executive Service Corps, 217
International Houses, 106–7, 307
International House of Tokyo, 26, 67, 87, 106, 107, 186, 443–44
International Monetary Fund, 218
International Review Group of Social Science Research on Population and Development (CELADE), 428
International Rice Research Institute, 74, 117, 186
International Union for the Scientific Study of Population, 44
International Youth Population Conference, 428
Interstate North (Atlanta), 217
Intrauterine device (IUD), 162, 164, 165

Jackson, C. D., 21, 121–22, 123
Jackson, Elmore, 399
Jackson, Jesse, 413
Jackson Hole Preserve, 214
Jamieson, Frank, 36, 38, 68, 91, 99, 204, 272, 274
Japan, 62–64, 87–89, 104–5
Japanese Land Reform Law of 1946, 64
Japan House, 452, 454–55

Japan Society, 3–4, 26, 77, 87, 88, 89, 90, 91, 97, 100, 101, 256, 259, 275, 452–56, 544, 561–62
Javits, Jacob, 93, 363
JDR 3rd Fund, 274, 390, 469
    Arts in Education program, 262, 265–66
    and Asian cultural work, 256–61, 445, 449, 544
    and Bicentennial celebration, 359, 361
    and performing arts, 261–66
    "Youth Task Force," 321–32
John Birch Society, 320
John Muir Institute for Environmental Studies, 407
Johnson, Eastman, 255, 273
Johnson, Lady Bird, 175, 215
Johnson, Lynda Bird, 235, 243
Johnson, Lyndon B., 167–66, 172, 173, 174–75, 176, 177–78, 212, 215, 235, 262, 264, 305, 306, 347–48, 396, 397, 400, 403–4
Johnson, Manning, 92
Johnson, Peter, 364, 391–92, 466, 544
Johnson, Philip, 101, 136, 153–54, 228–29
Johnson, U. Alexis, 368
Johnson administration, 342
Johnston, Paul, 338
John XXIII (Pope), 158, 167
Joint Commission on Rural Reconstruction, 70
Jones, Roger, 48–49, 57, 58, 61, 372
Jonsson, Erik, 352
Jordan, Vernon, 356
Josephs, Devereux C., 123, 133, 155–56, 157, 203, 247, 263
Juilliard Musical Trust, 130–31
Juilliard School of Music, 123, 130–31, 134, 139, 154–55
    See also Lincoln Center for the Performing Arts

Kahn, Ayub, 164
Katz, Stanley, 490
Keidanren, 150–51
Keiser, David, 155
Kennan, George, 47–49, 54, 260
Kennedy, Edward, 447
Kennedy, Jacqueline, 148–49, 231
Kennedy, John F., 58–59, 61, 148–50, 166–67, 188, 212, 215, 262, 305, 310
Kennedy, Joseph P., 133
Kennedy, Robert, 150, 244, 296, 306
Kennedy administration, 188, 158–59, 210, 240
Kennedy Foundation, 149–50

Kenya, 165, 238–39
Kenyatta, Jomo, 165, 238–39
Kerr, Clark, 188, 189, 190
Kettering Foundation, 361
Kimball, Lindsley, 185, 189, 207
King, Martin Luther, Jr., 279, 306, 314
Kintner, Robert, 275
Kirk, Dudley, 43
Kirk, Grayson, 99, 101, 102
Kirkland, Lane, 295
Kirstein, Lincoln, 123, 124, 126–28, 129–30, 140, 143–45, 146, 249
Kishi, Nobusuke, 77
Kissick, Tom, 271
Kissinger, Henry, 203, 511, 513, 520
Kiyosato Educational Experimental Project, 83
Klutznick, Philip, 377
Knisely, Gary, 363
Knowles, John, 362, 544
Kohler, Foy, 368
Korean Development Institute, 446
Korean National Museum, 445
Korean National Theater, 445
Korean War, 62
Kosygin, Aleksei N., 176
Kreps, Juanita, 387, 390, 391
Kuhn, Loeb, 33
Kykuit, 205, 494–95, 500

Ladejinsky, Wolf, 64, 65–66, 67, 69, 72, 76, 114
La Guardia, Fiorello, 12, 126
Lamontagne, Ray, 163, 167, 171–72, 173, 177, 240, 274–75, 277, 280–82, 302, 310, 397, 401, 404, 407, 425, 434, 447
Landry, Lionel, 461
Lane, Fitz Hugh, 253, 254
Lansdale, Edward G., 114
Lapham, Lewis, 81–82
Lasker, Mary, 175
Lasky, Victor, 510–11
Lattimore, Owen, 93–94, 95
Laura Spelman Rockefeller Memorial (LSRM), 193–94
Lazarsfeld, Paul, 162
Lee, Ivy, 5
Lee, Sherman, 224, 231, 251–54, 260, 443, 470, 472–73, 480, 544, 551
Lee, Tai Young, 446
Lefkowitz, Louis, 339
Legion of Honor Museum (San Francisco), 477–78
Lelewer, David, 323, 401–2, 407, 410–12, 414, 416, 417, 419, 422, 423, 425, 434

L'Enfant Plaza (Washington, D.C.), 217
Lesko, Monica, 543
LeVant, Jack I., 350
Levinson, A. J., 466
Lewis, A. B., 74
Lewis, John, 368, 369, 451
Life (magazine), 86, 264
Lilienthal, David, 406
Lilley, Robert, Jr., 325, 329
Lilley, Robert, Sr., 325
Lilly Foundation, 361
Lincoln Center for the Performing Arts, 136–37, 138–39, 214, 468, 562
    architects, 136, 153–54
    artistic program, 154–56
    construction of, 153–54
    Exploratory Committee for, 125, 128–33
    foreign contributors, 150–52
    fund-raising for, 146–53, 328
    JDR's involvement with, 124–25, 128–29, 138, 146–53, 156–57, 249–50, 290, 328
    library for, 132
    need for, 121–23
    Rockefeller Foundation involvement with, 122–124, 186
Lincoln Square Urban Renewal Project, 121
Lindsay, John V., 144–45, 146, 243
Linowitz, Sol, 356
Littauer School, 48, 49, 50, 52–53, 58
Lleras Camargo, Alberto, 173, 400
Lleras Restrepo, Carlos, 173
Lobbies, philanthropic, 294
Lockwood, John, 36, 38, 68, 91, 97, 114, 141, 142, 156, 204, 248, 272, 274, 293, 489
Loeb, Robert F., 187, 188
Logue, Edward, 511
London School of Economics, 12
Long, Russell, 293, 376, 381
Look (magazine), 201, 319, 426
Loomis-Chaffee School, 468
Loomis School, 247
Lourie, Donald, 56
Lovett, Robert, 188
Lowry, W. McNeil, 182
Loy, Myrna, 334
Lubis, Mochtar, 116
Lucas, Patricia, 544
Luce, Henry, 90, 203
Lynch, Thomas, 39
Lynes, Russell, 227–28, 229

Maass, Arthur, 58, 59
MacArthur, Douglas, 66

McCarran, Pat, 92, 94
McCarthy, Eugene, 306
McCarthy, Joseph, 47, 56, 92, 94
McCarthyism, 47, 53, 292, 366, 369
McCloskey, William J., 255
McCloy, John J., 77, 187, 216, 295
McCormack, Elizabeth, 377, 378, 381, 386, 523
McCormick, Edith Rockefeller, 148
McCracken, Robert J., 243
McCray, Porter, 257–61, 266
MacDonald, Malcolm, 78, 238
MacDonald, Ramsay, 78
McEachron, David, 454, 456
MacFadyen, John, 263
McGinley, Lawrence J., 131, 133, 146
McGovern, George, 244
McKeever, Porter, 377, 381, 386, 389–90, 391–92, 399, 400, 430, 432, 446, 448, 470, 473, 476–77, 544
McKelway, Benjamin, 188
McLean, Donald H., Jr., 27, 33, 34, 35–36, 38, 40, 44, 76, 91, 97, 102, 160, 163, 230, 256, 259, 266, 274–75, 280, 303, 392, 434, 439, 451–52, 457, 545
and International Houses, 108, 110, 111
and Japanese economy, 63, 68, 71, 73, 74–75
and Magsaysay awards, 112–13, 115, 117, 119
and Rockefeller Public Service Awards (RPSA), 47–51, 58, 59–61
"Thoughts on the Far East," 90–91
McLean, Joseph, 53–54
McLeod, Scott, 56
McNamara, Robert, 352, 398, 435
McNerney, Walter, 386, 391
McNulty, John W., 163–64, 169, 274–75, 310, 312
MacPherson, Harry, 173
Maffrey, August, 96, 101
Magsaysay, Jesús, 115
Magsaysay, Ramón, 67, 111–12
memorial awards, 112–19, 214
Mahoney, David J., 349–50
Mainichi Shimbun (newspaper), 444
Malaysia, 64
Malcolm X housing project, 343
Mali, Katherine, 466
Malik, Adam, 176
Malkin, Maurice, 92
Malraux, André, 150
Malthus, Thomas Robert, 24
Manhattan School of Music, 131

Mansfield, Mike, 238, 454
Marcinkus, Paul, 169–70
Marcos, Ferdinand, 118, 176
Maremont Foundation, 339
Marsh, John, 362
Marshall, Alton G., 511
Marshall, Burke, 356
Martha Baird Rockefeller Fund for Music, 131
Martin, William McChesney, 245
Maslow, Abraham, 316
Mason, Edward S., 48, 49, 50, 52, 54
Massachusetts Institute of Technology, 34, 52–53
Mathias, Charles M., 352, 363
Matsumoto, Mitsao, 237
Matsumoto, Shigeharu, 66–67, 83, 86, 87, 88, 108, 111, 150–51, 243, 443–44
Mauldin, W. Parker, 43, 435, 436, 437, 438
Mauzé, Jean, 206
May, Cordelia Scaife, 162
May, Stacy, 63, 66, 68, 69, 71, 74
Maynard, George W., 255
Mazzola, John, 156
Mboya, Tom, 238
Meade, Margaret, 279, 356
Meany, George, 356
Mecca Temple, 126
Mellon family, 162
Mellon Foundation, 461
Meloy, Daniel, 453
Menon, V. K. Krishna, 108
Merchant, Livingston, 281, 368
Merton, Robert K., 162
Metropolitan Club (Washington, D.C.), 281–83
Metropolitan Museum of Art, 470
Metropolitan Opera Association, 144
Metropolitan Opera Company (New York), 120, 126, 127, 128, 129, 130, 135–36, 139, 154
See also Lincoln Center for the Performing Arts
Mettler, Reuben, 326, 356
Michaels, George, 403
Michener, James, 90
Milbank, Tweed, 120, 272
Milbank Memorial Fund, 43
Miles, Rufus, 370
Miller, Arjay, 352
Miller, Mitch, 334
Millikan, Max, 52
Mills, Wilbur, 293, 376, 377
Milton, David, 206, 239
Miro, Carmen, 428
Mitchell, James, 48
Mitchell, John, 348

Mitsubishi Estate Company, 3, 4, 5
Mitsui, Takasumi, 84
Model, Jean, 232
Moe, Henry Allen, 188, 263
Montgomery, Robert, 276, 280
Moore, Arch, 244
Moore, Hugh, 159
Moore, Preston, 339, 343
Morocco, 174
Morris, Newbold, 123, 126, 127, 129, 130, 141, 142, 145–46
Morris, Richard, 544
Morrow, Hugh, 209, 316, 511
Morse, Wayne, 93
Moscone, George, 481
Moses, Robert, 120–22, 124, 131, 133, 141–42
Mosher, Arthur T., 74, 256–57, 282, 448–52
Mott Foundation, 183
Mt. Holyoke College, 322
Moyer, Raymond, 71
Moyers, Bill, 171, 173, 177, 231, 295, 356, 406
Moynihan, Daniel Patrick, 279, 343–44, 405, 406–12, 415, 418
Munro, Dana, 50, 53–54
Murphy, J. Morden, 101
Murphy, James ("Robin"), 211
Murphy, Margaretta Fitler ("Happy"), 211
Murphy, Robert, 113–14
Murray, Tom, 60
Murray, W. E., 113
Museum of Modern Art (MOMA), 12, 214, 227–29, 233, 246, 257–58, 470
Mutual Defense Assistance Program, 65
Myers, William I., 64, 66, 67, 68–70, 71, 72, 73, 74, 187

Nagako (empress of Japan), 454–55
Nasser, Gamal Abdel, 165, 277
Nathan, Robert, 372, 545, 546
National Academy of Public Administration, 361
National Academy of Sciences, 33
National Broadcasting Company (NBC), 16
National Civil Service League, 58
National Committee for the Bicentennial Era (NCBE), 362–64
National Committee on United States–China Relations, 447
National Council on Philanthropy, 391
National Cultural Center (Washington, D.C.), 149, 262, 265
National Endowment for the Arts, 264, 265, 479

National Endowment for the Humanities, 264, 360
National Foundation on the Arts and Humanities, 264
National Institute of Public Affairs, 59
National Institute of Social Sciences, 273, 305
National Institutes of Health, 55
National Training Laboratories, 280
National Trust for Historic Preservation, 501
Negro Family: The Case for National Action, The (Moynihan), 405
Nehru, Jawaharlal, 67–68, 78–79, 108
Nelson, Otto L., Jr., 133
Nelson, Warren O., 43
Nepal, 174
Nevins, Allan, 152
New Deal, 11, 21
Newman, Walter, 480
Newsom, Earl, 81, 274, 276
Newsweek (magazine), 204, 309, 324, 361
New York Boys' Club, 320
New York City
    Board of Estimate, 149
    Housing Commission, 335
New York City Ballet, 123, 129, 140, 141, 144
    See also Lincoln Center for the Performing Arts
New York City Housing Partnership, 335
New York City Opera, 130, 135–36, 145
New York City Symphony, 127
New York Economic Club, 166
New Yorker, The (magazine), 327–31
New York Herald Tribune (newspaper), 264
New York Journal-American (newspaper), 201
New York Philharmonic Society, 121, 128, 129, 139
    See also Lincoln Center for the Performing Arts
New York Public Library, 132, 139
New York State Council on the Arts, 263
New York Times, 13, 39, 67, 94, 124, 161, 249, 292, 317, 324, 343, 361, 419, 550
    "100 Neediest Cases," 226
New York Times Magazine, 380, 383
New York World's Fair, 142, 144
Ngo Dinh Diem, 77
Niarchos, Stavros, 150–51
Nielsen, Waldemar, 92, 182–84, 195–97, 292, 297, 390, 523

1934 Trusts, 11, 247, 467–68, 491
1952 Trusts, 16, 247, 503–4
Nixon, Richard M., 60, 177, 209–10,
　　215, 244, 265, 348–49, 352,
　　353–54, 356–57, 361, 376
　and China, 447–48
　and Nelson Rockefeller, 507–9
　and the Population Commission,
　　395–96, 400, 404, 405–7, 409–
　　10, 416–20
Nixon administration, 297, 301, 341,
　　369, 404–12, 415–20
Notestein, Frank, 32–33, 34–35, 36,
　　39, 40, 41, 44, 45, 81, 159, 398,
　　425, 434–37, 442
　as president of Population Council,
　　160–67, 171, 177, 403
Noyes, Charles, 91, 96, 114
Nyerere, Julius, 238

O'Brien, Donal C., Jr., 274, 469, 475,
　　497–501, 544
O'Connor, Frank, 212
Office of Population Research, 32, 33
Office of the Coordinator of Inter-
　　American Affairs (OCIAA), 15
Olivarez, Grace, 413
Onassis, Aristotle, 151
O'Neill, Abby M., 214
"One Per Cent Plan" group (Cleve-
　　land), 293
Oppenheimer, J. Robert, 87
Oranges in Tissue Paper (McCloskey),
　　255
Organization of American States
　　(OAS), 167
Organization of Petroleum Exporting
　　Countries (OPEC), 429
Osborn, Fairfield, 34, 40, 41–42, 43–44
Osborn, Frederick, 33, 34–35, 39, 40,
　　41, 42, 73, 159–60
Overby, Andrew N., 456
Overton, Douglas, 73, 87, 88, 89, 96,
　　99, 150, 452, 453
Overton, Leonard, 99, 100

Pace, Frank, 54
Pacific Affairs (journal), 94
Packwood, Robert, 406, 412
Paddock, Paul, 398
Paddock, William, 398
Pakistan, 65, 71, 81–82, 164
Papp, Joseph, 356
Pardee, Irving H., 206
Park, Jin Hwan, 445
Park, Kim Sung, 444–45
Parran, Thomas, 34, 39, 187
Parvin, Albert, 297
Parvin Foundation, 297

Pathfinder Fund, 428
Patman, Wright, 292–93, 296
Patterson, Franklin, 322–24
Paul, Eva, 20
Paulekiute, Jievute, 20
Paul VI (Pope), 168–70, 175
Peaceable Kingdom (Hicks), 255, 273
Peace Corps, 159, 240, 320, 321
Peale, Charles Willson, 255
Peale, Raphaelle, 255
Pease, Clifford, 435, 436
Pei, I. M., 473, 475
Pell, Claiborne, 264, 363
Pendleton Act of 1883, 56
People's Bicentennial Commission
　　(PBC), 349, 350
Percy, Charles H., 203, 241, 242, 409
Percy, Sharon. See Rockefeller,
　　Sharon
Performing Arts: Problems and Pros-
　　pects, The (Schickel), 264
Persico, Joseph, 316–17, 484, 487,
　　507, 511, 513
Peterson, Elizabeth, 232
Peterson, Merrill, 362
Peterson, Peter G., 295–99
Peterson, Russell, 428
Peterson Commission on Foundations
　　and Private Philanthropy,
　　295–99, 375, 376, 404
Peto, John F., 255
Phelps Memorial Hospital, 246, 468
Philanthropy, 289–99
Philharmonic Hall, 136, 145, 154, 249
　See also Lincoln Center for the Per-
　　forming Arts
Philippine-American Chamber of
　　Commerce, 90
Philippines, 64–65, 67, 71
　and Magsaysay awards, 111–19
Phillips, Russell, 118
Phillips Exeter Academy, 84–85, 247
Pifer, Alan, 182, 295, 378
Pinza, Ezio, 205
Piotrow, Phyllis, 40, 419
Pius XII (Pope), 44
Planned Parenthood, 34, 39, 174
Playboy (magazine), 320
Plimpton, Calvin, 323
Plimpton, Francis T. P., 329
Pocantico estate, 8, 12, 17–18, 47,
　　205, 206, 211, 493–501, 559–61
Population and Development Review
　　(journal), 441
Population and overpopulation, 31–32,
　　158–59, 214
　political support for interest in,
　　166–69
　and "War on Hunger," 174

Population and overpopulation *(cont.)*
World Leaders Statement on,
171–77, 398–99, 421
See also Commission on Population
Growth and the American
Future; Population Council
Population Bomb, The (Ehrlich), 398,
407
Population Commission. *See* Commission on Population Growth and
the American Future
Population Council, 38, 39–45, 64, 72,
75, 159–64, 247, 259, 407, 421,
468, 562
difficulties after World Population
Conference, 438–42
and World Population Conference,
423–24, 434–38
Population Education, Inc., 414, 419,
426–27
Population Tribune, 428
Population Trust Fund, 400
See also United Nations Fund for
Population Activities
Porter, Elsa, 368
Powell, Adam Clayton, 39
President's Advisory Committee on
Governmental Reorganization,
20
President's Commission on Juvenile
Delinquency and Youth Crime,
241
President's Committee to Study the
United States Military Assistance Program, 44–45
Price, Don K., 48
Princeton University, 11, 24, 32, 33,
34, 53, 84, 247, 307, 468
Center for International Studies, 63
Institute for Advanced Study, 47
Office of Population Research, 160
Woodrow Wilson School of Public
and International Affairs, 50–51,
53, 366–67, 368–73, 546
Pringle, Richard, 71
Products of Asia, 104–5
Profiles in Courage (Kennedy), 310
Progressive (magazine), 350
Progressive Era, 289
Project Interface, 327
Project on Human Sexual Development, 426–27
Project Rehab, 340–41
Prospects for America—The Rockefeller Panel Reports, 203
Public Administration Clearing House,
48

"Quantico technique," 202–3

Radhakrishnan, Sarvepalli, 108, 111
Ragan, James F., Jr., 337–39
Ramón Magsaysay Award Foundation
(RMAF), 115–19
early discussions for, 112–15
Ramsey, Christian N., Jr., 413
Ravenholt, Albert, 112–13, 115, 117,
119
Ravenholt, Marjorie, 112, 115, 117,
119
Ravenholt, Reimert T., 174
Rayburn, Sam, 59
RCA Building, 8, 271–74
Reader's Digest (magazine), 390
Reagan, Ronald, 447, 508
Reece, B. Carroll, 94–95
Reed, Ingrid, 371–72, 373, 374, 545
Rees, Edward H., 58
Reid, Alistair, 331
Reischauer, Edwin O., 50, 85, 88, 96,
150–51, 451, 454
Reisman, David, 87
Repertory Theater Association, 132,
139
Republican Party, 56, 209, 212, 303,
507
Reston, James, 161
Richardson, Edgar P., 253–55, 478,
479
Richardson, Elliot, 359
Rifkin, Jeremy, 349
Riis, Jacob, 335
Ripon Society, 327
Riverside Church, 468, 474
Robb, Catherine, 232
Robb, Charles S., 235
Roberts, Elizabeth, 426–27, 544
Robinson, Bill "Bojangles," 335
Rock, John, 168, 466
Rockefeller, Abby Aldrich, 8–9, 233
children of, 9–10
death of, 15–16, 232
Rockefeller, Abby ("Babs"), 9, 18–19,
161–62, 206, 209, 213, 239,
403, 487, 495, 504
Rockefeller, Abby (Babs's daughter),
504
Rockefeller, Abby (David's daughter),
505
Rockefeller, Alida Davison, 211–12,
226, 234, 236, 243, 244–46,
306, 308, 316, 391, 465, 478,
505
Rockefeller, Barbara ("Bobo"), 19–20,
201, 495
Rockefeller, Blanchette, 22, 40, 76–77,
78–79, 82–84, 86, 99, 108, 112,
114, 115, 116, 151–52, 170, 173,
211–12, 218, 221, 250, 251,

271, 302, 316, 322, 323, 351, 430,
443, 466, 474, 478, 481, 506
children, 224–26, 236, 238
family life, 223–27
marriage to JDR, 22, 223–27, 230–
33
and the Museum of Modern Art
(MOMA), 227–30, 233, 258, 470
Rockefeller, David, 9–11, 12, 118,
125, 211, 216–18, 455
and brothers, 213–15, 218
and Chase Manhattan Bank, 19,
216–17
contributions to Nelson's campaigns,
209
and father's wealth, 17–18, 208, 495
and Lincoln Center, 151–52
and Population Council, 43, 162
public interest in, 201
and Rockefeller Brothers' Fund, 203
and Rockefeller Center, 17, 493
and Rockefeller University, 489
Trilateral Commission, 462
and the Urban Coalition, 334, 335
and World War II, 14
Rockefeller, David, Jr., 503, 504, 505,
506
Rockefeller, Faith, 232
Rockefeller, Hope, 78, 83, 85, 112,
116, 226, 236, 237–39, 465, 505
Rockefeller, Jamie, 244
Rockefeller, Jay. See Rockefeller, John
D., IV
Rockefeller, John D. (Senior), 4, 5–7,
152, 181, 273, 289, 334, 474,
494
Rockefeller, John D. (Junior), 5, 474
and the arts, 125
at Brown University, 6
children of, 9–13, 17–19, 25–26,
206–8, 219–20, 502–3
and Colonial Williamsburg, 12, 18,
25–26, 205
death of, 208
and death of Abby, 15–16
disposition of wealth, 15–18, 208,
491–92, 504
and father's wealth, 6–7
Fosdick's biography of, 205–6
and the Great Depression, 12
and Lincoln Center, 134
marriage to Martha Baird Allen,
18–19, 205
and the Metropolitan Opera Company, 121–22
philanthropy, 6–8, 205–6, 289, 290
Pocantico estate, 494–96
and Rockefeller Center, 12, 16–17,
492

and Rockefeller Foundation, 12,
181, 185
and Rockefeller Public Service
Awards (RPSA), 55–56
staff and advisors, 273, 485–86
and urban housing, 334–35
Rockefeller, John D., 3rd (JDR), 9–11
and abortion rights, 401–3, 415–19,
466
and the Agricultural Development
Council (ADC), 75, 259, 448–
52, 468, 545
art collections, 250–56, 273, 443,
469, 471–81
Asian travels, 66–68, 76–89, 443–46
and the Asia Society, 101–3, 207,
214, 274, 328, 456–62, 463,
468, 469–77, 544
and Bicentennial of the American
Revolution, 346–47, 351–65
Bicentennial speeches, 354–55,
357–59
and brothers, 213–15, 217, 219–20,
221–22, 270–71, 316
children, 224–26, 238–41, 245–46
and City Center, 126–27
and Colonial Williamsburg, 12, 18,
23–24, 25–26, 32, 105, 207,
234–35, 242–43
Conference on Population Problems, 33–37
contributions to Nelson's campaigns,
209
Council on Economic and Cultural
Affairs, 72–75
and the Cousins, 232, 505–6
and cultural work in Asia, 256–61
on "culture," 105–6
death of, 549–53
death of father, 208
death of mother, 16
disposition of wealth, 246–48, 463,
467–69
early career, 22–27
family life, 223–27
and father, 11–12, 18, 25–27, 207–8
frugality, 269–71
and the Great Depression, 12
and Harrar, 192–95
health, 463–65, 542–43
and integration of social clubs,
281–83
interest in euthanasia, 465–67
in Japan, 82–84, 104–5, 443–44
and Japan Society, 3–4, 26, 77, 87,
88, 89, 90, 91, 97, 100, 101,
256, 259, 275, 452–56, 544
judgment, 31
liberalism of, 302–5

Rockefeller, John D., 3rd (cont.)
    and Lincoln Center. See Lincoln
        Center for the Performing Arts
    and Lyndon B. Johnson, 167–66,
        172, 173, 174–75, 176, 177–79
    marriage to Blanchette, 22, 223–27,
        230–33
    and national service concept, 320–
        21
    and nature of philanthropy, 289–99,
        375–76, 383–85
    and Nelson, 300, 303, 316, 499–500,
        531–39
    and Nelson's marriage to Happy,
        211–12
    and Notestein, 160
    offered ambassadorship to Indone-
        sia, 80–81
    offered ambassadorship to Japan,
        301–2, 309, 318
    office in RCA building, 271–74
    "Opportunities in the Broad Field of
        Population" (agenda), 37
    personal caution, 303–5
    personality, 268–69, 277, 279, 281,
        283–85
    personal staff and advisors, 163–64,
        272–81, 303–4
    Policy and Planning Committee, 99,
        274–77
    Population Commission, 395–96
    Population Council. See Population
        Council
    "profile" in The New Yorker,
        327–31
    public interest in, 201, 268–69
    as public speaker, 277–78
    and Rockefeller Center, 12, 17,
        271–74, 493
    and Rockefeller Foundation (RF),
        12, 23, 24, 25, 27, 32, 75,
        180–81, 195–97, 276, 290
    Rockefeller Public Service Awards
        (RPSA), 46–61, 207, 247,
        366–74, 545–46
    and Rusk, 185–87
    The Second American Revolution,
        313–17, 318, 346–47, 444
    on sex and sex education, 319–20
    social life, 230–31
    Society for the Family of Man Gold
        Medal award, 305–6
    speeches on population control,
        165–66
    speech on youth movement, 308–9
    and "third sector" activism,
        333–34, 346, 365, 366, 375–76,
        546, 567
    and urban housing, 334–45

    and the Vietnam War, 304–5
    will, 463, 467–69, 554–55
    women friends of, 231–33
    World Leaders Statement on
        population control, 171–77,
        399, 421
    and World War II, 14–15
    writings, 278–79, 310–17
    and "youth revolution," 305, 306–9,
        312–17, 318–19
    "Youth Task Force," 321–32
Rockefeller, John D., IV (Jay), 78, 83,
        84–86, 163, 181, 208, 211–12,
        224–26, 233, 236, 239–41, 248,
        316, 464–65, 505, 551–53, 567
    in West Virginia, 241–44
Rockefeller, John D., V, 465
Rockefeller, Larry, 505, 506
Rockefeller, Laura, 232, 505
Rockefeller, Laurance Spelman, 9–11,
        12, 33, 40, 117–18, 125, 205,
        211, 243, 510–11
    and brothers, 213–15
    conservation interests, 215
    contributions to Nelson's campaigns,
        209
    death of father, 208
    and father's wealth, 17–18, 495
    public interest in, 201
    and Rockefeller Brothers' Fund,
        203, 204
    and Rockefeller Brothers, Inc., 19
    and Rockefeller Center, 16–17, 493
    and Rock Resorts, 215–16
    and urban housing, 335–36, 338
    and Virgin Islands National Park, 19
    and World War II, 14–15
Rockefeller, Lucy, 505
Rockefeller, Margaretta Fitler Murphy
        ("Happy"), 211, 510
Rockefeller, Marilyn, 504
Rockefeller, Marion, 232, 505
Rockefeller, Martha Baird, 161–62,
        205, 208–9, 211, 214, 485–86,
        489, 496
Rockefeller, Mary French, 19
Rockefeller, Mary (Tod), 210, 211, 231
Rockefeller, Michael Clark, 259
Rockefeller, Nelson Aldrich, 9–11, 12,
        36, 64, 147, 327, 452
    and abortion rights, 403, 416
    behavior and disposition following
        vice presidency, 483–84
    and Bicentennial celebration, 352–
        54
    and brothers, 213–15, 221–22
    death of, 501, 554
    divorce, 210
    eulogy for Winthrop, 487

and father's wealth, 17–18, 208, 495, 509–10
federal assignments, 20–22, 201, 202–4
governorship of New York, 138, 141–42, 204–5, 209, 210–11, 212, 244, 263, 335, 508
and JDR's liberalism, 300, 303, 316
and Magsaysay awards, 112–13, 114, 115, 116, 118
marriage to Margaretta Fitler Murphy ("Happy"), 211–12
and Martha Baird, 208–9
and Museum of Modern Art, 12, 214, 227
and Nixon, 507–9
presidential campaigns, 177, 209–10, 212
and Pocantico estate, 498, 499–500
public interest in, 201
and Rockefeller archives, 488
and Rockefeller Brothers' Fund, 202–3, 262, 530–39
and Rockefeller Center, 16–17, 202, 493
and the U.S. State Department, 21, 53
and urban housing, 335
and vice presidency of the United States, 455, 508–13
Rockefeller, Neva, 232, 505
Rockefeller, Peggy, 218, 232, 505, 544
Rockefeller, Richard, 505
Rockefeller, Rodman, 496, 505
Rockefeller, Sandra, 224–26, 236–37, 465
Rockefeller, Sharon, 226, 240, 241–44, 465, 506
Rockefeller, Steven, 232, 505, 506
Rockefeller, William, 494
Rockefeller, Winthrop, 99–11, 12, 243, 354
    in Arkansas, 19–20, 218, 219
    and brothers, 213–15, 219–20
    death of, 486–87
    disposition of wealth, 504
    divorces, 20, 220–21, 494
    drinking problem, 219
    father's opinion of, 206–7, 219–20
    and father's wealth, 17–18, 495
    marriage to Barbara "Bobo" Sears, 19, 201
    marriage to Jeanette Edris, 218–19
    and Pocantico estate, 495, 498
    political career, 219–20
    public interest in, 201
    and Rockefeller Center, 17
    and World War II, 14
Rockefeller, Winthrop Paul, 20, 219, 504
Rockefeller Archive Center, 273, 334, 487–90, 544
Rockefeller Brothers, Inc., 19
Rockefeller Brothers' Fund (RBF), 13, 17, 33, 34, 41, 74, 91, 126, 194, 208, 213–14, 218, 272, 274, 276, 320, 377, 447, 449, 459, 485, 486, 492, 499, 503, 508, 519–25, 556–57
    Creel Committee, 525–29, 540–41
    Magsaysay awards, 113–18, 207, 214
    and Museum of Modern Art (MOMA), 214, 258
    and Population Council, 161
    and Rockefeller Archive Center, 488, 489–90
    Special Study projects, 202–3, 261, 262
    struggle for control of, 530–39
    and urban housing, 336, 338
Rockefeller Center, 3, 4, 5, 7, 8, 12, 16–17, 120, 125–26, 272, 491–93, 557–59
Rockefeller-Cohen Report, 400, 403–4
Rockefeller Cousins, 482–83, 487, 496–97, 503–6, 516–18
    See also specific names, e.g.: Rockefeller, John D., IV
Rockefeller Family Fund (RFF), 504
Rockefeller Foundation (RF), 6, 12, 23, 24, 25, 27, 32, 34, 173, 276, 362
    archives, 488, 489–50
    assets (1968), 181
    board of directors, 187–88
    and the CIA, 96–100, 186
    and Conference on Population Problems, 35–37
    and Cox Committee Hearings, 93–95, 186
    General Education Board, 95, 191–92, 310
    Harrar as president of, 189–92
    Harrar's program for, 192–97
    International Health Division, 32, 186
    and International Houses, 107, 109–10, 111, 186
    International Rice Research Institute, 74, 186
    and JDR, 12, 23, 24, 25, 27, 32, 75, 180–81, 195–97, 290
    Laura Spelman Rockefeller Memorial (LSRM), 193–94

Rockefeller Foundation *(cont.)*
 and Lincoln Center, 123, 130, 134,
  146–47, 151, 186
 Natural Sciences and Agriculture
  Division, 33, 68–70
 Nielsen on, 184
 and population issues, 32–38, 161,
  397, 398
 and Reece Committee hearings, 95,
  186, 290
 Rusk as president of, 185–87
 and Southeast Asia, 68–70, 304
 and urban housing, 335
Rockefeller Institute for Medical
  Research, 6, 217
 See also Rockefeller University
Rockefeller Panel Reports, 203
Rockefeller Public Service Awards
  (RPSA), 46–61, 174, 207, 247,
  275, 366–74, 545–46, 563–64
*Rockefellers: An American Dynasty,
  The* (Collier and Horowitz),
  483, 514–18
Rockefeller Sanitary Commission, 6,
  310
Rockefeller University, 6, 33, 42, 162,
  217, 488, 489
Rock Resorts, Inc., 19, 215–16, 272
Rodino, Peter, 512
Roe v. *Wade*, 402, 419, 422, 427, 466
Rogers, Carl, 316
Rogers, Richard, 146
Roman Catholic Church, 32, 39, 44,
  45, 158, 164, 167, 168–71, 401,
  403, 416–17
Romney, George, 212, 243, 378
Ronan, William J., 145, 204, 511
Roosevelt, Eleanor, 87
Roosevelt, Franklin D., 15, 204
Rose, Frederick, 461
Rosoff, Sidney, 466
Rossow, Jerry, 427
Rostow, Walt W., 173
Roth, William, 545
Ruckelshaus, William, 359–60
Rudel, Julius, 146
Ruder, Bill, 276, 278, 302, 321, 328,
  331, 351, 362, 389, 391, 435,
  465
Rusk, Dean, 27, 35, 36–37, 48, 69, 94,
  95, 96, 99, 100–101, 113, 180,
  240, 301
 and International Houses, 108, 109–
  10, 186
 and Lincoln Center, 122, 123, 186
 and population control, 162, 168,
  170–71, 175
 as president of Rockefeller Foundation, 185–87

and Rockefeller Brothers' Fund,
  203
 as Secretary of State, 188, 460
Ruttan, Vernon, 451

Saarinen, Aline, 227
Saarinen, Eero, 136
Sabbatical leave, 48–49
 See also Rockefeller Public Service
  Awards (RPSA)
Salas, Rafael, 400, 424
Salk, Jonas, 356
Saltzman, Charles, 282–83
Salyer, Steve, 426, 428–29, 430, 435
Sanford, Terry, 263, 356
Sanger, Margaret, 24, 41, 44, 159
Sanwa Bank (Osaka), 84
Sasaki, Hideo, 498
Saturday Evening Post (magazine), 13,
  81
Saturday Review (magazine), 309
Saunders, Bertha, 252
Scaife family, 162
Scalapino, Robert, 447
Scheuer, James, 412
Schickel, Richard, 264, 310
Schroeder, Patricia, 363
Schubart, Mark, 123
Schultz, Theodore W., 43
Schuman, William, 123, 124, 131,
  154–56
Schwartz, Hilda G., 474
Science and Survival (Commoner), 398
Scrivner, Robert W., 293, 522
Sears, Richard, 20
Sebald, William J., 114
Second American Revolution, The
  (Rockefeller) 313–17, 318, 346–
  47, 444
Segal, Sheldon, 43, 162, 435, 436
Seidman, Oscar, 55
Sen, B. R., 165, 400
Sex and sex education, 319–20, 414–15
Sex Information and Education Coun-
  cil of the United States
  (SIECUS), 320, 426
Shapiro, Irving, 387
Shapiro, Isaac, 453–54, 544
Sherbert, Paul C., 101, 458
*Ship and an Approaching Storm Off
  Camden, Maine* (Lane), 253
Shirazu, Jiro, 84
Shriver, R. Sargent, 149, 240
Shulman, Marshall D., 55, 56
Shultz, George, 376, 377
Shuman, James B., 316
Siciliano, Rocco, 60
Siegesmund, Carl, 273
Sierra Club, 397

Sihanouk, Prince Norodom, 79
Silent Spring (Carson), 397
Silverstein, Leonard, 376
Simon, John, 385–86
Simon, Paul, 363
Simon, William, 376, 377, 381, 386, 387
Simons, Harold, 343
Sleepy Hollow Restorations, Inc., 500
Sloan Foundation, 189
Smith, Al, 204
Smith, Datus, 260, 266, 275, 280, 295, 310–12, 325, 377, 389, 407, 447, 457, 460, 462, 471, 473, 475
Smith, Jean, 149–50
Smith, Stephen, 149–50
Smith College, 247, 322
Smithsonian Institution, 479
Society for the Family of Man Gold Medal award, 305–6
Society for the Right to Die, 466–67
Socony–Vacuum, 43
Southeast Asia, 64–65, 304
Southeast Asia Development Advisory Group (SEADAG), 459–61
South Korea, 65, 165, 444–46
Soviet Union, 23, 32, 175–76, 203
Spector, Melbourne L., 348, 350, 359
Spellman, Francis (Cardinal), 112
Spelman Fund, 47
Spencer, David, 238
Spencer, Hope. *See* Rockefeller, Hope
Spencer, John, 238–39, 243
Spofford, Charles, 120, 122, 123, 124, 129–30, 132, 133, 134, 136, 140, 143, 155–56, 157
    and performing arts, 262, 263
    and Rockefeller Brothers' Fund, 203
Sproul, Robert, 187
Staats, Elmer, 372
Standard Oil Company, 4
Standard Oil of New Jersey, 148, 335
Standard Vacuum Oil Company, 78
Stanford University, 245–46, 306
Stans, Maurice, 411
Stanton, Frank, 188, 231, 263, 356, 362
State Councils on the Arts, 263
State Theater, 143–44, 145–46, 153, 154
    See also Lincoln Center for the Performing Arts
Sterling, J. E. Wallace, 245, 348, 352
Stevens, Roger, 131, 264–65
Stevenson, Adlai, 99, 231
Stewart, James L., 452–53
Stewart, Walter, 180, 185

Stinchfield, Frank, 463
Stoddard, George D., 133
Stokes, Donald F., 370, 371, 545
Stratton, Julius, 295
Strauss, Lewis, 33, 34, 38, 39
Strong, Maurice, 424
Suharto, 176
Sukarno, 71, 78, 79
Sulzberger, Arthur, 187
Surrey, Stanley S., 380
Sweden, 172
Swift, Jerry, 323, 325–31
Swift, Paul "Porky," 325, 331

Taeuber, Irene, 33, 34
Tait, Joyce, 543
Taiwan, 65, 90, 165
Talbot, Phillips, 71, 73, 74, 96, 100, 101, 231, 256, 260, 448, 460–62, 471, 473, 476
Tanaka, Tokujiro, 84
Tarbell, Ida, 483
Tax Reform Act of 1969, 298, 368, 375, 377, 378, 382, 484–85, 521–22
Tax Reform Act of 1976, 382
Taylor, Arthur, 461
Taylor, George, 273
Taylor, Howard, 162
Taylor, Maxwell, 150, 153
Technical Cooperation Administration, 65
Teller, Edward, 203
Templer, Gerald, 67
Tenement Reform Law of 1901, 335
Teresa, Mother, 116
Terkel, Studs, 392
Thailand, 63, 71, 165
This Endangered Planet (Falk), 398
This Week (magazine), 177
Thomas, J. Parnell, 92
Thompson, Llewellyn, 368
Tie Line, 327
Tietze, Christoper, 44, 162, 403
Tillich, Paul, 87
Time (magazine), 12, 21, 205–6, 309, 324, 361
Time, Inc., 16
Tito (Josip Broz), 173
Tocqueville, Alexis de, 333, 355, 384
"Today" (television program), 264
Toffler, Alvin, 263–64
Tokyo Marine Insurance Company, 84
Toynbee, Arnold, 165
Trilateral Commission, 462
Truman, Harry S, 21, 54, 57
Truman administration, 92
Truman Doctrine, 65
Trust Committees, 11
Tuason, Pedro, 115

Tully, Alice, 153
Tunisia, 164–65, 172
Turkey, 165
Twentieth-Century Fund, 264
Twilight (Church), 253
Tydings, Joseph, 412

Udall, Stewart, 171
Uichango, Leopold, 115
Ullman, Al, 381, 386
United Arab Republic, 165, 172
United Nations, 23
  Asian leaders at, 76
  and population control, 32, 44, 159,
    165, 173–74, 176, 397, 398–400
  World Health Organization, 165
United Nations Association (UNA),
  399, 421
United Nations Development Program
  (UNDP), 399–400
UNESCO, 31–32
United Nations Fund for Population
  Activities (UNFPA), 400
UN World Population Year, 421
U.S. Air Force, 86
U.S. Army
  Officer Candidate School, 14
  Special Forces, 240
U.S. Atomic Energy Commission, 33
U.S. Committee for Borobudur, 448
U.S. Congress, 59–60
  and Bicentennial celebration, 348,
    350–51, 363
  Cox Committee, 92–94, 95, 186
  House Judiciary Committee, 511–12
  House Un-American Activities Com-
    mittee, 92
  and population issues, 168, 407–8
  Reece Committee, 94–95, 186
  Senate Finance Committee, 297
  Senate Government Operations
    Committee, 92
  Senate Internal Security Commit-
    tee, 92, 94
  Senate Watergate Hearings, 356–57
  Special Subcommittee on the Arts,
    263
  Ways and Means Committee, 296,
    297
U.S. Department of Agriculture, 71
U.S. Department of Health, Educa-
  tion, and Welfare (HEW), 21
U.S. Department of Housing and
  Urban Development (HUD),
  337–44
U.S. Department of State, 27, 48, 51
  Assistant Secretary for Latin Ameri-
    can Affairs, 20

  Bureau of Cultural Affairs, 258
  Foreign Service, 47, 52, 368
  International Information Adminis-
    tration (IIA), 51–53
  Jay Rockefeller at, 86, 240, 241
  JDR and, 47–48, 51–53, 77
  Nelson Rockefeller and, 20, 21
  Office of War Information, 51
  Policy Planning Staff, 48
  and population control, 170–71
U.S. Immigration and Naturalization
  Service, 133
U.S. Information Agency (USIA), 21,
  53
U.S. Navy, 55
  Bureau of Naval Personnel, 15
  JDR in, 14–15, 47
  Laurance Rockefeller in, 14–15
U.S. Supreme Court, 402, 419, 421,
  427, 466
U.S. Treasury Department
  Advisory Committee on Philan-
    thropy, 386, 388–89
  and charitable contributions, 291
  Internal Revenue Service (IRS), 39–
    41, 73, 95, 97, 293–94
  See also Filer Commission on Pri-
    vate Philanthropy and Public
    Needs; Peterson Commission on
    Foundations and Private
    Philanthropy
University Club, 282–83
University Grants Commission (India),
  108
University of California at Berkeley,
  106
University of Chicago, 6, 296
  International House at, 106
University of Massachusetts
  (Amherst), 322–24
University of Michigan, 166
University of North Carolina, 166
University of Paris, 106
University of Pittsburgh, 34
University of the Philippines, 74
University of Virginia, 361
Urban Coalition, 217, 334, 335–36
Urban Home Ownership Corporation
  (UHO), 336–45
U Thant, 173–74, 176, 400
Utley, Freda, 92

Valentiner, Wilhelm, 254
Vance, Cyrus, 356, 387
Van de Velde, Robert W., 55, 56, 57,
  58, 59–60, 366–68, 369
van Dusen, Henry P., 187, 465
Vassar College, 236, 246–47

Veiller, Lawrence, 335
Vietnam, 77, 304–5
Vietnam War, 304–5, 322, 332, 429
Virgin Islands National Park, 19
VISTA, 320, 321
Vittachi, Tarzie, 116
Vivian Beaumont Theater, 136, 154
   See also Lincoln Center for the Per-
     forming Arts
Vogt, William, 34
Voss, James, 452, 454

Wadsworth, Homer, 427
Wagner, Robert, 77, 121, 132, 141–42
Wald, Lillian, 335
Waldman, Ray, 417
Wallace, Lila Acheson, 460, 477
Warfield, William, 208
Warner, John, 351, 360, 362, 363
Warren, Earl, 279, 352
Warren, William, 295
Washburn, Gordon, 102, 461, 470,
   471
Washington Post (newspaper), 350,
   361, 550–51
Watanabe, Tadao, 84
Watergate, 350, 356–57, 359, 360–61
Wattleton, Faye, 544
Watts riot, 334
Waugh, Theodore, 542–43
*Way to Rehema's House: An East Afri-
   can Diary, The* (Spencer), 239
Weaver, Robert, 342
Weaver, Warren, 33, 34, 36–37, 68,
   69, 70, 71, 185, 189
Webb and Knapp, Inc., 133
Weil, Frank, 133
Weinberger, Casper, 428, 433–34
Weisblat, Abraham M., 74, 256, 257,
   258, 426, 448, 449
Welfare Council (New York City), 39
Westoff, Charles C., 412, 413–14, 434
Whalen, Grover, 142
Whalen, Richard, 149
Wharton, Clifton R., Jr., 74, 282,
   448–49, 451
White, Ian, 477–80
Whitehead, Robert, 132
White House Conference on Youth,
   327, 346
White House Council on the Arts,
   262
White House International Coopera-
   tion Year, 170
Whitney Museum, 479
Wien, Lawrence, 157, 390
Wilkins, Roy, 356
Wilkinson, Gerald, 67

Williamsburg. *See* Colonial
   Williamsburg
Williamsburg Conferences, 462
Wilson, Charles, 54
Wilson, Malcolm, 204
Winrock Farms, 218, 219
Winrock Livestock Project, 545
Winslow, Joseph, 58, 61
Winthrop Rockefeller Foundation,
   218
Wirtz, Willard, 171, 361
Wolfson, Louis, 297
Wolfson Family Foundation, 296
Wolper, David, 362
Wood, Grant, 255
Wood, Robert, 369
Woodcock, Leonard, 356
Woodrow Wilson School of Public and
   International Affairs, 50–54,
   57–58
Woods, George, 188, 399, 412
Woodworth, Lawrence N., 293–94,
   376, 386
Works Progress Administration, Music
   Project, 125–26
World Bank, 218
World Leaders Statement on popula-
   tion control, 171–77, 399, 421
World Population Conference (1974),
   422, 423–24, 427–32
   Draft World Plan of Action, 429–34
   Encounter for Journalists, 428
   JDR's speech at, 432–34
World's Fair (1964), 142, 154
Wriggins, Howard, 461
Wriston, Henry, 99
Wyeth, Andrew, 255

Yale University, 86
   Institute for Policy and Social Stud-
     ies, 385–86
Yankelovich, Daniel, 316, 321–22,
   332
Yen, James Y. C., 70–71, 72, 116
Ylvisaker, Paul, 321–22, 323, 380, 426
Yoo, Duk Hyung, 445
Yoshimura, Junzo, 454
Young, Edgar B., 26–27, 63, 91, 96–
   98, 101, 124, 163, 274, 275,
   303, 391
   and Arts in Education program, 262,
     265–66
   and Lincoln Center, 123, 124,
     126–27, 130, 133, 135, 136,
     140, 153, 155, 156, 274
Young, Kenneth T., 260, 275, 458–61
Young, Martin, 55
Young, Philip, 60

"Youth and the Establishment: A
   Unique Opportunity" (Rockefel-
   ler), 323–24
"Youth and the Establishment" survey
   (Yankelovich), 322
"Youth-establishment dialogues,"
   325–27, 331
"Youth, Love and Sex: The New
   Chivalry" (Rockefeller), 319–20

"Youth revolution," 305, 306–9,
   312–17, 318–19, 331–32
Yugoslavia, 173

Zablocki, Clement, 171
Zeidenstein, George, 438–42, 544
Zeidenstein, Sondra, 426
Zero population growth (ZPG),
   409